Lecture Notes in Computer Science 9036

Commenced Publication in 1973
Founding and Former Series Editors:
Gerhard Goos, Juris Hartmanis, and Jan van Leeuwen

Advanced Research in Computing and Software Science

Subline of Lecture Notes in Computer Science

More information about this series at http://www.springer.com/series/7410

Riccardo Focardi · Andrew Myers (Eds.)

Principles of Security and Trust

4th International Conference, POST 2015
Held as Part of the European Joint Conferences
on Theory and Practice of Software, ETAPS 2015
London, UK, April 11–18, 2015
Proceedings

 Springer

Editors
Riccardo Focardi
Ca' Foscari University
Venice
Italy

Andrew Myers
Cornell University
Ithaca
New York
USA

Lecture Notes in Computer Science
ISBN 978-3-662-46665-0   ISBN 978-3-662-46666-7   (eBook)
DOI 10.1007/978-3-662-46666-7

Library of Congress Control Number: 2015933999

LNCS Sublibrary: SL4 – Security and Cryptology

Springer Heidelberg New York Dordrecht London
© Springer-Verlag Berlin Heidelberg 2015

Printed on acid-free paper

Springer-Verlag GmbH Berlin Heidelberg is part of Springer Science+Business Media
(www.springer.com)

Foreword

ETAPS 2015 was the 18th instance of the European Joint Conferences on Theory and Practice of Software. ETAPS is an annual federated conference that was established in 1998, and this year consisted of six constituting conferences (CC, ESOP, FASE, FoSSaCS, TACAS, and POST) including five invited speakers and two tutorial speakers. Prior to and after the main conference, numerous satellite workshops took place and attracted many researchers from all over the world.

ETAPS is a confederation of several conferences, each with its own Program Committee and its own Steering Committee (if any). The conferences cover various aspects of software systems, ranging from theoretical foundations to programming language developments, compiler advancements, analysis tools, formal approaches to software engineering, and security. Organizing these conferences into a coherent, highly synchronized conference program enables the participation in an exciting event, having the possibility to meet many researchers working in different directions in the field, and to easily attend talks at different conferences.

The six main conferences together received 544 submissions this year, 152 of which were accepted (including 10 tool demonstration papers), yielding an overall acceptance rate of 27.9%. I thank all authors for their interest in ETAPS, all reviewers for the peer-reviewing process, the PC members for their involvement, and in particular the PC Co-chairs for running this entire intensive process. Last but not least, my congratulations to all authors of the accepted papers!

ETAPS 2015 was greatly enriched by the invited talks by Daniel Licata (Wesleyan University, USA) and Catuscia Palamidessi (Inria Saclay and LIX, France), both unifying speakers, and the conference-specific invited speakers [CC] Keshav Pingali (University of Texas, USA), [FoSSaCS] Frank Pfenning (Carnegie Mellon University, USA), and [TACAS] Wang Yi (Uppsala University, Sweden). Invited tutorials were provided by Daniel Bernstein (Eindhoven University of Technology, the Netherlands and the University of Illinois at Chicago, USA), and Florent Kirchner (CEA, the Alternative Energies and Atomic Energy Commission, France). My sincere thanks to all these speakers for their inspiring talks!

ETAPS 2015 took place in the capital of England, the largest metropolitan area in the UK and the largest urban zone in the European Union by most measures. ETAPS 2015 was organized by the Queen Mary University of London in cooperation with the following associations and societies: ETAPS e.V., EATCS (European Association for Theoretical Computer Science), EAPLS (European Association for Programming Languages and Systems), and EASST (European Association of Software Science and Technology). It was supported by the following sponsors: Semmle, Winton, Facebook, Microsoft Research, and Springer-Verlag.

The organization team comprised:

- General Chairs: Pasquale Malacaria and Nikos Tzevelekos
- Workshops Chair: Paulo Oliva
- Publicity chairs: Michael Tautschnig and Greta Yorsh
- Members: Dino Distefano, Edmund Robinson, and Mehrnoosh Sadrzadeh

The overall planning for ETAPS is the responsibility of the Steering Committee. The ETAPS Steering Committee consists of an Executive Board (EB) and representatives of the individual ETAPS conferences, as well as representatives of EATCS, EAPLS, and EASST. The Executive Board comprises Gilles Barthe (satellite events, Madrid), Holger Hermanns (Saarbrücken), Joost-Pieter Katoen (Chair, Aachen and Twente), Gerald Lüttgen (Treasurer, Bamberg), and Tarmo Uustalu (publicity, Tallinn). Other members of the Steering Committee are: Christel Baier (Dresden), David Basin (Zurich), Giuseppe Castagna (Paris), Marsha Chechik (Toronto), Alexander Egyed (Linz), Riccardo Focardi (Venice), Björn Franke (Edinburgh), Jan Friso Groote (Eindhoven), Reiko Heckel (Leicester), Bart Jacobs (Nijmegen), Paul Klint (Amsterdam), Jens Knoop (Vienna), Christof Löding (Aachen), Ina Schäfer (Braunschweig), Pasquale Malacaria (London), Tiziana Margaria (Limerick), Andrew Myers (Boston), Catuscia Palamidessi (Paris), Frank Piessens (Leuven), Andrew Pitts (Cambridge), Jean-Francois Raskin (Brussels), Don Sannella (Edinburgh), Vladimiro Sassone (Southampton), Perdita Stevens (Edinburgh), Gabriele Taentzer (Marburg), Peter Thiemann (Freiburg), Cesare Tinelli (Iowa City), Luca Vigano (London), Jan Vitek (Boston), Igor Walukiewicz (Bordeaux), Andrzej Wąsowski (Copenhagen), and Lenore Zuck (Chicago).

I sincerely thank all ETAPS SC members for all their hard work to make the 18th edition of ETAPS a success. Moreover, thanks to all speakers, attendants, organizers of the satellite workshops, and to Springer for their support. Finally, many thanks to Pasquale and Nikos and their local organization team for all their efforts enabling ETAPS to take place in London!

January 2015   Joost-Pieter Katoen

Preface

This volume contains the papers presented at POST 2015: 4th Conference on Principles of Security and Trust, held during April 16–17, 2015 in London, UK. Principles of Security and Trust is a broad forum related to the theoretical and foundational aspects of security and trust. Papers of many kinds are welcome: new theoretical results, practical applications of existing foundational ideas, and innovative theoretical approaches stimulated by pressing practical problems.

POST was created in 2012 to combine and replace a number of successful and long-standing workshops in this area: Automated Reasoning and Security Protocol Analysis (ARSPA), Formal Aspects of Security and Trust (FAST), Security in Concurrency (SecCo), and the Workshop on Issues in the Theory of Security (WITS). A subset of these events met jointly as an event affiliated with ETAPS 2011 under the name Theory of Security and Applications (TOSCA).

There were 57 submissions to POST 2015, including 55 research papers and two tool demonstration papers. Each submission was reviewed by three Program Committee members, who in many cases solicited the help of outside experts to review the papers. Electronic discussion was used to decide which papers to select for the program. The papers that appear in this volume may differ from the initial submissions; it is expected that some will be further revised and submitted for publication in refereed archival journals.

The Committee decided to accept 17 papers. In addition to these papers, the volume includes a contribution from the POST invited speaker Catuscia Palamidessi, who is also one of the ETAPS unifying speakers.

We would like to thank the members of the Program Committee, the External Reviewers, the POST Steering Committee, the ETAPS Steering Committee, and Local Organizing Committee, who all contributed to the success of POST 2015. We also thank all authors of submitted papers for their interest in POST and congratulate the authors of accepted papers. Finally, we gratefully acknowledge the use of EasyChair for organizing the submission process, the Program Committee's work, and the preparation of this volume.

January 2015

Riccardo Focardi
Andrew Myers

Organization

Program Committee

Pedro Adão	SQIG, IST, Lisboa, Portugal
Alessandro Armando	DIBRIS - University of Genoa, Italy
David Basin	ETH Zurich, Switzerland
Lujo Bauer	Carnegie Mellon University, USA
Karthikeyan Bhargavan	Inria, France
James Cheney	University of Edinburgh, UK
Stephen Chong	Harvard University, USA
Veronique Cortier	CNRS, Loria, France
Riccardo Focardi	Università Ca' Foscari, Venezia, Italy
Joshua Guttman	Worcester Polytechnic Institute, USA
Somesh Jha	University of Wisconsin, USA
Ralf Kuesters	University of Trier, Germany
Boris Köpf	IMDEA Software Institute, Spain
Peeter Laud	Cybernetica AS, Estonia
Ninghui Li	Purdue University, USA
Matteo Maffei	CISPA, Saarland University, Germany
Sergio Maffeis	Imperial College London, UK
Heiko Mantel	Technische Universität Darmstadt, Germany
Andrew Myers	Cornell University, USA
David Naumann	Stevens Institute of Technology, USA
Tamara Rezk	Inria, France
Mark Ryan	University of Birmingham, UK
Pierangela Samarati	Università degli Studi di Milano, Italy
Graham Steel	Cryptosense, France

Additional Reviewers

Arapinis, Myrto	Denzel, Michael
Carbone, Roberto	Dougherty, Daniel
Cheval, Vincent	Eigner, Fabienne
Chowdhury, Omar	Foresti, Sara
Chudnov, Andrey	Fragoso Santos, José
Costa, Gabriele	Fredrikson, Matt
Davidson, Drew	Gay, Richard
De Capitani Di Vimercati, Sabrina	Gazeau, Ivan
De Carli, Lorenzo	Hammer, Christian
Delignat-Lavaud, Antoine	Harris, William

Hu, Jinwei
Jia, Limin
Kordy, Piotr
Kremer, Steve
Laur, Sven
Liu, Jia
Livraga, Giovanni
Lortz, Steffen
Melissen, Matthijs
Mohammadi, Esfandiar
Novakovic, Chris
Perner, Matthias
Pironti, Alfredo
Radomirovic, Sasa
Rafnsson, Willard

Rausch, Daniel
Rowe, Paul
Sasse, Ralf
Schneider, David
Solhaug, Bjørnar
Strub, Pierre-Yves
Torabi Dashti, Mohammad
Traverso, Riccardo
Truderung, Tomasz
Van Der Meyden, Ron
Weber, Alexandra
Willemson, Jan
Yu, Jiangshan
Zalienscu, Eugen

Contents

Hardware and Physical Security

Privacy and Voting

Invited Contribution

Invited Contribution

Quantitative Approaches to the Protection of Private Information: State of the Art and Some Open Challenges

Catuscia Palamidessi

INRIA Saclay and LIX, École Polytechnique

Privacy is a broad concept affecting a variety of modern-life activities. As a consequence, during the last decade there has been a vast amount of research on techniques to protect privacy, such as communication anonymizers [9], electronic voting systems [8], Radio-Frequency Identification (RFID) protocols [13] and private information retrieval schemes [7], to name a few.

Until some years ago, the prevailing technology for privacy protection was k-anonymity [17,16]. Similarly to other techniques like ℓ-diversity, k-anonymity is based on the principle of modifying opportunely the so-called quasi-identifier attributes so that for every combination of quasi-identifier values in the data set, there are at least k individuals with these values. The idea is that in this way, each individual would be concealed in a group of at least k individuals with the same characteristics. The problem is that this technique requires the set of the quasi-identifier to be static, fixed in advance, and to be the same for all the individuals. However, as the amount of publicly available information about individuals grows, the distinction between quasi-identifier and non-quasi-identifier attributes fades away: Any information that distinguishes one person from another can be used to re-identify the person. For instance, any behavioral or transactional profile like movie viewing histories, consumption preferences, shopping habits, browsing patterns, etc. Furthermore, while many attributes may not be uniquely identifying on their own, in combination with others any attribute can be identifying. Due to these shortcomings, anonymity techniques, and more in general, the privacy protection paradigm based on de-identifying the data, have proved mostly ineffective against the emergence of powerful re-identification algorithms based on background knowledge, cross-correlation between databases, and analysis of the network structure. For instance, Narayanan and Shmatikov [15] conducted research on two large social networks, Flickr and Twitter, and demonstrated that, by using their algorithm, one third of the users who were members of both networks could be recognized in the completely anonymous Twitter graph with only 12% error rate!

In recent years, a new framework for privacy, called *differential privacy* (DP) has become increasingly popular in the area of statistical databases [10,12,11]. The idea is that, first, the access to the data should be allowed only through a query-based interface. Second, it should not be possible for the adversary to *distinguish*, from the answer to the query, whether a *certain individual is present or not* in the database. Formally, the *likelihood* of obtaining a certain answer should not change too much (i.e., more than a factor e^ϵ, where ϵ is a parameter)

R. Focardi and A. Myers (Eds.): POST 2015, LNCS 9036, pp. 3–7, 2015.
DOI: 10.1007/978-3-662-46666-7_1

when the individual joins (or leaves) the database. This is achieved by adding *random noise* to the answer, resulting in a trade-off between the privacy of the mechanism and the utility of the answer: the stronger privacy we wish to achieve, the more the answer needs to be perturbed, thus the less useful it is. One of the important features of DP is that it does not depend on the side information available to the adversary. Related to this, another important advantage is that DP is robust with respect to composition attacks: by combining the results of several queries, the level of privacy of every mechanism necessarily decreases, but with DP it declines in a controlled way. This is a feature that can only be achieved with randomized mechanisms: With deterministic methods, such as *k-anonymity*, composition attacks may be catastrophic.

DP has proved to be a solid foundation for privacy in statistical databases. Various people have also tried to extend it to other domains. However, there are some inherent limitations that make it inadequate in several practical cases. First, DP assumes that the disclosed information is produced by aggregating the data of multiple individuals. However, many privacy applications involve only a single individual, making differential privacy inapplicable. Second, even when multiple individuals are involved, DP assumes that full range of possible values of an individual needs to be *completely protected*. In applications where perturbations in an individual's value lead to a non-negligible change in the result, this requirement is impractical since the noise that we need to add is so big that the result becomes useless. In such cases, we wish to adapt our privacy definition, to only partially protect the user's data (which is often sufficient), while lowering the noise to obtain an acceptable level of utility. Third, DP focuses on the worst-case, since it requires the likelihood property to be satisfied for every possible database and every possible result. There are situations, however, where an average notion (weighed with the probabilities) would be more suitable for measuring the risk. For example, an insurance company protecting credit cards will be interested in knowing the probability that a card is compromised (and the corresponding expected loss) in order to decide what fee to apply. And an individual user may want to know the probability of a privacy breach in order to decide whether it is worth employing some costly counter-measures.

Finally, differential privacy needs some care when handling correlated data. In such situation, in fact, the adversary can filter out some of the noise by statistical reasoning. The best solution offered so far to this problem is to assign a *privacy budget*, and subtract from this budget a certain amount at every release of information.

In our team, we have addressed some of these issues by defining an extended DP framework in which the indistinguishability requirement is based on an arbitrary notion of distance (d_x-privacy, [5]). In this way we can naturally express (protection against) privacy threats that cannot be represented with the standard notion, leading to new applications of the differential privacy framework. In particular, we have explored applications in geolocation [3,4] and smart metering [5]. In the context of geolocation, the problem of the correlated data becomes particularly relevant when we consider traces, which usually are composed of a large amount of highly related points. We addressed this issue using *prediction functions* [6], obtaining encouraging results.

A different approach for measuring privacy is to employ techniques from *quantitative information flow* (QIF). Such techniques aim at quantifying the *leakage of secret information* through the observation of some public event, and have been successfully applied in several application contexts, such as programs, anonymity protocols, side channels attacks, etc. A common approach in this area is to use notions from information theory to measure the correlation between secret and observable information, the most prominent examples being Shannon and min-entropy. In contrast to differential privacy, these approaches typically provide average measures.

An important limitation of these entropy-based measures is that they treat secrets as atomic data, ignoring the structure and the relationship between the secrets. This structure is crucial for privacy applications: in geo-location systems, for instance, the *distance* between secrets (which are locations) plays a crucial role in defining the concept of privacy within a certain area.

Another limitation, common to both QIF and DP measures, is that they ignore several parameters that should play a fundamental role in an effective and realistic analysis of the privacy risk. First of all they ignore that the inference of the confidential information may have a cost for the adversary, which may considerably reduce the risk of an attack. Such cost can be, for example, in terms of computational resources or of some kind of deterrent. Furthermore, they ignore the gain that the adversary may obtain by acquiring the confidential data, and which is not necessarily the same for all the data (the credit card of Bill Gates is probably more worth than that of an average person...). Dually, they ignore the amount of damage that the user may suffer from the privacy breach, and that can be different depending on the data, or on the user.

The recently developed *g*-leakage framework [2,14,1] proposes a unified solution to the above issues by introducing the notion of *gain function*, which allows to express the gain of the adversary when guessing a secret. This richer definition of leakage has opened the way to new research directions.

Another shortcoming of the current approaches to privacy is that they are only applicable when the public information is well delimited and acquired in finite in time. Unfortunately, in most situation the source of public information is not necessarily bound, and some additional information can always be revealed in the future. At present, there are no techniques to verify privacy guarantees in situations in which the revelation of public information is not bound in time. This is a serious limitation, especially given that most of the systems which we use nowadays have an interactive nature, and usually are not under the control of the user.

In our team, we have started exploring a possible approach to this problem by defining a generalized version of the bisimulation distance based on the Kantorovich metric. In contrast to the standard bisimulation distance, which is additive and therefore not suitable to capture properties such as differential privacy, our framework considers the Kantorovich lifting on arbitrary metrics.

We have applied this framework to the particular case of the d_x-privacy, and provided an efficient method to compute it based on a dual form of the Kantorovich lifting. However, for other notions of leakage the quest for an efficient implementation remains open, as well as that of a generalized dual form.

References

1. Alvim, M.S., Chatzikokolakis, K., McIver, A., Morgan, C., Palamidessi, C., Smith, G.: Additive and multiplicative notions of leakage, and their capacities. In: IEEE 27th Computer Security Foundations Symposium, CSF 2014, Vienna, Austria, July 19-22, pp. 308–322. IEEE (2014)
2. Alvim, M.S., Chatzikokolakis, K., Palamidessi, C., Smith, G.: Measuring information leakage using generalized gain functions. In: Proceedings of the 25th IEEE Computer Security Foundations Symposium (CSF), pp. 265–279 (2012)
3. Andrés, M.E., Bordenabe, N.E., Chatzikokolakis, K., Palamidessi, C.: Geo-indistinguishability: differential privacy for location-based systems. In: Proceedings of the 20th ACM Conference on Computer and Communications Security (CCS 2013), pp. 901–914. ACM (2013)
4. Bordenabe, N.E., Chatzikokolakis, K., Palamidessi, C.: Optimal geo-indistinguishable mechanisms for location privacy. In: Proceedings of the 21th ACM Conference on Computer and Communications Security, CCS 2014 (2014)
5. Chatzikokolakis, K., Andrés, M.E., Bordenabe, N.E., Palamidessi, C.: Broadening the Scope of Differential Privacy Using Metrics. In: De Cristofaro, E., Wright, M. (eds.) PETS 2013. LNCS, vol. 7981, pp. 82–102. Springer, Heidelberg (2013)
6. Chatzikokolakis, K., Palamidessi, C., Stronati, M.: A Predictive Differentially-Private Mechanism for Mobility Traces. In: De Cristofaro, E., Murdoch, S.J. (eds.) PETS 2014. LNCS, vol. 8555, pp. 21–41. Springer, Heidelberg (2014)
7. Chor, B., Goldreich, O., Kushilevitz, E., Sudan, M.: Private information retrieval. In: Proceedings of the 36th Annual Symposium on Foundations of Computer Science, pp. 41–50. IEEE (1995)
8. Delaune, S., Kremer, S., Ryan, M.: Verifying privacy-type properties of electronic voting protocols. Journal of Computer Security 17(4), 435–487 (2009)
9. Dingledine, R., Mathewson, N., Syverson, P.F.: Tor: The second-generation onion router. In: Proceedings of the 13th USENIX Security Symposium, pp. 303–320. USENIX (2004)
10. Dwork, C.: Differential Privacy. In: Bugliesi, M., Preneel, B., Sassone, V., Wegener, I. (eds.) ICALP 2006. LNCS, vol. 4052, pp. 1–12. Springer, Heidelberg (2006)
11. Dwork, C.: A firm foundation for private data analysis. Communications of the ACM 54(1), 86–96 (2011)
12. Dwork, C., Lei, J.: Differential privacy and robust statistics. In: Mitzenmacher, M. (ed.) Proceedings of the 41st Annual ACM Symposium on Theory of Computing (STOC), Bethesda, MD, USA, May 31-June 2, pp. 371–380. ACM (2009)
13. Juels, A.: Rfid security and privacy: A research survey. IEEE Journal on Selected Areas in Communications 24(2), 381–394 (2006)
14. McIver, A., Morgan, C., Smith, G., Espinoza, B., Meinicke, L.: Abstract Channels and Their Robust Information-Leakage Ordering. In: Abadi, M., Kremer, S. (eds.) POST 2014 (ETAPS 2014). LNCS, vol. 8414, pp. 83–102. Springer, Heidelberg (2014)

15. Narayanan, A., Shmatikov, V.: De-anonymizing social networks. In: Proceedings of the 30th IEEE Symposium on Security and Privacy, pp. 173–187. IEEE Computer Society (2009)
16. Samarati, P.: Protecting respondents' identities in microdata release. IEEE Trans. Knowl. Data. Eng. 13(6), 1010–1027 (2001)
17. Samarati, P., Sweeney, L.: Generalizing data to provide anonymity when disclosing information (abstract). In: ACM (ed.) PODS 1998. Proceedings of the ACM SIGACT–SIGMOD–SIGART Symposium on Principles of Database Systems, Seattle, Washington, June 1-3, pp. 188–188. ACM Press (1998)

Information Flow and Security Types

IFC Inside: Retrofitting Languages with Dynamic Information Flow Control

Stefan Heule[1], Deian Stefan[1], Edward Z. Yang[1], John C. Mitchell[1], and Alejandro Russo[2],[**]

[1] Stanford University, Stanford, USA
[2] Chalmers University, Gothenburg, Sweden

Abstract. Many important security problems in JavaScript, such as browser extension security, untrusted JavaScript libraries and safe integration of mutually distrustful websites (mash-ups), may be effectively addressed using an efficient implementation of information flow control (IFC). Unfortunately existing fine-grained approaches to JavaScript IFC require modifications to the language semantics and its engine, a non-goal for browser applications. In this work, we take the ideas of coarse-grained dynamic IFC and provide the theoretical foundation for a language-based approach that can be applied to any programming language for which external effects can be controlled. We then apply this formalism to server- and client-side JavaScript, show how it generalizes to the C programming language, and connect it to the Haskell LIO system. Our methodology offers design principles for the construction of information flow control systems when isolation can easily be achieved, as well as compositional proofs for optimized concrete implementations of these systems, by relating them to their isolated variants.

1 Introduction

Modern web content is rendered using a potentially large number of different components with differing provenance. Disparate and untrusting components may arise from browser extensions (whose JavaScript code runs alongside website code), web applications (with possibly untrusted third-party libraries), and mashups (which combine code and data from websites that may not even be aware of each other's existence.) While just-in-time combination of untrusting components offers great flexibility, it also poses complex security challenges. In particular, maintaining data privacy in the face of malicious extensions, libraries, and mashup components has been difficult.

Information flow control (IFC) is a promising technique that provides security by tracking the flow of sensitive data through a system. Untrusted code is confined so that it cannot exfiltrate data, except as per an information flow policy. Significant research has been devoted to adding various forms of IFC to different kinds of programming languages and systems. In the context of the web, however, there is a strong motivation to preserve JavaScript's semantics and avoid JavaScript-engine modifications, while retrofitting it with dynamic information flow control.

[**] Work partially done while at Stanford.

© Springer-Verlag Berlin Heidelberg 2015
R. Focardi and A. Myers (Eds.): POST 2015, LNCS 9036, pp. 11–31, 2015.
DOI: 10.1007/978-3-662-46666-7_2

The Operating Systems community has tackled this challenge (e.g., in [1]) by taking a *coarse-grained* approach to IFC: dividing an application into coarse computational units, each with a single label dictating its security policy, and only monitoring communication between them. This coarse-grained approach provides a number of advantages when compared to the fine-grained approaches typically employed by language-based systems. First, adding IFC does not require intrusive changes to an existing programming language, thereby also allowing the reuse of existing programs. Second, it has a small runtime overhead because checks need only be performed at isolation boundaries instead of (almost) every program instruction (e.g., [2]). Finally, associating a single security label with the entire computational unit simplifies understanding and reasoning about the security guarantees of the system, without reasoning about most of the technical details of the semantics of the underlying programming language.

In this paper, we present a framework which brings coarse-grained IFC ideas into a language-based setting: an information flow control system should be thought of as multiple instances of completely isolated language runtimes or *tasks*, with information flow control applied to inter-task communication. We describe a formal system in which an IFC system can be designed once and then applied to any programming language which has control over external effects (e.g., JavaScript or C with access to hardware privilege separation). We formalize this system using an approach by Matthews and Findler [3] for combining operational semantics and prove non-interference guarantees that are independent of the choice of a specific target language.

There are a number of points that distinguish this setting from previous coarse-grained IFC systems. First, even though the underlying semantic model involves communicating tasks, these tasks can be coordinated together in ways that simulate features of traditional languages. In fact, simulating features in this way is a useful *design tool* for discovering what variants of the features are permissible and which are not. Second, although completely separate tasks are semantically easy to reason about, real-world implementations often blur the lines between tasks in the name of efficiency. Characterizing what optimizations are permissible is subtle, since removing transitions from the operational semantics of a language can break non-interference. We partially address this issue by characterizing isomorphisms between the operational semantics of our abstract language and a concrete implementation, showing that if this relationship holds, then non-interference in the abstract specification carries over to the concrete implementation.

Our contributions can be summarized as follows:

- We give formal semantics for a core coarse-grained dynamic information flow control language free of non-IFC constructs. We then show how a large class of target languages can be combined with this IFC language and prove that the result provides non-interference. (Sections 2 and 3)
- We provide a proof technique to show the non-interference of a concrete semantics for a potentially optimized IFC language by means of an isomorphism and show a class of restrictions on the IFC language that preserves non-interference. (Section 4)

– We have implemented an IFC system based on these semantics for Node.js, and we connect our formalism to another implementation based on this work for client-side JavaScript [4]. Furthermore, we outline an implementation for the C programming language and describe improvements to the Haskell LIO system that resulted from this framework. (Section 5)

In the extended version of this paper we give all the relevant proofs and extend our IFC language with additional features [5].

2   Retrofitting Languages with IFC

Before moving on to the formal treatment of our system, we give a brief primer of information flow control and describe some example programs in our system, emphasizing the parallel between their implementation in a multi-task setting, and the traditional, "monolithic" programming language feature they simulate.

Information flow control systems operate by associating data with *labels*, and specifying whether or not data tagged with one label l_1 can flow to another label l_2 (written as $l_1 \sqsubseteq l_2$). These labels encode the desired security policy (for example, confidential information should not flow to a public channel), while the work of specifying the semantics of an information flow language involves demonstrating that impermissible flows cannot happen, a property called *non-interference* [6]. In our coarse-grained floating-label approach, labels are associated with tasks. The task label—we refer to the label of the currently executing task as the *current label*—serves to protect everything in the task's scope; all data in a task shares this common label.

As an example, here is a program which spawns a new isolated task, and then sends it a mutable reference:

$$\textbf{let } i = {}_\text{TI}\lfloor\textbf{sandbox } (\textbf{blockingRecv } x, \_ \textbf{ in } {}^\text{IT}\lceil \, ! \, {}_\text{TI}\lfloor x \rfloor \rceil) \rfloor$$
$$\textbf{in } {}_\text{TI}\lfloor\textbf{send } {}^\text{IT}\lceil i \rceil \; l \; {}^\text{IT}\lceil\textbf{ref true}\rceil\rfloor$$

For now, ignore the tags ${}_\text{TI}\lfloor \, \cdot \, \rfloor$ and ${}^\text{IT}\lceil \, \cdot \, \rceil$: roughly, this code creates a new **sandbox**ed task with identifier i which waits (**blockingRecv**, binding x with the received message) for a message, and then **sends** the task a mutable reference (**ref true**) which it labels l. If this operation actually shared the mutable cell between the two tasks, it could be used to violate information flow control if the tasks had differing labels. At this point, the designer of an IFC system might add label checks to mutable references, to check the labels of the reader and writer. While this solves the leak, for languages like JavaScript, where references are prevalently used, this also dooms the performance of the system.

Our design principles suggest a different resolution: when these constructs are treated as isolated tasks, each of which have their own heaps, it is obviously the case that there is no sharing; in fact, the sandboxed task receives a dangling pointer. Even if there is only one heap, if we enforce that references not be shared, the two systems are morally equivalent. (We elaborate on this formally in Section 4.) Finally, this semantics strongly suggests that one should restrict the types of data which may be passed between tasks (for example, in JavaScript, one might only allow JSON objects to be passed between tasks, rather than general object structures).

Existing language-based, coarse-grained IFC systems [7, 8] allow a sub-computation to temporarily raise the floating-label; after the sub-computation is done, the floating-label is restored to its original label. When this occurs, the enforcement mechanism must ensure that information does not leak to the (less confidential) program continuation. The presence of exceptions adds yet more intricacies. For instance, exceptions should not automatically propagate from a sub-computation directly into the program continuation, and, if such exceptions are allowed to be inspected, the floating-label at the point of the exception-raise must be tracked alongside the exception value [7–9]. In contrast, our system provides the same flexibility and guarantees with no extra checks: tasks are used to execute sub-computations, but the mere definition of isolated tasks guarantees that (a) tasks only transfer data to the program continuation by using inter-task communication means, and (b) exceptions do cross tasks boundaries automatically.

2.1 Preliminaries

Our goal now is to describe how to take a **target language** with a formal operational semantics and combine it with an *information flow control language*. For example, taking ECMAScript as the target language and combining it with our IFC language should produce the formal semantics for the core part of COWL [4]. In this presentation, we use a simple, untyped lambda calculus with mutable references and fixpoint in place of ECMAScript to demonstrate some the key properties of the system (and, because the embedding does not care about the target language features); we discuss the proper embedding in more detail in Section 5.

Notation We have typeset nonterminals of the target language using **bold font** while the nonterminals of the IFC language have been typeset with *italic font*. Readers are encouraged to view a color copy of this paper, where target language nonterminals are colored **red** and IFC language nonterminals are colored *blue*.

2.2 Target Language: Mini-ES

In Fig. 1, we give a simple, untyped lambda calculus with mutable references and fixpoint, prepared for combination with an information flow control language. The presentation is mostly standard, and utilizes Felleisen-Hieb reduction semantics [10] to define the operational semantics of the system. One peculiarity is that our language defines an evaluation context $\mathbf{E}$, but, the evaluation rules have been expressed in terms of a different evaluation context $\mathcal{E}_\Sigma$; Here, we follow the approach of Matthews and Findler [3] in order to simplify combining semantics of multiple languages. To derive the usual operational semantics for this language, the evaluation context merely needs to be defined as $\mathcal{E}_\Sigma [\mathbf{e}] \triangleq \Sigma, \mathbf{E} [\mathbf{e}]$. However, when we combine this language with an IFC language, we reinterpret the meaning of this evaluation context.

$v ::= \lambda x.e \mid \textbf{true} \mid \textbf{false} \mid \textbf{a}$

$e ::= v \mid x \mid e\,e \mid \textbf{if } e \textbf{ then } e \textbf{ else } e \mid \textbf{ref } e \mid !e \mid e := e \mid \textbf{fix } e$

$E ::= [\cdot]_T \mid E\,e \mid v\,E \mid \textbf{if } E \textbf{ then } e \textbf{ else } e \mid \textbf{ref } E \mid !E \mid E := e \mid v := E \mid \textbf{fix } E$

$e_1; e_2 \qquad\qquad \triangleq (\lambda x.e_2)\,e_1 \text{ where } x \notin \mathcal{FV}(e_2)$

$\textbf{let } x = e_1 \textbf{ in } e_2 \triangleq (\lambda x.e_2)\,e_1$

T-APP   T-IFTRUE

$\mathcal{E}_\Sigma\,[(\lambda x.e)\,v] \rightarrow \mathcal{E}_\Sigma\,[\{v\,/\,x\}\,e]$ $\qquad\qquad$ $\mathcal{E}_\Sigma\,[\textbf{ if true then } e_1 \textbf{ else } e_2] \rightarrow \mathcal{E}_\Sigma\,[e_1]$

Fig. 1. λ_{ES}: simple untyped lambda calculus extended with booleans, mutable references and general recursion. For space reasons we only show two representative reduction rules; full rules can be found in the extended version of this paper.

In general, we require that a target language be expressed in terms of some global machine state Σ, some evaluation context E, some expressions e, some set of values v and a *deterministic* reduction relation on full configurations $\Sigma \times E \times e$.

2.3 IFC Language

As mentioned previously, most modern, dynamic information flow control languages encode policy by associating a label with data. Our embedding is agnostic to the choice of labeling scheme; we only require the labels to form a lattice [11] with the partial order $\sqsubseteq$, join $\sqcup$, and meet $\sqcap$. In this paper, we simply represent labels with the metavariable l, but do not discuss them in more detail. To enforce labels, the IFC monitor inspects the current label before performing a read or a write to decide whether the operation is permitted. A task can only write to entities that are at least as sensitive. Similarly, it can only read from entities that are less sensitive. However, as in other floating-label systems, this current label can be raised to allow the task to read from more sensitive entities at the cost of giving up the ability to write to others.

In Fig. 2, we give the syntax and *single-task* evaluation rules for a minimal information flow control language. Ordinarily, information flow control languages are defined by directly stating a base language plus information flow control operators. In contrast, our language is purposely minimal: it does not have sequencing operations, control flow, or other constructs. However, it contains support for the following core information flow control features:

- First-class labels, with label values l as well as operations for computing on labels ($\sqsubseteq$, $\sqcup$ and $\sqcap$).
- Operations for inspecting (**getLabel**) and modifying (**setLabel**) the current label of the task (a task can only increase its label).
- Operations for non-blocking inter-task communication (**send** and **recv**), which interact with the global store of per-task message queues Σ.
- A sandboxing operation used to spawn new isolated tasks. In concurrent settings **sandbox** corresponds to a fork-like primitive, whereas in a sequential setting, it more closely resembles computations which might temporarily raise the current floating-label [7, 12].

These operations are all defined with respect to an evaluation context $\mathcal{E}_{\Sigma}^{i,l}$ that represents the context of the current task. The evaluation context has three important pieces of state: the global message queues Σ, the current label l and the task ID i.

We note that first-class labels, tasks (albeit named differently), and operations for inspecting the current label are essentially universal to all floating-label systems. However, our choice of communication primitives is motivated by those present in browsers, namely **postMessage** [13]. Of course, other choices, such as blocking communication or labeled channels, are possible.

These asynchronous communication primitives are worth further discussion. When a task is sending a message using **send**, it also labels that message with a label l' (which must be at or above the task's current label l). Messages can only be received by a task if its current label is at least as high as the label of the message. Specifically, receiving a message using **recv** x_1, x_2 **in** e_1 **else** e_2 binds the message and the sender's task identifier to local variables x_1 and x_2, respectively, and then executes e_1. Otherwise, if there are no messages, that task continues its execution with e_2. We denote the filtering of the message queue by $\Theta \preceq l$, which is defined as follows. If Θ is the empty list **nil**, the function is simply the identity function, i.e., $\textbf{nil} \preceq l = \textbf{nil}$, and otherwise:

$$((l', i, e), \Theta) \preceq l = \begin{cases} (l', i, e), (\Theta \preceq l) & \text{if } l' \sqsubseteq l \\ \Theta \preceq l & \text{otherwise} \end{cases}$$

This ensures that tasks cannot receive messages that are more sensitive than their current label would allow.

2.4   The Embedding

Fig. 3 provides all of the rules responsible for actually carrying out the embedding of the IFC language within the target language. The most important feature of this embedding is that every task maintains its own copy of the target language global state and evaluation context, thus enforcing isolation between various tasks. In more detail:

- We extend the values, expressions and evaluation contexts of both languages to allow for terms in one language to be embedded in the other, as in [3]. In the target language, an IFC expression appears as $_{\text{TI}}\lfloor e \rfloor$ ("Target-outside, IFC-inside"); in the IFC language, a target language expression appears as $^{\text{IT}}\lceil e \rceil$ ("IFC-outside, target-inside").
- We reinterpret $\mathcal{E}$ to be evaluation contexts on task lists, providing definitions for $\mathcal{E}_{\Sigma}$ and $\mathcal{E}_{\Sigma}^{i,l}$. These rules only operate on the first task in the task list, which by convention is the only task executing.
- We reinterpret $\rightarrow$, an operation on a single task, in terms of $\hookrightarrow$, operation on task lists. The correspondence is simple: a task executes a step and then is rescheduled in the task list according to schedule policy α. Fig. 4 defines two concrete schedulers.

$$v ::= i \mid l \mid \textbf{true} \mid \textbf{false} \mid \langle\rangle \qquad\qquad \otimes \;\; ::= \sqsubseteq \mid \sqcup \mid \sqcap$$
$$e ::= v \mid x \mid e \otimes e \mid \textbf{getLabel} \mid \textbf{setLabel}\ e \mid \textbf{taskId} \mid \textbf{sandbox}\ e$$
$$\mid \textbf{send}\ e\ e\ e \mid \textbf{recv}\ x, x\ \textbf{in}\ e\ \textbf{else}\ e$$
$$E ::= [\cdot]_I \mid E \otimes e \mid v \otimes E \mid \textbf{setLabel}\ E \mid \textbf{send}\ E\ e\ e \mid \textbf{send}\ v\ E\ e \mid \textbf{send}\ v\ v\ E$$
$$\theta ::= (l, i\ e) \qquad\qquad \Theta ::= \textbf{nil} \mid \theta, \Theta \qquad\qquad \Sigma ::= \emptyset \mid \Sigma\,[i \mapsto \Theta]$$

I-GETTASKID

$$\mathcal{E}_\Sigma^{i,l}\,[\textbf{taskId}] \to \mathcal{E}_\Sigma^{i,l}\,[i]$$

I-GETLABEL

$$\mathcal{E}_\Sigma^{i,l}\,[\textbf{getLabel}] \to \mathcal{E}_\Sigma^{i,l}\,[l]$$

I-LABELOP
$$[\![l_1 \otimes l_2]\!] = v$$

$$\mathcal{E}_\Sigma^{i,l}\,[l_1 \otimes l_2] \to \mathcal{E}_\Sigma^{i,l}\,[v]$$

I-SEND
$$l \sqsubseteq l' \qquad \Sigma(i') = \Theta \qquad \Sigma' = \Sigma\,[i' \mapsto (l', i, v), \Theta]$$
$$\mathcal{E}_\Sigma^{i,l}\,[\textbf{send}\ i'\ l'\ v] \to \mathcal{E}_{\Sigma'}^{i,l}\,[\langle\rangle]$$

I-RECV
$$(\Sigma(i) \preceq l) = \theta_1, ..., \theta_k, (l', i', v) \qquad \Sigma' = \Sigma\,[i \mapsto (\theta_1, ..., \theta_k)]$$
$$\mathcal{E}_\Sigma^{i,l}\,[\textbf{recv}\ x_1, x_2\ \textbf{in}\ e_1\ \textbf{else}\ e_2] \to \mathcal{E}_{\Sigma'}^{i,l}\,[\{v\,/\,x_1, i'\,/\,x_2\}\ e_1]$$

I-NORECV
$$\Sigma(i) \preceq l = \textbf{nil} \qquad \Sigma' = \Sigma\,[i \mapsto \textbf{nil}]$$
$$\mathcal{E}_\Sigma^{i,l}\,[\textbf{recv}\ x_1, x_2\ \textbf{in}\ e_1\ \textbf{else}\ e_2] \to \mathcal{E}_{\Sigma'}^{i,l}\,[e_2]$$

I-SETLABEL
$$l \sqsubseteq l'$$
$$\mathcal{E}_\Sigma^{i,l}\,[\textbf{setLabel}\ l'] \to \mathcal{E}_\Sigma^{i,l'}\,[\langle\rangle]$$

Fig. 2. IFC language with all single-task operations

$$v ::= \cdots \mid {}^{\text{IT}}\lceil \mathbf{v} \rceil \qquad \mathbf{v} ::= \cdots \mid {}_{\text{TI}}\lfloor v \rfloor \qquad \mathcal{E}_{\boldsymbol{\Sigma}}\,[\mathbf{e}] \triangleq \Sigma; \langle \boldsymbol{\Sigma}, E[\mathbf{e}]_{\mathbf{T}} \rangle_l^i, \ldots$$
$$e ::= \cdots \mid {}^{\text{IT}}\lceil \mathbf{e} \rceil \qquad \mathbf{e} ::= \cdots \mid {}_{\text{TI}}\lfloor e \rfloor \qquad \mathcal{E}_\Sigma^{i,l}\,[e] \triangleq \Sigma; \langle \boldsymbol{\Sigma}, E[e]_I \rangle_l^i, \ldots$$
$$E ::= \cdots \mid {}^{\text{IT}}\lceil \mathbf{E} \rceil \qquad \mathbf{E} ::= \cdots \mid {}_{\text{TI}}\lfloor E \rfloor \qquad \mathcal{E}\,[e] \to \Sigma; t, \ldots \triangleq \mathcal{E}\,[e] \xrightarrow{\alpha} \Sigma; \alpha_{\text{step}}(t, \ldots)$$

I-SANDBOX
$$\Sigma' = \Sigma\,[i' \mapsto \textbf{nil}]$$
$$\boldsymbol{\Sigma}' = \kappa\,(\boldsymbol{\Sigma}) \qquad t_1 = \langle \boldsymbol{\Sigma}, E[i'] \rangle_l^i \qquad t_{\text{new}} = \langle \boldsymbol{\Sigma}', e \rangle_l^{i'} \qquad \text{fresh}(i')$$
$$\Sigma; \langle \boldsymbol{\Sigma}, E[\textbf{sandbox}\ e]_I \rangle_l^i, \ldots \xrightarrow{\alpha} \Sigma'; \alpha_{\text{sandbox}}(t_1, \ldots, t_{\text{new}})$$

I-DONE

$$\Sigma; \langle \boldsymbol{\Sigma}, v \rangle_l^i, \ldots \xrightarrow{\alpha} \Sigma; \alpha_{\text{done}}(\langle \boldsymbol{\Sigma}, v \rangle_l^i, \ldots)$$

I-NOSTEP
$$\Sigma; t, \ldots \not\xrightarrow{\ }$$

$$\Sigma; t, \ldots \xrightarrow{\alpha} \Sigma; \alpha_{\text{noStep}}(t, \ldots)$$

I-BORDER

$$\mathcal{E}_\Sigma^{i,l}\,\left[{}^{\text{IT}}\lceil {}_{\text{TI}}\lfloor e \rfloor \rceil\right] \to \mathcal{E}_\Sigma^{i,l}\,[e]$$

T-BORDER

$$\mathcal{E}_{\boldsymbol{\Sigma}}\,\left[{}_{\text{TI}}\lfloor {}^{\text{IT}}\lceil e \rceil \rfloor\right] \to \mathcal{E}_{\boldsymbol{\Sigma}}\,[e]$$

Fig. 3. The embedding $L_{\text{IFC}}(\alpha, \lambda)$, where $\lambda = (\boldsymbol{\Sigma}, \mathbf{E}, \mathbf{e}, \mathbf{v}, \to)$

$$
\begin{aligned}
\mathrm{RR}_{\mathrm{step}}(t_1, t_2, \ldots) &= t_2, \ldots, t_1 \\
\mathrm{RR}_{\mathrm{done}}(t_1, t_2, \ldots) &= t_2, \ldots \\
\mathrm{RR}_{\mathrm{noStep}}(t_1, t_2, \ldots) &= t_2, \ldots \\
\mathrm{RR}_{\mathrm{sandbox}}(t_1, t_2, \ldots) &= t_2, \ldots, t_1
\end{aligned}
\qquad
\begin{aligned}
\mathrm{SEQ}_{\mathrm{step}}(t_1, t_2, \ldots) &= t_1, t_2, \ldots \\
\mathrm{SEQ}_{\mathrm{noStep}}(t_1, t_2, \ldots) &= t_1, t_2, \ldots \\
\mathrm{SEQ}_{\mathrm{done}}(t) &= t \\
\mathrm{SEQ}_{\mathrm{done}}(t_1, t_2, \ldots) &= t_2, \ldots \\
\mathrm{SEQ}_{\mathrm{sandbox}}(t_1, t_2, \ldots, t_n) &= t_n, t_1, t_2, \ldots
\end{aligned}
$$

Fig. 4. Scheduling policies (concurrent round robin on the left, sequential on the right)

- Finally, we define some rules for scheduling, handling sandboxing tasks (which interact with the state of the target language), and intermediating between the borders of the two languages.

The I-SANDBOX rule is used to create a new isolated task that executes separately from the existing tasks (and can be communicated with via **send** and **recv**). When the new task is created, there is the question of what the target language state of the new task should be. Our rule is stated generically in terms of a function κ. Conservatively, κ may be simply thought of as the identity function, in which case the semantics of **sandbox** are such that the state of the target language is *cloned* when sandboxing occurs. However, this is not necessary: it is also valid for κ to remove entries from the state. In Section 4, we give a more detailed discussion of the implications of the choice of κ, but all our security claims will hold regardless of the choice of κ.

The rule I-NOSTEP says something about configurations for which it is not possible to take a transition. The notation $c \overset{\alpha}{\nrightarrow}$ in the premise is meant to be understood as follows: If the configuration c cannot take a step by any rule other than I-NOSTEP, then I-NOSTEP applies and the stuck task gets removed.

Rules I-DONE and I-NOSTEP define the behavior of the system when the current thread has reduced to a value, or gotten stuck, respectively. While these definitions simply rely on the underlying scheduling policy α to modify the task list, as we describe in Sections 3 and 6, these rules (notably, I-NOSTEP) are crucial to proving our security guarantees. For instance, it is unsafe for the whole system to get stuck if a particular task gets stuck, since a sensitive thread may then leverage this to leak information through the termination channel. Instead, as our example round-robin (RR) scheduler shows, such tasks should simply be removed from the task list. Many language runtime or Operating System schedulers implement such schedulers. Moreover, techniques such as instruction-based scheduling [14, 15] can be further applied close the gap between specified semantics and implementation.

As in [3], rules T-BORDER and I-BORDER define the syntactic boundaries between the IFC and target languages. Intuitively, the boundaries respectively correspond to an upcall into and downcall from the IFC runtime. As an example, taking λ_{ES} as the target language, we can now define a blocking receive (inefficiently) in terms of the asynchronous **recv** as series of cross-language calls:

$$
\mathbf{blockingRecv}\ x_1, x_2\ \mathbf{in}\ e \triangleq {}^{\mathrm{IT}}\lceil \mathbf{fix}\ (\lambda k._{\mathrm{TI}} \lfloor \mathbf{recv}\ x_1, x_2\ \mathbf{in}\ e\ \mathbf{else}\ {}^{\mathrm{IT}}\lceil k \rceil \rfloor) \rceil
$$

For any target language λ and scheduling policy α, this embedding defines an IFC language, which we will refer to as $L_{\mathrm{IFC}}(\alpha, \lambda)$.

3   Security Guarantees

We are interested in proving non-interference about many programming languages. This requires an appropriate definition of this notion that is language agnostic, so in this section, we present a few general definitions for what an information flow control language is and what non-interference properties it may have. In particular, we show that $L_{\mathrm{IFC}}(\alpha, \lambda)$, with an appropriate scheduler α, satisfies non-interference [6], without making any reference to properties of λ. We state the appropriate theorems here, and provide the formal proofs in the extended version of this paper.

3.1   Erasure Function

When defining the security guarantees of an information flow control, we must characterize what the *secret inputs* of a program are. Like other work [12, 16–18], we specify and prove non-interference using *term erasure*. Intuitively, term erasure allows us to show that an attacker does not learn any sensitive information from a program if the program behaves identically (from the attackers point of view) to a program with all sensitive data "erased". To interpret a language under information flow control, we define a function ε_l that performs erasures by mapping configurations to erased configurations, usually by rewriting (parts of) configurations that are more sensitive than l to a new syntactic construct •. We define an information flow control language as follows:

Definition 1 (Information flow control language). *An information flow control language L is a tuple $(\Delta, \hookrightarrow, \varepsilon_l)$, where Δ is the type of machine configurations (members of which are usually denoted by the metavariable c), $\hookrightarrow$ is a reduction relation between machine configurations and $\varepsilon_l : \Delta \to \varepsilon(\Delta)$ is an erasure function parametrized on labels from machine configurations to erased machine configurations $\varepsilon(\Delta)$. Sometimes, we use V to refer to set of terminal configurations in Δ, i.e., configurations where no further transitions are possible.*

Our language $L_{\mathrm{IFC}}(\alpha, \lambda)$ fulfills this definition as $(\Delta, \overset{\alpha}{\hookrightarrow}, \varepsilon_l)$, where $\Delta = \Sigma \times$ List(t). The set of terminal conditions V is $\Sigma \times t_V$, where $t_V \subset t$ is the type for tasks whose expressions have been reduced to values.[1] The erased configuration $\varepsilon(\Delta)$ extends Δ with configurations containing •, and Fig. 5 gives the precise definition for our erasure function ε_l. Essentially, a task and its corresponding message queue is completely erased from the task list if its label does not flow to the attacker observation level l. Otherwise, we apply the erasure function homomorphically and remove any messages from the task's message queue that are more sensitive than l.

The definition of an erasure function is quite important: it captures the attacker model, stating what can and cannot be observed by the attacker. In our case, we assume that the attacker cannot observe sensitive tasks or messages, or even the

---

[1] Here, we abuse notation by describing types for configuration parts using the same metavariables as the "instance" of the type, e.g., t for the type of task.

$$\varepsilon_l(\Sigma; ts) = \varepsilon_l(\Sigma); \text{filter } (\lambda t.t = \bullet) \text{ (map } \varepsilon_l \ ts)$$

$$\varepsilon_l(\langle \mathbf{\Sigma}, e \rangle_{l'}^i) = \begin{cases} \bullet & l' \not\sqsubseteq l \\ \langle \varepsilon_l(\mathbf{\Sigma}), \varepsilon_l(e) \rangle_{l'}^i & \text{otherwise} \end{cases}$$

$$\varepsilon_l(\Sigma \, [i \mapsto \Theta]) = \begin{cases} \varepsilon_l(\Sigma) & l' \not\sqsubseteq l, \text{ where } l' \text{ is the label of thread } i \\ \varepsilon_l(\Sigma) \, [i \mapsto \varepsilon_l(\Theta)] & \text{otherwise} \end{cases}$$

$$\varepsilon_l(\Theta) = \Theta \preceq l \qquad\qquad \varepsilon_l(\emptyset) = \emptyset$$

Fig. 5. Erasure function for tasks, queue maps, message queues, and configurations. In all other cases, including target-language constructs, ε_l is applied homomorphically. Note that $\varepsilon_l(e)$ is always equal to e (and similar for $\mathbf{\Sigma}$) in this simple setting. However, when the IFC language is extended with more constructs as shown in Section 6, then this will no longer be the case.

number of such entities. While such assumptions are standard [18, 19], our definitions allow for stronger attackers that may be able to inspect resource usage.[2]

3.2   Non-interference

Given an information flow control language, we can now define non-interference. Intuitively, we want to make statements about the attacker's observational power at some security level l. This is done by defining an equivalence relation called l-equivalence on configurations: an attacker should not be able to distinguish two configurations that are l-equivalent. Since our erasure function captures what an attacker can or cannot observe, we simply define this equivalence as the syntactic-equivalence of erased configurations [18].

Definition 2 (l-equivalence). *In a language $(\Delta, \hookrightarrow, \varepsilon_l)$, two machine configurations $c, c' \in \Delta$ are considered l-equivalent, written as $c \approx_l c'$, if $\varepsilon_l(c) = \varepsilon_l(c')$.*

We can now state that a language satisfies non-interference if an attacker at level l cannot distinguish the runs of any two l-equivalent configurations. This particular property is called termination sensitive non-interference (TSNI). Besides the obvious requirement to not leak secret information to public channels, this definition also requires the termination of public tasks to be independent of secret tasks. Formally, we define TSNI as follows:

Definition 3 (Termination Sensitive Non-Interference (TSNI)). *A language $(\Delta, \hookrightarrow, \varepsilon_l)$ satisfies termination sensitive non-interference if for any label l, and configurations $c_1, c_1', c_2 \in \Delta$, if*

$$c_1 \approx_l c_2 \qquad and \qquad c_1 \hookrightarrow^* c_1' \tag{1}$$

then there exists a configuration $c_2' \in \Delta$ such that

$$c_1' \approx_l c_2' \qquad and \qquad c_2 \hookrightarrow^* c_2' \ . \tag{2}$$

---

[2] We believe that we can extend $L_{\text{IFC}}(\alpha, \lambda)$ to such models using the resource limits techniques of [20]. We leave this extension to future work.

In other words, if we take two l-equivalent configurations, then for every intermediate step taken by the first configuration, there is a corresponding number of steps that the second configuration can take to result in a configuration that is l-equivalent to the first resultant configuration. By symmetry, this applies to all intermediate steps from the second configuration as well.

Our language satisfies TSNI under the round-robin scheduler RR of Fig. 4.

Theorem 1 (Concurrent IFC language is TSNI). *For any target language* λ, $L_{IFC}(\mathrm{RR}, \lambda)$ *satisfies TSNI.*

In general, however, non-interference will not hold for an arbitrary scheduler α. For example, $L_{\mathrm{IFC}}(\alpha, \lambda)$ with a scheduler that inspects a sensitive task's current state when deciding which task to schedule next will in general break non-interference [21, 22].

However, even non-adversarial schedulers are not always safe. Consider, for example, the sequential scheduling policy SEQ given in Fig. 4. It is easy to show that $L_{\mathrm{IFC}}(\mathrm{SEQ}, \lambda)$ does not satisfy TSNI: consider a target language similar to λ_{ES} with an additional expression terminal $\Uparrow$ that denotes a divergent computation, i.e., $\Uparrow$ always reduces to $\Uparrow$ and a simple label lattice $\{\mathsf{pub}, \mathsf{sec}\}$ such that $\mathsf{pub} \sqsubseteq \mathsf{sec}$, but $\mathsf{sec} \not\sqsubseteq \mathsf{pub}$. Consider the following two configurations in this language:

$$c_1 = \Sigma; \langle \Sigma_1, {}^{\mathrm{IT}}\lceil \textbf{ if false then } \Uparrow \textbf{ else true} \rceil \rangle^1_{\mathsf{sec}}, \langle \Sigma_2, e \rangle^2_{\mathsf{pub}}$$
$$c_2 = \Sigma; \langle \Sigma_1, {}^{\mathrm{IT}}\lceil \textbf{ if true then } \Uparrow \textbf{ else true} \rceil \rangle^1_{\mathsf{sec}}, \langle \Sigma_2, e \rangle^2_{\mathsf{pub}}$$

These two configurations are pub-equivalent, but c_1 will reduce (in two steps) to $c'_1 = \Sigma; \langle \Sigma_1, {}^{\mathrm{IT}}\lceil \textbf{true} \rceil \rangle^2_{\mathsf{pub}}$, whereas c_2 will not make any progress. Suppose that e is a computation that writes to a pub channel,[3] then the sec task's decision to diverge or not is directly leaked to a public entity.

To accommodate for sequential languages, or cases where a weaker guarantee is sufficient, we consider an alternative non-interference property called termination insensitive non-interference (TINI). This property can also be upheld by sequential languages at the cost of leaking through (non)-termination [23].

Definition 4 (Termination insensitive non-interference (TINI)). *A language* $(\Delta, V, \hookrightarrow, \varepsilon_l)$ *is termination insensitive non-interfering if for any label l, and configurations $c_1, c_2 \in \Delta$ and $c'_1, c'_2 \in V$, it holds that*

$$(c_1 \approx_l c_2 \ \wedge \ c_1 \hookrightarrow^* c'_1 \ \wedge \ c_2 \hookrightarrow^* c'_2) \implies c'_1 \approx_l c'_2$$

TINI states that if we take two l-equivalent configurations, and both configurations reduce to final configurations (i.e., configurations for which there are no possible further transitions), then the end configurations are also l-equivalent. We highlight that this statement is much weaker than TSNI: it only states that terminating programs do not leak sensitive data, but makes no statement about non-terminating programs.

---

[3] hough we do not model labeled channels, extending the calculus with such a feature is straightforward, see Section 6.

As shown by compilers [24, 25], interpreters [2], and libraries [12, 17], TINI is useful for sequential settings. In our case, we show that our IFC language with the sequential scheduling policy SEQ satisfies TINI.

Theorem 2 (Sequential IFC language is TINI). *For any target language* λ, $L_{IFC}(\text{SEQ}, \lambda)$ *satisfies TINI.*

4   Isomorphisms and Restrictions

The operational semantics we have defined in the previous section satisfy non-interference by design. We achieve this general statement that works for a large class of languages by having different tasks executing completely isolated from each other, such that every task has its own state. In some cases, this strong separation is desirable, or even necessary. Languages like C provide direct access to memory locations without mechanisms in the language to achieve a separation of the heap. On the other hand, for other languages, this strong isolation of tasks can be undesirable, e.g., for performance reasons. For instance, for the language λ_{ES}, our presentation so far requires a separate heap per task, which is not very practical. Instead, we would like to more tightly couple the integration of the target and IFC languages by reusing existing infrastructure. In the running example, a concrete implementation might use a single global heap. More precisely, instead of using a configuration of the form $\Sigma; \langle \Sigma_1, e_1 \rangle_{l_1}^{i_1}, \langle \Sigma_2, e_2 \rangle_{l_2}^{i_2} \cdots$ we would like a single global heap as in $\Sigma; \Sigma; \langle e_1 \rangle_{l_1}^{i_1}, \langle e_2 \rangle_{l_2}^{i_2}, \ldots$

If the operational rules are adapted naïvely to this new setting, then non-interference can be violated: as we mentioned earlier, shared mutable cells could be used to leak sensitive information. What we would like is a way of characterizing safe modifications to the semantics which preserve non-interference. The intention of our single heap implementation is to permit efficient execution while *conceptually maintaining isolation between tasks* (by not allowing sharing of references between them). This intuition of having a different (potentially more efficient) concrete semantics that behaves like the abstract semantics can be formalized by the following definition:

Definition 5 (Isomorphism of information flow control languages). *A language* $(\Delta, \hookrightarrow, \varepsilon_l)$ *is isomorphic to a language* $(\Delta', \hookrightarrow', \varepsilon'_l)$ *if there exist total functions* $f : \Delta \to \Delta'$ *and* $f^{-1} : \Delta' \to \Delta$ *such that* $f \circ f^{-1} = id_\Delta$ *and* $f^{-1} \circ f = id_{\Delta'}$. *Furthermore,* f *and* f^{-1} *are functorial (e.g., if* x' R' y' *then* $f(x')$ R $f(y')$*) over both l-equivalences and* $\hookrightarrow$.

If we weaken this restriction such that f^{-1} *does not have to be functorial over* $\hookrightarrow$, *we call the language* $(\Delta, \hookrightarrow, \varepsilon_l)$ *weakly isomorphic to* $(\Delta', \hookrightarrow', \varepsilon'_l)$.

Providing an isomorphism between the two languages allows us to preserve (termination sensitive or insensitive) non-interference as the following two theorems state.

Theorem 3 (Isomorphism preserves TSNI). *If* L *is isomorphic to* L' *and* L' *satisfies TSNI, then* L *satisfies TSNI.*

Proof. Shown by transporting configurations and reduction derivations from L to L', applying TSNI, and then transporting the resulting configuration, l-equivalence and multi-step derivation back.   □

Only weak isomorphism is necessary for TINI. Intuitively, this is because it is not necessary to back-translate reduction sequences in L' to L; by the definition of TINI, we have both reduction sequences in L by assumption.

Theorem 4 (Weak isomorphism preserves TINI). *If a language L is weakly isomorphic to a language L', and L' satisfies TINI, then L satisfies TINI.*

Proof. Shown by transporting configurations and reduction derivations from L to L', applying TINI and transporting the resulting equivalence back using functoriality of f^{-1} over l-equivalences.   □

Unfortunately, an isomorphism is often too strong of a requirement. To obtain an isomorphism with our single heap semantics, we need to mimic the behavior of several heaps with a single actual heap. The interesting cases are when we sandbox an expression and when messages are sent and received. The rule for sandboxing is parametrized by the strategy κ (see Section 2), which defines what heap the new task should execute with. We have considered two choices:

- When we sandbox into an empty heap, existing addresses in the sandboxed expression are no longer valid and the task will get stuck (and then removed by I-NOSTEP). Thus, we must rewrite the sandboxed expression so that all addresses point to fresh addresses guaranteed to not occur in the heap. Similarly, sending a memory address should be rewritten.
- When we clone the heap, we have to copy everything reachable from the sandboxed expression and replace all addresses correspondingly. Even worse, the behavior of sending a memory address now depends on whether that address existed at the time the receiving task was sandboxed; if it did, then the address should be rewritten to the existing one.

Isomorphism demands we implement this convoluted behavior, despite our initial motivation of a more efficient implementation.

4.1   Restricting the IFC Language

A better solution is to forbid sandboxed expressions as well as messages sent to other tasks to contain memory addresses in the first place. In a statically typed language, the type system could prevent this from happening. In dynamically typed languages such as λ_{ES}, we might restrict the transition for **sandbox** and **send** to only allow expressions without memory addresses.

While this sounds plausible, it is worth noting that we are modifying the IFC language semantics, which raises the question of whether non-interference is preserved. This question can be subtle: it is easy to remove a transition from a language and invalidate TSNI. Intuitively if the restriction depends on secret data, then a public thread can observe if some other task terminates or not, and from that obtain information about the secret data that was used to restrict the transition. With this in mind, we require semantic rules to get restricted only based on information observable by the task triggering them. This ensures that non-interference is preserved, as the restriction does not depend on confidential information. Below, we give the formal definition of this condition for the abstract IFC language $L_{IFC}(\alpha, \lambda)$.

Definition 6 (Restricted IFC language). *For a family of predicates $\mathcal{P}$ (one for every reduction rule), we call $L_{IFC}^{\mathcal{P}}(\alpha, \lambda)$ a restricted IFC language if its definition is equivalent to the abstract language $L_{IFC}(\alpha, \lambda)$, with the following exception: the reduction rules are restricted by adding a predicate $P \in \mathcal{P}$ to the premise of all rules other than* I-NOSTEP. *Furthermore, the predicate P can depend only on the erased configuration $\varepsilon_l(c)$, where l is the label of the first task in the task list and c is the full configuration.*

By the following theorem, the restricted IFC language with an appropriate scheduling policy is non-interfering.

Theorem 5. *For any target language λ and family of predicates $\mathcal{P}$, the restricted IFC language $L_{IFC}^{\mathcal{P}}(\mathrm{RR}, \lambda)$ is TSNI. Furthermore, the IFC language $L_{IFC}^{\mathcal{P}}(\mathrm{SEQ}, \lambda)$ is TINI.*

In the extended version of this paper we give an example how this formalism can be used to show non-intereference of an implementation of IFC with a single heap.

5   Real World Languages

Our approach can be used to retrofit any language for which we can achieve isolation with information flow control. Unfortunately, controlling the external effects of a real-world language, as to achieve isolation, is language-specific and varies from one language to another.[4] Indeed, even for a single language (e.g., JavaScript), how one achieves isolation may vary according to the language runtime or embedding (e.g., server and browser).

In this section, we describe several implementations and their approaches to isolation. In particular, we describe two JavaScript IFC implementations building on the theoretical foundations of this work. Then, we consider how our formalism could be applied to the C programming language and connect it to a previous IFC system for Haskell.

5.1   JavaScript

JavaScript, as specified by ECMAScript [26], does not have any built-in functionality for I/O. For this language, which we denote by λ_{JS}, the IFC system $L_{IFC}(\mathrm{RR}, \lambda_{JS})$ can be implemented by exposing IFC primitives to JavaScript as part of the runtime, and running multiple instances of the JavaScript virtual machine in separate OS-level threads. Unfortunately, this becomes very costly when a system, such as a server-side web application, relies on many tasks.

---

[4] Though we apply our framework to several real-world languages, it is conceivable that there are languages for which isolation cannot be easily achieved.

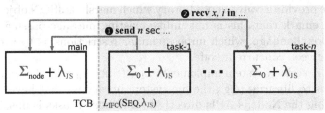

Fig. 6. This example shows how our trusted monitor (left) is used to mediate communication between two tasks for which IFC is enforced (right)

Luckily, this issue is not unique to our work—browser layout engines also rely on isolating code executing in separate iframes (e.g., according to the same-origin policy). Since creating an OS thread for each iframe is expensive, both the V8 and SpiderMonkey JavaScript engines provide means for running JavaScript code in isolation within a single OS thread, on disjoint sub-heaps. In V8, this unit of isolation is called a *context*; in SpiderMonkey, it is called a *compartment*. (We will use these terms interchangeably.) Each context is associated with a global object, which, by default, implements the JavaScript standard library (e.g., `Object`, `Array`, etc.). Naturally, we adopt contexts to implement our notion of tasks.

When JavaScript is embedded in browser layout engines, or in server-side platforms such as Node.js, additional APIs such as the Document Object Model (DOM) or the file system get exposed as part of the runtime system. These features are exposed by extending the global object, just like the standard library. For this reason, it is easy to modify these systems to forbid external effects when implementing an IFC system, ensuring that important effects can be reintroduced in a safe manner.

Server-side IFC for Node.js: We have implemented $L_{\text{IFC}}(\text{SEQ}, \lambda_{\text{JS}})$ for Node.js in the form of a library, without modifying Node.js or the V8 JavaScript engine. Our implementation[5] provides a library for creating new tasks, i.e., contexts whose global object only contains the standard JavaScript library and our IFC primitives (e.g., **send** and **sandbox**). When mapped to our formal treatment, **sandbox** is defined with $\kappa(\Sigma) = \Sigma_0$, where Σ_0 is the global object corresponding to the standard JavaScript library and our IFC primitives. These IFC operations are mediated by the trusted library code (executing as the main Node.js context), which tracks the state (current label, messages, etc.) of each task. An example for **send**/**recv** is shown in Fig. 6. Our system conservatively restricts the kinds of messages that can be exchanged, via **send** (and **sandbox**), to string values. In our formalization, this amounts to restricting the IFC language rule for **send** in the following way:

$$
\text{JS-SEND}
$$
$$
l \sqsubseteq l' \qquad \Sigma\,(i') = \Theta \qquad \Sigma' = \Sigma\,[i' \mapsto (l', i, v), \Theta]
$$
$$
e = {}^{\text{IT}}\lceil e\rceil \qquad \mathcal{E}_\Sigma\,[\texttt{typeOf(e)} \; \texttt{===} \; \texttt{"string"}] \to \mathcal{E}_\Sigma\,[\texttt{true}]
$$
$$
\Sigma; \langle \Sigma, E[\textbf{send}\; i'\; l'\; v]_I\rangle_l^i, \ldots \hookrightarrow \Sigma'; \alpha_{\text{step}}(\langle \Sigma, E[\langle\rangle]_I\rangle_l^i, \ldots)
$$

---

[5] Available at `http://github.com/deian/espectro`

Of course, we provide a convenience library which marshals JSON objects to/from strings. We remark that this is not unlike existing message-passing JavaScript APIs, e.g., `postMessage`, which impose similar restrictions as to avoid sharing references between concurrent code.

While the described system implements $L_{\text{IFC}}(\text{SEQ}, \lambda_{\text{JS}})$, applications typically require access to libraries (e.g., the file system library `fs`) that have external effects. Exposing the Node.js APIs directly to sandboxed tasks is unsafe. Instead, we implement libraries (like a labeled version of `fs`) as message exchanges between the sandboxed tasks (e.g., task-1 in Fig. 6) and the main Node.js task that implements the IFC monitor. While this is safer than simply wrapping unsafe objects, which can potentially be exploited to access objects outside the context (e.g., as seen with ADSafe [27]), adding features such as the `fs` requires the code in the main task to ensures that labels are properly propagated and enforced. Unfortunately, while imposing such a proof burden is undesirable, this also has to be expected: different language environments expose different libraries for handling external I/O, and the correct treatment of external effects is application specific. We do not extend our formalism to account for the particular interface to the file system, HTTP client, etc., as this is specific to the Node.js implementation and does not generalize to other systems.

Client-side IFC: This work provides the formal basis for the core part of the COWL client-side JavaScript IFC system [4]. Like our Node.js implementation, COWL takes a coarse-grained approach to providing IFC for JavaScript programs. However, COWL's IFC monitor is implemented in the browser layout engine instead (though still leaving the JavaScript engine unmodified).

Furthermore, COWL repurposes existing contexts (e.g., iframes and pages) as IFC tasks, only imposing additional constraints on how they communicate. As with Node.js, at its core, the global object of a COWL task should only contain the standard JavaScript libraries and `postMessage`, whose semantics are modeled by our JS-SEND rule. However, existing contexts have objects such as the DOM, which require COWL to restrict a task's external effects. To this end, COWL mediates any communication (even via the DOM) at the context boundary.

Simply disallowing all the external effects is overly-restricting for real-world applications (e.g., pages typically load images, perform network requests, etc.). In this light, COWL allows safe network communication by associating an implicit label with remote hosts (a host's label corresponds to its origin). In turn, when a task performs a request, COWL's IFC monitor ensures that the task label can flow to the remote origin label. While the external effects of COWL can be formally modeled, we do not model them in our formalism, since, like for the Node.js case, they are specific to this system.

5.2 Haskell

Our work borrows ideas from the LIO Haskell coarse-grained IFC system [12, 18]. LIO relies on Haskell's type system and monadic encoding of effects to achieve isolation and define the IFC sub-language. Specifically, LIO provides the `LIO` monad as a way of restricting (almost all) side-effects. In the context of our framework, LIO can be understood as follows: the *pure subset* of Haskell is the target language, while the monadic subset of Haskell, operating in the LIO monad, is the IFC language.

Unlike our proposal, LIO originally associated labels with exceptions, in a similar style to fine-grained systems [7, 8]. In addition to being overly complex, the interaction of exceptions with clearance (which sets an upper bound on the floating label, see the extended version of this paper) was incorrect: the clearance was restored to the clearance at point of the catch. Furthermore, pure exceptions (e.g., divide by zero) always percolated to trusted code, effectively allowing for denial of service attacks. The insights gained when viewing coarse-grained IFC as presented in this paper led to a much cleaner, simpler treatment of exceptions, which has now been adopted by LIO.

5.3   C

C programs are able to execute arbitrary (machine) code, access arbitrary memory, and perform arbitrary system calls. Thus, the confinement of C programs must be imposed by the underlying OS and hardware. For instance, our notion of isolation can be achieved using Dune's hardware protection mechanisms [28], similar to Wedge [28, 29], but using an information flow control policy. Using page tables, a (trusted) IFC runtime could ensure that each task, implemented as a lightweight process, can only access the memory it allocates—tasks do not have access to any shared memory. In addition, ring protection could be used to intercept system calls performed by a task and only permit those corresponding to our IFC language (such as **getLabel** or **send**). Dune's hardware protection mechanism would allow us to provide a concrete implementation that is efficient and relatively simple to reason about, but other sandboxing mechanisms could be used in place of Dune.

In this setting, the combined language of Section 2 can be interpreted in the following way: calling from the target language to the IFC language corresponds to invoking a system call. Creating a new task with the **sandbox** system call corresponds to *forking* a process. Using page tables, we can ensure that there will be no shared memory (effectively defining $\kappa(\Sigma) = \Sigma_0$, where Σ_0 is the set of pages necessary to bootstrap a lightweight process). Similarly, control over page tables and protection bits allows us to define a **send** system call that copies pages to our (trusted) runtime queue; and, correspondingly, a **recv** that copies the pages from the runtime queue to the (untrusted) receiver. Since C is not memory safe, conditions on these system calls are meaningless. We leave the implementation of this IFC system for C as future work.

6   Extensions and Limitations

While the IFC language presented thus far provides the basic information flow primitives, actual IFC implementations may wish to extend the minimal system with more specialized constructs. For example, COWL provides a labeled version of the XMLHttpRequest (XHR) object, which is used to make network requests.

Our system can be extended with constructs such as labeled values, labeled mutable references, clearance, and privileges. For space reasons, we provide details of this, including the soundness proof with the extensions, in the appendix of the extended version of this paper. Here, we instead discuss a limitation of our formalism: the lack of external effects.

Specifically, our embedding assumes that the target language does not have any primitives that can induce external effects. As discussed in Section 5, imposing this restriction can be challenging. Yet, external effects are crucial when implementing more complex real-world applications. For example, code in an IFC browser must load resources or perform XHR to be useful.

Like labeled references, features with external effects must be modeled in the IFC language; we must reason about the precise security implications of features that otherwise inherently leak data. Previous approaches have modeled external effects by internalizing the effects as operations on labeled channels/references [18]. Alternatively, it is possible to model such effects as messages to/from certain labeled tasks, an approach taken by our Node.js implementation. These "special" tasks are trusted with access to the unlabeled primitives that can be used to perform the external effects; since the interface to these tasks is already part of the IFC language, the proof only requires showing that this task does not leak information. Instead of restricting or wrapping unsafe primitives, COWL allow for controlled network communication at the context boundary. (By restricting the default XHR object, for example, COWL allows code to communicate with hosts according to the task's current label.)

7   Related Work

Our information flow control system is closely related to the coarse-grained information systems used in operating systems such as Asbestos [30], HiStar [1], and Flume [31], as well as language-based *floating-label IFC systems* such as LIO [12], and Breeze [7], where there is a monotonically increased label associated with threads of execution. Our treatment of termination-sensitive and termination-insensitive interference originates from Smith and Volpano [32, 33].

One information flow control technique designed to handle legacy code is secure multi-execution (SME) [34, 35]. SME runs multiple copies of the program, one per security level, where the semantics of I/O interactions is altered. Bielova et al. [36] use a transition system to describe SME, where the details of the underlying language are hidden. Zanarini et al. [37] propose a novel semantics for programs based on interaction trees [38], which treats programs as black-boxes about which nothing is known, except what can be inferred from their interaction with the environment. Similar to SME, our approach mediates I/O operations; however, our approach only runs the program once.

One of the primary motivations behind this paper is the application of information flow control to JavaScript. Previous systems retrofitted JavaScript with fine-grained IFC [2, 9]. While fine-grained IFC can result in fewer false alarms and target legacy code, it comes at the cost of complexity: the system must accommodate the entirety of JavaScript's semantics [2]. By contrast, coarse-grained approaches to security tend to have simpler implications [39, 40].

The constructs in our IFC language, as well as the behavior of inter-task communication, are reminiscent of distributed systems like Erlang [41]. In distributed systems, isolation is required due to physical constraints; in information flow control, isolation is required to enforce non-interference. Papagiannis et al. [42] built an information flow control system on top of Erlang that shares some similarities to ours. However, they do not take a floating-label approach (processes can find out when sending a message failed due to a forbidden information flow), nor do they provide security proofs.

There is limited work on general techniques for retrofitting arbitrary languages with information flow control. However, one time-honored technique is to define a fundamental calculus for which other languages can be desugared into. Abadi et al. [43] motivate their core calculus of dependency by showing how various previous systems can be encoded in it. Tse and Zdancewic [44], in turn, show how this calculus can be encoded in System F via parametricity. Broberg and Sands [45] encode several IFC systems into Paralocks. However, this line of work is primarily focused on static enforcements.

8   Conclusion

In this paper, we argued that when designing a coarse-grained IFC system, it is better to start with a fully isolated, multi-task system and work one's way back to the model of a single language equipped with IFC. We showed how systems designed this way can be proved non-interferent without needing to rely on details of the target language, and we provided conditions on how to securely refine our formal semantics to consider optimizations required in practice. We connected our semantics to two IFC implementations for JavaScript based on this formalism, explained how our methodology improved an exiting IFC system for Haskell, and proposed an IFC system for C using hardware isolation. By systematically applying ideas from IFC in operating systems to programming languages for which isolation can be achieved, we hope to have elucidated some of the core design principles of coarse-grained, dynamic IFC systems.

Acknowledgements. We thank the POST 2015 anonymous reviewers, Adriaan Larmuseau, Sergio Maffeis, and David Mazières for useful comments and suggestions. This work was funded by DARPA CRASH under contract #N66001-10-2-4088, by the NSF, by the AFOSR, by multiple gifts from Google, by a gift from Mozilla, and by the Swedish research agencies VR and the Barbro Oshers Pro Suecia Foundation. Deian Stefan and Edward Z. Yang were supported by the DoD through the NDSEG.

References

[1] Zeldovich, N., Boyd-Wickizer, S., Kohler, E., Mazières, D.: Making information flow explicit in HiStar. In: OSDI (2006)

[2] Hedin, D., Birgisson, A., Bello, L., Sabelfeld, A.: JSFlow: Tracking information flow in JavaScript and its APIs. In: SAC (2014)

[3] Matthews, J., Findler, R.B.: Operational semantics for multi-language programs. In: POPL (2007)

[4] Stefan, D., Yang, E.Z., Marchenko, P., Russo, A., Herman, D., Karp, B., Mazières, D.: Protecting users by confining JavaScript with COWL. In: OSDI (2014)

[5] Heule, S., Stefan, D., Yang, E.Z., Mitchell, J.C., Russo, A.: Ifc inside: Retrofitting languages with dynamic information flow control (2015), http://cowl.ws/ifc-inside.pdf

[6] Goguen, J., Meseguer, J.: Security policies and security Models. In: SP (1982)

[7] Hritcu, C., Greenberg, M., Karel, B., Pierce, B.C., Morrisett, G.: All your IFCException are belong to us. In: SP (2013)

[8] Stefan, D., Russo, A., Mitchell, J.C., Mazières, D.: Flexible dynamic information flow control in the presence of exceptions. Arxiv preprint arXiv:1207.1457 (2012)

[9] Hedin, D., Sabelfeld, A.: Information-flow security for a core of javascript. In: CSF (2012)

[10] Felleisen, M., Hieb, R.: The revised report on the syntactic theories of sequential control and state. TCS 103 (1992)

[11] Denning, D.E.: A lattice model of secure information flow. Commun. ACM 19 (1976)

[12] Stefan, D., Russo, A., Mitchell, J.C., Mazières, D.: Flexible dynamic information flow control in Haskell. In: Haskell (2011)

[13] W3C: HTML5 web messaging (2012), http://www.w3.org/TR/webmessaging/

[14] Stefan, D., Buiras, P., Yang, E.Z., Levy, A., Terei, D., Russo, A., Mazières, D.: Eliminating cache-based timing attacks with instruction-based scheduling. In: ESORICS (2013)

[15] Buiras, P., Levy, A., Stefan, D., Russo, A., Mazières, D.: A library for removing cache-based attacks in concurrent information flow systems. In: TGC (2013)

[16] Li, P., Zdancewic, S.: Arrows for secure information flow. TCS 411 (2010)

[17] Russo, A., Claessen, K., Hughes, J.: A library for light-weight information-flow security in Haskell. In: Haskell (2008)

[18] Stefan, D., Russo, A., Buiras, P., Levy, A., Mitchell, J.C., Mazières, D.: Addressing covert termination and timing channels in concurrent information flow systems. In: ICFP (2012)

[19] Boudol, C.: Noninterference for concurrent programs. In: ICALP (2001)

[20] Yang, E.Z., Mazières, D.: Dynamic space limits for Haskell. In: PLDI (2014)

[21] Russo, A., Sabelfeld, A.: Securing Interaction between threads and the scheduler. In: CSFW (2006)

[22] Barthe, G., Rezk, T., Russo, A., Sabelfeld, A.: Security of multithreaded programs by compilation. In: ESORICS (2007)

[23] Askarov, A., Hunt, S., Sabelfeld, A., Sands, D.: Termination-insensitive noninterference leaks more than just a bit. In: ESORICS (2008)

[24] Myers, A.C., Zheng, L., Zdancewic, S., Chong, S., Nystrom, N.: Jif: Java Information Flow. Software release (2001), Located at http://www.cs.cornell.edu/jif

[25] Simonet, V.: The Flow Caml system (2003), Software release at http://cristal.inria.fr/~simonet/soft/flowcaml/

[26] Ecma International: ECMAScript language specification (2014),
     http://www.ecma.org/
[27] Taly, A., Mitchell, J.C., Miller, M.S., Nagra, J.: Automated analysis of security-critical javascript apis. In: SP (2011)
[28] Belay, A., Bittau, A., Mashtizadeh, A., Terei, D., Mazières, D., Kozyrakis, C.: Dune: Safe user-level access to privileged CPU features. In: OSDI (2012)
[29] Bittau, A., Marchenko, P., Handley, M., Karp, B.: Wedge: Splitting applications into reduced-privilege compartments. In: NSDI (2008)
[30] Efstathopoulos, P., Krohn, M., VanDeBogart, S., Frey, C., Ziegler, D., Kohler, E., Mazières, D., Kaashoek, F., Morris, R.: Labels and event processes in the Asbestos operating system. In: SOSP (2005)
[31] Krohn, M., Yip, A., Brodsky, M., Cliffer, N., Kaashoek, M.F., Kohler, E., Morris, R.: Information flow control for standard OS abstractions. In: SOSP (2007)
[32] Smith, G., Volpano, D.: Secure information flow in a multi-threaded imperative language. In: POPL (1998)
[33] Volpano, D., Smith, G.: Eliminating covert flows with minimum typings. In: CSFW (1997)
[34] Devriese, D., Piessens, F.: Noninterference through secure multi-execution. In: SP (2010)
[35] Rafnsson, W., Sabelfeld, A.: Secure multi-execution: fine-grained, declassification-aware, and transparent. In: CSF (2013)
[36] Bielova, N., Devriese, D., Massacci, F., Piessens, F.: Reactive non-interference for a browser model. In: NSS (2011)
[37] Zanarini, D., Jaskelioff, M., Russo, A.: Precise enforcement of confidentiality for reactive systems. In: CSF (2013)
[38] Jacobs, B., Rutten, J.: A Tutorial on (Co)Algebras and (Co)Induction. EATCS 62 (1997)
[39] Yip, A., Narula, N., Krohn, M., Morris, R.: Privacy-preserving browser-side scripting with BFlow. In: EuroSys (2009)
[40] De Groef, W., Devriese, D., Nikiforakis, N., Piessens, F.: FlowFox: a web browser with flexible and precise information flow control. In: CCS (2012)
[41] Armstrong, J.: Making reliable distributed systems in the presence of software errors (2003)
[42] Papagiannis, I., Migliavacca, M., Eyers, D.M., Sh, B., Bacon, J., Pietzuch, P.: Enforcing user privacy in web applications using Erlang. In: W2SP (2010)
[43] Abadi, M., Banerjee, A., Heintze, N., Riecke, J.: A Core Calculus of Dependency. In: POPL (1999)
[44] Tse, S., Zdancewic, S.: Translating dependency into parametricity. In: ICFP (2004)
[45] Broberg, N., Sands, D.: Paralocks: Role-based information flow control and beyond. In: POPL (2010)

Very Static Enforcement of Dynamic Policies

Bart van Delft[1], Sebastian Hunt[2], and David Sands[1]

[1] Chalmers University of Technology, Sweden
[2] City University London

Abstract. Security policies are naturally dynamic. Reflecting this, there has been a growing interest in studying information-flow properties which change during program execution, including concepts such as declassification, revocation, and role-change.

A static verification of a dynamic information flow policy, from a semantic perspective, should only need to concern itself with two things: 1) the dependencies between data in a program, and 2) whether those dependencies are consistent with the intended flow policies as they change over time. In this paper we provide a formal ground for this intuition. We present a straightforward extension to the principal flow-sensitive type system introduced by Hunt and Sands (POPL '06, ESOP '11) to infer both end-to-end dependencies and dependencies at intermediate points in a program. This allows typings to be applied to verification of both static and dynamic policies. Our extension preserves the principal type system's distinguishing feature, that type inference is independent of the policy to be enforced: a single, generic dependency analysis (typing) can be used to verify many different dynamic policies of a given program, thus achieving a clean separation between (1) and (2).

We also make contributions to the foundations of dynamic information flow. Arguably, the most compelling semantic definitions for dynamic security conditions in the literature are phrased in the so-called knowledge-based style. We contribute a new definition of knowledge-based progress insensitive security for dynamic policies. We show that the new definition avoids anomalies of previous definitions and enjoys a simple and useful characterisation as a two-run style property.

1 Introduction

Information flow policies are security policies which aim to provide end-to-end security guarantees of the form "information must not flow from this source to this destination". Early work on information flow concentrated on static, multi-level policies, organising the various data sources and sinks of a system into a fixed hierarchy. The policy determined by such a hierarchy (a partial order) is simply that information must not flow from a to b unless $a \sqsubseteq b$.

1.1 Dynamic Policies

Since the pioneering work of Denning and Denning [DD77], a wide variety of information-flow policies and corresponding enforcement mechanisms have been proposed. Much of the recent work on information-flow properties goes beyond the static, multi-level security policies of earlier work, considering instead more sophisticated, dynamic

© Springer-Verlag Berlin Heidelberg 2015
R. Focardi and A. Myers (Eds.): POST 2015, LNCS 9036, pp. 32–52, 2015.
DOI: 10.1007/978-3-662-46666-7_3

forms of policy which permit different flows at different points during the excecution of a program. Indeed, this shift of focus better reflects real-world requirements for security policies which are naturally dynamic.

For example, consider a request for sensitive employee information made to an employer by a regulatory authority. In order to satisfy this request it may be necessary to temporarily allow the sensitive information to flow to a specific user in the Human Resources department. In simplified form, the essence of this example is captured in Figure 1.

```
// x → a
out x on a;
// x ↛ a
out 2 on a;
```

Fig. 1.

Here x contains the sensitive information, channel a represents the HR user, and the policy is expressed by the annotations x → a (x *may* flow to a) and x ↛ a (x *must not* flow to a). It is intuitively clear that this program complies with the policy.

Consider two slightly more subtle examples, in each of which revocation of a permitted flow depends on run-time data:

```
1  /*Program A*/         /*Program B*/
2  // x,y → a            // x → a
3  out x on a;           out x on a;
4  if (y > 0) {          if (x > 0) {
5      out 1 on a;           out 1 on a;
6      // x ↛ a              // x ↛ a
7  }                     }
8  out 2 on a;           out 2 on a;
9  out 3 on a;           out 3 on a;
```

In program A, the revocation of x → a is controlled by the value of y, whereas in program B it is controlled by the value of x itself. Note that the policy for A explicitly allows y → a so the conditional output (which reveals information about y) appears to be permissible. In program B the conditional output reveals information about x itself, but this happens *before* the revocation. So should program B be regarded as compliant? We argue that it should not, as follows. Consider "the third output" of program B as observed on channel a. Depending on the initial value of x, the observed value may be either 2 (line 8) or 3 (line 9). Thus this observation reveals information about x and, in the cases where revocation occurs, the observation happens *after* the revocation.

Unsurprisingly, increasing the sophistication of policies also increases the challenge of formulating good semantic definitions, which is to say, definitions which both match our intuitions about what the policies mean and can form the basis of formal reasoning about correctness.

At first sight it might seem that increasing semantic sophistication should also require increasingly intricate enforcement mechanisms. However, all such mechanisms must somehow solve the same two distinct problems:

1. Determine what data dependencies exist between the various data sources and sinks manipulated by the program.
2. Determine whether those dependencies are consistent with the flows permitted by the policy.

Ideally, the first of these problems would be solved independently of the second, since dependencies are a property of the code, not the policy. This would allow reuse at two levels: a) reuse of the same dependency analysis mechanisms and proof techniques for different *types* of policy; b) reuse of the dependency properties for a given program across verification of multiple *alternative* policies (whether of the same type or not).

In practice, enforcement mechanisms are typically not presented in a way which cleanly separates the two concerns. Not only does this hamper the reuse of analysis mechanisms and proof techniques, it also makes it harder to identify the *essential* differences between different approaches.

Central Contribution. We take a well-understood dependency type system for a simple while-language, originally designed to support enforcement of static policies, and extend it in a straightforward way to a language with output channels (§ 5). We demonstrate the advantages of a clean separation between dependency analysis and policy enforcement, by establishing a generic soundness result (§ 6) for the type system which characterises the meaning of types as dependency properties. We then show how the dependency information derived by the type system can be used to verify compliance with dynamic policies. Note that this means that the core analysis for enforcement can be done even before the policy is known: we dub this *very static* enforcement. More significantly, it opens the way to reuse dependency analyses across verification of multiple types of information flow policy (for example, it might be possible to use the dependency analyses from advanced slicing tools such as JOANA [JOA] and Indus [Ind]).

Foundations of Dynamic Flow Policies. Although it was not our original aim and focus, we also make some contributions of a more foundational nature, and our paper opens with these (§2–§4). The semantic definition of security which we use is based on work of Askarov and Chong [AC12], and we begin with their abstract formulation of dynamic policies (§2). In defining security for dynamic policies, they made a convincing case for using a family of attackers of various strengths, following an observation that the intuitively strongest attacker (who never forgets anything that has been observed) actually places weaker security demands on the system than we would want. On the other hand they observe that the family of *all* attackers contains pathological attacker behaviours which one certainly does not wish to consider. Due to this they do not give a characterisation of the set of all *reasonable* attackers against which one should protect. We make the following two foundational contributions:

Foundational Contribution 1. We focus (§3.3) on the pragmatic case of *progress insensitive* security (where slow information leakage is allowed through observation of computational progress [AHSS08]). We argue for a new definition of progress insensitive security (Def 11), which unconditionally grants all attackers knowledge of computational progress. With this modification to the definition from [AC12], the problematic examples of pathological attackers are eliminated, and we have a more complete definition of security. Consequently, we are able to prove security in the central contribution of the paper *for all attackers*.

Foundational Contribution 2. The definitions of security are based on characterising attacker knowledge and how it changes over time relative to the changing policy. As argued previously e.g., [BS09], this style of definition forms a much more intuitive basis for a semantics of dynamic policies than using two-run characterisations. However, two-run formulations have the advantage of being easier to use in proofs. We show (§4) that our new knowledge-based progress-insensitive security definition enjoys a simple two-run characterisation. We make good use of this in our proof of correctness of our central contribution.

2 The Dynamic Policy Model

In this section we define an abstract model of computation and a model of dynamic policies which maps computation histories to equivalence relations on stores.

2.1 Computation and Observation Model

Computation Model. The computation model is given by a labelled transition system over *configurations*. We write $\langle c, \sigma \rangle \xrightarrow{\alpha} \langle c', \sigma' \rangle$ to mean that configuration $\langle c, \sigma \rangle$ evaluates in one step to configuration $\langle c', \sigma' \rangle$ with label α. Here c is a *command* and $\sigma \in \Sigma$ is a *store*. In examples and when we instantiate this model the store will be a mapping from program variables to values.

The label α records any output that happens during that step, and we have a distinguished label value ϵ to denote a silent step which produces no output. Every non-silent label α has an associated channel $\mathsf{channel}(\alpha) \in Chan$ and a value $\mathsf{value}(\alpha)$. Channels are ranged over by a and values by v. We abbreviate a sequence of evaluation steps

$$\langle c_0, \sigma_0 \rangle \xrightarrow{\alpha_1} \langle c_1, \sigma_1 \rangle \xrightarrow{\alpha_2} \cdots \xrightarrow{\alpha_n} \langle c_n, \sigma_n \rangle$$

as $\langle c_0, \sigma_0 \rangle \to^n \langle c_n, \sigma_n \rangle$. We write $\langle c_0, \sigma_0 \rangle \to^* \langle c', \sigma' \rangle$ if $\langle c_0, \sigma_0 \rangle \to^n \langle c', \sigma' \rangle$ for some $n \geq 0$. We write the projection of a single step $\langle c, \sigma \rangle \xrightarrow{\alpha} \langle c', \sigma' \rangle$ to some channel a as $\langle c, \sigma \rangle \xrightarrow{\beta}_a \langle c', \sigma' \rangle$ where $\beta = v$ if $\mathsf{channel}(\alpha) = a$ and $\mathsf{value}(\alpha) = v$, and $\beta = \epsilon$ otherwise, that is, when α is silent or an output on a channel different from a.

We abbreviate a sequence of evaluation steps

$$\langle c_0, \sigma_0 \rangle \xrightarrow{\beta_1}_a \langle c_1, \sigma_1 \rangle \xrightarrow{\beta_2}_a \cdots \xrightarrow{\beta_n}_a \langle c_n, \sigma_n \rangle$$

as $\langle c_0, \sigma_0 \rangle \xrightarrow{t}_a^n \langle c_n, \sigma_n \rangle$ where t is the trace of values produced on channel a with every silent ϵ filtered out. We write $\langle c_0, \sigma_0 \rangle \xrightarrow{t}_a \langle c', \sigma' \rangle$ if $\langle c_0, \sigma_0 \rangle \xrightarrow{t}_a^n \langle c', \sigma' \rangle$ for some $n \geq 0$, and we omit the final configuration in contexts where it is not relevant, e.g. $\langle c, \sigma \rangle \xrightarrow{t}_a$. We use $|t|$ to denote the length of trace t.

Attacker's Observation Model. We follow the standard assumption that the command c is known to the attacker. We assume a passive attacker which aims to extract information about an input store σ by observing outputs. As in [AC12], the attacker is able only to observe a *single* channel. A generalisation to multi-channel attackers (which would also allow colluding attackers to be modelled) is left for future work.

2.2 Dynamic Policies

A flow policy specifies a limit on how much information an attacker may learn. A very general way to specify such a limit is as an equivalence relation on input stores.

Example 1. Consider a store with variables x and y. A simple policy might state that the attacker should only be able to learn the value of x. It follows that all stores which agree on the value of x should look the same to the attacker. This is expressed as the equivalence relation $\sigma \equiv \rho$ iff $\sigma(x) = \rho(x)$.

A more complicated policy might allow the attacker to learn the value of some arbitrary expression e on the initial store, e.g. $x = y$. This is expressed as the equivalence relation $\sigma \equiv \rho$ iff $\sigma(e) = \rho(e)$.

Definition 1 (Policy). *A policy P maps each channel to an equivalence relation $\equiv$ on stores. We write P_a for the equivalence relation that P defines for channel a.*

As defined, policies are static. A dynamic policy changes while the program is running and may dictate a different P for each point in the execution. Here we assume that the policy changes *synchronously* with the execution of the program. That is, the active policy can be deterministically derived from the execution history so far.

Definition 2 (Execution History). *An execution history $\mathcal{H}$ of length n is a transition sequence $\langle c_0, \sigma_0 \rangle \xrightarrow{\alpha_1} \langle c_1, \sigma_1 \rangle \xrightarrow{\alpha_2} \ldots \xrightarrow{\alpha_n} \langle c_n, \sigma_n \rangle$.*

Definition 3 (Dynamic Policy). *A dynamic policy D maps every execution history $\mathcal{H}$ to a policy $D(\mathcal{H})$. We write $D_a(\mathcal{H})$ for the equivalence relation that is defined by $D(\mathcal{H})$ for channel a, that is to say, $D_a(\mathcal{H}) = P_a$ where $P = D(\mathcal{H})$.*

Most synchronous dynamic policy languages in the literature determine the current policy based solely on the store σ_n in the final configuration of the execution history [AC12, BvDS13]. Definition 3 allows in principle for more flexible notions of dynamic policies, as they can incorporate the full execution history to determine the policy at each stage of an execution (similar to the notion of conditional noninterference used by [GM84, Zha12]). However, our enforcement does assume that the dynamic policy can be statically approximated per program point, which arguably is only feasible for policies in the style of [AC12, BvDS13]. Such approximations can typically be improved by allowing the program to branch on policy-related queries.

Since programs are deterministic, an execution history of length n is uniquely determined by its initial configuration $\langle c_0, \sigma_0 \rangle$. We use this fact to simplify our definitions and proofs:

Definition 4 (Execution Point). *An execution point is a triple (c_0, σ_0, n) identifying the point in execution reached after n evaluation steps starting from configuration $\langle c_0, \sigma_0 \rangle$. Such an execution point is considered well-defined iff there exists $\langle c_n, \sigma_n \rangle$ such that $\langle c_0, \sigma_0 \rangle \rightarrow^n \langle c_n, \sigma_n \rangle$.*

Lemma 1. *Each well-defined execution point (c_0, σ_0, n) uniquely determines an execution history $\mathcal{H}(c_0, \sigma_0, n)$ of length n starting in configuration $\langle c_0, \sigma_0 \rangle$.*

In the rest of the paper we rely on this fact to justify a convenient abuse of notation, writing $D(c_0, \sigma_0, n)$ to mean $D(\mathcal{H}(c_0, \sigma_0, n))$.

3   Knowledge-Based Security Conditions

Recent works on dynamic policies, including [AC12, BDLG11, BNR08, BS10], make use of so-called *knowledge-based* security definitions, building on the notion of gradual release introduced in [AS07]. This form of definition seems well-suited to provide intuitive semantics for dynamic policies. We focus in particular on the attacker-parametric model from Askarov and Chong in [AC12].

Suppose that the input state to a program is σ. In the knowledge-based approach, an attacker's knowledge of σ is modelled as a *knowledge set* K, which may be any set of states such that $\sigma \in K$. Note that the larger the knowledge set, the less certain is the attacker of the actual value of σ, so a smaller K means more precise knowledge. (Sometimes, as we see below, it can be more intuitive to focus on the complement $\overline{K}$, which is the set of a-priori possible states which the attacker is able to *exclude*, since this set, which we will call the *exclusion knowledge*, grows as the attacker learns more).

Now suppose that the currently active policy is $\equiv$. The essential idea in any knowledge-based semantics is to view the equivalence classes of $\equiv$ as placing upper bounds on the attacker's knowledge. In the simplest setting, if the actual input state is σ and the attacker's knowledge set is K, we require:

$$K \supseteq \{\sigma' \mid \sigma' \equiv \sigma\}$$

Or, in terms of what the attacker is able to exclude:

$$\overline{K} \subseteq \{\rho \mid \rho \not\equiv \sigma\} \tag{1}$$

How then do we determine the attacker's knowledge? Suppose an attacker knows the program c and observes channel a. Ignoring covert channels (timing, power, etc) an obvious approach is to say that the attacker's knowledge is simply a function of the trace t observed so far:

$$k(t) = \{\rho \mid \langle c, \rho \rangle \xrightarrow{t}_a\} \tag{2}$$

We define the exclusion knowledge as the complement of this: $ek(t) = \overline{k(t)}$. Note that, as a program executes and more outputs are observed, the attacker's exclusion knowledge can only increase; if $\langle c, \sigma \rangle \xrightarrow{t \cdot v}_a$ then $ek(t) \subseteq ek(t \cdot v)$, since, if ρ can already be excluded by observation of t (because c cannot produce t when started in ρ), then it will still be excluded when $t \cdot v$ is observed (if c cannot produce t it cannot produce any extension of t either).

But this simple model is problematic for dynamic policies. Suppose that the policies in effect when t and $t \cdot v$ are observed are, respectively $\equiv_1$ and $\equiv_2$. Then it seems that we must require both $ek(t) \subseteq \{\rho \mid \rho \not\equiv_1 \sigma\}$ and $ek(t \cdot v) \subseteq \{\rho \mid \rho \not\equiv_2 \sigma\}$. As observed above, it will always be the case that $ek(t) \subseteq ek(t \cdot v)$, so we are forced to require $ek(t) \subseteq \{\rho \mid \rho \not\equiv_2 \sigma\}$. In other words, the observations that we can permit at any given moment are constrained not only by the policy currently in effect but also by all policies which will be in effect in the future. This makes it impossible to have dynamic policies which revoke previously permitted flows (or, at least, pointless; since all revocations would apply retrospectively, the earlier "permissions" could never be exercised).

Askarov and Chong's solution has two key components, outlined in the following two sections.

3.1 Change in Knowledge

Firstly, recognising that policy changes should not apply retrospectively, we can relax (1) to constrain only how an attacker's knowledge should be allowed to *increase*, rather than its absolute value. The increase in attacker knowledge going from t to $t \cdot v$ is given by the set difference $ek(t \cdot v) - ek(t)$. So, instead of (1), we require:

$$ek(t \cdot v) - ek(t) \subseteq \{\rho \mid \rho \not\equiv \sigma\} \tag{3}$$

where $\equiv$ is the policy in effect immediately before the output v. (Some minor set-theoretic rearrangement gives the equivalent

$$k(t \cdot v) \supseteq k(t) \cap \{\sigma' \mid \sigma' \equiv \sigma\}$$

which is the form of the original presentation in [AC12].)

3.2 Forgetful Attackers

Focussing on change in knowledge addresses the problem of retrospective revocation but it creates a new issue. Consider the following example.

Example 2. The program in Figure 2 produces the same output many times, but only the first output is permitted by the policy. Assume that the value of x is 5. Before the first output, the exclusion knowledge of an observer on channel a is the empty set. After the first output the observer's exclusion knowledge is increased to include those stores σ where $\sigma(\mathrm{x}) \neq 5$. This is allowed by the policy at that point.

By the time the second output occurs, the policy prohibits any further flows from x. However, since the attacker's exclusion knowledge *already* provides complete knowledge of x, the second output does not actually change the attacker's exclusion knowledge at all, so (3) is satisfied (since $ek(t \cdot v) = ek(t)$). Thus a policy semantics based on (3) would accept this program even though it continues to leak the value of x *long* after the flow has been revoked.

Askarov and Chong address this by revisiting the assumption that an attacker's knowledge is necessarily determined by the simple function of traces (2) above. Consider an attacker which *forgets* the value of the first output in example 2. For this attacker, the second output would come as a revalation, revealing the value of x all over again, in violation of the policy. Askarov and Chong thus arrive at the intriguing observation that security against a more powerful attacker, one who remembers everything that happens, does not imply security against a less resourceful attacker, who might forget parts of the observations made.

```
// x → a
out x on a;
// x ↛ a
while (true)
    out x on a;
```

Fig. 2.

Forgetful attackers are modelled as deterministic automata.

Definition 5 (Forgetful Attacker ▷ § III.A [AC12]). *A forgetful attacker is a tuple $A = (S_A, s_0, \delta_A)$ where S_A is the set of attacker states; $s_0 \in S_A$ is the initial state; and $\delta_A : S_A \times Val \rightarrow S_A$ the (deterministic) transition function describing how the attacker's state changes due to the values that the attacker observes.*

We write $A(t)$ for the attacker's state after observing trace t:

$$A(\epsilon) = s_0$$
$$A(t \cdot v) = \delta_A(A(t), v)$$

A forgetful attacker's knowledge after trace t is defined as the set of all initial stores that produce a trace which would result in the same attacker state $A(t)$:

Definition 6 (Forgetful Attacker Knowledge ▷ § III.A [AC12]).

$$k(A, c, a, t) = \{\rho \mid \langle c, \rho \rangle \xrightarrow{t'}_a \wedge A(t') = A(t)\}$$

(Note that, in preparation for the formal definition of the security condition, program c and channel a now appear as explicit parameters.)

The proposed security condition is still essentially as given by (3), but now relative to a specific choice of attacker. Stated in the notation and style of the current paper, the formal definition is as follows.

Definition 7 (Knowledge-Based Security ▷ Def. 1 [AC12]). *Command c is secure for policy D against an attacker A on channel a for initial store σ if for all traces t and values v such that $\langle c, \sigma \rangle \xrightarrow{t}{}_a^n \langle c', \sigma' \rangle \xrightarrow{v}{}_a^1$ we have*

$$ek(A, c, a, t \cdot v) - ek(A, c, a, t) \subseteq \{\rho \mid \rho \not\equiv \sigma\}$$

where $\equiv\, = D_a(c, \sigma, n)$.

Having relativised security to the power of an attacker's memory, it is natural to consider the strong notion of security that would be obtained by requiring Def. 7 to hold for all choices of A. However, as shown in [AC12], this exposes a problem with the model: there are attackers for which even well-behaved programs are insecure according to Def. 7.

Example 3. Consider again the first example from the Introduction (Section 1.1). Here, for simplicity, we assume that the variable x is boolean, taking value 0 or 1.

It is intuitively clear that this program complies with the policy. However, as observed in [AC12], if we instantiate Def. 7 with the forgetful attacker displayed, the attacker's exclusion knowledge increases with the second output when $x = 0$.

After observing the value 0, the attacker's state is $A(0) = q_0$. Since $A(\epsilon) = q_0$, the exclusion knowledge is still the empty set. After the second observation, only stores where $x = 0$ could have led to state q_2, so the exclusion knowledge increases at a point where the policy does not allow it.

This example poses a question which (so far as we are aware) remains unanswered: if we base a dynamic policy semantics on Def.7, for *which set* of attackers should we require it to hold?

In the next section we define a progress-insensitive variant of Def.7. For this variant it seems that security against all attackers *is* a reasonable requirement and in Section 6 we show that progress-insensitive security against all attackers is indeed enforced by our type system.

3.3 Progress Insensitive Security

Since [VSI96], work on the formalisation and enforcement of information-flow policies has generally distinguished between two flavours of security: *termination-sensitive* and *termination-insensitive*. Termination-sensitive properties guarantee that protected information is neither revealed by its influence on input-output behaviour nor by its influence on termination behaviour. Termination-insensitive properties allow the latter flows and thus provide weaker guarantees. For systems with incremental output (as opposed to batch-processing systems) it is more appropriate to distinguish between *progress-sensitive* and *progress-insensitive* security. Progress-insensitive security ignores progress-flows, where a flow is regarded as a progress-flow if the information that it reveals can be inferred solely by observing *how many* outputs the system produces.

Two examples of programs with progress-flows are as follows:

Example 4. Programs containing progress-flows:

```
// Program A            // Program B
out 1 on a;             out 1 on a;
while (x == 8) skip;    if (x != 8) out 2 on a;
out 2 on a;
```

Let σ and ρ differ only on the value of x: $\sigma(x) = 4$ and $\rho(x) = 8$. Note that, if started in σ, both programs produce a trace of length 2 (namely, the trace $1 \cdot 2$) whereas, if started in ρ, the maximum trace length is 1. Thus, for both programs, observing just the length of the trace produced can reveal information about x. Note that, since termination is not an observable event in the semantics, A and B are actually observably equivalent; we give the two variants to emphasise that progress-flows may occur even in the absence of loops.

In practice, most enforcement mechanisms only enforce progress-insensitive security. This is a pragmatic choice since (a) it is hard to enforce progress-sensitive security without being overly restrictive (typically, all programs which loop on protected data will be rejected), and (b) programs which leak solely via progress-flows, leak slowly [AHSS08].

Recall that Knowledge-Based Security (Def. 7) places a bound on the increase in an attacker's knowledge which is allowed to arise from observation of the next output event. Askarov and Chong show how this can be weakened in a natural way to provide a progress-insensitive property, by artificially strengthening the supposed previous knowledge to already include progress knowledge. Their definition of progress knowledge is as follows:

Definition 8 (AC Progress Knowledge ▷ § III.A [AC12]).

$$k^+(A, c, a, t) = \{\rho \mid \langle c, \rho \rangle \xrightarrow{t' \cdot v}_a \wedge A(t') = A(t)\}$$

Substituting this (actually, its complement) in the "previous knowledge" position in Def. 7 provides Askarov and Chong's notion of progress-insensitive security:

Definition 9 (AC Progress-Insensitive (ACPI) Security ▷ Def. 2 [AC12]). *Command c is AC Progress-Insensitive secure for policy D against an attacker A on channel a for initial store σ if for all traces t and values v such that $\langle c, \sigma \rangle \xrightarrow{t}_a^n \langle c', \sigma' \rangle \xrightarrow{v}_a^1$ we have*

$$ek(A, c, a, t \cdot v) - ek^+(A, c, a, t) \subseteq \{\rho \mid \rho \not\equiv \sigma\}$$

where $\equiv \, = D_a(c, \sigma, n)$.

Now consider again programs A and B above. These are examples of programs where the *only* flows are progress-flows. In general, we say that a program is *quasi-constant* if there is some fixed (possibly infinite) trace t such that every trace produced by the program is a prefix of t, regardless of the choice of initial store. Thus, for a quasi-constant program, the only possible observable variation in behaviour is trace length, so all flows are progress-flows. Since PI security is intended explicitly to allow progress-flows, we should expect all quasi-constant programs to satisfy PI security, regardless of the choice of policy and for all possible attackers. But, for Def. 9, this fails to hold, as shown by the following counterexample.

Example 5. Consider the program and attacker below. The attacker is a very simple bounded-memory attacker which remembers just the last output seen and nothing else (not even whether it has seen any previous outputs).

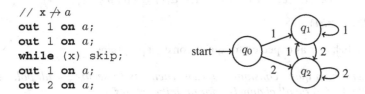

```
// x ↛ a
out 1 on a;
out 1 on a;
while (x) skip;
out 1 on a;
out 2 on a;
```

Clearly, the program is quasi-constant. However, it is *not* ACPI secure for the given attacker. To see this, suppose that x = 0 and consider the trace $t = 1 \cdot 1 \cdot 1$. The attacker has no knowledge at this point ($ek(t)$ is the empty set) since it does not know whether it has seen one, two or three 1's. It is easily verified that $ek^+(t)$ is also the empty set for this attacker (intuitively, giving this attacker progress knowledge in the form k^+ doesn't help it, since it still does not know which side of the loop has been reached). But $ek(t \cdot 2)$ is *not* the empty set, since in state q_2 the attacker is able to exclude all stores for which x = 1, thus ACPI security is violated.

What has gone wrong here? The attacker itself seems reasonable. We argue that the real problem lies in the definition of $k^+(A, c, a, t)$. As defined, this is the knowledge that A would have in state $A(t)$ if given just the additional information that c can produce at least one more output. But this takes no account of any *previous* progress knowledge which might have been forgotten by A. (Indeed, the above attacker forgets nearly all such previous progress knowledge.) As a consequence, the resulting definition of PI security mistakenly treats some increases in knowledge as significant, even though they arise purely because the attacker has forgotten previously available progress knowledge.

Our solution will be to re-define progress knowledge to include what the attacker would know *if it had been keeping count*. To this end, for any attacker $A = (S, s_0, \delta)$ we define a counting variant $A^\omega = (S^\omega, s_0^\omega, \delta^\omega)$, such that $S^\omega \subseteq S \times N$, $s_0^\omega = (s_0, 0)$ and $\delta^\omega((s, n), v) = (\delta(s, v), n + 1)$. In general, A^ω will be at least as strong an attacker as A:

Lemma 2. *For all A, c, a, t:*

1. $k(A^\omega, c, a, t) \subseteq k(A, c, a, t)$
2. $ek(A, c, a, t) \subseteq ek(A^\omega, c, a, t)$

Proof. It is is easily seen that $A^\omega(t) = (q, n) \Rightarrow A(t) = q$. Thus $A^\omega(t') = A^\omega(t) \Rightarrow A(t') = A(t)$, which establishes part 1. Part 2 is just the contrapositive of part 1.

Our alternative definition of progress knowledge is then:

Definition 10 (Full Progress Knowledge).

$$k^\#(A, c, a, t) = \{\rho \mid \langle c, \rho \rangle \xrightarrow{t' \cdot v}_a \wedge A^\omega(t') = A^\omega(t)\}$$

Our corresponding PI security property is:

Definition 11 (Progress-Insensitive (PI) Security). *Command c is progress-insensitive secure for policy D against an attacker A on channel a for initial store σ if for all traces t and values v such that $\langle c, \sigma \rangle \xrightarrow{t}_a^n \langle c', \sigma' \rangle \xrightarrow{v}_a^1$ we have*

$$ek(A, c, a, t \cdot v) - ek^\#(A, c, a, t) \subseteq \{\rho \mid \rho \not\equiv \sigma\}$$

where $\equiv\, = D_a(c, \sigma, n)$.

This definition behaves as expected for quasi-constant programs:

Lemma 3. *Let c be a quasi-constant program. Then c is PI secure for all policies D against all attackers A on all channels a for all initial stores σ.*

Proof. It suffices to note that, from the definitions, if $t \cdot v$ is a possible trace for c and c is quasi-constant, $ek^\#(A, c, a, t) = ek(A^\omega, c, a, t \cdot v)$. The result follows by Lemma 2.

As a final remark in this section, we note that there is a class of attackers for which ACPI and PI security coincide. Say that A is *counting* if it always remembers at least how many outputs it has observed. Formally:

Definition 12 (Counting Attacker). *A is counting if $A(t) = A(t') \Rightarrow |t| = |t'|$.*

Now say that attackers A and A' are isomorphic (written $A \cong A'$) if $A(t_1) = A(t_2) \leftrightarrow A'(t_1) = A'(t_2)$ and note that none of the attacker-parametric security conditions distinguish between isomorphic attackers (in particular, knowledge sets are always equal for isomorphic attackers). It is easily verified that $A \cong A^\omega$ for all counting attackers. It is then immediate from the definitions that ACPI security and PI security coincide for counting attackers.

4   Progress-Insensitive Security as a Two-Run Property

Our aim in this section is to derive a security property which guarantees (in fact, is equivalent to) PI security for all attackers, and in a form which facilitates the soundness proof of our type system. For this we seek a property in "two run" form.

First we reduce the problem by establishing that it suffices to consider just the counting attackers.

Lemma 4. *Let c be a command. Then, for any given policy, channel and initial store, c is PI secure against all attackers iff c is PI secure against all counting attackers.*

Proof. Left to right is immediate. Right to left, it suffices to show that

$$ek(A, c, a, t \cdot v) - ek^\#(A, c, a, t) \subseteq ek(A^\omega, c, a, t \cdot v) - ek^\#(A^\omega, c, a, t)$$

Since $A^\omega \cong (A^\omega)^\omega$, we have $ek^\#(A^\omega, c, a, t) = ek^\#(A, c, a, t)$. It remains to show that $ek(A, c, a, t \cdot v) \subseteq ek(A^\omega, c, a, t \cdot v)$, which holds by Lemma 2.

Our approach is now essentially to unwind Def. 11. Our starting point for the unwinding is:

$$ek(A, c, a, t \cdot v) - ek^\#(A, c, a, t) \subseteq \{\rho \mid \rho \not\equiv \sigma\}$$

where $\equiv$ is the policy in effect at the moment the output v is produced. Simple set-theoretic rearrangement gives the equivalent:

$$\{\sigma' \mid \sigma' \equiv \sigma\} \cap k^\#(A, c, a, t) \subseteq k(A, c, a, t \cdot v)$$

Expanding the definitions, we arrive at:

$$\rho \equiv \sigma \wedge \langle c, \rho \rangle \xrightarrow{t' \cdot v'}_a \wedge A^\omega(t') = A^\omega(t) \Rightarrow \exists s. \langle c, \rho \rangle \xrightarrow{s}_a \wedge A(s) = A(t \cdot v)$$

By Lemma 4, we can assume without loss of generality that A is counting, so we can replace $A^\omega(t') = A^\omega(t)$ by $A(t') = A(t)$ on the lhs. Since A is counting, we know that $|t| = |t'|$ and $|s| = |t \cdot v|$, hence $|s| = |t' \cdot v'|$. Now, since c is deterministic and both s and $t' \cdot v'$ start from the same ρ, it follows that $s = t' \cdot v'$. Thus we can simplify the unwinding to:

$$\rho \equiv \sigma \wedge \langle c, \rho \rangle \xrightarrow{t' \cdot v'}_a \wedge A(t') = A(t) \Rightarrow A(t' \cdot v') = A(t \cdot v)$$

Now, suppose that this holds for A and that $v' \neq v$. Let q be the attacker state $A(t') = A(t)$ and let r be the attacker state $A(t' \cdot v') = A(t \cdot v)$. Since $|t| \neq |t \cdot v|$ and A is counting, we know that $q \neq r$. Then we can construct an attacker A' from A which leaves q intact but splits r into two distinct states r_v and $r_{v'}$. But then security will fail to hold for A', since $A'(t' \cdot v') = r_v \neq r_{v'} = A'(t \cdot v)$. So, since we require security to hold for all A, we may strengthen the rhs to $A(t' \cdot v') = A(t \cdot v) \wedge v = v'$. Then, given $A(t') = A(t)$, since A is a deterministic automaton, it follows that $v = v' \Rightarrow A(t' \cdot v') = A(t \cdot v)$, hence the rhs simplifies to just $v = v'$ and the unwinding reduces to:

$$\rho \equiv \sigma \wedge \langle c, \rho \rangle \xrightarrow{t' \cdot v'}_a \wedge A(t') = A(t) \Rightarrow v' = v$$

Finally, since A now only occurs on the lhs, we see that there is a distinguished counting attacker for which the unwinding is harder to satisfy than all others, namely the attacker $A_\#$, for which $A_\#(t') = A_\#(t)$ iff $|t'| = |t|$. Thus the property will hold for all A iff it holds for $A_\#$ and so we arrive at our two-run property:

Definition 13 (Two-Run PI Security). *Command c is two-run PI secure for policy D on channel a for initial store σ if whenever $\langle c, \sigma \rangle \xrightarrow{t}_a^n \langle c_n, \sigma_n \rangle \xrightarrow{v}_a^1$ and $\rho \equiv \sigma$ and $\langle c, \rho \rangle \xrightarrow{t' \cdot v'}_a$ and $|t'| = |t|$, then $v' = v$, where $\equiv \; = D_a(c, \sigma, n)$.*

Theorem 1. *Let c be a command. For any given policy, channel and initial store, c is PI secure against all attackers iff c is two-run PI secure.*

Proof. This follows from the unwinding of the PI security definition, as shown above.

5 A Dependency Type System

Within the literature on enforcement of information flow policies, some work is distinguished by the appearance of explicit dependency analyses. In the current paper we take as our starting point the flow-sensitive type systems of [HS11, HS06], due to the relative simplicity of presentation. Other papers proposing similar analyses include [CHH02], [AB04], [AR80] and [BBL94]. Some of the similarities and differences between these approaches are discussed in [HS06].

The original work of [HS06] defines a family of type systems, parameterised by choice of a multi-level security lattice, and establishes the existence of principal typings within this family. The later work of [HS11] defines a single system which produces *only* principal types. In what follows we refer to the particular flow-sensitive type system defined in [HS11] as FST.

The typings derived by FST take the form of an environment Γ mapping each program variable x to a set $\Gamma(x)$ which has a direct reading as (a conservative approximation to) the set of dependencies for x. All other types derivable using the flow-sensitive type systems of [HS06] can be recovered from the principal type derived by FST. Because principal types are simply dependency sets, they are not specific to any particular security hierarchy or policy. This is the basis of the clean separation we are able to achieve between analysis and policy verification in what follows.

Consider the simple program shown in Figure 3. The type inferred for this program is Γ, where $\Gamma(x) = \{\}$, $\Gamma(y) = \{y, z\}$, $\Gamma(z) = \{z\}$. From this typing we can verify, for example, any static policy using a security lattice in which $level(z) \sqsubseteq level(y)$.

```
x := z + 1;
z := x;
if (z > 0)
    y := 1;
x := 0;
```

Fig. 3.

FST is defined only for a simple language which does not include output statements. This makes it unsuitable for direct application to verification of dynamic policies, so in the current paper we describe a straightforward extenion of FST to a language with output statements. We then show how the inferred types can be used to enforce policies such as those in [AC12] and [BvDS13], which appear very different from the simple static, multi-level policies originally targeted.

5.1 Language

We instantiate the abstract computation model of Section 2.1 with a simple while-language with output channels, shown in Figure 4. We let $x \in PVar$ range over program variables, $a \in Chan$ range over channels (as before) and $p \in PPoint$ range over program points. Here non-silent output labels have the form (a, v, p), $\mathsf{channel}(a, v, p) = a$, and $\mathsf{value}(a, v, p) = v$.

The language is similar to the one considered in [AC12], except for the absence of input channels. Outputs have to be annotated with a program point p to bridge between the dependency analysis and the policy analysis, described in Section 6.

5.2 Generic Typing

Traditional type systems for information flow assume that all sensitive inputs to the system (here: program variables) are associated with a security level. Expressions in the command to be typed might combine information with different security levels. To

Values $v ::= n$ Expressions $e ::= v \mid x$
Commands $c ::= \texttt{skip} \mid c_1; c_2 \mid x := e \mid \texttt{if } e \, c_1 \, c_2 \mid \texttt{while } e \, c \mid \texttt{out } e \texttt{ on } a \, @ \, p$

$$\langle \texttt{skip}; c, \sigma \rangle \xrightarrow{\epsilon} \langle c, \sigma \rangle \qquad \frac{\langle c_1, \sigma \rangle \xrightarrow{\alpha} \langle c_1', \sigma' \rangle}{\langle c_1; c_2, \sigma \rangle \xrightarrow{\alpha} \langle c_1'; c_2, \sigma' \rangle} \qquad \frac{\sigma(e) = v}{\langle x := e, \sigma \rangle \xrightarrow{\epsilon} \langle \texttt{skip}, \sigma' \rangle}$$

$$\frac{\sigma(e) = v}{\langle \texttt{out } e \texttt{ on } a \, @ \, p, \sigma \rangle \xrightarrow{(a,v,p)} \langle \texttt{skip}, \sigma' \rangle} \qquad \langle \texttt{while } e \, c, \sigma \rangle \xrightarrow{\epsilon} \langle \texttt{if } e \, (c; \texttt{while } e \, c) \, \texttt{skip}, \sigma \rangle$$

$$\frac{\sigma(e) \neq 0}{\langle \texttt{if } e \, c_1 \, c_2, \sigma \rangle \xrightarrow{\epsilon} \langle c_1, \sigma \rangle} \qquad \frac{\sigma(e) = 0}{\langle \texttt{if } e \, c_1 \, c_2, \sigma \rangle \xrightarrow{\epsilon} \langle c_2, \sigma \rangle}$$

Fig. 4. Language and semantics

ensure that all expressions can be typed, the security levels are therefore required to form at least a join-semilattice, or in some cases a full lattice. The type system then ensures no information of a (combined) level l_1 can be written to a program variable with level l_2 unless $l_1 \sqsubseteq l_2$.

The system FST from Hunt and Sands [HS11] differs from these type systems in two ways. Firstly, it does not require intermediate assignments to respect the security lattice ordering. As an observer is assumed to only see the final state of the program, only the final value of a variable must not depend on any information which is forbidden by the lattice ordering. For example, suppose $level(y) \sqsubseteq level(z) \sqsubseteq level(x)$ but $level(x) \not\sqsubseteq level(z)$ and consider the first two assignments in the example from Fig. 3.

$$x = z + 1; \quad z = x;$$

A traditional type system would label this command as insecure because of the assignment $z = x$ and the fact that $level(x) \not\sqsubseteq level(z)$, even though the value of z after this assignment does not depend on the initial value of x at all. FST however is *flow-sensitive* and allows the security label on x to vary through the code.

Secondly, and more significantly, by using the powerset of program variables as security lattice, FST provides a *principal typing* from which all other possible typings can be inferred.

Thus the typing by FST is generic: a command needs to be typed only once and can then be verified against any static information-flow policy. Since the ordering among labels is not relevant while deriving the typing, FST is also able to verify policies which are not presented in the shape of a security lattice, but any relational '*may-flow*' predicate between security labels can be verified.

5.3 Generic Typing for Dynamic Policies

We now present an extended version of FST which includes an additional typing rule for outputs. All the original typing rules of FST remain unchanged.

Intuitively, an output on a channel is like the final assignment to a variable in the original FST, that is, its value can be observed. Since types are sets of dependencies, we could simply type an output channel as the union of all dependencies resulting from all output statements for that channel. This would be sound but unduly imprecise: the only flows permitted would be those permitted by the policy *at all times*, in effect requiring us to conservatively approximate each dynamic policy by a static one. But we can do better than this.

The flow-sensitivity of FST means that a type derivation infers types at intermediate program points which will, in general, be different from the top-level type inferred for the program. These intermediate types are not relevant for variables, since their intermediate values are not observable. But the outputs on channels at intermediate points *are* observable, and so intermediate channel types *are* relevant. Therefore, for each channel we record in Γ distinct dependency sets for each program point at which an output statement on that channel occurs. Of course, this is still a static approximation of runtime behaviour. While our simple examples of dynamic policies explicitly associate policy changes to program points, for real-world use more expressive dynamic policy languages may be needed. In Section 2.2 we formally define the semantics of a dynamic policy as an arbitrary function of a program's execution history, which provides a high degree of generality. However, in order to apply a typing to the verification of such a policy, it is first necessary to conservatively approximate the flows permitted by the policy at each program point of interest (Definition 16).

Let X be the dependency set for the channel-a output statement at program point p. The meaning[1] of X is as follows:

> Let σ be a store such that execution starting in σ arrives at p, producing the i'th output on a. Let ρ be any store which agrees with σ on all variables in X and also eventually produces an i'th output on a (not necessarily at the same program point). Then these two outputs will be equal.

Two key aspects of our use of program points should be highlighted:

1. While the intended semantics of X as outlined above does not require corresponding outputs on different runs to be produced at the same program point, the X that is inferred by the type system *does* guarantee this stronger property. Essentially this is because (in common with all similar analyses) the type system uses control-flow dependency as a conservative proxy for the semantic dependency property of interest.
2. Our choice of program point to distinguish between different ouputs on the same channel is not arbitrary; it is essentially forced by the structure of the original type system. As noted, program point annotations simply allow us to record in the final typing exactly those intermediate dependency sets which are already inferred by the underlying flow-sensitive system. While it would be possible in principle to make even finer distinctions (for example, aiming for path-sensitivity rather than just flow-sensitivity) this would require fundamental changes to the type system.

The resulting type system is shown in Figure 5. We now proceed informally to motivate its rules. Definitions and proofs of formal soundness are presented in Section 6.

The type system derives judgements of the form $\vdash \{c\}\Gamma$, where $\Gamma : Var \to 2^{Var}$ is an environment mapping variables to a set of dependencies. The variables we consider are $Var = PVar \cup CPoint \cup \{\texttt{pc}\} \cup Chan$ with $CPoint = Chan \times PPoint$. We consider the relevance of each kind of variable in turn.

---

[1] This is progress-insensitive dependency (see Section 3). A progress-sensitive version can be defined in a similar way.

TS-SKIP $\vdash \{\texttt{skip}\}\, \Gamma_{id}$ TS-ASSIGN $\vdash \{\texttt{x} := e\}\, \Gamma_{id}\, [\texttt{x} \mapsto fv(e) \cup \{\texttt{pc}\}]$

TS-SEQ $\dfrac{\vdash \{c_1\}\Gamma_1 \qquad \vdash \{c_2\}\Gamma_2}{\vdash \{c_1\, ;\, c_2\}\, \Gamma_2; \Gamma_1}$

TS-IFELSE

$$\dfrac{\vdash \{c_i\}\Gamma_i \qquad \vdash \Gamma_i' = \Gamma_i; \Gamma_{id}[\texttt{pc} \mapsto \{\texttt{pc}\} \cup fv(e)] \qquad i = 1, 2}{\vdash \{\texttt{if } e\ c_1\ c_2\}\, (\Gamma_1' \cup \Gamma_2')[\texttt{pc} \mapsto \{\texttt{pc}\}]}$$

TS-WHILE

$$\dfrac{\vdash \{c\}\Gamma_c \qquad \Gamma_f = (\Gamma_c; \Gamma_{id}[\texttt{pc} \mapsto \{\texttt{pc}\} \cup fv(e)])^*}{\vdash \{\texttt{while } e\ c\}\, \Gamma_f\, [\texttt{pc} \mapsto \{\texttt{pc}\}]}$$

TS-OUTPUT

$\vdash \{\texttt{out } e \texttt{ on } a\, @\, p\}\Gamma_{id}[a_p \mapsto fv(e) \cup \{\texttt{pc}, a, a_p\}; a \mapsto \{\texttt{pc}, a\}]$

Fig. 5. Type System

- As program variables $PVar$ form the inputs to the command, these are the dependencies of interest in the typing of a command. For program variables themselves, $\Gamma(\texttt{x})$ are the dependencies for which a different initial value might result in a different final value of $\texttt{x}$.
- Pairs of channels and program points $(a, p) \in CPoint$ are denoted as a_p. The dependencies $\Gamma(a_p)$ are those program variables for which a difference in initial value might cause a difference in the value of any observation that can result from an output statement for channel a with annotation p.
- Whenever the program counter $\texttt{pc} \in \Gamma(\texttt{x})$ this indicates that this command potentially changes the value of program variable $\texttt{x}$. Similar, if $\texttt{pc} \in \Gamma(a)$ then c might produce an output on channel a and if $\texttt{pc} \in \Gamma(a_p)$ then c might produce an output on a caused by a statement annotated with p. We use the program counter to catch implicit flows that may manifest in these ways.
- We use $Chan$ to capture the latent flows described in example program B in the introduction. The dependencies $\Gamma(a)$ are those program variables for which a difference in initial value might result in a different number of outputs produced on channel a by this command. This approach to address latent flows was first introduced in [AC12] as *channel context bounds*.

We first explain the notation used in the unchanged rules from FST before turning our attention to the new TS-OUTPUT rule. All concepts have been previously introduced in [HS11].

The function $fv(e)$ returns the free variables in expression e. The identity environment Γ_{id} maps each variable to the singleton set of itself, that is $\Gamma_{id}(x) = \{x\}$ for all $x \in Var$. Sequential composition of environments is defined as:

$$\Gamma_2; \Gamma_1(x) = \bigcup_{y \in \Gamma_2(x)} \Gamma_1(y)$$

Intuitively, $\Gamma_2; \Gamma_1$ is as Γ_2 but substituting the dependency relations already established in Γ_1. We overload the union operator for environments: $(\Gamma_1 \cup \Gamma_2)(x) = \Gamma_1(x) \cup \Gamma_2(x)$. We write Γ^* for the fixed-point of Γ, used in TS-WHILE:

$$\Gamma^* = \bigcup_{n \geq 0} \Gamma^n \qquad \text{where } \Gamma^0 = \Gamma_{id} \text{ and } \Gamma^{n+1} = \Gamma^n; \Gamma$$

It is only in the typing TS-OUTPUT of the output command that the additional channel and program point dependencies are mentioned; this underlines our statement that extending FST to target dynamic policies is straightforward.

We explain the changes to Γ_{id} in TS-OUTPUT in turn. For a_p, clearly the value of the output and thus the observation is affected by the program variables occuring in the expression e. We also include the program counter pc to catch implicit flows; if we have a command of the form if e (out 1 on a @ p) (out 2 on a @ q) the output at a_p is affected by the branching decision, which is caught in TS-IFELSE.

We include the channel context bounds a for the channel on which this output occurs to capture the latent flows of earlier conditional outputs, as demonstrated in the introduction. Observe that by the definition of sequential composition of environments, we only add those dependencies for conditional outputs that happened *before* this output, since it cannot leak information about the absence of future observations.

Finally, we include the dependencies of output point a_p itself. By doing so the dependency set of a_p becomes *cumulative*: with every sequential composition (including those used in Γ^*) the dependency set of a_p only grows, as opposed to the dependencies of program variables. This makes us sum the dependencies of all outputs on channel a annotated with the same program point, as we argued earlier.

The mapping for channel context bounds a is motivated in a similar manner. The pc is included since the variables affecting whether this output occurs on channel a are the same as those that affect whether this statement is reached. Note that we are over-approximating here, as the type system adds the dependencies of e in

$$\text{if } e \text{ (out 1 on } a \text{ @ } p_1) \text{ (out 2 on } a \text{ @ } p_2)$$

to context bounds a, even though the number of outputs is always one.

Like for a_p, we make a depend on itself, thus accumulating all the dependencies that affect the number of outputs on channel a.

As the TS-OUTPUT rule does not introduce more complex operations than already present, the type system has the same complexity as FST. That is, the type system can be used to construct a generic type in $O(nv^3)$ where n is the size of the program and v the number of variables in *Var*.

6   Semantic Soundness and Policy Compliance

We present a soundness condition for the type system, and show that the type system is sound. We then describe how the derived generic typings can be used to check compliance with a dynamic policy that is approximated per program point. We begin by showing how an equivalence relation on stores can be created from a typing:

Definition 14. *We write* $=_{\Gamma(x)}$ *for the equivalence relation corresponding to the typing* Γ *of variable* $x \in Var$, *defined as* $\sigma =_{\Gamma(x)} \rho$ *iff* $\sigma(y) = \rho(y)$ *for all* $y \in \Gamma(x)$.

As we are using $\Gamma(a_p)$ as the approximation of dependencies for an observation, the soundness of the PI type system is similar to the PI security for dynamic policies, except that we take the equivalence relation as defined by $\Gamma(a_p)$ rather than the policy D_a.

Definition 15 (PI Type System Soundness). *We say that the typing $\vdash\{c\}\Gamma$ is sound iff for all σ, ρ, if $\langle c, \sigma\rangle \xrightarrow{t}_a \langle c_\sigma, \sigma'\rangle \xrightarrow{(a,v,p)}$ and $\langle c, \rho\rangle \xrightarrow{t'}_a \langle c_\rho, \rho'\rangle \xrightarrow{v'}_a$ and $|t| = |t'|$ then $\sigma =_{\Gamma(a_p)} \rho \Rightarrow v = v'$.*

Theorem 2. *All typings derived by the type system are sound.*

The proof for Theorem 2 can be found in Appendix A of [DHS15].

To link the typing and the actual dynamic policy, we rely on an analysis that is able to approximate the dynamic policy per program point. A sound approximation should return a policy that is at least as restrictive as the actual policy for any observation on that program point.

Definition 16 (Dynamic Policy Approximation). *A dynamic policy approximation $A : CPoint \to 2^{\Sigma \times \Sigma}$ is a mapping from channel and program point pairs to an equivalence relation on stores. The approximation A on command c, written $c : A$, is sound for dynamic policy D iff, for all σ if $\langle c, \sigma\rangle \to^n \langle c', \sigma'\rangle \xrightarrow{(a,v,p)}$ then $A(a_p)$ is coarser than $D_a(c, \sigma, n)$.*

We now arrive at the main theorem in this section. Given a typing $\vdash\{c\}\Gamma$, we can now easily verify for command c its compliance with *any* soundly approximated dynamic policy, by simply checking that the typing's policy is at least as restrictive as the approximated dynamic policy for every program point.

Theorem 3 (PI Dynamic Policy Compliance). *Let $c : A$ be a sound approximation of dynamic policy D. If $\vdash\{c\}\Gamma$ and $=_{\Gamma(a_p)}$ is coarser than $A(a_p)$ for all program points a_p, then c is two-run PI secure for D on all channels and for all initial stores.*

Proof. Given a store σ such that $\langle c, \sigma\rangle \xrightarrow{t}_a^n \langle c_\sigma, \sigma'\rangle \xrightarrow{(a,v,p)}$ and a store ρ such that $\langle c, \rho\rangle \xrightarrow{t'}_a \langle c_\rho, \rho'\rangle \xrightarrow{v'}_a$ and $|t| = |t'|$ and $\sigma D_a(c, \sigma, n)\rho$, we need to show that $v = v'$. Since $c : A$ is a sound approximation of D, we have that $\sigma A(a_p)\rho$ and as $=_{\Gamma(a_p)}$ is coarser than $A(a_p)$ we also have $\sigma =_{\Gamma(a_p)} \rho$. Which by Theorem 2 gives us that $v = v'$.

Corollary 1. *If the conditions of Theorem 3 are met, then c is PI secure for D for all attackers. This is immediate by Theorem 1.*

7 Related Work

In this section we consider the related work on security for dynamic policies and on generic enforcement mechanisms for information-flow control. We already discuss the knowledge-based definitions by Askarov and Chong [AC12] in detail in Section 3.

The generality of expressing dynamic policies per execution point can be identified already in the early work by Goguen and Meseguer [GM82]. They introduce the notion of conditional noninterference as a relation that should hold per step in the system, provided that some condition on the execution history holds. Conditional noninterference has been recently revisited by Zhang [Zha12] who uses unwinding relations to present a collection of properties that can be verified by existing proof assistants.

Broberg and Sands [BS09] developed another knowledge-based definition of security for dynamic policies which only dealt with the attacker with perfect recall. The approach was specialised to the specific dynamic policy mechanism Paralocks [BS10] which uses part of the program state to vary the ordering between security labels.

Balliu et al. [BDLG11] introduce a temporal epistemic logic to express information flow policies. Like our dynamic policies, the epistemic formulas are to be satisfied per execution point. Dynamic policies can be individually checked by the ENCOVER tool [BDLG12].

The way in which we define dynamic policies matches exactly the set of synchronous dynamic policies: those policies that deterministically determine the active policy based on an execution point. Conversely, an asynchronously changing policy cannot be deterministically determined from an execution point, but is influenced by an environment external to the running program.

There is relatively little work on the enforcement of asynchronous dynamic policies. Swamy et al. [SHTZ06] present the language RX where policies are define in a role-based fashion, where membership and delegation of roles can change dynamically. Hicks et al. [HTHZ05] present an extension to the DLM model, allowing the acts-for hierarchy among principals to change while the program is running.

Both approaches however need a mechanism to synchronise the policy changes with the program in order to enforce information-flow properties. RX uses transactions which can rollback when a change in policy violates some of the flows in it, whereas the work by Hicks et al. inserts automatically derived coercions that force run-time checks whenever the policy changes.

A benefit of our enforcement approach is that commands need to be analysed only once to be verified against multiple information-flow policies. This generality can also be found in the work by Stefan et al. [SRMM11] presenting LIO, a Haskell library for information-flow enforcement which is also parametric in the security policy. The main differences between our approach and theirs is that LIO's enforcement is dynamic rather than static, while the enforced policies are static rather than dynamic.

8 Conclusions

We extended the flow-sensitive type system from [HS06] to provide for each output channel individual dependency sets per point in the program and demonstrated that this is sufficient to support dynamic information flow policies. We proved the type system sound with respect to a straightforward two-run property which we showed sufficient to imply knowledge-based security conditions.

As our approach allows for the core of the analysis to be performed even before the policy is known, this enables us to reuse the results of the dependency analysis across the verification of multiple types of policies. An interesting direction for future research could be on the possibility to use the dependency analyses performed by advanced slicing tools such as JOANA [JOA] and Indus [Ind].

Acknowledgements. This work is partly funded by the Swedish agencies SSF and VR.

References

[AB04]   Amtoft, T., Banerjee, A.: Information Flow Analysis in Logical Form. In: Giacobazzi, R. (ed.) SAS 2004. LNCS, vol. 3148, pp. 100–115. Springer, Heidelberg (2004)

[AC12]   Askarov, A., Chong, C.: Learning is change in knowledge: Knowledge-based security for dynamic policies. In: Computer Security Foundations Symposium, pp. 308–322. IEEE (2012)

[AHSS08] Askarov, A., Hunt, S., Sabelfeld, A., Sands, D.: Termination-Insensitive Noninterference Leaks More Than Just a Bit. In: Jajodia, S., Lopez, J. (eds.) ESORICS 2008. LNCS, vol. 5283, pp. 333–348. Springer, Heidelberg (2008)

[AR80]   Andrews, G.R., Reitman, R.P.: An axiomatic approach to information flow in programs. TOPLAS 2(1), 56–75 (1980)

[AS07]   Askarov, A., Sabelfeld, A.: Gradual release: Unifying declassification, encryption and key release policies. In: Proc. IEEE Symp. on Security and Privacy, pp. 207–221 (May 2007)

[BBL94]   Banâtre, J.-P., Bryce, C., Le Métayer, D.: Compile-time detection of information flow in sequential programs. In: Gollmann, D. (ed.) ESORICS 1994. LNCS, vol. 875, pp. 55–73. Springer, Heidelberg (1994)

[BDLG11] Balliu, M., Dam, M., Le Guernic, G.: Epistemic temporal logic for information flow security. In: Programming Languages and Analysis for Security, PLAS 2011, pp. 6:1–6:12. ACM (2011)

[BDLG12] Balliu, M., Dam, M., Le Guernic, G.: Encover: Symbolic exploration for information flow security. In: 2012 IEEE 25th Computer Security Foundations Symposium (CSF), pp. 30–44. IEEE (2012)

[BNR08]   Banerjee, A., Naumann, D., Rosenberg, S.: Expressive declassification policies and modular static enforcement. In: Proc. IEEE Symp. on Security and Privacy, pp. 339–353. IEEE Computer Society (2008)

[BS09]   Broberg, N., David, S.: Flow-Sensitive Semantics for Dynamic Information Flow Policies. In: Programming Languages and Analysis for Security (2009)

[BS10]   Broberg, N., Sands, D.: Paralocks – role-based information flow control and beyond. In: Symposium on Principles of Programming Languages. ACM (2010)

[BvDS13] Broberg, N., van Delft, B., Sands, D.: Paragon for Practical Programming with Information-Flow Control. In: Shan, C.-c. (ed.) APLAS 2013. LNCS, vol. 8301, pp. 217–232. Springer, Heidelberg (2013)

[CHH02]   Clark, D., Hankin, C., Hunt, S.: Information flow for Algol-like languages. Journal of Computer Languages 28(1), 3–28 (2002)

[DD77]   Denning, D.E., Denning, P.J.: Certification of programs for secure information flow. Comm. of the ACM 20(7), 504–513 (1977)

[DHS15]   van Delft, B., Hunt, S., Sands, D.: Very Static Enforcement of Dynamic Policies. Technical Report 1501.02633, arXiv (2015)

[GM82]   Goguen, J.A., Meseguer, J.: Security policies and security models. In: Proc. IEEE Symp. on Security and Privacy, April 1982, pp. 11–20 (April 1982)

[GM84]   Goguen, J.A., Meseguer, J.: Unwinding and inference control. In: Proc. IEEE Symp. on Security and Privacy, pp. 75–86 (April 1984)

[HS06]   Hunt, S., Sands, D.: On Flow-sensitive Security Types. In: Symposium on Principles of Programming Languages, pp. 79–90. ACM (2006)

[HS11]   Hunt, S., Sands, D.: From Exponential to Polynomial-Time Security Typing via Principal Types. In: Barthe, G. (ed.) ESOP 2011. LNCS, vol. 6602, pp. 297–316. Springer, Heidelberg (2011)

[HTHZ05] Hicks, M., Tse, S., Hicks, B., Zdancewic, S.: Dynamic updating of information-flow policies. In: Foundations of Computer Security Workshop, pp. 7–18 (2005)

[Ind] Indus homepage, `http://indus.projects.cis.ksu.edu/` (accessed: January 09, 2015)

[JOA] JOANA homepage, `http://pp.ipd.kit.edu/projects/joana/` (accessed: January 09, 2015)

[SHTZ06] Swamy, N., Hicks, M., Tse, S., Zdancewic, S.: Managing Policy Updates in Security-Typed Languages. In: Proceedings of the 19th IEEE Workshop on Computer Security Foundations (2006)

[SRMM11] Stefan, D., Russo, A., Mitchell, J.C., Mazières, D.: Flexible dynamic information flow control in Haskell. In: Proceedings of the 4th ACM Symposium on Haskell (2011)

[VSI96] Volpano, D., Smith, G., Irvine, C.: A sound type system for secure flow analysis. J. Computer Security 4(3), 167–187 (1996)

[Zha12] Zhang, C.: Conditional Information Flow Policies and Unwinding Relations. In: Bruni, R., Sassone, V. (eds.) TGC 2011. LNCS, vol. 7173, pp. 227–241. Springer, Heidelberg (2012)

The Foundational Cryptography Framework

Adam Petcher[1,2] and Greg Morrisett[1]

[1] Harvard University, Cambridge, Massachusetts, USA
{apetcher,greg}@seas.harvard.edu
[2] MIT Lincoln Laboratory, Lexington, Massachusetts, USA

Abstract. We present the Foundational Cryptography Framework (FCF) for developing and checking complete proofs of security for cryptographic schemes within a proof assistant. This is a general-purpose framework that is capable of modeling and reasoning about a wide range of cryptographic schemes, security definitions, and assumptions. Security is proven in the computational model, and the proof provides concrete bounds as well as asymptotic conclusions. FCF provides a language for probabilistic programs, a theory that is used to reason about programs, and a library of tactics and definitions that are useful in proofs about cryptography. The framework is designed to leverage fully the existing theory and capabilities of the Coq proof assistant in order to reduce the effort required to develop proofs.

Keywords: Cryptography, Protocol Verification, Proof Assistant, Coq.

1 Introduction

Cryptographic algorithms and protocols are becoming more numerous, specialized, and complicated. As a result, it is likely that security vulnerabilities will slip by peer review. To address this problem, some cryptographers [7][16] have proposed an increased level of rigor and formality for cryptographic proofs. It is our hope that eventually, cryptographers will be able to describe cryptographic schemes and security proofs using a formal language, and the proofs can be checked automatically by a highly trustworthy mechanized proof checker.

To enable such mechanically-verified proofs, we have developed The Foundational Cryptography Framework (FCF). This framework embeds into the Coq proof assistant [17] a simple probabilistic programming language to allow the specification of cryptographic schemes, security definitions, and assumptions. The framework also includes useful theory, tactics, and definitions that assist with the construction of proofs of security. Once complete, the proof can be checked by the Coq proof checker. Facts proven in FCF include the security of El Gamal encryption [14], and of the encryption scheme described in Section 4 of this paper. We have also proven the security and correctness of the "tuple-set" construction of [11], and shown how this primitive can be used to construct a searchable symmetric encryption scheme supporting single keyword queries. This is a complex and sophisticated construction with a proof of over 15000

© Springer-Verlag Berlin Heidelberg 2015
R. Focardi and A. Myers (Eds.): POST 2015, LNCS 9036, pp. 53–72, 2015.
DOI: 10.1007/978-3-662-46666-7_4

lines of Coq code which includes a pair of core arguments involving more than 30 intermediate games.

FCF is heavily influenced by CertiCrypt [6], which was later followed by Easy-Crypt [5]. CertiCrypt is a framework that is built on Coq, and allows the development of mechanized proofs of security in the computational model for arbitrary cryptographic constructions. Unfortunately, proof development in CertiCrypt is time-consuming, and the developer must spend a disproportionate amount of time on simple, uninteresting goals. To address these limitations, the group behind CertiCrypt developed EasyCrypt, which has a similar semantics and logic, and uses the Why3 framework and SMT solvers to improve proof automation. EasyCrypt takes a huge step forward in terms of usability and automation, but it sacrifices some trustworthiness due to that fact that the trusted computing base is larger and the basis of the mechanization is a set of axiomatic rules.

FCF is a *foundational* framework like CertiCrypt, in which the rules used to prove equivalence of programs (or any fact) are mechanized proofs derived from the semantics or other core definitions. An important difference between CertiCrypt and FCF is that CertiCrypt uses a deep embedding of a probabilistic programming language whereas FCF uses a shallow embedding (similar to [19]). The shallow embedding allows us to easily extend the language, and to make better use of Coq's tactic language and existing automated tactics to reduce the effort required to develop proofs. The result is a framework that is foundational and easily extensible, but in which proof development effort is greatly reduced.

2 Design Goals

Based on our experience working with EasyCrypt, we formulated a set of idealized design goals that a practical mechanized cryptography framework should satisfy. We believe that FCF achieves many of these goals, though there is still some room for improvement, as discussed in Section 5.

Familiarity. Security definitions and descriptions of cryptographic schemes should look similar to how they would appear in cryptography literature, and a cryptographer with no knowledge of programming language theory or proof assistants should be able to understand them. Furthermore, a cryptographer should be able to inspect and understand the foundations of the framework itself.

Proof Automation. The system should use automation to reduce the effort required to develop a proof. Ideally, this automation is extensible, so that the developer can produce tactics for solving new kinds of goals.

Trustworthiness. Proofs should be checked by a trustworthy procedure, and the core definitions (*e.g.*, programming language semantics) that must be inspected in order to trust a proof should be relatively simple and easy to understand.

Extensibility. It should be possible to directly incorporate any existing theory that has been developed for the proof assistant. For example, it should be possible to directly incorporate an existing theory of lattices in order to support cryptography that is based on lattices and their related assumptions.

Concrete Security. The security proof should provide concrete bounds on the probability that an adversary is able to defeat the scheme. Concrete bounds provide more information than asymptotic statements, and they inform the selection of values for system parameters in order to achieve the desired level of security in practice.

Abstraction. The system should support abstraction over types, procedures, proofs, and modules containing any of these items. Abstraction over procedures and primitive types is necessary for writing security definitions, and for reasoning about adversaries in a natural way. The inclusion of abstraction over proofs and structures adds a powerful mechanism for developing sophisticated abstract arguments that can be reused in future proofs.

Code Generation. The system should be able to generate code containing the procedures of the cryptographic scheme that was proven secure. This code can then be used for basic testing, prototyping, or as an executable model to which future implementations will be compared during testing.

3   Framework Components

In a typical cryptographic proof, we specify cryptographic schemes, security definitions, and (assumed) hard problems, and then we prove a reduction from a properly-instantiated security definition to one or more problems that are assumed to be hard. In other words, we assume the existence of an effective adversary against the scheme in question, and then prove that we can construct a procedure that can effectively solve a problem that is assumed to be hard. This reduction results in a contradiction that allows us to conclude that an effective adversary against the scheme cannot exist.

The cryptographic schemes, security definitions, and hard problems are probabilistic, and FCF provides a common probabilistic programming language (Section 3.1) for describing all three. Then we provide a denotational semantics (Section 3.1) that allows reasoning about the probability distributions that correspond to programs in this language. This semantics assigns a numeric value to an event in a probability distribution, and it also allows us to conclude that two distributions are equivalent and we can replace one with the other (which supports the game-hopping style of [7]).

It can be cumbersome to work directly in the semantics, so we provide a theory of distributions (Section 3.2) that can be used to prove that distributions are related by equality, inequality or "closeness." A program logic (Section 3.3) is also provided to ease the development of proofs involving state or looping behavior. To reduce the effort required to develop a proof, the framework provides a library of tactics (Section 3.4) and a library of common program elements with associated theory (Section 3.4). The equational theory, program logic, tactics, and programming library greatly simplify proof development, yet they are all derived from the semantics of the language, and using them to complete a proof does not reduce the trustworthiness of the proof.

By combining all of the components described above, a developer can produce a proof relating the probability that some adversary defeats the scheme to the probability that some other adversary is able to solve a problem that is assumed to be hard. This is a result in the *concrete setting*, in which probability values are given as expressions, and certain problems are assumed to be hard for particular constructed adversaries. In such a result, it may be necessary to inspect an expression describing a probability value to ensure it is sufficiently "small," or to inspect a procedure to ensure it is in the correct complexity class. FCF provides additional facilities to obtain more traditional asymptotic results, in which these procedures and expressions do not require inspection. A set of asymptotic definitions (Section 3.5) allows conclusions such as "this probability is negligible" or "this procedure executes a polynomial number of queries." In order to apply an assumption about a hard problem, it may be necessary to prove that some procedure is efficient in some sense. So FCF provides an extensible notion of efficiency (Section 3.5) and a characterization of non-uniform polynomial time Turing machines.[1]

3.1   Probabilistic Programs

We describe probabilistic programs using Gallina, the purely functional programming language of Coq, extended with a computational monad in the spirit of Ramsey and Pfeffer [20], that supports drawing uniformly random bit vectors. Listing 2 contains an example of a valid FCF program that implements a one-time pad on bit vectors. This program accepts a bit vector argument x, samples a random bit vector of length c (where c is a constant declared outside of this function) and assigns the result to variable p, then returns $p \oplus x$.

The syntax of the language is defined by an inductive type called Comp and is shown in Listing 1. At a high-level, Comp is an embedded domain-specific language that inherits the host language Gallina, and extends it with operations for generating and working with random bits.

The most notable primitive operation is Rnd, which produces n uniformly random bits. The Repeat operation repeats a computation until some decidable predicate holds on the value returned. This operation allows a restricted form of non-termination that is sometimes useful (*e.g.*, for sampling natural numbers in a specified range). The operations Bind and Ret are the standard monadic constructors, and allow the construction of sequences of computations, and computations from arbitrary Gallina terms and functions, respectively. However, note that the Ret constructor requires a proof of decidable equality for the underlying return type, which is necessary to provide a computational semantics as seen later in this section. In the remainder of this paper, we will use a more natural notation for these constructors: $\{0,1\}^n$ is equivalent to (Rnd n), $x \xleftarrow{\$} c; f$ is

---

[1] The current release of the FCF code for version 8.4 of Coq is available from http://people.seas.harvard.edu/~apetcher/FCF_14.10.14.zip

```
Inductive Comp : Set -> Type :=
| Ret : forall {A : Set}
  {H: EqDec A}, A -> Comp A
| Bind : forall {A B : Set}, Comp
  B
  -> (B -> Comp A) -> Comp A
| Rnd : forall n, Comp (Bvector n)
| Repeat : forall {A : Set}, Comp
  A
  -> (A -> bool) -> Comp A.
```

Listing 1. Probabilistic Computation Syntax

```
Definition OTP (x : Bvector c) :
  Comp (Bvector c)
  := p <-$ {0, 1}^c; ret (p xor x)
```

Listing 2. An Example of a Probabilistic Program

$$[\![ret\ a]\!] = 1_{\{a\}}$$

$$[\![x \overset{\$}{\leftarrow} c; f\ x]\!] = \lambda x. \sum_{b \in \mathrm{supp}([\![c]\!])} ([\![f\ b]\!]\ x) * ([\![c]\!]\ b)$$

$$[\![\{0,1\}^n]\!] = \lambda x.\ 2^{-n}$$

$$[\![\text{Repeat}\ c\ P]\!] = \lambda x. (1_P\ x) * ([\![c]\!]\ x) * \left(\sum_{b \in P} ([\![c]\!]\ b) \right)^{-1}$$

Fig. 1. Semantics of Probabilistic Computations

the same as (Bind c (fun x ⇒ f)), and ret e is (Ret _ e). The framework includes an ASCII form of this notation used in Listing 2. In the case of Ret, the notation serves to hide the proof of decidable equality, which is irrelevant to the programmer and is usually constructed automatically by proof search.

FCF uses a (mostly) *shallow embedding*, in which functions in the object language are realized using functions in the metalanguage. In contrast, CertiCrypt uses a *deep embedding*, in which the data type describing the object language includes constructs for specifying and calling functions, as well as all of the primitives such as bit-vectors and xor.

We have found that there are key benefits to shallow embedding. The primary benefit is that we immediately gain all of the capability of the metalanguage, including (in the case of Coq) dependent types, higher-order functions, modules, *etc*. Another benefit is that it is very simple to include any necessary theory in a security proof, and all of the theory that has been developed in the proof assistant can be directly utilized. One benefit that is specific to Coq (and other proof assistants with this property) is that Gallina functions are necessarily terminating, and Coq provides some fairly complex mechanisms for proving that a function terminates. By combining this restriction on functions with additional restrictions on Repeat, we can ensure that a computation (eventually) terminates, and that this computation corresponds with a distribution in which the total probability mass is 1.

On the other hand, the shallow embedding approach does have some drawbacks. The main drawback is that a Gallina function is opaque; we can only reason about a Gallina function based on its input/output behavior. The most significant effect of this limitation is that we cannot directly reason about the computational complexity of a Gallina function. We address this issue in Section 3.5.

The denotational semantics of a probabilistic computation is shown in Figure 1. The denotation of a term of type Comp A is a function in $A \to \mathbb{Q}$ which should be interpreted as the probability mass function of a distribution on A. In FCF, all distributions are discrete and have finite support. In Figure 1, 1_S is the indicator function for set S. So the denotation of `ret a` is a function that returns 1 when the argument is definitionally equal to a, and 0 otherwise. We can view the denotation of $x \xleftarrow{\$} c; f\, c$ as a marginal probability of the joint distribution formed by c and f. We know the probability of all events in c, but we only know the probability of events in f conditioned on events in c, so we can compute the probability of any event in this marginal distribution using the law of total probability. The fact that random bits are uniform and independent is encoded in the denotation of $\{0,1\}^n$, which is a function that ignores the argument and returns the probability that any n-bit value is equal to a randomly chosen n-bit value. The probability that `Repeat` $c\, P$ produces x is the conditional probability of x given P in c—which is equivalent to the function shown in Figure 1.

It is important to note that this language is purely functional, but the monadic style gives programs an imperative appearance. This appearance supports the *Familiarity* design goal since cryptographic definitions and games are typically written in an imperative style.

It is sometimes necessary to include some state in a cryptographic definition or proof. This can be easily accomplished by layering a state monad on top of `Comp`. However, this simple approach does not allow the development of definitions in which an adversary has access to an oracle that must maintain some hidden state across multiple interactions with the adversary. The definition could not simply pass the state to the adversary, because then the adversary could inspect or modify it. So FCF provides an extension to `Comp` for probabilistic procedures with access to a stateful oracle. The syntax of this extended language (Listing 3) is defined in another inductive type called `OracleComp`, where `OracleComp A B C` is a procedure that returns a value of type `C`, and has access to an oracle that takes a value of type `A` and returns a value of type `B`.

```
Inductive OracleComp :  Set -> Set -> Set -> Type :=
| OC_Query : forall (A B : Set), A -> OracleComp A B B
| OC_Run : forall (A B C A' B' S : Set), EqDec S -> EqDec B -> EqDec A ->
    OracleComp A B C -> S -> (S -> A -> OracleComp A' B' (B * S)) ->
    OracleComp A' B' (C * S)
| OC_Ret : forall A B C, Comp C -> OracleComp A B C
| OC_Bind : forall A B C C', OracleComp A B C ->
    (C -> OracleComp A B C') -> OracleComp A B C'.
```

Listing 3. Computation with Oracle Access Syntax

The `OC_Query` constructor is used to query the oracle, and `OC_Run` is used to run some program under a different oracle that is allowed to access the current oracle. The `OC_Bind` and `OC_Ret` constructors are used for sequencing and for promoting terms into the language, as usual. In the rest of this paper, we overload the sequencing and `ret` notation in order to use them for `OracleComp` as well as `Comp`. We use `query` and `run`, omitting the additional types and decidable equality proofs, as notation for the corresponding constructors of `OracleComp`.

The denotation of an `OracleComp` is a function from an oracle and an oracle state to a `Comp` that returns a pair containing the value provided by the `OracleComp` and the final state of the oracle. The type of an oracle that takes

$$[\![query\ a]\!] = \lambda o\ s.(o\ s\ a)$$
$$[\![run\ c'\ s'\ o']\!] = \lambda o\ s.[\![c'(\lambda x\ y.[\![(o'(fst\ x)\ y)\ o\ (snd\ x)]\!])\ (s',s)]\!]$$
$$[\![ret\ c]\!] = \lambda o\ s.x \xleftarrow{\$} c; ret\ (x,s)$$
$$[\![x \xleftarrow{\$} c; f\ x]\!] = \lambda o\ s.[x,s'] \xleftarrow{\$} [\![c\ o\ s]\!]; [\![(f\ x)\ o\ s']\!]$$

Fig. 2. Semantics of Computations with Oracle Access

an A and returns a B is `(S -> A -> Comp(B * S))` for some type S which holds the state of the oracle. The denotational semantics is shown in Figure 2.

3.2 (In)Equational Theory of Distributions

A common goal in a security proof is to compare two distributions with respect to some particular value (or pair of values) in the distributions. To assist with such goals, we have provided an (in)equational theory for distributions. This theory contains facts that can be used to show that two probability values are equal, that one is less than another, or that the distance between them is bounded by some value. For simplicity of notation, equality is overloaded in the statements below in order to apply to both numeric values and distributions. When we say that two distributions (represented by probability mass functions) are equal, as in $D_1 = D_2$, we mean that the functions are extensionally equal, that is $\forall x, (D_1\ x) = (D_2\ x)$.

Theorem 1 (Monad Laws).
$$[\![a \xleftarrow{\$} ret\ b; fa]\!] = [\![(f\ b)]\!] \qquad [\![a \xleftarrow{\$} c; ret\ a]\!] = [\![c]\!]$$
$$[\![a \xleftarrow{\$} (b \xleftarrow{\$} c_1; c_2\ b); c_3\ a]\!] = [\![b \xleftarrow{\$} c_1; a \xleftarrow{\$} c_2\ b; c_3\ a]\!]$$

Theorem 2 (Commutativity).
$$[\![a \xleftarrow{\$} c_1; b \xleftarrow{\$} c_2; c_3\ a\ b]\!] = [\![b \xleftarrow{\$} c_2; a \xleftarrow{\$} c_1; c_3\ a\ b]\!]$$

Theorem 3 (Distribution Irrelevance). *For well-formed computation c,*
$$(\forall x \in supp([\![c]\!]), [\![f\ x]\!]y = v) \Rightarrow [\![a \xleftarrow{\$} c; f\ a]\!]y = v$$

Theorem 4 (Distribution Isomorphism). *For any bijection f,*
$$\forall x \in supp([\![c_2]\!]), [\![c_1]\!](f\ x) = [\![c_2]\!]x$$
$$\wedge\ \forall x \in supp([\![c_2]\!]), [\![f_1\ (f\ x)]\!]\ v_1 = [\![f_2\ x]\!]v_2$$
$$\Rightarrow [\![a \xleftarrow{\$} c_1; f_1\ a]\!]\ v_1 = [\![a \xleftarrow{\$} c_2; f_2\ a]\!]\ v_2$$

Theorem 5 (Identical Until Bad).
$$[\![a \xleftarrow{\$} c_1; ret\ (B\ a)]\!] = [\![a \xleftarrow{\$} c_2; ret\ (B\ a)]\!]\wedge$$
$$[\![a \xleftarrow{\$} c_1; ret\ (P\ a, B\ a)]\!](x, false) = [\![a \xleftarrow{\$} c_2; ret\ (P\ a, B\ a)]\!](x, false) \Rightarrow$$
$$|\ [\![a \xleftarrow{\$} c_1; ret\ (P\ a)]\!]\ x - [\![a \xleftarrow{\$} c_2; ret\ (P\ a)]\!]\ x\ | \leq [\![a \xleftarrow{\$} c_1; ret\ (B\ a)]\!]\ true$$

The meaning and utility of many of the above theorems is direct (such as the standard monad properties in Theorem 1), but others require some explanation. Theorem 3 considers a situation in which the probability of some event y in $[\![f\,x]\!]$ is the same for all x produced by computation c. Then the distribution $[\![c]\!]$ is irrelevant, and it can be ignored. This theorem only applies to *well-formed* computations: A well-formed computation is one that terminates with probability 1, and therefore corresponds to a valid probability distribution.

Theorem 4 is a powerful theorem that corresponds to the common informal argument that two random variables "have the same distribution." More formally, assume distributions $[\![c_1]\!]$ and $[\![c_2]\!]$ assign equal probability to any pair of events $(f\,x)$ and x for some bijection f. Then a pair of sequences beginning with c_1 and c_2 are denotationally equivalent as long as the second computations in the sequences are equivalent when conditioned on $(f\,x)$ and x. A special case of this theorem is when f is the identity function, which allows us to simply "skip" over two semantically equivalent computations at the beginning of a sequence.

Theorem 5, also known as the "Fundamental Lemma" from [7], is typically used to bound the distance between two games by the probability of some unlikely event. Computations c_1 and c_2 produce both a value of interest and an indication of whether some "bad" event happened. We use (decidable) predicate B to extract whether the bad event occurred, and projection P to extract the value of interest. If the probability of the "bad" event occurring in c_1 and c_2 is the same, and if the distribution of the value of interest is the same in c_1 and c_2 when the bad event does not happen, then the distance between the probability of the value of interest in c_1 and and c_2 is at most the probability of the "bad" event occurring.

3.3   Program Logic

The final goal of a cryptographic proof is always some relation on probability distributions, and in some cases it is possible to complete the proof entirely within the equational theory described in 3.2. However, when the proof requires reasoning about loops or state, a more expressive theory may be needed in order to discharge some intermediate goals. For this reason, FCF includes a program logic that can be used to reason about changes to program state as the program executes. Importantly, the program logic is related to the theory of probability distributions through completeness and soundness theorems which allow the developer to derive facts about distributions from program logic facts, and vice-versa.

The core logic is a Probabilistic Relational Postcondition Logic (PRPL), that behaves like a Hoare logic, except there are no preconditions. The definition of a PRPL specification is given in Definition 1. In less formal terms, we say that computations p and q are related by the predicate Φ if both p and q are marginals of the same joint probability distribution, and Φ holds on all values in the support of that joint distribution.

Definition 1 (PRPL Specification). *Given* $p : \text{Comp } A$ *and* $q : \text{Comp } B$,

$$p \sim q\{\Phi\} \Leftrightarrow \begin{pmatrix} \exists\,(d : \text{Comp } (A \ast B)), \forall(x, y) \in supp(\llbracket d \rrbracket), \Phi\,x\,y\,\wedge \\ \llbracket p \rrbracket = \llbracket x \xleftarrow{s} d; \text{ret } (fst\,x) \rrbracket \wedge \llbracket q \rrbracket = \llbracket x \xleftarrow{s} d; \text{ret } (snd\,x) \rrbracket \end{pmatrix}$$

Using the PRPL, we can construct a Probabilistic Relational Hoare Logic (PRHL) which includes a notion of precondition for functions that return computations as shown in Definition 2. The resulting program logic is very similar to the Probabilistic Relational Hoare Logic of EasyCrypt [5], and it has many of the same properties.

Definition 2 (PRHL Specification). *Given* $p : A \rightarrow \text{Comp } B$ *and* $q : C \rightarrow \text{Comp } D$, $\{\Psi\}p \sim q\{\Phi\} \Leftrightarrow \forall a\,b, \Psi\,a\,b \Rightarrow (p\,a) \sim (q\,b)\{\Phi\}$.

Several theorems are provided along with the program logic definitions to simplify reasoning about programs. In order to use the program logic, one only needs to apply the appropriate theorem, so it is not necessary to produce the joint distribution described in the definition of a PRPL specification unless a suitable theorem is not provided. Theorems are provided for reasoning about the basic programming language constructs, interactions between programs and oracles, specifications describing equivalence, and the relationship between the program logic and the theory of probability distributions. Some of the more interesting program logic theorems are described below.

Theorem 6 (Soundness/Completeness).

$$p \sim q\{\lambda\,a\,b.a = x \Leftrightarrow b = y\} \Leftrightarrow \llbracket p \rrbracket\,x = \llbracket q \rrbracket\,y$$
$$p \sim q\{\lambda\,a\,b.a = x \Rightarrow b = y\} \Leftrightarrow \llbracket p \rrbracket\,x \leq \llbracket q \rrbracket\,y$$

Theorem 7 (Sequence Rule).

$$p \sim q\{\Phi'\} \Rightarrow \{\Phi'\}r \sim s\{\Phi\} \Rightarrow (x \xleftarrow{s} p; r\,x) \sim (x \xleftarrow{s} q; s\,x)\{\Phi\}$$

Theorem 8 (Oracle Equivalence). *Given an* $\text{OracleComp } c$, *and a pair of oracles,* o *and* p *with initial states* s *and* t,

$$\Phi = \lambda\,x\,y.(fst\,x) = (fst\,y) \wedge P\,(snd\,x)(snd\,y) \Rightarrow$$
$$(\forall a\,s'\,t', P\,s'\,t' \Rightarrow (o\,s'\,a) \sim (p\,t'\,a)\{\Phi\}) \Rightarrow P\,s\,t \Rightarrow (\llbracket c \rrbracket\,o\,s) \sim (\llbracket c \rrbracket\,p\,t)\{\Phi\}$$

Theorem 6 relates judgments in the program logic to relations on probability distributions. Theorem 7 is the relational form of the standard Hoare logic sequence rule, and it supports the decomposition of program logic judgments. Theorem 8 allows the developer to replace some oracle with an observationally equivalent oracle. There is also a more general form of this theorem (omitted for brevity) in which the state of the oracle is allowed to go bad. This more general theorem can be combined with Theorem 5 to get "identical until bad" results for program/oracle interactions.

3.4   Tactics and Programming Library

The framework includes several tactics that can be used to transform goals using the facts in Sections 3.2 and 3.3. An example proof in section 4 uses the comp_simp, inline_first and comp_skip tactics. These tactics simplify programs (e.g. by applying left identity to remove unnecessary ret statements), pull out nested statements by applying associativity, and remove identical statements at the beginning of a pair of programs, respectively. Also included is a more sophisticated tactic called dist_compute that attempts to automatically discharge goals involving simple computations.

FCF also includes a library containing useful programming structures and their related theory. For example, the library includes several sampling routines, such as drawing a natural number from a specified range; drawing an element from a finite list, set, or group; or sampling from an arbitrary Bernoulli distribution. These sampling routines are all computations based on the Rnd statement provided by the language, and each routine is accompanied by a theory establishing that the resulting distribution is correct. The CompFold package contains *higher-order* functions for folding and mapping a computation over a list. This package uses the program logic extensively, and many of the theorems take a specification on a pair of computations as an argument, and produce a specification on the result of folding/mapping those computations over a list. The package also contains theorems about typical list and loop manipulations such as appending, flattening, fusion/fission and order permutation.

3.5   Asymptotic Theory and Efficient Procedures

Using the tools described in the previous sections, it is possible to complete a proof of security in the *concrete setting*. That is, the probability that an adversary wins a game is given as an expression which may include some value (or set of values) η that we can interpret as the security parameter. To get a typical asymptotic security result, we must show that this expression, when viewed as a function of η, is negligible. To assist with these sorts of conclusions, FCF provides a library of asymptotic definitions and theory.

An additional challenge is that the expression in the concrete security result may contain a value describing the probability that some other procedure wins some other game. We can apply a standard security assumption to conclude that this value is negligible in η, but in order to do so we need to show that the procedure is in the appropriate complexity class. FCF utilizes an extensible notion of complexity, and it includes a simple predicate that accepts non-uniform worst-case polynomial time Turing machines. This predicate is constructed using a concrete cost model that assigns numeric costs to particular Coq functions, Comp values, and OracleComp values. The cost model for Gallina functions is necessarily axiomatic, since there is no way to directly reason about intensional properties of Coq functions. It includes axioms for some primitive operations as well as a set of combinators for determining the cost of more complicated functions. A proof must assume additional cost axioms for the set of functions used by constructed adversaries, which is relatively small in practice. The axioms need to be carefully inspected to ensure they accurately describe the desired complexity class, though a similar kind of inspection is needed to ensure the faithfullness of a cost model for a deeply-embedded language.

3.6 Code Extraction

FCF provides a code extraction mechanism that includes a strong guarantee of equivalence between a model of a probabilistic program and the code extracted from that model. We developed a small-step operational semantics that describes the behavior of these computations on a traditional machine (in which the memory contains values rather than probability distributions). This operational semantics (omitted for brevity) is an oracle machine that is given a finite list of bits representing the "random" input, and it describes how a computation takes a single step to produce a new computation, a final value, or fails due to insufficient input bits.

To show that this semantics is correct, we consider $[c]_n$, the multiset of results obtained by running a program c under this semantics on the set of all input lists of length n. We can view $[c]_n$ as a distribution, where the mass of some value a in the distribution is the proportion of input strings that cause the program to terminate with value a. The statement of equivalence between the semantics is shown in Theorem 9.

Theorem 9. *If c is well-formed, then* $\lim_{n\to\infty} [c]_n = [\![c]\!]$

FCF contains a proof of Theorem 9 as a validation of the operational semantics used for extraction. Now that we have an operational semantics, we can simply use the standard Coq extraction mechanism to extract it along with the model of interest and all supporting types and functions. Of course, the trustworthiness of the extracted code depends on the correctness of Coq's extraction mechanism. Gallina does not allow infinite recursion, so the framework includes OCaml code that runs a computation under the operational semantics until a value is obtained. The final step is instantiating any abstract types and functions with appropriate OCaml code. This extraction mechanism does not produce production-quality code, but the code could be used for purposes related to prototyping and testing.

This alternate semantics also provides other benefits. Because limits are unique, if two programs are equivalent under the operational semantics, then they are also equivalent under the denotational semantics. This allows us to prove equivalence of two programs using the operational semantics when it is more convenient to do so. Another benefit is that the operational semantics can be considered to be the basic semantics for computations, and the denotational semantics no longer needs to be trusted. Some may prefer this arrangement, since the operational semantics more closely resembles a typical model of computation, and may be easier to understand and inspect. The operational semantics can also be used as a basis for a model of computation used to determine whether programs are efficient.

4 Security Proof Construction

This section uses an example to describe the process of constructing a proof of security using the general process described at the beginning of Section 3.

We consider a simple encryption scheme constructed from a pseudorandom function (PRF), and we prove that ciphertexts produced by this scheme are indistinguishable under chosen plaintext attack (IND-CPA). This example proof is relatively simple, yet it contains many elements that one would find in a typical cryptographic argument, and so it allows us to exercise all of the key functionality of the framework. A more complex mechanized proof (*e.g.*, the proof of [11]) may have more intermediate games and a different set of arguments to justify game transformations, but the structure is similar to the proof that follows. The omitted details of the proof can be found in the longer form of this paper available at http://arxiv.org/abs/1410.3735.

4.1 Concrete Security Definitions

In FCF, security definitions are used to describe properties that some construction is proven to have, as well as problems that are assumed to be hard. In the PRF encryption proof, we use the definition of a PRF to assume that such a PRF exists, and we use that assumption to prove that the construction in question has the IND-CPA property. A concrete security definition typically contains some game and an expression that describes the *advantage* of some adversary – *i.e.*, the probability that the adversary will "win" the game.

The game used to define the concrete security of a PRF is shown in Listing 4. Less formally, we say that f is a PRF for some adversary A if A cannot effectively distinguish f from a random function. So this means that we expect that PRF_Advantage is "small" as long as A is an admissible adversary.

The function f_oracle simply puts the function f in the form of an oracle, though a very simple one with no state and with deterministic behavior. The procedure RndR_func is an oracle implementing a random function constructed using the provided computation RndR. The expressions involving A use a coercion in Coq to invoke the denotational semantics for OracleComp, and therefore ensure that A can query the oracle but has no access to the state of the oracle.

At a high level, this definition involves two games describing two different "worlds" in which the adversary may find himself. In one world (PRF_G_A) the adversary interacts with the PRF, and in the other (PRF_G_B) the adversary interacts with a random function. In each game, the adversary interacts with the oracle and then outputs a bit. The advantage of the adversary is the difference between the probability that he outputs 1 in world PRF_G_A and the probability that he outputs 1 in world PRF_G_B. If f is a PRF, then this advantage should be small.

The concrete security definition for IND-CPA encryption is shown in Listing 6. In this definition, KeyGen and Encrypt are the key generation and encryption procedures. The adversary comprises two procedures, A1 and A2 with different signatures, and the adversary is allowed to share arbitrary state information between these two procedures. This definition uses a slightly different style than the PRF definition—there is one game and the "world" is chosen at random within that game. Then the adversary attempts to determine which world was chosen.

```
Variable Key D R : Set.
Variable RndKey : Comp Key.
Variable RndR : Comp R.
Variable A : OracleComp D R bool.
Variable f : Key -> D -> R.

Definition f_oracle(k: Key)(x: unit)
  (d : D) : Comp (R * unit) :=
  ret (f k d, tt).
Definition PRF_G_A : Comp bool :=
  k <-$ RndKey;
  [b, _] <-$2 A (f_oracle k) tt;
  ret b.
Definition PRF_G_B : Comp bool :=
  [b, _] <-$2 A (RndR_func) nil;
  ret b.
Definition PRF_Advantage :=
  | Pr[PRF_G_A] - Pr[PRF_G_B] |.
```

Listing 4. PRF Concrete Security Definition

```
Variable eta : nat.
Variable f : Bvector eta ->
  Bvector eta -> Bvector eta.

Definition PRFE_KeyGen :=
  {0, 1} ^ eta.
Definition PRFE_Encrypt
  (k : Key )(p : Plaintext) :=
  r <-$ {0, 1} ^ eta;
  ret (r, p xor (f k r)).
Definition PRFE_Decrypt
  (k : Key)(c : Ciphertext) :=
  (snd c) xor (f k (fst c)).
```

Listing 5. Encryption using a PRF

```
Variable Plaintext Ciphertext Key
  State : Set.
Variable KeyGen : Comp Key.
Variable Encrypt : Key -> Ciphertext
  -> Comp Plaintext.
Variable A1 : OracleComp
  Plaintext Ciphertext
  (Plaintext * Plaintext * State).
Variable A2 : State -> Ciphertext ->
  OracleComp Plaintext Ciphertext
  bool.

Definition EncryptOracle
  (k: Key)(x: unit)(p: Plaintext) :=
  c <-$ Encrypt k p;
  ret (c, tt).
Definition IND_CPA_SecretKey_G :=
  key <-$ KeyGen ;
  [b, _] <-$2
  (
    [p0, p1, s_A] <--$3 A1;
    b <--$$ {0, 1};
    pb <- if b then p1 else p0;
    c <--$$ Encrypt key pb;
    b' <--$ A2 s_A c;
    $ ret eqb b b'
  )
  (EncryptOracle key) tt;
  ret b.
Definition
  IND_CPA_SecretKey_Advantage :=
  | Pr[IND_CPA_SecretKey_G] - 1/2 |.
```

Listing 6. IND-CPA Concrete Security Definition

In Listing 6, the game produces an encryption oracle from the Encrypt function and a randomly-generated encryption key. Then the remainder of the game, including the calls to A1 and A2, may interact with that oracle. The code for this definition includes some additional notation (different arrows and extra $ symbols) that is only used to provide hints to the Coq parser and does not change the behavior of the program.

4.2 Construction

The construction, like the security definitions, can be modeled in a very natural way. Of course, one must take care to ensure that the construction has the correct signature as specified in the desired security property. The PRF encryption construction is shown in Listing 5.

In the PRF Encryption construction, we assume a nat called eta (η) which will serve as the security parameter. The encryption scheme is based on a function f, and the scheme will only be secure if f is a PRF. The type of keys and plaintexts is bit vectors of length eta, and the type of ciphertexts is pairs of these bit vectors. The decryption function is included for completeness, but it is not needed for this security proof.

4.3   Sequence of Games

The sequence of games represents the overall strategy for completing the proof. In the case of PRF Encryption, we want to show that the probability that the adversary will correctly guess the randomly chosen "world" is close to $1/2$. We accomplish this by instantiating the IND-CPA security definition with the construction, and then transforming this game, little by little, until we have a game in which this probability is exactly $1/2$. Each transformation may add some concrete value to the bounds, and we want to ensure that the sum of these values is small.

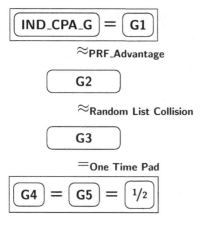

Fig. 3. Sequence of Games Diagram

```
Definition PRFE_Encrypt_OC (x : unit)
  (p : Plaintext) : OracleComp
  (Bvector eta) (Bvector eta)
  (Ciphertext * unit) :=
  r <--$$ {0,1} ^ eta;
  pad <--$ OC_Query r;
  $ (ret (r, p xor pad, tt)).

Definition PRF_A : OracleComp
  (Bvector eta) (Bvector eta) bool :=
  [a, n] <--$2 OC_Run A1
       PRFE_Encrypt_OC tt;
  [p0, p1, s_A] <-3 a;
  b <--$$ {0,1}; r <--$$ {0,1}^eta;
  pb <- if b then p1 else p0;
  pad <--$ OC_Query r;
  c <- (r, pb xor pad);
  z <--$ OC_Run (A2 s_A c)
       PRFE_Encrypt_OC n;
  [b',_] <-2 z; $ ret (eqb b b').
```

Listing 7. The Constructed Adversary Against the PRF

The diagram in Figure 3 shows the entire sequence of games, as well as the relationship between each pair of games in the sequence. In this diagram, two games are related by = if they are identical, and by $\approx$ if they are close. When the equivalence is non-trivial, the diagram gives an argument for the equivalence, which implies a bound on the distance between the games when they are not equal. The intermediate game code is omitted for brevity, but a detailed description of each game transformation follows.

We begin by instantiating the IND-CPA definition with the construction and simplifying to produce game G1. This equivalence is obvious, and the proof can be completed using Coq's `reflexivity` tactic.

Next we replace the function f with a random function, and the distance between G1 and G2 is exactly the advantage of some adversary against a PRF. The adversary against the PRF (Listing 7) is constructed from A1 and A2. PRFE_Encrypt_OC is an encryption oracle that interacts with the PRF as an oracle. PRF_A provides this encryption oracle to A1 and A2 (the two adversary procedures in the IND-CPA definition) using the OC_Run operation. This proof can be completed by performing simple manipulations and then unifying with PRF_Advantage.

Now we replace the random function output used to encrypt the challenge ciphertext with a bit vector selected completely at random to produce game G3. We show that G2 and G3 are "close" by demonstrating that these games are "identical until bad" in the sense of Theorem 5. The "bad" event of interest is the event that the randomly-generated PRF input used to encrypt the challenge plaintext is also used to encrypt some other value during the interaction between the adversary and the encryption oracle. There are two separate adversary procedures, and each one is capable of encountering r during its interaction with the oracle. To get an expression for the probability of the "bad" event, we assume natural numbers q_1 and q_2, and that A1 performs at most q_1 queries and A2 performs at most q_2 queries. FCF includes a library module called RndInList that includes general-purpose arguments related to the probability of encountering a randomly selected value in a list of a certain length, and the probability of encountering a certain value in a list of randomly-generated elements of a certain length. Using these arguments, we conclude that the distance between G2 and G3 is $q_1/2^\eta + q_2/2^\eta$.

The previous equivalences are proven using the program logic described in Section 3.3. Once the random functions are removed, there are no more issues related to state, and the remainder of the proof can be completed by reasoning on the probability distributions using the theory from Section 3.2.

In G3, the encryption of the challenge plaintext is by one-time pad, so we can replace the resulting ciphertext with a randomly-chosen value to produce G4. FCF contains a generic one-time-pad argument that we can apply to show that G3 is equivalent to G4. This step is relatively simple so we include the full code of the proof (Listing 8) for illustration. The one-time pad argument expects the game to be in a particular form, so we develop another intermediate game (G3_1), and we start by proving that G3 is equivalent to G3_1. These games only differ by associativity, so a simple repeated proof script establishes their equivalence. The second proof in Listing 8 focuses on the appropriate context, and then applies the one-time pad argument for xor. The custom tactics used in this proof are described in Section 3.4.

```
Theorem G3_G3_1_equiv:
  Pr[G3] == Pr[G3_1].

  unfold G3, G3_1.
  repeat (comp_simp;
    inline_first;
    comp_skip).
Qed.

Theorem G3_1_G4_equiv:
  Pr[G3_1] == Pr[G4].

  unfold G3_1, G4.
  do 4 (comp_skip;
    comp_simp).
  apply xor_OTP_eq.
  reflexivity.
Qed.
```

Listing 8. Proof of Equivalence of G3 and G4

In G4, the challenge bit is independent of all other values in the game, so we can move the sampling of this bit to the end of the game to produce G5. The proof of equivalence is by repeated application of the commutativity theorem (Theorem 2).

Finally, we develop the proof that the adversary wins Game 5 with probability exactly 1/2. This proof proceeds by discarding all of the statements in the game before the coin flip. Then what remains is a very simple game that flips a coin and compares the result to a fixed value. A provided tactic can automatically determine that the probability that this game returns *true* is 1/2.

By combining the equivalences of each pair of intermediate games, we get the final concrete security result shown in Listing 9. It is important to note that the statement of this theorem does not reference any of the intermediate games. The sequence of games was only a tool that we used to get the final result, and this sequence does not need to be inspected in order to trust the result.

```
Theorem PRFE_IND_CPA_concrete :
  IND_CPA_SecretKey_Advantage PRFE_KeyGen PRFE_Encrypt A1 A2 <=
  PRF_Advantage ({0,1}^eta) ({0,1}^eta) f PRF_A + (q1 / 2^eta + q2 / 2^eta).
```

Listing 9. Concrete Security Result

This completes the proof of security in the concrete setting. We have also developed an asymptotic security proof based on this result, but a discussion of this proof is omitted for brevity.

5   Comparison to EasyCrypt

This section attempts to evaluate FCF against the design goals listed in Section 2, and to contrast with both CertiCrypt and EasyCrypt.

All three of these frameworks provide concrete bounds, so this criterion is not discussed further. And, all three frameworks use a relatively familiar syntax for security definitions and constructions. We believe that, based on our experience working with cryptographers, they can easily understand these definitions (*e.g.*, Listing 4) after spending a few minutes familiarizing themselves with the notation.

Regarding proof automation, FCF lies somewhere between CertiCrypt and EasyCrypt. EasyCrypt achieves a significant level of automation by using SMT solvers to discharge simple logical goals, but higher-level goals still need to be addressed manually by applying tactics. FCF achieves a similarly high level of automation through the use of existing and custom Coq tactics. These tactics are not as powerful as modern SMT solvers, so the developer may need to manually address some goals in FCF that would be discharged automatically in EasyCrypt. However, the semantics of programs in FCF is computational, so Coq is able to immediately compute an expression describing the probability distribution for any program. This allows some simple equivalences to be discharged immediately using the semantics and tactics provided by FCF.

Regarding trust in *extensional properties*, FCF and CertiCrypt are foundational, meaning that the program logic is constructed definitionally from the semantics. In contrast, the relationship between EasyCrypt's semantics and program logic is not mechanized. The trusted computing base of EasyCrypt includes the EasyCrypt front end (the OCaml code that implements EasyCrypt) and the Why3 verification condition generator and one or more SMT solvers (if the proof includes a tactic that invokes the SMT solvers), whereas the TCB of FCF and CertiCrypt includes only the Coq type checker. EasyCrypt provides no support for reasoning about *intensional properties* such as execution time, whereas

CertiCrypt and FCF do, though FCF provides this suport using a trusted set of axioms.

EasyCrypt and CertiCrypt are based on simply-typed, first-order languages which are deeply-embedded into higher-order languages. This design makes it difficult to directly support abstraction, extension, and reuse, though these frameworks include elements which support these goals to some extent. In contrast, FCF uses a shallow embedding and the advanced features of Coq, such as dependent types, modules, notation, and higher-order functions, to support abstraction, extensiblity, and reuse. We believe that having such a rich language for describing games, assumptions, and arguments is critical for scaling to larger protocols.

FCF supports code generation with a semantics that is proven to be equivalent to the semantics used to reason about the probabilistic behavior of programs. That is, a program extracted from an FCF model is guaranteed to produce the correct probability distribution when the input bits provided to it are uniformly distributed, assuming the extraction mechanism of Coq preserves meaning. There has been some initial work [3] in producing implementations that correspond to EasyCrypt models, but there is no formal relationship between the semantics of the implementation and the semantics used to reason about the model.

EasyCrypt and FCF solve the same problem in slightly different ways and with different sets of strengths and weaknesses. It is too early to tell which sorts of proofs will benefit from one approach over the other.

6 Related Work

There has been a large amount of work in the area of verifying cryptographic schemes in recent years. In this section we will describe some of this related work, focusing on systems that attempt to establish security in the computational model. CertiCrypt [6] and EasyCrypt [5] have been thoroughly discussed previously in this paper.

There are several other examples of frameworks for cryptographic security proofs implemented within proof assistants. The most similar work is that of Nowak [19], who was the first to develop proofs of cryptography in Coq using a shallow embedding in which programs have probability distributions as their denotations. FCF builds on this work by adding more tools for modeling and reasoning such as procedures with oracle access (Section 3.1), a program logic (Section 3.3), and asymptotic reasoning (Section 3.5).

The work of [2] is a Coq library utilizing a deeply-embedded imperative programming language. This library is a predecessor to CertiCrypt, and it includes some important elements that were later adopted by CertiCrypt. Notably, the probabilistic programming language in this work is given a semantics in which program states are distributions, and the semantics describes how these distributions are transformed by each command in the language. Though this library lacks some of the features of CertiCrypt such as oracles, unrestricted loops, and the Probabilistic Relational Hoare Logic.

Verypto [9] is a fully-featured framework built on Isabelle [18] that includes a deep embedding of a functional programming language. To allow state information to remain hidden from adversaries, Verypto provides ML-style references, in contrast to the oracle system provided by FCF. To date, Verypto has only been used to prove the security of simple constructions, but this work uses an interesting approach that deserves more exploration.

CryptoVerif [10] is a tool based on a concurrent, probabilistic process calculus that is only able to prove properties related to secrecy and authenticity. CryptoVerif is highly automated to the extent that it will even attempt to locate intermediate games, and so proof development in CryptoVerif requires far less effort compared to FCF or EasyCrypt. However, there are a large number of proofs that could be completed in FCF or EasyCrypt that are impossible in CryptoVerif due to its specialized nature and lack of interactive proof development features.

Refinement types [8] have been used by Fournet et al [15] to develop proofs of security for cryptographic schemes in the computational model. In this system, a security property is specified as an ideal functionality (in the sense of the real/ideal paradigm), and constructions have these properties by assumption. This approach allows the proofs of security to be fairly simple, but many important facts are assumed rather than mechanized, and no concrete security claims are proved.

Computational soundness [1] provides another mechanism for verifying cryptographic schemes. This approach attempts to derive security in the computational model from security in the symbolic model by showing that any likely execution trace in the computational model also exists in the symbolic model. It is possible to mechanize such a proof as described in [4]. This approach is limited to classes of schemes for which computational soundness results have been discovered. Another limitation with this approach is that it can only produce proofs in the asymptotic setting—there is no way to prove concrete security claims.

Protocol Composition Logic (PCL) [12] provides a logic and proof system for verifying cryptographic schemes in the symbolic model. The system is based on a process calculus and allows reasoning about the results of individual protocol steps. More recent work [13] has extended this logic to allow for proofs in the computational model. In computational PCL, formulas are interpreted against probability distributions on traces and a formula is true if it holds with overwhelming probability. This approach is similar to computational soundness in that low-probability traces are ignored, and proofs of concrete security claims are impossible.

7   Conclusion and Future Work

Our contribution is a complete mechanized framework for specifying and checking cryptographic proofs within a proof assistant. Our framework compares favorably to the current state of the art, and provides many new benefits, such as extensibility through a foundational approach, a powerful language for describing schemes and arguments, and the ability to extract excutable code. Next we intend to demonstrate the scalability of FCF by describing a mechanized proof of security of a complex searchable symmetric encryption scheme ([11]).

References

1. Abadi, M., Rogaway, P.: Reconciling two views of cryptography. In: Watanabe, O., Hagiya, M., Ito, T., van Leeuwen, J., Mosses, P.D. (eds.) TCS 2000. LNCS, vol. 1872, pp. 3–22. Springer, Heidelberg (2000), http://dl.acm.org/citation.cfm?id=647318.723498
2. Affeldt, R., Tanaka, M., Marti, N.: Formal proof of provable security by game-playing in a proof assistant. In: Susilo, W., Liu, J.K., Mu, Y. (eds.) ProvSec 2007. LNCS, vol. 4784, pp. 151–168. Springer, Heidelberg (2007), http://dl.acm.org/citation.cfm?id=1779394.1779408
3. Almeida, J.B., Barbosa, M., Barthe, G., Dupressoir, F.: Certified computer-aided cryptography: Efficient provably secure machine code from high-level implementations. In: Proceedings of the 2013 ACM SIGSAC Conference on Computer and Communications Security, CCS 2013, pp. 1217–1230. ACM, New York (2013), http://doi.acm.org/10.1145/2508859.2516652
4. Backes, M., Unruh, D.: Computational soundness of symbolic zero-knowledge proofs against active attackers. In: 21st IEEE Computer Security Foundations Symposium, CSF 2008, pp. 255–269 (June 2008), preprint on IACR ePrint 2008/152
5. Barthe, G., Grégoire, B., Heraud, S., Béguelin, S.Z.: Computer-aided security proofs for the working cryptographer. In: Rogaway, P. (ed.) CRYPTO 2011. LNCS, vol. 6841, pp. 71–90. Springer, Heidelberg (2011)
6. Barthe, G., Grégoire, B., Zanella Béguelin, S.: Formal certification of code-based cryptographic proofs. In: 36th ACM SIGPLAN-SIGACT Symposium on Principles of Programming Languages, POPL 2009, pp. 90–101. ACM (2009), http://dx.doi.org/10.1145/1480881.1480894
7. Bellare, M., Rogaway, P.: Code-based game-playing proofs and the security of triple encryption. Cryptology ePrint Archive, Report 2004/331 (2004), http://eprint.iacr.org/
8. Bengtson, J., Bhargavan, K., Fournet, C., Maffeis, S., Gordon, A.D.: Refinement types for secure implementations. In: 21st IEEE Computer Security Foundations Symposium (CSF 2008), pp. 17–32. IEEE (2008)
9. Berg, M.: Formal Verification of Cryptographic Security Proofs. Ph.D. thesis, Saarland University (2013), http://www.infsec.cs.uni-saarland.de/~berg/publications/thesis-berg.pdf
10. Blanchet, B.: Computationally sound mechanized proofs of correspondence assertions. In: 20th IEEE Computer Security Foundations Symposium (CSF 2007), pp. 97–111. IEEE, Venice (2007)
11. Cash, D., Jarecki, S., Jutla, C., Krawczyk, H., Roşu, M.-C., Steiner, M.: Highly-Scalable Searchable Symmetric Encryption with Support for Boolean Queries. In: Canetti, R., Garay, J.A. (eds.) CRYPTO 2013, Part I. LNCS, vol. 8042, pp. 353–373. Springer, Heidelberg (2013)
12. Datta, A., Derek, A., Mitchell, J.C., Roy, A.: Protocol composition logic (PCL). Electronic Notes in Theoretical Computer Science 172, 311–358 (2007)

13. Datta, A., Derek, A., Mitchell, J.C., Turuani, M.: Probabilistic polynomial-time semantics for a protocol security logic. In: Caires, L., Italiano, G.F., Monteiro, L., Palamidessi, C., Yung, M. (eds.) ICALP 2005. LNCS, vol. 3580, pp. 16–29. Springer, Heidelberg (2005)
14. Elgamal, T.: A public key cryptosystem and a signature scheme based on discrete logarithms. IEEE Transactions on Information Theory 31(4), 469–472 (1985)
15. Fournet, C., Kohlweiss, M., Strub, P.Y.: Modular code-based cryptographic verification. In: Chen, Y., Danezis, G., Shmatikov, V. (eds.) ACM Conference on Computer and Communications Security, pp. 341–350. ACM (2011)
16. Halevi, S.: A plausible approach to computer-aided cryptographic proofs. Cryptology ePrint Archive, Report 2005/181 (2005), http://eprint.iacr.org/
17. The Coq development team: The Coq proof assistant reference manual. LogiCal Project (2004), version 8.0, http://coq.inria.fr
18. Nipkow, T., Paulson, L.C., Wenzel, M.: Isabelle/HOL. LNCS, vol. 2283. Springer, Heidelberg (2002)
19. Nowak, D.: A framework for game-based security proofs. Cryptology ePrint Archive, Report 2007/199 (2007), http://eprint.iacr.org/
20. Ramsey, N., Pfeffer, A.: Stochastic lambda calculus and monads of probability distributions. In: Proceedings of the 29th ACM SIGPLAN-SIGACT Symposium on Principles of Programming Languages, POPL 2002, pp. 154–165. ACM, New York (2002), http://doi.acm.org/10.1145/503272.503288

On the Flow of Data, Information, and Time

Martín Abadi[1] and Michael Isard[2]

[1] University of California, Santa Cruz, California, USA
[2] Microsoft Research*, Mountain View, California, USA

Abstract. We study information flow in a model for data-parallel computing. We show how an extant notion of virtual time can help guarantee information-flow properties. For this purpose, we introduce functions that express dependencies between inputs and outputs at each node in a dataflow graph. Each node may operate over a distinct set of virtual times—so, from a security perspective, it may have its own classification scheme. A coherence criterion ensures that those local dependencies yield global properties.

1 Introduction

The flow of data generally entails the flow of information, whose understanding is often essential for the performance and correctness of dataflow computations. For example, knowing that two dataflow computations on different input batches do not interfere with one another can open opportunities for asynchronous, overlapped execution. It may perhaps also contribute to ensuring that sensitive inputs do not leak through public outputs, that untrusted data does not taint trusted results, and other security and privacy properties.

Therefore, modern platforms for data-parallel computing sometimes track dependencies, at least coarsely, primarily in order to enable efficient implementations. For instance, Spark maintains dependencies between Resilient Distributed Datasets [17], representing their lineage. Naiad [11] associates messages and other events with virtual times [4]; the partial order of virtual times, which need not correspond to the order of execution, determines whether one event can potentially result in another event.

Of course, understanding the flow of information does not necessarily mean the same in data-parallel computing and in security and privacy. In particular, covert communication channels are seldom a concern for data-parallel computing. Furthermore, at least at present, systems for data-parallel computing typically leverage strong trust assumptions: most systems code is trusted, and even the environment is often assumed to be somewhat benign.

Nevertheless, we explore the idea that models and systems for data-parallel computing can offer substantial information-flow control. We focus on concepts and facilities for information-flow control, rather than on their applications. Specifically, we consider the computational model that underlies Naiad, called

---

* Most of this work was done at Microsoft Research. M. Abadi is now at Google.

© Springer-Verlag Berlin Heidelberg 2015
R. Focardi and A. Myers (Eds.): POST 2015, LNCS 9036, pp. 73–92, 2015.
DOI: 10.1007/978-3-662-46666-7_5

timely dataflow. We find that, after a modest strengthening (and a change of perspective), timely dataflow offers information-flow properties that resemble familiar ones from the security literature.

As indicated above, timely dataflow supports partially ordered virtual times. These virtual times may be viewed as analogous to security levels or classifications. Furthermore, timely dataflow considers the question of whether one event at a given virtual time t and location l in a dataflow graph could result in another event at a virtual time t' and location l' in the same graph. The expectation that an event at (l, t) cannot result in an event at (l', t') "in the past" is analogous to conditions on flows across security levels, but weaker. So we identify alternative concepts and properties that, although consistent with timely dataflow, lead to non-interference guarantees.

One somewhat unusual aspect of the resulting framework is that it allows the use of different sets of virtual times (that is, different sets of security levels) in different parts of a system. For example, virtual times inside loops may have coordinates that correspond to loop counters, and can distinguish data from different loop iterations that may be processed simultaneously; those coordinates do not make sense outside loops. From a security viewpoint, virtual times in different parts of a computation may reflect the classification schemes of different organizations, or the classification schemes appropriate to the different kinds of data being processed. While simple levels like "Public" and "Secret" are allowed, there is no built-in assumption or requirement that they mean and are treated the same everywhere. Moreover, each neighborhood of a dataflow graph could have its own custom levels. Finally, a virtual time may be a tuple that includes both structural information (such as loop counters) and other facets, such as secrecy and integrity levels. We define a criterion that ensures the coherence of the use of levels.

Our main results enable us to reason about systems organized as dataflow graphs, and to characterize the information that each node in such a graph may obtain. As a small example (to which we return in Section 5.4), consider a system that receives and processes messages that each pertain to one of two users U_1 and U_2. Suppose that a particular node p_0 in this system forwards data about each user to a different destination, p_1 or p_2 respectively. We abstract p_0's behavior by stating that its messages to p_1 do not depend on its inputs about U_2, and symmetrically its messages to p_2 do not depend on its inputs about U_1. We make such statements directly, formulating them in terms of virtual times; in other approaches, analogous statements might be encoded in type annotations. From p_0's properties and the topology of the dataflow graph we may then derive that p_1 learns nothing from the inputs about U_2, and that p_2 learns nothing from the inputs about U_1. More generally, our work provides an approach for establishing information-flow properties of a dataflow system from properties of individual nodes and the topology of the system.

The next section is a review of the relevant aspects of the model of computation that we consider. Section 3 introduces auxiliary concepts: frontiers, filtering, and reordering. Section 4 defines and studies the machinery for specifying dependency information at the level of individual nodes. Section 5 presents lemmas and our main results, including the coherence criterion and the non-interference guarantees. Section 6 concludes. Although this paper aims to be self-contained, it stems from a larger effort to understand, improve, and apply timely dataflow. Section 6 briefly discusses aspects of this effort relevant to security and some directions for further work. Because of space constraints, proofs are omitted.

2   Model of Computation

This section reviews the setting for our work. As explained in Section 6, it is a fragment of the full timely dataflow model, which was introduced in the context of Naiad [11] and whose formal study is the subject of another paper, currently in preparation. Here, therefore, we do not describe the model in full detail, focusing instead on the main ideas and aspects relevant to our present purposes.

As in other dataflow models (e.g., [5]), programs are organized as directed graphs, in which nodes do the processing and messages travel on edges. We write P for the set of nodes (or processors) and E for the set of edges (or channels). We refer to both nodes and edges as locations. For simplicity, we assume that the source $src(e)$ and the destination $dst(e)$ of each edge e are distinct nodes; however, in general, graphs may contain cycles. We write M for the set of messages, and M^* for the set of finite sequences of messages.

Each message m is associated with a virtual time $time(m)$. The virtual times form a partial order (not necessarily linear, not necessarily a lattice), which we write $(T, \leq)$. There is no built-in requirement that the order of processing of messages correspond in any way to their virtual times.

We can describe the state of a system as a mapping from nodes to their local states plus a mapping from edges to their contents. We write $LocState(p)$ for the local state of node p, and Σ_{Loc} for the set of local states; we are not concerned with the specifics of how local state is organized. We write $Q(e)$ for the finite sequence of messages on edge e.

A local history for a node p is a finite sequence $\langle\langle s, (e_1, m_1), \ldots, (e_k, m_k)\rangle\rangle$ that starts with an initial local state s that satisfies a given predicate $Initial(p)$, and is followed by (zero, one, or more) pairs of the form (e_i, m_i), which indicate the messages that the node has received and the corresponding edges. We write $Histories(p)$ for the set of local histories of p.

We assume that initially each node p is in a local state that satisfies $Initial(p)$, and for each edge e we let $Q(e)$ contain an arbitrary finite sequence of messages, so as to get computations started. (This detail constitutes a minor variation from other presentations of timely dataflow, in which computations can get started by other means.) Thereafter, at each step of computation (atomically, for simplicity), a node that has messages on incoming edges picks one of them, processes it, and places messages on its output edges. The processing is defined by a function $g_1(p)$ for each node p, which we apply to p's local state s and to a pair (e, m), and which produces a tuple that contains a new state s' and finite sequences of messages $\mu_1, \ldots, \mu_k$ on p's output edges $e_1, \ldots, e_k$, respectively. We write:

$$g_1(p)(s, (e, m)) = (s', \langle e_1 \mapsto \mu_1, \ldots, e_k \mapsto \mu_k \rangle)$$

where $\langle e_1 \mapsto \mu_1, \ldots, e_k \mapsto \mu_k \rangle$ is the function that maps e_1 to μ_1, ..., e_k to μ_k. Iterating this function $g_1(p)$, we obtain a function $g(p)$ which takes as input an entire local history h and produces a new state s' and the cumulative finite sequences of messages $\mu_1, \ldots, \mu_k$ for the output edges $e_1, \ldots, e_k$, as follows:

- $g(p)(\langle\!\langle s \rangle\!\rangle) = (s, \langle e_1 \mapsto \emptyset, \ldots, e_k \mapsto \emptyset \rangle)$,
- if $g(p)(h) = (s', \langle e_1 \mapsto \mu_1, \ldots, e_k \mapsto \mu_k \rangle)$ and $g_1(p)(s', (d, m)) = (s", \langle e_1 \mapsto \mu_1', \ldots, e_k \mapsto \mu_k' \rangle)$, then $g(p)(h \cdot (d, m)) = (s", \langle e_1 \mapsto \mu_1 \cdot \mu_1', \ldots, e_k \mapsto \mu_k \cdot \mu_k' \rangle)$.

As in this definition, we write $\emptyset$ for the empty sequence and $\langle\!\langle a_0, a_1, \ldots \rangle\!\rangle$ for a sequence that contains $a_0, a_1, \ldots$, and we use $\cdot$ both for adding elements to sequences and for appending sequences. We let $\Pi_{\mathrm{Loc}}(s', \langle e_1 \mapsto \mu_1, \ldots, e_k \mapsto \mu_k \rangle) = s'$ and $\Pi_{e_i}(s', \langle e_1 \mapsto \mu_1, \ldots, e_k \mapsto \mu_k \rangle) = \mu_i$ for $i = 1 \ldots k$.

The overall specification of a system denotes a set of allowed sequences of states. Each of the sequences starts in an initial state, and every pair of consecutive states is either identical (a "stutter") or related by a step of computation. We add an auxiliary state function H (a history variable [1]) in order to track local histories: $H(p)$ represents p's local history; thus, each state is defined by values for the state functions $LocState$, Q, and H. We express the specification in TLA [8], in Figure 1, with the following notations. A primed state function (Q', $LocState'$, or H') in an action refers to the value of the state function in the "next" state (the state after the action); $\square$ is the temporal-logic operator "always"; given an action N and a list of expressions $v_1, \ldots, v_k$, $[N]_{v_1, \ldots, v_k}$ abbreviates $N \vee ((v_1' = v_1) \wedge \ldots \wedge (v_k' = v_k))$.

We call $ISpec$ the complete specification, $InitProp$ the initial conditions, and $MessR$ the action that represents a step of computation. When Q_0 is a (state-independent) function from E to M^*, we also write $ISpec(Q_0)$ for the conjunction of $ISpec$ with $\forall e \in E.Q(e) = Q_0(e)$, which says that the initial values of the queues are as given by Q_0.

The definition of the action $MessR$ describes how a node p dequeues a message m and reacts to it, producing messages. This action is a relaxed version of a simpler action that we call $Mess$ (hence the name $MessR$) and according to which p takes a message from the head of $Q(e)$, so $Q(e) = m \cdot Q'(e)$. (The head of a queue is to the left, the tail to the right.) According to $MessR$, on the other hand, p is allowed to take any message m in $Q(e)$ such that there is no message n ahead of m with $time(n) \leq time(m)$; so, for some u and v, $Q(e) = u \cdot m \cdot v$, $Q'(e) = u \cdot v$, and u does not contain any message n with $time(n) \leq time(m)$. Thus, queues are not strictly FIFO. This relaxation can be useful in support of optimizations, as it can allow more messages for a given time to be processed together. It is also important for work on fault-tolerance in which we are currently engaged, and seems attractive in the present context as well. (See Section 5.)

$$InitProp \triangleq \begin{pmatrix} \forall p \in P.LocState(p) \in Initial(p) \\ \wedge \\ \forall e \in E.Q(e) \in M^* \\ \wedge \\ \forall p \in P.H(p) = \langle\!\langle LocState(p) \rangle\!\rangle \end{pmatrix}$$

$$MessR \triangleq \exists p \in P.MessR1(p)$$

$$MessR1(p) \triangleq \begin{pmatrix} \exists m \in M.\exists e \in E \text{ such that } p = dst(e).\exists u, v \in M^*. \\ Q(e) = u{\cdot}m{\cdot}v \wedge Q'(e) = u{\cdot}v \\ \wedge \\ \forall n \in u.time(n) \not\leq time(m) \\ \wedge \\ Mess2(p, e, m) \end{pmatrix}$$

$$Mess2(p, e, m) \triangleq \begin{pmatrix} let \\ \{e_1, \ldots, e_k\} = \{d \in E \mid src(d) = p\}, \\ s = LocState(p), \\ (s', \langle e_1 {\mapsto} \mu_1, \ldots, e_k {\mapsto} \mu_k \rangle) = g_1(p)(s, (e, m)) \\ in \\ LocState'(p) = s' \\ \wedge \\ Q'(e_1) = Q(e_1){\cdot}\mu_1 \ldots Q'(e_k) = Q(e_k){\cdot}\mu_k \\ \wedge \\ H'(p) = H(p){\cdot}(e, m) \\ \wedge \\ \forall q \in P \neq p.LocState'(q) = LocState(q) \\ \wedge \\ \forall d \in E - \{e, e_1, \ldots, e_k\}.Q'(d) = Q(d) \\ \wedge \\ \forall q \in P \neq p.H'(q) = H(q) \end{pmatrix}$$

$$ISpec \triangleq InitProp \wedge \Box[MessR]_{LocState, Q, H}$$

$$ISpec(Q_0) = ISpec \wedge \forall e \in E.Q(e) = Q_0(e)$$

Fig. 1. The specification

3   Frontiers, Filtering, and Other Auxiliary Concepts

We introduce a few auxiliary notions, namely frontiers, filtering, and reordering.

3.1   Frontiers

A subset S of T is *downward closed* if and only if, for all t and t', $t \in S$ and $t' \le t$ imply $t' \in S$. We call such a subset a *frontier*, and write F for the set of frontiers; we often let f range over frontiers. When $S \subseteq T$, we write $Close_{\downarrow}(S)$ for the downward closure of S (the least frontier that contains S).

As indicated in the Introduction, we may view virtual times as security levels. From that perspective, a frontier is a set of security levels S such that if S includes one level it includes all lower levels. For example, in multi-level security (MLS), such a set S might arise as the set of levels of the objects that a subject at a given level can read.

3.2   Filtering

We introduce *filtering* operations on histories and on sequences of messages. These filtering operations keep or remove all elements whose times are in a given frontier. Thus, they are analogous to the *purge* functions that appear in security models. (See, for example, McLean's survey [9, Section 2.2.1].)

Given a local history h and a frontier f, we write $h@f$ for the subsequence of h obtained by removing (filtering out) all events (d, m) such that $time(m) \notin f$. More precisely, $h@f$ is defined inductively by:

- $\langle\!\langle s \rangle\!\rangle @ f = \langle\!\langle s \rangle\!\rangle$,
- $(h \cdot (d, m)) @ f = (h @ f) \cdot (d, m)$ if $time(m) \in f$ and $(h \cdot (d, m)) @ f = h @ f$ otherwise.

Similarly, when u is a sequence of messages, we write $u@f$ for the subsequence obtained by removing those messages whose times are not in f. Finally, given a sequence of messages u and a frontier f, we write $u\overline{@}f$ for the subsequence of u consisting only of messages whose times are not in f.

3.3   Reordering

We define a relation $\hookrightarrow$ on finite sequences of messages: it is the least reflexive and transitive relation such that, for $u, v \in M^*$ and $m_1, m_2 \in M$, if $time(m_1) \not\le time(m_2)$ then $u \cdot m_1 \cdot m_2 \cdot v \hookrightarrow u \cdot m_2 \cdot m_1 \cdot v$. We call it the *reordering* relation.

This relation is a counterpart at the level of message sequences to the reordering that happens in message processing according to action *MessR* of Figure 1. It is therefore helpful for analyzing that specification and its implementations.

3.4   Subtraction

Subtraction for message sequences $(-)$ is defined inductively by:

$$u - \emptyset = u$$
$$u - m \cdot v = (u - m) - v$$
$$(m \cdot u - m) = u$$
$$(m' \cdot u - m) = m' \cdot (u - m) \text{ for } m' \neq m$$
$$\emptyset - m = \emptyset$$

The last clause $(\emptyset - m = \emptyset)$ appears in order to make subtraction a total operation. In our uses of subtraction, we sometimes ensure explicitly that it does not apply.

3.5   Some Properties of Filtering and Reordering

We state a few properties of filtering and reordering. Throughout, f, f_1, f_2, f_3 range over frontiers; u, v, w range over message sequences; h ranges over histories.

Proposition 1. If $f_1 = f_2 \cap f_3$ then $h@f_1 = h@f_2@f_3$.

Proposition 2. If $u \hookrightarrow v$ then $u@f \hookrightarrow v@f$.

Proposition 3. If $u \hookrightarrow v$ then $(u - w) \hookrightarrow (v - w)$.

Proposition 4. If $u \hookrightarrow v \cdot w$ then $(u - v@f) \hookrightarrow v@f \cdot w$.

Proposition 5. If $u@f = u'@f$, then $(u - v@f)@f = (u' - v@f)@f$.

The last two propositions (Propositions 6 and 7) are useful in reasoning with the action *MessR* because they provide methods for establishing that, for a sequence u and element m, there is no element n with $time(n) \leq time(m)$ to the left of m in u (in a prefix v). They say, respectively, that it suffices to consider any reordering u' of u or any sequence u' that coincides with u on some frontier f such that $time(m) \in f$.

Proposition 6. If $u \hookrightarrow u'$, $u' = v' \cdot m \cdot w'$, and $time(n) \not\leq time(m)$ for all n in v', then there exist v and w such that $u = v \cdot m \cdot w$, and $time(n) \not\leq time(m)$ for all n in v.

Proposition 7. If $u@f = u'@f$, $u' = v' \cdot m \cdot w'$, $time(m) \in f$, and $time(n) \not\leq time(m)$ for all n in v', then there exist v and w such that $u = v \cdot m \cdot w$, and $time(n) \not\leq time(m)$ for all n in v.

4   From Timeliness to Determination

Time domains and the could-result-in relation are central to timely dataflow. Although we do not need a formal definition of these notions for our present purposes, we review them informally in this section, in order to motivate our new definitions. While the could-result-in relation focuses on whether one event might trigger another event (directly or indirectly), we are interested in whether a history or a part of a history suffices for determining an output. These two questions are closely related, as we show. We treat the latter via *frontier transformers*, which are functions that map frontiers for inputs to frontiers for outputs and which we introduce and study in this section.

4.1   Time Domains

Timely dataflow does not require that all nodes deal with the same set of virtual times. In particular, the set T may be the disjoint union of multiple sets T_p, which we call *time domains*, one for each node p in a dataflow graph. Node p may expect inputs with times in set T_p and produce outputs with times in the sets appropriate for their recipients.

For example, in Naiad, nodes for loop ingress expect inputs with times of the form $(t_1, \ldots, t_k)$, and produce outputs with an extra coordinate, set to 0: $(t_1, \ldots, t_k, 0)$. Nodes for loop egress expect inputs with times of the form $(t_1, \ldots, t_k, t_{k+1})$, and drop the last coordinate on outputs. Nodes for loop feedback expect inputs with times of the form $(t_1, \ldots, t_k)$, and increment the last coordinate of these times. In all cases, the appropriate value of k is determined by the nesting depth of the loop.

Beyond these standard examples, it is possible, at least in principle, for programmers to define custom nodes, with their own ideas about virtual times. Thus, a custom node may consume inputs with times 1 and 2, but, somehow, produce results with times "Public" and "Secret"; or a custom node may consume inputs with times "Public" and "Secret", but produce results with finer classifications, such as "(Secret,A)" or "(Secret,B)", where "A" and "B" might indicate compartments, retention policies, or other properties of interest..

For simplicity, we proceed with the assumption that all inputs of a node are in the same time domain, but the outputs on each outgoing edge may be in a different time domain. It is straightforward to accommodate inputs in different time domains by inserting relay nodes that translate across time domains on incoming edges.

4.2   The Could-result-in Relation

When one event at a given virtual time t and location l in a dataflow graph can potentially result in another event at a virtual time t' and location l' in the same graph, we say that (l, t) could-result-in (l', t'). We write this relation $(l, t) \rightsquigarrow (l', t')$. For example, suppose that whenever node p receives any message m with $time(m) = 1$ on incoming edge d, p outputs a message n with $time(n) = 2$

on outgoing edge e; in this case we would have that $(d, 1) \rightsquigarrow (e, 2)$. In Naiad, the could-result-in relation is exploited for supporting completion notifications, which tell a node when it will no longer see messages for a given time. It also allows an implementation to reclaim resources that correspond to pairs (l, t) at which no more events are possible.

Informally, we expect that an event at (l, t) cannot result in an event at (l', t') "in the past". Naiad relies on this property in some of its algorithms. It holds rather obviously for most nodes, since, in response to an input at time t, most nodes would produce outputs at the same time t. However, defining "in the past" is delicate across time domains; fortunately, the approach that we develop in this paper does not require it.

As suggested in the Introduction, the expectation that an event cannot result in another event "in the past" is somewhat analogous to conditions on flows across security levels. For example, one may generally expect that a "low-integrity" event cannot cause a "high-integrity" event, except perhaps in trusted system components. Obviously, however, this property is not quite equivalent to a non-interference guarantee, or to other strong guarantees defined in the security literature [9]. Even if an input on edge d at time 2 may not trigger an output on edge e at time 1 for a node p, so we do not have $(d, 2) \rightsquigarrow (e, 1)$, the input at time 2 may affect the contents of future messages at time 1, if p is stateful and sends such messages in response to future inputs at times 0 and 1. Thus, inputs at time 2 may interfere with outputs at time 1.

4.3   Frontier Transformers

Going beyond what the could-result-in relation can express, knowing whether subsets of inputs determine subsets of outputs can be useful for a variety of purposes. We are finding it valuable in the context of current work on fault-tolerance. It is also clearly valuable for security, in which we often want, for instance, that "Public" inputs determine "Public" outputs, or that "Trusted" inputs determine "Trusted" outputs.

Formally, for each edge $e \in E$, we assume a function $\phi(e)$ that maps frontiers to frontiers (so, $\phi(e)$ is a frontier transformer). Its main intended property is Condition 1 which says that h gives rise to a message on e in $\phi(e)(f)$ if and only if so does $h@f$, and with messages in the same order and multiplicity.

Condition 1. *For all $f \in F$, if $g(p)(h) = (\ldots, \langle \ldots e_i \mapsto \mu_i \ldots \rangle)$ and $g(p)(h@f) = (\ldots, \langle \ldots e_i \mapsto \mu_i' \ldots \rangle)$ then $\mu_i @ \phi(e_i)(f) = \mu_i' @ \phi(e_i)(f)$.*

For many simple nodes, $\phi(e)$ may be the identity function for all outgoing edges e. On the other hand, the identity function is not always appropriate, particularly (but not only) when a node produces outputs in a different time domain than its inputs. Some of the nodes described in Section 4.1 exemplify this point. Entering a loop at depth $k+1$, inputs to an ingress node in a frontier f determine outputs for all times $\{(t_1, \ldots, t_k, t_{k+1}) \mid (t_1, \ldots, t_k) \in f\}$. In a loop at depth k, inputs to a feedback node in a frontier f determine outputs in

$\{(t_1, \ldots, t_k + 1) \mid (t_1, \ldots, t_k) \in f\}$. As another simple example, when T consists of two unrelated points t_1 and t_2 that represent private data for two users U_1 and U_2, we may have a node with outgoing edges e_1 and e_2 that demultiplexes data for U_1 and U_2, so that $\phi(e_1)(\{t_1\}) = T$ and $\phi(e_2)(\{t_2\}) = T$.

The function ϕ need not be as accurate as possible. In particular, $\phi(e)$ could always be completely uninformative (as small as possible), with $\phi(e)(f) = \emptyset$ for all $f \neq T$ and $\phi(e)(T) = T$. However, a more informative ϕ is typically more helpful, and generally easy to find.

In this paper, we do not investigate how to check that a node actually satisfies Condition 1 for a given ϕ. Section 6 returns briefly to this subject.

4.4   Relating ϕ to $\leadsto$

With the aim of clarifying the relation between ϕ and $\leadsto$, we argue that $\leadsto$ is included in ϕ at each node. More precisely, if an event at a node p at time t_1 could-result-in an event at time t_2 on one of the outgoing edges e, and t_2 is in $\phi(e)(f)$ for some frontier f, then t_1 is in f. For example, if f includes only the security level "Public", and $\phi(e)$ is simply the identity function, this property entails that if an event at p at time t_1 could-result-in a message on e at the level "Public", then t_1 is also in f and hence equals "Public".

Proposition 8. *Assume that ϕ satisfies Condition 1. Suppose $src(e) = p$ and $(p, t_1) \leadsto (e, t_2)$. Then, for all f, if $t_2 \in \phi(e)(f)$ then $t_1 \in f$.*

This proposition relies on the following property of $\leadsto$: if $(p, t_1) \leadsto (e, t_2)$ and $src(e) = p$ then there exist a history h for p, a state s such that

$$g(p)(h) = (s, \ldots)$$

and an event (d, m) such that $t_1 \leq time(m)$ and

$$g_1(p)(s, (d, m)) = (\ldots, \langle \ldots e \mapsto \mu \ldots \rangle)$$

where some element of μ has time $\leq t_2$. In this paper we simply assume this property; the proof that it actually holds requires a definition of $\leadsto$, which we omit.

4.5   A Special Case of Condition 1

In the security literature, non-interference properties are sometimes expressed in terms of single levels (e.g., outputs at level "Trusted" are determined by inputs at level "Trusted", or outputs to a user U are determined by U's inputs), rather than in terms of sets of levels analogous to frontiers. McLean's survey [9], for example, phrases purging functions and non-interference in terms of individual users, while the classic article by Goguen and Meseguer [3] refers to groups of users.

We therefore investigate the power of a special case of Condition 1 in which the frontier f is not arbitrary but rather consists of (the downward closure of) a single time. Such a special case is often sufficient, and sometimes equivalent to the full Condition 1. In particular, when $(T, \leq)$ is a finite linear order, the only frontiers are $\emptyset$ and the sets of the form $Close_{\downarrow}(\{t\})$ for some $t \in T$.

Condition 2 captures this special case. It specializes Condition 1 to f of the form $Close_{\downarrow}(\{t\})$, for $t \in T$. It does not require that $\phi(e_i)(f)$ be of the same form.

Condition 2. *For all $t \in T$, if $f = Close_{\downarrow}(\{t\})$, $g(p)(h) = (\ldots, \langle \ldots e_i \mapsto \mu_i \ldots \rangle)$, and $g(p)(h@f) = (\ldots, \langle \ldots e_i \mapsto \mu_i' \ldots \rangle)$ then $\mu_i@\phi(e_i)(f) = \mu_i'@\phi(e_i)(f)$.*

We generally adopt Condition 1 rather than Condition 2, because Condition 2 is strictly weaker than Condition 1. The following small but tricky example illustrates this point. Perhaps with the security literature in mind (e.g., [2]), one may imagine that a lattice structure for the set of times T would help, and specifically that it would enable us to represent an arbitrary frontier f by the least upper bound of its elements. However, a variant of the example shows that Condition 2 is strictly weaker than Condition 1 even if T is a very simple distributive lattice.

Example 1. Suppose that T consists of three unrelated elements a, b, and c, and a fourth element d below b and c but not a.

The example concerns a simple node p that ignores its initial state. It has a single input edge e and a single output edge e', for which we take $\phi(e')(f) = f$. Moreover, the node ignores the contents of input messages, considering only their times. It also ignores all input messages at times b and c. As output, it may produce $\emptyset$, $\langle\!\langle m_b, m_c \rangle\!\rangle$, or $\langle\!\langle m_c, m_b \rangle\!\rangle$, where m_b and m_c are distinct, fixed messages with $time(m_b) = b$ and $time(m_c) = c$. So the function $g(p)$ for this node can be regarded as mapping a sequence of (a and d) times for input messages to $\emptyset$, $\langle\!\langle m_b, m_c \rangle\!\rangle$, or $\langle\!\langle m_c, m_b \rangle\!\rangle$. We write $\bar{g}$ for this mapping, and define it as follows:

$$\bar{g}(a^*) = \emptyset$$
$$\bar{g}(a^+ \cdot d \cdot u) = \langle\!\langle m_b, m_c \rangle\!\rangle$$
$$\bar{g}(d \cdot u) = \langle\!\langle m_c, m_b \rangle\!\rangle$$

where u is an arbitrary sequence of a's and d's. It is straightforward to define a function $g_1(p)$ that induces a function $g(p)$ that corresponds to $\bar{g}$.

Let $f = \{b, c, d\}$. Condition 1 fails for this f. We have that $\bar{g}((a \cdot d)@f) = \bar{g}(d) = \langle\!\langle m_c, m_b \rangle\!\rangle$, so $\bar{g}((a \cdot d)@f)@f = \langle\!\langle m_c, m_b \rangle\!\rangle$, while $\bar{g}(a \cdot d) = \langle\!\langle m_b, m_c \rangle\!\rangle$, so $\bar{g}(a \cdot d)@f = \langle\!\langle m_b, m_c \rangle\!\rangle$, hence

$$\bar{g}((a \cdot d)@f)@f \neq \bar{g}(a \cdot d)@f$$

On the other hand, in the special case of frontiers of the form $Close_{\downarrow}(\{t\})$, where $t \in T$, Condition 1 holds:

- For $t = a$: For all u, $\bar{g}(u@Close_{\downarrow}(\{a\})) = \emptyset$, and $\bar{g}(u)$ never contains a message at time a, so

$$\bar{g}(u@Close_{\downarrow}(\{a\}))@Close_{\downarrow}(\{a\}) = \bar{g}(u)@Close_{\downarrow}(\{a\})$$

- For $t = b$: For all u, $\bar{g}(u@Close_\downarrow(\{b\})) = \langle\!\langle m_c, m_b\rangle\!\rangle$ if u contains a d, and is $\emptyset$ otherwise; so $\bar{g}(u@Close_\downarrow(\{b\}))@Close_\downarrow(\{b\}) = \langle\!\langle m_b\rangle\!\rangle$ if u contains a d, and is $\emptyset$ otherwise. On the other hand, $\bar{g}(u) = \langle\!\langle m_c, m_b\rangle\!\rangle$ or $\langle\!\langle m_b, m_c\rangle\!\rangle$ if u contains a d, and is $\emptyset$ otherwise; so $\bar{g}(u)@Close_\downarrow(\{b\}) = \langle\!\langle m_b\rangle\!\rangle$ if u contains a d, and is $\emptyset$ otherwise. Therefore, in all cases,

$$\bar{g}(u@Close_\downarrow(\{b\}))@Close_\downarrow(\{b\}) = \bar{g}(u)@Close_\downarrow(\{b\})$$

- For $t = c$: This case is exactly analogous to that of $t = b$.
- For $t = d$: For all u, $\bar{g}(u)@Close_\downarrow(\{d\}) = \emptyset$, so

$$\bar{g}(u@Close_\downarrow(\{d\}))@Close_\downarrow(\{d\}) = \bar{g}(u)@Close_\downarrow(\{d\})$$

The partial order of times, as defined above, is not a lattice. We can, however, give a variant of the example in which it is. We modify the partial order by placing a above b and c (and therefore above d as well); we do not modify the function $\bar{g}$. The argument that Condition 1 fails for the frontier $\{b, c, d\}$ but holds for $Close_\downarrow(\{t\})$ when $t \in \{b, c, d\}$ is exactly as above. It remains to check that Condition 1 holds for $Close_\downarrow(\{t\})$ when $t = a$.

- For $t = a$: For all u, $\bar{g}(u@Close_\downarrow(\{a\})) = \bar{g}(u)$, so

$$\bar{g}(u@Close_\downarrow(\{a\}))@Close_\downarrow(\{a\}) = \bar{g}(u)@Close_\downarrow(\{a\})$$

4.6 Another Perspective on ϕ and Its Properties

Intuitively, we may expect ϕ to have additional properties beyond Condition 1, and such properties are sometimes useful for working with ϕ. For example, we may expect that, for all e, $\phi(e)(T) = T$, since the initial state of a node and its inputs (and their exact interleaving) determine its outputs. We may also expect $\phi(e)$ to be monotonic, since intuitively knowing more of the input cannot remove information about the output. Furthermore, given a function $\phi(e)$ that is not necessarily monotonic, we could define a new monotone function $\phi'(e)$ by

$$\phi'(e)(f) = \cup_{f' \subseteq f}\phi(e)(f')$$

Finally, we may expect that $\phi(e)$ distributes over intersections. This property implies both $\phi(e)(T) = T$ and the monotonicity of $\phi(e)(T)$. We formulate it as follows:

Condition 3. *For all $e \in E$, for any index set X and family of frontiers f_x for $x \in X$, $\phi(e)(\cap_{x \in X} f_x) = \cap_{x \in X}\phi(e)(f_x)$.*

In the remainder of this section, we present another way of looking at frontier transformers. While $\phi(e)$ may be seen as going from inputs to outputs, the alternative perspective is based on reasoning in the opposite direction, from outputs to inputs. We show that the two perspectives yield equivalent results; in our opinion, this equivalence makes frontier transformers (and Condition 3) even more compelling.

Suppose that, for a node p and an outgoing edge e, we are given a function R_0 from times to frontiers, with the property (informally) that knowing p's inputs at $R_0(t)$ suffices for knowing its outputs on e at t. This function induces a monotone function $R(t) = \cup_{t' \leq t} R_o(t')$, with the property that knowing p's inputs at $R(t)$ suffices for knowing its outputs on e up to t, as the following condition asserts.

Condition 4. *If $g(p)(h) = (\ldots, \langle \ldots e_i \mapsto \mu_i \ldots \rangle)$ and $g(p)(h@R(t)) = (\ldots, \langle \ldots e_i \mapsto \mu'_i \ldots \rangle)$ then $\mu_i @ (Close_\downarrow(\{t\})) = \mu'_i @ (Close_\downarrow(\{t\}))$.*

Going forward, we prefer to work with R rather than R_0, because we have not set out the notation to work directly with R_0, and because knowing the output only at a time t and not at the times below t may sometimes be useless, in particular in the context of differential computation [10]. The fact that R is (or may be) generated from some function R_0 is reflected in the following monotonicity condition.

Condition 5. *If $t' \leq t$ then $R(t') \subseteq R(t)$.*

Every function R induces a function $\phi(e)$, and conversely every function $\phi(e)$ induces a function R, as follows. Let us write $\mathcal{F}$ for the function that maps R to $\phi(e)$ and $\mathcal{G}$ for the function that goes in the opposite direction. For $\rho : T \to F$ and $\psi : F \to F$, we set:

$$\mathcal{F}(\rho)(f) = \{t \mid \rho(t) \subseteq f\}$$

and

$$\mathcal{G}(\psi)(t) = \cap\{f \mid t \in \psi(f)\}$$

We obtain that the conditions on $\phi(e)$ and those on R are exactly equivalent, and that the functions $\mathcal{F}$ and $\mathcal{G}$ are anti-monotone and inverses of each other:

Proposition 9.

- If $\phi(e) = \mathcal{F}(R)$ and R satisfies Conditions 4 and 5 then $\phi(e)$ satisfies Conditions 1 and 3.
- Conversely, if $R = \mathcal{G}(\phi(e))$ and $\phi(e)$ satisfies Conditions 1 and 3 then R satisfies Conditions 4 and 5.

Proposition 10.

- If $\phi(e)(f) \subseteq \phi'(e)(f)$ for all f, then $\mathcal{G}(\phi'(e))(t) \subseteq \mathcal{G}(\phi(e))(t)$ for all t.
- If $R(t) \subseteq R'(t)$ for all t, then $\mathcal{F}(R')(f) \subseteq \mathcal{F}(R)(f)$ for all f.

Proposition 11.

- For all f, $\phi(e)(f) = \mathcal{F}(\mathcal{G}(\phi(e)))(f)$.
- For all t, $R(t) = \mathcal{G}(\mathcal{F}(R))(t)$.

The following example illustrates that Condition 3 is needed in order for us to obtain $\phi(e)(f) = \mathcal{F}(\mathcal{G}(\phi(e)))(f)$, as we do in Proposition 11. Distributivity over finite intersections would not suffice.

Example 2. Suppose that the set of times T consists of the integers (including the negative ones), and that $\phi(e)(f) = T$ if $f \neq \emptyset$ and $\phi(e)(\emptyset) = \emptyset$. Note that $\phi(e)$ distributes over all finite intersections but not over all infinite intersections. We obtain that $\mathcal{G}(\phi(e))(t) = \cap\{f \mid t \in \phi(e)(f)\} = \emptyset$, since $t \in \phi(e)(f)$ for all non-empty f, but the intersection of all non-empty f is empty. Further, we obtain that $\mathcal{F}(\mathcal{G}(\phi(e)))(f) = \{t \mid \mathcal{G}(\phi(e))(t) \subseteq f\} = \{t \mid \emptyset \subseteq f\} = T$, for all f. In sum, $\mathcal{F}(\mathcal{G}(\phi(e)))$ is strictly bigger than $\phi(e)$ in this example.

From a semantics perspective, a frontier is a predicate, and a frontier transformer $\phi(e)$ is a predicate transformer. Curiously, our predicate transformers go from inputs to outputs; generally the opposite is true. Nevertheless, much of the material in this section is part of the general theory of predicate transformers (e.g. [12, p. 83]), not specific to our setting. An exception is the correspondence between Conditions 1 and 4, in Proposition 9.

5   Main Results

In this section we present our main results. We start with an informal discussion of the results which leads to a few definitions, continue with some auxiliary lemmas, then state our main theorem.

Throughout, we assume a function ϕ that satisfies Condition 1. This condition is purely local: it refers to the behavior of each node in isolation. In this section, we use it in order to obtain global guarantees for an entire system.

5.1   Informal Discussion and Definitions

Our main theorem considers the messages that each node p receives within a frontier $D(p)$, possibly a different frontier for each node. Initially, however, let us consider the simple case in which $T = \{\text{"Public"}, \text{"Secret"}\}$, with "Public" $\leq$ "Secret", and $D(p) = \{\text{"Public"}\}$ for all p. In this case, we can derive that each node's history is independent of any secrets, even if queues may contain secrets initially and even if nodes can generate secrets in response to public messages.

More precisely, suppose that $\sigma = \langle\!\langle s_0, s_1, \ldots \rangle\!\rangle$ is a behavior of the system with initial values for the queues Q_0. Suppose further that HQ_0 is such that $HQ_0(e)@\{\text{"Public"}\} = Q_0(e)@\{\text{"Public"}\}$ for all e, that is, that Q_0 and HQ_0 coincide on public messages. Then there exists an alternative behavior $\hat{\sigma} = \langle\!\langle \hat{s}_0, \hat{s}_1, \ldots \rangle\!\rangle$ with initial values HQ_0 such that, if p has respective histories h and $\hat{h}$ in two corresponding states s_i and $\hat{s}_i$, then $h@\{\text{"Public"}\} = \hat{h}@\{\text{"Public"}\}$. In this alternative behavior, each node has no information about messages outside "Public", not even that they exist at all.

Recall that, in Section 2, the definition of the action *MessR* says that, given a sequence of messages $u \cdot m \cdot v$, a node p is allowed to process m when there is no message n ahead of m (so, in u) with $time(n) \leq time(m)$. Although motivated by other applications, this specification of *MessR* seems attractive from an information-flow perspective. It enables a system to produce the same behavior at $time(m)$ independently of data at higher and unrelated levels. For example, given the queue $n \cdot m$ where $time(n) =$ "Secret" and $time(m) =$ "Public", the node p can process m as though n was not there.

Going beyond the special case where D is constant across nodes, we would want that a node p gets no information about messages outside $D(p)$ from messages in $D(p)$. For this purpose, we would assume that Q_0 and HQ_0 coincide on $D(p)$ for edges going into p, and would reason that for every behavior σ with Q_0 there is an alternative behavior $\hat{\sigma}$ with HQ_0 that yields the same histories filtered to $D(p)$ at each node p. Thus, messages at $D(p)$ are fixed, and those outside $D(p)$ differ between σ and $\hat{\sigma}$.

However, not all possible mappings of nodes to frontiers constitute reasonable values for D. For instance, suppose that $D(p) = \{$"Public"$\}$, $D(q) = \{$"Public", "Secret"$\}$, and p has sent some messages to q on a direct edge e from p to q. Any secrets that p has sent to q will be apparent in q's history, and corresponding actions at p must be present in any alternative behavior. Such examples suggest that, when there is an edge from p to q, perhaps we should require that $D(q) \subseteq D(p)$.

Still, this requirement is not quite satisfactory in that it does not consider the dependence of p's outputs on e on p's inputs. Treating this dependence via the function ϕ, we amend the requirement to $D(q) \subseteq \phi(e)(D(p))$. Thus, the frontier at q is included in the frontier determined on e by the frontier at p.

In sum, we arrive at the following definitions:

- We say that a function D from P to F is *coherent* if, whenever $p, q \in P$, $e \in E$, $src(e) = p$, and $dst(e) = q$, $D(q) \subseteq \phi(e)(D(p))$.
- We say that two functions Q_0 and HQ_0 from E to M^* are *equivalent up to D*, and write $Q_0 \simeq HQ_0$, if for all $q \in P$ and $e \in E$ with $q = dst(e)$, $Q_0(e)@D(q) = HQ_0(e)@D(q)$.

We have studied weaker but sound requirements in which we consider not only the static graph topology but also what messages are actually sent. We have also studied the possibility of D being state-dependent, as explained in Section 6. In this paper we do not develop those more sophisticated variants, for simplicity.

5.2   Lemmas

Our first auxiliary lemma relates g, local states, queues, and local histories. It relies on definitions of properties Inv_{LocH} and Inv_{QH}, which it asserts are invariants. Property Inv_{LocH} says that the local state of a node is the local state obtained by applying g to its history. Property Inv_{QH} similarly relates the contents of a queue $Q(e)$ to what is obtained by applying g to the history of e's source. We do not quite have $\Pi_e g(p)(H(p)) = Q(e)$, however, for three reasons:

- the initial value of $Q(e)$ must be added ahead of the result of applying g to the history of e's source, on the left of this equation;
- the messages that e's destination has consumed, which are in its history, must be added ahead of $Q(e)$, on the right;

– finally, reorderings are possible, because of the definition of *MessR*, so we should use a reordering relation rather than an equality.

We arrive at the following definitions and lemma:

– Let Inv_{LocH} be

$$\forall p \in P.\Pi_{\mathrm{Loc}}g(p)(H(p)) = LocState(p)$$

– Let Inv_{QH} be:

$$\forall p, q \in P, e \in E \text{ such that } src(e) = p \wedge dst(e) = q.$$
$$(Q_0(e)\cdot\Pi_e g(p)(H(p))) \hookrightarrow (\langle m \mid (e, m) \in H(q)\rangle\cdot Q(e))$$

– Let Inv_{LocQH} be the conjunction of Inv_{LocH} and Inv_{QH}.

Lemma 1. *$ISpec(Q_0)$ implies $\Box Inv_{\mathrm{LocQH}}$.*

Our second lemma is motivated by the definition of HQ in Section 5.3 below. There, we consider a sequence of messages defined as a subtraction. The lemma implies that the subtraction never resorts to the clause $\emptyset - m = \emptyset$; in other words, the sequence from which we are subtracting contains all the elements of the sequence that we are subtracting, and with at least the same multiplicity.

Lemma 2. *Assume that $Q_0 \simeq HQ_0$ and that D is coherent. Let $p = src(e)$ and $q = dst(e)$. Let $\mu = HQ_0(e)\cdot\Pi_e g(p)(H(p)@D(p))$ and $\nu = \langle m \mid (e, m) \in H(q)\rangle$. Then $ISpec(Q_0)$ implies $\Box(\mu\cdot u - \nu@D(q)) = (\mu - \nu@D(q))\cdot u$, for all u.*

5.3   Main Theorem

Our main theorem relies on a way of mapping one state to another state. Specifically, given state functions *LocState*, Q, and H, we define new state functions *HLocState*, HQ, and HH. We then show that if a behavior satisfies $ISpec(Q_0)$ then the behavior induced by the mapping satisfies $ISpec(HQ_0)$.

As in other work with TLA (e.g., [8, Section 8.9.4]), we phrase the theorem in terms of formulas and substitutions rather than in terms of behaviors. For any expression *Exp*, we write $\overline{Exp}$ for the result of applying the substitution $[HLocState/LocState, HH/H, HQ/Q]$ to *Exp*.

We let:

$$HLocState(p) = \Pi_{\mathrm{Loc}}g(p)(H(p)@D(p))$$

$$HQ(e) = HQ_0(e)\cdot\Pi_e g(p)(H(p)@D(p)) - \langle m \mid (e, m) \in H(q)\rangle@D(q)$$
$$\text{where } p = src(e), q = dst(e)$$

$$HH(p) = H(p)@D(p)$$

According to these definitions, *HLocState(p)* is obtained by applying $g(p)$, much as in Inv_{LocH}, but filtering the history with $D(p)$. Intuitively, *HLocState(p)* is intended to be the local state that p would reach if it only saw messages with times in $D(p)$. Similarly $HQ(e)$ aims to describe the contents of $Q(e)$ in an alternative reality in which the source of e would see only messages with times in $D(p)$ and the destination of e would only consume messages in $D(q)$. Its definition has many of the same ingredients as Inv_{QH}. Finally, $HH(p)$ is simply the part of p's local history that is limited to messages with times in $D(p)$.

We obtain:

Theorem 1. *Assume that $Q_0 \simeq HQ_0$ and that D is coherent. Then $ISpec(Q_0)$ implies $ISpec(HQ_0)$.*

The following corollary reformulates the theorem in terms of a behavior σ and an alternative behavior $\hat{\sigma}$. It also considers the case where the local history of some node p in σ contains only messages with times in $D(p)$. The corollary states that the node would have exactly the same history in the alternative behavior $\hat{\sigma}$. Thus, the history does not allow p to differentiate σ and $\hat{\sigma}$.

Corollary 1. *Assume that $Q_0 \simeq HQ_0$ and that D is coherent. For every behavior $\sigma = \langle\!\langle s_0, s_1, \ldots \rangle\!\rangle$ that satisfies $ISpec(Q_0)$ there exists a behavior $\hat{\sigma} = \langle\!\langle \hat{s}_0, \hat{s}_1, \ldots \rangle\!\rangle$ that satisfies $ISpec(HQ_0)$ and such that, for all $p \in P$, if $H(p)$ has the value h in s_i then it has the value $h@D(p)$ in $\hat{s}_i$.*

If in addition, for some $p \in P$, σ satisfies $\Box(H(p) = H(p)@D(p))$, then $H(p)$ has the same sequence of values in σ and in $\hat{\sigma}$.

While differences in models make precise comparisons difficult, the properties that these results express resemble non-interference and its possibilistic variants, such as restrictiveness [9, Section 2.2.2]. For instance, restrictiveness talks about adding or deleting "high-level inputs" to a system trace; in our results, the change from Q_0 to HQ_0 can essentially serve that purpose.

5.4   A Small Example

We close this section with an application of Theorem 1 and Corollary 1. It is a trivial exercise, but illustrates how the results can be instantiated.

Consider a simple graph with nodes p_0, p_1, and p_2, with edges e_1 and e_2 from p_0 to p_1 and p_2, respectively, plus an inert node q with an edge e_0 from q to p_0. Initially, $Q(e_0)$ contains messages for two unrelated times t_1 and t_2 that represent private data for two users U_1 and U_2 (as in Section 4.3); $Q(e_1)$ and $Q(e_2)$ are initially empty. Suppose that p_0 demultiplexes the payload of those messages, applies to them a state-independent function, and strips the time information which is not needed at p_1 and p_2. Formally, all of p_0's outputs are in a third, unrelated time *null*.

We still have $\phi(e_1)(\{t_1\}) = T$ and $\phi(e_2)(\{t_2\}) = T$, and we also have $\phi(e_1)(\{t_2\}) = \emptyset$ and $\phi(e_2)(\{t_1\}) = \emptyset$. Since q has no incoming edges, we can take $\phi(e_0)(f) = T$ for all f.

Therefore, we can satisfy the coherence criterion for the function D by letting $D(q) = T$, $D(p_0) = \{t_1\}$, $D(p_1) = T$, and $D(p_2) = \emptyset$. Suppose further that

σ is a behavior of the system with the given initial messages in $Q(e_0)$. Then, according to Corollary 1, there exists another behavior $\hat{\sigma}$ with the same initial messages in $Q(e_0)$ at time t_1 but arbitrary ones at time t_2 (because $D(p_0) = \{t_1\}$). Moreover, $Q(e_1)$ is initially empty in $\hat{\sigma}$ (because $D(p_1) = T$), but the initial contents of $Q(e_2)$ are arbitrary (because $D(p_2) = \emptyset$). It follows from Corollary 1 that the local history at p_1 is identical in σ and $\hat{\sigma}$. In other words, this local history does not allow p_1 to infer anything about which messages at time t_2 are initially present on e_0.

Some alternative choices of D also satisfy the coherence criterion but lead to different results, in particular showing that, symmetrically, p_2 cannot infer anything about which messages at time t_1 are initially present on e_0.

6   Conclusion

In this paper, we study how a dataflow model of computation, timely dataflow, can offer information-flow properties. The required enhancements include the use of functions that express dependencies between inputs and outputs at each node. They are consistent with the possibility that each node operates over a distinct set of virtual times. We leave for further work the enforcement or checking of those dependencies. In the context of Naiad, programming conventions have sometimes been used for ensuring the expected properties of the could-result-in relation; those could probably be extended and codified into information-flow type systems or other static analyses. We also leave for further work the study of declassification and of quantitative information-flow properties, which should be helpful in applications. Although Naiad remains a research artifact, it is already a substantial, efficient system on which non-trivial applications have been developed, but not, to date, with consideration of security and privacy properties. Beyond Naiad, more broadly, there seems to be growing interest in mandatory access control, information-flow control, and their applications in modern data-parallel systems (e.g., [13,6]).

As mentioned in the Introduction, this work stems from a larger effort to understand, improve, and apply timely dataflow. We close this paper with a brief discussion of some of our recent and ongoing work, and how it relates to security.

Section 2 is based on the original description of the timely dataflow model of computation in the context of Naiad [11], and on another paper (in preparation) that studies the model in more generality and detail. In particular, the model includes completion notifications, which tell a node when it will no longer see messages for a given time, and which require a careful definition and analysis of the could-result-in relation. Other features of the model include external input and output channels. We omit these aspects of timely dataflow here, in order to simplify the presentation of this paper, though we have considered their information-flow aspects. Interestingly, completion notifications introduce flows of information "at a distance" (not necessarily from neighbor to neighbor in a dataflow graph), via the run-time system that tracks the progress of the computation and delivers those notifications.

A further paper (also in preparation) explores fault-tolerance in the timely dataflow model. Over the years, connections between non-interference and fault-tolerance have been identified (e.g., [16,15,14]); perhaps it is time to revisit them. Much of the machinery that we present in this paper arose in our work on fault-tolerance, in a more general, more dynamic form. In particular, there, the function D that maps a node to a set of times is state-dependent, rather than static. "Undo computing" [7], which restores system integrity after an intrusion by undoing changes made by an adversary while preserving legitimate user actions, may be an intriguing area of application for this ongoing work.

Acknowledgments. We are grateful to our coauthors on work on Naiad for discussions that led to this paper, and to Gordon Plotkin for pointing out the connection with predicate transformers.

References

1. Abadi, M., Lamport, L.: The existence of refinement mappings. Theoretical Computer Science 82(2), 253–284 (1991)
2. Denning, D.E.: A lattice model of secure information flow. Communications of the ACM 19(5), 236–243 (1976)
3. Goguen, J.A., Meseguer, J.: Security policies and security models. In: IEEE Symposium on Security and Privacy, pp. 11–20 (1982)
4. Jefferson, D.R.: Virtual time. ACM Transactions on Programming Languages and Systems 7(3), 404–425 (1985)
5. Kahn, G.: The semantics of simple language for parallel programming. In: IFIP Congress, pp. 471–475 (1974)
6. Khan, S.M., Hamlen, K.W., Kantarcioglu, M.: Silver lining: Enforcing secure information flow at the cloud edge. In: 2014 IEEE International Conference on Cloud Engineering, pp. 37–46 (2014)
7. Kim, T., Wang, X., Zeldovich, N., Kaashoek, M.F.: Intrusion recovery using selective re-execution. In: 9th USENIX Symposium on Operating Systems Design and Implementation, pp. 89–104 (2010)
8. Lamport, L.: Specifying Systems, The TLA+ Language and Tools for Hardware and Software Engineers. Addison-Wesley (2002)
9. McLean, J.: Security models. In: Marciniak, J. (ed.) Encyclopedia of Software Engineering. Wiley & Sons (1994)
10. McSherry, F., Murray, D.G., Isaacs, R., Isard, M.: Differential dataflow. In: CIDR 2013, Sixth Biennial Conference on Innovative Data Systems Research (2013)
11. Murray, D.G., McSherry, F., Isaacs, R., Isard, M., Barham, P., Abadi, M.: Naiad: A timely dataflow system. In: ACM SIGOPS 24th Symposium on Operating Systems Principles, pp. 439–455 (2013)
12. Plotkin, G.: Domains, the so-called Pisa notes (1983), http://homepages.inf.ed.ac.uk/gdp/publications/Domains_a4.ps.
13. Roy, I., Setty, S.T.V., Kilzer, A., Shmatikov, V., Witchel, E.: Airavat: Security and privacy for MapReduce. In: Proceedings of the 7th USENIX Symposium on Networked Systems Design and Implementation, pp. 297–312 (2010)

14. Rushby, J.: Partitioning for avionics architectures: Requirements, mechanisms, and assurance. NASA Contractor Report CR-1999-209347, NASA Langley Research Center (June 1999)
15. Simpson, A., Woodcock, J., Davies, J.: Safety through security. In: Proceedings of the 9th International Workshop on Software Specification and Design, pp. 18–24. IEEE Computer Society (1998)
16. Weber, D.G.: Formal specification of fault-tolerance and its relation to computer security. In: Proceedings of the 5th International Workshop on Software Specification and Design, pp. 273–277. ACM (1989)
17. Zaharia, M., Chowdhury, M., Das, T., Dave, A., Ma, J., McCauly, M., Franklin, M.J., Shenker, S., Stoica, I.: Resilient distributed datasets: A fault-tolerant abstraction for in-memory cluster computing. In: Proceedings of the 9th USENIX Symposium on Networked Systems Design and Implementation, pp. 15–28 (2012)

Risk Assessment and Security Policies

Pareto Efficient Solutions
of Attack-Defence Trees

Zaruhi Aslanyan and Flemming Nielson

DTU Compute, Technical University of Denmark, Denmark
{zaas,fnie}@dtu.dk

Abstract. Attack-defence trees are a promising approach for representing threat scenarios and possible countermeasures in a concise and intuitive manner. An attack-defence tree describes the interaction between an attacker and a defender, and is evaluated by assigning parameters to the nodes, such as probability or cost of attacks and defences. In case of multiple parameters most analytical methods optimise one parameter at a time, e.g., minimise cost or maximise probability of an attack. Such methods may lead to sub-optimal solutions when optimising conflicting parameters, e.g., minimising cost while maximising probability.

In order to tackle this challenge, we devise automated techniques that optimise all parameters at once. Moreover, in the case of conflicting parameters our techniques compute the set of all optimal solutions, defined in terms of Pareto efficiency. The developments are carried out on a new and general formalism for attack-defence trees.

Keywords: Attack-defence trees, attack trees, countermeasures, security assessment, Pareto efficiency, multiple criteria.

1 Introduction

Nowadays fast growing technologies influence our everyday life and increase our productivity. Unfortunately, we witness with alarming frequency that they also increase the risk of physical and cyber attacks to a wide range of targets, from personal devices to systems of public concern. The growing number of threats demands a thorough investigation of the security properties of a system when deployed in a given environment. To this end, various formal graphical models have been studied.

Fault trees, introduced in the early 1980's, are one of the first and most prominent graphical representations for analysing the safety of a system. They represent a system failure in terms of the failure of its components [1].

Fault trees inspired a similar approach to security. In 1991, Weiss used trees in security analysis and presented threat-logic trees as a graphical attack-modelling technique [2]. Later, in 1999, Schneier introduced *attack trees* as a tool to evaluate the security of complex systems in a structured, hierarchical way. Attack trees allow to analyse the possible attack scenarios and reason about the security of

© Springer-Verlag Berlin Heidelberg 2015
R. Focardi and A. Myers (Eds.): POST 2015, LNCS 9036, pp. 95–114, 2015.
DOI: 10.1007/978-3-662-46666-7_6

the whole system in a formal, methodical way, by splitting a complex goal into sub-goals and basic attacks [3]. However, attack trees evaluate only the attacker's behaviour and do not consider possible defences undertaken to avoid the attacks.

To overcome this limitation, further extensions of attack trees for capturing the defender's behaviour have been studied. Such extensions have been explored in several dimensions. Some enrich an attack tree model by integrating appropriate defender's actions against specific attacks only at leaf level [4], while others combine attack and defence models and present a methodology to compute specific parameters [5]. Kordy [6] introduced a more general tool, called attack-defence trees, to represent the interaction between an attacker and a defender.

Attack-defence trees are extensions of attack trees with countermeasures. They illustrate in a graphical way the possible actions an attacker can perform in order to attain a given goal, and the feasible countermeasures a defender can undertake to counter such actions. Attack-defence trees are used for analysing attack-defence scenarios. Analyses are performed by considering specific aspects or properties of the scenario. The evaluation assigns values to the parameters of the leaves and the tree is traversed from the leaves to the root.

Most analyses of attack-defence trees focus on one specific aspect of the system, such as feasibility or cost of an attack or a defence. They do not consider multiple parameters and the subsequent need for optimising all of them at once. Moreover, optimisation of multiple parameters might lead to incomparable values, in which case such methods may result in sub-optimal solutions. However, in many real-life scenarios a single parameter might not be adequate for the analysis of complex attack-defence scenarios.

In order to address multi-parameter optimisation of attack-defence trees, we present evaluation techniques that characterise the leaves of a tree with more than one parameter, such as the success probability *and* the cost of an attack. Our techniques compute different aspects of the scenario and handle multiple parameters, thus optimising all of them at once. Multi-parameter optimisation becomes necessary in case of conflicting parameters, as there is no single best solution but rather a set of optimal solutions. We handle conflicting parameters by computing the set of efficient solutions, defined in terms of Pareto efficiency. Thus, Pareto efficiency handles the multi-criteria optimisation problem, as well as parameters with incomparable values.

Our developments are performed on a new language-based formalism for attack-defence trees. Furthermore, we study the issue in both Boolean and probabilistic settings. For each such setting, we first consider the problem of feasibility of the attack or the defence, and then we extend our techniques to compute optimal attacks or defences in presence of multiple costs. Moreover, for each case, we first define the solution considering all possible player interactions, obtaining a natural but exponential characterisation. Then, we improve dramatically on the complexity devising an algorithmic evaluation that is linear in the size of the tree and yet sound for an expressive sub-class of models.

Organisation of the paper. In Sect. 2 we introduce our formalism for attack-defence trees and provide evaluation techniques for feasibility queries. Sect. 3 extends the model with a single cost and presents evaluation techniques for computing minimum cost. We extend the single cost model to multiple costs in Sect. 4. The results of evaluation are discussed on a case study for a Radio-Frequency Identification system managing goods in a warehouse. We describe related work in Sect. 5 and conclude in Sect. 6.

2   Formal Model of Attack-Defence Trees

In the following, we present our formalism for attack-defence trees. We start by defining the syntax and the terminology used throughout the paper. Then, we describe the evaluation techniques for investigating the feasibility of attacks and defences both in Boolean and probabilistic settings. The Boolean case is thoroughly explained in Sect. 2.2. The developments are generalised to the probabilistic setting in Sect. 2.3.

2.1   Syntax and Well-Formednes

Syntax and intended semantics. We construe an attack-defence tree as an interaction between two players (denoted by τ), the proponent ($\tau = p$) and the opponent ($\tau = o$), in the wake of [6]. A player can be either an attacker or a defender. We associate the proponent with the player at the root, and the opponent with the opposite player. Each player has an associated goal, such as minimising or maximising the overall probability of an attack or a defence.

The root of the tree represents the main goal of an attack-defence scenario for a given player τ. The leaves represent the basic actions that a player can perform to achieve his/her goal. The internal nodes show how those actions can be combined. In order to simplifying the technical developments, we assume that the players' actions are independent.

The abstract syntax of an attack-defence tree t is presented in Table 1. A tree is either a leaf or the application of a tree operator to one or two sub-trees.

Based on the player type, a leaf a is either a basic action of the proponent or of the opponent. We denote the set of proponent's and opponent's basic actions by Act_p and Act_o, respectively. We assume that these two sets are disjoint, $Act_p \cap Act_o = \emptyset$. We denote by Act the set of all basic actions, $Act = Act_p \cup Act_o$.

There are two special types of leaves; $\&_{\text{true}}$ represents a trivially-successful action, and $\&_{\text{false}}$ represents a trivially-failed action.

As standard in the literature, tree operators include conjunction and disjunction, while we introduce negation and a novel construct for player alternation. The conjunction operator $t = \&_\wedge(t_1, t_2)$ requires that the goals of t_1, t_2 are achieved in order for the goal of t to be achieved. The disjunction operator $t = \&_\vee(t_1, t_2)$ requires that the goal of at least one sub-tree is achieved in order for the goal of t to be achieved.

The negation operator $t = \&_\neg(t')$ requires that the goal of the sub-tree t' is not achieved in order for the goal of t to be achieved. This operator negates the goal

Table 1. The type system for defining well-formed trees

$$t ::= a \mid \&_\wedge(t_1, t_2) \mid \&_\vee(t_1, t_2) \mid \&_\neg(t) \mid \&_\sim(t) \mid \&_{\text{true}} \mid \&_{\text{false}}$$

$$\vdash a : p \text{ if } a \in Act_p \qquad\qquad \vdash a : o \text{ if } a \in Act_o$$

$$\frac{\vdash t_1 : \tau \;\; \vdash t_2 : \tau}{\vdash \&_\wedge(t_1, t_2) : \tau} \quad \frac{\vdash t_1 : \tau \;\; \vdash t_2 : \tau}{\vdash \&_\vee(t_1, t_2) : \tau} \quad \frac{\vdash t : \tau}{\vdash \&_\neg(t) : \tau} \quad \frac{\vdash t : \tau}{\vdash \&_\sim(t) : \tau'} \tau' = \tau^{-1}$$

of t' and leaves the player unchanged. Such an operator allows to analyse a wider range of attack and defence scenarios, including the cases of unrecoverable and conflicting actions, thus making trees more flexible and expressive. For instance, cutting a communication wire might be unrecoverable, and after having cut a wire a player might not be able to communicate with a given device.

The changing player operator $t = \&_\sim(t')$ changes the goal of t' by changing the type of the player. Note that in this case the goal belongs to the opposite player. For instance, if t' belongs to an attacker with the corresponding goal (e.g., minimising), then the tree t belongs to a defender with the corresponding goal (e.g., maximising). Thus, the changing player operator flips the player from an attacker to a defender and vice versa, as highlighted by the side-condition of the corresponding rule, where $p^{-1} = o$ and $o^{-1} = p$.

The syntax of Table 1 is overly liberal for it does not associate players to nodes. The simple type system, showed in the second section of the table, enforces such association defining a well-formedness condition. We denote by $Tree_\tau$ the set of well-formed attack-defence trees whose root belongs to a player τ. Based on the type of the player, we have $Tree_p$ when τ is the proponent and $Tree_o$ when τ is the opponent and $Tree = Tree_p \cup Tree_o$. In the following, we will refer to them as attack-defence trees or simply trees. Moreover, we introduce below the notion of polarity consistency, to be exploited in the technical developments.

Polarity-Consistent Tree. We say that an action a occurs negatively in a tree, if a is under an odd number of negations. Otherwise, we say that an action a occurs positively. Such *polarities* are denoted with the symbols $-$ and $+$, respectively.

Definition 1. *An attack-defence tree t is polarity-consistent iff there is no action that occurs both positively and negatively in t.*

A sufficient (but not necessary) condition for polarity-consistency is that all actions are "uniformly good" or "uniformly bad" for the proponent. If t is a polarity-consistent tree, then the polarity of each action is uniquely determined.

Running Example. Let us introduce an example that we will develop throughout the paper. We consider a fragment of a Radio-Frequency Identification (RFID) system managing goods in a warehouse, studied in [7]. Particularly, we consider an attacker (proponent) whose goal consists in removing the RFID tags from

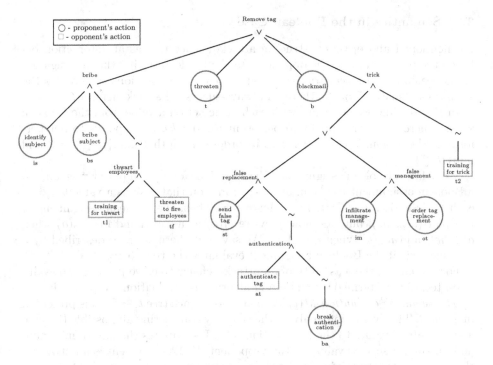

Fig. 1. Attack-defence tree for removing tag

goods with the help of an insider. In order to enable a direct comparison with the evaluation techniques in the literature, our attack-defence tree does not contain negation. We will see, however, that as far as the calculation is concerned, negation would be treated similarly to the changing player operator.

In order to attain the goal, the attacker can "bribe", "threaten", "blackmail", or "trick" the insider. For bribing a person the attacker has to "identify a corruptible subject" and "bribe the subject". The defender (opponent) can protect against bribery by "thwarting employees", which can be done by "training for security" and by "threatening to fire the employees".

In case the attacker decides instead to "trick" the insider by placing a fake tag, they can either "send false replacement tags" or give a "false management order" to do it. The latter can be done by "infiltrating the management" and "ordering replacement tags". To fight such attacks, the defender can provide the employees with "training for trick".

The corresponding attack-defence tree is given in Figure 1. We decorate internal nodes with labels to keep track of sub-goals, hence making the tree more informative and human-readable. We label the leaves to refer to them easily.

The t, displayed in Figure 1, is represented by the following syntactic term:
$$t = \&_\vee(\&_\wedge(\text{is}, \&_\wedge(\text{bs}, \&_\sim(\&_\wedge(\text{t1,tf})))),$$
$$\&_\vee(t, \&_\vee(b, \&_\wedge(\&_\vee(\&_\wedge(\text{st}, \&_\sim(\&_\wedge(\text{at}, \&_\sim(\text{ba})))), \&_\wedge(\text{im,ot})), \&_\sim(\text{t2})))))$$

2.2 Semantics in the Boolean Case

As mentioned above, we construe an attack-defence tree as an interaction between the proponent and the opponent. In the Boolean setting the investigation of the feasibility of a scenario is related to answering questions such as "Is the scenario satisfiable?" or "Is there an always-successful attack/defence?".

In this setting, we associate with each basic action a value from the Boolean set $\mathbb{B}$, where *true* corresponds to performing and *false* corresponds to not performing the action. We consider $\mathbb{B}$ to be ordered such that $\max\{tt, ff\} = tt$ and $\min\{tt, ff\} = ff$.

We define a Boolean assignment of basic actions for a given player τ as follows: a Boolean assignment m_τ is an arbitrary function that assigns a value $b \in \mathbb{B}$ to each basic action $a \in Act_\tau$; $m_\tau : Act_\tau \to \mathbb{B}$. Thus, the Boolean assignment m is a pair (m_p, m_o), but we allow to write $m(a)$ as a shorthand for $m_p(a)$ when $a \in Act_p$ and $m_o(a)$ when $a \in Act_o$. We say that the main goal described by a tree succeeds if the Boolean assignment evaluates the tree to *true*.

For evaluating the feasibility of an attack-defence tree, we present two evaluation techniques, termed semantic and algorithmic evaluations respectively.

The semantic evaluation $M(t)$ of an attack-defence tree $t \in Tree_p$ is presented in Table 2. The evaluation analyses the tree t by considering all possible Boolean assignments of values to the basic actions of t. It computes the pair of minimum and maximum success values of the proponent. If the proponent is an attacker, then it computes the minimum and the maximum values of an attack. Otherwise, it computes the minimum and maximum values of a defence. We observe that if the main goal of the scenario (represented by the root of the tree) is successful for the proponent, then it is not successful for the opponent. Similarly, if the proponent wants to maximise the success of the main goal, then the opponent wants to minimise it. Thus, the players have opposite goals. We integrate this consideration into our technique by minimising the value of t over all opponent's Boolean assignments m_o, and then maximising it over all proponent's Boolean assignments m_p. This is illustrated in the second component of $M(t)$ in Table 2, which computes the maximum success value of the proponent. The first component of $M(t)$ computes the minimum success value of the proponent. Therefore, the computation maximises the value over all m_o's and then minimises it over all m_p's.

The analysis $\mathcal{B}[\![t]\!]m$ of the tree t, displayed in the second part of the Table 2, is performed recursively on the structure of t. Observe that even though the negation and changing player operators work on the same assignment m, the former only changes the polarity of a tree whereas the latter changes the optimisation objective by swapping the players.

The result of the semantic evaluation, when the proponent is an attacker, is interpreted as follows.

- If both the minimum and the maximum values of t are *false* (ff, ff), then the system is always secure despite the attacker's actions.

Table 2. The Boolean semantic evaluation of an attack-defence tree

$$M(t) = (\min\{\max\{\mathcal{B}[\![t]\!](m_p, m_o) \mid m_o \text{ Boolean assignment}\} \mid m_p \text{ Boolean assignment}\},$$
$$\max\{\min\{\mathcal{B}[\![t]\!](m_p, m_o) \mid m_o \text{ Boolean assignment}\} \mid m_p \text{ Boolean assignment}\})$$

$$\begin{aligned}
\mathcal{B}[\![a]\!]m &= m(a) \\
\mathcal{B}[\![\&_\wedge(t_1, t_2)]\!]m &= \mathcal{B}[\![t_1]\!]m \wedge \mathcal{B}[\![t_2]\!]m \\
\mathcal{B}[\![\&_\vee(t_1, t_2)]\!]m &= \mathcal{B}[\![t_1]\!]m \vee \mathcal{B}[\![t_2]\!]m \\
\mathcal{B}[\![\&_\neg(t)]\!]m &= \neg\mathcal{B}[\![t]\!]m \\
\mathcal{B}[\![\&_\sim(t)]\!]m &= \neg\mathcal{B}[\![t]\!]m \\
\mathcal{B}[\![\&_{\text{true}}]\!]m &= tt \\
\mathcal{B}[\![\&_{\text{false}}]\!]m &= ff
\end{aligned}$$

- If the minimum value of t is *false* and the maximum value of t is *true* (ff, tt), then the system is vulnerable. In other words, there exist actions (a Boolean assignment m) such that an attack on the system is feasible.
- If both the minimum and the maximum values of t are *true* (tt, tt), then the system is flawed. In other words, despite the attacker's actions (for all Boolean assignments m) an attack on the system is always successful.

The result is interpreted likewise, when the proponent is a defender.

The semantic evaluation characterises the analysis in a natural way, for it explicitly considers all the interactions interwoven in a tree in terms of assignments to the leaves. Nonetheless, it gives rise to an exponential computation already in the Boolean case, the satisfiability problem being NP-complete. Therefore, evaluation techniques that enjoy a lower complexity are needed. In particular, we face the problem of defining those restrictions on attack-defence trees under which the more efficient methods are sound with respect to the semantic evaluation, our gold standard.

The algorithmic evaluation $INT(t)$ of an attack-defence tree $t \in Tree_p$ is presented in Table 3. Similarly to the semantic evaluation, it computes the pair of minimum and maximum success values of the proponent. It considers the values of basic actions and propagates them up to the root. The propagation is performed according to the rules given in Table 3. The first rule assigns the minimum and the maximum success values to the actions based on the player type. Observe that, as the players have opposite goals, the success values are also opposite. The next four rules define the computation for operators. Conjunction and disjunction are treated in the standard way, hence let us focus on the negation and changing player operators. Both operators change the goal of the player. The negation operator negates the goal without changing the player, while the changing player operator changes the goal by changing the player. Thus, in both rules we first swap the minimum and maximum values, and then apply negation. The last two rules are independent from the players and represent always successful and failed actions.

The semantic and algorithmic evaluations might lead to different results, as we can see by considering the attack-defence tree $t = \&_\wedge(a, \&_\neg(a))$, where $a \in Act_p$.

Table 3. The Boolean algorithmic evaluation of an attack-defence tree

$$
\begin{aligned}
INT(a) &= \begin{cases} (\mathit{ff}, \mathit{tt}) & \text{if } a \in Act_p \\ (\mathit{tt}, \mathit{ff}) & \text{if } a \in Act_o \end{cases} \\
INT(\&_\wedge(t_1, t_2)) &= let\ (min_i, max_i) = INT(t_i), i \in \{1, 2\} \\
&\quad in\ (min_1 \wedge min_2, max_1 \wedge max_2) \\
INT(\&_\vee(t_1, t_2)) &= let\ (min_i, max_i) = INT(t_i), i \in \{1, 2\} \\
&\quad in\ (min_1 \vee min_2, max_1 \vee max_2) \\
INT(\&_\neg(t)) &= let\ (min, max) = INT(t) \\
&\quad in\ (\neg max, \neg min) \\
INT(\&_\sim(t)) &= let\ (min, max) = INT(t) \\
&\quad in\ (\neg max, \neg min) \\
INT(\&_{\text{true}}) &= (\mathit{tt}, \mathit{tt}) \\
INT(\&_{\text{false}}) &= (\mathit{ff}, \mathit{ff})
\end{aligned}
$$

The result of the semantic evaluation is $M(t) = (\mathit{ff}, \mathit{ff})$, while the results of the algorithmic evaluation is $INT(t) = (\mathit{ff}, \mathit{tt})$. However, observe that t is not polarity-consistent. As a matter of fact, if we restrict to polarity-consistent trees, then the two evaluations are equivalent.

Theorem 1. *If $t \in Tree$ is a polarity-consistent tree, then $M(t) = INT(t)$.*

The semantic evaluation considers all possible Boolean assignments m, thus being exponential in the size of t. The implementation of the algorithmic evaluation consists in a bottom-up traversal of t, and thus is linear in the size of the tree. Therefore, in case of polarity-consistent trees, our method offers a dramatic improvement in performance hence in scalability. This is in line with the development of, e.g., [8].

2.3 Semantics in the Probabilistic Case

The probabilistic setting generalises the Boolean one. In the following, we give a brief explanation of the setting and the evaluations, focusing on the novelties and omitting redundant details.

In the probabilistic setting, we consider the interval $[0, 1]$, where 1 corresponds to success and 0 corresponds to failure. The questions tackled in the probabilistic setting are, e.g., "What is the maximum probability of an attack?" or "How vulnerable is the system to the attack?".

In the remainder of the paper, we shall restrict our investigation to linear trees, inspired by Girard's linear logic [9] and defined as follows:

Definition 2. *An attack-defence tree t is linear iff no action occurs twice in t.*

The notion of linearity is stronger than polarity-consistency, as the latter does not forbid to have multiple occurrences of the same action with the same polarity. Let us focus on the occurrences of an action a in the following polarity-consistent tree: $t = \&_\vee(\&_\wedge(a, b), \&_\wedge(a, c))$. In the tree t the action a is performed once but

Table 4. The probabilistic semantic evaluation of an attack-defence tree

$$M(t) = (\min\{\max\{\mathcal{P}[\![t]\!](m_p, m_o) \,|\, m_o \text{ Boolean assignment}\} \,|\, m_p \text{ Boolean assignment}\},$$
$$\max\{\min\{\mathcal{P}[\![t]\!](m_p, m_o) \,|\, m_o \text{ Boolean assignment}\} \,|\, m_p \text{ Boolean assignment}\})$$

$$\mathcal{P}[\![a]\!]m \quad = \begin{cases} M_2(a) & \text{if } m(a) = tt \\ M_1(a) & \text{if } m(a) = f\!f \end{cases}$$

$$\mathcal{P}[\![\&_\wedge(t_1, t_2)]\!]m = \mathcal{P}[\![t_1]\!]m \cdot \mathcal{P}[\![t_2]\!]m$$
$$\mathcal{P}[\![\&_\vee(t_1, t_2)]\!]m = 1 - (1 - \mathcal{P}[\![t_1]\!]m) \cdot (1 - \mathcal{P}[\![t_2]\!]m)$$
$$\mathcal{P}[\![\&_\neg(t)]\!]m \quad = 1 - \mathcal{P}[\![t]\!]m$$
$$\mathcal{P}[\![\&_\sim(t)]\!]m \quad = 1 - \mathcal{P}[\![t]\!]m$$
$$\mathcal{P}[\![\&_{\text{true}}]\!]m \quad = 1$$
$$\mathcal{P}[\![\&_{\text{false}}]\!]m \quad = 0$$

occurs more than once, and the success of each sub-tree containing a depends on the actions b, c. However, observe that in t the actions of sub-trees $\&_\wedge(a, b)$ and $\&_\wedge(a, c)$ are not independent. The assumption of linearity ensures independence of actions, thereby guaranteeing the soundness of the computations explained below.

We assume that each basic action $a \in Act$ has two associated success probabilities; success probability $M_1(a)$ in case of not performing a, and success probability $M_2(a)$ in case of performing a, such that $M_1(a) < M_2(a)$. For instance, an attacker might succeed to disable a security camera with a given probability M_2, or the security camera might be disabled due to some external conditions with a given probability M_1, which for the attacker will be the probability of succeeding without performing the action. We consider the Boolean assignment m_τ as defined in the previous section, $m_\tau : Act_\tau \to \mathbb{B}$, and assume that an action a has a probability of success $M_1(a)$ if $m(a)$ is *false* and has a probability of success $M_2(a)$ if $m(a)$ is *true*. Choosing $M_1(a) = 0$ and $M_2(a) = 1$ coincides with the Boolean case.

The evaluation of attack-defence trees in the probabilistic setting follows the development for the Boolean setting: first, we characterise the solution to our problem in a top-down fashion, and then we investigate what limitations on the model allow to devise an algorithmic approach with lower complexity.

The semantic evaluation $M(t)$ of an attack-defence tree $t \in Tree_p$ is illustrated in Table 4. It computes the minimum and the maximum success probability of a scenario by analysing the tree t over all Boolean assignments from which the probability values are inferred. Observe that also here the players have opposite goals, e.g., the proponent wants to maximise the overall probability of success, while the opponent wants to minimise it.

The result of the computation, when the proponent is an attacker, is interpreted as follows. The maximum success probability p shows the existence of an attack with probability p. In this case, we say that the system is p-vulnerable.

The algorithmic evaluation $INT(t)$ of an attack-defence tree $t \in Tree_p$ is given in Table 5. It traverses the tree from the leaves to the root and propagates

Table 5. The probabilistic algorithmic evaluation of an attack-defence tree

$$INT(a) \quad = \begin{cases} (M_1(a), M_2(a)) & \text{if } a \in Act_p \\ (M_2(a), M_1(a)) & \text{if } a \in Act_o \end{cases}$$

$INT(\&_\wedge(t_1, t_2)) = let \ (min_i, max_i) = INT(t_i), i \in \{1, 2\}$
$\qquad\qquad\qquad in \ (min_1 \cdot min_2, max_1 \cdot max_2)$

$INT(\&_\vee(t_1, t_2)) = let \ (min_i, max_i) = INT(t_i), i \in \{1, 2\}$
$\qquad\qquad\qquad in \ (1 - (1 - min_1) \cdot (1 - min_2), 1 - (1 - max_1) \cdot (1 - max_2))$

$INT(\&_\neg(t)) \quad = let \ (min, max) = INT(t)$
$\qquad\qquad\qquad in \ (1 - max, 1 - min)$

$INT(\&_\sim(t)) \quad = let \ (min, max) = INT(t)$
$\qquad\qquad\qquad in \ (1 - max, 1 - min)$

$INT(\&_{\text{true}}) \quad = (1, 1)$

$INT(\&_{\text{false}}) \quad = (0, 0)$

Table 6. The values of probability and cost for the basic actions of the example

Label	Name of the Node	M_1	M_2	c
is	identify subject	0.2	0.8	80
bs	bribe subject	0	0.7	100
t1	training for thwart	0.1	0.3	0
tf	threaten to fire employees	0.1	0.4	0
t	threaten	0	0.7	160
b	blackmail	0	0.7	150
st	send false tag	0	0.5	50
at	authenticate tag	0.1	0.7	0
ba	break authentication	0.1	0.6	85
im	infiltrate management	0	0.5	70
ot	order tag replacement	0	0.6	0
t2	training for trick	0.1	0.4	0

the values of the basic actions. Similarly to the Boolean case, as the negation and changing player operators change the goal of the player, we first swap the minimum and maximum values before applying negation.

The restriction of linear trees is adequate for showing the equivalence of the two evaluations.

Theorem 2. *If $t \in Tree$ is a linear tree, then $M(t) = INT(t)$.*

Hence, in the probabilistic setting linearity allows to scale from an exponential to a linear complexity.

Running Example. Consider the attack-defence tree t presented in Figure 1. Observe that t is a linear tree, thus we can apply the algorithmic evaluation for computing the maximum probability of success at the root. Table 6 lists possible probability values for basic actions (the last column is for later reference). Providing a realistic estimate is a research topic in itself and falls outside the scope of this work. Following the algorithmic computation, at the root we obtain $INT(t) = (0, 0.97)$, that is, the system is 0.97 vulnerable.

3   Attack-Defence Trees with Cost

In this section we extend our evaluation techniques by considering a single cost for basic actions. We evaluate the minimum cost of an attack or defence in the Boolean and probabilistic settings. Similarly to the previous section, the Boolean case is thoroughly explained in Sect. 3.1. The developments are generalised to the probabilistic setting in Sect. 3.2.

3.1   Cost in the Boolean Case

In the following, we extend the model of attack-defence trees described in Sect. 2.2 with a single cost for basic actions. Therefore, each basic action is associated with a pair of Boolean and cost values.

When we consider costs, we can focus on questions such as "What is the minimum cost of an attack?" or "How much does it cost to protect a system in a given scenario?". Observe that such questions are player-dependent, meaning that the model is evaluated from a given player's perspective. Since we assumed that the basic actions are independent, we need to consider one player's values only. For instance, for computing the minimum cost of an attack we need only the cost of the attacker's actions and do not require the cost of the defender's actions. Thus, in our evaluation techniques we consider only the cost of the proponent's actions, and do not consider the cost of the opponent's actions.

In the following we consider the set $D = \mathbb{B} \times \mathbb{R}_{\geq 0}$. In order to link the cost parameter to the existing model in the Boolean setting, we assume that each basic action of the proponent $a \in Act_p$ has two associated costs (non-negative real numbers). One is the cost of not performing a (0 in the following), the other is the cost c of performing a. We set both costs of the opponent actions to 0.

Extending the model with costs and evaluating the pairs of success *and* cost values lead to multi-parameter optimisation. Moreover, such pairs are incomparable in case the goal of a player is to maximise one parameter while minimising the other. In order to address multi-parameter optimisation in the case of incomparable values, we resort to Pareto efficiency and define two functions for computing the sets of Pareto efficient solutions. A solution is called Pareto efficient if it is not dominated by any other solution in the ordering relation [10].

We assume that the goal of the proponent is to maximise the success value while minimising the cost of an attack or defence. In order to compute the set of pairs of efficient solutions, where we want to maximise the first argument while minimising the second, we define function MR^{+-}. The function computes the set of all pairs that have higher value for the first argument *or* lower value for the second argument with respect to the other pairs in the set.

$$MR^{+-}(Z) = \{(x,y) \in Z \mid \forall (x',y') \in Z : x' \sqsupseteq x \wedge y' \sqsubseteq y \Rightarrow x' = x \wedge y' = y\}$$
$$= \{(x,y) \in Z \mid \forall (x',y') \in Z : (x \sqsupseteq x' \vee y \sqsubset y') \wedge (x \sqsupset x' \vee y \sqsubseteq y')\}$$

where $Z \subseteq D$.

Note that the sign "+" indicates the maximisation and the sign "-" indicates the minimisation, and their position refer to the parameter of the maximisation/minimisation.

In Sect. 2.2 we discussed how the negation and changing player operators change the goal, e.g., maximisation is turned into minimisation. Thus, if the proponent's goal is to maximise the success value and minimise the cost of an attack or defence, then under negation the goal is to minimise the success value and minimise the cost of an attack or defence. Observe that the goal for the cost does not change, as we assume to deal with rational players. Therefore, we define function MR^{--} to compute the set of all pairs that have lower values for both arguments with respect to the other pairs in the set.

$$MR^{--}(Z) = \{(x, y) \in Z \mid \forall (x', y') \in Z : x' \sqsubseteq x \land y' \sqsubseteq y \Rightarrow x' = x \land y' = y\}$$
$$= \{(x, y) \in Z \mid \forall (x', y') \in Z : (x \sqsubseteq x' \lor y \sqsubset y') \land (x \sqsubset x' \lor y \sqsubseteq y')\}$$

where $Z \subseteq D$.

Observe that the "+" symbol in MR^{+-} corresponds to the outer-most max operator in Table 2, and the first "-" symbol in MR^{--} corresponds to the outer-most min operator.

Following the previous developments, we present two evaluation techniques.

The semantic evaluation $M(t, A)$ of an attack-defence tree $t \in Tree_p$ and a set of actions A is illustrated in Table 7. It computes a pair, where the first argument is a set computed by the function MR^{--} and consists of all pairs that have lower success value and lower cost of the proponent actions compared to other pairs, and the second argument is the set computed by the function MR^{+-} and consists of all pairs that have higher success value and lower cost of the proponent actions compared to other pairs.

As we discussed in Sect. 2.2, if the proponent wants to maximise the success of the main goal, then the opponent wants to minimise it. In other words, the players affect the computation of the success value of the main goal in opposite ways, e.g., when one wants to maximise, the other wants to minimise and vice versa. The functions MR^{--} and MR^{+-} evaluate the success values based on the goal of the proponent. In order to consider the effect of the opponent with the opposite goal, we define functions $f_1^{m_p}(t)$ and $f_2^{m_p}(t)$ given in Table 7. The functions compute respectively the maximum and minimum success values over all Boolean assignments m_o for a given Boolean assignment m_p.

As the costs of the opponent's actions are 0 and do not influence the overall cost of the proponent, we consider only the cost of the proponent. The cost is represented with the concept of a budget, denoted by b_p, for associating with each success value the corresponding budget of the proponent and the Boolean assignment m_p. The budget $b_p \in \mathbb{R}_{\geq 0}$ takes values from 0 to infinity in an increasing manner. For a given budget b_p we take m_p such that the cost of the proponent for m_p is not greater than b_p, and the corresponding success value for m_p is computed. The cost for a given m_p is computed with the function *cost*, defined in Table 7.

Table 7. The Boolean semantic evaluation of an attack-defence tree with cost

$$M(t, A) = (MR^{--}(\{ (f_1^{m_p}(t), b_p) \mid cost(m_p, A) \le b_p\}),$$
$$MR^{+-}(\{ (f_2^{m_p}(t), b_p) \mid cost(m_p, A) \le b_p\}))$$

$$f_1^{m_p}(t) = \max\{\mathcal{B}[\![t]\!](m_p, m_o) \mid m_o \text{ Boolean assignment}\}$$
$$f_2^{m_p}(t) = \min\{\mathcal{B}[\![t]\!](m_p, m_o) \mid m_o \text{ Boolean assignment}\}$$

$$cost(m_p, A) = \sum_{a \in A} \begin{cases} c(a), & \text{if } m_p(a) = tt \\ 0, & \text{if } m_p(a) = ff \end{cases}$$

The result of the semantic evaluation is a pair of sets of Pareto efficient solutions for the given optimisation criteria of the goal.

The algorithmic evaluation $INT(t)$ for an attack-defence tree $t \in Tree_p$ is given in Table 8. It again computes a pair, where the first argument consists of all pairs that have lower success value and cost of the proponent actions, and the second argument consists of all pairs that have higher success value and lower cost of the proponent actions. Such sets are computed in the bottom-up fashion, defined by the rules presented in Table 8. The rules extend the ones for the success value computation, presented in Sect. 2.2, Table 3.

The first rule assigns the sets MR^{--} and MR^{+-} to the basic actions. Observe that the cost of not performing the proponent's actions, as well as both costs of the opponent's actions, is 0. The rules for conjunction and disjunction use the common computation for success values and sum the costs. The negation and changing player operators evaluate the success value as described in Sect. 2.2, while leaving the cost unchanged. The last two rules correspond to always successful and failed actions, which are independent from the players, and thus have a cost equal to 0. Applying the functions MR^{--} and MR^{+-} in each rule of the evaluation allows to reduce the size of the sets in each step.

We denote by $yield(t) \subseteq Act$ the set of actions that are in the leaves of t. By considering the polarity-consistent tree $t = \&_\wedge(\&_\vee(a, b), \&_\vee(a, \&_\sim(c)))$, where $a, b \in Act_p, c \in Act_o$, $c(a) = 2$ and $c(b) = 1$, we see that the two evaluation techniques lead to different results. The semantic evaluation gives the result $M(t, yield(t)) = (\{(ff, 0)\}, \{(ff, 0), (tt, 2)\})$, while the algorithmic evaluation gives the result $INT(t) = (\{(ff, 0)\}, \{(ff, 0), (tt, 3)\})$.

Therefore, the assumption of polarity consistency, considered in the Boolean case in Sect. 2.2, is no longer adequate when dealing with the notion of cost. In order to show the equivalence of the two evaluations we resort to a stronger assumption of linearity.

Theorem 3. *If $t \in Tree$ is a linear tree, then $M(t, yield(t)) = INT(t)$.*

We measure complexity of the two evaluation methods by calculating the number of set operations. The semantic evaluation is exponential in the size of t, as it considers all Boolean assignments. The algorithmic evaluation is linear and hence presents a dramatic improvement in the case of linear trees.

Table 8. The Boolean algorithmic evaluation of an attack-defence tree with cost

$$INT(a) \quad = \begin{cases} (MR^{--}(\{(f\!f,0),(tt,c(a))\}), \\ MR^{+-}(\{(f\!f,0),(tt,c(a))\})) & \text{if } a \in Act_p \\ (MR^{--}(\{(tt,0)\}), MR^{+-}(\{(f\!f,0)\})) & \text{if } a \in Act_o \end{cases}$$

$$INT(\&_\wedge(t_1,t_2)) = let \ (V_i,W_i) = INT(t_i), i \in \{1,2\}$$
$$in \ (MR^{--}(\{(b \wedge b',c+c') \mid (b,c) \in V_1,(b',c') \in V_2\}),$$
$$MR^{+-}(\{(b \wedge b',c+c') \mid (b,c) \in W_1,(b',c') \in W_2\}))$$

$$INT(\&_\vee(t_1,t_2)) = let \ (V_i,W_i) = INT(t_i), i \in \{1,2\}$$
$$in \ (MR^{--}(\{(b \vee b',c+c') \mid (b,c) \in V_1,(b',c') \in V_2\}),$$
$$MR^{+-}(\{(b \vee b',c+c') \mid (b,c) \in W_1,(b',c') \in W_2\}))$$

$$INT(\&_\neg(t)) \quad = let \ (V,W) = INT(t)$$
$$in \ (MR^{--}(\{(\neg b,c) \mid (b,c) \in W\}), MR^{+-}(\{(\neg b,c) \mid (b,c) \in V\}))$$

$$INT(\&_\sim(t)) \quad = let \ (V,W) = INT(t)$$
$$in \ (MR^{--}(\{(\neg b,c) \mid (b,c) \in W\}), MR^{+-}(\{(\neg b,c) \mid (b,c) \in V\}))$$

$$INT(\&_{\text{true}}) \quad = (\{(tt,0)\}, \{(tt,0)\})$$

$$INT(\&_{\text{false}}) \quad = (\{(f\!f,0)\}, \{(f\!f,0)\})$$

3.2 Cost in the Probabilistic Case

In this section we briefly generalise our development to the probabilistic setting, concentrating on the differences with respect to the Boolean setting.

In the probabilistic setting the cost-related questions are the same as in the Boolean setting, and the same observation regarding the cost to the proponent and to the opponent applies. Here we consider the set $D = [0,1] \times \mathbb{R}_{\geq 0}$. The cost is integrated to the basic actions in the same way. Thus, to extend the probabilistic model with costs, we assume that each basic action of the proponent player $a \in Act_p$ has two associated costs, 0 in case of not performing a, and c in case of performing a. We set both costs of the opponent's actions equal to 0.

As in the Boolean case, by considering probability *and* cost and focusing on maximising the first while minimising the other, we face a multi-parameter optimisation issue with incomparable values. Similarly to the Boolean setting, we provide two evaluation techniques based on Pareto efficiency by considering the functions MR^{--} and MR^{+-}. We compute the set of Pareto efficient solutions for answering questions such as "What is the maximum probability and the minimum cost of an attack?".

The semantic evaluation $M(t,A)$ of an attack-defence tree $t \in Tree_p$ and a given set A is illustrated in Table 9. The evaluation follows the corresponding one for the Boolean case, described in the Sect. 3.1. The only difference is that the tree t is evaluated over the Boolean assignments by considering the probabilistic analysis $\mathcal{P}[\![t]\!]$ instead of the Boolean $\mathcal{B}[\![t]\!]$ one (and considering the corresponding

Table 9. The probabilistic semantic evaluation of an attack-defence tree with cost

$$M(t, A) = (MR^{--}(\{ (f_1^{m_p}(t), b_p) \mid cost(m_p, A) \leq b_p\}),$$
$$MR^{+-}(\{ (f_2^{m_p}(t), b_p) \mid cost(m_p, A) \leq b_p\}))$$

$$f_1^{m_p}(t) = \max\{\mathcal{P}[\![t]\!](m_p, m_o) \mid m_o \text{ Boolean assignment}\}$$
$$f_2^{m_p}(t) = \min\{\mathcal{P}[\![t]\!](m_p, m_o) \mid m_o \text{ Boolean assignment}\}$$

$$cost(m_p, A) = \sum_{a \in A} \begin{cases} c(a), & \text{if } m_p(a) = tt \\ 0, & \text{if } m_p(a) = ff \end{cases}$$

probabilistic values for each action). The result of the evaluation is the pair of the sets MR^{--} and MR^{+-}, corresponding to the set of Pareto efficient solutions.

The algorithmic evaluation $INT(t)$ for a tree $t \in Tree_p$ is given in Table 10. It traverses the tree from the leaves to the root according to the rules presented in Table 10. The rules follow the corresponding ones of the Boolean setting.

Analogously to the previous section, we shall restrict to linear trees in order to show the equivalence of the two evaluations.

Theorem 4. If $t \in Tree$ is a linear tree, then $M(t, yield(t)) = INT(t)$.

Again, a syntactic restriction allows to develop a sound evaluation technique that is linear in the size of the tree as opposed to the exponential complexity that characterises the general case.

Running Example. Consider the linear attack-defence tree t discussed in Figure 1. Table 6 lists possible values for probability and cost for basic actions.

In order to detect the attacks with maximum probability of success and minimum cost, we apply the algorithmic evaluation. At the root we obtain: $INT(t) = (\{(0,0)\}, \text{"The plot in Figure 2"}\})$. The overall result of the evaluation, i.e., the set of efficient solutions for the goal representing the Pareto frontier of the problem, is displayed in Figure 2. The probability of successful attacks ranges from 0 to 0.97 and the corresponding cost ranges from 0 to 695. The intermediate points on the Pareto frontier indicate other optimal solutions. We can conclude that the system under study is (p,c)-vulnerable for all the incomparable pairs in the Pareto frontier. In particular, the attack is not trivially attainable (all pairs with probability greater than zero require a cost greater than zero).

4 Attack-Defence Trees with Multiple Cost

In this section we extend further the model to deal with multiple costs for basic actions. Observing that the Boolean setting is a special case of the probabilistic one, in the following we describe the extended model only in the probabilistic setting, focusing on the extensions with respect to a single cost model.

Table 10. The probabilistic algorithmic evaluation of an attack-defence tree with cost

$$INT(a) = \begin{cases} (MR^{--}(\{(M_1(a),0),(M_2(a),c(a))\}), \\ MR^{+-}(\{(M_1(a),0),(M_2(a),c(a))\})) & \text{if } a \in Act_p \\ (MR^{--}(\{(M_2(a),0)\}),MR^{+-}(\{(M_1(a),0)\})) & \text{if } a \in Act_o \end{cases}$$

$$INT(\&_\wedge(t_1,t_2)) = let\ (V_i,W_i) = INT(t_i), i \in \{1,2\}$$
$$in\ (MR^{--}(\{(p \cdot p',c+c') \mid (p,c) \in V_1, (p',c') \in V_2\}),$$
$$MR^{+-}(\{(p \cdot p',c+c') \mid (p,c) \in W_1, (p',c') \in W_2\}))$$

$$INT(\&_\vee(t_1,t_2)) = let\ (V_i,W_i) = INT(t_i), i \in \{1,2\}$$
$$in\ (MR^{--}(\{(1-(1-p)(1-p'),c+c') \mid (p,c) \in V_1, (p',c') \in V_2\}),$$
$$MR^{+-}(\{(1-(1-p)(1-p'),c+c') \mid (p,c) \in W_1, (p',c') \in W_2\}))$$

$$INT(\&_\neg(t)) = let\ (V,W) = INT(t)$$
$$in\ (MR^{--}(\{(1-p,c) \mid (p,c) \in W\}),MR^{+-}(\{(1-p,c) \mid (p,c) \in V\}))$$

$$INT(\&_\sim(t)) = let\ (V,W) = INT(t)$$
$$in\ (MR^{--}(\{(1-p,c) \mid (p,c) \in W\}),MR^{+-}(\{(1-p,c) \mid (p,c) \in V\}))$$

$$INT(\&_{true}) = (\{(1,0)\},\{(1,0)\})$$

$$INT(\&_{false}) = (\{(0,0)\},\{(0,0)\})$$

We consider the set $D = [0,1] \times \mathbb{R}^n_{\geq 0}$. We assume that each basic action of the proponent $a \in Act_p$ has a vector of n associated costs, a vector of 0's in case of not performing a, and a vector $\gamma : Act_p \to \mathbb{R}^n_{\geq 0}$ in case of performing a. When adding costs we resort to point-wise summation of vectors. We set the cost of the opponent's actions to vectors of 0's.

Analogously to the previous sections, we deal with a multi-parameter optimisation with incomparable values. We give two evaluation techniques by using Pareto efficiency. In order to generalise the functions MR^{--} and MR^{+-}, defined in the previous section, we introduce polarity modifications of the comparison operators as follows: $\sqsupseteq^+$ is $\sqsupseteq$, $\sqsupset^+$ is $\sqsupset$, $\sqsupseteq^-$ is $\sqsubseteq$ and $\sqsupset^-$ is $\sqsubset$. The sign "+" corresponds to the maximisation of the parameters and keeps the operator as it is, while the sign "−" corresponds to the minimisation of the parameters, therefore it changes the operator.

We define a general frontier function, where $s_i \in \{+,-\}$ and $Z \subseteq D$, as follows:

$$MR^{s_0,\cdots,s_n}(Z) = \{(x_0,\cdots,x_n) \in Z \mid \forall(x'_0,\cdots,x'_n) \in Z :$$
$$x'_0 \sqsupseteq^{s_0} x_0 \wedge \cdots \wedge x'_n \sqsupseteq^{s_n} x_n \Rightarrow x'_0 = x_0 \wedge \cdots \wedge x'_n = x_n\}$$
$$= \{(x_0,\cdots,x_n) \in Z \mid \forall(x'_0,\cdots,x'_n) \in Z :$$
$$((x_0 \sqsupseteq^{s_0} x'_0) \vee (x_1 \sqsupset^{s_1} x'_1) \vee \cdots \vee (x_n \sqsupset^{s_n} x'_n)) \wedge \cdots$$
$$\cdots \wedge ((x_0 \sqsupset^{s_0} x'_0) \vee (x_1 \sqsupset^{s_1} x'_1) \vee \cdots \vee (x_n \sqsupseteq^{s_n} x'_n))\}$$

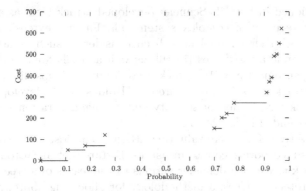

Fig. 2. Pareto efficient solutions for the attack-defence tree t

The function $MR^{s_0, \cdots, s_n}$ computes the efficient solutions for multiple parameters by maximising the parameter values if $s_i = +$ and minimising it if $s_i = -$. Note that each $\sqsupseteq^{s_i}$ is in fact a total order (on [0,1] or $\mathbb{R}_{\geq 0}$) and hence $\neg(x'_i \sqsupseteq^{s_i} x_i)$ is equivalent to $x_i \sqsupseteq^{s_i} x'_i$ (as in Sect. 3). Observe that with this notation we get MR^{--} when we take $n = 1$ and $s_0 = s_1 = -$, and we get MR^{+-} when we take $n - 1$ and $s_0 = +, s_1 = -$.

The definition of the semantic and algorithmic evaluations closely follows that of the corresponding ones in the Sect. 3.2. Similarly, we show their equivalence by restricting to linear trees.

For better understanding the extension to multiple costs, let us explain the rule for conjunction in the algorithmic evaluation. The rule is as follows:

$$
\begin{aligned}
INT(\&_\wedge(t_1, t_2)) = \; &let \; (V_i, W_i) = INT(t_i), i \in \{1, 2\} \\
&in \; (MR^{--\cdots-}(\{(p \cdot p', c_1 + c'_1, \cdots, c_n + c'_n) \mid \\
&\qquad (p, c_1, \cdots, c_n) \in V_1, (p', c'_1, \cdots, c'_n) \in V_2\}), \\
&\quad MR^{+-\cdots-}(\{(p \cdot p', c_1 + c'_1, \cdots, c_n + c'_n) \mid \\
&\qquad (p, c_1, \cdots, c_n) \in W_1, (p', c'_1, \cdots, c'_n) \in W_2\}))
\end{aligned}
$$

First, it computes all possible combinations of pairs from both sub-trees t_1 and t_2 by multiplying probabilities and summing costs. Then, it applies functions $MR^{\cdots}$ in order to get the Pareto efficient solutions. This is sound due to the point-wise ordering of the set.

5 Related Work

We now expand on the comparison with related work given in Sect. 1. Different graphical approaches have been studied, for evaluating the security of a system. A historical overview on existing graph-based approaches for security threats is given by Piètre-Cambacédès and Boussou [11]. Moreover, Kordy et al. summarise the existing methodologies for analysing attack and defence scenarios in [12].

As we mentioned in Sect. 1, Schneier developed attack trees as an approach to analyse the security of complex systems [3]. Further extensions of attack trees based on Schneier's model have been considered, such as attack graphs [13,14] and dynamic attack trees [15,16], as well as tools for modelling [17,18] and generating automatically [19] attack trees. Mauw and Oostdijk give a formal semantics of attack trees in [20]. Moreover, Buldas et al. developed a multi-parameter attack tree model for security analysis against rational attacks [21], subsequently extended in [22,23,24].

While attack trees focus on evaluating attack scenarios, other tree-structure representations incorporate countermeasures. Bistarelli et al. introduced an extension of attack trees with defender actions to the leaves of a tree [4]. Edge et al. proposed protection trees, a methodology for allocating appropriate protections against specified attacks such that the success probability of the defender is maximised [25]. Zonouz et al. [26] and Roy et al. [5] proposed a methodology for attack and defence modelling that combines analytical methods of attack and defence trees. They capture attacks and countermeasures at any node of a tree.

Finally, Kordy et al. [6] formalised attack-defence trees as an intuitive model for presenting attacks and countermeasures in a single view. For evaluating attack-defence trees the typical bottom-up approach of attack trees is extended. Attack-defence trees are interpreted with various semantics to answer questions such as the vulnerability of the system to an attack or the minimum cost of an attack [6]. Most evaluations [6,27,28] analyse a specific aspect of a scenario and do not consider trees with multiple parameters.

Further developments on attack-defence trees have been carried out, such as studying the relationship between such trees and two-player games [8] and combining the tree methodology with Bayesian networks for analysing probabilistic measures of attack-defence trees with dependent actions [28].

6   Conclusion

The growing centrality of technology requires a thorough investigation of the security properties of complex systems with respect to cyber and physical attacks, as well as consideration of possible defences undertaken to counter such attacks.

Attack-defence trees are a useful tool to study attack-defence scenarios and present the interaction between an attacker and a defender in an intuitive way. Moreover, such models are relied on to develop quantitative analyses of attacks and defences. Many evaluation methods consider one-parameter trees or analyse multi-parameter trees focusing on one specific aspect of the scenario, such as probability of success or cost. Nonetheless, in case of multi-parameter models, conflicting objectives may lead to incomparable values, which require to optimise all parameters at once on pain of computing sub-optimal solutions.

In order to tackle this issue, we have presented evaluation techniques for multi-parameter attack-defence trees that optimise all parameters at once, leveraging the concept of Pareto efficiency. Our developments have been carried out on a new language-based formalism for attack-defence trees, which extends standard trees with negation and with a novel operator for player alternation. In this language, the interaction between an attacker and a defender is made explicit by associating a player to each node thanks to a simple type system. We have called *proponent* the player at the root and *opponent* the other player.

We have developed analyses of attack-defence scenarios both in the Boolean and in the probabilistic settings, investigating aspects such as the feasibility and the cost of an attack or a defence. For each case we have illustrated the natural semantic evaluation technique as well as an algorithmic evaluation which enjoys a dramatic improvement in complexity, and we have proven under which conditions the latter can be relied on in place of the former. Both methods characterise the goal of the scenario with a set of Pareto efficient solutions.

Our current methods focus on the players independently: for evaluating the cost of the proponent p, we set the cost of the opponent to 0 and assign a budget to p. In future work, we plan to extend the model with a budget for the opponent, so as to compute the optimal solutions for both players at once.

Acknowledgment. Part of the research leading to these results has received funding from the European Union Seventh Framework Programme (FP7/2007-2013) under grant agreement no. 318003 (TRE$_S$PASS). Special thanks to Roberto Vigo and Alessandro Bruni for valuable comments and inspiring discussions.

References

1. Vesely, W., Roberts, N., Haasl, D., Goldberg, F.: Fault Tree Handbook. Number v. 88 in Fault Tree Handbook. Systems and Reliability Research, Office of Nuclear Regulatory Research, U.S. Nuclear Regulatory Commission (1981)
2. Weiss, J.D.: A system security engineering process. In: Proceedings of the 14th National Computer Security Conference, pp. 572–581 (1991)
3. Schneier, B.: Attack Trees: Modeling Security Threats. Dr. Dobb's Journal of Software Tools 24(12), 21–29 (1999)
4. Bistarelli, S., Fioravanti, F., Peretti, P.: Defense trees for economic evaluation of security investments. In: Availability, Reliability and Security, pp. 416–423 (2006)
5. Roy, A., Kim, D.S., Trivedi, K.S.: Attack countermeasure trees (ACT): Towards unifying the constructs of attack and defense trees. Security and Communication Networks 5(8), 929–943 (2012)
6. Kordy, B., Mauw, S., Radomirović, S., Schweitzer, P.: Foundations of attack–defense trees. In: Degano, P., Etalle, S., Guttman, J. (eds.) FAST 2010. LNCS, vol. 6561, pp. 80–95. Springer, Heidelberg (2011)
7. Bagnato, A., Kordy, B., Meland, P.H., Schweitzer, P.: Attribute decoration of attack-defense trees. IJSSE 3(2), 1–35 (2012)
8. Kordy, B., Mauw, S., Melissen, M., Schweitzer, P.: Attack-defense trees and two-player binary zero-sum extensive form games are equivalent. In: Alpcan, T., Buttyán, L., Baras, J.S. (eds.) GameSec 2010. LNCS, vol. 6442, pp. 245–256. Springer, Heidelberg (2010)
9. Girard, J.Y.: Linear logic: Its syntax and semantics. In: Proceedings of the Workshop on Advances in Linear Logic, pp. 1–42. Cambridge University Press (1995)
10. Legriel, J., Le Guernic, C., Cotton, S., Maler, O.: Approximating the pareto front of multi-criteria optimization problems. In: Esparza, J., Majumdar, R. (eds.) TACAS 2010. LNCS, vol. 6015, pp. 69–83. Springer, Heidelberg (2010)

11. Piètre-Cambacédès, L., Bouissou, M.: Beyond attack trees: Dynamic security modeling with boolean logic driven markov processes (BDMP). In: Eighth European Dependable Computing Conference, EDCC-8 2010, pp. 199–208 (2010)
12. Kordy, B., Piètre-Cambacédès, L., Schweitzer, P.: Dag-based attack and defense modeling: Don't miss the forest for the attack trees. CoRR abs/1303.7397 (2013)
13. Sheyner, O., Haines, J.W., Jha, S., Lippmann, R., Wing, J.M.: Automated generation and analysis of attack graphs. In: IEEE S&P 2002, pp. 273–284 (2002)
14. Jha, S., Sheyner, O., Wing, J.M.: Two formal analyses of attack graphs. In: 15th IEEE Computer Security Foundations Workshop (CSFW-15 2002), pp. 49–63 (2002)
15. Arnold, F., Hermanns, H., Pulungan, R., Stoelinga, M.: Time-dependent analysis of attacks. In: Abadi, M., Kremer, S. (eds.) POST 2014. LNCS, vol. 8414, pp. 285–305. Springer, Heidelberg (2014)
16. Khand, P.: System level security modeling using attack trees. In: Computer, Control and Communication, IC4 2009, pp. 1–6 (2009)
17. Amenaza: SecurITree, http://www.amenaza.com
18. Isograph: AttackTree+, http://www.isograph.com/software/attacktree/
19. Vigo, R., Nielson, F., Riis Nielson, H.: Automated Generation of Attack Trees. In: 27th Computer Security Foundations Symposium (CSF 2014), pp. 337–350. IEEE (2014)
20. Mauw, S., Oostdijk, M.: Foundations of attack trees. In: Won, D.H., Kim, S. (eds.) ICISC 2005. LNCS, vol. 3935, pp. 186–198. Springer, Heidelberg (2006)
21. Buldas, A., Laud, P., Priisalu, J., Saarepera, M., Willemson, J.: Rational Choice of Security Measures Via Multi-Parameter Attack Trees. In: López, J. (ed.) CRITIS 2006. LNCS, vol. 4347, pp. 235–248. Springer, Heidelberg (2006)
22. Jürgenson, A., Willemson, J.: Computing exact outcomes of multi-parameter attack trees. In: Meersman, R., Tari, Z. (eds.) OTM 2008, Part II. LNCS, vol. 5332, pp. 1036–1051. Springer, Heidelberg (2008)
23. Jürgenson, A., Willemson, J.: On fast and approximate attack tree computations. In: Kwak, J., Deng, R.H., Won, Y., Wang, G. (eds.) ISPEC 2010. LNCS, vol. 6047, pp. 56–66. Springer, Heidelberg (2010)
24. Buldas, A., Lenin, A.: New efficient utility upper bounds for the fully adaptive model of attack trees. In: Das, S.K., Nita-Rotaru, C., Kantarcioglu, M. (eds.) GameSec 2013. LNCS, vol. 8252, pp. 192–205. Springer, Heidelberg (2013)
25. Edge, K., Dalton, G., Raines, R., Mills, R.: Using attack and protection trees to analyze threats and defenses to homeland security. In: MILCOM 2006, pp. 1–7. IEEE (2006)
26. Zonouz, S.A., Khurana, H., Sanders, W.H., Yardley, T.M.: RRE: A game-theoretic intrusion response and recovery engine. In: DSN 2009, pp. 439–448 (2009)
27. Kordy, B., Pouly, M., Schweitzer, P.: Computational aspects of attack-defense trees. In: Bouvry, P., Kłopotek, M.A., Leprévost, F., Marciniak, M., Mykowiecka, A., Rybiński, H. (eds.) SIIS 2011. LNCS, vol. 7053, pp. 103–116. Springer, Heidelberg (2012)
28. Kordy, B., Pouly, M., Schweitzer, P.: A probabilistic framework for security scenarios with dependent actions. In: Albert, E., Sekerinski, E. (eds.) IFM 2014. LNCS, vol. 8739, pp. 256–271. Springer, Heidelberg (2014)

Analysis of XACML Policies with SMT

Fatih Turkmen[1], Jerry den Hartog[1], Silvio Ranise[2], and Nicola Zannone[1]

[1] Eindhoven University of Technology, Eindhoven, The Netherlands
[2] Fondazione Bruno Kessler (FBK) Trento, Italy

Abstract. The eXtensible Access Control Markup Language (XACML) is an extensible and flexible XML language for the specification of access control policies. However, the richness and flexibility of the language (along with the verbose syntax of XML) come with a price: errors are easy to make and difficult to detect when policies grow in size. If these errors are not detected and rectified, they result in serious data leakage and/or privacy violations leading to significant legal and financial consequences. To assist policy authors in the analysis of their policies, several policy analysis tools have been proposed based on different underlying formalisms. However, most of these tools either abstract away functions over non-Boolean domains (hence they cannot provide information about them) or produce very large encodings which hinder the performance. In this paper, we present a generic policy analysis framework that employs SMT as the underlying reasoning mechanism. The use of SMT does not only allow more fine-grained analysis of policies but also improves the performance. We demonstrate that a wide range of security properties proposed in the literature can be easily modeled within the framework. A prototype implementation and its evaluation are also provided.

1 Introduction

Access rules governing sensitive data such as patient health records or financial transactions are usually encoded in a policy that is enforced by the authorization system. Correctness of access control policies is crucial for organizations to prevent authorization violations or fraud which can result in serious data leakage and/or privacy violations leading to significant legal and financial consequences (e.g., financial and reputation loss). In this work, we consider policies expressed in eXtensible Access Control Markup Language (XACML) [20]. XACML provides an extensible and flexible language that allows the specification of structured policies in which policies specified by different authorities can be combined together. However, policy specification in XACML is known to be a difficult and error-prone task [10,13]. This richness and flexibility along with its verbose syntax make it difficult to determine whether policies work as intended. Therefore, automated tools are needed to assist policy authors in analyzing their policies to detect and correct errors before policies are deployed.

This need has spurred the development of several methods and tools for the verification of policy specifications at design time using formal reasoning [5,8,10,12,13]. The security properties being verified can express requirements

© Springer-Verlag Berlin Heidelberg 2015
R. Focardi and A. Myers (Eds.): POST 2015, LNCS 9036, pp. 115–134, 2015.
DOI: 10.1007/978-3-662-46666-7_7

on the policies but also on relations between policies. A requirement on a policy could specify (types of) access requests that should (not) be granted by the policy. An updated policy being compared with the original to ensure the update is 'safe' is an example of a requirement on the relation between policies. Here 'safe' could be expressed in being as permissive/restrictive as another policy as is done in policy refinement [5] and subsumption [13]. Despite a large variety in security properties that one may need to check, existing policy analysis tools often support only a restricted set of properties due to the (lack of) expressiveness of the formalization employed by the tool and the capabilities offered by the underlying reasoner.

Advances in propositional satisfiability (SAT) research [11] make SAT solvers an attractive underlying reasoner in policy analysis [13]. SAT allows efficient reasoning about propositional logic formula and many access control policies and security properties can be naturally modeled in propositional logic. However, SAT solvers do not natively support reasoning on predicates over non-Boolean variables and functions which frequently appear in access control policies and, in particular, in XACML policies. For instance, SAT does not allow a straightforward reasoning on temporal constraints such as *request-time* > 13:20, which can play an important role in the correctness of a policy and thus in the security of the system. Such non-Boolean expressions are usually left uninterpreted [13] which restricts analysis capabilities. Alternatives that support fine-grained policy analysis can lead to excessively large encodings of the policy. The analyst is forced to choose a trade-off between performance and accuracy by introducing bounds on the domains.

In this paper, we consider SAT modulo theories (SMT) [6] as the underlying reasoning method for the analysis of XACML policies. SMT enables the use of theories, such as linear arithmetic and equality, to reason about the satisfiability of first order formulas. SMT is a natural extension to SAT in which SMT solvers employ tailored reasoners when solving non-Boolean predicates in the input formula. The use of SMT makes it possible to perform a more fine-grained analysis than existing SAT-based policy analysis tools allow.

The contributions of this paper are thus as follows:

- A novel policy analysis framework which makes it possible to verify access control policies against a large range of security properties.
- A fine-grained analysis of access control policies by performing reasoning on non-Boolean predicates, e.g. arithmetic functions on numeric attributes.
- A prototype implementation of the framework and its extensive evaluation using a number of well-known security properties taken from the literature.

The remainder of the paper provides an overview of XACML and SMT in Section 2, and an encoding of XACML policies in SMT in Section 3. Our analysis framework that uses this encoding for policy analysis is given in Section 4. Section 5 presents a prototype of our framework with experimental results. Section 6 discusses related work, and Section 7 provides conclusions.

2   Preliminaries

In this section we shortly recall key points of XACML and SMT.

2.1   XACML

XACML [20] is an OASIS standard for the specification of access control policies. It provides an attribute-based language that allows the specification of composite policies. In this work, we focus on the core specification of XACML v3 [20] (without obligations).

Three policy elements are provided by XACML: *policy sets*, *policies* and *rules*. A policy set consists of policy sets and policies; policies in turn consist of rules. If policy element p_1 is nested in policy element p_2 we say that p_1 is a *child policy element* of p_2 and that p_2 is the *parent policy element* of p_1. Each policy element has a (possibly empty) *target* which defines (restricts) the applicability of the policy element in terms of attributes characterizing the subject, the resource, the action to be performed on the resource, and the environment. Intuitively, the target identifies the set of access requests that the policy element applies to. In addition, rules specify an *effect* element that defines whether the requested actions should be allowed (*Permit*) or denied (*Deny*), and can be associated with *conditions* to further restrict their applicability.

If an access request matches both the target and conditions of a rule, the rule is applicable to the request and yields the decision specified by its effect element. Otherwise, the rule is not applicable, and a *NotApplicable* decision is returned. If an error occurs during evaluation, an *Indeterminate* decision is returned. XACML v3 also introduces an extended set of *Indeterminate* values to allow a fine-grained combination of decisions: *Indeterminate{P}*, *Indeterminate{D}* and *Indeterminate{PD}*. Intuitively, these *Indeterminate* decisions indicate the evaluation result of a policy element if the error not occurred.

To combine decisions obtained from the evaluation of different applicable policy elements, XACML provides a number of combining algorithms [20]: permit-overrides, deny-overrides, deny-unless-permit, permit-unless-deny, first-applicable and only-one-applicable.[1] Intuitively, these algorithms define procedures to evaluate composite policies based on the order of the policy elements and priorities between decisions.

Next we present a sample XACML policy in a concise form that we will use as a running example through the paper.

Example 1. *A user is allowed to create an object of type "transaction" only if his credit balance (credit) is higher than the value of the transaction itself (value) and banking costs (cost). Transactions can only be created during working days (i.e., Monday, Tuesday, Wednesday, Thursday, Friday) within the time interval*

---

[1] Combining algorithms permit-overrides and deny-overrides are defined over the *Indeterminate* extended set, while the other algorithms are defined over a single *Indeterminate* decision value. Combining algorithm only-one-applicable can only be used to combine policy sets and policies.

08:00-18:00. One way to model this policy is to represent (the negation of) these constraints as Deny *rules and then to combine the resulting rules using* deny-overrides *(dov):*

$p[\text{dov}]$:   resource-type $=$ *"transaction"* $\wedge$ action-id $=$ *"create"*
$r_1[Deny]$:   value $+$ cost $>$ credit
$r_2[Deny]$:   current-day $\notin \{Mo, Tu, We, Th, Fr\} \vee$
                current-time $< 08{:}00 \vee$ current-time $> 18{:}00$
$r_3[Permit]$: **true**

where **true** *is used to indicate that the target of the policy element matches every access request. We assume that attributes* value, cost, credit, current-time *and* current-day *are further constrained with function* one-and-only *so that a policy element returns* Indeterminate *if multiple values are provided for them.*

2.2   Satisfiability Modulo Theories

SMT [6] is a generalization of SAT in which Boolean variables can be replaced by constraints from a variety of theories. To specify SMT formulas, we follow an extended version of the SMT-LIB (v2) standard (http://www.smtlib.org) which is based on many-sorted first order logic. In the remainder, we assume the usual syntactic (e.g., sort, constant, predicate and function symbols, terms, atoms, literals, Boolean connectives, quantifiers, and formulas) and semantic (e.g., structure, satisfaction, model, and validity) notions of many-sorted first order logic; see [9] for formal definitions.

A theory $\mathcal{T}$ consists of a signature and a class of models. Intuitively, the signature fixes the vocabulary to build formulas and the class of models gives the meaning of the symbols in the vocabulary. As an example, consider the theory of an enumerated data-type: the signature consists of a single sort symbol and n constants corresponding to the elements in the enumeration; the class of models contains all structures interpreting the sort symbol as a set of cardinality n. For Linear Arithmetic over the Integers (LAI), the signature consists of the numerals (corresponding to the integers), binary addition, and the usual ordering relations; the class of models contains the standard model of the integers in which only linear constraints are considered. For the theory of uninterpreted functions, the signature consists of a finite set of symbols and the equality sign; the class of models contains all those structures interpreting the equality sign as a congruence relation and the other symbols in the signature as arbitrary constants, functions, or relations.

A formula φ is $\mathcal{T}$-*satisfiable* (or *satisfiable modulo* $\mathcal{T}$) iff there exists a structure $\mathcal{M}$ in the class of models of $\mathcal{T}$ and a valuation ϕ (i.e., a mapping from the variables that are not in the scope of a quantifier in the formula to the elements in the domains of $\mathcal{M}$) satisfying φ (in symbols, $\mathcal{M}, \phi \models \varphi$). A formula φ is $\mathcal{T}$-*valid* (or *valid modulo* $\mathcal{T}$) iff for every structure $\mathcal{M}$ in the class of models of $\mathcal{T}$ and every valuation ϕ, we have that $\mathcal{M}, \phi \models \varphi$. Notice that a formula φ is $\mathcal{T}$-valid iff the negation of φ (i.e., $\neg\varphi$) is $\mathcal{T}$-unsatisfiable.

Checking the satisfiability of conjunctions of literals (i.e., atoms or their negations) modulo certain theories – e.g., the theory of uninterpreted functions, theories of enumerated data-types, and Linear Arithmetic over the Integers – is well-known to be decidable [6]. These results imply the decidability of checking the satisfiability of quantifier-free formulas modulo the same theories. This is so as it is always possible to transform arbitrary Boolean combinations of atoms into disjunctive normal form (DNF), i.e. in a disjunction of conjunctions of literals. Unfortunately, the transformation to DNF may be computationally expensive and generate an exponentially larger formula [9]. For this reason, even if checking the satisfiability of conjunctions of literals modulo certain theories is polynomial (as it is the case for the theory of uninterpreted functions), checking the satisfiability of quantifier-free formulas modulo the same theories becomes NP-hard. While these theoretical limitations are unavoidable, modern SMT solvers have developed a wealth of heuristics to scale and handle very large formulas with arbitrary Boolean structures. The interested reader is pointed to [6] for a thorough introduction.

The situation is further complicated by two possible sources of problems. First, several verification problems (such as the XACML policy analysis problems considered in this paper) require to consider more than one theory to model various aspects of the situation under scrutiny. Under suitable assumption on the component theories, it is possible to build theory solvers capable of checking the satisfiability of conjunctions of literals in combinations of theories by modularly re-using the theory solvers of the component theories. However, the complexity of checking the satisfiability of conjunctions of literals in the combination can be much higher than that of modulo the individual theories. For instance, there exists a combination of two theories with polynomial satisfiability problem whose combination becomes NP-complete [22]. The second source of problems is the presence of quantifiers in the proof obligations generated by certain verification tools (as it is the case of some of the policy analysis problems considered in this work). In fact, the decidability of quantifier-free formulas does not extend to quantified formulas. For instance, checking the satisfiability of quantified formulas modulo the theory of uninterpreted functions is undecidable since one can encode the satisfiability problem for arbitrary first-order formulas whose undecidability is well-known [9]. Despite this and other negative results, several efforts have been put in identifying classes of quantified formulas whose satisfiability is decidable by integrating instantiation or quantifier-elimination procedures in SMT solvers; see, e.g., [6] for pointers to relevant work.

3 Encoding XACML Policies in SMT

In this section, we first present our formalization of XACML policies that allows us to represent policies in terms of predicates. We then show how the obtained predicates can be used to define SMT formulas.

3.1   XACML Formalization

An access control schema $\langle Att, Dom \rangle$ defines the vocabulary used for specifying access control policies. Here Att is a set of attributes $a_1, \ldots, a_n$, Dom gives the corresponding attribute domains $Dom_{a_1}, \ldots, Dom_{a_n}$ and we refer to set $2^{Dom_{a_1}} \times \ldots \times 2^{Dom_{a_n}}$ as the *policy space* specified within the schema. The elements of the policy space are called *attribute assignments*. An attribute assignment maps attributes to a (possibly empty) set of values in their domains. An *access request* $\langle a_1 = v_{1_i}, \ldots, a_n = v_{n_k} \rangle$ (with $v_{1_i} \in Dom_{a_1}, \ldots, v_{n_k} \in Dom_{a_n}$) specifies an attribute assignment, provided the values for those attributes are not assigned the empty set (multiple attribute/value pairs with the same attribute indicate multiple values are assigned to that attribute). Hereafter, $\mathcal{R}$ denotes the set of all possible access requests, i.e. the policy space.

Each policy element in XACML has a target that specifies *applicability constraints* in terms of attribute assignments. Applicability constraints are used to divide the policy space in three disjoint sub-spaces: the *Applicable* space AS_A, the *Indeterminate* space AS_{IN}, and the *NotApplicable* space AS_{NA}. These sub-spaces respectively represent access requests for which the policy's target matches the request, checking whether the target matches the request produces an error, and the target does not match the request. We represent the applicability space of a policy element as $\langle AS_A, AS_{IN} \rangle$ with an access request req in the set AS_{NA} (in symbols, $req \in AS_{NA}$) iff $req \notin AS_A \cup AS_{IN}$. An access request is evaluated against a policy element only if it matches the target of policy element's parent. Based on this observation, we flatten a XACML policy by propagating its applicability constraints in a top-down fashion from the root policy element to rules.

Definition 1. *Let p be a policy where $\langle AS_A^T, AS_{IN}^T \rangle$ is the applicability space induced by its target. The applicability space of p is inductively given by:*

$$\langle AS_A^p, AS_{IN}^p \rangle = \begin{cases} \langle AS_A^T, AS_{IN}^T \rangle & \text{if p is a root policy} \\ \langle AS_A^T \cap AS_A^q, (AS_{IN}^T \cap AS_A^q) \cup AS_{IN}^q \rangle & \text{if q is the parent of p} \end{cases}$$

For the root policy (i.e., the policy that does not have a parent policy element), the applicability space is that induced by its target. For policies that do have a parent the applicability space of the parent is also taken into account so the parents applicability is iteratively propagated to all its child policies. Thus, a rule has an applicability space which is determined by the applicability constraints in its target and by the applicability constraints in the target of all its ancestor policy elements. Note that, as for any target AS_A^T and AS_{IN}^T are disjoint, a straightforward inductive arguments shows that AS_A^p and AS_{IN}^p are also disjoint.

Example 2. *Consider the policy in Example 1. Below we represent the applicability constraints ac_i defined from the target of every policy element:*

ac_0 : *"transaction"* $\in$ resource-type

ac_1 : *"create"* $\in$ action-id

ac_2 : $\bigwedge_{d \in \{Mo,Tu,We,Th,Fr\}} d \notin$ current-day

ac_3 : $\forall v \in$ current-time $v > 18{:}00$

ac_4 : $\forall v \in$ current-time $v < 8{:}00$

ac_5 : $\forall v_1 \in$ credit, $v_2 \in$ cost, $v_3 \in$ value $(v_1 < v_2 + v_3)$

$ac_6, ..., ac_{10}$: $att = \emptyset \vee \exists v_1, v_2 \in att.(v_1 \neq v_2 \wedge v_1 \in att \wedge v_2 \in att)$

where att is current-day, current-time, credit, cost, *and* value *in* ac_6, ac_7, ac_8, ac_9, *and* ac_{10}, *respectively. Constraints* $ac_6, ..., ac_{10}$ *address* Indeterminate *cases by requiring att to be either empty or to contain at least two distinct elements (denoted by* v_1 *and* v_2*). The applicability space induced by the target of rule* r_i, $\langle AS_A^{T_i}, AS_{IN}^{T_i} \rangle$, *can be represented as follows (for the sake of simplicity, we represent sets of access requests as the applicability constraints that render them):*

T_1 : $\langle ac_5 \cap (ac_8 \cup ac_9 \cup ac_{10}), ac_8 \cup ac_9 \cup ac_{10} \rangle$

T_2 : $\langle (ac_2 \cup ac_3 \cup ac_4) \cap \overline{(ac_6 \cup ac_7)}, ac_6 \cup ac_7 \rangle$

T_3 : $\langle \mathcal{R}, \emptyset \rangle$

Policy p has applicability space $\langle ac_0 \cap ac_1, \emptyset \rangle$*; this space has to be propagated to rules. Thus, the applicability space* $\langle AS_A^{r_i}, AS_{IN}^{r_i} \rangle$ *of rule* r_i *is:*

r_1 : $\langle ac_0 \cap ac_1 \cap ac_5 \cap (ac_8 \cup ac_9 \cup ac_{10}), (ac_8 \cup ac_9 \cup ac_{10}) \cap (ac_0 \cap ac_1) \rangle$

r_2 : $\langle ac_0 \cap ac_1 \cap (ac_2 \cup ac_3 \cup ac_4) \cap \overline{(ac_6 \cup ac_7)}, (ac_6 \cup ac_7) \cap (ac_0 \cap ac_1) \rangle$

r_3 : $\langle ac_0 \cap ac_1, \emptyset \rangle$

Based on the possible decisions in XACML, the policy space can be partitioned into four disjoint subsets DS_P, DS_D, DS_{IN} and DS_{NA} by using rule effects and applicability constraints. These subsets represent the classes of access requests that evaluate to same access decision: *Permit, Deny, Indeterminate* and *NotApplicable*, respectively. We denote the decision space of a policy as $\langle DS_P, DS_D, DS_{IN} \rangle$. If an access request does not fall in $DS_P \cup DS_D \cup DS_{IN}$, then it falls in DS_{NA}. The decision space of a rule can be derived from its effect and applicability constraints.

Definition 2. *Let* $\langle AS_A, AS_{IN} \rangle$ *be the applicability space of a rule r and* Effect *its effect. The decision space of r, denoted* $\langle DS_P, DS_D, DS_{IN} \rangle$*, is*

$$DS_P = \begin{cases} AS_A & \text{if Effect} = \text{Permit} \\ \emptyset & \text{otherwise} \end{cases}$$

$$DS_D = \begin{cases} AS_A & \text{if Effect} = \text{Deny} \\ \emptyset & \text{otherwise} \end{cases}$$

$$DS_{IN} = AS_{IN}$$

In order to obtain the decision space of the root policy element, the decision space of child policy elements have to be recursively combined in a bottom-up fashion according to specified combining algorithms. As noted in Section 2.1 some combining algorithms use an extended decision set in which the *Indeterminate* space is subdivided into three parts. For these we extend the decision space accordingly. Here, we show the decision space of a policy with respect to deny-overrides as an example. The other combining algorithms can be defined in a similar way. Let $\langle DS_P^{p_1}, DS_D^{p_1}, DS_{IN(P)}^{p_1}, DS_{IN(D)}^{p_1}, DS_{IN(PD)}^{p_1} \rangle$ and

$\langle DS_P^{p_2}, DS_D^{p_2}, DS_{IN(P)}^{p_2}, DS_{IN(D)}^{p_2}, DS_{IN(PD)}^{p_2} \rangle$ be the (extended) decision spaces of policy elements p_1 and p_2, respectively. We are interested in the decision space $\langle DS_P^p, DS_D^p, DS_{IN}^p \rangle$ of a policy p which combines policy elements p_1 and p_2 using deny-overrides. The decision spaces induced by deny-overrides can be defined as follows:

$$DS_D^p = DS_D^{p_1} \cup DS_D^{p_2}$$

$$DS_{IN(PD)}^p = \Big((DS_{IN(PD)}^{p_1} \cup DS_{IN(PD)}^{p_2}) \cup (DS_{IN(D)}^{p_1} \cap (DS_{IN(P)}^{p_2} \cup DS_P^{p_2}))$$

$$\cup (DS_{IN(D)}^{p_2} \cap (DS_{IN(P)}^{p_1} \cup DS_P^{p_1})) \Big) \setminus DS_D^p$$

$$DS_{IN(D)}^p = (DS_{IN(D)}^{p_1} \cup DS_{IN(D)}^{p_2}) \setminus (DS_D^p \cup DS_{IN(PD)}^p)$$

$$DS_P^p = (DS_P^{p_1} \cup DS_P^{p_2}) \setminus (DS_D^p \cup DS_{IN(PD)}^p \cup DS_{IN(D)}^p)$$

$$DS_{IN(P)}^p = (DS_{IN(P)}^{p_1} \cup DS_{IN(P)}^{p_2}) \setminus (DS_D^p \cup DS_{IN(PD)}^p \cup DS_{IN(D)}^p \cup DS_P^p)$$

Intuitively, the representation above defines the priorities between decision spaces. The *Deny* space of the parent policy element is the union of the *Deny* space of child policy elements, i.e. the former evaluates to *Deny* if at least one child policy element evaluates to *Deny*. Then, *Indeterminate{PD}* has priority over *Indeterminate{D}*; in turn *Indeterminate{D}* has priority over *Permit*, which has priority over *Indeterminate{P}*. The overall *Indeterminate* space can be obtained as the union of the three *Indeterminate* spaces, i.e. $DS_{IN}^p = DS_{IN(PD)}^p \cup DS_{IN(D)}^p \cup DS_{IN(P)}^p$.

Example 3. *Consider the policy in Example 1 and the applicability space of the rules forming it in Example 2. Decision space of rule r_i $\langle DS_P^{r_i}, DS_D^{r_i}, DS_{IN}^{r_i} \rangle$ is*

$r_1 : \langle \emptyset, ac_0 \cap ac_1 \cap ac_5 \cap (ac_8 \cup ac_9 \cup ac_{10}), (ac_8 \cup ac_9 \cup ac_{10}) \cap (ac_0 \cap ac_1) \rangle$

$r_2 : \langle \emptyset, ac_0 \cap ac_1 \cap (ac_2 \cup ac_3 \cup ac_4) \cap \overline{(ac_6 \cup ac_7)}, (ac_6 \cup ac_7) \cap (ac_0 \cap ac_1) \rangle$

$r_3 : \langle ac_0 \cap ac_1, \emptyset, \emptyset \rangle$

The decision space of the overall policy $\langle DS_P, DS_D, DS_{IN} \rangle$ can be obtained by combining the decision space of the rules as shown above (by derivation order):

$$DS_D^p = ac_0 \cap ac_1 \cap$$
$$\Big((ac_5 \cap (ac_8 \cup ac_9 \cup ac_{10})) \cup ((ac_2 \cup ac_3 \cup ac_4) \cap \overline{(ac_6 \cup ac_7)}) \Big)$$

$$DS_{IN}^p = \big(ac_0 \cap ac_1 \cap (ac_8 \cup ac_9 \cup ac_{10} \cup ac_6 \cup ac_7) \big) \setminus DS_D^p$$

$$DS_P^p = (ac_0 \cap ac_1) \setminus (DS_D^p \cup DS_{IN}^p)$$

where notation $\overline{S}$ is used to denote the complement of set S.

3.2 Policies as SMT Formulas

The expressions presented in the previous section can be straightforwardly translated to many-sorted first-order formulas over the attributes in Att and a theory $\mathcal{T}$ specifying the algebraic structures of the values of Att in Dom. This allows us to encode the decision space of a policy using SMT formulas.

Definition 3. *Given an XACML policy p and a background theory $\mathcal{T}$, the representation of p in SMT is a tuple $\langle \mathcal{F}_P, \mathcal{F}_D, \mathcal{F}_{IN} \rangle$ where $\mathcal{F}_P$, $\mathcal{F}_D$ and $\mathcal{F}_{IN}$ are many sorted first-order formulas encoding Permit, Deny, Indeterminate decision spaces of p respectively with some of their terms interpreted in $\mathcal{T}$.*

When talking about deciding satisfiability of a policy p in SMT, we refer to $\mathcal{T}$-satisfiability of the formulas $\mathcal{F}_P$, $\mathcal{F}_D$ and $\mathcal{F}_{IN}$. Since decision spaces DS_P, DS_D and DS_{IN} are pair-wise disjoint, their satisfiability is mutually exclusive.

The background theories needed for the analysis of a policy are determined from the policy's applicability constraints. In order to do this, we map classes of common XACML functions to certain background theories that can be used to encode the applicability constraints constructed from them.

Most of the logical functions of XACML (i.e., *or, and, not*) do not require any specific background theory. Some applicability constraints involving equality predicates of attributes with finite domains can be modeled by the theory of enumerated data types in which attribute values are represented as 0-ary function symbols within an appropriate signature Σ. Other constraints involving equality predicates require the theory of equality with uninterpreted functions. This theory does not impose any constraint on the way the symbols in the signature are interpreted. Thus, the predicates that are not supported by any theory can be left uninterpreted and analyzed using the theory of "uninterpreted functions". The theory of equality with uninterpreted functions can be used to support XACML functions for which a dedicated theory is not available such as XPath-based functions. Constraints defined using arithmetic and numeric comparison functions (e.g., $ac_3, \ldots, ac_5$ in Example 2) require the theory of linear arithmetic. Applicability constraints defined over strings, bag and sets may require dedicated theories. For instance, constraints defined using comparison functions over strings and string conversion functions can be modeled with the theory of strings [26]; constraints defined over bag and set functions (e.g., $ac_6, \ldots, ac_{10}$) can be modeled with the theories of arrays [15] and cardinality constraints on sets [24].

Finally, observe that a background theory can be a combination of different theories as it is the case of Example 2 in which the cost of a transaction depends on its value. This dependence can be represented by a function f which is left uninterpreted since we are not interested in specifying exactly how the cost must be derived from the value of the transaction. By abstracting the actual details of f, the applicability constraint ac_5 can be represented as (credit $<$ f(value) $+$ value) and interpreted within a combined background theory of linear arithmetic and uninterpreted functions.

4   XACML Policy Analysis

The previous section describes an encoding of XACML policies as SMT formulas. In this section we use this encoding to represent *policies analysis problems*, i.e. for a collection of policies checking various properties expressed in so called *queries*. We first introduce the query language and then give example query formulas for different policy properties from the literature.

Definition 4. *Let $\langle Att, Dom \rangle$ be the access control scheme and $\mathcal{T}$ a background theory with signature Σ. A policy analysis problem is a tuple $\langle Q, (p_1, \ldots, p_n) \rangle$*

where $p_1, \ldots, p_n$ are policies expressed in SMT with respect to $\mathcal{T}$ and Q is a (policy) query. A query Q is a formula of the form

$$Q = P_i \mid D_i \mid IN_i \mid g(t_1, \ldots, t_k) \mid \neg Q \mid Q_1 \vee Q_2 \mid \ldots$$
$$\mid (\forall x : \sigma \; Q) \mid (\exists x : \sigma \; Q) \mid \nu x.Q \mid Q\langle a_1 = v_{1_j}, \ldots, a_n = v_{n_k}\rangle$$

where P_i, D_i and IN_i (for $i = 1, \ldots, n$) are new symbols representing the Permit, Deny and Indeterminate spaces of policy p_i (they thus represent $\mathcal{F}_P^{p_i}$, $\mathcal{F}_D^{p_i}$ and $\mathcal{F}_{IN}^{p_i}$ respectively, see also query semantics below), g is a Σ-atom over terms $t_1, \ldots, t_k$ such that each term t is either a variable denoting attributes from Att or built using function symbols in Σ, and logical operators are defined as usual where Q_1 and Q_2 are also queries. In quantified formulas, i.e. $(\forall x : \sigma \; Q)$ and $(\exists x : \sigma \; Q)$, σ ranges over sort symbols in the theory $\mathcal{T}$. $\nu x.Q$ represents the restriction of a variable x in Q (i.e., $\nu x.Q \equiv Q[x/y]$ with y a fresh variable), $Q\langle a_1 = v_{1_j}, \ldots, a_n = v_{n_k}\rangle$ represents the instantiation of a policy with a request with $v_{1_j} \in Dom_{a_1}, \ldots, v_{n_k} \in Dom_{a_n}$.

Note that construct $\nu x.Q$ is used to restrict the scope of the substitution of a variable x to a subformula Q of the query. This construct allows us to encode properties comparing a number of policies, in which some policies are instantiated with a request while other policies are instantiated with a different request (see below for examples of such properties). $Q\langle a_1 = v_{1_j}, \ldots, a_n = v_{n_k}\rangle$ is logically equivalent to $Q \wedge v_{1_j} \in a_1 \wedge \ldots \wedge v_{n_k} \in a_n$.

The basic query P_i encodes (inclusion in) the *Permit* space of policy p_i; it is satisfiable if any request is permitted by p_i. Similarly, D_i and IN_i represent the *Deny* and *Indeterminate* spaces of p_i respectively. Constraints such as **Alice** $\in$ subject-id, $\forall v \in$ current-time $v < 18{:}00$ etc., are used to instantiate the subject or the time of the query. The predicates can also capture relations between different policies (see examples below).

Example 4. *Let p_1, p_2 be two policies, and $\langle P_1, D_1, IN_1 \rangle$ and $\langle P_2, D_2, IN_2 \rangle$ their SMT representation, respectively. Below we present some example queries.*

- *$(P_1 \rightarrow P_2)$: any request permitted by p_1 is also permitted by p_2.*
- *ν subject-id.$(P_1\langle$subject-id $=$ **Alice**$\rangle) \wedge \nu$ subject-id.$(D_1\langle$subject-id $=$ **Bob**$\rangle)$: some request is permitted by p_1 for Alice but denied for Bob.*
- *$(P_1 \wedge D_2)\langle$subject-id $=$ **Alice**$\rangle$: some request of Alice is permitted by p_1 but denied by p_2.*
- *$P_1\langle$subject-id $=$ **Alice**, resource-type $=$ **transaction**, action-id $=$ **create**$\rangle$: policy p_1 allows Alice to create a transaction.*

Definition 5. *Let $\langle Q, (p_1, \ldots, p_n)\rangle$ be a policy analysis problem, $\mathcal{T}$ a background theory with signature Σ, and $\mathcal{M}$ a structure for signature Σ. Let $\langle \mathcal{F}_P^{p_i}, \mathcal{F}_D^{p_i}, \mathcal{F}_{IN}^{p_i}\rangle$ be the encoding of policy p_i in SMT with some or all terms interpreted in $\mathcal{T}$. We say that $\langle Q, (p_1, \ldots, p_n)\rangle$ is satisfiable with respect to $\mathcal{T}$ if the formula*

$$Q \wedge \bigwedge_{i=1}^{n} (P_i \leftrightarrow \mathcal{F}_P^{p_i}) \wedge (D_i \leftrightarrow \mathcal{F}_D^{p_i}) \wedge (IN_i \leftrightarrow \mathcal{F}_{IN}^{p_i})$$

is $\mathcal{T}$-satisfiable. Otherwise, we say that it is unsatisfiable.

In the remainder of this section, we demonstrate that our framework can model various types of policy properties proposed in the literature.

Policy Refinement and Subsumption Organizations often need to update their security policies to comply with new regulations or to adapt changes in their business model. Nonetheless, they might have to ensure that the new policies preserve (refine) the intention of the original policies. Different definitions of policy refinement have been proposed in the literature. Backes et al. [5] propose a notion of policy refinement based on the idea that *"one policy refines another if using the first policy automatically also fulfills the second policy"*. Intuitively, a policy refines another policy if whenever the latter returns *Permit* (or *Deny*) the first policy returns the same decision. This can be formalized in our framework as follows. Let p_1, p_2 be two policies with decision space $\langle P_1, D_1, IN_1 \rangle$ and $\langle P_2, D_2, IN_2 \rangle$ respectively. Policy p_2 is a refinement of p_1 iff the following formula is $\mathcal{T}$-valid

$$(P_1 \rightarrow P_2) \wedge (D_1 \rightarrow D_2) \tag{1}$$

Hughes and Bultan [13] present a stronger notion of policy refinement called policy subsumption. In addition to constraining *Permit* and *Deny* spaces as in refinement, subsumption also imposes constraints on the *Indeterminate* space. Formally, policy p_1 subsumes policy p_2 iff the following formula is $\mathcal{T}$-valid

$$(P_1 \rightarrow P_2) \wedge (D_1 \rightarrow D_2) \wedge (IN_1 \rightarrow IN_2) \tag{2}$$

Note that our framework is general enough to express other notions of policy refinement, for instance imposing constraints only on the *Permit* space or on the *Deny* space. In the next example, we demonstrate the notion of policy refinement presented in [5] with respect to background theory *linear arithmetic*.

Example 5. *Consider the XACML policy in Example 1. Suppose that the policy is updated by omitting the cost of the transaction in rule r_1:*

$$r_1'[Deny] : \mathsf{value} > \mathsf{credit}$$

We want to check whether the new policy is a refinement of the original policy. It is easy to verify that (1) does not hold if the cost of the transaction is higher than the credit minus the value of the service. Therefore, the new policy is not a refinement of the original policy.

Change-impact Change-impact analysis [10] aims to analyze the impact of changes to policies. Intuitively, change-impact analysis is the counterpart of policy refinement, in which the goal is to extract the differences between two policies. Differently from policy refinement, changes of the *NotApplicable* space should also be considered in change-impact analysis. Let p_1, p_2 be two policies with decision space $\langle P_1, D_1, IN_1 \rangle$ and $\langle P_2, D_2, IN_2 \rangle$ respectively. We are interested in finding the access requests for which the decisions returned by p_1 and

p_2 are different. This policy analysis problem consists of finding access requests that satisfy the following formula:

$$(P_1 \rightarrow \neg P_2) \vee (D_1 \rightarrow \neg D_2) \vee (IN_1 \rightarrow \neg IN_2) \tag{3}$$
$$\vee (\neg (P_1 \vee D_1 \vee IN_1) \rightarrow (P_2 \vee D_2 \vee IN_2))$$

where $\neg(P_1 \vee D_1 \vee IN_1)$ represents the *NotApplicable* space.·

Attribute Hiding An attribute hiding attack is a situation in which a user is able to obtain a more favorable authorization decision by hiding some of her attributes [8]. Attribute hiding attack is a threat exploiting the non-monotonicity of access control systems such as XACML. Differently from the previous policy properties that can be expressed solely in terms of *Permit*, *Deny* and *Indeterminate* spaces of the policies, attribute hiding is about changing the request: a request that is previously denied is permitted by hiding some attributes or attribute-value pairs. In particular, we call *partial attribute hiding* attack the situation in which a user hides a single attribute-value pair. Let $req = \langle a_1 = v_{1_i}, \ldots, a_n = v_{n_k} \rangle$ with $v_{1_i} \in Dom_{a_1}, \ldots, v_{n_k} \in Dom_{a_n}$ be a request denied by a policy p (i.e., a solution of D_p), and $a_{j_m} = v_{j_m}$ an attribute-value pair occurring in req ($1 \leq j \leq n$) and $v_{j_m} \in Dom_{a_j}$. A policy is vulnerable to partial attribute hiding attack if the request obtained by suppressing $a_j = v_{j_m}$ from req is permitted by p (i.e., a solution of P_p). The property representing the absence of partial attribute hiding attack can be encoded as follows:

$$\nu a.(D_p \langle a = v \rangle) \rightarrow \neg P_p \tag{4}$$

where we use restriction to ensure that the request is only applied to the left part of the formula. A more generalized version of attribute hiding attack is *general attribute hiding* where a user completely suppresses information about one attribute. The property representing the absence of general attribute hiding attack can be encoded as follows:

$$\nu a.(D_p \langle a = v_1, \ldots, a = v_n \rangle) \rightarrow \neg P_p \tag{5}$$

We use an example policy from [8] to discuss the analysis of attribute hiding.

Example 6. *Consider two competing companies, A and B. To protect confidential information from competitors, company A defines the following policy:*

$$p[\text{dov}] : \textbf{true}$$
$$r_1[Deny] : \text{confidential} = true \wedge \text{employer} = B$$
$$r_2[Permit] : \textbf{true}$$

The first rule (r_1) of the policy denies employees of company B to access confidential information while the second rule (r_2) grants access to every requests.

*The two rules are combined using deny-overrides combining algorithm (dov).
Now consider the following access requests:*

$$req_1 = \langle \text{employer} = A, \text{confidential} = true \rangle$$
$$req_2 = \langle \text{employer} = A, \text{employer} = B, \text{confidential} = true \rangle$$
$$req_3 = \langle \text{confidential} = true \rangle$$

*Rule r_1 is only applicable to request req_2 and thus the request is denied. Rule r_2 is
applicable to the remaining requests and thus access is granted for requests req_1
and req_3. However, if the subject can hide some information from the request,
for instance, reducing req_2 to req_1 by suppressing element employer $= B$ from
the request (partial attribute hiding) or to req_3 by suppressing attribute employer
from the request (general attribute hiding), then she would be allowed to access
confidential information leading to a violation of the conflict of interest requirement. Note that we assume that attribute confidential is under the control of the
system and cannot be hidden by the user.*

Scenario-finding Scenario finding queries [10,19] aim to find attribute assignments that represent scenarios in which a sought behavior occurs. They are especially useful to obtain request instances of certain decision types (e.g., *permit*)
which are otherwise difficult to obtain manually. Examples of scenario finding
queries include checking whether a policy ever permits (some) users to perform
certain actions or denies certain actions under given circumstances. Scenario
finding can also be used to check whether a policy is compliant with well-known
security principles. For instance, a XACML policy implementing role-based access control can be checked for the separation of duty principle or a XACML
policy implementing Chinese Wall policy can be checked if it correctly implements conflict of interest classes.

Scenario finding does not have a fixed form of encoding as the previous properties since it is formulated by the user according to selected decision space.

Example 7. *In the context of Example 2 a policy author may want to check
whether the policy permits any access request before 18:00 on Saturday. We can
encode this query as follows:*

$$P \wedge \text{current-day} = Saturday \wedge \text{time} < 18{:}00$$

Many types of scenario finding queries can be formulated and analyzed within
existing XACML analysis tools. However, most of these tools leave non-Boolean
functions (i.e., Σ-terms of form $f(t_1, \ldots, t_n)$) uninterpreted. In contrast, SMT
enables to reason on those attributes using a suitable underlying background
theory. For instance, an SMT solver can find an assignment for an attribute
"age" that satisfies a Linear Arithmetic constraint age < 18.

5   Evaluation

In this section we evaluate our SMT-based policy analysis framework by means
of a prototype implementation. In the evaluation we use two sets of experiments,

one comparing our SMT-based solution to SAT-based techniques and one showing our prototype can be used on realistic policies. Our experimental testbed consists of a 64-bit (virtual) machine with 16GB of RAM and 3.40GHz quad-core CPU running Ubuntu.

5.1 Prototype Implementation

To support the analysis of XACML policies described in the previous section, we have implemented *X2S* [25], a formal policy analysis tool. *X2S* employs Z3 [18], an SMT-LIB v2 compliant tool that supports efficient reasoning in a wide range of background theories, as the underlying solver. *X2S* accepts both XACML v2 and v3 policies and supports a large fraction of standard XACML functions. It consists of two main components. The first component, the *SMT Translator*, first translates XACML policies provided by the user into SMT formulas using the encoding presented in Section 3. Next the user is prompted to enter a query expressed in the language defined in Section 4 which is also translated and added to SMT specification. The second component, the *Report Generator*, presents the results of the analysis by providing an interface to the SMT solver.

Our prototype can enumerate models as required for certain queries such as *change impact*. We perform this by incrementally adding a new constraint representing the negation of the obtained model to the original formula. However, there may be infinitely many models satisfying a formula with certain expression types. To help alleviate this problem, we try to avoid models that do not "significantly" differ from those already considered with respect attribute assignments. In particular, we do this in the treatment of arithmetic expressions by fixing the assignments of (arithmetic) variables in a model to the first values found. For instance, if the first solution of the arithmetic expression $att_1 < att_2$ assigns 4 and 5 to the attributes respectively, then we fix these assignments by adding new (conjunctive) constraints $att_1 = 4$ and $att_2 = 5$ to the original formula.

5.2 Experiments 1: SAT vs. SMT

Consider a user wanting to validate and possibly update a set of policies collected over time and from different contributors. For example, a building manager wants to verify the policy governing the access to a certain building in which right to enter depend on the current time and date and/or membership of a group; or a bank manager wants to verify the bank policy for transfers which depend on the balance of accounts, size of the transfer, etc. The main advantage of our SMT approach over a SAT based solution is that it allows direct reasoning with non-Boolean values. For example, one can use the background theories for basic sets (i.e., the theory of arrays) and linear arithmetic (LAI). To perform this analysis in SAT one has to encode everything in Boolean terms. With some limitations we can encode LAI constraints in SAT using order encoding [21] where each expression of the form $x \leq c$ is represented by a different Boolean variable. Membership expressions in the set theory can be encoded in SAT using a similar approach where the relation between a variable and a value from its domain is represented with a different Boolean variable for each value.

Ideally, the user's validation tool would be able to give real-time feedback on their edits, or at the very least, respond promptly to a validation query. When analyzing with SAT, users needs to find a suitable trade-off between the precision and the efficiency as well as the scalability of the analysis; for example instead of the time only distinguishing 'morning' from 'afternoon' or hour of the day. Choosing what granularity is suitable for what attribute is a difficult, laborious and error-prone task requiring the user to closely investigate all constraints. Too low granularity may lead to missing errors in the policies. Yet, the more fine grained the analysis is, the larger the SAT encoding. Our experiments below confirm that increasing the granularity quickly become very costly performance wise. Our SMT-based approach does not need to restrict the granularity.

To illustrate the effect of granularity on the analysis we distinguish course grained analysis using a 'small' domain (e.g., morning/afternoon for time, and day of the week for date), an analysis with some detail through a 'medium' (M) size domain (e.g., minutes in an hour, days in a month) and a detailed analysis using a 'large' (L) domain (e.g., minute in a day, day of a year). We analyze policies and properties from the examples in Section 4. We check policy refinement (PR), policy subsumption (PS), change-impact (CI) analysis, both partial (P-AH) and global (G-AH) Attribute Hiding, and finally scenario finding (SF). We analyze each with our prototype and three different SAT solvers; zchaff [17], lingeling [7] and Z3 itself to obtain a fair comparison as certain solvers are optimized for certain types of problems. We use size 10 to represent small domains, 100 for medium domains and 500 for large domains (they may need to be much larger but this size already shows the clear advantage of our SMT solution). Note that we aim at a comparison in orders of magnitude rather than an in-depth and comprehensive performance analysis. For small domains all solutions are able to complete the analysis quickly with limited resources; they are fast enough for real-time feedback during editing. For the medium and large domains the results are provided in Table 1. The first column specifies the property (**P**) analyzed. The second column (**Q**) gives the class of formula used; finding a counter-example ($\neg \mathcal{F}$) or a satisfying assignment ($\mathcal{F}$). The other columns present the results in terms of number of variables used in the encoding, memory allocation[2] and required computation time for the SAT solvers with M(edium) and L(arge) domain size, and SMT.

Compared to the number of many-sorted first order variables in SMT encoding, the number of Boolean variables in SAT encoding is quite large due to the mapping of non-Boolean domains to Boolean variables. For instance, the SMT encoding of the policy query for verifying policy refinement requires 12 variables. These variables are used to specify the attributes defined in the policy as well as the Boolean variables representing one-and-only constraints on the arithmetic variables (Example 1). In contrast, 591 Boolean variables are needed to encode the same policy query in SAT when a medium size domain is considered. The

---

[2] We used a memory profiler for measuring the memory usage.

Table 1. Evaluation Results of Example Properties with SAT vs SMT Encoding

		#Vars			Memory(MB)							Time(s)						
		SAT		SMT	Z3-SAT		zchaff		lingeling		SMT	Z3-SAT		zchaff		lingeling		SMT
P	**Q**	M	L		M	L	M	L	M	L		M	L	M	L	M	L	
PR	¬$\mathcal{F}$	591	2191	12	84	459	99	340	23	555	0.3	1.6	99.7	~0	3.3	20.5	>100	~0
PS	¬$\mathcal{F}$	909	2509	12	303	240	377	1159	82	2054	0.3	3.9	6.1	~0	12.4	65.5	>100	~0
CI	$\mathcal{F}$	1409	3009	12	88	231	650	1087	133	1513	0.5	0.3	9.1	~0	19.1	36.5	45.5	~0
P-AH	¬$\mathcal{F}$	24	15	3	0.1	0.1	0.1	0.1	~0	~0	0.3	~0	~0	~0	~0	~0	~0	~0
G-AH	¬$\mathcal{F}$	12	12	4	~0	~0	0.1	0.1	~0	~0	0.3	~0	~0	~0	~0	~0	~0	~0
SF	$\mathcal{F}$	511	1718	12	13	328	92	409	14	356	0.3	~0	1.2	~0	13.4	0.2	7.3	~0

memory allocated by the SMT solver needed in analyzing the example policies was always less than 1MB for all properties while SAT solver requires several orders of magnitude more memory. The time necessary to prove (or disprove) that the property holds was negligible (~10ms) for all SMT cases. Analysis with SAT solvers performs far worse with the growth of the domain size as can be noted from the table. For instance, for scenario finding analysis with a large domain, the best performing SAT solver (Z3) took ~1.2s which is several orders of magnitude slower than the analysis with SMT (which took 7ms). The exception is the case of attribute hiding analysis where the SAT solvers offer performance similar to SMT. This is expected since our example policy for attribute hiding does not include complicated predicates and the available predicates can be easily represented in propositional logic. Note that in our experiments for the case of change-impact analysis, we obtained only one model since we prune the uninteresting assignments of arithmetic variables (i.e. value, credit and cost). Finally, we also observe a performance variation between different SAT solvers. We believe this is due to the fact that certain solvers are better tailored to certain types of problems.

In conclusion, even with these relatively simple policies, performance quickly becomes impractical using SAT based solvers while the SMT approach could even be used for real-time feedback while editing a policy. In the next section, we test our approach with some more complex and realistic policies.

5.3   Experiments 2: Real-World Policies

In this second set of experiments, we analyze four realistic policies with our prototype in order to obtain insights about its performance in real-world settings. The policy GradeMan is a simplified version of the access control policy used to regulate access to grades at Brown university and the Continue-a policy is used to manage a conference management system. Both policies are from [10] and consist mainly of string equality predicates. IN4STARS is an in-house policy defined in the context of a project on intelligence interoperability. It contains various user-defined functions that are used to determine the privileges of users according to their clearance. All these three policies are XACML v2 policies. Our final test policy, KMarket, is a sample policy to manage authorizations in

Table 2. Evaluation Results for Real-world Policies

Policy	#PSet	#Policy	#Rule	Time(ms)					
				PR	PS	CI	P-AH	G-AH	SF
IN4STARS	3	4	11	24	28	1717	7	7	10
KMarket	1	3	12	36	12	2525	13	12	10
GradeMan	11	5	5	40	30	2424	10	9	17
Continue-a	111	266	298	91	87	2929	33	21	43

an on-line trading application from [1]. It contains simple arithmetic operations such as less-than and is written in XACML v3.

We performed policy refinement, subsumption and change-impact analysis by modifying the value of a single, randomly chosen attribute in the original policy. The number of models has been limited to 100 during change-impact analysis. For scenario finding, we look for an assignment of attributes (i.e. model) that is permitted by the input policy. Our findings are summarized in Table 2 in which we report the characteristics of policies (e.g., the number of policy elements in the XACML policy) and the time taken by our prototype to answer queries.

Analyzing the policies included in our experiments takes less than 100ms for all properties except Change-impact which makes feedback during policy editing feasible. Change-impact analysis, however, brings the time up to 3s as it requires the enumeration of models in the SMT formula. Another important observation in the experiments is the efficiency of dealing with expressions with non-Boolean attributes; we have not observed a significant performance difference between the analysis of KMarket which contains linear arithmetic expressions and Grade-Man which consists of very simple expressions. Finally, the result of Continue-a analysis (a policy with around 300 rules) indicates that the time needed for analysis with SMT of larger policies increases but not necessary as quickly as the policy grows. This result is not surprising since the analysis of a policy with our approach not only depends on the size of the policy but also the type of expressions contained in them.

We believe the experimental results of this and the previous section demonstrate that our approach can be used in practice to analyze realistic policies at a more fine-grained level than the one permitted by the use of SAT solvers with no significant performance penalty.

6   Related Work

When XACML policies grow in number and size, or are updated to address new security requirements, it is difficult to verify their correctness due to XACML's rich and verbose syntax. To assist policy authors in the analysis of XACML policies, several policy analysis tools have been proposed. One of the most prominent tools for policy analysis is Margrave [10]. Margrave uses multi-terminal binary decision diagrams (MTBDDs) as the underlying representation of XACML policies. The nodes of an MTBDD represent Boolean variables encoding the attribute-values pairs in the policy. The terminal nodes represent the possible decisions (i.e., *NotApplicable*, *Permit* or *Deny*). Given an assignment of Boolean values to the variables, a path from the root to a terminal node according to the variable values indicates the result of the policy under that assignment. Margrave uses MTBDDs to support two types of analysis: policy querying, which analyzes access requests evaluated to a certain decision, and change-impact analysis, which is used to compare policies. Another policy analysis tool that employs BDDs for the encoding of XACML policies is XAnalyzer [12]. XAnalyzer uses a policy-based segmentation technique to detect and resolve policy anomalies such as redundancy and conflicts. Compared to our approach, BDD-based approaches allow the verification of XACML policies against a limited range of properties. In addition, these approaches encode only a fragment of XACML with simple constraints [13].

An alternative to Margrave, and in general to BDD-based approaches, is presented in [13] where policies and properties are encoded as propositional formulas and analyzed using a SAT solver. However, SAT solvers cannot handle non-Boolean variables; most XACML functions are thus left uninterpreted limiting the capability of the analysis. EXAM [16] combines the use of SAT solvers and MTBDD to reason on various policy properties. In particular, EXAM supports three classes of queries: *metadata* (e.g., policy creation date), *content* (e.g., number of rules) and *effect* (e.g., evaluation of certain requests). Policies and queries are expressed as Boolean formulas. These formulas are converted to MTBDDs and then combined into a single MTBDD for analysis.

Other formalisms have also been used for the analysis of XACML policies. For instance, Kolovski et al. [14] use description logic (DL) to formalize XACML policies and employs off-the-shelf DL reasoners for policy analysis. The use of DL reasoners enables the analysis on a wide subset of XACML in a more expressive manner but also hinders the performance. Ramli et al. [23] and Ahn et al. [2] present a formulation of policy analysis problems similar to ours in answer set programming (ASP). However, these approaches have drawbacks due to intrinsic limitations of ASP. Unlike SMT, ASP does not support quantifiers, and cannot easily express constraints such as Linear Arithmetic. Indeed, in ASP the grounding (i.e., instantiation of variables with values) of Linear Arithmetic constraints either yield very large number of clauses (integers) or is not supported (reals).

In summary, the approaches discussed above lack the inherent benefits of SMT: either background theories are not supported so that the attributes involved in most XACML functions cannot be analyzed at a finer level, or the performance of analysis deteriorates very quickly.

While the use of SMT for the analysis of XACML policies is new to our knowledge, there are few recent proposals that exploit SMT solvers for the analysis of policies specified in different access control models. The work in [3] shares with our approach the use of SMT solvers to support the analysis of polycies. The main difference is in the input language: instead of using XACML, Arkoudas et al. [3] adopts a sophisticated logical framework, which can handle XACML policies (such as Continue) indirectly by translating them to expressions of the logical framework to which the available analyses (such as those considered in this paper) can be applied. In contrast, our technique generates proof obligations to be discharged by SMT solvers directly from XACML policies. Another example of SMT techniques supporting the analysis of policies is [4] in which SMT solvers are used to detect conflicts and redundancies in RBAC. Here, rules specifying constraints on the assignment/activation of roles are encoded as SMT formulas with certain background theories such as enumerated data types and Linear Arithmetic over the reals/integers. Although these proposals show the potentiality of SMT for policy analysis, the policy specifications considered in such proposals are rather simple. In this work we make an additional step by showing that SMT is able to deal with real world XACML policies.

7   Conclusions

In this paper, we presented an SMT-based analysis framework for policies specified in XACML. The use of SMT does not only enable wider coverage of XACML compared to existing analysis tools but also presents significant performance gains in terms of allocated memory and computational time. As demonstrated in the paper, several security policy properties found in the literature can be easily encoded and checked within our framework. In our prototype, we use various background theories to encode a large fraction of XACML functions, allowing a fine-grained analysis of XACML policies. SMT function symbols encoding XACML functions for which a specific background theory is not available (e.g., XPath-based and regular-expression-based functions) are left uninterpreted. With the development of new background theories, policy analysis problems using those predicates can be represented and solved efficiently. Our experiments show that our framework enables efficient policy analysis and can be used in practice. As future work, we plan to extend the performance analysis of our prototype against a larger set of real-world policies.

Acknowledgments. This work has been partially funded by the EDA project IN4STARS2.0, the EU FP7 project AU2EU, the ARTEMIS project ACCUS, and the Dutch national program COMMIT under the THeCS project.

References

1. Balana: Open source xacml 3.0 implementation (January 2013), http://xacmlinfo.org/category/balana/
2. Ahn, G.J., Hu, H., Lee, J., Meng, Y.: Representing and reasoning about web access control policies. In: COMPSAC, pp. 137–146 (2010)
3. Arkoudas, K., Chadha, R., Chiang, C.J.: Sophisticated access control via SMT and logical frameworks. ACM TISSEC 16(4), 17 (2014)
4. Armando, A., Ranise, S.: Automated and efficient analysis of role-based access control with attributes. In: Cuppens-Boulahia, N., Cuppens, F., Garcia-Alfaro, J. (eds.) DBSec 2012. LNCS, vol. 7371, pp. 25–40. Springer, Heidelberg (2012)

5. Backes, M., Karjoth, G., Bagga, W., Schunter, M.: Efficient comparison of enterprise privacy policies. In: SAC, pp. 375–382 (2004)
6. Barrett, C.W., Sebastiani, R., Seshia, S.A., Tinelli, C.: Satisfiability modulo theories. In: Handbook of Satisfiability, pp. 825–885. IOS Press (2008)
7. Biere, A.: Lingeling essentials, A tutorial on design and implementation aspects of the the SAT solver lingeling. In: POS, p. 88 (2014)
8. Crampton, J., Morisset, C.: PTaCL: A Language for Attribute-Based Access Control in Open Systems. In: Degano, P., Guttman, J.D. (eds.) POST 2012. LNCS, vol. 7215, pp. 390–409. Springer, Heidelberg (2012)
9. Enderton, H.B.: A Mathematical Introduction to Logic. Academic Press (1972)
10. Fisler, K., Krishnamurthi, S., Meyerovich, L.A., Tschantz, M.C.: Verification and change-impact analysis of access-control policies. In: ICSE, pp. 196–205 (2005)
11. Gomes, C.P., Kautz, H., Sabharwal, A., Selman, B.: Satisfiability Solvers. In: Handbook of Knowledge Representation, Foundations of Artificial Intelligence, vol. 3, pp. 89–134. Elsevier (2008)
12. Hu, H., Ahn, G.J., Kulkarni, K.: Discovery and Resolution of Anomalies in Web Access Control Policies. TDSC 10(6), 341–354 (2013)
13. Hughes, G., Bultan, T.: Automated verification of access control policies using a SAT solver. STTT 10(6), 503–520 (2008)
14. Kolovski, V., Hendler, J.A., Parsia, B.: Analyzing web access control policies. In: WWW, pp. 677–686 (2007)
15. Kröning, D., Weissenbacher, G.: A Proposal for a Theory of Finite Sets, Lists, and Maps for the SMT-Lib Standard. In: Pro. International Workshop on Satisfiability Modulo Theories (2009)
16. Lin, D., Rao, P., Bertino, E., Li, N., Lobo, J.: Exam: A comprehensive environment for the analysis of access control policies. Int. J. Inf. Sec. 9(4), 253–273 (2010)
17. Moskewicz, M.W., Madigan, C.F., Zhao, Y., Zhang, L., Malik, S.: Chaff: Engineering an efficient SAT solver. In: DAC, pp. 530–535 (2001)
18. de Moura, L., Bjørner, N.S.: Z3: An Efficient SMT Solver. In: Ramakrishnan, C.R., Rehof, J. (eds.) TACAS 2008. LNCS, vol. 4963, pp. 337–340. Springer, Heidelberg (2008)
19. Nelson, T.: First-order Models For Configuration Analysis. Ph.D. thesis, Worcester Polytechnic Institute (2013)
20. OASIS XACML Technical Committee: eXtensible Access Control Markup Language (XACML) (2013)
21. Petke, J., Jeavons, P.: The Order Encoding: From Tractable CSP to Tractable SAT. In: Sakallah, K.A., Simon, L. (eds.) SAT 2011. LNCS, vol. 6695, pp. 371–372. Springer, Heidelberg (2011)
22. Pratt, V.R.: Two easy theories whose combination is hard. Tech. rep. MIT (1977)
23. Kencana Ramli, C.D.P., Nielson, H.R., Nielson, F.: XACML 3.0 in Answer Set Programming. In: Albert, E. (ed.) LOPSTR 2012. LNCS, vol. 7844, pp. 89–105. Springer, Heidelberg (2013)
24. Suter, P., Steiger, R., Kuncak, V.: Sets with cardinality constraints in satisfiability modulo theories. In: Jhala, R., Schmidt, D. (eds.) VMCAI 2011. LNCS, vol. 6538, pp. 403–418. Springer, Heidelberg (2011)
25. Turkmen, F., den Hartog, J., Zannone, N.: Analyzing Access Control Policies with SMT. In: Proceedings of the ACM Conference on Computer and Communications Security, pp. 1508–1510. ACM (2014)
26. Zheng, Y., Zhang, X., Ganesh, V.: Z3-str: A Z3-based string solver for web application analysis. In: ESEC/SIGSOFT FSE, pp. 114–124 (2013)

Protocols

Automatically Checking Commitment Protocols in ProVerif without False Attacks

Tom Chothia[1], Ben Smyth[2], and Chris Staite[1]

[1] School of Computer Science, University of Birmingham, UK
[2] Mathematical and Algorithmic Sciences Lab, France Research Center, Huawei Technologies Co. Ltd., France

Abstract. ProVerif over-approximates the attacker's power to enable verification of processes under replication. Unfortunately, this results in ProVerif finding false attacks. This problem is particularly common in protocols whereby a participant commits to a particular value and later reveals their value. We introduce a method to reduce false attacks when analysing secrecy. First, we show how inserting phases into non-replicated processes enables a more accurate translation to Horn clauses which avoids some false attacks. Secondly, we generalise our methodology to processes under replication. Finally, we demonstrate the applicability of our technique by analysing BlueTooth Simple Pairing. Moreover, we propose a simplification of this protocol that achieves the same security goal.

1 Introduction

State space exploration has emerged as a leading verification technique [25] and, in this context, Abadi & Fournet [2] propose the applied pi calculus – an extension of the pi calculus – to reason with cryptographic protocols. Unfortunately, proving security in this context is undecidable [21], due to several sources of unboundedness, including, messages of arbitrary length and the possibility of an unbounded number of sessions. Accordingly, state-of-the-art automated reasoning techniques focus on sound, but incomplete, methodologies, which may report false attacks and do not always terminate.

Blanchet [8,9,10] translates applied pi calculus processes to Horn clauses and uses resolution of Horn clauses to reason with secrecy and authentication properties, these results have been implemented in ProVerif [15]. ProVerif has been successfully used to automatically analyse cryptographic protocols from a variety of applications domains, including, key exchange [1,10,29], electronic voting [20,5,4] and trusted computing [18,19,28], for example. However, Blanchet's translation to Horn clauses over-approximates the attacker's power and, therefore, ProVerif may report false attacks; as highlighted by Blanchet [12, §2.2]:

---

* A long version of this paper and ProVerif source code supporting this paper are available from `http://www.cs.bham.ac.uk/~tpc/projects/falseattacks`.

© Springer-Verlag Berlin Heidelberg 2015
R. Focardi and A. Myers (Eds.): POST 2015, LNCS 9036, pp. 137–155, 2015.
DOI: 10.1007/978-3-662-46666-7_8

"false attacks occur typically for protocols that first need to keep data secret, then publish them later in the protocol. In that situation, the Horn clause model considers that the attacker can re-inject the secret in the early part of the run, which is not possible in reality."

This behaviour is typical of protocols in which participants commit to a value and later reveal it, such as the BlueTooth Simple Pairing protocol [22,23], which we analyse in Section 6. In this paper, we introduce techniques for analysing secrecy that avoids some false attacks.

1.1   Our Contribution in Context of Existing Work

Let us consider the following process, proposed by Allamigeon & Blanchet [3, §3.2]:

$$\nu\, n.c(x).\overline{c}\langle n\rangle.\text{if } x = n \text{ then } \overline{c}\langle s\rangle \tag{P1}$$

Process P1 generates a fresh bound name n, binds a message input to variable x, outputs the name n, tests if the message bound to x is equal to n, and outputs the free name s, if the test succeeds. It follows intuitively that an attacker that does not know s in advance, cannot derive s from Process P1, that is, we have secrecy($\{c\}, s$) : P1. However, the Horn clauses generated by Blanchet's translation of P1 include:

$$\texttt{attacker}(x) \Rightarrow \texttt{attacker}(n)$$
$$\texttt{attacker}(n) \Rightarrow \texttt{attacker}(s)$$

Hence, ProVerif cannot prove secrecy($\{c\}, s$) : P1, because the Horn clauses permit the following false attack: knowledge of an arbitrary term M implies knowledge of n and knowledge of n implies knowledge of s. This is due to an over-approximation: the Horn clauses model the process $\nu\, n.!c(x).\overline{c}\langle n\rangle.\text{if } x = n$ then $\overline{c}\langle s\rangle$, rather than P1. It follows that the Horn clauses do not enforce that a message input must be received *before* the bound name n is output. Intuitively, such false attacks can be avoided by ensuring that the translation preserves temporal order of message inputs and outputs. We shall achieve this objective using Blanchet, Abadi & Fournet's notion of *phases* [13, §8]. Phases, denoted $t\!:\!P$, ensure which parts of concurrent processes are active at a particular time.

Inserting phases into a process can stop false attack, e.g., we can add a phase into process P1:

$$0\!:\!\nu\, n.c(x).1\!:\!\overline{c}\langle n\rangle.\text{if } x = n \text{ then } \overline{c}\langle s\rangle \tag{P2}$$

The semantics of phases ensure that P2 is a sound approximation of P1. However, the Horn clauses generated by Blanchet's translation of P2 to Horn clauses are more precise:

$$\texttt{attacker}(x) \Rightarrow \texttt{attacker}'(x)$$
$$\texttt{attacker}(x) \Rightarrow \texttt{attacker}'(n)$$
$$\texttt{attacker}(n) \Rightarrow \texttt{attacker}'(s)$$

Indeed, ProVerif can use these Horn clauses to prove secrecy($\{c\}, s$) : P2 and, since P2 is a sound approximation of P1, we have secrecy($\{c\}, s$) : P1.

We define a compiler (Section 3) that inserts phases into a restricted class of processes such that Blanchet's translation from compiled processes to Horn clauses enforces order. We prove the soundness of our methodology:

secrecy holds in the original process
iff secrecy holds in the compiled process

This technique is limited to proving secrecy of names which are not under the scope of a replication and we overcome this limitation using an alternative notion of secrecy.

The class of secrecy properties which can be considered using Blanchet's definition [10, Section 3.1] is limited, for example, we cannot consider secrecy of an arbitrary session secret s in the process $!\nu\, s.P$, that is, we cannot consider if an instance of $\nu\, s.P$ leaks s. This problem can be overcome by abstraction, in particular, Blanchet [10, §2.3] proposes the following solution. Extend the set of function symbols with the binary constructor e and the binary destructor d, let the set of rewrite rules def$(d) = \{d(x, e(x,y)) \to y\}$, and modify $!\nu\, s.P$ such that $e(s, m)$ is published at the end of every *successful* session of $\nu\, s.P$, where m is a free name not known by the attacker. It follows that the modified process preserves secrecy of m iff $!\nu\, s.P$ preserves secrecy of s, hence, we have a methodology to consider the secrecy of bound names.

We consider (Section 4) a definition for secrecy of bound names which does not require abstraction and introduce a new proof technique: given a process P, name s, and fresh name s', we have

secrecy of the bound name s in $!\nu\, s.P$
iff secrecy of the bound name s' in $\nu\, s'.(P\{s'/s\}) \mid !\nu\, s.P$
iff secrecy of the free name s' in $P\{s'/s\} \mid !\nu\, s.P$

In the context of these results, we describe how our compiler can be applied to avoid false attacks, in particular, we can prove security results for secrets under the scope of a replication.

We demonstrate the applicability of our technique by analysing three protocols (Sections 5 & 6): a toy extension of the Needham-Schroeder protocol in which one of the participants reveals their nonce at the end of a successful run, the Bluetooth Simple Pairing [22,23], and a simplification of the Bluetooth Simple Pairing that we propose. ProVerif finds false attacks against each of these protocols, whereas our techniques allow us to prove security.

Pairing protocols typically use a low-entropy, human-verifiable string, derived from a high-entropy shared secret, to authenticate protocol participants and protect against impersonation attacks. Given that the string is low-entropy, strings derived from distinct secrets may collide and an attacker that can predict collisions can launch impersonation attacks. Accordingly, pairing protocols must ensure that deriving collisions is computationally expensive. The Bluetooth Simple

Pairing protocol defends against such attacks by making both parties commit to particular values before the low-entropy string can be calculated; this deprives an attacker of the opportunity to carry out a brute force attack to find a collision.

We develop theory to enable protocols that are vulnerable to collision attacks to be accurately modelled in the applied pi calculus. Accordingly, our analysis of Bluetooth Simple Pairing is more precise than an earlier analysis by Chang & Shmatikov [17], which ignores collision attacks, and so would incorrectly find the protocol to be secure even if the steps that stop impersonation attacks were removed. We also present a simplified version of the Bluetooth Simple Pairing protocol, which achieves the same secrecy goals with fewer steps, and we use our analysis method to show that it is secure.

The key contributions of this paper are:

- A framework for avoiding some false attacks when analysing secrecy.
- A definition for secrecy of bound names.
- A method to captured collision attacks.
- A demonstration of how BlueTooth Simple Pairing defends against collision attacks.
- A simplified pairing protocol.

Hence, our paper advances automated analysis techniques.

2   Background: Applied pi Calculus

We adopt Blanchet's dialect [10] of the applied pi calculus [2,27], which is suited to automated reasoning using Blanchet's ProVerif [15]. The dialect uses the notion of configurations proposed by Baudet [7] to avoid structural equivalence, which simplifies security definitions and subsequent proofs.

The calculus assumes an infinite set of *names*, an infinite set of *variables*, and a finite set of *function symbols* (*constructors* and *destructors*), each with an associated arity. We write f for a constructor, g for a destructor; constructors are used to build terms whereas destructors are used to manipulate terms in processes. *Terms* range over names, variables, and applications of constructors to terms. *Substitutions* $\{M/x\}$ replace the variable x with the term M. Arbitrarily large substitutions can be written as $\{M_1/x_1, \ldots, M_n/x_n\}$ and the letters σ and τ range over substitutions. We write $M\sigma$ for the result of applying σ to the variables of M.

The signature Σ is equipped with a finite set of equations of the form $M = N$ and we derive an equational theory from this set by reflexive, symmetric and transitive closure, closure under the application of constructors, closure under substitution of terms for variables, and closure under bijective renaming of names. We write $\Sigma \vdash M = N$ for an equality modulo the equational theory and $\Sigma \vdash M \neq N$ for an inequality modulo the equational theory. (We write $M = N$ and $M \neq N$ for syntactic equality and inequality, respectively.)

The semantics of a destructor g of arity l is given by a finite set $\text{def}(g)$ of rewrite rules $g(M'_1, \ldots, M'_l) \to M'$, where $M'_1, \ldots, M'_l, M'$ are terms that contain only constructors and variables; the variables of M' must be bound in $M'_1, \ldots, M'_l$ and variables are subject to renaming. The value $g(M_1, \ldots, M_l)$ is defined if and only if there exists a substitution σ and a rewrite rule $g(M'_1, \ldots, M'_l) \to M'$ in $\text{def}(g)$ such that $M_i = M'_i\sigma$ for all $i \in \{1, \ldots, l\}$, and in this case $g(M_1, \ldots, M_l)$ is defined as $M'\sigma$.

The grammar for terms and *processes* is presented in Figure 1, where t is a non-negative integer representing a global clock. The process *let* $x = g(M_1, ..., M_l)$ *in* P *else* Q tries to evaluate $g(M_1, ..., M_l)$; if this succeeds (that is, if $g(M_1, ..., M_l)$ is defined), then x is bound to the result and P is executed, otherwise, Q is executed. The statement let $x = g(M_1, \ldots, M_l)$ in P else Q may be abbreviated as let $x = g(M_1, \ldots, M_l)$ in P, when Q is 0. The syntax does not include the conditional if $M = N$ then P else Q, but this can be defined as let $x = \text{eq}(M, N)$ in P else Q, where x is a fresh variable, eq is a binary destructor, and $\text{def}(\text{eq}) = \{\text{eq}(x, x) \to x\}$; we always include eq in our set of function symbols. For convenience, we may write if $M = N$ then P else Q for let $x = \text{eq}(M, N)$ in P else Q and if $M = N$ then P for let $x = \text{eq}(M, N)$ in P. In Figure 1, we extend Blanchet's syntax [10] with Blanchet, Abadi & Fournet's notion of *phases* [13, §8], denoted $t : P$, which ensures a process $t : P$ is only active during time t.

Fig. 1. Syntax for terms and processes

$M, N ::=$	terms
x, y, z	variables
a, b, c, k, s	names
$f(M_1, \ldots, M_n)$	constructor application
$D ::= g(M_1, \ldots, M_n)$	destructor application
$P, Q ::=$	processes
0	nil
$\overline{M}\langle N \rangle.P$	output
$M(x).P$	input
$P \mid Q$	parallel composition
$!P$	replication
$\nu a.P$	restriction
let $x = D$ in P else Q	term evaluation
$t : P$	phase

The sets of free and bound names, respectively variables, in process P are denoted by $\text{fn}(P)$ and $\text{bn}(P)$, respectively $\text{fv}(P)$ and $\text{bv}(P)$. We also write $\text{fn}(M)$ and $\text{fv}(M)$ for the sets of names and variables in term M. A process P is closed if it has no free variables. A context C is a process with a hole and we obtain $C[P]$ as the result of filling C's hole with P. An evaluation context is a context whose hole is not in the scope of a replication, an input, an output, or a term evaluation.

The operational semantics (Figures 2) for the applied pi-calculus are defined by reduction ($\rightarrow$) on *configurations*. A configuration $\mathcal{C}$ is a pair $E, \mathcal{P}$ such that E is a finite set of names, and $\mathcal{P}$ is a finite multiset of pairs of closed process. The set E contains all the free names in $\mathcal{P}$, and is extended to include any names introduced during reduction, namely, those names introduced by $(E, \mathcal{P} \cup \{t : \nu a; P\}) \rightarrow (E \cup \{a'\}, \mathcal{P} \cup \{t : P\{a'/a\}\})$. A sequence of reductions, denoted $\mathcal{C}_1 \rightarrow \mathcal{C}_2 \rightarrow \cdots \rightarrow \mathcal{C}_n$, is called a *trace*. We occassionally write $\rightarrow^*$ for the reflexive and transitive closure of $\rightarrow$.

Fig. 2. Operational semantics

$$E, \mathcal{P} \cup \{t : 0\} \rightarrow E, \mathcal{P} \qquad \text{(RED NIL)}$$

$$E, \mathcal{P} \cup \{t : !P\} \rightarrow E, \mathcal{P} \cup \{t : !P, t : P\} \qquad \text{(RED REPL)}$$

$$E, \mathcal{P} \cup \{t : (P \mid Q)\}) \rightarrow E, \mathcal{P} \cup \{t : P, t : Q\} \qquad \text{(RED PAR)}$$

$$E, \mathcal{P} \cup \{t : \nu a.P\} \rightarrow E \cup \{a'\}, \mathcal{P} \cup \{t : P\{a'/a\}\} \qquad \text{(RED RES)}$$
for some name $a' \notin E$

$$E, \mathcal{P} \cup \{t : \overline{N}\langle M \rangle.P, t : N(x).Q\} \rightarrow E, \mathcal{P} \cup \{t : P, t : Q\{M/x\}\} \qquad \text{(RED I/O)}$$

$$E, \mathcal{P} \cup \{t : \text{let } x = D \text{ in } L\} \rightarrow E, \mathcal{P} \cup \{t : P\{M/x\}\} \qquad \text{(RED DESTR 1)}$$
if there exists M such that $D \rightarrow M$

$$E, \mathcal{P} \cup \{t : \text{let } x = D \text{ in } P \text{ else } Q\}) \rightarrow E, \mathcal{P} \cup \{t : Q\} \qquad \text{(RED DESTR 2)}$$
if there is no M such that $D \rightarrow M'$

$$E, \mathcal{P} \cup \{t : t' : P\} \rightarrow E, \mathcal{P} \cup \{t' : P\} \qquad \text{(RED ORDER)}$$
if $t < t'$

Given a process P in the applied pi-calculus without phases and a set of names *Init*, the configuration *Init*, $\{0 : P\}$ will reduce using our semantics in exactly the same way as the configuration *Init*, $\{P\}$ using Blanchet's semantics [10]. We note that Blanchet, Abadi & Fournet [13, §8], who introduce phases, assume any process without phases is assumed to run in phase zero. In this paper, we wish to distinguish between processes in phase zero and processes without phases, so we always make the phases explicit, except in case studies where we adopt Blanchet, Abadi & Fournet's convention for brevity.

3   Secrecy of Free Names

We recall (Definition 1) Blanchet's formalisation [10] of knowledge derivable from a trace – that is, a reduction on a configuration – as any names which are output.

Definition 1. *Let $\mathcal{T} = E_0, \mathcal{P}_0 \rightarrow^* E', \mathcal{P}'$ be a trace, n be a name, and Init be a finite set of names. We write* attacker$(Init, n) : \mathcal{T}$ *if $\mathcal{T}$ contains a reduction $E, \mathcal{P} \cup \{t:\overline{c}\langle n\rangle.P, t:c(x).Q\} \rightarrow E, \mathcal{P} \cup \{t:P, t:Q\{n/x\}\}$ for some $E, \mathcal{P}, P, Q, x, t$ and $c \in Init$.*

It follows naturally that a configuration preserves the secrecy of a name if no (adversarial) process added to the configuration can generate a trace which permits the name to be derived. We recall (Definition 2) Blanchet's definition [10] for secrecy of free names.

Definition 2. *Let $\mathcal{C} = E, \mathcal{P}$ be a configuration, n be a name and Init be a finite set of names, where* fn$(\mathcal{P}) \subseteq E$. *We write* secrecy$(Init, n) : \mathcal{C}$ *if for all processes Q such that* fn$(Q) \subseteq Init$ *there is no trace $\mathcal{T} = E \cup Init \cup \mathrm{fn}(n), \mathcal{P} \cup \{Q\} \rightarrow^* E', \mathcal{P}'$ such that* attacker$(Init, n) : \mathcal{T}$ *for some E' and $\mathcal{P}'$.*

Let P be a closed process, n be a name, and Init be a finite set of names. We write secrecy$(Init, n) : P$ *if* secrecy$(Init, n) : \mathrm{fn}(P), \{P\}$.

Definition 2 facilitates the analysis of secrecy when the secret is a free name and Section 4 proposes a definition which supposes the secret is bound.

As discussed in Section 1.1, we encounter false attacks when analysing secrecy of free names and we overcome this problem in the remainder of this section.

3.1 Our Compiler: Phases Improve Horn Clause Generation

As demonstrated in Section 1.1, false attacks can be avoided by inserting phases into processes. Formally, we insert phases using function δ:

Definition 3. *Given a set of names Init and a process, we define δ as follows:*

$$\delta(Init, P) = \{P\} \cup \{C[1:M(x).P'] : P = C[M(x).P']\}$$
$$\cup \{C[1:\overline{M}\langle N\rangle.P'] : P = C[\overline{M}\langle N\rangle.P'] \wedge \mathrm{fn}(M) \cap Init = \emptyset\}$$

Function δ outputs a set of processes representing all ways of inserting a phase into P such that the phase appears immediately before an input or an output on a private channel[1].

The insertion of one phase does not generally result in a sound abstraction. For instance, process P2 | 0:!P1 is not a sound approximation of 0:P1 | 0:!P1, because the phase in P2 prevents the instance of n generated by P2 being input by 0:P1. This problem can be overcome by ensuring that all inputs and outputs are available in either phase 0 or phase 1, which can be achieved using our compiler (Definition 4). For simplicity, we restrict our compiler to multisets of processes $\mathcal{P} = \{0:L, 0:!L_1, \ldots, 0:!L_m\}$, where $L, L_1, \ldots, L_m$ are *linear processes* (Figure 3) and ProVerif discovers false attacks arising from process L. This is sufficient to avoid the false attacks discovered in the examples in this paper.

---

[1] Outputs on public channels can be received by the environment in phase 0 and replayed in phase 1, therefore function δ does not insert phases immediately before outputs on public channels.

Fig. 3. Syntax for linear processes

$L ::=$	linear processes
0	nil
$\overline{M}\langle N\rangle.L$	output
$M(x).L$	input
$\nu\, a.L$	restriction
let $x = g(M_1,\ldots,M_n)$ in L else 0	destructor application

Definition 4. *Given a set of names Init and a multiset of process* $\mathcal{P} = \{0 : L, 0\!:\!!L_1,\ldots,0\!:\!!L_m\}$, *we define* Δ *as follows:*

$$\Delta(\mathit{Init},\mathcal{P}) = \left\{ \{P\} \cup \mathcal{Q} \;\middle|\; P \in \delta(\mathit{Init},0\!:\!L) \wedge \mathcal{Q} = \bigcup_{1\leq i\leq m} \delta(\mathit{Init},0\!:\!!L_i) \right\}$$

The compiler tries to avoid false attacks by inserting a phase into process L (in a different place for each member of the set produced by Δ). To ensure that all of the original reductions are still possible, our compiler also generates a copy of every other process with a phase in every necessary position.

3.2   Automated Reasoning without False Attacks

Our compiler is designed such that Blanchet's translation from compiled processes to Horn clauses ensures that the clauses abide by an ordering, thereby avoiding the false attacks described in Section 1.1, whilst preserving secrecy:

Theorem 1. *Given a name s, sets of names E and Init and a multiset of processes* $\mathcal{P} = \{0\!:\!L, 0\!:\!!L_1,\ldots,0\!:\!!L_m\}$, *such that* $s \notin \bigcup_{1\leq i\leq n}(\mathrm{fn}(L_i) \cup \mathrm{bn}(L_i))$ *and* $\mathrm{fn}(\mathcal{P}) \subseteq E$, *we have for all* $\mathcal{Q} \in \Delta(\mathit{Init},\mathcal{P})$ *that:*

$$\mathrm{secrecy}(\mathit{Init},s) : E, \mathcal{P} \Leftrightarrow \mathrm{secrecy}(\mathit{Init},s) : E, \mathcal{Q}$$

The proof of Theorem 1 appears in the long version of this paper. We demonstrate an application of Theorem 1 with reference to processes P1 and P2:

Example 1. Let $C = 0 : \nu\, n.c(x).\_$ and witness that $0 : \mathrm{P1} = C[\overline{c}\langle n\rangle.\text{if } x = n \text{ then } \overline{c}\langle s\rangle]$ and $\mathrm{P2} = C[1\!:\!\overline{c}\langle n\rangle.\text{if } x = n \text{ then } \overline{c}\langle s\rangle]$, i.e., $\{\mathrm{P2}\} \in \Delta(\{c\},\{\mathrm{P1}\})$. We have $\mathrm{secrecy}(\{c\},s) : \{c,s\},\{0\!:\!\mathrm{P1}\} \Leftrightarrow \mathrm{secrecy}(\{c\},s) : \{c,s\},\{\mathrm{P2}\}$ by Theorem 1, hence, $\mathrm{secrecy}(\{c\},s) : (0\!:\!\mathrm{P1}) \Leftrightarrow \mathrm{secrecy}(\{c\},s) : \mathrm{P2}$ by Definition 2. Moreover, since ProVerif can prove $\mathrm{secrecy}(\{c\},s) : \mathrm{P2}$, we have the desired result, namely $\mathrm{secrecy}(\{c\},s) : (0\!:\!\mathrm{P1})$.

4   Secrecy of Bound Names

We adapt the notion of knowledge derivable from a trace (Definition 1) to consider names which are bound by the trace's initial configuration.

Definition 5. *Let* $\mathcal{T} = E_0, \mathcal{P}_0 \to^* E_1, \mathcal{P}_1$ *be a trace,* n *be a name, and Init be a finite set of names. We write* $\widehat{\text{attacker}}(Init, n) : \mathcal{T}$ *if* $\mathcal{T}$ *contains the following reductions*

$$E, \mathcal{P} \cup \{t : \nu\, n.P\} \to E \cup \{n'\}, \mathcal{P} \cup \{t : P\{n'/n\}\}$$
$$\to^* E', \mathcal{P}' \cup \{s : \overline{c}\langle n'\rangle.P', s : c(x).Q'\}$$
$$\to E', \mathcal{P}' \cup \{s : P', s : Q'\{n'/x\}\}$$

where $c \in Init$ *and some* $E, E', \mathcal{P}, \mathcal{P}', P, P', Q', n', x, s$ *and* t.

Intuitively, a trace $\mathcal{T}$ satisfies $\widehat{\text{attacker}}(Init, n) : \mathcal{T}$ if n is bound by the trace's initial configuration, n is renamed to n' and, subsequently, n' is outputted.

It follows naturally from Definition 5 that a configuration preserves secrecy of a bound name if no (adversarial) process added to the configuration can generate a trace which permits the name to be derived.

Definition 6. *Let* $\mathcal{C} = E, \mathcal{P}$ *be a configuration,* n *be a name and Init be a set of names, where* $\text{fn}(\mathcal{P}) \subseteq E$. *We write* $\widehat{\text{secrecy}}(Init, n) : \mathcal{C}$ *if for all processes* Q *such that* $\text{fn}(Q) \subseteq Init$ *and* $n \notin \text{bn}(Q)$, *there is no trace* $\mathcal{T} = E \cup Init, \mathcal{P} \cup \{Q\} \to^*$ $E', \mathcal{P}'$ *such that* $\widehat{\text{attacker}}(Init, n) : \mathcal{T}$ *for some* E' *and* $\mathcal{P}'$.

Let P *be a closed process,* n *be a name and Init be a finite set of names, where* $n \in \text{bn}(P)$. *We write* $\widehat{\text{secrecy}}(Init, n) : P$ *if* $\widehat{\text{secrecy}}(Init, n) : \text{fn}(P), \{P\}$.

We remark that $\widehat{\text{secrecy}}(Init, n) : P$ guarantees secrecy of every bound name n in P. It follows that $\widehat{\text{secrecy}}(Init, n) : (s : \nu\, n.Q \mid t : \nu\, n.R)$ implies $\widehat{\text{secrecy}}(Init, n) :$ $(s : \nu\, n.Q \mid t : \nu\, m.(R\{m/n\}) \land \widehat{\text{secrecy}}(Init, m) : (s : \nu\, n.Q \mid t : \nu\, m.(R\{m/n\}))$, for example.

Secrecy of bound names is not new. ProVerif can already check the secrecy of bound names, however, the corresponding theoretical definition has not been published. (Blanchet [11] has confirmed that Definition 6 corresponds to the secrecy of bound names notion used by ProVerif.) In addition, Ryan & Smyth [27, §3.1] propose a definition for secrecy of bound names in the applied pi calculus, however, their definition is restricted to bound names which do not appear under the scope of replication and we do not impose such a restriction. The false attacks we encounter when analysing secrecy of free names similarly occur when analysing secrecy of bound names, for instance, ProVerif cannot prove $\widehat{\text{secrecy}}(\{c\}, s) : \{c\}, \{0 : !\nu\, s.\text{P1}\}$. In the remainder of this section we overcome this problem.

4.1   A Proof Technique for Secrecy of Bound Names

It follows from our semantics and the definition of bound secrecy that: if $t : !\nu\, n.P$ does not preserve the secrecy of n, then there exists an instance of $\nu\, n.P$ that leaks n, when running in parallel with $!\nu\, n.P$. We now show that it is sufficient to rename n with some fresh name m in an instance of $\nu\, n.P$ and consider secrecy of the m in $t : \nu\, m.(P\{m/n\}) \mid !\nu\, n.P)$.

Theorem 2. *Given a name s, sets of names E and Init, process P and multiset of processes $\mathcal{P}$ such that $s \notin \mathrm{bn}(P) \cup \mathrm{bn}(\mathcal{P})$ and $\mathrm{fn}(\mathcal{P}) \cup (\mathrm{fn}(P) \setminus \{s\}) \subseteq E$, we have, for all fresh names s', that:*

$$\widehat{\mathrm{secrecy}}(Init, s) : E, \mathcal{P} \cup \{t \colon !\nu\, s.P\} \iff$$
$$\widehat{\mathrm{secrecy}}(Init, s') : E, \mathcal{P} \cup \{t \colon !\nu\, s.P, t \colon \nu\, s'.(P\{s'/s\})\}$$

The proof of Theorem 1 appears in the long version of this paper.

4.2   Secrecy of Bound and Free Names Coincide

Secrecy of bound and free names coincide when the secret is not under replication.

Proposition 1. *Given a name s, sets of names E and Init, process P and multiset of processes $\mathcal{P}$ such that $s \notin \mathrm{bn}(P) \cup \mathrm{bn}(\mathcal{P}) \cup \mathrm{fn}(\mathcal{P}) \cup Init \cup E$ and $\mathrm{fn}(\mathcal{P}) \cup (\mathrm{fn}(P) \setminus \{s\}) \subseteq E$, we have:*

$$\widehat{\mathrm{secrecy}}(Init, s) : E, \mathcal{P} \cup \{t \colon \nu\, s.P\} \iff \mathrm{secrecy}(Init, s) : E \cup \{s\}, \mathcal{P} \cup \{t \colon P\}$$

Proof sketch. We note that $E, \mathcal{P} \cup \{t \colon \nu\, s.P\} \to E \cup \{s'\}, \mathcal{P} \cup \{t \colon P\{s'/s\}\}$, for a fresh name s' and that $\mathrm{secrecy}(Init, s) : E \cup \{s\}, \mathcal{P} \cup \{t \colon P\}$ iff $\mathrm{secrecy}(Init, s') : E \cup \{s'\}, \mathcal{P} \cup \{t \colon P\{s'/s\}\}$. Therefore, given a trace that causes free secrecy to fail to hold for the R.H.S we can add the new name declaration to produce a trace that causes secrecy to fail for the L.H.S. Conversely, given a trace that causes secrecy to fail for the L.H.S., removing the new name declaration will give us a trace that causes secrecy to fail for the R.H.S. □

A similar equivalence does not hold when the secret is under replication, as the following example demonstrates:

Example 2. For instance, suppose $P = \overline{a}\langle s \rangle \mid a(x).a(y).\text{if } x = y \text{ then } \overline{c}\langle s \rangle$ and $Init = \{c\}$, we have $\widehat{\mathrm{secrecy}}(Init, s) : (0 \colon !\nu\, s.P)$ but not $\mathrm{secrecy}(Init, s) : (0 \colon !P)$, since:

$$
\begin{aligned}
E, \{0 \colon !P, 0 \colon c(z)\} \to\to\ & E, \{0 \colon !P, 0 \colon P, 0 \colon P, 0 \colon c(z)\} & \text{by (\textsc{Red Repl})} \\
\to\to\ & E, \{0 \colon !P, 0 \colon \overline{a}\langle s \rangle, 0 \colon \overline{a}\langle s \rangle, Q, Q, 0 \colon c(z)\} & \text{by (\textsc{Red Par})} \\
\to\to\ & E, \mathcal{P} \cup \{0 \colon \text{if } s = s \text{ then } \overline{c}\langle s \rangle, 0 \colon c(z)\} & \text{by (\textsc{Red I/O})} \\
\to\ & E, \mathcal{P} \cup \{0 \colon \overline{c}\langle s \rangle, 0 \colon c(z)\} & \text{by (\textsc{Red Destr 1})} \\
\to\ & E, \mathcal{P} \cup \{0 \colon 0, 0 \colon 0\{s/z\}\} & \text{by (\textsc{Red I/O})}
\end{aligned}
$$

where $E = \{a, c, s\}$, $Q = 0 \colon a(x).a(y).\text{if } x = y \text{ then } \overline{c}\langle s \rangle$ and $\mathcal{P} = \{0 \colon !P, 0, 0, Q\}$.

4.3   Automated Reasoning without False Attacks

The following corollary allows us to reduce the false attacks encountered when analysing secrecy of bound names.

Corollary 1. *Given a name s, sets of names E and $Init$, and a multiset of processes $\mathcal{P} = \{0 : !\nu\, s.L, 0 : !L_1, \ldots, 0 : !L_m\}$, such that $s \notin \text{bn}(L) \cup \bigcup_{1 \le i \le n}(\text{fn}(L_i) \cup \text{bn}(L_i))$ and $\text{fn}(\mathcal{P}) \subseteq E$, we have for all fresh names s' and $\mathcal{Q} \in \Delta(Init, \mathcal{P} \cup \{L\{s'/s\}\})$ that:*

$$\widehat{secrecy}(Init, s) : E, \mathcal{P} \Leftrightarrow secrecy(Init, s') : E \cup \{s'\}, \mathcal{Q}$$

Proof. We have:

$\widehat{secrecy}(Init, s) : E, \mathcal{P}$
$\Leftrightarrow \widehat{secrecy}(Init, s') : E, \{0 : \nu\, s'.(L\{s'/s\})\} \cup \mathcal{P}$ by Theorem 2
$\Leftrightarrow secrecy(Init, s') : E \cup \{s'\}, \{0 : L\{s'/s\}\} \cup \mathcal{P}$ by Proposition 1   □
$\Leftrightarrow secrecy(Init, s') : E \cup \{s'\}, \mathcal{Q}$ by Theorem 1

We demonstrate an application of Corollary 1 by evaluating $\widehat{secrecy}(\{c\}, s)$: $\{c\}, \{!\nu\, s.P1\}$:

Example 3. Witness that $\nu\, s.P1 = C[c(x).\bar{c}\langle n\rangle.\text{if } x = n \text{ then } \bar{c}\langle s\rangle]$, where $C = \nu\, n.\_$, but there is no other context C, process L and terms M and x such that $\nu\, s.P1 = C[M(x).L]$. In addition, there is no context C, process L and terms M, N such that $\nu\, s.P1 = C[\overline{M}\langle N\rangle.L] \wedge \text{fn}(M) \cap \{c\} = \emptyset$. It follows that $\delta(\{c\}, \nu\, s.0 : P1) = \{0 : !\nu\, s.P1, 0 : !\nu\, s.1 : c(x).\bar{c}\langle n\rangle.\text{if } x = n \text{ then } \bar{c}\langle s\rangle\}$. Let $\mathcal{Q} = \delta(\{c\}, 0 : \nu\, s.P1) \cup \{P3\}$, where P3 is defined as follows:

$$0 : \nu\, n.c(x).1 : \bar{c}\langle n\rangle.\text{if } x = n \text{ then } \bar{c}\langle s'\rangle \tag{P3}$$

Since $P1\{s'/s\} = C[\bar{c}\langle n\rangle.\text{if } x = n \text{ then } \bar{c}\langle s'\rangle]$, where $C = \nu\, n.c(x).\_$, we have P3 $\in \delta(\emptyset, 0 : P1\{s'/s\})$ and it follows that $\mathcal{Q} \in \Delta(\{c\}, \{0 : P1\{s'/s\}, 0 : !\nu\, s.P1\})$. We have $\widehat{secrecy}(\{c\}, s)$: $\{c\}, \{0 : !\nu\, s.P1\} \Leftrightarrow secrecy(\{c\}, s')$: $\{c, s'\}, \mathcal{Q}$ by Corollary 1 and, since ProVerif can prove $secrecy(\{c\}, s) : \mathcal{Q}$, we have the desired result $\widehat{secrecy}(\{c\}, s) : \{c\}, \{!\nu\, s.P1\}$.

5   Case Study I: Needham-Schroeder Protocol

For our first case study, we compose the Needham-Schroeder protocol [26] with a symmetric encryption scheme to derive a secure channel.

Needham-Schroeder protocol. The Needham-Schroeder protocol [26] is intended to generate a session key shared between two participants. We assume the participants are Alice and Bob, to prevent Lowe's man-in-the-middle attack[2] [24]. The protocol proceeds as follows. First, Alice generates a nonce and outputs

---

[2] Lowe's attack works as follows: an attacker engages Alice in a session of the protocol and impersonates Alice to Bob in a parallel session. The attack can be thwarted by assuming that Alice will only run the protocol with Bob, rather than any other principal.

the nonce encrypted with Bob's public key. Secondly, Bob decrypts Alice's ciphertext using his private key to recover Alice's nonce, generates a nonce, and outputs the pair of nonces encrypted with Alice's public key. Finally, Alice decrypts Bob's ciphertext using her private key to recover the pair of nonces and outputs Bob's nonce encrypted with Bob's public key. The rationale behind the protocol is that: since only Bob can recover Alice's nonce, only he can output the encrypted pair of nonces, moreover, since only Alice can recover Bob's nonce, only she can output his encrypted nonce; it follows that the two nonces are only known to Alice and Bob.

Symmetric encryption scheme. Symmetric encryption enables a secret to be shared between two participants. We consider the following symmetric encryption scheme. Given an identifier, key, and secret as input, the initiator outputs the identifier paired with the secret encrypted with the key. Upon receipt of such a pair, the interlocutor uses the key associated with the initiator's identifier to decrypt the ciphertext. It follows from our description that the initiator's secret can only be known by the key holders.

We compose the Needham-Schroeder protocol and symmetric encryption scheme to derive a secure channel[3]. The Needham-Schroeder protocol is used to generate a pair of nonces and these nonces are used by the symmetric encryption scheme as follows: Alice's nonce is used as the identifier and Bob's nonce is used as the key. Intuitively, the composition ensures that Alice's secret is known only to Alice and Bob, because Bob's nonce is only known to Alice and Bob.

5.1   Applied pi Calculus Model

We construct a signature Σ to capture the primitives modelling cryptographic operators and constants: $\Sigma = \{\mathsf{fst}, \mathsf{snd}, \mathsf{pk}, \mathsf{pair}, \ \mathsf{adec}, \mathsf{aenc}, \mathsf{sdec}, \mathsf{senc}\}$, where $\mathsf{fst}, \mathsf{snd}, \mathsf{pk}$ are unary functions and $\mathsf{adec}, \mathsf{aenc}, \mathsf{sdec}, \mathsf{senc}$ are binary functions. We equip the signature with the following rewrite rules:

$$\{\mathsf{fst}(\mathsf{pair}(x,y)) \to x, \ \mathsf{snd}(\mathsf{pair}(x,y)) \to y,$$
$$\mathsf{adec}(x, \mathsf{aenc}(\mathsf{pk}(x), y)) \to y, \ \mathsf{sdec}(x, \mathsf{senc}(x, y)) \to y\}.$$

Our signature and associated rewrite rules allow us to model: asymmetric encryption, pairing, and symmetric encryption.

We define the participants, Alice and Bob, in our composition of the Needham-Schroeder protocol with a symmetric encryption scheme (Figure 4). Hence, the complete composition is modelled by the configuration $E_{\mathsf{NSL}}, \mathcal{P}_{\mathsf{NSL}} = \{c, k_A, k_B\}$, $\{!\nu\, s.A, !B, !\overline{c}\langle\mathsf{pk}(k_A)\rangle, !\overline{c}\langle\mathsf{pk}(k_B)\rangle\}$ (which are implicitly assumed to be running in phase 0).

---

[3] This example was inspired by discussion with Blanchet & Cortier [14].

Fig. 4. Processes modelling Alice and Bob in the Needham-Schroeder protocol

$A = \nu\, n_A.$
$\quad \bar{c}\langle \mathsf{aenc}(\mathsf{pk}(k_B), n_A)\rangle.$
$\quad c(x_{\mathsf{ciph}}).$
$\quad \mathsf{let}\ x_{\mathsf{pair}} = \mathsf{adec}(k_A, x_{\mathsf{ciph}})\ \mathsf{in}$
$\quad \mathsf{let}\ y_{\mathsf{nonce}} = \mathsf{fst}(x_{\mathsf{pair}})\ \mathsf{in}$
$\quad \mathsf{if}\ y_{\mathsf{nonce}} = n_A\ \mathsf{then}$
$\quad \mathsf{let}\ x_{\mathsf{nonce}} = \mathsf{snd}(x_{\mathsf{pair}})\ \mathsf{in}$
$\quad \bar{c}\langle \mathsf{aenc}(\mathsf{pk}(k_B), x_{\mathsf{nonce}})\rangle.$
$\quad (* \text{ end key exchange } *)$
$\quad \bar{c}\langle \mathsf{pair}(n_A, \mathsf{senc}(x_{\mathsf{nonce}}, s))\rangle)$

$B = c(y_{\mathsf{ciph}}).$
$\quad \mathsf{let}\ y_{\mathsf{nonce}} = \mathsf{adec}(k_B, y_{\mathsf{ciph}})\ \mathsf{in}$
$\quad \nu\, n_B.$
$\quad \bar{c}\langle \mathsf{aenc}(\mathsf{pk}(k_A), \mathsf{pair}(y_{\mathsf{nonce}}, n_B)))\rangle.$
$\quad c(y'_{\mathsf{ciph}}).$
$\quad \mathsf{let}\ x_{\mathsf{nonce}} = \mathsf{adec}(k_B, y'_{\mathsf{ciph}})\ \mathsf{in}$
$\quad \mathsf{if}\ x_{\mathsf{nonce}} = n_B\ \mathsf{then}$
$\quad c(y_{\mathsf{pair}}).$
$\quad \mathsf{let}\ y'_{\mathsf{nonce}} = \mathsf{fst}(y_{\mathsf{pair}})\ \mathsf{in}$
$\quad \mathsf{if}\ y_{\mathsf{nonce}} = y'_{\mathsf{nonce}}\ \mathsf{then}$
$\quad \mathsf{let}\ y''_{\mathsf{ciph}} = \mathsf{snd}(y_{\mathsf{pair}})\ \mathsf{in}$
$\quad \mathsf{let}\ y_{\mathsf{secret}} = \mathsf{sdec}(n_B, y''_{\mathsf{ciph}})\ \mathsf{in}\ 0$

5.2 Analysis

We would like to analyse $\widehat{\mathsf{secrecy}}(\{c\}, s) : E_{\mathsf{NSL}}, \mathcal{P}_{\mathsf{NSL}}$ using ProVerif. However, the Horn clauses generated by Blanchet's translation of $\mathcal{P}_{\mathsf{NSL}}$ result in Horn clauses which model the process $\mathcal{P}_{\mathsf{NSL}}$ with a replication after the name restriction $\nu\, n_A$. Unfortunately, secrecy does not hold in this process, because the attacker can learn n_A during one run of the protocol and simulate Bob during a second run to learn Alice's secret s. Indeed, ProVerif finds such an attack. However, this is a false attack, because the protocol states that Alice should use a fresh nonce for every session of the protocol. This false attack can be avoided using our results.

By Corollary 1, to prove $\widehat{\mathsf{secrecy}}(\{c\}, s) : E_{\mathsf{NSL}}, \mathcal{P}_{\mathsf{NSL}}$ it is sufficient to prove $\mathsf{secrecy}(Init, s') : E \cup \{s'\}, \mathcal{Q}$, where $\mathcal{Q} \in \Delta(\{c\}, \mathcal{P}_{\mathsf{NSL}} \cup \{A\{s'/s\}\})$. Let us construct a suitable $\mathcal{Q}$. By definition of Δ (Definition 4), we have $\mathcal{Q} = \{L\} \cup \bigcup_{P \in \mathcal{P}_{\mathsf{NSL}}}\{!R \mid R \in \delta(Init, P)\}$ for some $L \in \delta(\emptyset, A\{s'/s\})$. Since $\mathcal{P}_{\mathsf{NSL}}$ does not contain any private channels, for all contexts C, processes L and terms M and N such that $\mathsf{fv}(M) \cap \{c\} = \emptyset$, we have $\nu\, s.A \neq C[\overline{M}\langle N\rangle.L']$, $B \neq C[\overline{M}\langle N\rangle.L']$, $\bar{c}\langle\mathsf{pk}(k_A)\rangle \neq C[\overline{M}\langle N\rangle.L']$, and $\bar{c}\langle\mathsf{pk}(k_B)\rangle \neq C[\overline{M}\langle N\rangle.L']$. Moreover, since $\bar{c}\langle\mathsf{pk}(k_A)\rangle$ and $\bar{c}\langle\mathsf{pk}(k_B)\rangle$ do not contain inputs, we have $\{!R \mid R \in \delta(Init, \bar{c}\langle\mathsf{pk}(k_A)\rangle)\} = \{!\bar{c}\langle\mathsf{pk}(k_A)\rangle\}$ and, similarly, $\{!R \mid R \in \delta(Init, \bar{c}\langle\mathsf{pk}(k_B)\rangle)\} = \{!\bar{c}\langle\mathsf{pk}(k_B)\rangle\}$. The set $\{!R \mid R \in \delta(Init, \nu\, s.A)\}$ contains $!\nu\, s.A$ and a modified version of $!\nu\, s.A$, namely, $!\nu\, s.A$ with a phase inserted before the input. The set $\{!R \mid R \in \delta(Init, B)\}$ contains $!B$ and three modified versions of $!B$, namely, $!B$ with a phase before each of the three inputs. We have a concrete definition of $\bigcup_{P \in \mathcal{P}_{\mathsf{NSL}}}\{!R \mid R \in \delta(Init, P)\}$ and we let $L \in \delta(\emptyset, A\{s'/s\})$ be $A\{s'/s\}$ with a phase inserted before the penultimate output. ProVerif can automatically verify that $\mathsf{secrecy}(Init, s') : E \cup \{s'\}, \mathcal{Q}$ holds (verification takes less than one second using ProVerif 1.86pl4 on Ubuntu 12.04.3 with 3.60GHz Intel Xeon E5-1620 and 8GB memory).

6   Case Study II: Bluetooth Simple Pairing

The Bluetooth Simple Pairing protocol [22,23] extends the (elliptic curve) Diffie-Hellman protocol to provide authenticated key exchange. There are a number of variations of this protocol, depending on the capabilities of the devices being paired, here we look at the "Numeric Comparison Protocol" that aims to securely pair devices that are capable of displaying a short number on a screen, and receiving an input from the user. The displays of the participants' devices provide a low-bandwidth, authenticated "out of band" channel, which is assumed to be untappable by the attacker. The bandwidth constraint of this out of band channel makes BlueTooth Pairing non-trivial.

The protocol (Figure 5) proceeds as follows. Alice and Bob establish a Diffie-Hellman key (Steps 1 & 2). Bob generates a nonce and outputs a commitment to his nonce (Step 3), Alice outputs a nonce (Step 4), and Bob reveals his nonce (Step 5). Alice and Bob each establish their transcript of values g^x, g^y, N_a, N_b and check that the first few characters of their transcripts – which we write as $\texttt{short}(g^x, g^y, N_a, N_b)$ – match using their out of band channel (Step 6). Alice and Bob can use the Diffie-Hellman key g^{xy}.

The rationale behind the protocol is that: checking the transcripts on an authenticated channel guarantees the key is shared between Alice and Bob. However, Alice and Bob are only required to check a few characters of the transcript, because the authenticated channel is low-bandwidth, which limits the number of characters that can be checked. Formally, we derive the low-entropy string of the characters that should be checked by applying function $\texttt{short}$ to the values g^x, g^y, N_a, N_b.

Fig. 5. BlueTooth Simple Pairing

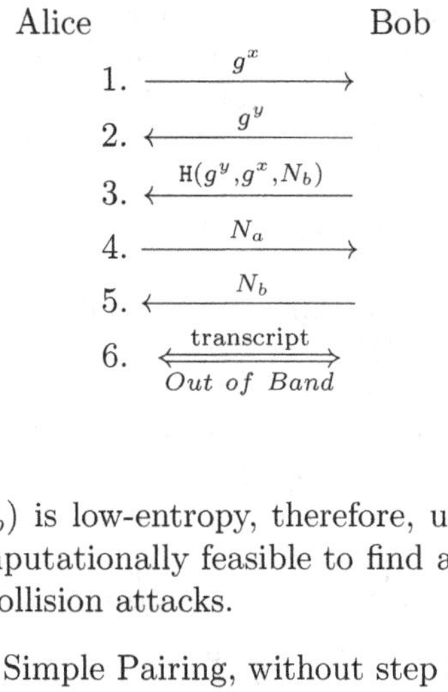

Collision attacks. String $\texttt{short}(g^x, g^y, N_a, N_b)$ is low-entropy, therefore, unlike computing a hash on g^x, g^y, N_a, N_b, it is computationally feasible to find a collision. The following example demonstrates collision attacks.

Example 4. Consider a variant of BlueTooth Simple Pairing, without step 3. In this protocol, the attacker can replace Alice's message g^x with g^z and Bob's message N_b with N_e such that $\texttt{short}(g^z, g^y, N_a, N_b) = \texttt{short}(g^x, g^z, N_a, N_e)$. (This would require the attacker to make many guesses for the nonce N_e.) Given that Alice and Bob would now see the same low-entropy string, the attacker can impersonate Alice.

Such an attack is prevented in BlueTooth Simple Pairing, by forcing both participants to commit to their nonces before they see the other participant's nonce. Alice must send her nonce first, and Bob must send a hash of this nonce before he sees Alice's Nonce. Alice will check that this nonce matches the hash between steps 5 and 6 of the protocol. This ensures that the attacker never has the opportunity to launch an impersonation attack.

We remark that collision attacks are conceptually different from guessing attacks against weak secrets [6,16], which occur when an attacker gets enough information from a protocol to verify a guess of a value, which is low entropy. The kind of brute force attack we describe here occurs when an attacker has some control over the inputs to a high-entropy function and needs to force the short code based on the output of that function to equal a certain value. In particular, if an attacker controls one input and knows the values of all the other inputs, the attacker can generated a large number of possible inputs and, by brute force, find an input of their own that makes the output of the function produce a value that matches any short code they wish.

6.1   Applied pi Calculus Model

Our model assumes that an attacker can generate sufficiently many transcripts such that distinct transcripts share the same first few characters. That is, given $\mathtt{short}(M_1, M_2, M_3, M_4)$, the adversary can compute $\mathtt{short}(N_1, N_2, N_3, N_4)$ such that $\mathtt{short}(M_1, M_2, M_3, M_4) = \mathtt{short}(N_1, N_2, N_3, N_4)$. Function $\mathtt{bruteforce}$ captures this. Moreover, we supplement $\mathtt{short}$ with $\mathtt{shortb}$ to enable automated analysis.

We construct a signature $\Sigma = \{\mathtt{g},\mathtt{f},\mathtt{sdec},\mathtt{senc},\mathtt{H},\mathtt{bruteforce},\mathtt{short},\mathtt{shortb}\}$, where $\mathtt{g}$ is a unary function, $\mathtt{sdec}$, $\mathtt{senc}$ and $\mathtt{f}$ are binary functions, $\mathtt{H}$ is a ternary function, and $\mathtt{bruteforce}$, $\mathtt{short}$ and $\mathtt{shortb}$ take four arguments. Function $\mathtt{H}$ represents a hash function, $\mathtt{sdec}$ and $\mathtt{senc}$ capture symmetric encryption, i.e., $\mathtt{def}(\mathtt{short}) = \{\mathtt{sdec}(x, \mathtt{senc}(x, y)) \rightarrow y\}$, and the purpose of the remaining functions is explained below.

Diffie-Hellman key agreement is modelled in the standard fashion [10, §9.1] using functions $\mathtt{f}$ and $\mathtt{g}$ and the following equation:

$$\mathtt{f}(x, \mathtt{g}(y)) = \mathtt{f}(y, \mathtt{g}(x))$$

which allows us to capture $(g^x)^y = (g^y)^x$. (A more general setting is beyond the scope of [10, §9.1].)

Function $\mathtt{shortb}$ is used to model a low-entropy string derived from its input. For instance, $\mathtt{shortb}(g^x, g^y, N_A, N_B)$ represents a low-entropy string derived from terms g^x, g^y, N_A, and N_B. To capture collision attacks, function $\mathtt{shortb}$ is not used directly (that is, we do not use $\mathtt{shortb}$ in processes), instead, destructor $\mathtt{short}$ is used and we map occurrences of $\mathtt{short}$ to $\mathtt{shortb}$ using the following rewrite rule:

$$\mathtt{short}(w, x, y, z) \rightarrow \mathtt{shortb}(w, x, y, z)$$

Moreover, we add the following rewrite rules to capture collisions:

$$\mathtt{short}(w, x, y, \mathtt{bruteforce}(w, x, y, \mathtt{shortb}(\hat{w}, \hat{x}, \hat{y}, \hat{z}))) \rightarrow \mathtt{shortb}(\hat{w}, \hat{x}, \hat{y}, \hat{z})$$
$$\mathtt{short}(w, x, \mathtt{bruteforce}(w, x, z, \mathtt{shortb}(\hat{w}, \hat{x}, \hat{y}, \hat{z})), z) \rightarrow \mathtt{shortb}(\hat{w}, \hat{x}, \hat{y}, \hat{z})$$
$$\mathtt{short}(w, \mathtt{bruteforce}(w, y, z, \mathtt{shortb}(\hat{w}, \hat{x}, \hat{y}, \hat{z})), y, z) \rightarrow \mathtt{shortb}(\hat{w}, \hat{x}, \hat{y}, \hat{z})$$
$$\mathtt{short}(\mathtt{bruteforce}(x, y, z, \mathtt{shortb}(\hat{w}, \hat{x}, \hat{y}, \hat{z})), x, y, z) \rightarrow \mathtt{shortb}(\hat{w}, \hat{x}, \hat{y}, \hat{z})$$

It follows from our rewrite rules that

$$\text{short}(M_1, M_2, M_3, M_4) \rightarrow \text{shortb}(M_1, M_2, M_3, M_4)$$

and

$$\text{short}(N_1, N_2, N_3, \text{bruteforce}(N_1, N_2, N_3, \text{shortb}(M_1, M_2, M_3, M_4)))$$
$$\rightarrow \text{shortb}(M_1, M_2, M_3, M_4))$$

i.e., terms $\text{short}(M_1, M_2, M_3, M_4)$ and $\text{short}(N_1, N_2, N_3, \text{bruteforce}(N_1, N_2, N_3, \text{shortb}(M_1, M_2, M_3, M_4)))$ collide.

The ProVerif source of this, and all our other examples, are available from the following URL: http://www.cs.bham.ac.uk/~tpc/projects/falseattacks.

6.2   Analysis

We analyse this protocol by adding in the exchange of a value at the end of the protocol using the key g^{xy} and testing for the secrecy of this value. Running our model in ProVerif we find that it results in a false attack, due to the commitment problem that was discussed above. The tool suggests that the attacker can send a dummy commitment value and then observe nonces N_a and N_b. The attacker can then use a brute forced value based on N_b and start the protocol again with a commitment to this new brute forced value, however, in this second run of the protocol Bob would be using a different N_b value and so the attack is a false one.

Applying Theorem 1 to transform the BlueTooth Protocol results in a model (available from the aforementioned URL) for which ProVerif can verify that the secrecy of *seckey* in less than a second, and so Theorem 1 then tells us that, in spite of the false attack, the original protocol is also secure. If we remove the check of the commitment sent in step 3 of the protocol, then ProVerif finds the attack in which the attacker performs a man in the middle attack using the bruteforce function to find a value which matches the short code sent between Alice and Bob.

6.3   Case Study III: The Simplified Simple Pairing Protocol

Our final case study proposes a simplified version of the Bluetooth Simple Pairing protocol (Figure 6). Our new protocol merges the tasks of the Diffie-Hellman exponents and the nonces. The out of band channel is used for confirmations of a short code based on the Diffie-Hellman key. We note that in the specification of the Bluetooth Simple Pairing protocol [23] the Diffie-Hellman steps of the protocol are presented as a method of stopping eavesdropping attacks, and the steps using the nonce values are presented quite separately as a method of stopping active attacks; the contribution of our protocol is to show that these steps can be merged. We also note that in the Bluetooth Simple Pairing protocol the channel is protected by the entropy of the secret Diffie-Hellman values and the nonces, whereas in our new protocol it is just protected by the entropy of the secret Diffie-Hellman values. Therefore, for our protocol to be secure, the secret Diffie-Hellman values must be high-entropy and fresh; this is not currently an explicit requirement stated in the Bluetooth specification.

Fig. 6. SSP: Simplified Simple Pairing

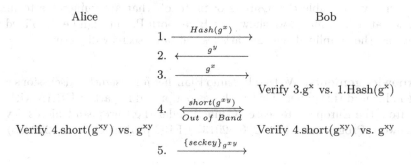

Our new protocol starts with Alice sending a commitment to a particular Diffie-Hellman exponent. Bob then sends his exponent and Alice replies by sending her's. Bob must check that the exponent he receives matches the commitment to avoid the brute force attack described above. Alice and Bob then compare the transcript of the key on their out of bound channel. The nonces used in the Bluetooth Simple Pairing protocol are no longer needed, as the freshness guarantees are now provided by the values x and y.

A brute force attack may be tried against the short string in this protocol. To allow this in our model, we adapt the rules for `bruteforce` and `short` to work against Diffie-Hellman exponents. In this case, the `short` function is applied to the `f` function i.e., `short(f(s,g(t)))` represents the short string generated from the Diffie-Hellman key `f(s,g(t))`.

Given `g(t)` and `M`, the attacker can derive a term `N` such that `short(f(N,g(t)))` = `short(M)`, and we write this `N` value as `bruteforce(g(t),M)` and capture the desired relation using the following rewrite rules:

$$\texttt{short}(x) \rightarrow \texttt{shortb}(x)$$
$$\texttt{short}(\texttt{f}(\texttt{bruteforce}(x, \texttt{shortb}(y)), x)) \rightarrow \texttt{shortb}(y)$$
$$\texttt{short}(y, \texttt{f}(\texttt{bruteforce}(y, \texttt{shortb}(x)))) \rightarrow \texttt{shortb}(x)$$

It follows from the above rules that given `g(t)` and `f(s,g(t))`, the attacker can derive `bruteforce(g(t),short(f(s,g(t))))` such that `short(f(bruteforce(g(t),` `short(f(s,g(t)))),g(t)))` = `short(f(s,g(t)))`, thereby modelling a brute force attack against the Diffie-Hellman exponents.

Analysing this scheme using ProVerif results in the discovery of a false attack, whereas Theorem 1 allows us to verify the secrecy of *seckey*.

7   Conclusion

We have shown how false atacks can be avoided when analysing secrecy with ProVerif. Our method works by inserting phases into processes such that they enforce an ordering on Horn clauses. We demonstrate the applicability of our methodology by analysing BlueTooth Pairing. This case study leads use to develop theory to enable the analysis of protocols that are vulnerable to impersonation attacks. Finally, we show that BlueTooth Pairing can be simplified and show that the simplified scheme satisfies the same secrecy objectives.

Acknowledgements. We thank Bruno Blanchet for insightful discussions which have influenced this paper. This work was performed in part at INRIA with support from the European Research Council under the European Union's Seventh Framework Programme (FP7/2007-2013) / ERC project *CRYSP* (259639).

References

1. Abadi, M., Blanchet, B., Fournet, C.: Just Fast Keying in the Pi Calculus. ACM Transactions on Information and System Security 10(3) (2007)
2. Abadi, M., Fournet, C.: Mobile values, new names, and secure communication. In: POPL 2001: 28th ACM SIGPLAN-SIGACT Symposium on Principles of Programming Languages, pp. 104–115. ACM Press (2001)
3. Allamigeon, X., Blanchet, B.: Reconstruction of Attacks against Cryptographic Protocols. In: CSFW 2005: 18th Computer Security Foundations Workshop, pp. 140–154. IEEE Computer Society (2005)
4. Arapinis, M., Cortier, V., Kremer, S., Ryan, M.: Practical everlasting privacy. In: Basin, D., Mitchell, J.C. (eds.) POST 2013. LNCS, vol. 7796, pp. 21–40. Springer, Heidelberg (2013)
5. Backes, M., Hriţcu, C., Maffei, M.: Automated Verification of Remote Electronic Voting Protocols in the Applied Pi-calculus. In: CSF 2008: 21st IEEE Computer Security Foundations Symposium, pp. 195–209. IEEE Computer Society (2008)
6. Baudet, M.: Deciding security of protocols against off-line guessing attacks. In: Proc. 12th ACM Conference on Computer and Communications Security (CCS 2005), pp. 16–25. ACM Press (2005)
7. Baudet, M.: Sécurité des protocoles cryptographiques: Aspects logiques et calculatoires. PhD thesis, Laboratoire Spécification et Vérification, ENS Cachan, France (2007)
8. Blanchet, B.: An efficient cryptographic protocol verifier based on Prolog rules. In: CSFW 2001: 14th IEEE Computer Security Foundations Workshop, pp. 82–96. IEEE Computer Society (2001)
9. Blanchet, B.: From Secrecy to Authenticity in Security Protocols. In: Hermenegildo, M.V., Puebla, G. (eds.) SAS 2002. LNCS, vol. 2477, pp. 342–359. Springer, Heidelberg (2002)
10. Blanchet, B.: Automatic Verification of Correspondences for Security Protocols. Journal of Computer Security 17(4), 363–434 (2009)
11. Blanchet, B.: Private email communication (November 12, 2012)

12. Blanchet, B.: Security Protocol Verification: Symbolic and Computational Models. In: Degano, P., Guttman, J.D. (eds.) Principles of Security and Trust. LNCS, vol. 7215, pp. 3–29. Springer, Heidelberg (2012)
13. Blanchet, B., Abadi, M., Fournet, C.: Automated verification of selected equivalences for security protocols. Journal of Logic and Algebraic Programming 75(1), 3–51 (2008)
14. Blanchet, B., Cortier, V.: Private email communication (November 13, 2012)
15. Blanchet, B., Smyth, B.: ProVerif: Automatic Cryptographic Protocol Verifier User Manual & Tutorial (2011), http://www.proverif.ens.fr/
16. Blanchet, B., Smyth, B., Cheval, V.: Proverif 1.88: Automatic cryptographic protocol verifier, user manual and tutorial (2013)
17. Chang, R., Shmatikov, V.: Formal analysis of authentication in bluetooth device pairing. In: Foundations of Computer Security and Automated Reasoning for Security Protocol Analysis (2007)
18. Chen, L., Ryan, M.: Attack, Solution and Verification for Shared Authorisation Data in TCG TPM. In: Degano, P., Guttman, J.D. (eds.) FAST 2009. LNCS, vol. 5983, pp. 201–216. Springer, Heidelberg (2010)
19. Delaune, S., Kremer, S., Ryan, M.D., Steel, G.: Formal analysis of protocols based on tpm state registers. In: CSF 2011: 24th IEEE Computer Security Foundations Symposium, pp. 66–80. IEEE (2011)
20. Delaune, S., Ryan, M.D., Smyth, B.: Automatic verification of privacy properties in the applied pi-calculus. In: Karabulut, Y., Mitchell, J., Herrmann, P., Jensen, C.D. (eds.) IFIPTM 2008: 2nd Joint iTrust and PST Conferences on Privacy, Trust Management and Security. IFIP, vol. 263, pp. 263–278. Springer, Heidelberg (2008)
21. Durgin, N.A., Lincoln, P., Mitchell, J.C., Scedrov, A.: Multiset rewriting and the complexity of bounded security protocols. Journal of Computer Security 12(2), 247–311 (2004)
22. Bluetooth Special Interest Group. Specification of the bluetooth system (2001)
23. Bluetooth Special Interest Group. Simple pairing whitepaper (2006)
24. Breaking, G.L.: Breaking and Fixing the Needham-Schroeder Public-Key Protocol using FDR. In: Margaria, T., Steffen, B. (eds.) TACAS 1996. LNCS, vol. 1055, pp. 147–166. Springer, Heidelberg (1996)
25. Meadows, C.: Open Issues in Formal Methods for Cryptographic Protocol Analysis. In: Gorodetski, V.I., Skormin, V.A., Popyack, L.J. (eds.) MMM-ACNS 2001. LNCS, vol. 2052, p. 21. Springer, Heidelberg (2001)
26. Needham, R.M., Schroeder, M.D.: Using Encryption for Authentication in Large Networks of Computers. Communications of the ACM 21(12), 993–999 (1978)
27. Ryan, M.D., Smyth, B.: Applied pi calculus. In: Cortier, V., Kremer, S. (eds.) Formal Models and Techniques for Analyzing Security Protocols, ch. 6. IOS Press (2011)
28. Smyth, B., Ryan, M.D., Chen, L.: Formal analysis of privacy in Direct Anonymous Attestation schemes (2012)
29. Zhao, F., Hanatani, Y., Komano, Y., Smyth, B., Ito, S., Kambayashi, T.: Secure Authenticated Key Exchange with Revocation for Smart Grid. In: ISGT 2012: 3rd IEEE Power & Energy Society Conference on Innovative Smart Grid Technologies, pp. 1–8 (2012)

Generalizing Multi-party Contract Signing

Sjouke Mauw[1] and Saša Radomirović[2]

[1] CSC/SnT, University of Luxembourg
`sjouke.mauw@uni.lu`
[2] Institute of Information Security, Dept. of Computer Science, ETH Zurich
`sasa.radomirovic@inf.ethz.ch`

Abstract. Multi-party contract signing (MPCS) protocols allow a group of signers to exchange signatures on a predefined contract. Previous approaches considered either completely linear protocols or fully parallel broadcasting protocols. We introduce the new class of DAG MPCS protocols which combines parallel and linear execution and allows for parallelism even within a signer role. This generalization is useful in practical applications where the set of signers has a hierarchical structure, such as chaining of service level agreements and subcontracting.

Our novel DAG MPCS protocols are represented by directed acyclic graphs and equipped with a labeled transition system semantics. We define the notion of *abort-chaining sequences* and prove that a DAG MPCS protocol satisfies fairness if and only if it does not have an abort-chaining sequence. We exhibit several examples of optimistic fair DAG MPCS protocols. The fairness of these protocols follows from our theory and has additionally been verified with our automated tool.

We define two complexity measures for DAG MPCS protocols, related to execution time and total number of messages exchanged. We prove lower bounds for fair DAG MPCS protocols in terms of these measures.

1 Introduction

A multi-party contract signing (MPCS) protocol is a communication protocol that allows a number of parties to sign a digital contract. The need for MPCS protocols arises, for instance, in the context of service level agreements (SLAs) and in supply chain contracting. In these domains (electronic) contract negotiations and signing are still mainly bilateral. Instead of negotiating and signing one multi-party contract, in practice, multiple bilateral negotiations are conducted in parallel [20]. Because negotiations can fail, parties may end up with just a subset of the pursued bilateral contracts. If a party is missing contracts with providers or subcontractors, it faces an *overcommitment* problem. If contracts with customers are missing, it has an *overpurchasing* problem [8]. Both problems can be prevented by using fair multi-party contract signing protocols.

Existing optimistic MPCS protocols come in two flavors. *Linear* MPCS protocols require that at any point in time at most one signer has enough information to proceed in his role by sending messages to other signers. *Broadcast* MPCS protocols specify a number of communication rounds in each of which all signers

© Springer-Verlag Berlin Heidelberg 2015
R. Focardi and A. Myers (Eds.): POST 2015, LNCS 9036, pp. 156–175, 2015.
DOI: 10.1007/978-3-662-46666-7_9

send or broadcast messages to each other. However, neither of the two kinds of protocols is suitable for SLAs or supply chain contracting. The reason is that in both domains, the set of contractors typically has a hierarchical structure, consisting of main contractors and levels of subcontractors. It is undesirable (and perhaps even infeasible) for the main contracting partners and their subcontractors to directly communicate with another partner's subcontractors. This restriction immediately excludes broadcast protocols as potential solutions and forces linear protocols to be impractically large.

In this paper we introduce MPCS protocol specifications that support arbitrary combinations of linear and parallel actions, even within a protocol role. The message flow of such protocols can be specified as a directed acyclic graph (DAG) and we therefore refer to them as *DAG* MPCS protocols.

A central requirement for MPCS protocols is *fairness*. This means that either all honest signers get all signatures on the negotiated contract or nobody gets the honest signers' signatures. It is well known that in asynchronous communication networks, a deterministic MPCS protocol requires a trusted third party (TTP) to achieve fairness [5]. *Optimistic* MPCS protocols [1] involve the TTP only when conflicts or faults occur and thus prevent the TTP from becoming a bottleneck. We focus on optimistic protocols in this paper.

DAG MPCS protocols not only allow for better solutions to the subcontracting problem, but also have further advantages over linear and broadcast MPCS protocols and we design three novel MPCS protocols that demonstrate this. One such advantage concerns communication complexity. Linear protocols can reach the minimal number of messages necessary to be exchanged in fair MPCS protocols at the cost of a high number of protocol "rounds". We call this the *parallel complexity*, which is a generalization of the round complexity measure for broadcast protocols, and define it in Section 4.3. Conversely, broadcast protocols can attain the minimal number of protocol rounds necessary for fair MPCS, but at the cost of a high message complexity. We demonstrate that DAG MPCS protocols can simultaneously attain best possible order of magnitude for both complexity measures.

As discussed in our related work section, the design of fair MPCS protocols has proven to be non-trivial and error-prone. We therefore not only prove our three novel DAG MPCS protocols to be fair, but we also derive necessary and sufficient conditions for fairness of any optimistic DAG MPCS protocol. These conditions can be implemented and verified automatically, but they are still non-trivial. Therefore, for a slightly restricted class of DAG protocols, we additionally derive a fairness criterion that is easy to verify.

Contributions. Our main contributions are (i) the definition of a syntax and interleaving semantics of DAG MPCS protocols (Section 4.1); (ii) the definition of the message complexity and parallel complexity of such protocols (Section 4.3); (iii) a method to derive a full MPCS specification from a *skeletal graph*, including the TTP logic (Section 5); (iv) necessary and sufficient conditions for fairness of DAG MPCS protocols (Section 6); (v) minimal complexity bounds for DAG

MPCS protocols (Section 7.1); (vi) novel fair MPCS protocols (Section 7.2); (vii) a software tool that verifies whether a given MPCS protocol is fair.[1]

2   Related Work

We build on the body of work that has been published in the field of fair optimistic MPCS protocols in asynchronous networks. The first such protocols were proposed by Baum-Waidner and Waidner [2], viz. a round-based broadcast protocol and a related round-based linear protocol. They showed subsequently [3] that these protocols are round-optimal. This is a complexity measure that is related to, but less general than, parallel complexity defined in the present paper.

Garay et al. [6] introduced the notion of *abuse-free* contract signing. They developed the technique of *private contract signature* and used it to create abuse-free two-party and three-party contract signing protocols. Garay and Mac-Kenzie [7] proposed MPCS protocols which were later shown to be unfair using the model checker Mocha and improved by Chadha et al. [4]. Mukhamedov and Ryan [17] developed the notion of *abort chaining attacks* and used such attacks to show that Chadha et al.'s improved version does not satisfy fairness in cases where there are more than five signers. They introduced a new optimistic MPCS protocol and proved fairness for their protocol by hand and used the NuSMV model checker to verify the case of five signers. Zhang et al. [21] have used Mocha to analyze the protocols of Mukhamedov and Ryan and of Mauw et al. [15].

Mauw et al. [15] used the notion of abort chaining to establish a lower bound on the message complexity of linear fair MPCS protocols. This complexity measure is generalized in the present paper to DAG MPCS protocols. Kordy and Radomirović [10] have shown an explicit construction for fair linear MPCS protocols. The construction covers in particular the protocols proposed by Mukhamedov and Ryan [17] and the linear protocol of Baum-Waidner and Waidner [2], but not the broadcast protocols. The DAG MPCS protocol model and fairness results developed in the present paper encompass both types of protocols. MPCS protocols combining linear and parallel behaviour have not been studied yet.

Apart from new theoretical insights to be gained from designing and studying DAG MPCS protocols, we anticipate interesting application domains in which multiple parties establish a number of related contracts, such as SLAs. Emerging business models like Software as a Service require a negotiation to balance a customer's requirements against a service provider's capabilities. The result of such a negotiation is often complicated by the dependencies between several contracts [13] and multi-party protocols may serve to mitigate this problem. Karaenke and Kirn [8] propose a multi-tier negotiation protocol to mitigate the problems of overcommitment and overpurchasing. They formally verify that the protocol solves the two observed problems, but do not consider the fairness problem. SLAs and negotiation protocols have also been studied in the multi-agent community. An example is the work of Kraus [11] who defines a multi-party

---

[1] Proofs of theorems and additional results including a description of the tool and a link to it are given in the extended version of this paper [14].

negotiation protocol in which agreement is reached if all agents accept an offer. If the offer is rejected by at least one agent, a new offer will be negotiated.

Another interesting application area concerns *supply chain contracting* [12]. A supply chain consists of a series of firms involved in the production of a product or service with potentially complex contractual relationships. Most literature in this area focuses on economic aspects, like pricing strategies. An exception is the recent work of Pavlov and Katok [9] in which fairness is studied from a game-theoretic point of view. The study of multi-party signing protocols and multi-contract protocols has only recently been identified as an interesting research topic in this application area [19].

3   Preliminaries

3.1   Multi-party Contract Signing

The purpose of a multi-party contract signing protocol is to allow a number of parties to sign a digital contract in a fair way. In this section we recall the basic notions pertaining to MPCS protocols. We use A to denote the set of signers involved in a protocol, $\mathfrak{C}$ to denote the contract, and T to denote the TTP.

A signer is considered *honest* (cf. Definition 5) if it faithfully executes the protocol specification. An MPCS protocol is said to be *optimistic* if its execution in absence of adversarial behaviour and failures and with all honest signers results in signed contracts for all participants without any involvement of T. Optimistic MPCS protocols consist of two subprotocols: the *main* protocol that specifies the exchange of *promises* and *signatures* by the signers, and the *resolve* protocol that describes the interaction between the agents and T in case of a failure in the main protocol. A promise made by a signer indicates the intent to sign $\mathfrak{C}$. A promise $\wp_P(m, x, Q, \text{T})$ can only be generated by signer $P \in A$. The content (m, x) can be extracted from the promise and the promise can be verified by signer $Q \in A$ and by T. A signature $\mathcal{S}_P(m)$ can only be generated by P and by T, if T has a promise $\wp_P(m, x, Q, \text{T})$. The content m can be extracted and the signature can be verified by anybody. Cryptographic schemes that allow for the above properties are digital signature schemes and private contract signatures [6].

MPCS protocols must satisfy at least two security requirements, namely *fairness* and *timeliness*. An optimistic MPCS protocol for contract $\mathfrak{C}$ is said to be *fair* for an honest signer P if whenever some signer $Q \neq P$ obtains a signature on $\mathfrak{C}$ from P, then P can obtain a signature on $\mathfrak{C}$ from all signers participating in the protocol. An optimistic MPCS protocol is said to satisfy *timeliness*, if each signer has a recourse to stop endless waiting for expected messages. The fairness requirement will be the guiding principle for our investigations and timeliness will be implied by the communication model together with the behaviour of the TTP. A formal definition of fairness is given in Section 6.

3.2   Graphs

Let $G = (V, E)$ with $E \subseteq V \times V$ be a directed acyclic graph. Let $v, w \in V$ be vertices. We say that v *causally precedes* w, denoted $v \prec w$, if there is a directed path from v to w in the graph. We write $v \preceq w$ for $v \prec w \vee v = w$. We extend *causal precedence* to the set $V \cup E$ as follows. Given two edges $(v, w), (v', w') \in E$, we say that (v, w) *causally precedes* (v', w') and write $(v, w) \prec (v', w')$, if $w \preceq v'$. Similarly, we write $v \prec (v', w')$ if $v \preceq v'$ and $(v, w) \prec v'$ if $w \preceq v'$. Let $x, y \in V \cup E$. If x causally precedes y we also say that y *causally follows* x. We say that a set $S \subseteq V \cup E$ is *causally closed* if it contains all causally preceding vertices and edges of its elements, i.e., $\forall x \in S, y \in V \cup E : y \prec x \implies y \in S$.

By $\text{in}(v) \subseteq E$ we denote the set of edges incoming to v and by $\text{out}(v) \subseteq E$ the set of edges outgoing from v. Formally, we have $\text{in}(v) = \{(w, v) \in E \mid w \in V\}$ and $\text{out}(v) = \{(v, w) \in E \mid w \in V\}$.

3.3   Assumptions

The communication between signers is asynchronous and messages can get lost or be delayed arbitrarily long. The communication channels between signers and the TTP T are assumed to be *resilient*. In order to simplify our reasoning, we assume that the channels between protocol participants are confidential and authentic. We consider the problem of delivering confidential and authentic messages in a Dolev-Yao intruder model to be orthogonal to the present problem setting.

We assume that $\mathfrak{C}$ contains the contract text along with fresh values (contributed by every signer) which prevent different protocol executions from generating interchangeable protocol messages. Furthermore we assume that $\mathfrak{C}$ contains all information that T needs in order to reach a decision regarding the contract in case it is contacted by a signer. This information contains the protocol specification, an identifier for T, identifiers for the signers involved in the protocol, and the assignment of signers to protocol roles in the protocol specification.

We assume the existence of a designated resolution process per signer which coordinates the various resolution requests of the signer's parallel threads. It will ensure that T is contacted at most once by the signer. After having received the first request from one of the signer's threads, this resolution process will contact T on behalf of the signer and store T's reply. This reply will be forwarded to all of the signer's threads whenever they request resolution.

4   DAG Protocols

Our DAG protocol model is a multi-party protocol model in an asynchronous network with a TTP and an adversary that controls a subset of parties.

4.1   Specification and Execution Model

A *DAG protocol specification* (or simply, a *protocol specification*) is a directed acyclic graph in which the vertices represent the state of a signer and the edges represent either a causal dependency between two states (an ε-edge) or the sending of a message. A vertex' outgoing edges can be executed in parallel. Edges labeled with *exit* denote that a signer contacts T.

Definition 1. *Let R be a set of roles such that $T \notin R$ and M a set of messages. Let ε and exit be two symbols, such that ε, exit $\notin M$. By M_ε^{exit} and R_T we denote the sets $M_\varepsilon^{exit} = M \cup \{\varepsilon, exit\}$ and $R_T = R \cup \{T\}$, respectively. A DAG protocol specification is a labeled directed acyclic graph $\mathcal{P} = (V, E, r, \mu, \delta)$, where*

1. *(V, E) is a directed acyclic graph;*
2. *$r: V \to R_T$ is a labeling function assigning roles to vertices;*
3. *$\mu: E \to M_\varepsilon^{exit}$ is an edge-labeling function that satisfies*
   (a) $\forall (v, v') \in E: \mu(v, v') = \varepsilon \implies r(v) = r(v')$,
   (b) $\forall (v, v') \in E: \mu(v, v') = exit \implies r(v') = T$;
4. *$\delta: M^* \to M$ is a function associated with exit-labeled edges.*

A message edge (v, v') specifies that $\mu(v, v') = m$ is to be sent from role $r(v)$ to role $r(v')$. An ε-edge (v, v') represents internal progress of role $r(v) = r(v')$ and allows to specify a causal order in the role's events. An exit edge denotes that a role can contact the TTP. The TTP then uses the function δ to determine a reply to the requesting role, based on the sequence of messages that it has received. In Section 5 exit messages and the δ function are used to model the resolve protocol of the TTP.

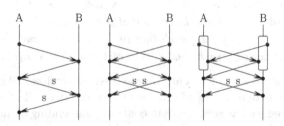

Fig. 1. Linear, broadcast, and the novel DAG MPCS protocols

We give three examples of DAG protocols in Figure 1, represented as Message Sequence Charts (MSCs). The dots denote the vertices, which we group vertically below their corresponding role names. Vertical lines in the MSCs correspond to ε-edges and horizontal or diagonal edges represent message edges. We mark edges labeled with signing messages with an "s" and we leave out the edge labels of promise messages. We do not display exit edges, they are implied by the MPCS protocol specification. A box represents the splitting of a role into two parallel threads, which join again at the end of the box. We revert to a traditional representation of labeled DAGs if it is more convenient (see, e.g., Figure 2).

The first protocol in Figure 1 is a classical linear 2-party contract signing protocol. It consists of one round of promises followed by a round of exchanging signatures. The second protocol is the classical broadcast protocol for two signers. It consists of two rounds of promises, followed by one round of signatures. The third protocol is a novel DAG protocol, showing the power of in-role parallelism. It is derived from the broadcasting protocol by observing that its fairness does not depend on the causal order of the first two vertices of each of the roles.

Let $\mathcal{P} = (V, E, r, \mu, \delta)$ be a protocol specification. The *restriction* of $\mathcal{P}$ to role P, denoted by $\mathcal{P}_P$, is the protocol specification $(V_P, E_P, r_P, \mu_P, \delta_P)$, where

$$E_P = \{(v, v') \in E \mid r(v) = P \vee r(v') = P\}, \quad V_P = \{v, v' \in V \mid (v, v') \in E_P\},$$
$$r_P(v) = r(v) \text{ for } v \in V_P, \quad \mu_P(e) = \mu(e) \text{ for } e \in E_P, \quad \text{and} \quad \delta_P = \delta.$$

The execution state of a protocol consists of the set of events, connected to vertices or edges, that have been executed.

Definition 2. *Let $\mathcal{P} = (V, E, r, \mu, \delta)$ be a protocol specification. A* state *of $\mathcal{P}$ is a set $s \subseteq V \cup E$. The set of states of $\mathcal{P}$ is denoted by $\mathcal{S}_\mathcal{P}$. The* initial state *of $\mathcal{P}$ is defined as $s_0 = \emptyset$.*

In order to give DAG protocols a semantics, we first define the *transition relation* between states of a protocol.

Definition 3. *Let $\mathcal{P} = (V, E, r, \mu, \delta)$ be a protocol specification, $L = \{\varepsilon, send, recv, exit\}$ the set of transition labels, and $s, s' \in \mathcal{S}_\mathcal{P}$ the states of $\mathcal{P}$. We say that $\mathcal{P}$ transitions with label α from state s into s', denoted by $s \overset{\alpha}{\leadsto} s'$, iff $s \neq s'$ and one of the following conditions holds*

1. *$\alpha = recv$ and $\exists v \in V$, such that $in(v) \subseteq s$ and $s' = s \cup \{v\}$,*
2. *$\alpha = send$ and $\exists m \in M, e \in E$, such that $\mu(e) = m$, and $s' = s \cup \{e\}$,*
3. *$\alpha = \varepsilon$ and $\exists e = (v, v') \in E$, such that $\mu(e) = \varepsilon$, $v \in s$ and $s' = s \cup \{e\}$,*
4. *$\alpha = exit$ and $\exists e \in E$, such that $\mu(e) = exit$ and $s' = s \cup \{e\}$.*

In Definition 3, receive events are represented by vertices, all other events by edges. By the first condition, a receive event can only occur if all events assigned to the incoming edges have occurred. In contrast, the sending of messages (second condition) can take place at any time. The third condition states that an ε-edge can be executed if the event on which it causally depends has been executed. Finally, like send events, an exit event can occur at any time. Every event may occur at most once, however. This is ensured by the condition $s' \neq s$.

The transitions model all possible behavior of the system. The behavior of honest agents in the system will be restricted as detailed in the following subsection. We denote sequences by $[a_0, a_1, \ldots, a_l]$ and the concatenation of two sequences σ_1, σ_2 by $\sigma_1 \cdot \sigma_2$.

Definition 4. *Let $\mathcal{P} = (V, E, r, \mu, \delta)$ be a protocol specification and $L = \{\varepsilon, send, recv, exit\}$ a set of labels. The* semantics *of $\mathcal{P}$ is the labeled transition system $(\mathcal{S}_\mathcal{P}, L, \leadsto, s_0)$, which is a graph consisting of vertices $\mathcal{S}_\mathcal{P}$ and edges $\leadsto$ with start state s_0. An* execution *of $\mathcal{P}$ is a finite sequence $\rho = [s_0, \alpha_1, s_1, \ldots, \alpha_l, s_l]$, $l \geq 0$, such that $\forall i \in \{0, \ldots, l-1\}$: $s_i \overset{\alpha_{i+1}}{\leadsto} s_{i+1}$. The set of all executions of $\mathcal{P}$ is denoted by $Exe(\mathcal{P})$.*

If $\rho = [s_0, \alpha_1, s_1, \ldots, \alpha_l, s_l]$ is an execution of $\mathcal{P}$ and $\mathcal{P}_P$ is the restriction to role P, then the *restricted* execution ρ_P is obtained inductively as follows.

1. $[s]_P = [s \cap (V_P \cup E_P)]$ for a state s.

$$2.\ ([s, \alpha, s'] \cdot \sigma)_P = \begin{cases} [s]_P \cdot \sigma_P & \text{if } [s]_P = [s']_P \\ [s]_P \cdot [\alpha] \cdot ([s'] \cdot \sigma)_P & \text{else.} \end{cases}$$

Commutativity of restriction and execution is asserted by the following lemma.

Lemma 1. *Let P be a protocol specification and P_P the restriction to role P. Then every restricted execution ρ_P is an execution of P_P.*

4.2   Adversary Model

An honest agent executes the protocol specification faithfully. The following definition specifies what this entails for a DAG protocol: the agent waits for the reception of all causally preceding messages before sending causally following messages, does not execute an *exit* edge attached to a vertex v if all messages at v have been received and never executes more than one *exit* edge (which in the context of MPCS protocols corresponds to contacting the TTP at most once), and does not send any messages which causally follow a vertex from which the *exit* edge was executed.

Definition 5. *Let P be a DAG protocol specification. An agent P is honest in an execution ρ of P, if all states s of the restricted execution ρ_P satisfy the following conditions:*

1. *s contains at most one exit edge.*
2. *If s contains no exit edge, then s is causally closed.*
3. *If s contains an exit edge $e = (v, w)$, $\mu(e) = exit$, then $v \notin s$ and $s \setminus \{e\}$ is causally closed.*

A dishonest agent is only limited by the execution model. Thus a dishonest agent can send its messages at any time and in any order, regardless of the causal precedence given in the protocol specification. A dishonest agent can execute multiple *exit* edges and may send and receive messages causally following an exit edge. Dishonest agents are controlled by a single adversary, their knowledge is shared with the adversary. The adversary can delay or block messages sent from one agent to another, but the adversary cannot prevent messages between agents and the TTP from being delivered eventually. All communication channels are authentic and confidential.

4.3   Communication Complexity

To define measures for expressing the communication complexity of DAG protocols, we introduce the notion of *closed executions*. A closed execution is a complete execution of the protocol by honest agents.

Definition 6. *Let $P = (V, E, r, \mu, \delta)$ be a protocol specification and $(S_P, L, \leadsto, s_0)$ be the semantics for P. Given $\rho = [s_0, \alpha_1, s_1, \ldots, \alpha_l, s_l] \in \text{Exe}(P)$, we say that ρ is closed if the following three conditions are satisfied*

1. s_i *is causally closed, for every* $0 \leq i \leq l$,
2. $\alpha_i \neq exit$, *for every* $1 \leq i \leq l$,
3. $\nexists \alpha \in L \setminus \{exit\}, s \in \mathcal{S}_\mathcal{P} : \rho \cdot [\alpha, s] \in \mathrm{Exe}(\mathcal{P})$.

The set of all closed executions of $\mathcal{P}$ *is denoted by* $\mathrm{Exe}_C(\mathcal{P})$.

Let $\rho = [s_0, \alpha_1, s_1, \ldots, \alpha_l, s_l]$ be an execution of a protocol $\mathcal{P}$. By $|\rho|_{send}$ we denote the number of labels α_i, for $1 \leq i \leq l$, such that $\alpha_i = send$.

Lemma 2. *For any two closed executions* ρ *and* ρ' *of a protocol* $\mathcal{P}$ *we have* $|\rho|_{send} = |\rho'|_{send}$.

The proof is given in [14]. The first measure expressing the complexity of a protocol $\mathcal{P}$ is called *message complexity*. It counts the overall number of messages that have been sent in a closed execution of a protocol $\mathcal{P}$.

Definition 7. *Let* $\mathcal{P}$ *be a protocol specification and let* $\rho \in \mathrm{Exe}_C(\mathcal{P})$. *The message complexity of* $\mathcal{P}$, *denoted by* $MC_\mathcal{P}$, *is defined as* $MC_\mathcal{P} = |\rho|_{send}$.

Lemma 2 guarantees that the message complexity of a protocol is well defined.

The second complexity measure is called *parallel complexity*. It represents the minimal time of a closed execution assuming that all events which can be executed in parallel are executed in parallel. The parallel complexity of a protocol is defined as the length of a maximal chain of causally related send edges.

Definition 8. *The* parallel complexity *of a protocol* $\mathcal{P}$, *denoted by* $PC_\mathcal{P}$, *is defined as*

$$PC_\mathcal{P} = \max_{n \in \mathbb{N}} \exists_{[e_1, e_2, \ldots, e_n] \in E^*} : \forall_{1 \leq i \leq n} : \mu(e_i) = send \wedge \forall_{1 \leq i < n} : e_i \prec e_{i+1}.$$

Example 1. The message complexity of the first protocol in Figure 1 is 4, which is known to be optimal for two signers [18]. Its parallel complexity is 4, too. The message complexity of the other two protocols is 6, but their parallel complexity is 3, which is optimal for broadcasting protocols with two signers [3].

5   DAG MPCS Protocols

We now define a class of optimistic MPCS protocols in the DAG protocol model.

5.1   Main Protocol

The key requirements we want our DAG MPCS protocol specification to satisfy, stated formally in Definition 9, are as follows. The messages exchanged between signers in the protocol are of two types, promises, denoted by $\wp()$, and signatures, denoted by $\mathcal{S}()$. Every promise contains information about the vertex from which it is sent. This is done by concatenating the contract $\mathfrak{C}$ with the vertex v the promise originates from and is denoted by $(\mathfrak{C}, v)$. The signers can contact the TTP at any time. This is modeled with exit edges: Every vertex $v \in V$ such that $r(v) \in A$ (the set of all signers) is adjacent to a unique vertex $v_T \in V$, $r(v_T) = T$. The communication with T is represented by δ. The set of vertices with outgoing signature messages is denoted by *SigSet*.

Definition 9. *Let* $\mathcal{P} = (V, E, r, \mu, \delta)$ *be a protocol specification,* $A \subset R$ *be a finite set of signers,* $\mathfrak{C}$ *be a contract, and* $SigSet \subseteq V$. $\mathcal{P}$ *is called a* DAG MPCS *protocol specification for* $\mathfrak{C}$, *if* [2]

1. $\exists! \, v_T \in V : r(v_T) = T \wedge \forall v \in V \setminus \{v_T\} : (v, v_T) \in E$,
2. $\forall v, w \in V : v \prec w \Rightarrow (v, w) \in E \vee \exists u \in V : v \prec u \prec w \wedge r(u) \in \{r(v), r(w)\}$,
3. $\forall (v, w) \in E : \mu(v, w) =$

$$
\begin{cases}
\varepsilon, & \text{if } r(v) = r(w), \\
exit, & \text{if } w = v_T, \\
\mathcal{S}_{r(v)}(\mathfrak{C}), & \text{if } v \in SigSet \wedge r(v) \neq r(w) \neq T, \\
\wp_{r(v)}(\mathfrak{C}, v, r(w), T), & \text{else.}
\end{cases}
$$

4. $\delta : M^* \to \{ \text{``abort''}, (\mathcal{S}_P(\mathfrak{C}))_{P \in A} \}$, *where* $(\mathcal{S}_P(\mathfrak{C}))_{P \in A}$ *denotes a list of signatures on* $\mathfrak{C}$, *one by each signer.*

We write $SigSet(\mathcal{P})$ *for the largest subset of* $SigSet$ *which satisfies*

$$
v \in SigSet(\mathcal{P}) \Rightarrow \exists w \in V : (v, w) \in E, \mu(v, w) \in M.
$$

The set $SigSet(\mathcal{P})$ *is called the* signing set.

We represent DAG MPCS protocols as *skeletal* graphs as shown in Figure 2a. The full graph, shown in Figure 2b, is obtained from the skeletal graph by adding all edges required by condition 2 of Definition 9 and extending μ according to condition 3. The ε edges are dashed in the graphs. The shaded vertices in the graphs indicate the vertices that are in the signing set. We define the *knowledge* $K(v)$ of a vertex v to be the set of message edges causally preceding v, and incoming to a vertex of the same role. The knowledge of a vertex represents the state right after its receive event.

$$
K(v) = \{(w, v') \in E \mid \mu(w, v') \in M, v' \preceq v, r(v') = r(v)\}
$$

We define the *pre-knowledge* $K_\prec(v)$ of a vertex v to be $K_\prec(v) = \{(w, v') \in K(v) \mid v' \prec v\}$. The pre-knowledge represents the state just *before* the vertex' receive event has taken place. We extend both definitions to sets $S \subseteq V$:

$$
K(S) = \bigcup_{v \in S} K(v) \quad \text{and} \quad K_\prec(S) = \bigcup_{v \in S} K_\prec(v).
$$

We define the *initial set* of $\mathcal{P}$, denoted $InitSet(\mathcal{P})$ to be the set of vertices of the protocol specification for which the pre-knowledge of the same role does not contain an incoming edge by every other role. Formally,

$$
v \in InitSet(\mathcal{P}) \iff \{r(w) \in A \mid (w, v') \in K_\prec(v)\} \cup \{r(v)\} \neq A
$$

The *end set* of $\mathcal{P}$, denoted $EndSet(\mathcal{P})$, is the set of vertices of the protocol specification at which the corresponding signer possesses all signatures.

$$
v \in EndSet(\mathcal{P}) \iff \{r(w) \in A \mid (w, v') \in K(v), w \in SigSet(\mathcal{P})\} \cup \{r(v)\} = A
$$

---

[2] We write $\exists!$ for unique existential quantification.

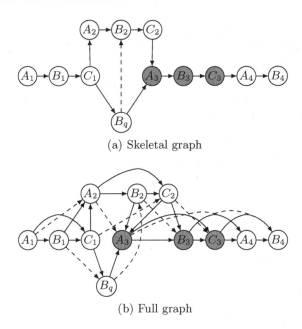

(a) Skeletal graph

(b) Full graph

Fig. 2. Skeletal and full representation of a DAG MPCS protocol

5.2 Resolve Protocol

Let $\mathcal{P} = (V, E, r, \mu, \delta)$ be a DAG MPCS protocol specification. The resolve protocol is a two-message protocol between a signer and the TTP T, initiated by the signer. The communication channels for this protocol are assumed to be resilient, confidential, and authentic. T is assumed to respond immediately to the signer. This is modeled in $\mathcal{P}$ via an exit edge from a vertex $v \in V \setminus \{v_T\}$ to the unique vertex $v_T \in V$. T's response is given by the δ function, $\delta : M^* \to \{\text{"abort"}, (S_P(\mathfrak{C}))_{P \in A}\}$. If $m_1, \ldots, m_n$ is the sequence of messages sent by the signers to T, then $\delta(m_1, \ldots, m_n)$ is T's response for the last signer in the sequence. The function will be stated formally in Definition 10.

We denote the resolve protocol in the following by $Res(\mathfrak{C}, v)$. The signer initiating $Res(\mathfrak{C}, v)$ is $r(v)$. He sends the list of messages assigned to the vertices in his pre-knowledge $K_{\prec}(v)$, prepended by $\wp_{r(v)}(\mathfrak{C}, v, r(v), T)$, to T. This demonstrates that $r(v)$ has executed all receive events causally preceding v. We denote $r(v)$'s message for T by p_v:

$$p_v = \big(\wp_{r(v)}(\mathfrak{C}, v, r(v), T), (\mu(w, v'))_{(w,v') \in K_{\prec}(v)}\big) \tag{1}$$

The promise $\wp_{r(v)}(\mathfrak{C}, v, r(v), T)$, which is the first element of p_v, is used by T to extract the contract $\mathfrak{C}$, to learn at which step in the protocol $r(v)$ claims to be, and to create a signature on behalf of $r(v)$ when necessary. All messages received from the signers are stored. T performs a deterministic decision procedure, shown in Algorithm 1, on the received message and existing stored messages and *immediately* sends back "abort" or the list of signatures $(S_P(\mathfrak{C}))_{P \in A}$.

Our decision procedure is based on [10, 17]. The input to the algorithm consists of a message m received by the T from a signer and state information which is maintained by T. T extracts the contract and the DAG MPCS protocol specification from m. For each contract $\mathfrak{C}$, T maintains the following state information. A list $Evidence_{\mathfrak{C}}$ of all messages received from signers, a set $I_{\mathfrak{C}}$ of vertices the signers contacted T from, a set $Dishonest_{\mathfrak{C}}$ of signers considered to be dishonest, and the last decision made $decision_{\mathfrak{C}}$. If T has not been contacted by any signer regarding contract $\mathfrak{C}$, then $decision_{\mathfrak{C}} =$ "abort". Else, $decision_{\mathfrak{C}}$ is equal to "abort" or the list $(\mathcal{S}_Q(\mathfrak{C})_{Q \in A})$ of signatures on $\mathfrak{C}$, one by each signer.

T verifies that the request is legitimate in that the received message m is valid and the requesting signer P is not already considered to be dishonest. If these preliminary checks pass, the message is appended to $Evidence_{\mathfrak{C}}$. This is described in Algorithm 1 in lines 1 through 9. The main part of the algorithm, starting at line 10, concerns the detection of signers who have continued the main protocol execution after executing the resolve protocol. If P has not received a promise from every other signer in the protocol (i.e. the if clause in line 10 is not satisfied), then T sends back the last decision made (line 17). This decision is an "abort" token unless T has been contacted before and decided to send back a signed contract. If P has received a promise from every other signer, T computes the set of dishonest signers (lines 11 through 13) by adding to it every signer which has carried out the resolve protocol, but can be seen to have continued the protocol execution (line 12) based on the evidence the TTP has collected. If P is the only honest signer that has contacted T until this point in time, the decision is made to henceforth return a signed contract.

Definition 10. *Let* $\mathcal{P} = (V, E, r, \mu, \delta)$ *be a DAG MPCS protocol specification and* δ_0 *the TTP decision procedure from Algorithm 1. Then* $\delta : M^* \rightarrow M$ *is defined for* $m_1, \ldots, m_n \in M$ *by*

$$\delta(m_1, \ldots, m_n) = \pi_1(\delta_1(m_1, \ldots, m_n)),$$

where π_1 *is the projection to the first coordinate and* δ_1 *is defined inductively by*

$$\delta_1() = (\text{"abort"}, \text{"abort"}, \emptyset, \emptyset, \emptyset)$$
$$\delta_1(m_1, \ldots, m_n) = \delta_0(m_n, \delta_1(m_1, \ldots, m_{n-1})).$$

Thus the δ function represents the response of the TTP in the $Res(\mathfrak{C}, v)$ protocol for all executions of $\mathcal{P}$.

6   Fairness

We say that a DAG MPCS protocol execution is fair for signer P if one of the following three conditions is true: (i) No signer has received a signature of P; (ii) P has received signatures of all other signers; (iii) P has not received an "abort" token from the TTP.

The key problem in formalizing these conditions is to capture under which circumstances the TTP responds with an "abort" token to a request by a signer.

Algorithm 1. TTP decision procedure δ_0

> **input** : $m, r, decision_{\mathfrak{C}}, Evidence_{\mathfrak{C}}, I_{\mathfrak{C}}, Dishonest_{\mathfrak{C}}$
> **output**: $r, decision_{\mathfrak{C}}, Evidence_{\mathfrak{C}}, I_{\mathfrak{C}}, Dishonest_{\mathfrak{C}}$

```
 1  if m ≠ (℘_P(𝕮, v, P, T), list) then
 2  │   r = "abort";
 3  └   return output;
 4  if P ∈ Dishonest_𝕮 ∨ ∀w ∈ V : m ≠ p_w ∨ ∃w' ∈ I_𝕮 : P = r(w') then
 5  │   Dishonest_𝕮 := Dishonest_𝕮 ∪ {P};
 6  │   r = "abort";
 7  └   return output;
 8  I_𝕮 := I_𝕮 ∪ {v};
 9  Evidence_𝕮 := (Evidence_𝕮, m);
10  if v ∉ InitSet(𝒫) then
11  │   for w ∈ I_𝕮 do
12  │   │   if w ≺ (w', x) ∈ K_≺(I_𝕮) ∧ r(w') = r(w) then
13  │   │   └   Dishonest_𝕮 := Dishonest_𝕮 ∪ {r(w)};
14  │   if ∀w ∈ I_𝕮 : r(w) ∉ Dishonest_𝕮 ⟹ r(w) = P then
15  │   └   decision_𝕮 := (𝒮_Q(𝕮))_{Q∈A};
16  r = decision_𝕮;
17  return output;
```

The TTP's response is dependent on the decision procedure which in turn depends on the order in which the TTP is contacted by the signers. Since the decision procedure is deterministic, it follows that the δ function can be determined for every execution $\rho = [s_0, \alpha_1, s_1, \ldots, s_n]$ by considering the pre-knowledge of the vertices from which the *exit* transitions are taken. Abusing notation, we will write $\delta(\rho)$ instead of $\delta(m_1, \ldots, m_k)$ where m_i are the messages sent to the TTP at the i-th *exit* transition in the execution.

Definition 11. *Let* T *be the TTP. An execution* $\rho = [s_0, \alpha_1, \ldots, s_n]$ *of* $\mathcal{P}$ *is fair for signer* P *if one of the following conditions is satisfied:*

1. *P has not sent a signature and no signer has received signatures from* T.

$$\delta(\rho) = \text{"abort"} \wedge \forall(v, w) \in s_n : r(v) = P, r(w) \neq P \Longrightarrow v \notin SigSet(\mathcal{P})$$

2. *P has received signatures from all other signers.*

$$\exists v \in s \cap EndSet(\mathcal{P}) : r(v) = P$$

3. *P has not received an "abort" token from* T.

$$\exists(v, w) \in s : r(v) = P \wedge r(w) = T \Rightarrow \delta([s_0, \ldots, s_k, exit, s_k \cup \{(v, w)\}]) \neq \text{"abort"}$$

If none of these conditions are satisfied, the execution is unfair for P.

Definition 12. *An MPCS protocol specification* $\mathcal{P}$ *is said to be fair, if every execution* ρ *of* $\mathcal{P}$ *is fair for all signers that are honest in* ρ.

6.1   Sufficient and Necessary Conditions

By the TTP decision procedure, T returns an "abort" token if contacted from a vertex $v \in InitSet(\mathcal{P})$. Thus a necessary condition for fairness is that an honest signer executes all steps of the initial set causally before all steps of the signing set that are not in the end set:

$$\forall v \in InitSet(\mathcal{P}), w \in SigSet(\mathcal{P}) \setminus EndSet(\mathcal{P}) : r(v) = r(w) \implies v \prec w \quad (2)$$

If P contacts T from a vertex $v \notin InitSet(\mathcal{P})$, then T responds with an "abort" token if it has already issued an "abort" token to another signer who is not in the set $Dishonest_{\mathfrak{C}}$. This condition can be exploited by a group of dishonest signers in an *abort chaining attack* [16]. The following definition states the requirements for a successful abort chaining attack. For ease of reading, we define the predicate $\mathrm{hon}(v, I)$. The predicate is true if there is no evidence (pre-knowledge) at the vertices in I that the signer $r(v)$ has sent a message at or causally after v:

$$\mathrm{hon}(v, I) \equiv \neg \exists (x, y) \in K_{\prec}(I) : v \prec (x, y) \wedge r(v) = r(x)$$

This is precisely the criterion used by T to verify honesty in Algorithm 1, line 12.

Definition 13. *Let $\mathfrak{C}$ be a contract and $l \leq |A|$. A sequence $(v_1, \ldots, v_l \mid s)$ over V is called an abort-chaining sequence (AC sequence) for $\mathcal{P}$ if the following conditions hold:*

1. *Signer $r(v_1)$ receives an abort token: $v_1 \in InitSet(\mathcal{P})$*
2. *No signer contacts T more than once: $\forall_{i \neq j}\, r(v_i) \neq r(v_j)$*
3. *The present and previous signer to contact T are considered honest by T:*

$$\forall i \leq l : \mathrm{hon}(v_i, \{v_1, \ldots, v_i\}) \wedge \mathrm{hon}(v_{i-1}, \{v_1, \ldots, v_i\})$$

4. *The last signer to contact T has not previously received all signatures:*

$$\forall v \prec v_l : r(v) = r(v_l) \implies v \notin EndSet(\mathcal{P})$$

5. *The last signer to contact T has sent a signature before contacting T or in a parallel thread:*

$$s \in SigSet(\mathcal{P}) \setminus EndSet(\mathcal{P}) : r(s) = r(v_l) \wedge v_l \not\preceq s$$

The AC sequence represents the order in which signers execute the resolve protocol with T. A vertex v_i in the sequence implies an exit transition via the edge (v_i, v_T) in the protocol execution. An abort chaining attack must start at a step in which T has no choice but to respond with an abort token due to lack of information. Condition 1 covers this. Each signer may run the resolve protocol at most once. This is covered by Condition 2. To ensure that T continues to issue "abort" tokens, Condition 3 requires that there must always be a signer which according to T's evidence has not continued protocol execution after contacting T. To complete an abort chaining attack, there needs to be a signer which has issued a signature (Condition 5), but has not received a signature (Conditions 4 and 5) and will not receive a signed contract from T because there is an honest signer (by Condition 3) which has received an "abort" token.

It is not surprising that a protocol with an AC sequence is unfair. However, the converse is true, too. The proof of this and the following theorems is given in [14].

Theorem 1. *Let $\mathcal{P}$ be a DAG MPCS protocol. Then $\mathcal{P}$ is fair if and only if it has no AC sequences.*

6.2 Fairness Criteria

Theorem 1 reduces the verification of fairness from analyzing all executions to verifying that there is no AC-sequence (Definition 13). This, however, is still difficult to verify in general. The following two results are tools to quickly assess fairness of DAG MPCS protocols. The first is an unfairness criterion and the second is a fairness criterion for a large class of DAG MPCS protocols.

The following theorem states that in a fair DAG MPCS protocol, the union of paths from the initial set to every vertex $v \in SigSet(\mathcal{P})$ must contain all permutations of all signers (other than $r(v)$) as subsequences. In the class of linear MPCS protocols, considered in [10], this criterion was both necessary and sufficient. We show in Example 2 below that this criterion is not sufficient for fairness of DAG MPCS protocols.

For $I \subseteq V$, $v \in V$, let path(I, v) be the set of all directed paths from a vertex in I to v and let seq$(I, v) = \{r(p) \in A^* \mid p \in \text{path}(I, v)\}$ be the sequences of signers corresponding to the paths from I to v, where $r(p) = (r(v_1), \ldots, r(v_k))$.

Theorem 2. *Let $k = |A|$. Let $\mathcal{P}$ be an optimistic fair DAG MPCS protocol,*

$$I = \{v \in InitSet(\mathcal{P}) \mid (v \prec w \wedge r(v) = r(w)) \Rightarrow w \notin InitSet(\mathcal{P})\}.$$

If $v \in SigSet(\mathcal{P})$, then for every permutation $(P_1, \ldots, P_{k-1})$ of signers in $A \setminus \{r(v)\}$, there exists a sequence in seq(I, v) which contains $(P_1, \ldots, P_{k-1})$ as a (not necessarily consecutive) subsequence.

The converse of the theorem is not true as the following example shows. In particular, this example demonstrates that the addition of a vertex to a fair DAG MPCS protocol does not necessarily preserve fairness.

Example 2. The protocol in Figure 3a is fair by the results of [10]. By Theorem 2, for every vertex $v \in SigSet(\mathcal{P})$ every permutation of signers in $A \setminus \{P\}$ occurs as a subsequence of a path in seq(I, v). The protocol in Figure 3b is obtained by adding the vertex B_q as a parallel thread of signer B. Thus the permutation property on the set of paths is preserved, yet the protocol is not fair: An AC sequence is $(B_q, C_3, A_4 | A_3)$. The vertex B_q is in $InitSet(\mathcal{P})$, the evidence presented to the TTP at C_3 includes the vertices causally preceding C_2, thus B is considered to be honest. The evidence presented by signer A at A_4 are the vertices causally preceding A_3 proving that B is dishonest, but C is honest. Thus A has sent a signature at A_3 but will not receive signatures from B and C.

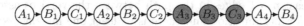

(a) A three-party MPCS protocol from a signing sequence [10].

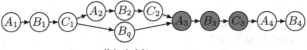

(b) Adding a vertex

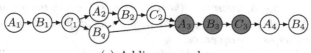

(c) Adding an ε edge.

Fig. 3. Skeletal graphs of fair protocols (a, c) and an unfair protocol (b)

If a protocol has no in-role parallelism, then the converse of Theorem 2 is true. Thus we have a simple criterion for the fairness of such protocols.

Theorem 3. *Let $\mathcal{P}$ be an optimistic DAG MPCS protocol without in-role parallelism. Let*

$$I = \{v \in InitSet(\mathcal{P}) \mid (v \prec w \land r(v) = r(w)) \Rightarrow w \notin InitSet(\mathcal{P})\}.$$

If all paths from I to $v \in SigSet(\mathcal{P})$ contain all permutations of $A \setminus \{r(v)\}$ then $\mathcal{P}$ is fair for $r(v)$.

Example 3. By adding a causal edge between vertex B_q and vertex B_2 of the protocol in Figure 3b, as shown in Figure 3c, we obtain again a fair protocol.

7   Protocols

In this section we illustrate the theory and results obtained in the preceding sections by proving optimality results and constructing a variety of protocols.

7.1   Minimal Complexity

We prove lower bounds for the two complexity measures defined in our model, viz. parallel and message complexity.

Theorem 4. *The minimal parallel complexity for an optimistic fair DAG MPCS protocol is $n + 1$, where n is the number of signers in the protocol.*

Proof. By Theorem 2, every permutation of signers in the protocol must occur as a subsequence in the set of paths from a causally last vertex in the initial set to a vertex in the signing set. Since a last vertex v in the initial set must have a non-empty knowledge $K(v)$, there must be a message edge causally preceding v.

There are at least $n - 1$ edges in the path between the vertices associated with the n signers in a permutation and there is at least one message edge outgoing from a vertex in the signing set. Thus a minimal length path for such a protocol must contain $n + 1$ edges.

The minimal parallel complexity is attained by the broadcast protocols of Baum-Waidner and Waidner [2].

Theorem 5. *The minimal message complexity for an optimistic fair DAG MPCS protocol is $\lambda(n) + 2n - 3$, where n is the number of signers in the protocol and $\lambda(n)$ is the length of the shortest sequence which contains all permutations of elements of an n-element set as subsequences.*

The minimal message complexities for $2 < n < 8$ are $n^2 + 1$. The minimal message complexities for $n \geq 10$ are smaller or equal to n^2.

Note that while broadcasting protocols have a linear parallel complexity, they have a cubic message complexity, since in each of the $n + 1$ rounds each of the n signers sends a message to every other signer. Linear protocols on the other hand have quadratic minimal message and parallel complexities. In the following we demonstrate that there are DAG protocols which attain a linear parallel complexity while maintaining a quadratic message complexity.

7.2   Protocol Constructions

Single Contractor, Multiple Subcontractors. A motivation for fair MPCS protocols given in [10] is a scenario where a single entity, here referred to as a contractor, would like to sign k contracts with k independent companies, in the following referred to as subcontractors. The contractor has an interest in either having all contracts signed or to not be bound by any of the contracts. The subcontractors have no contractual obligations towards each other. It would therefore be advantageous if there is no need for the subcontractors to directly communicate with each other.

The solutions proposed in [10] are linear protocols. Their message and parallel complexities are thus quadratic. Linear protocols can satisfy the requirement that subcontractors do not directly communicate with each other only by greatly increasing the message and parallel complexities.

The protocol we propose here is a DAG, its message complexity is $2(n+1)(n-1)$ and its parallel complexity is $2n + 2$ for n signers. It therefore combines the low parallel complexity typically attained by broadcasting protocols with the low message complexity of linear protocols. Additionally, the protocol proposed does not require any direct communication between subcontractors.

Figure 4a shows a single contractor with three subcontractors. The protocol can be subdivided into five rounds, one round consisting of the subcontractors sending a message to the contractor followed by the contractor sending a message

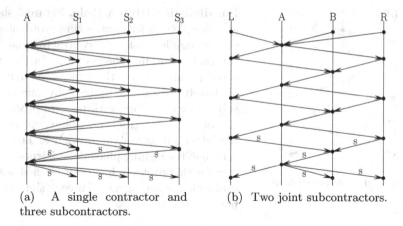

(a) A single contractor and three subcontractors.

(b) Two joint subcontractors.

Fig. 4. Two examples of fair DAG MPCS protocols

to the subcontractors. In the first four rounds promises are sent, in the final round signatures are sent. The protocol can be easily generalized to more than three subcontractors. For every subcontractor added, one extra round of promises needs to be included in the protocol specification.

The protocol is fair by Theorem 3. The MSC shown in Figure 4a resembles the skeletal graph from which it was built. The message contents can be derived by computing the full graph according to Condition 2 of Definition 9. The result is as follows. In each round of the protocol, each of the subcontractors sends to the contractor a promise for the contractor and for each of the other subcontractors. The contractor then sends to each of the subcontractors all of the promises received and his own promise. The final round is performed in the same manner, except that promises are replaced by signatures.

Two Contractors with Joint Subcontractors. Figure 4b shows a protocol where two contractors want to sign a contract involving two subcontractors. The subcontractors are independent of each other.

After the initial step, where all signers send a promise to the first contractor A, there are three protocol rounds, one round consisting of the contractor A sending promises to the two subcontractors L and R in parallel which in turn send promises to the second contractor B. A new round is started with the second contractor sending the promises received with his own promise to contractor A.

This protocol, too, can be generalized to several independent subcontractors. For every subcontractor added, one extra protocol round needs to be included in the protocol specification and each protocol step of the subcontractors executed analogously.

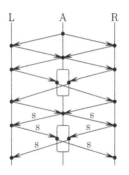

Fig. 5. In-role parallelism

Parallelism within a Role. Figure 5 shows an example of a subcontracting protocol with in-role parallelism for the contractor role. The contractor initiates the protocol. In the indicated parallel phase, the contractor may immediately forward a promise by one of the subcontractors along with his own promise to the other subcontractor without waiting for the latter subcontractor's promise. The same is true in the signing phase. The fairness property for this protocol has been verified with a tool which tested fairness for each signer in all possible executions.

8   Conclusion

We have identified fair subcontracting as a challenging new problem in the area of multi-party contract signing. We have made first steps towards solving this problem by introducing DAG MPCS protocols and extending existing fairness results from linear protocols to DAG protocols. For three typical subcontracting configurations we propose novel DAG MPCS protocols that perform well in terms of message complexity and parallel complexity. Fairness of our protocol schemes follows directly from our theoretical results and we have verified it for concrete protocols with our automatic tool.

There are a number of open research questions related to fair subcontracting that we haven't addressed. We mention two. The first concerns the implementation of multi-contracts. In our current approach we consider a single abstract contract shared by all parties. However, in practice such a contract may consist of a number of subcontracts that are accessible to the relevant signers only. How to cryptographically construct such contracts and what information these contracts should share is not evident. Second, a step needs to be made towards putting our results into practice. Given the application domains identified in this paper, we must identify the relevant signing scenarios and topical boundary conditions in order to develop dedicated protocols for each application area.

Acknowledgement. We thank Barbara Kordy for her many helpful comments on this paper.

References

1. Asokan, N.: Fairness in electronic commerce. PhD thesis, Univ. of Waterloo (1998)
2. Baum-Waidner, B., Waidner, M.: Optimistic asynchronous multi-party contract signing. Research Report RZ 3078 (#93124), IBM Zurich Research Laboratory, Zurich, Switzerland (November 1998)

3. Baum-Waidner, B., Waidner, M.: Round-optimal and abuse free optimistic multi-party contract signing. In: Welzl, E., Montanari, U., Rolim, J.D.P. (eds.) ICALP 2000. LNCS, vol. 1853, pp. 524–535. Springer, Heidelberg (2000)
4. Chadha, R., Kremer, S., Scedrov, A.: Formal analysis of multi-party contract signing. In: CSFW 2004, p. 266. IEEE, Washington, DC (2004)
5. Even, S., Yacobi, Y.: Relations among public key signature systems. Technical Report 175, Computer Science Dept. Technion, Haifa, Isreal (March 1980)
6. Garay, J.A., Jakobsson, M., MacKenzie, P.D.: Abuse-free optimistic contract signing. In: Wiener, M. (ed.) CRYPTO 1999. LNCS, vol. 1666, pp. 449–466. Springer, Heidelberg (1999)
7. Garay, J.A., MacKenzie, P.D.: Abuse-free multi-party contract signing. In: Jayanti, P. (ed.) DISC 1999. LNCS, vol. 1693, pp. 151–166. Springer, Heidelberg (1999)
8. Karaenke, P., Kirn, S.: Towards model checking & simulation of a multi-tier negotiation protocol for service chains. In: Int. Found. for Autonomous Agents and Multiagent Systems AAMAS 2010, pp. 1559–1560 (2010)
9. Katok, E., Pavlov, V.: Fairness in supply chain contracts: a laboratory study. J. of Operations Management 31, 129–137 (2013)
10. Kordy, B., Radomirović, S.: Constructing optimistic multi-party contract signing protocols. In: CSF 2012, pp. 215–229. IEEE Computer Society (2012)
11. Kraus, S.: Automated negotiation and decision making in multi-agent environments. In: ACM Multi-agent Systems and Applications, pp. 150–172 (2001)
12. Krishnan, H., Winter, R.: The economic foundations of supply chain contracting. Foundations and Trends in Technology, Information and Operations Management 5(3-4), 147–309 (2012)
13. Lu, K., Yahyapour, R., Yaqub, E., Kotsokalis, C.: Structural optimisation of reduced ordered binary decision diagrams for SLA negotiation in IaaS of cloud computing. In: Liu, C., Ludwig, H., Toumani, F., Yu, Q. (eds.) ICSOC 2012. LNCS, vol. 7636, pp. 268–282. Springer, Heidelberg (2012)
14. Mauw, S., Radomirović, S.: Generalizing Multi-party Contract Signing. CoRR, abs/1501.03868 (Extended version.) (2015), http://arxiv.org/abs/1501.03868
15. Mauw, S., Radomirović, S., Dashti, M.T.: Minimal message complexity of asynchronous multi-party contract signing. In: CSF 2009, pp. 13–25. IEEE (2009)
16. Mukhamedov, A., Ryan, M.D.: Improved multi-party contract signing. In: Dietrich, S., Dhamija, R. (eds.) FC 2007 and USEC 2007. LNCS, vol. 4886, pp. 179–191. Springer, Heidelberg (2007)
17. Mukhamedov, A., Ryan, M.D.: Fair multi-party contract signing using private contract signatures. Inf. Comput. 206(2-4), 272–290 (2008)
18. Schunter, M.: Optimistic Fair Exchange. Phd thesis, Universität des Saarlandes (2000)
19. Seifert, R., Zequiera, R., Liao, S.: A three-echelon supply chain with price-only contracts and sub-supply chain coordination. Int. J. of Production Economics 138, 345–353 (2012)
20. Yaqub, E., Wieder, P., Kotsokalis, C., Mazza, V., Pasquale, L., Rueda, J., Gómez, S.G., Chimeno, A.: A generic platform for conducting SLA negotiations. In: Service Level Agreements for Cloud Computing, pp. 187–206. Springer (2011)
21. Zhang, Y., Zhang, C., Pang, J., Mauw, S.: Game-based verification of contract signing protocols with minimal messages. Innovations in Systems and Software Engineering 8(2), 111–124 (2012)

Leakiness is Decidable for Well-Founded Protocols*

Sibylle Fröschle

OFFIS & University of Oldenburg, 26121 Oldenburg, Germany
froeschle@informatik.uni-oldenburg.de

Abstract. A limit to algorithmic verification of security protocols is posed by the fact that checking whether a security property such as secrecy is satisfied is undecidable in general. In this paper we introduce the class of well-founded protocols. It is designed to exclude what seems to be common to all protocols used in undecidability proofs: the protocol syntax ensures that honest information cannot be propagated unboundedly without the intruder manipulating it. We show that the secrecy property of leakiness is decidable for well-founded protocols.

Consider the INSECURITY problem that stands behind classical protocol verification: Given a protocol P and an attack goal G, is there a run of protocol P controlled by the Dolev-Yao intruder that obtains G? This problem is well-known to be undecidable in general [13,17]. One can distinguish between two directions to restrict the problem to analyse the decidability border.

One direction is to restrict the sources of infinity the Dolev-Yao intruder can make use of: an attack may involve messages of unbounded size, an unbounded number of freshly generated data, and an unbounded number of sessions. This direction is well-investigated and many positive results have been obtained. INSECURITY turns out to be NP-complete when the number of sessions is bounded [23,7], and EXPTIME-complete when both the number of freshly generated data and the message size is bounded [12,14]. INSECURITY remains undecidable when only one of these two restrictions is imposed. A recent survey of this area can be found in [14].

The second direction for borderline investigations is to leave the sources of infinity a priori unconstrained, but impose restrictions on the message format. In [10,9] INSECURITY was shown to be PTIME decidable for *ping-pong* protocols. These protocols have a very restricted message format that makes it possible to formalize them by a form of context-free grammars. More directly motivated by protocol verification, works by Lowe [18] and Ramanujam and Suresh [20,22,21] investigate decidability when imposing conditions that make encrypted messages context-explicit. The idea is that such protocols merely satisfy the prudent engineering practice recommended by Abadi and Needham [1]. These works achieve

---

* This work is partially supported by the *Niedersächsisches Vorab* of the Volkswagen Foundation and the Ministry of Science and Culture of Lower Saxony as part of the *Interdisciplinary Research Center on Critical Systems Engineering for Socio-Technical Systems*.

R. Focardi and A. Myers (Eds.): POST 2015, LNCS 9036, pp. 176–195, 2015.
DOI: 10.1007/978-3-662-46666-7_10

decidability results for the problem of non-secrecy without temporary secrets, which we call LEAKINESS here.

Our Contribution. In this paper, we tackle the decidability of context-explicit protocols 'from the top', trying to pinpoint in an abstract manner why the usual undecidability reductions do not carry over to such protocols. More concretely, we introduce the class of *well-founded protocols*. It is designed to exclude what seems to be common to all protocols used in undecidability results: the message format allows that honest information can be propagated unboundedly without the intruder manipulating it. We prove that LEAKINESS is decidable for well-founded protocols. Our class strictly contains those of [18,20,22,21].

Related Work. In [18] Lowe obtains a small model property (from which decidability of LEAKINESS is immediate) by a condition that requires that encrypted components are textually distinct, and that each encrypted component includes all protocol roles. Together this ensures that every encryption that occurs in a protocol run can be uniquely assigned to a protocol position and the set of agents involved in the run. The *structured* protocols of [20] introduce a condition that is similar to the first part of Lowe's: between any two terms that occur in distinct communications, no encrypted subterm of one can be unified with a subterm of the other. In the full version of this paper [22] the authors obtain NEXPTIME decidability of LEAKINESS for their class of *context-explicit* protocols: these protocols are structured and in addition require that each encryption to be sent out is tagged by a freshly generated nonce. This ensures that each instantiation of an encryption can be traced back to exactly one session. In [21] Ramanujam and Suresh obtain decidability of LEAKINESS for their *tagged* protocols. These are essentially an instance of their context-explicit protocols: the structured condition is implemented by using constants to identify encrypted subterms; they also require the additional dynamic tagging with freshly generated nonces. The novelty of [21] lies in the fact that the result also works for untyped messages, and hence, unbounded message length.

The three results [18,22,21] have in common that they establish a small model property: if there is an attack then there is a small attack and the problem reduces to checking protocol runs with a bounded number of events. The three works do not allow composed keys nor blind forwarding of ciphertexts. Since [18] and [22] work with a typed algebra together with the latter this means that the message size is bounded, and decidability follows from the small model property. [21] lifts the typing restriction, and thereby admits messages of unbounded size. In addition to the small model property it is shown that if there is an attack then there is a well-typed attack.

In [2] Arapinas and Duflot provide a general approach for bounding the size of messages in an attack: they introduce a condition of well-formedness and show that a protocol admits an attack iff it admits a well-typed attack for a particular typing system that bounds message size. They also show that the tagging scheme of Blanchet and Podelski [3] implements well-formedness. The tagging system is light in that it only introduces a different constant in each encryption. The tagging system is used in [3] to enforce termination of a resolution-based verification method. (The verification method is approximate so this does not give a decidability result.) In [5] the approach of [2] is extended to equivalence checking and a more general typing system. As an application decidability of trace equivalence for tagged protocols is obtained for a fixed number of nonces. The setting admits symmetric encryption and assumes session identifiers.

Dougherty and Guttman are first to apply the idea of context-explicitness in a rich algebraic setting [11]. They introduce a class of lightweight Diffie-Hellman protocols with simple signatures. The simple signatures are defined by requiring an ordering on the occurrences of signatures in a protocol to be acyclic. They obtain a small model property for their class, which together with other algebraic results leads to decidability of their security goals for lightweight Diffie-Hellman protocols.

Synopsis. In Section 1 we present the necessary definitions. In Section 2 we introduce *well-founded protocols* motivated by a notion of *honest causality*, and prove their characteristic property. In Section 3 we introduce a normal form for intruder deductions and protocol runs, so-called *well-structured source trees and bundles*. We obtain two structural insights on well-structured bundles. In Section 4 this allows us to transform *honest cause components* of non-leaky bundles into bundles. The transformation also works for minimal leaky bundles and preserves leaks. Altogether, this means that the size of minimal leaky bundles is bounded by the size of honest cause components. (Indeed, this holds for protocols in general.) For well-founded protocols we obtain a bound on the size of honest cause components, and thereby of minimal leaky bundles. With this decidability is immediate. The ideas behind this work were presented at [15]. A full version of the paper can be found on the web page of the author.

1   Preliminaries

Terms and Messages. Let $Atoms$ be a set of atomic messages or *atoms*, and $AVars$ a set of variables for atoms. Then $ATerms = Atoms \cup AVars$ is the set of atomic terms. The set of atoms, and variables for atoms respectively, can be be further structured into several atomic message types. Here we only assume a set of agent names $Agents \subset Atoms$, and a set of variables for agent names $Vars_{Agents}$ respectively. Set $Terms_{Agents} = Agents \cup Vars_{Agents}$. Moreover, let $Vars$ be a set of variables to present any message.

The set of *terms*, denoted by $Terms$, is generated from the set of basic terms $ATerms \cup Vars$ by the following operators:

- $priv(ag)$ where $ag \in Terms_{Agents}$,
- $\langle t_1, t_2 \rangle$ where $t_1, t_2 \in Terms$,
- $\{t\}_k$ where $t \in Terms$ and $k \in ATerms$,
- $\{|t|\}_{ag}$ where $t \in Terms$ and $ag \in Terms_{Agents}$.

$priv(ag)$ depicts the private key of agent ag, $\langle t_1, t_2 \rangle$ represents the concatenation of terms t_1 and t_2, $\{t\}_k$ models the symmetric encryption of t by atomic key k, and $\{t\}_{ag}$ stands for the asymmetric encryption of t with the public key of agent ag. As usual we equate the public keys of agents with their names.

Given two terms t_1, t_2, we write $t_1 \sqsubseteq t_2$ if t_1 is a subterm of t_2. We also define a relation $\sqsubseteq_s$ to express when a term t_1 is *source-contained* in a term t_2. This is inductively defined as follows:

- $t \sqsubseteq_s a$ where $a \in ATerms$ iff $t = a$,
- $t \sqsubseteq_s priv(ag)$, iff $t = priv(ag)$ or $t = ag$,
- $t \sqsubseteq_s \langle t_1, t_2 \rangle$ iff $t = \langle t_1, t_2 \rangle$ or $t \sqsubseteq_s t_1$ or $t \sqsubseteq_s t_2$,
- $t \sqsubseteq_s \{t'\}_k$ iff $t = \{t'\}_k$ or $t \sqsubseteq_s t'$,
- $t \sqsubseteq_s \{t'\}_{ag}$ iff $t = \{t'\}_{ag}$ or $t \sqsubseteq_s t'$.

A *message* is a ground, i.e., variable-free term. A *message template* is a term that does not contain any elements of *Atoms*. We denote the set of messages by *Mesg* and the set of message templates by *TMesg*. A *ground substitution* is a function that assigns messages to variables such that the types are preserved.

$$\frac{x \quad y}{\langle x, y \rangle} \; C_{pair} \qquad \frac{\langle x, y \rangle}{x} \; D_{pair_1} \qquad \frac{\langle x, y \rangle}{y} \; D_{pair_2}$$

$$\frac{x \quad y_a}{\{x\}_{y_a}} \; C_{senc} \qquad \frac{\{x\}_{y_a} \quad y_a}{x} \; D_{senc}$$

$$\frac{x \quad y_{ag}}{\{x\}_{y_{ag}}} \; C_{aenc} \qquad \frac{\{x\}_{y_{ag}} \quad priv(y_{ag})}{x} \; D_{aenc}$$

where $x, y \in Vars$, $y_a \in AVars$, and $y_{ag} \in Vars_{Agents}$.

Fig. 1. The Dolev-Yao intruder deduction system $\mathcal{I}_{DY}$

Intruder Deduction Capabilities. We assume the deduction capabilities of the standard Dolev-Yao intruder, modelled by the inference system $\mathcal{I}_{DY}$ depicted in Fig. 1. The rules of inference fall into matching composition and decomposition rules. The composition rules model the intruder's ability to build new messages from messages he has already deduced while the decomposition rules capture when he can decompose deduced messages into their parts.

Let T be a set of terms, and u be a term. We say u is *deducible* from T in $\mathcal{I}_{DY}$, written $u \in \mathcal{DY}(T)$, iff there is a proof tree of $T \vdash u$ in $\mathcal{I}_{DY}$. A *proof* of $T \vdash u$ in an inference system $\mathcal{I}$ is a proof tree Π such that:

- Every leaf of Π is labelled with a term v such that $v \in T$.
- For every node labelled with v_0 having n children labelled with $v_1, \ldots, v_n$, there is an instance of an inference rule with conclusion v_0 and premises $v_1, \ldots, v_n$. We say that Π ends with this instance if the node is the root of Π.
- The root is labelled with u.

Let Π be a proof tree of $T \vdash u$. Let n be a node of Π. We write $lab(n)$ for the label of n. We denote the subtree that is rooted in n by $subtree(n)$. Clearly, it is a proof tree of $T \vdash lab(n)$. We denote the root node of Π by $root(\Pi)$, and the set of leaves of Π by $leaves(\Pi)$. We denote by $Concl(\Pi)$ the label of the root of Π, and by $Hyp(\Pi)$ the set of labels of the leaves of Π. If Π only contains instances of decomposition rules we say Π is a *decomposition tree*, and if it only contains instances of composition rules a *composition tree* respectively. The *size* of a proof tree is the number of its nodes. A proof tree of $T \vdash u$ is *minimal* if there is no other proof tree of $T \vdash u$ with size strictly smaller than Π.

Protocol Specifications. A *protocol* is a pair $P = (roles_P, script_P)$, where $roles_P$ is a finite set of *roles*, and $script_P$ is a function that maps every role in $roles_P$ to a *role script*. Given $r \in roles_P$, $script_P(r)$ is a finite sequence

$$p_1 M_1 \ p_2 M_2 \ \ldots \ p_n M_n$$

where $n \geq 1$, and for every $i \in [1, n]$, $p_i \in \{+, -\}$ and M_i is a message template, i.e. a term without any atom. A term prefixed with a '+' is thought to be sent, and a term prefixed with a '−' to be received respectively. For $i \in [1, n]$ define $fresh_r(i)$ to be the set $\{x \in Vars \mid p_i = `+` \ \& \ x \sqsubseteq M_i \ \& \ \forall j \in [1, i[, x \not\sqsubseteq M_j\}$. We require the following three axioms:

r1 $p_1 = `-`$, and $\exists A \in Vars_{Agents} \exists M_1' \in TMesg. \ M_1 = A \ \lor \ M_1 = \langle A, M_1' \rangle$,
r2 $\forall i \in [1, n]$, $fresh_r(i) \subseteq AVars$, and
r3 $\forall i \in [1, n]$, if $p_i = `+`$ then
$$\{M_j \mid j \in [1, i[\ \& \ p_j = `-`\} \cup \{priv(A)\} \cup fresh_r(i) \vdash M_i \ ,$$
where A is given as in axiom (r1).

Role scripts will be interpreted as follows. The ownership of the session will be defined by the agent name to be received in the first component of the first message. This is the reason behind Axiom (r1). If a variable appears for the first time in a message pattern to be received then any value that respects the sort of the variable can be matched to it. If a variable appears for the first time in a message pattern to be sent then a fresh value will be assigned to it at this step. Axiom (r2) ensures that only atoms can be freshly generated. The received or freshly generated value is henceforward understood to be bound to the variable. Axiom (r3) ensures that each message to be sent can be assembled from the messages already received, the private key of the owner of the session, and the atoms to be freshly generated at this step. Our interpretation that variables that first appear in a message pattern to be sent are assumed to be freshly generated is no restriction: public session parameters such as agent names can be received in a message to be sent by the intruder. Our use of message templates is no restriction either: constants can be modelled by types with one element or via adapting the definitions so that agents have prior knowledge of constants.

Example 1. The Needham-Schroeder Public Key (NSPK) Protocol [19] is informally described by the message exchange shown on the left below. Formally, it is specified by $P = (roles_P, script_P)$, where $roles_P = \{A, B\}$, and $script_P(A)$ and $script_P(B)$ are defined as follows.

		A	B
1. $A \longrightarrow B : \{\!|N_A, A|\!\}_B$	1	$-A, B$	$-B, A$
2. $B \longrightarrow A : \{\!|N_A, N_B|\!\}_A$	2	$+\{\!|N_A, A|\!\}_B$	$-\{\!|N_A, A|\!\}_B$
3. $A \longrightarrow B : \{\!|N_B|\!\}_B$	3	$-\{\!|N_A, N_B|\!\}_A$	$+\{\!|N_A, N_B|\!\}_A$
	4	$+\{\!|N_B|\!\}_B$	$-\{\!|N_B|\!\}_B$

Strands and Bundles. We now define protocol executions in terms of the strand space model (e.g. [16]). More precisely, we work with a variation of the strand space model: first, our definition of bundle will not make use of the usual intruder strands but uses deduction trees whose leaves are mapped to output events. Second, we add a total order to the concept of bundle, which means we have available the execution order of events as well as the causal relationship between them. In the following, assume a fixed protocol $P = (roles_P, script_P)$.

A *strand* represents an instantiation of a role script of the protocol or a prefix thereof. (We admit prefixes to be able to model incomplete protocol sessions; a situation that naturally arises in a snapshot of a protocol execution.) Formally, a *strand* of P is a totally ordered labelled graph $s = (E, \Rightarrow, l)$ where

- $E = \{(s, 1), \ldots, (s, n)\}$, $n > 0$,
- $(s, i) \Rightarrow (s, j)$ iff $j = i + 1$,
- $l : E \to \{+, -\} \times Mesg$, and

there are $r \in roles_P$, a prefix of $script_P(r)$ of the form $p_1 M_1 \ p_2 M_2 \ \ldots \ p_n M_n$, and a ground substitution σ such that for all $i \in [1, n]$ we have:

S1 $l(s, i) = p_i M_i \sigma$,
S2 if $x \in fresh_r(i)$ then
    (a) for all $j \in [1, i[$, $x\sigma \not\sqsubseteq M_j \sigma$,
    (b) for all $x' \in fresh_r(i)$, $x\sigma = x'\sigma$ implies $x = x'$.

Observe how the two axioms ensure that s can indeed be understood as an instantiation of the partial role script via σ. Axiom (S1) ensures that the signed message is an instance of the respective signed message template. Axiom (S2) guarantees that if an atom is to be freshly generated for message M_i then (a) it does not occur earlier on the strand, and (b) it is distinct from all other atoms freshly generated for message M_i.

We call E the set of *events of s*. Given an event e of s, we call the first component of $l(e)$ the *sign of e*, written $sign(e)$, and the second component the *message of e*, written $msg(e)$. If $sign(e) = $ '+', we call e an *output event*, and if $sign(e) = $ '−' an *input event* respectively. We say atom a *originates on event* (s, i) if (s, i) is an output event, $a \sqsubseteq msg(s, i)$, and for all $j \in [1, i[$, $a \not\sqsubseteq msg(s, j)$. In our technical framework we have the following convenient fact:

Proposition 2. *Let s be a strand such that s is a (partial) instance of $r \in roles_P$ via substitution σ. For all events (s, i) of s we have: $x \in fresh_r(i)$ iff $x\sigma$ originates on (s, i).*

We assume a special strand *init*, which consists of a finite set of output events that models the intruder's initial knowledge he has prepared for the protocol run. We assume that he has available at least his own private key, denoted by $priv(i)$, and an atom of each atomic type. By abuse of notation we usually consider this strand as one event *init*.

An *ordered strand space of P* is a pair $\mathcal{S} = (S, <)$ where S is a set of strands of P, and $<$ is a total order on the events of S such that

S1 $init \in S$,
S2 $\Rightarrow \subseteq <$, and
S3 $init < e$ for every event $e \neq init$.

Axiom (S1) models that the intruder is always expected to prepare some initial knowledge. Axiom (S2) expresses that if e' precedes e in a session then e' must have happened before e. Axiom (S3) expresses that the intruder generates all atoms he will use in the attack in advance.

In the context of an ordered strand space $\mathcal{S} = (S, <)$, we denote the set of events of S by E, the set of input events by E_{in}, and the set of output events by E_{out} respectively. Given $e \in E$, the *downwards closure of e in $\mathcal{S}$* is defined by $e \Downarrow = \{e' \mid e' \leq e\}$, and the *strict downwards closure of e in $\mathcal{S}$* by $e \downarrow = \{e' \mid e' < e\}$. When $\mathcal{S}$ is not uniquely determined by the context we also use $e \Downarrow_\mathcal{S}$, and $e \downarrow_\mathcal{S}$ respectively.

Let $\mathcal{S}$ be an ordered strand space. A *source (proof) tree wrt $\mathcal{S}$* is a pair (Π, src) where Π is a proof tree, and $src : leaves(\Pi) \rightarrow E_{out}$ is a map from the leaf nodes of Π to the output events of $\mathcal{S}$ such that $src(n_l) = e$ implies $lab(n_l) = msg(e)$. Given a message m, we say (Π, src) is a source tree for m wrt $\mathcal{S}$ if $Concl(\Pi) = m$.

A bundle represents a snapshot of a protocol execution. Formally, a *bundle* of P is a tuple $B = (\mathcal{S}, \{(\Pi_e, src_e)\}_{e \in E_{in}})$ where

- $\mathcal{S} = (S, <)$ is an ordered strand space of P, and
- $\forall e \in E_{in}, (\Pi_e, src_e)$ is a source tree for $msg(e)$ wrt $e \downarrow$

such that

B1 every atom a occurring in S has a unique origin in S: there is exactly one event $e \in E$ such that a originates on e.

The required family of source trees ensures that the message of every input event can be deduced by the intruder from the messages of the previous output events (including the intruder's own event *init*.) Axiom (B1) together with Prop. 2 ensures that if an atom is thought to be freshly generated on some strand then on any other strand it has to be received before it can be sent. Given an atom a that occurs in $\mathcal{S}$, define the *origin* of a, denoted by $origin(a)$, to be the unique event on which a originates as guaranteed by Axiom (B1).

Define $\rightarrow \subseteq E_{out} \times E_{in}$ by: $e \rightarrow e'$ iff there is a leaf $n_l \in \Pi_{e'}$ such that $src_{e'}(n_l) = e$. It is easy to check that $\rightarrow \subseteq <$. We denote the relation $\rightarrow \cup \Rightarrow$ by $\prec_1$. $\prec_1$ expresses *immediate causality*: if $e \rightarrow e'$ then e is an immediate cause of e' due to the intruder deduction causality between messages captured by the intruder to deduce a message that is then injected by him into a protocol session. If $e \Rightarrow e'$ then e is an immediate cause of e' due to the execution order causality within a protocol session. The transitive closure of $\prec_1$, denoted by $\prec$, is a strict order, which captures *causality*. It is compatible with the execution order $<$: we have $\prec \subseteq <$, and hence, $\prec$ is a strict order.

A *bundle skeleton* of P is an ordered strand space $\mathcal{S}$ of P that can be extended to form a bundle, i.e., there is a family of source trees $\{(\Pi_e, src_e)\}_{e \in E_{in}}$ such that $(\mathcal{S}, \{(\Pi_e, src_e)\}_{e \in E_{in}})$ is a bundle of P.

We carry over our notations E, E_{in}, E_{out}, $e \Downarrow$, and $e \downarrow$ from ordered strand spaces to bundles and bundle skeletons in the obvious way. Moreover, we write $\mathcal{DY}(\mathcal{S})$ and $\mathcal{DY}(B)$ short for $\mathcal{DY}(M)$, where M is the set of messages of output events of $\mathcal{S}$, and B respectively.

The Leakiness Problem. We now define the secrecy problem as formulated by Ramanujam and Suresh (e.g. [22]). We call the problem *leakiness* to avoid confusion with other notions of secrecy. We also slightly generalize it to include leaks of private keys. Informally, a protocol run is considered to be *leaky* if (1) some atom is secret at some intermediate state of the run but known to the intruder at the end of the run, or (2) the private key of some agent other than the intruder is known to the intruder at the end of the run. The *leakiness problem* is then to check whether a protocol has a leaky run.

Let P be a protocol, and $\mathcal{S}$ be a bundle skeleton of P. An atom a *originates secretly* in $\mathcal{S}$ if $a \notin \mathcal{DY}(origin(a) \Downarrow)$. We say an atom a is a *leak* in $\mathcal{S}$ if a originates secretly in $\mathcal{S}$ but $a \in \mathcal{DY}(\mathcal{S})$. We say a private key $priv(ag)$ is a *leak* in $\mathcal{S}$ if $ag \neq i$ but $priv(ag) \in \mathcal{DY}(\mathcal{S})$. $\mathcal{S}$ is *leaky* if there is a leak in $\mathcal{S}$ and *non-leaky* otherwise. These notions carry over to bundles in the usual way.

LEAKINESS:
Given: A protocol P.
Decide: Is there a bundle B of P such that B is leaky?

2   Honest Causality and Well-Founded Protocols

Well-founded protocols are defined to syntactically exclude what is common to all protocols used in undecidability results: that honest information can be propagated unboundedly without the intruder manipulating it. First, we define two core concepts, *honest encryptions* and *source paths*. Based on these concepts we formalize the idea of unmanipulated information propagation in terms of a relation $\prec_h$, called *honest causality*. This will lead us to our definition of *well-founded protocols* We then confirm that for well-founded protocols the *honest causal depth* of each bundle is indeed bounded by the depth of the protocol. Finally, we define the concept of *honest cause components*.

Honest Encryptions and Source Paths. Let M be a set of messages the intruder has available at some stage of a protocol run. We wish to single out those encryptions that he can deduce but that he cannot analyse nor synthesize. We call them the *honest encryptions wrt M* since they must have come from an honest agent.

Given a set of messages M, an *honest encryption wrt M* is a message $h \in \mathcal{DY}(M)$ such that

1. h is a symmetric encryption $\{m\}_k$ such that $k \notin \mathcal{DY}(M)$, or
2. h is a public key encryption $\{\!|m|\!\}_{ag}$ such that $m \notin \mathcal{DY}(M)$.

We denote the set of honest encryptions wrt M by $HEnc(M)$. Given a strand space S, we write $HEnc(S)$ short for $HEnc(M)$, where $M = \{msg(e) \mid e \in E_{out}\}$.

Let m be a message, and Π be a proof tree. Say m is source-contained in the conclusion of Π. We are interested in tracing back where m originates from in the deduction. We translate this into the concept of *source path*. Given a message m, and a proof tree Π, we define a path π of Π to be an *intermediate source path of m in Π* iff

> *Base case:* $\pi = n_r$ such that n_r is the root of Π, and $m \sqsubseteq_s lab(n_r)$, or
> *Inductive case:* $\pi = \pi'n$ such that π' is an intermediate source path of m in Π, and one of the following holds with respect to the last node n' of π' and the rule instance it is conclusion of:

$$\frac{c_1 : m_1 \qquad [c_2 : m_2]}{n' : m'} \; R$$

1. $R = C_{pair}$, n is the left child c_1, and $m \sqsubseteq_s m_1$,
2. $R = C_{pair}$, n is the right child c_2, and $m \sqsubseteq_s m_2$,
3. $R = C_{senc}$ or C_{aenc}, n is the left child c_1, and $m \sqsubseteq_s m_1$,
4. $R = D_{pair_i}$ for $i = 1$, or 2, or
5. $R = D_{senc}$ or D_{aenc}, and n is the left child c_1.

We say π is a *soure path of m in Π* if it is a maximal intermediate source path of m in Π.

Proposition 3. *Let m be a message, Π be a proof tree, and π be a source path of m in Π. For all nodes n of π, we have $m \sqsubseteq_s lab(n)$.*

Note that if there are several occurrences of m in $Concl(\Pi)$ then there can be several source paths of m in Π. A source path will trace back m either to a leaf, or to the conclusion of a composition node. Since atoms and private keys cannot be composed they can always be traced back to leaves. Moreover, if m is an honest encryption wrt $Hyp(\Pi)$ then it can also be traced back to leaves since it can neither be composed nor decomposed.

Proposition 4. *Let M be a set of messages, m a message, and Π a proof tree of $M \vdash m$. If $h \in HEnc(M)$ such that $h \sqsubseteq_s m$ then there is a source path π of h in Π such that π ends in a leaf.*

Honest Causality. Let P be a protocol, and let $B = (S, <, \{(\Pi_e, src_e)\}_{e \in E_{in}})$ be a bundle of P. We define a relation $\to_h \subseteq E_{out} \times E_{in}$ as follows: $e' \to_h e$ iff there is $h \in HEnc(e\downarrow)$ such that there is a source path of h in Π_e ending in a leaf node n_l with $src_e(n_l) = e'$.

We denote the relation $\to_h \cup \Rightarrow$ by $\prec_h^1$. $\prec_h^1$ expresses that information is propagated unmanipulated directly from one protocol event to another. If $e' \Rightarrow e$ this is so because e' precedes e in a protocol session. If $e' \to_h e$ this is so because an encryption is passed from e' to e in unmanipulated form: because it can neither be analysed nor synthesized by the intruder at that point. The transitive closure of $\prec_h^1$, denoted by $\prec_h$, is a strict order, which captures unmanipulated information propagation. We call it *honest causality*. It is straightforward to check that $\prec_h$ is a strict order.

Given an event $e \in E$, we define the *honest causal depth of* e, written $depth_{\prec_h}(e)$, inductively as follows: if e is minimal wrt $\prec_h$ then $depth_{\prec_h}(e) = 0$; otherwise $depth_{\prec_h}(e) = 1 + \max\{depth_{\prec_h}(e') \mid e' \prec_h^1 e\}$. The *honest causal depth* of B, denoted by $depth_{\prec_h}(B)$, is given by $\max\{depth_{\prec_h}(e) \mid e \in E\}$.

Well-Founded Protocols. We now design a protocol class, which satisfies: given a protocol P of the class, there is $n \in \mathsf{Nat}$ such that for every bundle B of P, $depth_h(B)$ is bounded by n. We base the definition on a preorder on protocol positions that captures *potential* unmanipulated information propagation.

Let P be a protocol. We define the set of *protocol positions* of P by $Pos = \{(r, i) \mid r \in roles_P \ \& \ 1 \leq i \leq |script_P(r)|\}$. Define the *output positions* of P by $Pos_{out} = \{(r, i) \in Pos \mid p_i = \text{`}+\text{'} \text{ in } script_P(r)\}$, and the *input positions* by $Pos_{in} = \{(r, i) \in Pos \mid p_i = \text{`}-\text{'} \text{ in } script_P(r)\}$ respectively.

First, define a relation $\Rightarrow_P \subseteq Pos \times Pos$ by $(r, i) \Rightarrow_P (r', j)$ iff $r = r'$ and $i < j$. Second, define a relation $\to_P \subseteq Pos_{out} \times Pos_{in}$, which describes when an enryption sent can possibly match an encryption received during a protocol run: $p \to_P p'$ iff there are substitutions σ and σ', and an encryption m_e such that $m_e \sqsubseteq msg(p)\sigma$, and $m_e \sqsubseteq msg(p')\sigma'$.

We denote the relation $\to_p \cup \Rightarrow_p$ by $\prec_p^1$. $p \prec_p^1 p'$ expresses that information might be passed in a protected manner directly from an instance of p to an instance of p'. If $p \Rightarrow_p p'$ then this is so because p precedes p' in a role script. If $p \to_p p'$ this is so because an encryption, which is possibly neither analysable nor composable by the intruder, might be sent from an instance of p to an instance of p'. The reflexive and transitive closure of $\prec_p^1$, denoted by $\preceq_p$, is a preorder that captures *potential* unmanipulated information propagation.

Definition 5. *We say a protocol P is* well-founded *iff $\prec_p^1$ is acyclic, or $\preceq_p$ is a partial order equivalently.*

Let P be a well-founded protocol. Given a position $p \in Pos$, we define the *depth of p*, written $depth_{\prec_p}(p)$, inductively as follows: if p is minimal wrt to $\prec_p$ then $depth_{\prec_p}(p) = 0$; otherwise $depth_{\prec_p}(p) = 1 + \max\{depth_{\prec_p}(p') \mid p' \prec_p^1 p\}$. The *depth of protocol P*, denoted by $depth(P)$, is given by $\max\{depth_{\prec_p}(p) \mid p \in Pos\}$.

Example 6. Recall the NSPK protocol from Example 1. It is easy to check that $\prec_p^1$ is acyclic, and hence, the NSPK protocol is well-founded. Moreover, observe that it has depth 6.

Example 7. The Woo and Lam protocol (c.f. [6]) is a flawed authentication protocol where B wants to verify that A is present with the help of a server S.

$$1.\ A \longrightarrow B : A$$
$$2.\ B \longrightarrow A : N_B$$
$$3.\ A \longrightarrow B : \{N_B\}_{sh(A,S)}$$
$$4.\ B \longrightarrow S : \{A, \{N_B\}_{sh(A,S)}\}_{sh(B,S)}$$
$$5.\ S \longrightarrow B : \{N_B\}_{sh(B,S)}$$

Formally, the protocol is specified by the following role scripts:[1]

	A	B	S
1	$-A, B, S$	$-B, A, S$	$-S, A, B$
2	$+A$	$-A$	$-\{A, \{N_B\}_{sh(A,S)}\}_{sh(B,S)}$
3	$-N_B$	$+N_B$	$+\{N_B\}_{sh(B,S)}$
4	$+\{N_B\}_{sh(A,S)}$	$-X$	
5		$+\{A, X\}_{sh(B,S)}$	
6		$-\{N_B\}_{sh(B,S)}$	

The Woo and Lam protocol is not well-founded: e.g., we have $(B,4) \Rightarrow_p$ $(B,5) \rightarrow_p (B,4)$, and $(S,2) \Rightarrow_p (S,3) \rightarrow_p (S,2)$. The first situation is an example of how blind copies always cause $\prec_p^1$ to be cyclic.

Example 8. The Otway-Rees protocol (c.f. [6]) establishes a shared secret between two agents with the help of a trusted server.

$$1.\ A \longrightarrow B : A, B, \{N_A, A, B\}_{sh(A,S)}$$
$$2.\ B \longrightarrow S : A, B, \{N_A, A, B\}_{sh(A,S)}, \{N_B, A, B\}_{sh(B,S)}$$
$$3.\ S \longrightarrow B : \{N_A, K_{AB}\}_{sh(A,S)}, \{N_B, K_{AB}\}_{sh(B,S)}$$
$$4.\ B \longrightarrow A : \{N_A, K_{AB}\}_{sh(A,S)}$$

Formally, it has the following role scripts:

	A	B	S
1	$-A, B, S$	$-B, A, S$	$-S, A, B$
2	$+A, B, \{N_A, A, B\}_{sh(A,S)}$	$-A, B, X$	$-A, B, \{N_A, A, B\}_{sh(A,S)}, \{N_B, A, B\}_{sh(B,S)}$
3	$-\{N_A, K_{AB}\}_{sh(A,S)}$	$+A, B, X, \{N_B, A, B\}_{sh(B,S)}$	$+\{N_A, K_{AB}\}_{sh(A,S)}, \{N_B, K_{AB}\}_{sh(B,S)}$
4		$-Y, \{N_B, K_{AB}\}_{sh(B,S)}$	
5		$+Y$	

It is easy to see that $\prec_p^1$ is cyclic due to blind copies: e.g., we have $(B,2) \Rightarrow_p$ $(B,3) \rightarrow_p (B,2)$ by substituting any encryption for X. Note that in this example blind copies are merely relayed from an input concatenation to an output concatenation, and the Dolev-Yao intruder could have provided the relaying himself. Hence, the following simplified formalization is adequate with respect to most analysis problems (including leakiness).

---

[1] Long-term shared keys $sh(A, B)$ can be added to our framework analogously to public keys.

	A		B		S
1	$-A, B, S$		$-B, A, S$		$-S, A, B$
2	$+A, B, \{N_A, A, B\}_{sh(A,S)}$		$-A, B$		$-A, B, \{N_A, A, B\}_{sh(A,S)}, \{N_B, A, B\}_{sh(B,S)}$
3	$-\{N_A, K_{AB}\}_{sh(A,S)}$		$+A, B, \{N_B, A, B\}_{sh(B,S)}$		$+\{N_A, K_{AB}\}_{sh(A,S)}, \{N_B, K_{AB}\}_{sh(B,S)}$
4			$-\{N_B, K_{AB}\}_{sh(B,S)}$		

It is easy to check that this transformed version is well-founded.

The examples are representative for other well-known authentication and key establishment protocols of the Clark/Jacob library [6] and the collection of Boyd and Mathuria [4]. Protocols for authentication and key establishment without a trusted third party are typically well-founded. For example, this also includes the corrected NSPK by Lowe, the ISO/IEC 9798-2 three pass mutual authentication protocol, and the revised Andrew protocol of Burrows et al. Protocols with a trusted third party typically involve that the server sends a ticket to one of the agents, who then passes it on to another agent. Since tickets formally lead to blind copies such protocols are not well-founded. However, many can be transformed into equivalent well-founded protocols similarly to the Otway-Rees protocol in Example 8. This includes Kerberos Version 5, Yahalom, and Bauer-Berson-Feiertag. Other protocols send the ticket in an encryption and will not allow this transformation. Examples are Needham-Schroeder Shared Key, and the Denning-Sacco protocol. Interestingly, it seems difficult to find real protocols without flaws that fail to be well-founded without this being due to blind copies.

The Characteristic. We are now ready to establish the characteristic of well-founded protocols P: *for every bundle B of P, the honest causal depth of B is bounded by the depth of P.* This follows from: More precisely, for every event e of B, the honest causal depth of e is bounded by the depth of the protocol position that is instantiated by e.

Lemma 9. *Let P be a well-founded protocol, and let B be a bundle of P. For all $e \in E$ we have: $depth_{\prec_h}(e) \leq depth_{\prec_p}(pos(e))$.*

Theorem 10. *Let P be a well-founded protocol. For all bundles B of P we have: $depth_{\prec_h}(B) \leq depth(P)$.*

Honest Cause Components. Let P be a protocol in general, and let $B = (S, <, \{\Pi_e, src_e\}_{e \in E_{in}})$ be a bundle of P. Given $e' \in E$, define the *honest cause set* of e' by $e' \Downarrow_h = \{e'' \mid e'' \preceq_h e'\}$, and the *strict honest cause set* of e' by $e' \downarrow_h = \{e'' \mid e'' \prec_h e'\}$ respectively. When B is not uniquely determined by the context we also use $e' \Downarrow_h^B$ and $e' \downarrow_h^B$. The *honest cause component induced by e'* is defined by $(S \upharpoonright E_C, < \upharpoonright E_C, \{\Pi_e, src_e\}_{e \in E_{in} \upharpoonright E_C})$ where $E_C = e' \Downarrow_h \cup \{init\}$.

3   Well-Structured Source Trees and Bundles

This section is about *well-structured* source trees and bundles. First we introduce two basic concepts, *bricks* and the *event of first deducibility* of a message. Then we provide the definition based on these concepts. We show that every bundle can be transformed into a well-structured bundle with the same underlying skeleton. Finally, we prove two structural lemmas: the BWS Lemma, and the WS Lemma respectively. The latter will allow us to transform honest cause components into bundles in Section 4. In the following, fix a protocol P.

Basic Concepts. Given a set of messages M, we wish to capture those messages that form the smallest units the intruder has available to build new messages. Such *bricks* are deducible atoms, private keys, and encryptions that can neither be analysed nor synthesized, i.e. honest encryptions. Formally, a *brick wrt* M is a message $b \in \mathcal{DY}(M)$ such that (1) b is an atom, (2) b is a private key, or (3) b is an honest encryption wrt M. We denote the *set of bricks wrt* M by $Bricks(M)$. Given an ordered strand space $\mathcal{S}$, we write $Bricks(\mathcal{S})$ short for $Bricks(M)$ where $M = \{msg(e) \mid e \in E_{out}\}$. We use $Bricks(e\downarrow)$, $Bricks(e\Downarrow)$, and $Bricks(B)$ with the analogous interpretation. Note that $Bricks(M)$ is not the same as the fringe of $analz(M)$: a public key encryption might be synthesizable by the intruder but not analyzable.

Let $\mathcal{S} = (S, <)$ be an ordered strand space. Given a message $m \in \mathcal{DY}(\mathcal{S})$, we single out the event e at which m becomes deducible for the first time wrt $<$. Formally, the *event of first deducibility of m wrt* $\mathcal{S}$, denoted by $efd_\mathcal{S}(m)$, is defined to be the event $e \in E$ such that $m \in \mathcal{DY}(e\Downarrow)$, and e is minimal wrt $<$, i.e. for all other events $e' \in E$ such that $m \in \mathcal{DY}(e'\Downarrow)$, $e < e'$.

Definition and Existence. The general idea behind well-structured bundles is this: if the intruder needs to deduce a message m at the current stage of the protocol run then he will compose m from units that are bricks at this stage; and he will deduce each thus employed brick b by a decomposition using the message of the event, say e, at which b has first become deducible in the protocol run, and units that have been available as bricks at the stage before e. And this is continued in an inductive fashion.

Assume an ordered strand space $\mathcal{S} = (S, <)$. We first define when a source tree is *brick-well-structured* wrt $\mathcal{S}$. This is the case when its conclusion, say b, is a brick wrt $\mathcal{S}$, and b is the result of a minimal decomposition of the message of $efd_\mathcal{S}(b)$, say e, and elements of $Bricks(e\downarrow)$. The latter are deduced by source trees that are brick-well-structured wrt $e\downarrow$ in an inductive fashion.

Let (Π, src) be a source tree wrt $\mathcal{S}$. Formally, we define when (Π, src) is *brick-well-structured wrt* $\mathcal{S}$ by induction on the size of $\mathcal{S}$ (i.e. the number of events of $\mathcal{S}$).

Base case $|\mathcal{S}| = 0$: There are no source trees wrt such $\mathcal{S}$.

Inductive case $|\mathcal{S}| > 0$: (Π, src) is *brick-well-structured wrt* $\mathcal{S}$ iff, setting $b = Concl(\Pi)$, $e = efd_\mathcal{S}(b)$, and $m = msg(e)$,

- there is a minimal proof tree Π_d of $Bricks(e\downarrow) \cup \{m\} \vdash b$ with leaves $l_1 : m, \ldots, l_j : m, l'_1 : b_1, \ldots, l'_k : b_k$ for some $j > 0$, $k \geq 0$, and
- for all $i \in [1, k]$, there is a brick-well-structured source tree (Π_i, src_i) with $Concl(\Pi_i) = b_i$ wrt $e\downarrow$,

such that

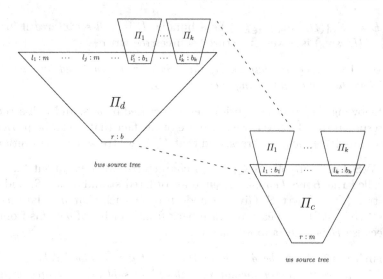

Fig. 2. Well-structured source trees

1. $b \in Bricks(\mathcal{S})$,
2. Π is the composition of $\Pi_d, \Pi_1, \ldots, \Pi_k$ by replacing for each $i \in [1, k]$ the leaf l'_i by the proof tree Π_i, and
3. $src = \{(l_i, e) \mid i \in [1, j]\} \cup \bigcup \{src_i \mid i \in [1, k]\}$.

We say a source tree (Π, src) is brick-well-structured for b wrt $\mathcal{S}$ if it is brick-well-structured wrt $\mathcal{S}$ and $Concl(\Pi) = b$.

A source tree with conclusion m is *well-structured wrt* $\mathcal{S}$ if it deduces m in two stages: first, it composes m from bricks wrt $\mathcal{S}$ in a minimal way; second, it deduces each employed brick b by a source tree that is *brick-well-structured wrt* $\mathcal{S}$. Let (Π, src) be a source tree wrt $\mathcal{S}$. Formally, we say (Π, src) is *well-structured wrt* $\mathcal{S}$ iff, setting $m = Concl(\Pi)$,

- there is a minimal proof tree Π_c of $Bricks(\mathcal{S}) \vdash m$ with leaves $l_1 : b_1, \ldots, l_k : b_k$ for some $k > 0$, and
- for all $i \in [1, k]$, there is a brick-well-structured source tree (Π_i, src_i) for b_i wrt $\mathcal{S}$

such that

1. Π is composed of $\Pi_c, \Pi_1, \ldots, \Pi_k$ by replacing for each $i \in [1, k]$ the leaf l_i by the proof tree Π_i, and
2. $src = \bigcup \{src_i \mid i \in [1, k]\}$.

We say a source tree (Π, src) is well-structured for m wrt $\mathcal{S}$ if it is well-structured wrt $\mathcal{S}$ and $Concl(\Pi) = m$.

Proposition 11. *Let $\mathcal{S}$ be an ordered strand space, and $m \in \mathcal{DY}(\mathcal{S})$. Then there is a well-structured source tree for m wrt $\mathcal{S}$.*

Let $B = (\mathcal{S}, \{(\Pi_e, src_e)\}_{e \in E_{in}})$ be a bundle. B is *well-structured* if for every $e \in E_{in}$, (Π_e, src_e) is a well-structured source tree wrt $e\!\downarrow$.

Theorem 12. *For every bundle B, there is a well-structured bundle B' such that B' has the same underlying skeleton as B.*

In the following, we abbreviate brick-well-structured by *bws*, and well-structured by *ws* respectively. Moreover, we make use of the fact that it can be proved that bws trees are decomposition trees, and that Π_c in ws trees is a composition tree.

The BWS Lemma. We now prove a characteristic lemma about bws source trees, called the *BWS Lemma*. Assume an ordered strand space $\mathcal{S}$, and a bws source tree (Π, src) wrt $\mathcal{S}$. Given a node n of Π such that n is labelled by a brick $b \in Bricks(\mathcal{S})$, it is easy to trace back from which leaf b stems from. This is so because Π is a decomposition tree.

Proposition 13. *Let n be a node of Π such that n is labelled by a brick $b \in Bricks(\mathcal{S})$. There is exactly one source path of b in $subtree(n)$. Moreover, it ends in a leaf. We call it $srcpath\!\uparrow_\Pi(n)$.*

The BWS Lemma says: either we can trace back the source of b to the event of first deducibility of b wrt $\mathcal{S}$, or we can exhibit a leak in $\mathcal{S}$. The latter is the case when b exists wrapped by an encryption at some stage of the run, but b becomes first deducible only at a later stage when the encryption can be decrypted by the intruder. We translate this into the tool of *leak witness situations*.

Definition 14. *Let $\mathcal{S}$ be an ordered strand space, and $e \in E$. We say a proof tree Π contains a leak witness situation wrt $\mathcal{S}$ and e iff Π contains*

1. *an instance of rule D_{senc}*

$$\frac{n_l : \{m\}_k \quad n_r : k}{n_p : m} \; D_{senc}$$

such that $\{m\}_k \in HEnc(e\!\downarrow)$ and $k \in \mathcal{DY}(e\!\Downarrow)$, or
2. *an instance of rule D_{aenc}*

$$\frac{n_l : \{\!|m|\!\}_{ag} \quad n_r : priv(ag)}{n_p : m} \; D_{aenc}$$

such that $\{\!|m|\!\}_{ag} \in HEnc(e\!\downarrow)$ and $priv(ag) \in \mathcal{DY}(e\!\Downarrow)$ respectively.

We call n_l the cipher node and n_r the d-key node of the leak witness situation.

Proposition 15. *Let $\mathcal{S}$ be a bundle skeleton, (Π, src) be a source tree wrt $\mathcal{S}$, and $e \in E$. If Π contains a leak witness situation wrt $\mathcal{S}$ and e then $\mathcal{S}$ is leaky. More precisely, the label of the d-key node is a leak at e.*

Lemma 16 (BWS Lemma). *Let $\mathcal{S}$ be a bundle skeleton, and let (Π, src) be a bws source tree wrt $\mathcal{S}$. For each node n of Π such that n is labelled by a brick $b \in Bricks(\mathcal{S})$ one of the following situations holds:*

1. $srcpath\uparrow_\Pi(n)$ ends in a leaf n_l such that $src(n_l) = efd_S(b)$, or
2. $srcpath\uparrow_\Pi(n)$ passes through a node n' such that n' is the cipher node of a leak witness situation wrt S and $efd_S(b)$.

The proof of the lemma proceeds by case analysis. Assume Π is of the format of Fig. 2, and set $\pi = srcpath_\Pi(n)$. There are three cases to consider: (1) π is entirely contained in Π_d and does not intersect with the roots of the Π_i; then the first situation can be shown to apply. (2) π starts in Π_d but passes through a Π_i. Then we can exhibit a leak witness situation at the transition from Π_d into Π_i, and the second situation applies. (3) π is entirely contained in one of the Π_i. Then we can argue by induction hypothesis.

By Prop. 15 a leak witness situation indeed implies a leak. Then we further obtain the corollary below, where the following fact yields a special case.

Proposition 17. *Let S be a non-leaky bundle skeleton. For all atoms $a \in \mathcal{DY}(S)$ we have: $efd_S(a) = origin_S(a)$.*

Corollary 18. *Let S be a non-leaky bundle skeleton, and let (Π, src) be a bws source tree wrt S. For each node n of Π such that n is labelled by a brick $b \in Bricks(S)$, we have: $srcpath\uparrow_\Pi(n)$ ends in a leaf n_l such that $src(n_l) = efd_S(b)$. Moreover, if b is an atom then $src(n_l) = origin_S(a)$.*

The WS Lemma. Let B be a ws bundle, and let (Π, src) be the source tree of some input event e of B. Assume Π is of the format of Fig. 2. The WS Lemma gives us insights about the source events of the leaves of Π.

Let n_l be a leaf of Π. Consider the largest path π that traces all ancestor nodes of n_l such that the first and only the first node of π is labelled by a brick wrt $e\downarrow$. Since n_l belongs to some bws source tree, say Π_i, the path π clearly exists. Call its first node n, and let the label of n be b. Since Π_i is a decomposition tree, π is a source path of b in $subtree(n)$. Hence, it coincides with $srcpath\uparrow_{\Pi_i}(n)$.

Proposition 19. *Let n_l be a leaf of Π, and let Π_i be the bws source tree within Π that n_l belongs to. n_l has an ancestor node n such that n is labelled by a brick $b \in Bricks(e\downarrow)$ and $srcpath\uparrow_{\Pi_i}(n)$ ends in n_l. We call n the special ancestor of n_l, denoted by $anc(n_l)$.*

Using the existence of $anc(n_l)$ we obtain the following statement about the source event of n_l:

Lemma 20 (WS Lemma). *Let B be a ws bundle, and let (Π, src) be the source tree of some input event e of B. Let n_l be a leaf of Π, and let b be the label of $anc(n_l)$. We have:*

1. *If b is an atom and B is non-leaky then $src(n_l) = origin_B(a)$.*
2. *If b is a private key and B is non-leaky then $b = priv(i)$, and $src(n_l) = init$.*
3. *If $b \in HEnc(e\downarrow)$ then $src(n_l) \prec_h e$.*

The first case is a consequence of Corollary 18. The second case is immediate. To see the third case assume $b \in HEnc(e\downarrow)$ and observe that n must be the root of Π_i (where Π_i is given as in Prop. 19). This is so since Π_i is a decomposition tree (hence b cannot be the left child of a decryption node), and we do not consider compositional keys (hence b cannot be the right child of a decryption node). Consider the path that traces all ancestor nodes of n in Π_c from the root. Since Π_c is a composition tree this path must be a source path of b. If we combine it with $srcpath_{\Pi_i}(n)$ we obtain a source path of b in Π that ends in n_l, and hence by definition $src(n_l) \to_h e$.

4   Transforming Honest Cause Components into Bundles

The main result of this section is this: given a ws bundle B, if B is minimal leaky then B coincides with the honest cause component induced by the last event of B. We achieve this as follows. Based on the WS Lemma we show how honest cause components of non-leaky ws bundles can be transformed into bundles. The transformation also works for minimal leaky bundles and preserves leakiness. Then by a minimality argument the main result stated above is immediate. In the following, fix a protocol P.

Let B be a non-leaky ws bundle, and C be an honest cause component of B. The only reason why, in general, C is not a bundle is that leaves in the source trees of C might have their sources outside of E_C, i.e. in $E_B \setminus E_C$. Let's take a closer look at this situation. Consider a source tree (Π_e, src_e) of C, and a leaf n_l of Π_e such that $src_e(n_l) \notin E_C$. By Prop. 19 we know that n_l has a special ancestor node n that is labelled by a brick b of $e\downarrow_B$. By Lemma 20 we further obtain that b must be an atom that does *not* originate on an event in C: if b is a private key then $src_e(n_l) = init$, which implies $src_e(n_l) \in E_C$, a contradiction; if $b \in HEnc(e\downarrow)$ then $src_e(n_l) \prec_h e$, which also implies $src_e(n_l) \in E_C$, a contradiction; if b is an atom then $src_e(n_l) = origin_B(a)$, and hence $origin_B(a) \notin E_C$ by our assumption $src_e(n_l) \notin E_C$.

Lemma 21. *Let B be a non-leaky ws bundle, and C be an honest cause component of B. Let (Π_e, src_e) be a source tree for some input event e of C. Then for all leaves n_l of Π_e with $src_e(n_l) \notin E_C$ we have: $anc(n_l)$ is labelled by an atom a with $origin_B(a) \notin E_C$.*

Since for such atoms we do not need to respect unique origination constraints wrt E_C we can substitute them by intruder atoms. Thereby we can transform C into a bundle. For the transformation we first define the concept of atom substitution. An *atom substitution* is a function $\alpha : A \to A'$ such that $A, A' \subseteq Atoms$ and the map preserves atomic types. We generalize atom substitutions α to proof trees and strands in the obvious way. Given a proof tree Π we write $\Pi\alpha$ for the result of applying α to all terms of Π. Given a strand s, we write $s\alpha$ for the result of applying α to all terms of s.

In Fig. 3 we provide the algorithm, *PruneSubst(C)*. We first define an atom substitution that substitutes every atom of C that does not originate in C by an

$PruneSubst(\Pi, src, \alpha)$

1. Traverse Π upwards from the root and for each encountered node n do:
   (a) if $lab(n) = a$ for some $a \in domain(\alpha)$ then do:
       i. $\Pi := \Pi \setminus \{subtree(c) \mid c \text{ is a child of } n\}$
       ii. $src := src \setminus \{(n, e') \mid (n, e') \in src \text{ for any } e'\}$
       iii. $src := src \cup \{(n, init)\}$
2. $\Pi := \Pi\alpha$

$PruneSubst(C)$

1. $\alpha = \{(a, c) \mid a \text{ is an atom of } C \text{ such that } origin_B(a) \notin E_C$
   $\& \ c \text{ is an atom known to the intruder of the same type as } a\}$.
2. For every input event e of C do $PruneSubst(\Pi_e, src_e, \alpha)$
3. For every strand s of C do $s := s\alpha$

Fig. 3. Algorithm $PruneSubst$

intruder atom. Then for every proof tree of an input event $e \in E_C$ we proceed as follows. We traverse the proof tree from the root upwards until we hit a node that is labelled by an atom to be substituted. We prune the tree so that such nodes become leaves. We assign $init$ to be the source of such new leaves. We then apply the atom substitution to the entire tree. Thereby $init$ provides indeed an appropriate source for the new leaves. Finally, we apply the substitution to the strands of C. By Lemma 21 we thereby eliminate all leaves that do not have their source in E_C. Moreover, since we only substitute atoms that do not originate in E_C unique origination constraints are not compromised. Together this ensures that the result is a bundle.

Theorem 22. *Let B be a non-leaky ws bundle, and let C be an honest cause component of B. Then $PruneSubst(C)$ is a bundle.*

Since minimal leaky bundles are non-leaky bundles with one additional output event the transformation carries over to minimal leaky bundles. Moreover, the transformation is not too strong in that it preserves leakiness. This is non-trivial to show and requires a variant of Lemma 21.

Theorem 23. *Let B be a minimal leaky ws bundle, and let C be the honest cause component of the last event of B. Then $PruneSubst(C)$ is a leaky bundle. (Indeed, it is also minimal leaky.)*

Now the main result is immediate: given B and C as above, B must coincide with C. Otherwise there is an event in B that is not in C. Then $PruneSubst(C)$ yields a leaky bundle that is smaller than B, a contradiction to the assumption that B is minimal leaky.

Corollary 24. *Let B be a minimal leaky ws bundle, and let C be the honest cause component of the last event of B. Then $B = C$.*

5   Main Result and Further Research

Theorem 25. LEAKINESS *is decidable for well-founded protocols.*

To decide LEAKINESS we only need to check whether there exists a minimal leaky bundle. By Theorem 12 it is sufficient to only consider minimal leaky *well-structured* bundles. By Corollary 24 their size is bounded by that of the honest cause components of ws bundles. For well-founded protocols the latter are bounded. This follows from Theorem 10, and the fact that the message size is bounded: we work with typed messages, and the definition of well-foundedness excludes blind copies. Altogether this means we only have to consider bundles of bounded size. As usual we can then work with a fixed alphabet, guess a candidate bundle, and check whether it is indeed a minimal leaky bundle.

For technical ease we have proved the result for a simple message algebra with symmetric and asymmetric encryption. It is straightforward to lift all concepts and proofs to include other cryptographic operations such as digital signatures, MACs, and cryptographic hash functions. Rather than only defining honest encryptions one can work with honest ciphertexts that fall into the corresponding subcases. Moreover, by the approach of Arapinas in [2] the decidability result can be lifted to an untyped message algebra.

Non-trivial extensions include generalizing the result to allow compositional keys and a restricted form of ciphertext forwarding that cannot be dealt with by the simple transformation suggested for Example 8. Now that the proof is in place we can also investigate which standard algebraic theories [8] can be plugged into the framework. One will only have to check that certain properties of honest ciphertexts are satisfied. That this is possible is also indicated by [11], where similar ideas are independently used to obtain decidability in the context of Diffie-Hellmann protocols.

We see our result on LEAKINESS as a major step towards obtaining decidability for a class of standard authentication properties. We hope that some of the insights of Dougherty and Guttman in [11] might help to achieve this. Their security problem is expressed as geometric sequents, and hence, is much more general than LEAKINESS; on the other hand, their proof relies on the fact that there are no temporary secrets. This is naturally given since their class of Diffie-Hellman protocols does not include encryption. Hence, a combination of the techniques might cover a wide class of protocols and security properties.

Acknowledgements. The author is very grateful to Joshua Guttman who has shepherded this paper. His comments and feedback have made this a much improved paper. The author would also like to thank the anonymous referees for their valuable comments.

References

1. Abadi, M., Needham, R.: Prudent engineering practice for cryptographic protocols. IEEE Trans. Softw. Eng. 22(1), 6–15 (1996)
2. Arapinis, M., Duflot, M.: Bounding messages for free in security protocols. In: Arvind, V., Prasad, S. (eds.) FSTTCS 2007. LNCS, vol. 4855, pp. 376–387. Springer, Heidelberg (2007)

3. Blanchet, B., Podelski, A.: Verification of Cryptographic Protocols: Tagging Enforces Termination. Theoretical Computer Science 333(1-2), 67–90 (2005), Special issue FoSSaCS 2003
4. Boyd, C., Mathuria, A.: Protocols for Authentication and Key Establishment. Springer (2003)
5. Chrétien, R., Cortier, V., Delaune, S.: Typing messages for free in security protocols: The case of equivalence properties. In: Baldan, P., Gorla, D. (eds.) CONCUR 2014. LNCS, vol. 8704, pp. 372–386. Springer, Heidelberg (2014)
6. Clark, J., Jacob, J.: A survey of authentication protocol literature: Version 1.0 (1997)
7. Comon-Lundh, H., Cortier, V., Zălinescu, E.: Deciding security properties for cryptographic protocols. application to key cycles. ACM Trans. Comput. Logic 11(9), 9:1–9:42 (2010)
8. Cortier, V., Delaune, S., Lafourcade, P.: A survey of algebraic properties used in cryptographic protocols. Journal of Computer Security 14(1), 1–43 (2006)
9. Dolev, D., Yao, A.C.-C.: On the security of public key protocols (extended abstract). In: FOCS, pp. 350–357 (1981)
10. Dolev, S., Even, S., Karp, R.M.: On the security of ping-pong protocols. Inform. and Control 55(1-3), 57–68 (1982)
11. Dougherty, D., Guttman, J.: Decidability for lightweight diffie-hellman protocols. In: CSF 2014, pp. 217–231. IEEE Computer Society (2014)
12. Durgin, N., Lincoln, P., Mitchell, J., Scedrov, A.: Multiset rewriting and the complexity of bounded security protocols. J. of Computer Security 12(2), 247–311 (2004)
13. Even, S., Goldreich, O.: On the security of multi-party ping-pong protocols. In: Symposium on the Foundations of Computer Science, pp. 4–39. IEEE Computer Society (1983)
14. Fröschle, S.: From Security Protocols to Security APIS: Foundations and Verification. To appear in the Information Security and Cryptography series of Springer
15. Fröschle, S.: On well-founded security protocols. In: Joint Workshop on Foundations of Computer Security and Formal and Computational Cryptography (FCS-FCC 2014) (2014)
16. Guttman, J.D., Thayer, F.J.: Authentication tests and the structure of bundles. Theor. Comput. Sci. 283(2), 333–380 (2002)
17. Heintze, N., Tygar, J.D.: A model for secure protocols and their compositions. IEEE Transactions on Software Engineering 22, 2–13 (1996)
18. Lowe, G.: Towards a completeness result for model checking of security protocols. Journal of Computer Security 7(1), 89–146 (1999)
19. Needham, R.M., Schroeder, M.D.: Using encryption for authentication in large networks of computers. Commun. ACM 21(12), 993–999 (1978)
20. Ramanujam, R., Suresh, S.P.: A decidable subclass of unbounded security protocols. In: WITS 2003, pp. 11–20 (2003)
21. Sarukkai, S., Suresh, S.P.: Tagging makes secrecy decidable with unbounded nonces as well. In: Pandya, P.K., Radhakrishnan, J. (eds.) FSTTCS 2003. LNCS, vol. 2914, pp. 363–374. Springer, Heidelberg (2003)
22. Ramanujam, R., Suresh, S.P.: Decidability of context-explicit security protocols. Journal of Computer Security 13(1), 135–165 (2005)
23. Rusinowitch, M., Turuani, M.: Protocol insecurity with finite number of sessions is NP-complete. In: CSFW 2001, pp. 174–187. IEEE Computer Society (2001)

Abstractions for Security Protocol Verification

Binh Thanh Nguyen and Christoph Sprenger

Institute of Information Security
Department of Computer Science, ETH Zurich, Switzerland

Abstract. We present a large class of security protocol abstractions with the aim of improving the scope and efficiency of verification tools. We propose typed abstractions, which transform a term's structure based on its type, and untyped abstractions, which remove atomic messages, variables, and redundant terms. Our theory improves on previous work by supporting a useful subclass of *shallow* subterm-convergent rewrite theories, user-defined types, and untyped variables to cover type flaw attacks. We prove soundness results for an expressive property language that includes secrecy and authentication. Applying our abstractions to realistic IETF protocol models, we achieve dramatic speedups and extend the scope of several modern security protocol analyzers.

1 Introduction

Security protocols play a central role in today's networked applications. Past experience has amply shown that informal arguments justifying the security of such protocols are insufficient. This makes security protocols prime candidates for formal verification. In the last two decades, research in formal security protocol verification has made enormous progress, which is reflected in many state-of-the-art tools including AVANTSSAR [1], ProVerif [6], Maude-NPA [14], Scyther [10], and Tamarin [21]. These tools can verify small to medium-sized protocols in a few seconds or less, sometimes for an unbounded number of sessions. Despite this success, they can still be challenged when verifying real-world protocols such as those defined in standards and deployed on the internet (e.g., TLS, IKE, and ISO/IEC 9798). Such protocols typically have messages with numerous fields, support many alternatives (e.g., cryptographic setups), and may be composed from more basic protocols (e.g., IKEv2-EAP).

Abstraction [7] is a standard technique to over-approximate complex systems by simpler ones for verification. Sound abstractions preserve counterexamples (or attacks in security terms) from concrete to abstracted systems. In the context of security protocols, abstractions are extensively used. Here, we only mention a few examples. First, the Dolev-Yao model is a standard (not necessarily sound) abstraction of cryptography. Second, many tools use abstractions to map the verification problem into the formalism of an efficient solver or reasoner. We call these *back-end* abstractions. For example, ProVerif [6] translates models in the applied pi calculus to a set of Horn clauses, SATMC [4] reduces protocol verification to SAT solving, and Paulson [24] models protocols as inductively

© Springer-Verlag Berlin Heidelberg 2015
R. Focardi and A. Myers (Eds.): POST 2015, LNCS 9036, pp. 196–215, 2015.
DOI: 10.1007/978-3-662-46666-7_11

defined trace sets. Finally, some abstractions aim at speeding up automated analysis by simplifying protocols within a given protocol model before feeding them to verifiers [18,22]. Our work belongs to this class of *front-end* abstractions.

Extending Hui and Lowe's work [18], we proposed in [22] a rich class of protocol abstractions and proved its soundness for a wide range of security properties. We used a type system to uniformly transform all terms of a given type (e.g., a pattern in a protocol role and its instances during execution) whereas [18] only covers ground terms. Our work [22] exhibits several limitations: (1) the theory is limited to the free algebra over a fixed signature; (2) all variables have strict (possibly structured) types, hence we cannot precisely model ticket forwarding or Diffie-Hellman exchanges. While the type system enables fine-grained control over abstractions (e.g., by discerning different nonces), it may eliminate realistic attacks such as type flaw attacks; (3) some soundness conditions involving quantifiers are hard to check in practice; and (4) it presents few experimental results for a single tool (SATMC) using abstractions that are crafted manually.

In this work, we address all the limitations above. First, we work with a useful subclass of *shallow* subterm-convergent rewrite theories modulo a set of axioms to model cryptographic operations. Second, we support untyped variables, user-defined types, and subtyping. User-defined types enable the grouping of similar atomic types (e.g., session keys) and adjusting the granularity of matching in message abstraction. Third, we have separated the removal of variables, atomic messages, and redundancies (new untyped abstractions) from the transformation of the message structure (typed abstractions). This simplifies the specifications and soundness proof of typed abstractions. Fourth, we provide effectively checkable syntactic criteria for the conditions of the soundness theorem. Finally, we extended Scyther [10] with fully automated support for our abstraction methodology. We validated our approach on an extensive set of realistic case studies drawn from the IKEv1, IKEv2, ISO/IEC 9798, and PANA-AKA standard proposals. Our abstractions result in very substantial performance gains. We have also obtained positive results for several other state-of-the-art verifiers (ProVerif, CL-Atse, OFMC, and SATMC) with manually produced abstractions.

Example: The IKEv2-mac Protocol. The Internet Key Exchange (IKE) family of protocols is part of the IPsec protocol suite for securing Internet Protocol (IP) communication. IKE establishes a shared key, which is later used for securing IP packets, realizes mutual authentication, and offers identity protection as an option. Its first version (IKEv1) dates back to 1998 [17]. The second version (IKEv2) [20] significantly simplifies the first one. However, the protocols in this family are still complex and contain a large number of fields.

Concrete protocol. As our running example, we present a member of the IKEv2 family, called IKEv2-mac (or IKE$_m$ for short), which sets up a session key using a Diffie-Hellman (DH) key exchange, provides mutual authentication based on MACs, and also offers identity protection. We use Cremers' models of IKE [11] as a basis for our presentation and experiments (see Section 4.2). Our starting point is the following concrete IKE$_m$ protocol between an initiator A and a responder B.

$\mathsf{IKE_m}(1)$. $A \to B : SPIa, o, sA1, g^x, Na$
$\mathsf{IKE_m}(2)$. $B \to A : SPIa, SPIb, sA1, g^y, Nb$
$\mathsf{IKE_m}(3)$. $A \to B : SPIa, SPIb, \{\!| A, B, AUTHa, sA2, tSa, tSb |\!\}_{SK}$
$\mathsf{IKE_m}(4)$. $B \to A : SPIa, SPIb, \{\!| B, AUTHb, sA2, tSa, tSb |\!\}_{SK}$

Here, $SPIa$ and $SPIb$ denote the *Security Parameter Indices* that determine cryptographic algorithms, o is a constant number, $sA1$ and $sA2$ are *Security Associations*, g is the DH group generator, x and y are secret DH exponents, Na and Nb are nonces, and tSa and tSb denote *Traffic Selectors* specifying certain IP parameters. $AUTHa$ and $AUTHb$ denote the authenticators of A and B and SK the session key derived from the DH key g^{xy}. These are defined as follows.

$$SK = \mathsf{kdf}(Na, Nb, g^{xy}, SPIa, SPIb)$$
$$AUTHa = \mathsf{mac}(\mathsf{sh}(A, B), SPIa, o, sA1, g^x, Na, Nb, \mathsf{prf}(SK, A))$$
$$AUTHb = \mathsf{mac}(\mathsf{sh}(B, A), SPIa, SPIb, sA1, g^y, Nb, Na, \mathsf{prf}(SK, B))$$

We model the functions mac, kdf, and prf as hash functions and use $\mathsf{sh}(A, B)$ and $\mathsf{sh}(B, A)$ to refer to the (single) long-term symmetric key shared by A and B.

We consider the following security properties: (P1) the secrecy of the DH key g^{xy}, which implies the secrecy of SK, and (P2) mutual non-injective agreement on the nonces Na and Nb and the DH half-keys g^x and g^y.

Abstraction. Our theory supports the construction of abstract models by removing inessential fields and operations. For example, in $\mathsf{IKE_m}$ we can remove: (i) the symmetric encryptions with the session key SK; then (ii) all atomic top-level fields except Na and Nb; (iii) all fields of SK except the DH key g^{xy}; and (iv) from the authenticators: the fields $SPIa$, $SPIb$, and $sA1$ and the application of prf including the agent names underneath. The resulting protocol is $\mathsf{IKE_m^2}$:

$\mathsf{IKE_m^2}(1)$. $A \to B : g^x, Na$ $\mathsf{IKE_m^2}(3)$. $A \to B : AUTHa$
$\mathsf{IKE_m^2}(2)$. $B \to A : g^y, Nb$ $\mathsf{IKE_m^2}(4)$. $B \to A : AUTHb$

where $SK = \mathsf{kdf}(g^{xy})$ and $AUTHa = \mathsf{mac}(\mathsf{sh}(A, B), o, g^x, Na, Nb, SK)$ for role A and $AUTHb = \mathsf{mac}(\mathsf{sh}(B, A), g^y, Nb, Na, SK)$ for role B.

Scyther verifies the properties (P1) and (P2) in 8.7s on the concrete and in 1.7s on an automatically generated abstract protocol (which is less intuitive than the one presented here). Our soundness results imply that the original protocol $\mathsf{IKE_m}$ also enjoys these properties. We chose the protocol $\mathsf{IKE_m}$ as running example for its relative simplicity compared to the other protocols in our case studies. In many of our experiments (Section 4.2), our abstractions (i) result in much more substantial speedups, or (ii) enable the successful unbounded verification of a protocol where it times out or exhausts memory on the original protocol.

2   Security Protocol Model

We define a term algebra $\mathcal{T}_\Sigma(V)$ over a signature Σ and a set of variables V in the standard way. Let Σ^n denote the symbols of arity n. We call the elements of Σ^0

atoms and write $\Sigma^{\geq 1}$ for the set of proper function symbols. For a fixed $\Sigma^{\geq 1}$, we will vary Σ^0 to generate different sets of terms, denoted by $\mathcal{T}(V, \Sigma^0)$, including terms in protocol roles, network messages, and types. We write $subs(t)$ for the set of subterms of t and define the size of t by $|t| = |subs(t)|$. We also define $vars(t) = subs(t) \cap V$. If $vars(t) = \emptyset$ then t is called *ground*. We denote the top-level symbol of a (non-variable) term t by $top(t)$ and the set of its symbols in $\Sigma^{\geq 1}$ by $ct(t)$. A position is a sequence of natural numbers. We denote the subterm of t at position p with $t|_p$ and write $t[u]_p$ for the term obtained by replacing $t|_p$ at position p by u. We also partition Σ into sets of public and private symbols, denoted by Σ_{pub} and Σ_{pri}. We assume Σ_{pub} includes pairing $\langle \cdot, \cdot \rangle$ which associates to the right, e.g., $\langle t, u, v \rangle = \langle t, \langle u, v \rangle \rangle$. We usually write, e.g., $\{\!| t, u, v |\!\}_k$ rather than $\{\!| \langle t, u, v \rangle |\!\}_k$. We define the *splitting* function by $split(\langle t, u \rangle) = split(t) \cup split(u)$ on pairs and $split(t) = \{t\}$ on other terms t. We call the elements of $split(t)$ the *fields* of t. For $n \in \mathbb{N}$, $\tilde{n}$ denotes $\{1, \ldots, n\}$.

The set of *message terms* is $\mathcal{M} = \mathcal{T}(V, \mathcal{A} \cup \mathcal{F} \cup \mathcal{C})$, where V, $\mathcal{A}$, $\mathcal{F}$, and $\mathcal{C}$ are pairwise disjoint infinite sets of variables, agents, fresh values, and constants.

2.1 Type System

We introduce a type system akin to [2] and extend it with subtyping. We define the set of atomic types by $\mathcal{Y}_{at} = \mathcal{Y}_0 \cup \{\alpha, msg\} \cup \{\beta_n \mid n \in \mathcal{F}\} \cup \{\gamma_c \mid c \in \mathcal{C}\}$, where α, β_n, and γ_c are the types of agents, the fresh value n, and the constant c, respectively. Moreover, msg is the type of all messages and $\mathcal{Y}_0$ is a disjoint set of user-defined types. The set of all types is then defined by $\mathcal{Y} = \mathcal{T}(\emptyset, \mathcal{Y}_{at})$.

We assume that all variables have an atomic type, i.e., $V = \{V_\tau\}_{\tau \in \mathcal{Y}_{at}}$ is a family of disjoint infinite sets of variables. Let $\Gamma: V \to \mathcal{Y}_{at}$ be such that $\Gamma(X) = \tau$ if and only if $X \in V_\tau$. We extend Γ to atoms by defining $\Gamma(a) = \alpha$, $\Gamma(n) = \beta_n$, and $\Gamma(c) = \gamma_c$ for $a \in \mathcal{A}$, $n \in \mathcal{F}$, and $c \in \mathcal{C}$, and then homomorphically to all terms $t \in \mathcal{M}$. We call $\tau = \Gamma(t)$ the *type of* t and sometimes also write $t : \tau$.

The subtyping relation $\preccurlyeq$ on types is defined by the following inference rules and by two additional rules (not shown) defining its reflexivity and transitivity.

$$\frac{\tau \in \mathcal{Y}}{\tau \preccurlyeq msg} \ S(msg) \qquad \frac{\tau_1 \preccurlyeq_0 \tau_2}{\tau_1 \preccurlyeq \tau_2} \ S(\preccurlyeq_0) \qquad \frac{\tau_1 \preccurlyeq \tau_1' \quad \cdots \quad \tau_n \preccurlyeq \tau_n'}{c(\tau_1, \ldots, \tau_n) \preccurlyeq c(\tau_1', \ldots, \tau_n')} \ S(c \in \Sigma^n)$$

Every type is a subtype of msg by the first rule. The second rule embeds a user-defined *atomic subtyping relation* $\preccurlyeq_0 \subseteq (\mathcal{Y}_{at} \setminus \{msg\}) \times \mathcal{Y}_0$, which relates atomic types (except msg) to user-defined atomic types in $\mathcal{Y}_0$. For simplicity, we require that $\preccurlyeq_0$ is a partial function. The third rule ensures that subtyping is preserved by all symbols. The set of subtypes of τ is $\tau{\downarrow} = \{\tau' \in \mathcal{Y} \mid \tau' \preccurlyeq \tau\}$.

2.2 Equational Theories

An *equation* over a signature Σ is an unordered pair $\{s, t\}$, written $s \simeq t$, where $s, t \in \mathcal{T}_\Sigma(V_{msg})$. An *equation presentation* $\mathcal{E} = (\Sigma, E)$ consists of a signature Σ and a set E of equations over Σ. The *equational theory* induced by $\mathcal{E}$ is the smallest Σ-congruence, written $=_E$, containing all instances of equations in E. We often identify $\mathcal{E}$ with the induced equational theory.

A *rewrite rule* is an oriented pair $l \rightarrow r$, where $vars(r) \subseteq vars(l) \subseteq \mathcal{V}_{msg}$. A *rewrite theory* is a triple $\mathcal{R} = (\Sigma, Ax, R)$ where Σ is a signature, Ax a set of Σ-equations, and R a set of rewrite rules. The rewriting relation $\rightarrow_{R,Ax}$ on $\mathcal{T}_\Sigma(V)$ is defined by $t \rightarrow_{R,Ax} t'$ iff there exists a non-variable position p in t, a rule $l \rightarrow r \in R$, and a substitution σ such that $t|_p =_{Ax} l\sigma$ and $t' = t[r\sigma]_p$. If $t \rightarrow^*_{R,Ax} t'$ and t' is irreducible, we call t' R,Ax-*normal* and also say that t' is a *normal form* of t. Under suitable termination, confluence, and coherence conditions (see [19] for definitions), one can decompose an equational theory (Σ, E) into a rewrite theory (Σ, Ax, R) where $Ax \subseteq E$ and, for all terms $t, u \in \mathcal{T}_\Sigma(V)$, we have $t =_E u$ iff $t{\downarrow}_{R,Ax} =_{Ax} u{\downarrow}_{R,Ax}$. Here, $t{\downarrow}_{R,Ax}$ denotes any normal form of t. In this paper, we work with decomposable equational theories.

A rewriting theory R is *subterm-convergent* if it is convergent and, for each $l \rightarrow r \in R$, r is either a proper subterm of l or ground and in normal form with respect to R. For our soundness result, we consider the subclass $\mathcal{S}$ of subterm-convergent rewrite theories where each rule in R has one of the following forms.

- (R1): $d(c(x_1, \ldots, x_n, t), u) \rightarrow x_j$, where $c, d \in \Sigma_{\mathsf{pub}}$, t, u are terms, $j \in \widetilde{n}$, and $x_1, \ldots, x_n$ are pairwise distinct variables with $x_i \notin vars(t, u)$ for all $i \in \widetilde{n}$.
- (R2): $d(c(x_1, \ldots, x_n)) \rightarrow x_j$, where $c, d \in \Sigma_{\mathsf{pub}}$, $j \in \widetilde{n}$, and $x_1, \ldots, x_n$ are pairwise distinct variables.
- (R3): $c(x_1, \ldots, x_n) \rightarrow x_j$ where $c \in \Sigma_{\mathsf{pub}}$, x_j is a variable with $j \in \widetilde{n}$, and x_i is a variable or an atom for all $i \in \widetilde{n}$.
- (R4): $l \rightarrow a$ for a constant a.

Intuitively, the first three forms enable different types of projection of a term's arguments. Rules R1 and R2 apply a destructor d to extract one of c's arguments. In rule R1 the destructor has two arguments. The terms t and u can be seen a pair of matching keys required to extract x_j. Rule R3 uses no destructor. Finally, R4 models rewriting a term to a constant. Since the rules (R1-R3) have limited depth, we call the class $\mathcal{S}$ of rewrite theories *shallow subterm-convergent*.

We also introduce a condition on the equations Ax of the rewrite theory.

Definition 1. *A rewrite theory (Σ, Ax, R) is well-formed if for all $\{s, t\} \in Ax$, we have (i) neither s nor t is a pair and (ii) $top(s) = top(t)$.*

We only consider equational theories that can be decomposed into a shallow subterm-convergent, well-formed rewrite theory. These are adequate to model many well-known cryptographic primitives as illustrated by the examples below.

Example 1. We model the protocols of our case studies (see Sections 1 and 4) in the rewrite theory $\mathcal{R}_{cs} = (\Sigma_{cs}, Ax_{cs}, R_{cs})$ where

$$\Sigma_{cs} = \{\mathsf{sh}, \mathsf{pk}, \mathsf{pri}, \mathsf{prf}, \mathsf{kdf}, \mathsf{mac}, \langle \cdot, \cdot \rangle, \pi_1, \pi_2, \{\!|\cdot|\!\}_\cdot, \{\!|\cdot|\!\}_\cdot^{-1}, \{\cdot\}_\cdot, \{\cdot\}_\cdot^{-1}, [\cdot]_\cdot, \mathsf{ver}\} \cup \Sigma_{cs}^0$$

contains function symbols for: shared, public, and private long-term keys (where $\Sigma_{\mathsf{pri}} = \{\mathsf{sh}, \mathsf{pri}\}$); hash functions prf, kdf, and mac; pairs and projections; symmetric and asymmetric encryption and decryption; and signing and verification.

The set of atoms Σ^0_{cs} is specified later. The set R_{cs} consists of rewrite rules for projections (type R2) and for decryption and signature verification (type R1):

$$\pi_1(\langle X, Y \rangle) \to X \qquad \{\!\{[X]_K\}\!\}^{-1}_K \to X \qquad \mathsf{ver}([X]_{\mathsf{pri}(K)}, \mathsf{pk}(K)) \to X$$
$$\pi_2(\langle X, Y \rangle) \to Y \qquad \{\!\{X\}_{\mathsf{pk}(K)}\}^{-1}_{\mathsf{pri}(K)} \to X$$

We have two equations in Ax_{cs}, namely, $\mathsf{exp}(\mathsf{exp}(g, X), Y) \simeq \mathsf{exp}(\mathsf{exp}(g, Y), X)$ to model Diffie-Hellman key exchange and $\mathsf{sh}(X, Y) \simeq \mathsf{sh}(Y, X)$.

Example 2. The theory of XOR is given by the following rewrite system where the rules are of types R2, R3 and R4. The rightmost rule ensures coherence [19].

$$X \oplus Y \simeq Y \oplus X \qquad\qquad X \oplus 0 \to X \quad X \oplus X \oplus Y \to Y$$
$$(X \oplus Y) \oplus Z \simeq X \oplus (Y \oplus Z) \quad X \oplus X \to 0$$

For our theoretical development, we consider an arbitrary but fixed shallow subterm-convergent and well-formed rewrite theory (Σ, Ax, R) that includes the function symbols and rewrite rules for pairing and projections.

We denote by $dom(g)$ and $ran(g)$ the domain and range of a function g. We now define well-typed substitutions, which respect subtyping.

Definition 2 (Well-typed substitutions). *A substitution θ is* well-typed *if $\Gamma((X\theta)\!\downarrow_{R,Ax}) \preccurlyeq \Gamma(X)$ for all $X \in dom(\theta)$.*

2.3 Protocols

For a set of terms T, we define the set of events $Evt(T) = \{\mathsf{snd}(t), \mathsf{rcv}(t) \mid t \in T\}$ and $term(ev(t)) = t$ for event $ev(t)$. A *role* is a sequence of events from $Evt(\mathcal{M})$.

Definition 3 (Protocol). *A protocol is a function $P : \mathcal{V}_\alpha \rightharpoonup Evt(\mathcal{M})^*$ mapping agent variables to roles. Let $\mathcal{M}_P = term(ran(P))$ be the set of protocol terms appearing in the roles of P, and let $\mathcal{V}_P$, $\mathcal{A}_P$, $\mathcal{F}_P$, and $\mathcal{C}_P$ denote the sets of variables, agents, fresh values, and constants in $\mathcal{M}_P$.*

*Example 3 (*IKE$_m$ *protocol).* We formalize the IKE$_m$ protocol from Section 1 in the rewrite theory of Example 1 as follows, using upper-case (lower-case) identifiers for variables (atoms). The atoms Σ^0_{cs} are composed of constants $C = \{g, o, sA1, sA2, tSa, tSb\}$ and fresh values $F = \{na, nb, x, y, sPIa, sPIb\}$. The variables and their types are $A, B : \alpha$, $Ga, Gb : msg$, $SPIa, SPIb, Na, Nb : nonce$ where *nonce* is a user-defined type that satisfies $\beta_n \preccurlyeq_0 nonce$ for all $n \in F$. We show here the initiator role A. The responder role B is dual.

$$\begin{aligned} \mathsf{IKE}_m(A) = \;&\mathsf{snd}(sPIa, o, sA1, \mathsf{exp}(g, x), na) \cdot \mathsf{rcv}(sPIa, SPIb, sA1, Gb, Nb) \cdot \\ &\mathsf{snd}(sPIa, SPIb, \{\!\{A, B, AUTHaa, sA2, tSa, tSb\}\!\}_{SKa}) \cdot \\ &\mathsf{rcv}(sPIa, SPIb, \{\!\{B, AUTHba, sA2, tSa, tSb\}\!\}_{SKa}) \end{aligned}$$

where the terms $SKa = \mathsf{kdf}(na, Nb, \mathsf{exp}(Gb, x), sPIa, SPIb)$ and

$$AUTHaa = \mathsf{mac}(\mathsf{sh}(A, B), sPIa, o, sA1, \mathsf{exp}(g, x), na, Nb, \mathsf{prf}(SKa, A))$$
$$AUTHba = \mathsf{mac}(\mathsf{sh}(A, B), sPIa, SPIb, sA1, Gb, Nb, na, \mathsf{prf}(SKa, B)).$$

represent the initiator A's view of the session key and of the authenticators.

$$\frac{u \in T}{T \vdash_E u} \; \text{Ax} \qquad \frac{T \vdash_E t' \quad t' =_E t}{T \vdash_E t} \; \text{Eq} \qquad \frac{T \vdash_E t_1 \quad \cdots \quad T \vdash_E t_n}{T \vdash_E f(t_1, \ldots, t_n)} \; \text{Comp} \, (f \in \Sigma_{\text{pub}}^{\geq 1})$$

Fig. 1. Intruder deduction rules (where $\Sigma_{\text{pub}}^{\geq 1} = \Sigma^{\geq 1} \cap \Sigma_{\text{pub}}$)

2.4   Operational Semantics

Let *TID* be a countably infinite set of thread identifiers. When we instantiate a role into a thread for execution, we mark its variables and fresh values with the thread identifier i. We define the instantiation $t^{\#i}$ of a term t for $i \in TID$ as the term where every variable or fresh value u is replaced by u^i. Constants and agents remain unchanged. Instantiation does not affect the type of a term.

We define by $T^{\#} = \{ t^{\#i} \mid t \in T \wedge i \in TID \}$ the set of instantiations of terms in a set T and abbreviate $T^{\flat} = T \cup T^{\#}$. For example, $\mathcal{M}^{\#}$ is the set of instantiated message terms, which we will use to instantiate roles into threads. We define the set of *network messages* exchanged during protocol execution by $\mathcal{N} = \mathcal{T}(\mathcal{V}^{\#}, \mathcal{A} \cup \mathcal{F}^{\#} \cup \mathcal{F}^{\bullet} \cup \mathcal{C})$, where $\mathcal{F}^{\bullet} = \{ n_k^{\bullet} \mid n \in \mathcal{F} \wedge k \in \mathbb{N} \}$ is the set of attacker-generated fresh values. Note that $\mathcal{M}^{\#} \subseteq \mathcal{N}$. We abbreviate $\mathcal{T} = \mathcal{M} \cup \mathcal{N}$.

We use a Dolev-Yao attacker model parametrized by an equational theory E. Its judgements are of the form $T \vdash_E t$ meaning that the intruder can derive term t from the set of terms T. The derivable judgements are defined in a standard way by the three deduction rules in Figure 1.

We define a transition system with states (tr, th, σ), where

- tr is a *trace* consisting of a sequence of pairs of thread identifiers and events,
- $th : TID \rightharpoonup dom(P) \times Evt(\mathcal{M}_P^{\#})^*$ are *threads* executing role instances, and
- $\sigma : \mathcal{V}^{\#} \rightharpoonup \mathcal{N}$ is a well-typed ground substitution from instantiated protocol variables to network messages such that $\mathcal{V}_P^{\#} \subseteq dom(\sigma)$.

The trace tr as well as the executing role instance are symbolic (with terms in $\mathcal{M}^{\#}$). The separate substitution σ instantiates these messages to (ground) network messages. The ground trace associated with such a state is $tr\sigma$.

The set $Init_P$ of initial states of protocol P contains all (ϵ, th, σ) satisfying

$$\forall i \in dom(th). \, \exists R \in dom(P). \, th(i) = (R, P(R)^{\#i})$$

where all terms in the respective protocol roles are instantiated. The substitution σ is chosen non-deterministically in the initial state.

The rules in Figure 2 define the transitions. In both rules, the first premise states that a send or receive event heads thread i's role. This event is removed and added together with the thread identifier i to the trace tr. The substitution σ remains unchanged. The second premise of *RECV* requires that the network message $t\sigma$ matching the term t in the receive event is derivable from the intruder's (ground) knowledge $IK(tr)\sigma \cup IK_0$. Here, $IK(tr)$ denotes the (symbolic) intruder knowledge derived from a trace tr as the set of terms in the send events on tr, i.e., $IK(tr) = \{ t \mid \exists i. \, (i, \mathsf{snd}(t)) \in tr \}$ and IK_0 denotes the intruder's (ground) initial knowledge. We assume $\mathcal{A} \cup \mathcal{C} \cup \mathcal{F}^{\bullet} \subseteq IK_0$ and IK_0 is R, Ax-normal. Note that the *SEND* rule implicitly updates this intruder knowledge.

$$th(i) = (R, \mathsf{snd}(t) \cdot tl)$$
$$(tr, th, \sigma) \rightarrow (tr \cdot (i, \mathsf{snd}(t)), th[i \mapsto (R, tl)], \sigma) \quad SEND$$

$$th(i) = (R, \mathsf{rcv}(t) \cdot tl) \quad IK(tr)\sigma \cup IK_0 \vdash_E t\sigma$$
$$(tr, th, \sigma) \rightarrow (tr \cdot (i, \mathsf{rcv}(t)), th[i \mapsto (R, tl)], \sigma) \quad RECV$$

Fig. 2. Operational semantics

2.5 Property Language

We use the same specification language as in [22] to express secrecy and authentication properties. Hence, we only sketch some of its elements and give examples. There are atomic formulas to express equality ($t = u$), the secrecy of a term ($secret(t)$), the occurrence of an event e by thread i in the trace ($steps(i, e)$), that thread i executes role R, and the honesty of other agents in the view of a thread i. Quantification is allowed over thread identifier variables. To achieve attack preservation, the predicate $secret(t)$ may occur only positively.

Example 4 (Properties of IKE$_m$*).* We express the secrecy of the Diffie-Hellman key $\exp(Gb, x)$ for role A of the protocol IKE$_m$ of Example 3 as follows.

$$\phi_s = \forall j. \ (role(j, A) \wedge honest(j, [A, B]) \wedge steps(j, \mathsf{rcv}(t_4))) \Rightarrow secret(\exp(Gb^j, x^j)).$$

where $t_4 = \langle sPIa, SPIb, \{\!| B, AUTHba, sA2, tSa, tSb |\!\}_{SKa} \rangle$ and $honest(j, [A, B])$ means that A and B are honest. We formalize non-injective agreement of A with B on the nonces na and nb and the DH half-keys $\exp(g, x)$ and $\exp(g, y)$ by

$$\phi_a = \forall j. \ (role(j, A) \wedge honest(j, [A, B]) \wedge steps(j, \mathsf{rcv}(t_4)))$$
$$\Rightarrow (\exists k. \ role(k, B) \wedge steps(k, \mathsf{snd}(\langle SPIa, sPIb, sA1, \exp(g, y), nb \rangle)) \wedge$$
$$\langle A^j, B^j, na^j, Nb^j, \exp(g, x^j), Gb^j \rangle = \langle A^k, B^k, Na^k, nb^k, Ga^k, \exp(g, y^k) \rangle).$$

3 Security Protocols Abstractions

We introduce our security protocol abstractions and illustrate their usefulness on our running example. We will present two types of protocol abstractions:

Typed abstractions transform a term's structure by reordering or removing fields and by splitting or removing cryptographic operations. The same transformations are applied to all terms of a given type and its subtypes.

Untyped abstractions complement typed ones with additional simplifications: the removal of unprotected atoms and variables and of redundant subterms.

Our main results are soundness theorems for these abstractions. They ensure that any attack on a given property of the original protocol translates to an attack on the abstracted protocol. As we will see, these results hold under certain conditions on the protocol and the property. Here, we focus on typed abstractions, but we will also briefly introduce the untyped ones (see [23] for details).

3.1   Typed Protocol Abstractions

Our typed abstractions are specified by a list of recursive equations subject to some conditions on their shape. We define their semantics in terms of a simple Haskell-style functional program. We use both pattern matching on terms and subtyping on types to select the equation to be applied to a given term. This ensures that terms of related types are transformed in a uniform manner.

Syntax. Let $\mathcal{W} = \{\mathcal{W}_\tau\}_{\tau \in \mathcal{Y}}$ be a family of *pattern variables* disjoint from $\mathcal{V}$. We define the set of *patterns* by $\mathcal{P} = \mathcal{T}(\mathcal{W}, \emptyset)$. A pattern $p \in \mathcal{P}$ is called *linear* if each (pattern) variable occurs at most once in p. We extend the typing function Γ to patterns by setting $\Gamma(X) = \tau$ if and only if $X \in \mathcal{W}_\tau$ and then lifting it homomorphically to all patterns. Our typed message abstractions are instances of the following recursive function specifications.

Definition 4. *A function specification* $F_f = (f, E_f)$ *consists of an unary function symbol* $f \notin \Sigma^1$ *and a list of equations*

$$E_f = [f(p_1) = u_1, \ldots, f(p_n) = u_n],$$

where each $p_i \in \mathcal{P}$ *is a linear pattern such that* $u_i \in \mathcal{T}_{\Sigma^{\geq 1} \cup \{f\}}(vars(p_i))$ *for all* $i \in \tilde{n}$, *i.e.,* u_i *consists of variables from* p_i *and function symbols from* $\Sigma^{\geq 1} \cup \{f\}$.

We use vectors (lists) of terms $\bar{t} = [t_1, \ldots, t_n]$ for $n > 0$. We define $set(\bar{t}) = \{t_1, \ldots, t_n\}$ and $\hat{f}(\bar{t}) = \langle f(t_1), \ldots, f(t_n) \rangle$, the elementwise application of a function f to a vector where the result is converted to a tuple (with the convention $\langle t \rangle = t$). We extend *split* to vectors by $split(\bar{t}) = split(set(\bar{t}))$. We define three sets of function symbols occurring in R and Ax as follows.

$$
\begin{aligned}
\mathsf{C_R} &= \{c \mid d(c(x_1, \ldots, x_n, t), u) \to x_j \in R\} \\
\mathsf{C_{Key}} &= \bigcup \{ct(t) \cup ct(u) \mid d(c(x_1, \ldots, x_n, t), u) \to x_j \in R\} \\
\mathsf{C_{Ax}} &= \bigcup \{ct(s) \cup ct(t) \mid \{s, t\} \in Ax\}
\end{aligned}
$$

The function $pp(c)$ returns the set of extractable indices of a function symbol c, i.e., $pp(c) = \{j \mid d(c(x_1, \ldots, x_n, t), u) \to x_j \in R \text{ or } d(c(x_1, \ldots, x_n)) \to x_j \in R\}$.

Definition 5 (Typed abstraction). *A function specification* $F_f = (f, E_f)$ *is a typed abstraction if each equation in* E_f *has the form*

$$f(c(p_1, \ldots, p_n)) = \langle e_1, \ldots, e_d \rangle$$

where for each $i \in \tilde{d}$ *we have either*

(a) $e_i = f(q)$ *such that* $q \in split(p_j)$ *for some* $j \in \tilde{n}$, *or*
(b) $e_i = c(\hat{f}(\overline{q_1}), \ldots, \hat{f}(\overline{q_n}))$ *such that* $set(\overline{q_j}) \subseteq split(p_j)$ *for all* $j \in \tilde{n}$, $c \neq \langle \cdot, \cdot \rangle$, *and* $c \in \mathsf{C_R}$ *implies* $\overline{q_n} = [p_n]$, *i.e.,* $\hat{f}(\overline{q_n}) = f(p_n)$.

Moreover, we require (i) for all $j \in pp(c)$ *we have* $split(p_j) \subseteq Q_j$ *where*

$$Q_j = \bigcup \{set(\overline{q_j}) \mid \exists i \in \tilde{d}. \, e_i = c(\hat{f}(\overline{q_1}), \ldots, \hat{f}(\overline{q_n}))\} \cup \{q \mid \exists i \in \tilde{d}. \, e_i = f(q)\}.$$

and (ii) if $c \in \mathsf{C_{Ax}} \cup \mathsf{C_{Key}}$ *then* $p_i = X_i : msg$ *for all* $i \in \tilde{n}$, $d = 1$ *and* $e_1 = c(f(X_1), \ldots, f(X_n))$ *is an instance of (b); we say* F_f *is homomorphic for* c.

Intuitively, the abstractions can only weaken the cryptographic protection of terms, but never strengthen it. Each equation in E_f maps a term with top-level symbol c to a tuple whose components have the form (a) or (b). Form (a) allows us to pull fields out of the scope of c, hence removing c's protection. Using form (b) we can reorder or remove fields in each argument of c. Form (b) is subject to two conditions. First, we disallow this form for pairs to obtain the simple shape $f(\langle p_1, p_2 \rangle) = \widehat{f}(\overline{q})$. Second, we cannot permit the reordering or removal of fields in key positions, i.e., in the last argument of $c \in C_R$. Moreover, by point (i), all fields of extractable arguments, i.e., elements of $split(p_j)$ for $j \in pp(c)$, must be present in some e_i and point (ii) requires that the abstraction is homomorphic for function symbols c occurring in axioms and in keys ($c \in C_{Ax} \cup C_{Key}$).

Example 5. We present a typed abstraction $F_f = (f, E_f)$ illustrating a representative selection of the possible message transformations. Suppose $X : \gamma_c$, $Y : nonce$, and $Z, U, V : msg$ and let E_f consists of the following three equations:

$$f(\langle X, Y, Z \rangle) = \langle f(Y), f(X), f(Z) \rangle$$
$$f(\mathsf{kdf}(X, Y, U, V)) = \langle \mathsf{kdf}(f(X), f(Y)), \mathsf{kdf}(f(U)) \rangle$$
$$f(\{\!|X, Y, Z|\!\}_U) = \langle \{\!|f(X), f(Y)|\!\}_{f(U)}, f(Y), \{\!|f(Z)|\!\}_{f(U)} \rangle$$

The patterns' types filter the matching terms: X and Y only match the constant c and a nonce, respectively. The first equation swaps the first two fields in n-tuples for $n \geq 3$. The second one splits a kdf hash into two, removing the field V. The last equation splits an encryption: the pair $\langle f(X), f(Y) \rangle$ and $f(Z)$ are encrypted separately with the key $f(U)$ and $f(Y)$ is pulled out of the encryption. Note that by condition (i) of Definition 5, we cannot directly remove plaintext fields from encryptions. To achieve this, we pull such fields out of encryptions to the top-level. This may require a combination of several abstractions if there are multiple layers of cryptographic protection. At the top-level, the fields are no longer protected and can be removed using untyped abstractions. In Section 4.1, we will discuss our heuristics to determine sequences of abstractions automatically.

Semantics. The semantics of a typed abstraction F_f is given by the Haskell-style functional program f (Program 1).[1] To ensure totality, we use the extended function specification $(f, E_f^+) = (f, E_f \cdot E_f^0)$, where $f(g(Z_1, \ldots, Z_n)) = g(f(Z_1), \ldots, f(Z_n)) \in E_f^0$ for each $g \in \Sigma^n$ with $n \geq 1$ such that $Z_i : msg$ for all $i \in \tilde{n}$, and $f(Z) = Z$ with $Z : msg$ is the last clause in E_f^0. We assume E_f and E_f^0 do not share variables. The **case** statement has a clause

$$p \mid \Gamma(t) \preccurlyeq \Gamma(p) \Rightarrow u$$

for each equation $f(p) = u$ of E_f^+. Such a clause is enabled if (1) the term t matches the pattern p, i.e., $t = p\theta$ for some substitution θ, and (2) its type $\Gamma(t)$ is a subtype of $\Gamma(p)$. The first enabled clause is executed. Hence, the equations

---

[1] We are overloading the symbol f here, but no confusion should arise.

fun $f(t) =$ **case** t **of**

$$\|_{(f(p)=u)\in E_f^+}\ p\mid \Gamma(t) \preccurlyeq \Gamma(p) \Rightarrow u$$

Program 1. Functional program f resulting from $F_f = (f, E_f)$

E_f^0 serve as fall-back clauses, which cover the terms not handled by E_f. In particular, the last clause $f(Z) = Z$ handles exactly the atoms and variables.

We extend f to events, event sequences, and traces by applying f to the terms they contain and to substitutions and protocols by applying f to the terms in their range. Similarly, we extend f to formulas ϕ of our property language by applying f to all terms occurring in ϕ.

Finding Abstractions. Finding abstractions is fully automated by our tool using a heuristic that we will describe in Section 4.1. However, the resulting abstractions can be counterintuitive. Therefore, we present here a simplified strategy that we apply to our running example below: We start by identifying the terms that appear in the $secret(\cdot)$ predicates and equations of the desired properties. Then we determine the cryptographic operations that are essential to achieve these properties and try to remove all other terms and operations.

Example 6 (from $\mathsf{IKE_m}$ *to* $\mathsf{IKE_m^1}$*).* In order to preserve the secrecy of the DH key $\exp(\exp(g, x), y)$ and the agreement on na, nb, $\exp(g, x)$, and $\exp(g, y)$, we have to keep either the mac or the symmetric encryption with SK (see Examples 3 and 4). We want to remove as many other fields and operations as possible (e.g., prf). We choose to remove the encryption as this allows us to later remove additional fields (e.g., $sA2$) using untyped abstractions. We keep o in $AUTHa$ to prevent unifiability with $AUTHb$ and hence potential false negatives. This leads us to the typed abstraction $F_1 = (f_1, E_1)$ where E_1 is defined by the equations

$$f_1(\{\!|X, Y|\!\}_Z) = \langle f_1(X), f_1(Y)\rangle$$
$$f_1(\mathsf{mac}(X_1, \ldots, X_8)) = \mathsf{mac}(\widehat{f}_1([X_1, X_3, X_5, X_6, X_7, X_8]))$$
$$f_1(\mathsf{mac}(Y_1, \ldots, Y_8)) = \mathsf{mac}(\widehat{f}_1([Y_1, Y_5, Y_6, Y_7, Y_8]))$$
$$f_1(\mathsf{kdf}(Z_1, \ldots, Z_5)) = \mathsf{kdf}(f_1(Z_3))$$
$$f_1(\mathsf{prf}(U, Z)) = f_1(U)$$

(where we omitted the homomorphic clauses for $\exp$ and $\langle \cdot, \cdot \rangle$) and $X : \alpha$, $X_3 : \gamma_o$, $Y_3 : nonce$, $Z_3 : \exp(msg, msg)$, $U : \mathsf{kdf}(msg)$ and all remaining pattern variables are of type msg. Applying f_1 to $\mathsf{IKE_m}$ we obtain $\mathsf{IKE_m^1}$. Here is the abstracted initiator role.

$$S_{\mathsf{IKE_m^1}}(A) = \mathsf{snd}(sPIa, o, sA1, \exp(g, x), na) \cdot \mathsf{rcv}(sPIa, SPIb, sA1, Gb, Nb)\cdot$$
$$\mathsf{snd}(sPIa, SPIb, A, B, AUTHaa, sA2, tSa, tSb)\cdot$$
$$\mathsf{rcv}(sPIa, SPIb, B, AUTHba, sA2, tSa, tSb)$$

with $SKa = \mathsf{kdf}(\exp(Gb, x))$, $AUTHaa = \mathsf{mac}(\mathsf{sh}(A, B), o, \exp(g, x), na, Nb, SKa)$, and $AUTHba = \mathsf{mac}(\mathsf{sh}(A, B), Gb, Nb, na, SKa)$. In a second step, we will remove most fields in the roles of $\mathsf{IKE_m^1}$ using untyped abstractions.

3.2   Soundness of Typed Abstractions

To justify the soundness of our abstractions, we show that any attack on a property ϕ of the original protocol P is reflected as an attack on the property $f(\phi)$ of the abstracted protocol $f(P)$. We decompose this into reachability preservation (RP) and an attack preservation (AP) as follows. We require that, for all reachable states (tr, th, σ) of P, there is a ground substitution σ' such that

(RP) $(f(tr), f(th), \sigma')$ is a reachable state of $f(P)$, and
(AP) $(tr, th, \sigma) \not\models \phi$ implies $(f(tr), f(th), \sigma') \not\models f(\phi)$.

These properties will require some assumptions about the protocol P, the formula ϕ, and the abstraction f. Before we formally state the soundness theorem, we will introduce and motivate these assumptions while sketching its proof. For the remainder of this subsection we assume arbitrary but fixed P, ϕ, F_f.

We start with two basic properties of abstractions. The first one, which we call the *substitution property*, states that $f(t\theta) = f(t)f(\theta)$ for well-typed R, Ax-normal substitutions θ. This does not hold in general. For example, suppose E_f contains the clauses $f(h(Y : \gamma_c)) = f(X)$ and $f(h(X : msg)) = h(f(X))$ in this order. Then the property is violated for $t = h(Z : msg)$ and $\theta = [c/Z]$. Thus, we must ensure that t and all its instance $t\theta$ are transformed uniformly, i.e., match the same clauses of E_f. We therefore require that (i) the patterns in E_f must not overlap and (ii) all recursive calls of f on composed terms during the transformation of t are handled by the clauses of E_f, without recourse to the fall-back clauses in E_f^0. This is formalized in the following two definitions where we denote the set of pattern types of a list of equations L by $\Pi(L) = \{\Gamma(p) \mid (f(p) = u) \in L\}$, we define $\Pi_f = \Pi(E_f)$, and let $Rec(F_f, t)$ be the set of terms u such that $f(u)$ is called in the computation of $f(t)$.

Definition 6. *A function specification F_f is pattern-disjoint if the types in Π_f are pairwise disjoint, i.e., $\Gamma(p_i)\!\downarrow \cap\ \Gamma(p_j)\!\downarrow = \emptyset$ for all $i, j \in \tilde{n}$ such that $i \neq j$.*

Definition 7 (Uniform domain). *We define the uniform domain of F_f by $udom(F_f) = \{t \in \mathcal{T} \mid \Gamma(Rec(F_f, t)) \subseteq \Pi_f\!\downarrow \cup \mathcal{Y}_{at}\}$.*

We will require that the protocol terms $t \in \mathcal{M}_P$ belong to this set, which ensures that their instances $t\theta$ with R, Ax-normal substitutions θ are transformed uniformly. We henceforth assume that F_f is pattern-disjoint. Note that the abstractions defined in Examples 5 and 6 are pattern-disjoint.

Theorem 1 (Substitution property). *Let $t \in udom(F_f)$ and θ be a well-typed and R, Ax-normal substitution. Then $f(t\theta) = f(t)f(\theta)$.*

The second basic property needed in our soundness proof is that abstractions preserve equality modulo E. We decompose this into the preservation of Ax-equality and of rewriting steps. Neither is preserved in general. To ensure this we need the following two definitions.

Definition 8 (R, Ax-closedness). *F_f is R, Ax-closed if the following holds: $t =_{Ax} u$ implies $\tau_t \preccurlyeq \tau$ if and only if $\tau_u \preccurlyeq \tau$, for all R, Ax-normal composed terms $t : \tau_t$ and $u : \tau_u$ and all $\tau \in \Pi(E_f^+)$.*

We henceforth assume that F_f is R, Ax-closed. In [23], we present a syntactic criterion for checking this. To achieve the preservation of rewriting steps under abstraction, we must ensure that, for all positions p in t where a rule $l \to r \in R$ is applicable, the redex $t|_p$ in t is transformed into a redex $f(t|_p)$ in $f(t)$ that still Ax-matches l. This is the purpose of the following definition.

Definition 9 (R, Ax-homomorphism). *We say that f is R, Ax-homomorphic for a term t if for all non-variable positions p in t and for all rules $l \to r \in R$ such that there exists a well-typed Ax-unifier of $t|_p$ and l, it holds that*

(i) *f is homomorphic for all $c \in ct(l)$,*
(ii) *f is homomorphic for $top(t|_{p'})$ and $top(t|_{p'}) \neq top(l')$ for all strict prefixes p' of p and rewrite rules $l' \to r' \in R$ such that $ct(l')$ is not a singleton.*

We define $rdom(F_f)$ to be the set of terms for which f is R, Ax-homomorphic.

Many interesting protocols P satisfy $\mathcal{M}_P \subseteq rdom(F_f)$, including those from our case studies. Since we must also cover redexes arising by instantiating protocol terms $t \in \mathcal{M}_P$, this definition employs Ax-unification rather than Ax-matching. The definition ensures that instantiations with R, Ax-normal substitutions and rewriting steps both preserve the membership of terms in $rdom(F_f)$.

Theorem 2 (Equality preservation). *Let t and u be terms such that $t, u \in rdom(F_f)$. Then $t =_E u$ implies $f(t) =_E f(u)$.*

Reachability preservation (RP) To achieve reachability preservation, we prove that every step of P can be simulated by a corresponding step of $f(P)$. In particular, to simulate receive events, we show that intruder deducibility is preserved under abstractions f (cf. second premise of rule $RECV$), i.e.,

$$T\theta, IK_0 \vdash_E u\theta \Rightarrow f(T)f(\theta{\downarrow}_{R,Ax}), f(IK_0) \vdash_E f(u)f(\theta{\downarrow}_{R,Ax}). \tag{1}$$

This property is also required to show the preservation of attacks on secrecy as part of (AP). We first establish deducibility preservation for ground terms:

Theorem 3 (Deducibility preservation). *Let $T \cup \{t\} \subseteq \mathcal{N}$ be a set of ground network messages such that $C \subseteq T$ and T is R, Ax-normal. Then $T \vdash_E t$ implies $f(T) \vdash_E f(t{\downarrow}_{R,Ax})$.*

We can now derive (1) by applying Theorems 3, 2 and 1 in this order, combined with applications of rule Eq and a cut property of intruder deduction. Summarizing, reachability preservation (RP) holds for $\mathcal{M}_P \subseteq udom(F_f) \cap rdom(F_f)$.

Attack Preservation (AP). We next define and explain the conditions on formulas needed to establish attack preservation. Let

- Sec_ϕ be the set of all terms t that occur in formulas $secret(t)$ in ϕ,
- Eq_ϕ be the set of pairs (t, u) such that the equation $t = u$ occurs in ϕ and $EqTerm_\phi = \{t, u \mid (t, u) \in Eq_\phi\}$ is the set of underlying terms, and
- Evt_ϕ be the set of events occurring in ϕ.

Let Eq_ϕ^+ the positively occurring equations in ϕ and similarly for Evt_ϕ.

Definition 10 (Safe formulas). ϕ *is safe for P and f if*

(i) $Sec_\phi \cup EqTerm_\phi \subseteq udom(F_f) \cap rdom(F_f)$,

(ii) $f(t\sigma) =_E f(u\sigma)$ *implies* $t\sigma =_E u\sigma$ *for all* $(t, u) \in Eq_\phi^+$ *and for all well-typed* R,Ax-*normal ground substitutions* σ, *and*

(iii) $f(t) = f(u)$ *implies* $t = u$, *for all* $e(t) \in Evt_\phi^+$ *and* $e(u) \in Evt(\mathcal{M}_P)$.

Condition (i) requires that F_f is uniform and R, Ax-homomorphic for the terms in secrecy statements and equalities. Condition (ii) expresses the injectivity of the abstraction on the terms in positively occurring equalities. This condition is required to preserve attacks on agreement properties. In other words, it prevents abstractions from fixing attacks on agreement by identifying two terms that differ in the original protocol. In the full version [23], we provide a syntactic criterion to check condition (ii) that avoids the universal quantification over substitutions. Condition (iii) is required for properties involving event orderings and *steps* predicates. It states that the abstraction must not identify an event occurring positively in the property with a distinct protocol event.

We now state the soundness theorem. Below, IK_0 and IK_0' respectively denote the intruder's initial knowledge associated with P and $f(P)$.

Theorem 4 (Soundness). *Suppose P, ϕ, and F_f satisfy (i) $f(IK_0) \subseteq IK_0'$, (ii) F_f is pattern-disjoint and R, Ax-closed, (iii) $\mathcal{M}_P \subseteq udom(F_f) \cap rdom(F_f)$, and ϕ is safe for P and f. Then, for all states (tr, th, σ) reachable in P, we have*

1. $(f(tr), f(th), f(\sigma \downarrow_{R,Ax}))$ *is a reachable state of $f(P)$, and*
2. $(tr, th, \sigma) \not\models \phi$ *implies* $(f(tr), f(th), f(\sigma \downarrow_{R,Ax})) \not\models f(\phi)$.

3.3   Untyped Abstractions

Typed abstractions offer a wide range of possibilities to transform cryptographic operations including subterm removal, splitting, and pulling fields outside a cryptographic operation. We complement these abstractions with two kinds of *untyped abstractions* that allow us to remove (1) unprotected atoms and variables of any type and (2) redundancy in the form of intruder-derivable terms. Untyped protocol abstractions are functions $g : \mathcal{T} \to \mathcal{T} \cup \{\mathsf{nil}\}$ where messages to be removed are mapped to nil. We remove events with nil arguments from the roles. Due to lack of space, we only sketch the definitions and give an example here. Full details and soundness results can be found in [23].

Atom/Variable Removal. The *removal abstraction* $rem_T : \mathcal{T} \to \mathcal{T} \cup \{\mathsf{nil}\}$ for a set T of atoms or variables is defined by

- $rem_T(u) = \mathsf{nil}$ if $u \in T^\flat$,
- $rem_T(\langle t_1, t_2 \rangle) = \begin{cases} rem_T(t_i) & \text{if } rem_T(t_{3-i}) = \mathsf{nil} \text{ for some } i \in \widetilde{2} \\ \langle rem_T(t_1), rem_T(t_2) \rangle & \text{otherwise} \end{cases}$
- $rem_T(t) = t$ for all other terms.

In order to preserve attacks, we have to restrict the removal of atoms and variables from a protocol term t to fields $u \in split(t)$ that appear only unprotected (clear) in t, i.e., such that $u \notin subs(t) \setminus split(t)$.

Example 7 (IKE$_m^1$ to IKE$_m^2$). We use atom/variable removal to simplify the protocol IKE$_m^1$. First, we recall the specification of role A of IKE$_m^1$.

$$S_{\mathsf{IKE}_m^1}(A) = \mathsf{snd}(sPIa, o, sA1, \exp(g, x), na) \cdot \mathsf{rcv}(sPIa, SPIb, sA1, Gb, Nb) \cdot$$
$$\mathsf{snd}(sPIa, SPIb, A, B, AUTHaa, sA2, tSa, tSb) \cdot$$
$$\mathsf{rcv}(sPIa, SPIb, B, AUTHba, sA2, tSa, tSb)$$

We remove the role names A and B, the constants o, $sA1$, $sA2$, tSa, tSb, the fresh value $sPIa$, and the variable $SPIb$ using an atom/variable removal abstraction. The result is the protocol IKE$_m^2$ whose initiator role is defined as follows.

$$S_{\mathsf{IKE}_m^2}(A) = \mathsf{snd}(\exp(g, x), na) \cdot \mathsf{rcv}(Gb, Nb) \cdot \mathsf{snd}(AUTHaa) \cdot \mathsf{rcv}(AUTHba)$$

We also apply the typed abstraction from Example 6 and the untyped abstraction here to the properties ϕ_s and ϕ_a of Example 4. These only affect the events in the *steps* predicates. The relevant soundness conditions are satisfied.

Redundancy Removal. A redundancy removal abstraction rd enables the elimination of redundancies within each role of a protocol. Intuitively, a protocol term t appearing in a role r can be abstracted to $rd(t)$ if t and $rd(t)$ are derivable from each other under the intruder knowledge T containing the terms preceding t in r and the initial knowledge IK_0. For example, we can simplify $r = \mathsf{snd}(t) \cdot \mathsf{rcv}(\langle t, u \rangle)$ to $\mathsf{snd}(t) \cdot \mathsf{rcv}(u)$. In contrast to atom/variable removal, redundancy removal can also remove composed terms. It is therefore a very effective ingredient for automatic abstraction, which we describe next.

4 Implementation and Experimental Results

We have implemented our abstraction methodology for the Scyther tool and tested it on a variety of complex protocols, mainly stemming from the IKE and ISO/IEC 9798 families. Scyther is an efficient verifier for security protocols. It supports verification for both a bounded and an unbounded number of threads. Protocols are specified by a set of linear role scripts. It also supports user-defined types. These features match our setting very well.

4.1 Abstraction Heuristics

Our tool computes a series of successively more abstract protocols. Each abstraction step consists of a typed abstraction followed by a redundancy and an atom/variable removal abstraction. A heuristic guides the automatic generation of the typed abstractions. These abstractions may be partially user-specified.

Central to our heuristic are the (sub)terms of Sec_ϕ and $EqTerm_\phi$ for a given property ϕ, which we call *essential terms*. The heuristic assigns *security labels*, c for confidentiality and a for authenticity, to cryptographic primitives as their intended security guarantees. These labels are inherited by subterms. Concretely, we label symmetric encryptions and MACs with c and a, asymmetric encryptions and hashes with c, and signatures with a. Based on this labeling, we decide which fields are pulled outside of or removed from the topmost cryptographic operations. The main criterion is that these transformations must preserve the following labeling properties of each essential term t: the presence of an a label on *some* occurrence of t and of c labels on *all* occurrences of t. The successive abstractions work from the outside to the inside of the original protocol's terms. The untyped abstractions simply remove all inessential top-level fields.

Example 8. We can simplify the term $\{\!|B, AUTHba, sA2, tSa, tSb|\!\}_{SKa}$ where $AUTHba = \mathsf{mac}(\mathsf{sh}(A, B), sPIa, SPIb, sA1, \underline{Gb}, \underline{Nb}, \underline{na}, \mathsf{prf}(SKa, B))$ of the $\mathsf{IKE_m}$ protocol from Example 3 in two successive abstraction steps as follows.

$$\{\!|B, AUTHba, sA2, tSa, tSb|\!\}_{SKa} \mapsto \langle B, AUTHba, sA2, tSa, tSb \rangle$$
$$AUTHba \mapsto \mathsf{mac}(\mathsf{sh}(A, B), \underline{Gb}, \underline{Nb}, \underline{na}, \mathsf{prf}(SKa, B))$$

In the first step, we pull the whole plaintext out of the encryption since the security labels of essential terms (underlined) are preserved by the mac. In the second step, we transform $AUTHba$ by keeping essential and removing inessential terms. Note that removing the term $u = \mathsf{prf}(SKa, B)$ or pulling it out of the mac would not preserve authenticity for the essential term x inside SKa. In a further step, we can simplify u by deleting inessential subterms and dropping prf.

Our abstractions are sound, but not complete. Therefore, we may encounter false negatives, i.e., spurious attacks. We carefully try to avoid these, for instance, by checking that abstractions do not introduce new pairs of unifiable terms. We currently do not check automatically whether an attack is spurious. Whenever an attack on a protocol P is found, we proceed to analyze (only) the failed properties on the next more concrete protocol in the series of abstractions.

4.2   Experimental Results

We have validated the effectiveness of our abstractions on 22 members of the IKE and ISO/IEC 9798 protocol families and on the PANA-AKA protocol [3]. We verify these protocols using five tools based on four different techniques: Scyther [10], CL-Atse [26], OFMC [5], SATMC [4], and ProVerif [6]. Only Scyther and ProVerif support verification of an unbounded number of threads. Due to lack of space, we present only a selection of 16 experimental results for Scyther (Table 1) and refer to the full version [23] for a complete account. Our models of the IKE and ISO/IEC 9798 protocols are based on Cremers' [8,9]. Since Scyther uses a fixed signature with standard cryptographic primitives and no equational theories, the IKE models approximate the DH theory by oracle roles.

We mark verified properties by ✓ and falsified ones by ×. An entry ✓/× means the property holds for one role but not for the other. Each row consists of two lines, corresponding to the analysis time without (line 1) and with (line 2)

Table 1. Experimental results. The time is in seconds. **No:** Number of abstractions. Properties: **S**ecrecy, **A**liveness, **W**eak agreement, and **N**on-injective agreement.

protocol	No	S	A	W	N	3	4	5	6	7	8	∞
IKEv1-pk-a22	1	✓			✓	18.48	82.93	249.55	554.09	1006.04	1734.85	TO
						0.83	1.26	2.08	3.47	5.96	10.28	TO
IKEv2-eap	5	✓			✓	TO	TO	TO	TO	TO	TO	TO
						78.35	798.44	4212.71	20911.20	TO	TO	TO
IKEv2-mac	5	✓			✓	1.85	4.91	6.72	8.07	8.42	8.49	8.70
						0.62	1.77	1.83	1.73	1.73	1.80	1.74
IKEv2-mactosig	4	✓			✓	11.65	141.37	1075.46	7440.81	TO	TO	TO
						2.89	12.38	24.54	38.68	53.36	65.07	77.68
IKEv2-sigtomac	5	✓			✓	6.15	33.19	65.05	115.34	204.93	206.45	237.34
						3.59	12.72	28.44	44.44	55.11	66.97	67.15
IKEv1-pk-m	2				×	48.62	269.92	507.40	869.23	16254.80	TO	TO
						0.04	0.05	0.05	0.05	0.05	0.05	TO
IKEv1-pk-m2	2				✓/×	18.26	274.87	4438.72	TO	TO	TO	TO
						1.48	7.79	32.75	110.32	339.93	963.08	TO
IKEv1-sig-m	2				×	0.34	0.45	0.45	0.45	0.45	0.46	0.44
						0.05	0.05	0.05	0.06	0.05	0.05	0.06
IKEv1-sig-m-perlman	2				×	2.86	13.99	40.78	67.83	72.08	72.15	109.03
						0.05	0.05	0.05	0.05	0.05	0.05	0.05
ISO/IEC 9798-2-5	1	✓				0.78	8.96	73.87	564.67	4214.22	TO	TO
						0.07	0.11	0.12	0.11	0.11	0.11	0.11
ISO/IEC 9798-2-6	1	✓				0.57	3.74	18.42	67.01	196.30	488.04	21278.58
						0.05	0.04	0.05	0.05	0.05	0.05	0.05
ISO/IEC 9798-3-6-1	2		✓		✓	43.08	802.95	8903.70	ME	ME	ME	ME
						0.13	0.18	0.19	0.19	0.19	0.19	0.19
ISO/IEC 9798-3-6-2	1		✓		✓	2.74	8.67	19.56	33.91	52.51	69.48	90.04
						0.12	0.15	0.15	0.15	0.15	0.15	0.15
ISO/IEC 9798-3-7-1	2		✓		✓	40.43	740.47	7483.36	16631.42	ME	ME	ME
						0.13	0.18	0.19	0.19	0.19	0.19	0.19
ISO/IEC 9798-3-7-2	1		✓		✓	2.38	7.71	16.68	26.99	35.06	49.49	TO
						0.22	0.32	0.33	0.33	0.33	0.33	0.33
PANA-AKA	5	✓	✓	✓	✓	5769.53	TO	TO	TO	TO	TO	TO
						0.10	0.10	0.10	0.10	0.10	0.10	0.10

abstraction for 3-8 or unboundedly many (∞) threads. The times were measured on a cluster of 12-core AMD Opteron 6174 processors with 64 GB RAM each. They include computing the abstractions (4-20 ms) and the verification itself.

Verification. For 8 of the 12 original protocols that are verified, an unbounded verification attempt results in a timeout (TO = 8h cpu time) or memory exhaustion (ME). In 6 of these, our abstractions enabled a verification in less than 0.4 seconds and in one case in 78 seconds. However, for the first two protocols, we still get a timeout. For the large majority of the bounded verification tasks, we significantly push the bound on the number of threads and achieve massive speedups. For example, our abstractions enable the verification of the complex nested protocols IKEv2-eap and PANA-AKA. Scyther verifies an abstraction of IKEv2-eap for up to 6 threads and, more strikingly, completes the unbounded verification of the simplified PANA-AKA in under 0.1 seconds whereas it can handle only 4 threads of the original. We also achieve dramatic speedups for many other protocols, most notably for IKEv1-pk-a22, ISO/IEC 9798-2-6, and ISO/IEC 9798-3-6-2. Moreover, the verification time for many abstracted protocols increases much more slowly than for their originals. We obtain almost constant verification times for the six ISO/IEC 9798 protocols, whereas the time significantly increases on some originals, e.g., for ISO/IEC 9798-3-6-1. For a few protocols, e.g., IKEv2-sigtomac and IKEv2-mac, the speedup is more modest.

Falsification. For rows marked by ×, the second line corresponds to falsification time for the most abstract model, which is much faster than on the original one. For example, for 8 threads of the IKEv1-pk-m protocol, we reduce falsification time from a timeout to 0.05 seconds. In the unbounded case, the speedup factors are 7 for IKEv1-sig-m and 2180 for IKEv1-sig-m-perlman. A manual analysis of the abstract attacks shows that none of them is spurious, suggesting that our measures to prevent them are effective. We expect that fast automatic detection of spurious attacks is feasible and will affect performance only negligibly.

Combination. For the IKEv1-pk-m2 protocol, the tool verifies non-injective agreement for one role and falsifies it for the other one. Surprisingly, we obtain a remarkable speedup even though the analysis of this protocol is done three times (for two abstract and the original models). Our abstractions push the feasibility bound from 5 to 8 threads. As the property is verified very quickly for one role on the most abstract model, it needs to be analyzed only for the other role at lower abstraction levels. This explains the remarkable speedups we obtain and therefore illustrates an advantage of our abstraction mechanism in this case.

5   Related Work and Conclusions

Hui and Lowe [18] define several kinds of abstractions similar to ours with the aim of improving the performance of the CASPER/FDR verifier. They establish soundness only for ground messages and encryption with atomic keys. We work in a more general model, cover additional properties, and treat the non-trivial issue of abstracting the open terms in protocol specifications. Other works [25,13,12] also propose a set of syntactic transformations, however without formally establishing their soundness. Using our results, we can, for instance, justify the soundness of the refinements in [13, Section 3.3]. Guttman [16,15] studies the preservation of security properties for a rich class of protocol transformations in the strand space model. His approach to property preservation is based on the simulation of protocol analysis steps instead of execution steps. Each such step explains the origin of a message. He does not have a syntactic soundness check.

In this work, we propose a set of syntactic protocol transformations that allows us to abstract realistic protocols and capture a large class of attacks. Unlike previous work [22,18], our theory and soundness results accommodate equational theories, untyped variables, user-defined types, and subtyping. These features allow us to accurately model protocols, capture type-flaw attacks, and adapt to different verification tools, e.g., those supporting equational theories such as ProVerif and CL-atse. We have extended Scyther with an abstraction module, which we validated it on various IKE and ISO/IEC 9798 protocols. We also tested our technique (with manually produced abstractions) on ProVerif, CL-atse, OFMC, and SATMC. Our experiments clearly show that modern protocol verifiers can substantially benefit from our abstractions, which often either enable previously unfeasible verification tasks or lead to dramatic speedups.

Our abstraction tool does not check for spurious attacks. We plan to add this functionality to complete the automatic abstraction-refinement process. We are also interested in generalizing the tool and supporting more protocol verifiers.

Acknowledgements. We thank Mathieu Turuani and Michael Rusinowitch for our discussions on the topic of this paper, Cas Cremers for his help with Scyther, David Basin, Ognjen Maric, and Ralf Sasse for their careful proof-reading, and the anonymous reviewers for their useful feedback. This work is partially supported by the EU FP7-ICT-2009 Project No. 256980, NESSoS: Network of Excellence on Engineering Secure Future Internet Software Services and Systems.

References

1. Armando, A., Arsac, W., Avanesov, T., Barletta, M., Calvi, A., Cappai, A., Carbone, R., Chevalier, Y., Compagna, L., Cuéllar, J., Erzse, G., Frau, S., Minea, M., Mödersheim, S., von Oheimb, D., Pellegrino, G., Ponta, S.E., Rocchetto, M., Rusinowitch, M., Torabi Dashti, M., Turuani, M., Viganò, L.: The AVANTSSAR platform for the automated validation of trust and security of service-oriented architectures. In: Flanagan, C., König, B. (eds.) TACAS 2012. LNCS, vol. 7214, pp. 267–282. Springer, Heidelberg (2012)
2. Arapinis, M., Duflot, M.: Bounding messages for free in security protocols. In: Arvind, V., Prasad, S. (eds.) FSTTCS 2007. LNCS, vol. 4855, pp. 376–387. Springer, Heidelberg (2007)
3. Arkko, J., Haverinen, H.: RFC 4187: Extensible authentication protocol method for 3rd generation authentication and key agreement (EAP-AKA) (2006), http://www.ietf.org/rfc/rfc4187
4. Armando, A., Compagna, L.: SAT-based model-checking for security protocols analysis. International Journal of Information Security 7(1), 3–32 (2008)
5. Basin, D.A., Mödersheim, S., Viganó, L.: OFMC: A symbolic model checker for security protocols. Int. J. Inf. Sec. 4(3), 181–208 (2005)
6. Blanchet, B.: An efficient cryptographic protocol verifier based on Prolog rules. In: CSFW, pp. 82–96. IEEE Computer Society (2001)
7. Cousot, P., Cousot, R.: Abstract interpretation: A unified lattice model for static analysis of programs by construction or approximation of fixpoints. In: Graham, R.M., Harrison, M.A., Sethi, R. (eds.) POPL, pp. 238–252. ACM (1977)
8. Cremers, C.: IKEv1 and IKEv2 protocol suites (2011), https://github.com/cascremers/scyther/tree/master/gui/Protocols/IKE
9. Cremers, C.: ISO/IEC 9798 authentication protocols (2012), https://github.com/cascremers/scyther/tree/master/gui/Protocols/ISO-9798

10. Cremers, C.J.F.: The Scyther tool: Verification, falsification, and analysis of security protocols. In: Gupta, A., Malik, S. (eds.) CAV 2008. LNCS, vol. 5123, pp. 414–418. Springer, Heidelberg (2008)

11. Cremers, C.: Key exchange in IPsec revisited: Formal analysis of IKEv1 and IKEv2. In: Atluri, V., Diaz, C. (eds.) ESORICS 2011. LNCS, vol. 6879, pp. 315–334. Springer, Heidelberg (2011)

12. Datta, A., Derek, A., Mitchell, J.C., Pavlovic, D.: Abstraction and refinement in protocol derivation. In: Proc. 17th IEEE Computer Security Foundations Workshop (CSFW) (2004)

13. Datta, A., Derek, A., Mitchell, J.C., Pavlovic, D.: A derivation system and compositional logic for security protocols. Journal of Computer Security 13, 423–482 (2005)

14. Escobar, S., Meadows, C., Meseguer, J.: Maude-NPA: Cryptographic protocol analysis modulo equational properties. In: Aldini, A., Barthe, G., Gorrieri, R. (eds.) FOSAD 2007. LNCS, vol. 5705, pp. 1–50. Springer, Heidelberg (2007)

15. Guttman, J.D.: Transformations between cryptographic protocols. In: Degano, P., Viganò, L. (eds.) ARSPA-WITS 2009. LNCS, vol. 5511, pp. 107–123. Springer, Heidelberg (2009)

16. Guttman, J.D.: Security goals and protocol transformations. In: Mödersheim, S., Palamidessi, C. (eds.) TOSCA 2011. LNCS, vol. 6993, pp. 130–147. Springer, Heidelberg (2012)

17. Harkins, D., Carrel, D.: The Internet Key Exchange (IKE) IETF RFC 2409 (Proposed Standard) (November 1998), http://www.ietf.org/rfc/rfc2409.txt

18. Hui, M.L., Lowe, G.: Fault-preserving simplifying transformations for security protocols. Journal of Computer Security 9(1/2), 3–46 (2001)

19. Jouannaud, J., Kirchner, H.: Completion of a set of rules modulo a set of equations. SIAM J. Comput. 15(4), 1155–1194 (1986)

20. Kaufman, C., Hoffman, P., Nir, Y., Eronen, P.: Internet Key Exchange Protocol Version 2 (IKEv2). IETF RFC 5996 (September 2010), http://tools.ietf.org/html/rfc5996

21. Meier, S., Schmidt, B., Cremers, C., Basin, D.: TAMARIN prover for the symbolic analysis of security protocols. In: Sharygina, N., Veith, H. (eds.) CAV 2013. LNCS, vol. 8044, pp. 696–701. Springer, Heidelberg (2013)

22. Nguyen, B.T., Sprenger, C.: Sound security protocol transformations. In: Basin, D., Mitchell, J.C. (eds.) POST 2013. LNCS, vol. 7796, pp. 83–104. Springer, Heidelberg (2013)

23. Nguyen, B.T., Sprenger, C.: Abstractions for security protocol verification. Tech. rep. Department of Computer Science, ETH Zurich (January 2015), http://dx.doi.org/10.3929/ethz-a-010347780

24. Paulson, L.: The inductive approach to verifying cryptographic protocols. J. Computer Security 6, 85–128 (1998)

25. Pavlovic, D., Meadows, C.: Deriving secrecy in key establishment protocols. In: Gollmann, D., Meier, J., Sabelfeld, A. (eds.) ESORICS 2006. LNCS, vol. 4189, pp. 384–403. Springer, Heidelberg (2006)

26. Turuani, M.: The CL-atse protocol analyser. In: Pfenning, F. (ed.) RTA 2006. LNCS, vol. 4098, pp. 277–286. Springer, Heidelberg (2006)

Hardware and Physical Security

Automated Backward Analysis
of PKCS#11 v2.20

Robert Künnemann

Department of Computer Science – TU Darmstadt, Germany

Abstract. The PKCS#11 standard describes an API for cryptographic operations which is used in scenarios where cryptographic secrets need to be kept secret, even in case of server compromise. It is widely deployed and supported by many hardware security modules and smart cards. A variety of attacks in the literature illustrate the importance of a careful configuration, as API-level attacks may otherwise extract keys.

Formal verification of PKCS#11 configurations requires the analysis of a system that contains mutable state, a problem that existing methods solved by either artificially restricting the number of keys, introducing model-specific over-approximation or performing proofs by hand. At Security & Privacy 2014, Kremer and Künnemann presented a variant of the applied pi calculus that handles global state and, in conjunction with the tamarin prover for protocol verification, allows for the precise analysis of protocols with state. Using this tool chain, we show secrecy of keys for a PKCS#11 configuration that makes use of features introduced in version 2.20 of the standard, including wrap and unwrap templates in an extensible model.

This configuration supports the creation of so-called wrapping keys for import and export of sensitive keys (e. g., for backup or transfer), and it permits the co-existence of sensitive keys and non-sensitive keys on the same device.

1 Introduction

The more complex a system is, the more difficult is assuring its security. Given the complexity of the runtime environment provided by multi-purpose computers, it appears reasonable to compute security-critical operations outside the computer that actually runs the protocol (and usually more than one protocol), and instead on a device which is *a*) smaller, and thus more amenable to verification, and *b*) designed with security in mind. In security-critical contexts, e. g., the cash machine network or the public key infrastructure, the use of such devices, so-called *security tokens*, is common practice. In case the (complex) system running the protocol is under adversarial control, i. e., in case of server compromise, cryptographic secrets are protected by the (smaller, and thus more secure) security token, and the fact that these secrets were never directly accessible, even to the server.

PKCS#11 defines a platform-independent API to security tokens, for example smart cards, but also hardware security modules (HSMs). HSMs are physical computing devices that can be attached directly to a server via Ethernet, USB or other services, providing logical and physical protection for sensitive information and algorithms.

© Springer-Verlag Berlin Heidelberg 2015
R. Focardi and A. Myers (Eds.): POST 2015, LNCS 9036, pp. 219–238, 2015.
DOI: 10.1007/978-3-662-46666-7_12

The fundamental security feature this standard provides is protecting the cryptographic values of keys marked as "sensitive" [22, Section 7]:

> Additional protection can be given to private keys and secret keys by marking them as "sensitive" [..]. Sensitive keys cannot be revealed in plaintext off the token [..].

Clulow's attack. It was discovered very soon that a faithful implementation of the standard violates this property. Clulow showed the following attack in 2003 [8], which serves as an introduction to the caveats in the design of PKCS#11. Keys are accessed via handles, hence indirectly. Some may be used for encryption and/or decryption, therefore an attacker that can access the token (e. g., in case of server compromise) can request the encryption of some message he supplies with a key of his choice, given that he knows the handle (which we will consider public) and that the key is configured to allow for encryption by setting an attribute 'encrypt' to true, analogously for decryption. Similarly, it is possible to *wrap* a key k_1 with another key k_2, that is, encrypt k_1 under k_2. This allows for backup, as well as for transfer. Given that k_2 is present on two security tokens A and B, one may wrap k_1 with k_2 on A (using two handles associated with k_1 and k_2, respectively) and *unwrap* the resulting cypher-text on B, using another handle to k_2. The scenario where k_2 is configured for wrapping *and* for decryption permits the attacker to request a wrapping of k_1 under k_2 and then decrypt the resulting cyphertext, thus obtaining the value of k_1 in the plain. The attack also applies when k_2 is wrapped under itself.

An 'incomplete' implementation of the standard, often called a *configuration* can thwart this attack by forbidding the same key to be used for wrapping and decryption. But there are other conflicts, e. g., between encryption and unwrapping. In the present paper, we propose a configuration and a method for verifying its security. We focus on attacks on the logical level, using only API calls that are (by themselves) perfectly harmless, as opposed to attacks on the implementation of cryptographic functionality [4].

Related Work. Building on the work of Longley and Rigby [20] and Bond and Anderson [5] on API attacks, several recent papers have investigated the security of APIs on the logical level adapting symbolic techniques for protocol analysis [6, 9, 11], finding many new attacks. There have also been academic proposals for new APIs [19, 10, 18]. While many attacks were found, a lot of effort was directed towards finding configurations that are secure, i. e., that preserve secrecy of keys.

In the analysis of PKCS#11 configurations, there are three major lines of work. The first one uses protocol verification techniques, regarding the security token as the (sole) participant in a protocol, with the adversary sending requests on the public network. Early results by Delaune, Kremer and Steel translated a given configuration into a satisfiability problem which is solved by model checking, providing secrecy of keys if the number of keys is known in advance [11]. This restriction was lifted in later work [14] by Fröschle and Steel, showing that a class of configurations can safely be abstracted by configurations that are *static* (i. e., a key's attribute cannot be changed) and showing that the latter is soundly over-approximated in a bounded model. This method is used in further work by Bortolozzo, Centenaro, Focardi and Steel to find attacks on security tokens using automatic reverse engineering and to show a configuration very similar to ours secure.

The second line of work uses a program verification approach, modelling security tokens in a first-order linear time logic with past operators. In contrast to the protocol verification approach, proofs have been conducted by hand (using a tableau proof method that proceeds by backward analysis), but provide support for advanced data structures introduced by PKCS#11, version 2.20, in particular wrap/unwrap templates. An *attribute template* is a set of attributes, but contains the attributes 'wrapping template' and 'unwrapping template' which themselves are pointers to attribute templates, resulting in a recursive data structure. In early work, Fröschele and Sommer show security, but only for keys with 'extractable' set to false [15], i. e., keys that cannot be wrapped at all. In more recent work, the authors added support for wrap/unwrap templates [13]. Positives result only cover the secrecy of trusted wrapping keys, but not of keys wrapped using these keys (as opposed to the results in the present paper, and in the work by Bortolozzo et al.). The proof is done by hand and covers about six pages [16].

The third line of work uses static analysis on the implementation of the security token [7]. Using security type-checking, a software implementation (written in a subset of C) of the wrap, unwrap, encrypt and decrypt functions was shown to preserve secrecy of sensitive keys against a Dolev-Yao attacker for a configuration that is functionally equal to the one presented here, but uses a default type for wrapped keys rather than wrap/unwrap templates. A generalised version of this framework proposes an imperative programming language with cryptographic operations and a centralised store mapping values (possibly handles) to pairs of key values and their ground types [2]. Mapping sets of PKCS#11 attributes to types, the generalised framework again allows for the analysis of PKCS#11, more specifically, PKCS#11 v2.20 using the configuration analysed in the present paper.

Contribution. The present work shares common ground with the first two lines of work. It follows a protocol verification approach and provides machine support, but relies on backward analysis rather than finite model checking. Therefore, the resulting model can be extended without breaking the soundness of the decision procedure (or introducing limitations to the number of keys), but provides a largely automated proof procedure although decidability cannot be guaranteed. The model is formulated in a variant of the applied pi calculus augmented with operators for state manipulation. This high-level protocol description language can be translated to multiset rewrite rules using the Sapic tool which has been proven sound and complete in prior work [17]. The generated multiset rewrite system can be verified using the tamarin prover [23], which is sound and complete as well. The constraint solving algorithm employed by the tamarin prover uses backward analysis. While various methods in the first line of work achieve security for an unbounded number of keys indirectly (using bounded analysis and an over-approximation specific to the modelling of the PKCS#11 API) [14, 6], this method supports an unlimited number of fresh values by default. For one, our model is closer to an actual implementation, containing locking operations as well as database lookup, but most importantly, our result requires no additional over-approximation. Hence, the security proof is machine-verifiable (relying on the correctness of the translation procedure [17] and the solving algorithm [23]) and the model extensible. The same holds for the third line of work, too (except that parallelism and hence locking is not supported). The type-checking approach is much faster and requires less manual intervention than our approach, but might not be able to type configurations that are actually secure. However, the configuration we show secure has been verified using type-checking [7, 2], hence the question of whether there actually is a more versatile policy that can be shown secure using backward analysis but is not amenable to security type-checking remains open.

The flexibility and precision of our modelling comes at the cost of losing some amount of automation. As the verification method is sound and complete, but is able to express the secrecy problem with unbounded nonces, which is undecidable [12], there is no guarantee that the tool terminates. In order to achieve termination, some intervention is necessary: Lemmas need to be used to cut branches in the proof attempt. The advantage is a result that applies to a version of PKCS#11 (2.20) with wrap/unwrap templates and an intuitive, extensible model. In the present proof, we have given 10 lemmas, 6 of which are at least partially guided when being used without any model-specific heuristics for the choice of goals in the proof. If we provide a (model-specific) heuristic, a proof is found without user intervention. The lemmas are model-specific, but not specific to the configuration we show secure (except for four trivial lemmas that speed up the proof, but could be left out). We note that the tool chain is sound and complete no matter which heuristic is used, i. e., even when the model is altered (e. g., to describe future versions of PKCS#11), if the heuristics are helpful in finding a proof, the result is correct.

The configuration of PKCS#11 we prove secure implements a policy with three kinds of keys: keys that are used to encrypt or decrypt payload and kept secret, keys that can wrap and unwrap the first kind of keys for backup and keys that can be read in the clear and are neither wrapped, nor used to wrap other keys but may encrypt/decrypt payload. Keys cannot change roles, which we consider a sensible best practice, thus this policy is static in the sense of [14].

This policy has been shown to provide secrecy of sensitive keys if implemented via restricting the wrap and unwrap commands [7] or via wrap/unwrap templates [2] using type-checking. As in these works, we show that non-sensitive keys (keys the attacker is allowed to read in the clear) do not impair the security of other keys.

2   The PKCS#11 Standard, v2.20

The PKCS#11 standard specifies a security API (this term was coined by Bond and Anderson [5]), that is, an API that separates trusted code operating on secret data from untrusted code. As in the case of PKCS#11, security APIs are often used to perform cryptographic computations. Separating the implementation of cryptographic operations from the rest of the system has the advantage that cryptographic secrets can be hidden *behind* the API, whilst the code only accesses these secrets indirectly, using handles. If the API gives access to an external piece of hardware, which is often the case, the hope is that malicious code is restricted to using the API. Smart cards and hardware security modules (HSMs) implementing PKCS#11 are much simpler than multi-purpose computers, and designed with security in mind, so the idea of "outsourcing" sensitive information and operations that depend on this information to a device that is easier to secure seems to be reasonable. However, a sound design of said API is essential in reaching this goal.

Table 1. Attributes relevant to key-management. Modifiable means that attributes may be modified after an object is created, or while it is copied, however, tokens may decide not to permit modification upon copying [22, Tab. 15, footnote 8, p. 66]. SO-only means the attribute can only be set by the SO.

name	modifiable	SO-only	comment
wrap (wrap)	yes	no	can be first argument for wrap
unwrap (unwrap)	yes	no	can be first argument for unwrap
encrypt (enc)	yes	no	can be used for encryption
decrypt (dec)	yes	no	can be used for decryption
sensitive (sens)	yes	no	value shall not be extracted (directly), but may be wrapped
extractable (extr)	yes	no	Value shall not be extracted (directly) or used as second argument to wrap
trusted (trus)	no	yes	has been generated by SO
wrap-with-trusted (wwt)	no	no	can only be wrapped by 'trusted' keys
wrap template (wt)	no	no	key that are wrapped need to match this template
unwrap template (ut)	no	no	template applied to keys after being imported by unwrap

PKCS#11 gives multiple applications access to several cryptographic devices via *slots* [22, p.14], abstracting away from their respective implementation technology, be it smart cards, PCMCIA cards, HSMs, etc. After a user, or an application, has established a *session* to a device (through a slot), they can identify either as a Security Officer (SO), or a normal user [22, p.15]. The role of the SO is to initialize a token and to set the normal user's PIN. The normal user cannot log in until the SO has set the normal user's PIN. Within a session, the user can manipulate *objects* stored on the token, such as keys and certificates. Objects are referred to by *handles*. The value of a handle does not reveal any information about the value of the key. Objects may be marked public and private. A normal user, if authenticated, can access public and private objects, otherwise only public objects. The SO can only access public objects, but perform operations the normal user cannot perform, such as setting the user's PIN.

Attributes. Objects may have attributes (besides being public or private), some of them specific to their class and type (public keys of type CKK_RSA have a public exponent, for example), and some general. The latter pertain to the key-management functions of PKCS#11, and are listed in Table 1. Real devices offer only a subset of the functionality specified by PKCS#11, partly due to security considerations: The PKCS#11 standards permits modifying the attributes wrap and dec, immediately giving rise to Clulow's attack, see p.220.

2.1 Modelling

Security APIs are a means to provide a higher level of assurance in case of server compromise. If the server is compromised, the user PIN can easily be intercepted and the attacker can establish a session with the device. Hence we model a network comprising only of a single PKCS#11 token, which does not perform any kind of authentication for normal users. The Dolev-Yao adversary is in full control over the network and is thus able to issue arbitrary requests. The PKCS#11 standard discusses security against server compromise and states that "none of the [these attacks] can compromise keys marked 'sensitive', since a key that is sensitive will always remain sensitive" [22, p. 31]. This does not hold true for PKCS#11 itself (cf. p. 220), but we will show a configuration of PKCS#11, for which this holds true.

This paper describes a formal model of the core key-management functionality in PKCS#11, therefore we left out message digesting functions, signature and MAC functions, as well as dual-purpose cryptographic functions (like C_DigestEncryptUpdate) and random number generation, as they do not pertain to the key and object management part of PKCS#11. Key-derivation (C_DeriveKey) allows for creating a new key object from a base key and could be considered key-management, but there is no cryptographic mechanism in PKCS#11 that supports wrap/unwrap as well as key derivation [22, Section 12]. Thus we consider this function outside the key-management core of PKCS#11. Note that encryption and decryption functions may allow for producing, or decrypting wrappings (as Clulow's attack shows), so they do pertain to the key-management part. We concentrate on encryption and decryption for single-part data, i. e., the functions for multi-part data C_EncryptInit, C_EncryptUpdate, C_EncryptFinal are left out in favour of C_Encrypt, as our focus lies on API-level attacks. The same holds for decryption functions. We furthermore ignored object management functions that reveal only information which the attacker, as the only user accessing the token, can compute anyway, such as C_GetObjectSize, C_GetAttributeValue, C_FindObjectsInit, C_-FindObjects and C_FindObjectsFinal. The function C_DestroyObject is disabled, since our modelling gives the adversary an unlimited amount of space to store keys, thus any attack can be transformed into an attack that does not delete objects. Previous works

Table 2. Object- and Key-management operations in PKCS#11 and our modelling. Function marked '(n.p.)' are not present.

function	description	process	comment
Object management functions			
C_CreateObject	creates an object	(n.p.)	forbidden by policy
C_CopyObject	creates a copy of an object	(n.p.)	not helpful to adversary (in this configuration)
C_DestroyObject	destroys an object	(n.p.)	not helpful to adversary
C_SetAttributeValue	modifies object's attribute	(n.p.)	forbidden by policy
Encryption/Decryption functions			
C_Encrypt	encrypts single-part data	encrypt	
C_Decrypt	decrypts single-part data	decrypt	
Key-management functions			
C_GenerateKey	generates a secret key	create	
C_GenerateKeyPair	generates a public / private key pair	(n.p.)	asymm. wrapping keys permits 'Trojan wrapped key attack'
C_WrapKey	wraps (encrypts) a key	wrap	
C_UnwrapKey	unwraps (decrypts) a key	unwrap	

[11, 14, 6, 15] have similar restrictions. The full list of functions is listed in Table 8 of the PKCS#11 standard [22, p. 27]. The rest of PKCS#11 is what we consider the core key-management part (Table 2). The configuration, while being more versatile than policies that were previously proposed, forbids certain operations that are potentially harmful. Another class of attacks Clulow discovered are "Trojan wrapped key attacks", where a public unwrapping key is used to introduce a wrapping key that the attacker knows the value of, by producing the wrapping outside the device. We conclude that our policy should not allow for asymmetric wrapping keys at all, and simplify the model by only regarding symmetric keys. Extending the model to cover asymmetric keys for non-key-management operations is straight-forward, but unlikely to lead to new insights with respect to the security of policies.

2.2 Proposed Configuration

In this section, we will discuss policies that have been proposed in previous work and introduce requirements that guided the design of the policy we will prove secure. We will argue that, given these requirements, there are only two secure policies.

The first requirement shall be that there are 'usage' keys, i. e., keys that may encrypt or sign payload. Since only encryption and decryption are relevant to key-management, we propose:

> Requirement A: There should be keys that can be used for encryption and decryption.

Delaune et al. have shown different policies secure, all of which have in common that wrap and unwrap are conflicting attributes [11]. Since wrapping keys are useful for backup and out-of-device-storage of keys, we could formulate the requirement that wrapping keys should be suitable for wrapping and unwrapping any key, however, we think that the backup, and possibly the distribution of 'usage' keys – in our model, keys used for encryption and decryption – is the main purpose of wrapping keys. Being able to wrap wrapping keys is useful, but only once it is established that usage keys can be wrapped.

> Requirement B: Wrapping keys should be able to wrap and unwrap keys that can be used for encryption and decryption.

Policies in related work often support the setting and unsetting of some attributes [15, 13], requiring attributes to be unmodifiable where needed. Many configurations describe policies by declaring conflicting attributes (pairs of attributes that are forbidden to be set at once) and sticky (unmodifiable when set) attributes. We argue for a different approach: security policies become much easier to understand and to design if the key is assigned a role upon creation, and cannot be altered in subsequent steps. In most cases, it is clear from the beginning which keys needs to be protected, setting a key to sensitive after it was ready to be exposed is clearly bad practice. The attributes wrap, unwrap, enc, dec, extr, trust have in common that an attacker becomes only less powerful in unsetting them. The opposite holds for wwt. Being able to alter wrapping/unwrapping templates is much less useful as it seems, as wrappings in

PKCS#11 carry no information about which wrapping template was used. Altering the wrapping template could be useful to define the class of keys that can be wrapped as the union of permitted wrapping templates but, as we will see, this class can be defined using a single wrapping template.

Requirement C: Policies should disable C_SetAttributeValue altogether.

Bortolozzo et al. proposed a policy that is static in that attributes cannot be altered after the creation of keys [6]. Ignoring templates where wrap, unwrap, enc and dec are false, they propose three templates:

1. Freshly generated keys can have wrap and unwrap set.
2. Freshly generated keys can have enc and dec set.
3. Keys imported with unwrap may have unwrap and encrypt set, but wrap and decrypt unset.

Intuitively, the third template means that keys 'degrade' when being backed up, that is, they cannot resume to their full functionality. The policy we analyse here differs in this regard: 'trusted' keys can be used to wrap 'usage' keys, which can be adequately restored.

Table 3. The templates using in the proposed policy. (A dot ● is present for each attribute that is set.)

name	wrap	unwrap	enc	dec	sens	extr	trus	wwt	wt	ut
trusted	●	●			●	●	●	●	usage	usage
usage			●	●	●			●	-	-
untrusted			●	●		●			-	-

These policies are incomparable; while the second policy supports lossless key-backup, the policy by Bortolozzo et al. allows for transferring wrapping keys between two PKCS#11 device A and B. Assume A and B have the same wrapping key set-up at the start (e. g., by the SO). A creates another wrapping key, which is wrapped using the common wrapping key, and unwrapped at B. Now A can use this second-level wrapping key to produce wrappings that B can import.

3   Preliminaries

Terms and equational theories. As usual in symbolic protocol analysis we model messages by abstract terms. Therefore we define an order-sorted term algebra with the sort *msg* and two incomparable subsorts *pub* and *fresh*. For each of these subsorts we assume a countably infinite set of names, FN for fresh names and PN for public names. Fresh names will be used to model cryptographic keys and nonces while public names model publicly known values. We furthermore assume a countably infinite set of variables for each sort s, $\mathcal{V}_s$ and let $\mathcal{V}$ be the union of the set of variables for all sorts. We write $u : s$ when the name or variable u is of sort s. Let Σ be a signature, i.e., a set of function symbols, each with an arity. We write f/n when function symbol f is of arity n. We denote by $\mathcal{T}_\Sigma$ the set of well-sorted terms built over Σ, PN, FN and $\mathcal{V}$. For a term t we denote by $names(t)$, respectively $vars(t)$ the set of names, respectively variables, appearing in t. The set of ground terms, i.e., terms without variables, is denoted by $\mathcal{M}_\Sigma$. When Σ is fixed or clear from the context we often omit it and simply write $\mathcal{T}$ for $\mathcal{T}_\Sigma$ and $\mathcal{M}$ for $\mathcal{M}_\Sigma$.

We equip the term algebra with an equational theory E, that is, a finite set of equations of the form $M = N$ where $M, N \in \mathcal{T}$. From the equational theory we define the binary relation $=_E$ on terms, which is the smallest equivalence relation containing equations in E that is closed under application of function symbols, bijective renaming of names and substitution of variables by terms of the same sort. Furthermore, we require E to distinguish different fresh names, i.e., $\forall a, b \in FN : a \neq b \Rightarrow a \neq_E b$.

Example 1. Symmetric encryption can be modelled using a signature

$$\Sigma = \{\, senc/2, sdec/2, true/0 \,\}$$

and an equational theory defined by

$$sdec(senc(m, k), k) = m.$$

For the rest of the paper we assume that E refers to some fixed equational theory and that the signature and equational theory always contain symbols and equations for pairing and projection, i.e., $\{\langle ., . \rangle, \mathsf{fst}, \mathsf{snd}\} \subseteq \Sigma$ and equations $\mathsf{fst}(\langle x, y \rangle) = x$ and $\mathsf{snd}(\langle x, y \rangle) = y$ are in E. We will sometimes use $\langle x_1, x_2, \ldots, x_n \rangle$ as a shortcut for $\langle x_1, \langle x_2, \langle \ldots, \langle x_{n-1}, x_n \rangle \ldots \rangle$.

We also use the usual notion of positions for terms. A position p is a sequence of positive integers and $t|_p$ denotes the subterm of t at position p.

Facts. We also assume an unsorted signature Σ_{fact}, disjoint from Σ. The set of *facts* is defined as

$$\mathcal{F} := \{F(t_1, \ldots, t_k) \mid t_i \in \mathcal{T}_\Sigma, F \in \Sigma_{fact} \text{ of arity } k\}.$$

Facts will be used both to annotate protocols, by the means of events, and for defining multiset rewrite rules. We partition the signature Σ_{fact} into *linear* and *persistent* fact symbols. We suppose that Σ_{fact} always contains a unary, persistent symbol !K and a linear, unary symbol Fr. Given a sequence or set of facts S we denote by $lfacts(S)$ the multiset of all linear facts in S and $pfacts(S)$ the set of all persistent facts in S. By notational convention facts whose identifier starts with '!' will be persistent. $\mathcal{G}$ denotes the set of ground facts, i.e., the set of facts that do not contain variables. For a fact f we denote by $ginsts(f)$ the set of ground instances of f. This notation is also lifted to sequences and sets of facts as expected.

Predicates. We assume an unsorted signature Σ_{pred} disjoint from Σ and Σ_{fact}. The set of *predicates* is defined as

$$\mathcal{P} := \{pr(t_1, \ldots, t_k) \mid t_i \in \mathcal{T}_\Sigma, pr \in \Sigma_{pred} \text{ of arity } k\}.$$

Predicates will be used to describe branching conditions in protocols. Each predicate is defined via a first-order formula over ground atoms of the form $t_1 \approx t_2$, i.e., the grammar for such formulae is

$$\langle\phi\rangle ::= t_1 \approx t_2 \mid \neg\phi \mid \phi_1 \wedge \phi_2 \mid \exists x.\phi$$

where t_1, t_2 are terms and $x \in \mathcal{V}$. For an n-ary predicate pr, $pr(x_1, ..., x_n)$ is defined by a formula ϕ_{pr} such that $fv(\phi_p) \subseteq x_1, ..., x_n$, where fv denotes the free variables in a formula, i.e., variables $v \in \mathcal{V}$ not bound by $\exists v$. The semantics of the first-order formulae is as usual where we interpret $\approx$ as $=_E$. We use $\sigma_1 \vee \sigma_2$ as short-hand for $\neg(\neg\sigma_1 \wedge \neg\sigma_2)$.

Example 2. A predicate $pr = can\_wrap$ is used to check whether the attributes associated to two handles (10 attributes each) allow for wrapping. For readability, we rename x_1 to $wrap_1$, x_{15} to $extr_2$, x_7 to $trus_1$ and x_{18} to wwt_2:

$$\sigma_{can\_wrap} := (wrap_1 \approx \text{'on'} \wedge extr_2 \approx \text{'on'}) \wedge$$
$$((wwt2 \approx \text{'off'}) \vee (wwt_2 \approx \text{'on'} \wedge trus_1 \approx \text{'on'}))$$

Substitutions. A substitution σ is a partial function from variables to terms. We suppose that substitutions are well-typed, i.e., they only map variables of sort s to terms of sort s, or of a subsort of s. We denote by $\sigma = \{^{t_1}/_{x_1}, \ldots, ^{t_n}/_{x_n}\}$ the substitution whose domain is $\mathbf{D}(\sigma) = \{x_1, \ldots, x_n\}$ and which maps x_i to t_i. As usual we homomorphically extend σ to apply to terms and facts and use a postfix notation to denote its application, e.g., we write $t\sigma$ for the application of σ to the term t. A substitution σ is grounding for a term t if $t\sigma$ is ground. Given function g we let $g(x) = \bot$ when $x \notin \mathbf{D}(x)$. When $g(x) = \bot$ we say that g is undefined for x. We define the function $f := g[a \mapsto b]$ with $\mathbf{D}(f) = \mathbf{D}(g) \cup \{a\}$ as $f(a) := b$ and $f(x) := g(x)$ for $x \neq a$.

Sets, sequences and multisets. We write $\mathbb{N}_n$ for the set $\{1, \ldots, n\}$. Given a set S we denote by S^* the set of finite sequences of elements from S and by $S^\#$ the set of finite multisets of elements from S. We use the superscript $^\#$ to annotate usual multiset operations, e.g., $S_1 \cup^\# S_2$ denotes the multiset union of multisets S_1, S_2. Given a multiset S we denote by $set(S)$ the set of elements in S. The sequence consisting of elements $e_1, \ldots, e_n$ will be denoted by $[e_1, \ldots, e_n]$ and the empty sequence is denoted

$$
\begin{aligned}
\langle P,Q\rangle ::=~ & 0 \\
\mid~ & P \mid Q \\
\mid~ & !P \\
\mid~ & \nu n:~fresh;~P \\
\mid~ & out(M, N);~P \\
\mid~ & in(M, N);~P \\
\mid~ & \text{if } Pred \text{ then } P \text{ [else } Q] \quad Pred \in \mathcal{P} \\
\mid~ & event~F~;~P \quad (F \in \mathcal{F})
\end{aligned}
$$

$$
\begin{aligned}
\langle P,Q\rangle ::=~ & \textit{(continued)} \\
\mid~ & insert~M,N;~P \\
\mid~ & delete~M;~P \\
\mid~ & lookup~M \text{ as } x \text{ in } P \text{ [else } Q] \\
\mid~ & lock~M;~P \\
\mid~ & unlock~M;~P \\
\mid~ & [L] \dashv A \mapsto [R];~P \quad (L, R, A \in \mathcal{F}^*)
\end{aligned}
$$

Fig. 1. Syntax, where $M, N \in \mathcal{T}$

by [ ]. Given a sequence S, we denote by $idx(S)$ the set of positions in S, i.e., $\mathbb{N}_n$ when S has n elements, and for $i \in idx(S)$ S_i denotes the ith element of the sequence. Set membership modulo E is denoted by $\in_E$ and defined as $e \in_E S$ if $\exists e' \in S. \; e' =_E e$. $\subset_E$ and $=_E$ are defined for sets in a similar way. Application of substitutions is lifted to sets, sequences and multisets as expected. By abuse of notation we sometimes interpret sequences as sets or multisets; the applied operators should make the implicit cast clear.

3.1 A Cryptographic pi Calculus with Explicit State

Syntax and Informal Semantics. The Sapic calculus is a variant of the applied pi calculus [1]. In addition to the usual operators for concurrency, replication, communication and name creation, it offers several constructs for reading and updating an explicit global state. The grammar for processes is described in Fig. 1.

0 denotes the terminal process. $P \mid Q$ is the parallel execution of processes P and Q and $!P$ the replication of P, allowing an unbounded number of sessions in protocol executions. The construct $\nu n; P$ binds the name $n \in FN$ in P and models the generation of a fresh, random value. Processes $out(M, N); P$ and $in(M, N); P$ represent the output, respectively input, of message N on channel M. Readers familiar with the applied pi calculus [1] may note that we opted for the possibility of pattern matching in the input construct, rather than merely binding the input to a variable x. The process if $Pred$ then P else Q will execute P or Q, depending on whether $Pred$ holds. For example, if $Pred = equal(M, N)$, and $\phi_{equal} = x_1 \approx x_2$, then if $equal(M, N)$ then P else Q will execute P if $M =_E N$ and Q otherwise. (In the following, we will use $M = N$ as short-hand for $equal(M, N)$.) The event construct is merely used for annotating processes and will be useful for stating security properties. For readability we sometimes omit to write else Q when Q is 0, as well as trailing 0 processes.

The remaining constructs are used for manipulating state and are new compared to the applied pi calculus. We offer two different mechanisms for state. The first construct is *functional* and allows to associate a value to a key. The construct insert M,N binds the value N to a key M. Successive inserts allow to change this binding. The delete M operation simply "undefines" the mapping for the key M. The lookup M as x in P else Q allows to retrieve the value associated to M, binding it to the variable x in P. If the mapping is undefined for M the process behaves as Q. The lock and unlock constructs allow to gain exclusive access to a resource M. This is essential for writing protocols where parallel processes may read and update a common memory. We additionally offer another kind of global state in form of a multiset of ground facts, as opposed to the previously introduced functional store. The purpose of this construct is to provide access to the underlying notion of state in tamarin, but we stress that it is distinct from the previously introduced functional state, and its use is only advised to expert users. It is not used in the present modelling.

The bound names of a process are those that are bound by νn. We suppose that all names of sort *fresh* appearing in the process are under the scope of such a binder. Free names must be of sort *pub*. A variable x can be bound in three ways: (i) by the construct lookup M as x, or (ii) $x \in vars(N)$ in the construct $in(M, N)$ and x is not under the scope of a previous binder, (iii) $x \in vars(L)$ in the construct $[L] \dashv A]\rightarrow [R]$ and x is not under the scope of a previous binder. While the construct lookup M as x always acts as a binder, the input and $[L] \prec[A] \mapsto[R]$ constructs do not rebind an already bound variable but perform pattern matching.

A process is ground if it does not contain any free variables. We denote by $P\sigma$ the application of the homomorphic extension of the substitution σ to P. As usual we suppose that the substitution only applies to free variables. We sometimes interpret the syntax tree of a process as a term and write $P|_p$ to refer to the subprocess of P at position p (where $|$, if and lookup are interpreted as binary symbols, all other constructs as unary).

Semantics

Frames and deduction. Before giving the formal semantics of our calculus we introduce the notions of frame and deduction. A *frame* consists of a set of fresh names $\tilde{n}$ and a substitution σ and is written $\nu\tilde{n}.\sigma$. Intuitively a frame represents the sequence of messages that have been observed by an adversary during a protocol execution and secrets $\tilde{n}$ generated by the protocol, a priori unknown to the adversary. Deduction models the capacity of the adversary to compute new messages from the observed ones.

Definition 1 (Deduction). *We define the deduction relation* $\nu\tilde{n}.\sigma \vdash t$ *as the smallest relation between frames and terms defined by the deduction rules in Figure 2.*

$$\dfrac{a \in FN \cup PN \quad a \notin \tilde{n}}{\nu\tilde{n}.\sigma \vdash a} \text{ DNAME} \qquad \dfrac{\nu\tilde{n}.\sigma \vdash t \quad t =_E t'}{\nu\tilde{n}.\sigma \vdash t'} \text{ DEQ}$$

$$\dfrac{x \in \mathbf{D}(\sigma)}{\nu\tilde{n}.\sigma \vdash x\sigma} \text{ DFRAME} \qquad \dfrac{\nu\tilde{n}.\sigma \vdash t_1 \cdots \nu\tilde{n}.\sigma \vdash t_n \quad f \in \Sigma^k}{\nu\tilde{n}.\sigma \vdash f(t_1, \ldots, t_n)} \text{ DAPPL}$$

Fig. 2. Deduction rules

Operational semantics. We can now define the operational semantics of our calculus. The semantics is defined by a labelled transition relation between process configurations. A *process configuration* is a 6-tuple $(\mathcal{E}, \mathcal{S}, \mathcal{S}^{\mathrm{MS}}, \mathcal{P}, \sigma, \mathcal{L})$ where

- $\mathcal{E} \subseteq FN$ is the set of fresh names generated by the processes;
- $\mathcal{S} : \mathcal{M}_\Sigma \to \mathcal{M}_\Sigma$ is a partial function modeling the functional store;
- $\mathcal{S}^{\mathrm{MS}} \subseteq \mathcal{G}^{\#}$ is a multiset of ground facts and models the multiset of stored facts;
- $\mathcal{P}$ is a multiset of ground processes representing the processes executed in parallel;
- σ is a ground substitution modeling the messages output to the environment;
- $\mathcal{L} \subseteq \mathcal{M}_\Sigma$ is the set of currently acquired locks.

The transition relation is defined by the rules described in Fig. 3. Transitions are labelled by sets of ground facts. For readability we omit empty sets and brackets around singletons, i.e., we write $\to$ for $\xrightarrow{\emptyset}$ and $\xrightarrow{f}$ for $\xrightarrow{\{f\}}$. We write $\to^*$ for the reflexive, transitive closure of $\to$ (the transitions that are labelled by the empty sets) and write $\xRightarrow{f}$ for $\to^* \xrightarrow{f} \to^*$. We can now define the set of traces, i.e., possible executions, that a process admits.

Definition 2 (Traces of P). *Given a ground process P we define the* set of traces of P *as*

$$traces^{pi}(P) = \left\{ [F_1, \ldots, F_n] \mid (\emptyset, \emptyset, \emptyset, \{P\}, \emptyset, \emptyset) \overset{F_1}{\Longrightarrow} (\mathcal{E}_1, \mathcal{S}_1, \mathcal{S}_1^{MS}, \mathcal{P}_1, \sigma_1, \mathcal{L}_1) \right.$$
$$\left. \overset{F_2}{\Longrightarrow} \ldots \overset{F_n}{\Longrightarrow} (\mathcal{E}_n, \mathcal{S}_n, \mathcal{S}_n^{MS}, \mathcal{P}_n, \sigma_n, \mathcal{L}_n) \right\}$$

3.2 Security Properties

The formalism used for defining security properties in the Sapic tool, which is used to define key secrecy as well as helping lemmas was introduced with the tamarin tool [23]. Security properties are described in an expressive two-sorted first-order logic. The sort *temp* is used for time points, $\mathcal{V}_{temp}$ are temporal variables.

Definition 3 (Trace formulas). *A trace atom is either false $\perp$, a term equality $t_1 \approx t_2$, a timepoint ordering $i \lessdot j$, a timepoint equality $i \doteq j$, or an action $F@i$ for a fact $F \in \mathcal{F}$ and a timepoint i. A trace formula is a first-order formula over trace atoms.*

As we will see in our case studies this logic is expressive enough to analyze a variety of security properties, including complex injective correspondence properties.

To define the semantics, let each sort s have a domain $\mathbf{D}(s)$. $\mathbf{D}(temp) = \mathcal{Q}$, $\mathbf{D}(msg) = \mathcal{M}$, $\mathbf{D}(fresh) = FN$, and $\mathbf{D}(pub) = PN$. A function $\theta : \mathcal{V} \to \mathcal{M} \cup \mathcal{Q}$ is a valuation if it respects sorts, that is, $\theta(\mathcal{V}_s) \subset \mathbf{D}(s)$ for all sorts s. If t is a term, $t\theta$ is the application of the homomorphic extension of θ to t.

Definition 4 (Satisfaction relation). *The satisfaction relation $(tr, \theta) \vDash \varphi$ between trace tr, valuation θ and trace formula φ is defined as follows:*

$$
\begin{aligned}
&(tr, \theta) \vDash \perp && never \\
&(tr, \theta) \vDash F@i && \textit{iff } \theta(i) \in idx(tr) \textit{ and } F\theta \in_E tr_{\theta(i)} \\
&(tr, \theta) \vDash i \lessdot j && \textit{iff } \theta(i) < \theta(j) \\
&(tr, \theta) \vDash i \doteq j && \textit{iff } \theta(i) = \theta(j) \\
&(tr, \theta) \vDash t_1 \approx t_2 && \textit{iff } t_1\theta =_E t_2\theta \\
&(tr, \theta) \vDash \neg\varphi && \textit{iff not } (tr, \theta) \vDash \varphi \\
&(tr, \theta) \vDash \varphi_1 \wedge \varphi_2 && \textit{iff } (tr, \theta) \vDash \varphi_1 \textit{ and } (tr, \theta) \vDash \varphi_2 \\
&(tr, \theta) \vDash \exists x : s.\varphi && \textit{iff there is } u \in \mathbf{D}(s) \textit{ such that} \\
&&& \qquad (tr, \theta[x \mapsto u]) \vDash \varphi
\end{aligned}
$$

When φ is a ground formula we sometimes simply write $tr \vDash \varphi$ as the satisfaction of φ is independent of the valuation.

Definition 5 (Validity, satisfiability). *Let $Tr \subseteq (\mathcal{P}(\mathcal{G}))^*$ be a set of traces. A trace formula φ is said to be* valid *for Tr, written $Tr \vDash^\forall \varphi$, if for any trace $tr \in Tr$ and any valuation θ we have that $(tr, \theta) \vDash \varphi$.*

A trace formula φ is said to be satisfiable *for Tr, written $Tr \vDash^\exists \varphi$, if there exist a trace $tr \in Tr$ and a valuation θ such that $(tr, \theta) \vDash \varphi$.*

Note that $Tr \vDash^\forall \varphi$ iff $Tr \nvDash^\exists \neg\varphi$. Given a ground process P we say that φ is valid, written $P \vDash^\forall \varphi$, if $traces^{pi}(P) \vDash^\forall \varphi$, and that φ is satisfied in P, written $P \vDash^\exists \varphi$, if $traces^{pi}(P) \vDash^\exists \varphi$.

Standard operations:

$$(\mathcal{E}, \mathcal{S}, \mathcal{S}^{\mathrm{MS}}, \mathcal{P} \cup^{\#} \{0\}, \sigma, \mathcal{L}) \quad \longrightarrow \quad (\mathcal{E}, \mathcal{S}, \mathcal{S}^{\mathrm{MS}}, \mathcal{P}, \sigma, \mathcal{L})$$

$$(\mathcal{E}, \mathcal{S}, \mathcal{S}^{\mathrm{MS}}, \mathcal{P} \cup^{\#} \{P|Q\}, \sigma, \mathcal{L}) \quad \longrightarrow \quad (\mathcal{E}, \mathcal{S}, \mathcal{S}^{\mathrm{MS}}, \mathcal{P} \cup^{\#} \{P, Q\}, \sigma, \mathcal{L})$$

$$(\mathcal{E}, \mathcal{S}, \mathcal{S}^{\mathrm{MS}}, \mathcal{P} \cup^{\#} \{!P\}, \sigma, \mathcal{L}) \quad \longrightarrow \quad (\mathcal{E}, \mathcal{S}, \mathcal{S}^{\mathrm{MS}}, \mathcal{P} \cup^{\#} \{!P, P\}, \sigma, \mathcal{L})$$

$$(\mathcal{E}, \mathcal{S}, \mathcal{S}^{\mathrm{MS}}, \mathcal{P} \cup^{\#} \{\nu a; P\}, \sigma, \mathcal{L}) \quad \longrightarrow \quad (\mathcal{E} \cup \{a'\}, \mathcal{S}, \mathcal{S}^{\mathrm{MS}}, \mathcal{P} \cup^{\#} \{P\{a'/a\}\}, \sigma, \mathcal{L})$$
$$\text{if } a' \text{ is fresh}$$

$$(\mathcal{E}, \mathcal{S}, \mathcal{S}^{\mathrm{MS}}, \mathcal{P}, \sigma, \mathcal{L}) \xrightarrow{K(M)} (\mathcal{E}, \mathcal{S}, \mathcal{S}^{\mathrm{MS}}, \mathcal{P}, \sigma, \mathcal{L}) \quad \text{if } \nu\mathcal{E}.\sigma \vdash M$$

$$(\dots, \mathcal{P} \cup^{\#} \{\mathrm{out}(M, N); P\}, \sigma, \mathcal{L}) \xrightarrow{K(M)} (\mathcal{E}, \mathcal{S}, \mathcal{S}^{\mathrm{MS}}, \mathcal{P} \cup^{\#} \{P\}, \sigma \cup \{^{N}/x\}, \mathcal{L})$$
$$\text{if } x \text{ is fresh and } \nu\mathcal{E}.\sigma \vdash M$$

$$(\dots, \mathcal{P} \cup^{\#} \{\mathrm{in}(M, N); P\}, \sigma, \mathcal{L}) \xrightarrow{K(\langle M, N\tau\rangle)} (\dots, \mathcal{P} \cup^{\#} \{P\tau\}, \sigma, \mathcal{L})$$
$$\text{if } \exists\tau. \, \tau \text{ is grounding for } N, \nu\mathcal{E}.\sigma \vdash M, \nu\mathcal{E}.\sigma \vdash N\tau$$

$$\begin{array}{l}(\dots, \mathcal{P} \cup^{\#} \{\mathrm{out}(M, N); P, \\ \quad \mathrm{in}(M', N'); Q\}, \sigma, \mathcal{L})\end{array} \quad \longrightarrow \quad (\mathcal{E}, \mathcal{S}, \mathcal{S}^{\mathrm{MS}}, \mathcal{P} \cup^{\#} \{P, Q\tau\}, \sigma, \mathcal{L})$$
$$\text{if } M =_E M' \text{ and } \exists\tau. \, N =_E N'\tau \text{ and } \tau \text{ grounding for } N'$$

$$\begin{array}{l}(\dots, \mathcal{P} \cup^{\#} \{\mathrm{if} \, pr(M_1, \dots, M_n) \\ \quad \mathrm{then} \, P \, \mathrm{else} \, Q\}, \sigma, \mathcal{L})\end{array} \quad \longrightarrow \quad (\mathcal{E}, \mathcal{S}, \mathcal{S}^{\mathrm{MS}}, \mathcal{P} \cup^{\#} \{P\}, \sigma, \mathcal{L})$$
$$\text{if } \phi_{pr}\{^{M_1}/x_1, \dots, {}^{M_n}/x_n\} \text{ is satisfied}$$

$$\begin{array}{l}(\dots, \mathcal{P} \cup^{\#} \{\mathrm{if} \, pr(M_1, \dots, M_n) \\ \quad \mathrm{then} \, P \, \mathrm{else} \, Q\}, \sigma, \mathcal{L})\end{array} \quad \longrightarrow \quad (\mathcal{E}, \mathcal{S}, \mathcal{S}^{\mathrm{MS}}, \mathcal{P} \cup^{\#} \{Q\}, \sigma, \mathcal{L})$$
$$\text{if } \phi_{pr}\{^{M_1}/x_1, \dots, {}^{M_n}/x_n\} \text{ is not satisfied}$$

$$(\dots, \mathcal{P} \cup^{\#} \{\mathrm{event}(F); P\}, \sigma, \mathcal{L}) \xrightarrow{F} (\mathcal{E}, \mathcal{S}, \mathcal{S}^{\mathrm{MS}}, \mathcal{P} \cup \{P\}, \sigma, \mathcal{L})$$

Operations on global state:

$$(\dots, \mathcal{P} \cup^{\#} \{\mathrm{insert} \, M, N; P\}, \sigma, \mathcal{L}) \longrightarrow (\mathcal{E}, \mathcal{S}[M \mapsto N], \mathcal{S}^{\mathrm{MS}}, \mathcal{P} \cup^{\#} \{P\}, \sigma, \mathcal{L})$$

$$(\dots, \mathcal{P} \cup^{\#} \{\mathrm{delete} \, M; P\}, \sigma, \mathcal{L}) \longrightarrow (\mathcal{E}, \mathcal{S}[M \mapsto \bot], \mathcal{S}^{\mathrm{MS}}, \mathcal{P} \cup^{\#} \{P\}, \sigma, \mathcal{L})$$

$$\begin{array}{l}(\dots, \mathcal{P} \cup^{\#} \{\mathrm{lookup} \, M \, \mathrm{as} \, x \\ \quad \mathrm{in} \, P \, \mathrm{else} \, Q\}, \sigma, \mathcal{L})\end{array} \longrightarrow (\mathcal{E}, \mathcal{S}, \mathcal{S}^{\mathrm{MS}}, \mathcal{P} \cup^{\#} \{P\{V/x\}\}, \sigma, \mathcal{L})$$
$$\text{if } \mathcal{S}(N) =_E V \text{ is defined and } N =_E M$$

$$\begin{array}{l}(\dots, \mathcal{P} \cup^{\#} \{\mathrm{lookup} \, M \, \mathrm{as} \, x \\ \quad \mathrm{in} \, P \, \mathrm{else} \, Q\}, \sigma, \mathcal{L})\end{array} \longrightarrow (\mathcal{E}, \mathcal{S}, \mathcal{S}^{\mathrm{MS}}, \mathcal{P} \cup^{\#} \{Q\}, \sigma, \mathcal{L})$$
$$\text{if } \mathcal{S}(N) \text{ is undefined for all } N =_E M$$

$$(\dots, \mathcal{P} \cup^{\#} \{\mathrm{lock} \, M; P\}, \sigma, \mathcal{L}) \longrightarrow (\mathcal{E}, \mathcal{S}, \mathcal{S}^{\mathrm{MS}}, \mathcal{P} \cup^{\#} \{P\}, \sigma, \mathcal{L} \cup \{M\})$$
$$\text{if } M \notin_E \mathcal{L}$$

$$(\dots, \mathcal{P} \cup^{\#} \{\mathrm{unlock} \, M; P\}, \sigma, \mathcal{L}) \longrightarrow (\mathcal{E}, \mathcal{S}, \mathcal{S}^{\mathrm{MS}}, \mathcal{P} \cup^{\#} \{P\}, \sigma, \mathcal{L} \setminus \{M' : M' =_E M\})$$

$$(\dots, \mathcal{P} \cup^{\#} \{[l \, \overset{\frown}{-[} a] \mapsto r]; P\}, \sigma, \mathcal{L}) \xrightarrow{a'} (\mathcal{E}, \mathcal{S}, \mathcal{S}^{\mathrm{MS}} \setminus lfacts(l') \cup^{\#} r', \mathcal{P} \cup^{\#} \{P\tau\}, \sigma, \mathcal{L})$$
$$\text{if } \exists\tau, l', a', r'.\tau \text{ grounding for } l \, \overset{\frown}{-[} a] \mapsto r, l' \, \overset{\frown}{-[} a'] \mapsto r' =_E (l \, \overset{\frown}{-[} a] \mapsto r)\tau,$$
$$lfacts(l') \subseteq^{\#} \mathcal{S}^{\mathrm{MS}}, pfacts(l') \subset \mathcal{S}^{\mathrm{MS}}$$

Fig. 3. Operational semantics

4   Model

In this section, we will introduce our model of a PKCS#11 token. The complete code is available at http://sapic.gforge.inria.fr/pkcs11templates.zip. We consider a security device that allows the creation of keys in its secure memory. The user can access the device via an API. If he creates a key, he obtains a handle, which he can use to let the device perform operations on his behalf. For each handle the device also stores a list of attributes, which define what operations are permitted for this handle. The goal is that the user can never gain knowledge of the key, as the user's machine might be compromised. We model the device by the following process (we use out(m) as a shortcut for out(c, m) for a public channel c):

$$P_{init}; !(P_{create} \mid P_{dec} \mid P_{enc} \mid P_{wrap} \mid P_{unwrap} \mid P_{get\_keyval}), \text{ where}$$

$P_{init} :=$
/*   *wrap, unwrap, enc, dec, sens, extr, trus, wwt, wt   , ut */*
insert   ⟨'template','trusted'⟩,
              ⟨ 'on', 'on', 'off','off','on','on', 'on', 'on','usage','usage'⟩;
insert   ⟨'template','usage'⟩,
              ⟨'off', 'off','on','on','on', 'on','off', 'on','undef','undef'⟩;
insert   ⟨'template','untrusted'⟩,
              ⟨'off', 'off','on','on','off', 'on','off', 'off','undef','undef'⟩;

This sets up the templates before starting operation in the replicated process. Key-generation is handled by P_{create}:

$P_{create} :=$ in(⟨'create',*atts,ptr*⟩);
lock 'device';
ν h; ν k;
lookup ⟨'template', *ptr*⟩ as *templ* in
if *permits*(*attwrap*(*templ*), [...], *attut*(*templ*),
              attwrap(*atts*),   [...], *attut*(*atts*)) then
     event *NewKey*(*h,k*,*attsens*(*atts*));
     insert ⟨'obj',*h*⟩, ⟨*k, atts* ⟩;
     event *WrapKey*(*h,k,attwrap*(*atts*)); event *DecKey*(*h,k, attdec* (*atts*));
     event *EncKey*(*h,k, attenc* (*atts*)); event *UnwrapKey*(*h,k,attunwrap*(*atts*));
     out(*h*) ;
     unlock 'device'

Upon reception of a key generation request with a list of attributes and a pointer to a template, the device is locked. Then, the device creates a new handle h and a key k. The pointer is retrieved from the database P_{init} has written to. The functions *attwrap*, to *attut* are simple deconstructors, *attwrap*, for example, extracts the first element from a list of 10 attributes (see Tab. 1). The predicate *permits* compares the attributes given by the adversary with the attributes stored with the template. In subsection 2.2, we have argued that templates should determine the key's attributes, hence *permits* is true if and only if the attributes including the pointers to the templates match exactly. To obtain a more permissive modelling, this predicate can be altered, e. g., to allow for certain attributes to be changed.

The creation of keys is logged as an event $\text{NewKey}(h, k, attsens(atts))$. If the third argument is 'on', this key is sensitive, i. e., secrecy needs to be preserved. Events are used to state security properties and helping lemmas. Next, the device stores the key that belongs to the handle by associating the pair $\langle$'key', $h\rangle$ to the value of the key k and the attributes. The events WrapKey to UnwrapKey are used to refer to the attributes of keys in helping lemmas and otherwise irrelevant. Finally, the handle is output and the device unlocked.

Remark 1. The predicate *permits* compares the attributes, including the pointers wt and ut, literally. Since our policy only accepts pointers to templates created by P_{init}, and since those are distinct, this is without loss of generality. Furthermore, the adversary has to provide the pointer to the template, which is without loss of generality, too, since the pointers are of sort *pub*.

If a handle has the 'dec' attribute set, it can be used for decryption:

$P_{dec} := \text{in}(\langle h, senc(m,k)\rangle);$
lock 'device';
lookup $\langle$'obj', $h\rangle$ as v in
    if $can\_decrypt(\ attwrap(tem(v)),\ [\ldots], attut(tem(v)))$ then
        if $key(v)=k$ then
            event $DecUsing(k,m);$ out$(m);$ unlock 'device'

The lookup stores the value associated to $\langle$'obj', $h\rangle$ in v. The predicate $can\_decrypt$ is satisfied, iff. the fourth argument, $attdec(tem(v))$ equals 'on'. The function symbol tem extracts the second element of a pair, it is defined by the equation $tem(\langle k, t\rangle) = t$. Similarly, $key(\langle k, t\rangle) = k$. If the key stored with this handle matches the key used to generate the encryption, the plain-text is output and the device unlocked.

If a key has the 'wrap' attribute set, it can be used to encrypt the value of a second key:

$P_{wrap} := \text{in}(\langle h1, h2\rangle);$
lock 'device';
lookup $\langle$'obj', $h1\rangle$ as $v1$ in
    lookup $\langle$'obj', $h2\rangle$ as $v2$ in
        if $can\_wrap(\ attwrap(tem(v1)), [\ldots], attut(tem(v1)),$
                    $attwrap(tem(v2)),\ [\ldots], attut(tem(v2)))$ then
            lookup $\langle$'template', $attwt(tem(v1))\rangle$ as wt in
                if $permits(\ attwrap(wt),\ [\ldots], attut(wt),$
                            $attwrap(tem(v2)),\ [\ldots], attut(tem(v2)))$ then
                    event $Wrap(key(v1),key(v2));$
                    out$(senc(key(v2), key(v1)));$
                    unlock 'device'

Given the two handles h_1 and h_2, the corresponding keys and attributes are retrieved. The predicate can_wrap is defined in Example 2 on page 228. If the template referred to by the entry 'wt' in the first key's attribute list permits wrapping the second key, i. e., it is equal to the second handle's attributes, then the encryption is output. The complete model including P_{enc}, P_{unwrap} and P_{get_keyval} can be found at http://sapic. gforge.inria.fr/pkcs11templates.zip.

Limitations. While being more detailed than previous works in terms of the attributes and commands supported, our model does have the following limitations: *Integrity of wrappings.* In our model, a wrapping can only be imported if it is an encryption of some message with a key that is on the device. In reality, this integrity property cannot be given. There are techniques that allow to account for malleability of cypher-texts in the symbolic model [3]. The current draft for version 2.40 indicates that authenticated encryption might be part of the future version of this standard [21] . *Multiple tokens.* We currently model a single token. By encapsulating the current process P in $\nu device$: $pub.P$ and prepending *device* to database keys, this situation could be modelled. *Copying keys, asymmetric keys, key derivation.* C_CopyObject, support for asymmetric keys and key-derivation are not modelled for various reasons explained in Section 2.1. While we conjecture copying objects could be enabled, and asymmetric keys as well as key-derivation keys be allowed as 'usage' keys, this is missing in the current model (as opposed to other related work [11, 7]).

5 Security Results for the Proposed Policy

The main security result is the secrecy of keys generated on the device that have been marked 'sensitive' upon creation, in our case, keys created with the templates 'trusted' or 'usage'. This is expressed by the following trace formula:

$$\neg(\exists h, k: msg, \ i, j: temp. \ \text{NewKey}(h, k, \text{'on'})@i \land \text{K}(k)@j)$$

The action NewKey refers to the event in the key-generation process P_{create}, which we introduced in Section 4. If the third argument is 'on', k has been created 'sensitive'. To derive the result, we have defined 9 helping lemmas, four of which are rather trivial, but help speeding up the proof. The first, dec_limits, establishes typing invariants, most importantly, it states that decrypt is not useful to the adversary: Any message obtained by decryption was either known to the adversary in advance, or a key that was created 'sensitive' or imported was leaked, or there was some key that had the attributes 'wrap' and 'dec' set at different points in time. The following four lemmas state that given the templates it is, e. g., not possible to create a key with 'trusted' as wrapping template. The lemma bad_keys states that a key that was created by unwrapping must earlier have been created on the device, unless something bad happened, i. e., either a sensitive key leaked, or a key had wrap and dec, or unwrap and enc set before. The latter two conflicts are known to cause attacks [8]. The following lemma no_key_is_wrap_and_-dec says that the first conflict can only occur if the second occurred before, or a sensitive key was leaked. Subsequently, it is shown the second conflict cannot occur, unless a key was leaked. The lemma cannot_obtain_key_ind is an inductive version of the security property cannot_obtain_key.

Table 4. Evaluation of our proof method with and without the model-specific heuristics, broken down into lemmas. Interaction is measured in terms of mouse clicks. The user choses the next proof goal out of a list in a web interface. The value was determined by counting occurrences of the keyword 'solve' in the file. The proof size is the number of case distinctions.

name	interaction		proof size	
	(w/o heur.)	(w/ heur.)	(w/o heur.)	(w/ heur.)
dec_limits	11	0	3394	2235
trusted_as_ut_impossible	0	0	4	4
untrusted_as_ut_impossible	0	0	4	4
untrusted_as_wt_impossible	0	0	4	4
trusted_as_wt_impossible	0	0	4	4
bad_keys	0	0	2988	683
no_key_is_wrap_and_dec_[..]	15	0	1177	2396
no_key_is_enc_and_unwrap	29	0	2669	352
cannot_obtain_key_ind	6	0	7306	14598
cannot_obtain_key	0	0	0	0

User intervention is necessary to find the proof when the tamarin prover is used with heuristics adapted to general Sapic output. They differ from the standard 'smart' heuristic only in that the actions corresponding to unlock operations and premises corresponding to the previous state in the execution are prioritized. Using a model-specific heuristic, it is possible to find the proof automatically. This heuristic prioritizes the resolution of insert operations with 'template' in the first argument (thereby moving the case distinction about which templates is used upwards in the proof tree) and deprioritizes the adversary's deduction of handles (as they are public anyway). With this heuristic, the complete proof is found within half an hour on a computation server with 24 Intel Xeon 2.67GHz cores and 50GB RAM. Experiments on desktop machines are planned. See Table 4 for more details. The manual part of the proof, transcripts of the complete proof and the tools used are available at http://sapic.gforge.inria.fr/pkcs11templates.zip.

6   Conclusion and Future Work

We have investigated a new method of verifying key secrecy in PKCS#11 configurations following the protocol verification approach. It requires manual effort in defining helping lemmas, but overcomes the need for a model-specific approximation techniques and models PKCS#11 in a precise and intuitive manner. In particular, our model supports features that have been added in version 2.20 of the standard. The upcoming [21] version 2.40 is available for public review and will support encryption with authenticated data, a mechanism that has long been requested and has the potential to remove the restriction to three-level policies outlined in Section 2.2 and allow for new policies. Future work on version 2.40 will benefit from the fact that our verification technique applies without model-specific approximation. The second contribution is a secure configuration of PKCS#11 that permits wrapping and unwrapping for backup purposes.

Besides adapting our model to the case of multiple tokens in the network, we plan to increase the degree of automation by refining the model-specific heuristic for the tamarin prover's constraint solving algorithm. The current heuristic is rather simple, but may be generalized. We stress that completeness and soundness of the tool chain are independent of the heuristic used, suggesting a tool chain without approximation but adapted heuristics as an alternative to ad-hoc approximations that does not necessarily provide decidability, but is more flexible with regard to extensions and less reliant on hand-written proofs.

Acknowledgements. This work was supported by the German Federal Ministry of Education and Research (BMBF) within EC SPRIDE.

References

[1] Abadi, M., Fournet, C.: Mobile Values, New Names, and Secure Communication. In: POPL 2001. ACM Press (2001)

[2] Adão, P., Focardi, R., Luccio, F.L.: Type-Based Analysis of Generic Key Management APIs. In: CSF, pp. 97–111. IEEE (2013)

[3] Ahmed, N., Jensen, C.D., Zenner, E.: Towards Symbolic Encryption Schemes. In: Foresti, S., Yung, M., Martinelli, F. (eds.) ESORICS 2012. LNCS, vol. 7459, pp. 557–572. Springer, Heidelberg (2012)

[4] Bardou, R., Focardi, R., Kawamoto, Y., Simionato, L., Steel, G., Tsay, J.-K.: Efficient Padding Oracle Attacks on Cryptographic Hardware. In: Safavi-Naini, R., Canetti, R. (eds.) CRYPTO 2012. LNCS, vol. 7417, pp. 608–625. Springer, Heidelberg (2012)

[5] Bond, M., Anderson, R.: API level attacks on embedded systems. IEEE Computer Magazine 34(10) (2001)

[6] Bortolozzo, M., et al.: Attacking and Fixing PKCS#11 Security Tokens. In: CCS 2010. ACM Press (2010)

[7] Centenaro, M., Focardi, R., Luccio, F.L.: Type-based analysis of key management in PKCS#11 cryptographic devices. Journal of Computer Security 21(6) (2013)

[8] Clulow, J.: On the security of PKCS #11. In: Walter, C.D., Koç, Ç.K., Paar, C. (eds.) CHES 2003. LNCS, vol. 2779, pp. 411–425. Springer, Heidelberg (2003)

[9] Cortier, V., Keighren, G., Steel, G.: Automatic Analysis of the Security of XOR-Based Key Management Schemes. In: Grumberg, O., Huth, M. (eds.) TACAS 2007. LNCS, vol. 4424, pp. 538–552. Springer, Heidelberg (2007)

[10] Cortier, V., Steel, G., Wiedling, C.: Revoke and let live: a secure key revocation API for cryptographic devices. In: CCS 2012. ACM (2012)

[11] Delaune, S., Kremer, S., Steel, G.: Formal Analysis of PKCS#11 and Proprietary Extensions. Journal of Computer Security 18(6) (2010)

[12] Durgin, N., et al.: Undecidability of Bounded Security Protocols. In: Workshop on Formal Methods and Security Protocols. IEEE (1999)

[13] Fröschle, S., Sommer, N.: Concepts and Proofs for Configuring PKCS#11. In: Barthe, G., Datta, A., Etalle, S. (eds.) FAST 2011. LNCS, vol. 7140, pp. 131–147. Springer, Heidelberg (2012)

[14] Fröschle, S., Steel, G.: Analysing PKCS#11 key management aPIs with unbounded fresh data. In: Degano, P., Viganò, L. (eds.) ARSPA-WITS 2009. LNCS, vol. 5511, pp. 92–106. Springer, Heidelberg (2009)

[15] Fröschle, S., Sommer, N.: Reasoning with past to prove PKCS#11 keys secure. In: Degano, P., Etalle, S., Guttman, J. (eds.) FAST 2010. LNCS, vol. 6561, pp. 96–110. Springer, Heidelberg (2011)

[16] Fröschle, S.B., Sommer, N.: When is a PKCS#11 configuration secure? Tech. rep. Reports of SFB/TR 14 AVACS 82, SFB/TR 14 AVACS (2011), https://vhome.offis.de/sibyllef/cryptokireport.pdf

[17] Kremer, S., Künnemann, R.: Automated analysis of security protocols with global state. In: Security and Privacy. IEEE Computer Society (2014)

[18] Kremer, S., Künnemann, R., Steel, G.: Universally Composable Key-Management. In: Crampton, J., Jajodia, S., Mayes, K. (eds.) ESORICS 2013. LNCS, vol. 8134, pp. 327–344. Springer, Heidelberg (2013)

[19] Kremer, S., Steel, G., Warinschi, B.: Security for Key Management Interfaces. In: CSF 2011, pp. 66–82. IEEE Computer Society (2011)

[20] Longley, D., Rigby, S.: An Automatic Search for Security Flaws in Key Management Schemes. Computers and Security 11(1) (March 1992)

[21] PKCS #11 Cryptographic Token Interface Base Specification Version 2.40, Committee Specification 01. OASIS Open (September 2014), http://docs.oasis-open.org/pkcs11/pkcs11-base/v2.40/cs01/pkcs11-base-v2.40-cs01.html

[22] PKCS #11: Cryptographic Token Interface Standard. RSA Security Inc. v2.20 (June 2004)

[23] Schmidt, B., et al.: Automated Analysis of Diffie-Hellman Protocols and Advanced Security Properties. In: CSF 2012. IEEE (2012)

A Safe Update Mechanism for Smart Cards

Kristian Beilke and Volker Roth

Freie Universität Berlin, Berlin, Germany
{kristian.beilke,volker.roth}@fu-berlin.de,
http://www.inf.fu-berlin.de/groups/ag-si/

Abstract. With the advent of the integration of smart card chips into national identity documents, the business model of replacing compromised smart cards becomes uneconomical. We propose a mechanism to safely apply updates to embedded systems, particularly high value smart cards, that are costly to replace. We identify the requirements for such a mechanism and describe how it can be implemented. Our mechanism achieves its properties at the expense of using moderately more non-volatile memory to store program code than contemporary smart cards. We have developed a Common Criteria protection profile package to abstractly describe such a mechanism and summarize it in this paper. The mechanism and the abstract description can be a starting point for a practical realization in consumer products.

1 Introduction

Updates have become an important part of a comprehensive security strategy. As the tedious and costly task of applying updates results in many unpatched systems, automatic or vendor controlled updates try to improve the situation. *One notable exception are smart cards.*

Smart cards are a special kind of computer. Regular computers are generally too complex to obtain assurance about their correctness. Smart cards are comparably simple devices with limited functionality. The assumption that underlies their use is that we can engineer them in a trustworthy fashion, that is, with few errors, if any, without backdoors, and with enough resilience against attacks. Compromising a smart card should be more expensive to an attacker than the possible gain.

Yet, our trust is a function of time. The sophistication of attacks grows the necessary know-how becomes more widely available over the Internet, and resources to attack systems become cheaper. Smart cards that were state of the art a few years ago do not hold up to today's standards such as BSI-CC-PP-0084 [7]. Steady improvements of hardware attacks [17] have diminished the technological advantage of manufacturers of security hardware to only a few years ahead of the attackers. At the same time, smart cards have found their way into products with expected lifetimes of up to ten years, for example, national identity documents [11]. These two factors, the increasing pace at which techniques are developed that chip away on smart card security, and the extended lifetime of

© Springer-Verlag Berlin Heidelberg 2015
R. Focardi and A. Myers (Eds.): POST 2015, LNCS 9036, pp. 239–258, 2015.
DOI: 10.1007/978-3-662-46666-7_13

smart card systems in the field, increase the likelihood of a critical security breach over the system's lifetime.

Apart from hardware attacks that can be defended against only if the attack was anticipated at design time, software and protocol vulnerabilities are a major attack vector. Such a vulnerability might go unnoticed for years, but when it is discovered, it might suddenly pose a grave risk. A recent example is the publication of the Heartbleed attack against openssl (CVE-2014-0160).

The industry response for low to medium value smart cards has been and still is card re-issuance. The vulnerable smart cards are invalidated and new ones are produced. Economically this only works, if the cards are cheap to replace. If the cost of replacing or re-issuing a card exceeds a certain threshold as is the case with modern identity documents, the investment into software updates will be justified. The same is true if a forced replacement leads to reputation damage or a loss of trust in the issuer or the smart card enabled system. This is the case for ID documents where a major part of the production cost are physical protection features against illegitimate reprints. Therefore we see a need for the provision of software updates on high value smart cards such as ID documents.

Software updates may not seem novel nor particularly challenging as a research topic but there are reasons why update mechanisms have not yet found their way into many of today's deployed smart card systems.

Many embedded systems such as smart phones, home routers, or set-top boxes provide user or vendor accessible interfaces that enable firmware updates. These can take the form of hardware debug interfaces or bootloaders. Usually the update mechanisms support a fail-safe *recovery mode* that is highly useful in cases where the regular update process fails and leaves the device in an unusable state. However, said recovery mechanisms can themselves be the target of attacks as was shown with industrial FPGA products [15]. The critical nature of most smart card applications leaves no room for such a loophole, and loosing deployed devices due to erroneous updates is not acceptable as this easily damages the issuer in an industry where trust is important.

Another reason that makes updates on smart cards difficult is certification, usually under the Common Criteria framework (CC) [2]. For certain high value applications such as electronic national identity documents it is required of the issuers to only use certified hardware and software products. Evaluations for high CC assurance classes are time-consuming and expensive. Once an IT product is certified, it cannot be changed at all without voiding its compliance to the certified state. Therefore, even small modifications require a re-certification of the entire implementation which in effort and cost is comparable to the original evaluation. Manufacturers having already sold their product have no incentives to bear the costs of re-certification due to an update. Therefore update mechanisms have not been included. One exception are virtual machine based cards such as Java Cards supporting the Global Platform standard [9]. They contain update mechanisms but they only target the application level. A replacement of cryptographic primitives which are part of the operating system or in a vendor supplied library is not possible short of re-implementing this functionality in the application. This is too limited in our view, as the application logic on smart cards only encompasses a rather small part of the code that an update should be applied to. We see the need to provide updates that include the applications, the OS, and parts of or even the complete firmware (device embedded software). The technical effort to provide the updates does not increase with the extended scope. The development and test effort is comparable. The problem of who bears the costs of re-evaluation remains.

Furthermore economic reasons prevented updates in the past. Smart cards had only small amounts of writable non-volatile memory (NVM) available. NVM is a comparably large structure inside the chip and size drives the cost of chips. Large parts of the software were placed in ROM and hence there was not much space to integrate new code. With the advent of FLASH memory based controllers this is changing rapidly. Some newer smart card products already are equipped with only a small amount of ROM and comparatively large FLASH based memories [1].

Our contribution. We outline a generic mechanism that enables fail-safe updates on smart cards and we analyze its safety and security. In particular, we show that the mechanism does not decrease the system's security. We summarize a CC Protection Profile package we have developed for an abstract update mechanism that is compatible to a current Protection Profile for high value application smart cards.

Paper organization. We begin with a detailed analysis of smart card-specific requirements for update mechanisms in Sect. 2 while Sect. 3 explains the threat model. We designed an approach that we believe meets the requirements and we describe it in Sect. 4. In Sect. 5 we evaluate how well existing update mechanisms fulfill the requirements as we discuss related work. Section 6 introduces the Common Criteria (CC) and the context wherein to place the CC Protection Profile Package which we describe in Sect. 7. After a discussion in Sect. 8 we offer our conclusions in Sect. 9.

2 Requirements for Smart Card Updates

In this section we derive the requirements for an update mechanism applicable to high value smart cards. We first depict a scenario of how an end user should experience the process. Based on that scenario and the threats we identify therein we list the requirements for an update mechanism and follow with notes about basic security objectives and considerations about functionality.

2.1 Update Scenario

Alice has been issued a personalized smart card. The card has multiple applications and can be used for multiple use cases including online authentication, proof of age, digital signatures, etc. The functions are protected by a PIN only known to Alice. The card has a validity period spanning multiple years.

Some years after issuance a flaw in one of the cryptographic algorithms used extensively by the card is discovered. Since the algorithm is implemented in a firmware level library which is compiled into the image and installed on the chip before personalization a simple ad hoc fix is not available. To prevent the necessity to reissue all affected cards the issuer in cooperation with the software manufacturers provides an update. The update must be applied to all affected smart cards before they may be used again.

There are two ways it can be applied. First, if the smart card is inserted in an official terminal, such as an ATM, the update is applied before the card will run any applications. Alice notices only a slight delay after which the regular use case is executed as usually. Second, Alice uses the smart card on a personal reader connected to a PC on which middleware software for the use of the card is running. This could be at Alice's home or even in public untrusted place, such as an internet cafe. In both cases the terminal and the middleware software as well as the whole PC are not trusted. The middleware only establishes a communication channel between the smart card and a server. The server provides the update. The channel is to be mutually authenticated, encrypted, and integrity protected. Inside the channel the update mechanism is executed. Again, after a little while the regular use case resumes and Alice can use the smart card with the update applied to the cryptographic library.

2.2   Requirements

The specific properties of smart cards and the environments in which they must operate lead to several requirements an update mechanism must meet. The following list of requirements are relevant to the use case at hand: updates on high value smart cards.

1. **Robustness:** As the environment is under the control of the user or even an attacker, an update process can be interrupted at any point of time before it completes. This could be caused by a sudden loss of power. The card must be able to handle such interruptions without leaving the software in an inconsistent state.
2. **Low level system updates:** Updates should not be limited to applications on the smart card but should allow the operating system and the device embedded software to be updated as well, including libraries with cryptographic core functionality.
3. **Security:** The mechanism shall not enable attackers to gain any new information from the card or to compromise its security. This means that the protections of a smart card with such an update mechanism are not lower than those of an otherwise identical smart card without the mechanism. Security in this context covers authenticity, confidentiality, and access control. Unauthorized updates and downgrades must be prevented.

2.3 Secure Updates in Detail

To guarantee the security of an in-the-field update mechanism the use of cryptographic primitives is mandatory to fulfill the following security goals:

- Correctness
  - all bytes are correctly transmitted, the update is complete and correct
  - the update is written to the correct location in memory
- Access Control
  - the update is from an authorized source
  - only an authorized entity can execute the update process
  - the update is protected while stored
- Communication Security
  - the update can not be modified in transit without detection
  - the update is transmitted confidentially

Whether and how these are implemented is application specific and has been explored before, for example by Abrahamsson [3]. We therefore do not elaborate on the details in this paper. We assume these primitives to be an integral part of the software that the updates are applied to. We focus our attention on the safety requirements 1. and 2. from Sect. 2.2 in this paper. However, we do describe how a downgrade protection can be implemented in Sect. 4.4.

2.4 The Software Split

The requirement to all low level updates results in an assignment of which code must be stored in what memory. Code stored in ROM is not changeable. The code in NVM can be updated. The simplest approach is to define the complete functionality needed to apply an update as part of the static code which can not be changed. In many embedded systems this is a reasonable idea. With smart cards this functionality comprises the majority of all available features as this needs communication, cryptography, access control and authentication. The only part left is the application logic which is comparably small.

Such a split stands in contradiction to our requirement to affect low level functionality with the updates. The static part of the software has to be minimal, so the largest part of the software, including the update mechanism, will be changeable through updates. Accordingly this means that the access control and authentication decisions must also be made by code that can be updated. We therefore require trust into the updates themselves. A malicious or malfunctioning update, that changes the security functions, can violate any safety or security properties we aim to achieve.

3 Threat Model and Security Objectives

Smart cards are trusted devices operated in untrusted environments. We must anticipate that an adversary may obtain multiple authentic copies of a smart card and that he may attack them in arbitrary ways, limited only by his resources, for example by means of:

1. invasive physical attacks such as micro-probing and reverse engineering,
2. semi- and non-invasive attacks such as fault induction, power and electro-magnetic analysis,
3. logical attacks that exploit implementation bugs, weaknesses in cryptographic protocols or insufficient operating system protection against untrusted code,
4. any combination of the above.

The inconvenient consequence is that a well-funded adversary will likely be able to uncover any secrets of a smart card eventually. Hence, security, and conse-quently the trust in a smart card system, is a function of time and of the value of the assets that the smart card system protects. The higher the value the more resources can the adversary invest and still obtain his payoff. These delibera-tions are part of any smart card system design and determine the extent to which protection mechanisms are integrated. Our work also depends on these deliberations as it builds on the security properties of a smart card's hardware and its software against state-of-the-art attacks.

In this paper, we focus on logical attacks on our update mechanism instead. These are any attack vectors our update mechanism adds to the pre-existing attack vectors on a smart card. In particular, if a smart card hardware is insecure with respect to an invasive attack then our update mechanism will certainly be insecure as well. A system is only as secure as its weakest link. Our security objective is to add update functionality to smart cards without making any link weaker than it already is. Towards this end, we identify a set of attack vectors that are specific to update systems. An adversary may attempt to

1. Bring the update mechanism into an invalid state, to cause an invalid state transition or to cause the mechanism to perform unauthorized computations
2. Cause the update mechanism to accept an update that is not authentic
3. Cause the update mechanism to accept an update that is authentic but obsolete, that is, to perform a downgrade.

Our informal security objective is the following:

> If a smart card hardware is secure and its operating system is secure and its operating system can verify the authenticity of an update and the update installs another secure operating system then the smart card system is *secure after the update*.

Furthermore, the smart card system is *safe* if its update installs an operating system that enables a subsequent update.

An attacker that can freely write to arbitrary memory locations does not need to attack the update mechanism. We therefore assume he can at best change random bytes to either 0x00 or 0xFF. This is the case when a NVM write operation is interrupted between the deletion of a page and the writing of new data. With modern hardware this should not be possible. The chip will buffer enough power to finish the write after a delete. Nevertheless we consider this as an attack. An attacker can also observe and manipulate any communication between the update provider and the smart card. An attack is considered a success if the attacker gains access to any confidential information or can abuse the functionality of the applications in any way not intended by the developer.

4   Safe Smart Card Updates

We detail an update mechanism that meets all requirements specified in Sect. 2. This does not mean that our mechanism necessarily meets *all conceivable requirements* that can be asked of an update mechanism. However it meets all requirements that we set as a goal for this stage of our research.

Whenever systems have the requirement of firmware updates that have to be applied by the end-user in an uncontrolled environment, similar solutions have been discovered. In systems where space has been available memory duplication and transactional behavior to switch between memory images has been used. This includes mainboards [12] and MCUs [10].

What is new with our work is the necessity to not only guarantee a recoverable system in case a failure occurs, but to guarantee an always working and secure system.

To achieve the stated goals we require additional storage space to hold two images instead of just one. One image holds the current system, that is, the image which must be updated. The other image will receive the new and updated version, which is about to become the current system. Once the other image is the current image, the previous image becomes the staging area for the next update. In the following, we describe how the transition occurs from one image to the other and informally prove its safety properties.

4.1   System Layout

We abstract from the practically available memory of a smart card in the following description. The functionality can be implemented on a ROM/EEPROM based card as well as on a purely FLASH based controller.

Our approach segments the smart card memory as follows. First, a minimal bootloader is mapped to a segment with the address where the smart card begins execution on power-on or whenever a reset occurs. The bootloader keeps its state v_0 in a small NVM segment, which may consist of a single memory word. Two more NVM segments called A and B contain system images. We refer to the images in these segments as image A or B depending on which segment they are in. Another small NVM segment v_1 contains state variables for each image. The images use them to communicate with the bootloader. The communication channel is one-way and one-shot, that is, the bootloader reads the contents of these variables into registers and clears the variables upon each boot. Additional segments can contain the applications and the application data, if such a partition is desired. All segments need to be written to and thus are located in NVM. Only the bootloader may be placed in ROM, if it is available. Upon power-on or reset, the memory access is set to read/write for the entire address space and execution begins at a specific address in the bootloader. Before the bootloader branches into an image, it removes write access to its state segment and configures further access restrictions based on which image it invokes. The following table summarized the access rights assignment by phase.

State	‖Loader	v_0	Segm. A	Segm. B	v_1	Apps	Data
Boot	r	rw	rw	rw	rw	rw	rw
boot_A	–	r	r	rw	w	rw	rw
boot_B	–	r	rw	r	w	rw	rw

Note that images are not allowed to write their own code, but they receive access rights that enable them to write the other image. A mandatory assumption is that the smart card supports memory protection mechanisms enforcing the access control restrictions as we have defined them. In Sect. 8 we discuss how existing mechanisms in smart cards can be used to that effect.

4.2   System States and State Transitions

From the bootloader's perspective, the system has two states. We illustrate these states and the associated state transitions in Fig. 1. State boot_A directly transfers control to the image in segment A and state boot_B does the same for the image in segment B. In state boot_A, segment A contains the current image, that is, the one in need of an update, whereas segment B is the staging area for the updated image. These roles are reversed in state boot_B. The bootloader

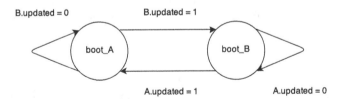

Fig. 1. The bootloader state transitions. The circles represent bootloader states. On every reset one of the transitions is made. The regular case if no update was written will not change the state but remain in either boot_A or boot_B using the transition to itself.

transitions from state boot_A to state boot_B in these steps:

1. **Normal operation** The bootloader is in state boot_A and there are no flags set. The bootloader transfers control to image A without changing state. Image A provides the facilities for regular operation and for writing an update to the other segment B.
2. **Writing the update** Image A processes an update request, writes the update to segment B and verifies its authenticity. Then it sets flag B.updated and instantly reboots. This signals the bootloader that an update is available in segment B.

3. **Changing the image** The bootloader is in state boot_A and flag B.updated is set. The bootloader changes its state to boot_B, clears all flags, and transfers control to image B.

The state transitions from state boot_B to state boot_A, and the phases that lead to these state changes, are symmetric to the ones we described before. The corresponding description can be obtained by substituting A for B and vice versa. Figure 2 illustrates the general behavior of the bootloader by means of a flowchart.

4.3   Safety Properties

We prove informally that our update mechanism is safe. The proof proceeds in four steps. We first argue informally that the system starts in a safe state. Then we show that, if the system is in a safe state then it will transition into another safe state, where each step is marked by a reset. Our proof hinges on the notion of a *safe image*. Note that each state transition is initiated by an internal or external reset that invokes the bootloader at a well-defined entry point. We therefore prove next that any finite number of external resets leads to a safe state. Finally, we show that all safe states are reachable from a safe state, which establishes liveliness and completes our proof.

Safe initial state. The initial state is determined by the factory settings of the smart card. We must assume that this is a safe state or else the system is obviously insecure.

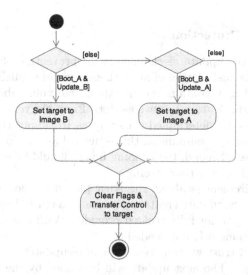

Fig. 2. The flowchart of the bootloader. Every reset puts the bootloader back into its start state. After transferring control, one of the images controls execution until another reset occurs or power is cut.

Safe state transitions. Let $x \in \{A, B\}$ be the current state and $x.z$ the variable z bound to state x. If $x = A$ then $\bar{x} = B$. Note that, whenever the system is in state boot_x, its state transitions are completely determined by the value of variable $\bar{x}$.updated. Furthermore, the bootloader transfers control to image x in this state , with r access permissions to segments x and $\bar{x}$ where $\bar{\bar{x}} = x$ and $\bar{A} = B$. In state boot_x, segment x also gets w rights on segment $\bar{x}$. Assume we are in state boot_x. A state transition occurs only if $\bar{x}$.updated $= 1$. Because image x is safe, it sets $\bar{x}$.updated $= 1$ only after it has written and verified image $\bar{x}$. Therefore, if $\bar{x}$.updated $= 1$ and image x is safe then so is image $\bar{x}$. Since x is safe the new state is safe.

External resets are safe. By our previous argument, state transitions on state variables that are zero transition only into safe states. Further note that, if a state variable is 1 then both states x and $\bar{x}$ are safe. Therefore, a reset at any time during the update leads to a safe state. From this we conclude that the system is safe if the adversary performs a finite number of resets.

All states are reachable. Let I_1 be a safe, that is, an authentic and correct, image that is installed on the smart card and let I_2, I_3, I_4 be authentic updates with increasing version numbers, that is, I_i is a legitimate update for I_j whenever $i > j$. By simulating the state machine described in Sect. 4.2 on updates I_2 to I_4 one finds that all states are reached from a safe state.

Final remarks. Obviously, all safety guarantees are void if the adversary can bypass the access control restrictions on the smart card memory.

4.4 Downgrade Protection

One aim to secure the update mechanism is the prevention of downgrades, that is, prohibition of the installation of an authentic update which is older than the running image and may contain known exploitable vulnerabilities. A practical implementation of this feature has two aspects. First, the version of the currently running image must be determined remotely as to supply the correct update. Although not a security requirement, this is needed for an effective management of the update process. Second, the running image should be able to determine if a provided update is newer than itself.

The latter requirement is about the trust placed in the update provider as opposed to trust in the update creator. We assume a trusted or authentic update could be provided by a not fully trusted provider. With full trust in the update provider this requirement is not needed.

In case of limited trust we can crate a chain of updates by embedding public keys into the images. The next update will be signed by the private key corresponding to the public key embedded in the previous image. This establishes a trust chain, were no update can be skipped.

4.5   Memory Attacks

The bootloader has very limited functionality as it only switches between images based on its state and flags set in NVM. An attacker might try to change these flags or the state with the intention to boot the older image containing exploitable vulnerabilities. For that matter the old image might be invalidated after a successful update. This would require the bootloader to contain code that checks if an image is valid. No matter how the invalidation is implemented, it has to be a write access to NVM, for which the bootloader had to check. Ultimately this has the same effect as the flag we already use. An attacker would have to control the content of NVM to attack this scheme. Making the flag a hard to produce bit pattern, distributing it in memory and even duplicating it so that an attack that flips bits in memory becomes very unlikely to be successful is sufficient. If we assume, that an adversary can write to NVM at will, he could just run any code of his choosing, breaking the smart cards security independent of the update mechanism.

If the bootloader discovers an invalid state or flag, it might assume an attack had taken place and disable the smart card, as is the case if the security sensors in the chip are activated due to hardware attacks. The point to take home is that such invalid state and flags can be detected.

4.6   Security Properties

Based on the threat of an attacker that can control the environment we analyze the security of our mechanism. We assume that the attacker can interrupt the process at any time of his choosing. We therefore have to consider all situations where an operation is carried out. We call the attackers action an interruption. An interruption will have the same effect as a regular reset. The smart card will resume operation with the start of the bootloader.

1. Interruption during image write and verification. Any interruption before the *updated* flag is set will simply void the update process. It is comparable to a situation where the update has not been done at all and has to be started from the beginning. This make the requirement to remotely determine the current version of the software important.
2. Interruption after setting the *update* flag. This has no effect as an reset is required for normal operation and the running image will do just that.
3. Interruption before the bootloader modifies its state. Such interruptions have no effect as no changes to NVM have been done.
4. Interruption between the bootloader state change and clearing of the flags. After the state has changed the new image is seen as activate. When the bootloader starts up again the still set *updated* flag is not considered as it is not relevant on the given state. Once the bootloader completes it will clear the flag.
5. Interruption after clearing the *update* flags. Again this has no effect as all actions the change the state are completed.

5   Comparison with Related Work

Reloading of executable code onto smart cards is not a new concept per se. Such functionality exists on some smart card platforms such as Global Platform [9]. However, they all have shortcomings regarding the requirements stated in Sect. 2. In what follows we give an overview of update mechanisms reported on in the literature and in standards specifications. We then analyze how these existing procedures match our requirements. Subsequently we evaluate how our mechanism differs from the existing ones and summarize the results in Table 1. For brevity we labeled the mechanisms with the first word from their name. Our mechanism is labeled **safe**.

Table 1. Matching of the requirements to existing smart card update schemes

Requirement	patch	live	multi-app	full	**safe**
1. Robustness	-	-	+	+	+
2. Low Level Updates	+	-	-	+	+
3. Security	?	?	+	-	+

- not supported, + supported, ? depends on implementation

5.1   Patching of ROM Based Code

The majority of today's high security smart cards are engineered with a basic operating system in ROM and *trampolines* in EEPROM. This means that at specific positions in its code in ROM, the operating system jumps to predefined positions in EEPROM. In the absence of patches the code in EEPROM merely returns to the position behind the jump in ROM. A patch overwrites the EEPROM code with new functions, and returns to a position behind the code that is obsoleted by the patch [14] in ROM. This is a viable solution as long as the designers correctly anticipate which code will need patching and precede it with a jump to EEPROM. This requires foresight and adapted tools that generate code with trampolines which makes this approach inflexible and complex to handle.

If a memory management unit (MMU) is available on the system then this enables a more flexible procedure. The MMU is configured to issue an interrupt whenever the execution reaches obsolete code. The interrupt handler then forces a branch into the code's replacement. This incurs some overhead but is also viable as long as the replaced code segments are not too many.

However, we have not found an assessment of these mechanisms' safety. They are used primarily in safe and controlled environments for completion, that is, to put finishing touches on cards before they are issued to end users.

5.2   Live Patching

The most direct method to patching resource constrained card-based systems is to modify the executable code while the system is running, for example, if the code is copied to RAM before it is executed. A fine-grained update mechanism of this kind for Java Cards is described by Noubissi et al. [13]. This approach is risky and provides no safety guarantees. It is generally used to patch only applications in order to avoid the risk of making the device inoperable. Allowing low level updates does require to control the complete state of the software such as in PROTEOS [8] which is overly complex.

5.3 Multi-application Cards

By design multi-application cards, for example Java Cards and MULTOS smart cards [4, 5] based on the Global Platform specification [9], have the ability to load and delete applications in the field. Deleting and reloading an application can be viewed as an update. However, this approach does not allow updates to the lower levels of the software.

5.4 Update Mechanisms from Other Domains

Safe update mechanisms play a vital role in many computer systems. Important examples that shall not go unmentioned are satellites and planetary probes. Once on their mission these devices cannot be recovered manually and need fail-safe procedures to update their software. They focus on the detection of misbehaving updates, rather than security.

Additionally, industry filed for and obtained patent protection for a number of approaches to update various types of systems. Abrahamsson summarizes and evaluates several of them in his thesis [3], followed by a description of his own proposal, which is a combination of the ones he analyzed. In several respects his solution is conceptually similar to ours described in Sect. 4, but its concrete design is not compatible with smart cards.

Full Reflash. A different class of embedded systems that requires updates are smart phones. They have evolved to a point where they could be considered general purpose computers. Usually, phones enable firmware updates by means of a bootloader and an update mode. When booted into this update mode the firmware can be replaced. Additionally, minor updates can be applied directly to the executable code in non-volatile memory while the device is running. The same approach is applied to the firmware on many embedded micro-controllers. In this case a debugger needs to be connected that enables direct access to the NVM. This has a direct security implication. As the focus is usually on recovering from errors, these mechanisms offer an increased attack surface.

5.5 Comparison

We summarized in Table 1 how well each smart card update mechanism matches our requirements. The classical and the live patching approach do not offer safety protections against failed updates. Multi-application cards and full-reflash have the required safety properties. This is due to the separation of the update mechanism from the code that is the subject of an update, and serves as a safety measure against errors and failures. In case of the full-reflash, a bootloader with an update or recovery mode updates the remainder of the system. In the case of a multi-application card, the OS handles the updating of applications.

Our safe update mechanism combines the safety properties of the full-reflash approach with the ability to make changes to the lower layers of the operating system and the device-embedded software. Its security properties depend on the implementation in the updateable image. They are as strong as in a similar smart card without the update mechanism. It therefore fulfills the identified requirements through the use of more NVM.

6   Safe Updates Protection Profile Package

A protection profile package is part of a protection profile which in turn is a document according to the Common Criteria (CC) framework. In this section we briefly introduce the CC and the protection profile on which our package is based. We then explain why we see the creation as worthwhile and what we try to achieve.

6.1   The Common Criteria Framework

The Common Criteria (CC) is an international standard (ISO/IEC 15408) for computer security certification. It is a formal approach to secure IT-products and used as the basis for government driven certification schemes. "The CC permits comparability between the results of independent security evaluations. The CC does so by providing a common set of requirements for the security functionality of IT products and for assurance measures applied to these IT products during a security evaluation. These IT products may be implemented in hardware, firmware or software." Consumers shall gain confidence in IT products through evaluation and the evaluation results may help consumers to determine whether IT products fulfill their needs.

When an IT-product is evaluated it is called the target of evaluation (TOE). The evaluation is conducted according to certain assurance requirements belonging to an evaluation assurance level (EAL). An EAL defines a set of assurance requirements. Seven hierarchical EAL levels exist, where every level includes all requirements of all lower levels. The evaluation checks conformance of a TOE to an security target (ST). The ST specifies the security functionality requirements (SFRs). All parts of the TOE needed to implement the SFRs are called the TOE security functionality (TSF). A catalog of SFRs is offered in the CC documents.

An ST describes a certain product. In contrast a protection profile (PP) specifies an implementation independent list of SFRs, or a class of TOEs. STs can claim compliance to a PP but they also may contain additional SFRs.

6.2   The Safe Updates Protection Profile Package

Many CC protection profiles for smart cards exist. The most important ones applicable to high value smart cards have been created by the major manufactures. They describe requirements for resistance against physical attacks and functional requirements of the software in the form of the device embedded software and the OS. A recent protection profile was published under the name BSI-CC-PP-0084 [7]. It defines requirements of a Security Integrated Circuit (IC) product to maintain the integrity of all memory and the confidentiality of the protected memory areas as well as maintain the correct execution of the software on the Security IC. Additionally BSI-CC-PP-0084 defines optional Loader packages that enable the loading of code and data onto the Security IC. These packages have a limited feature set, not specifying any requirements of how an update mechanism is supposed to work. We created a package that extends the Loader packages from BSI-CC-PP-0084 with functional requirements for safe updates with the special attention to in-the-field updates. Our package defines the TOE with the ability to load confidentiality and integrity protected updates through a loader with access control, while keeping the TOE operational despite failed update processes.

6.3   Goals

The creation of a protection profile is aimed to define a minimum of abstract requirements for smart cards that support updates while deployed. Such smart cards incorporate hardware security features. But the architectures from different manufacturers posses different features. Some have full MMUs, some duplicate all calculations in hardware, and others contain various sensors against attacks. We derived the requirements for updates from experiences with different state-of-the-art smart card products from NXP and Infineon as well as from requests of card-issuers for secure updates. Next to the security functions required for smart card applications, there must be support for (1) a loader component, (2) access control to the loader, (3) a trusted channel between the loader and the update provider, (4) robustness, (5) a way for the update provider to determine the current version of the software running on the smart card.

The loader manages the NVM to store the updates and integrate them into the software. This includes checking the update for completeness, integrity, and handling memory encryption where applicable.

The second function enforces the security policy for access to the loader. Only designated update providers shall be trusted to access the loader.

The third function serves to protect the transferred update for integrity and confidentiality by using a trusted channel. Both ends should be mutually authenticated to determine the authenticity of the update provider and the smart card. The trusted channel is bound to these entities and uses encryption and integrity checking.

The fourth function guarantees that smart cards are not unintentionally rendered inoperable during an update. This could be the case due to a power loss or an attacker trying to manipulate the process.

The last function serves management purposes. Since some smart card might not be used frequently, they might miss multiple updates. If these updates have dependencies on each other, the update provider must be able to determine the currently running version on the smart card, that is, the correct order of updates to be installed.

6.4   Package

As smart card chips are used in a wide range of products with different requirements, the protection profiles should contain the basic requirements for all products. Special functions such as updates, which are only relevant to a subset of all compliant products, are placed in an package to which compliance is optional. We therefore specified a package instead of a full protection profile.

6.5   Related Work

Smart cards used for national identity cards in Germany have to be evaluated under Common Criteria. The protection profile to which the security targets had to comply to until recently was the BSI-CC-PP-0035 [6] which covers the hardware of a Security IC and optionally the Security IC Dedicated Software (IC firmware) and libraries. The operating system and applications are usually covered by an additional protection profile that was composed on top of BSI-CC-PP-0035. In the beginning of 2014 BSI-CC-PP-0035 was superseded by BSI-CC-PP-0084 [7], a modernized version that also covers additional optional packages for extended security functionality.

The two packages that allow loading of code are "Loader dedicated for usage in secured environment only" and "Loader dedicated for usage by authorized users only". The second loader package incorporates the functionality of the first and adds access control as well as a trusted channel requirement to access the loader. In combination these packages provide the functional requirements of a loader that supports the first three functions we see as essential for updates.

Both packages fail to specify what we see as essential requirements for safety and robustness. They also fail to specify how the current state of the software on the smart card can be determined. Without further functional requirements any method of allowing arbitrary writes into NVM by an authorized user does qualify as an update mechanism. We presume this is due to the fact, that even tho none of the existing mechanisms has yet been standardized their inclusion should be allowed in future products without favoring the solution of one particular manufacturer over another. Unfortunately this might lead to bad solutions in an traditional closed industry. This motivated the creation of the package "Safe Loader".

7   Overview of the Package Safe Loader

This section gives details about the package and how we modeled certain security objectives with SFRs.

7.1 Architecture and Functions

The protection profile package *Safe Loader* describes security requirements used for in-the-field Software Updates. The package augments the Protection Profile BSI-CC-PP-0084 [7] (hereafter *"original PP"*) with the additional functionality to load software. The original PP defines a Security IC product in the form of a composite TOE. It describes a combination of a Security Integrated Circuit (Security IC) with a Card Operating System (COS) and Embedded Software. .

The TOE provides functionality to download data into non volatile memory (NVM). This functionality will be called loader in the following. The common patch process of the TOE has not been used during operational use in the smart card life cycle. The loader extends the use to life cycle phases after delivery of the TOE, during its operational usage. It enables updates in an environment not necessarily controlled by a trusted party but by the end user or even by an attacker. Therefore the update mechanism requires special protection measures and safety properties such that a continued safe operational state can be guaranteed. The same loader can also be used in earlier life cycle phases of the TOE, if applicable.

The loader affects data and code stored in non-volatile memory. The affected data and code includes parts of the firmware (IC-Dedicated Software), the COS (Embedded Software), and the applications which make up the software of the TOE in the original PP.

7.2 Security Objectives and SFRs

To address the security objectives of the TOE we defined security functional requirements. As this package extends the loader packages from BSI-CC-PP-0084 [7] with the security objectives, we only outline the security objectives that were not included in the BSI-CC-PP-0084. They can be placed in two groups: (i) integrity of the software, and (ii) version information. The integrity of the software objective aims to guarantee that in no condition the update mechanism leaves the system in an inconsistent state. This is modeled through a recovery function, that requires either a successful update or a recovery to a consistent state, as well as failure of functions with the preservation of a secure state.

The version information objective is matched by requirements for a command to prove the identity of the TSF itself and the export of a fingerprint of the TOE implementation in response to such a command.

7.3 Modeling of Safety Properties

The safety property of the update mechanism guarantees that no kind of interruption can bring the software into an insecure and inconsistent state. The security functional requirements to enforce this behavior have been modeled with FPT_RCV.4 (Function recovery) and FPT_FLS.1 (Failure with preservation of secure state).

FPT_FLS.1 requires the TOE in the case it detects an unsuccessful installation of downloaded software to preserve a secure state. Any failure condition, such as a failed integrity check on the image written or downloaded will abort the mechanism and leave to current image unchanged.

FPT_RCV.4 requires the TOE that the function to install a software update has the property to either complete successfully or recover to a consistent and secure state. This is the transaction of switching between the images after writing and verifying them has been completed.

The transactional behavior of the switching, which recovers to a secure state on any error, and the fail safe behavior of the remaining steps of the update mechanism result in only safe transitions between secure states.

8   Discussion

In this section, we analyze certain hardware requirements for practical realizations on smart card hardware. We argue which features we deem necessary and which we see as useful but not necessarily required. We then match our practical algorithm description to the protection profile package. Lastly we discuss how the protection profile package can be used.

Memory Access. The security of our update mechanism depends on memory protection mechanisms to restrict access to the memory regions the bootloader uses. In its simplest form this is realized through operating system access control alone. A better method is hardware supported memory protection, for example, in the form of a memory protection unit (MPU) or a memory management unit (MMU) that the bootloader configures in connection with hierarchical protection domains in the CPU. In this way image write access and flag modify access to the correct regions can be allowed while access to the protected regions and the bootloader code triggers an interrupt. Not all smart card chips include an MPU, even fewer include an MMU. An alternative yet effective mechanism with similar functionality is described by Smith and Weingart [16]. Their mechanism uses a hardware memory controller with a "ratchet" functionality. On every reset or boot, the running code has complete access privileges. Every time control is transferred to code that is less trustworthy, the ratchet is increased and thereby protects certain areas of memory from access. The ratchet cannot be decreased except by a reboot which will transfer control to the trusted code, that is, the bootloader. This scheme is simpler to implement in a microcontroller architecture than a complete MPU or MMU and protection rings.

Additional Hardware Support. In the described form the safe update mechanism can be implemented on any system supporting a bootloader. One possible improvement is hardware support for the switching between memory images. Implementing the functionality that makes up the transaction during the switch between the images in hardware has the advantage of decreasing the amount of critical operations. At the same time this can remove the necessity of a separate bootloader. If the hardware would switch the mapping of memory with a special command, only one image would be available in the memory map. This lessens the requirement for special memory protections.

Implementation. A practical realization of the safe update algorithm consists of a small bootloader and a memory mapping that provides disjunct memory areas for the images. The bootloader implements the flag checking and switching and has to know the starting addresses of the images to transfer control. It also needs to read and write NVM.

The update writing code as well as all security for access control and authentication of the update provider and the update is part of the image itself. Since the necessary functionality is in most cases already available in a smart card OS, the image will not be enlarged significantly. The access control decisions can be modeled by the ISO/IEC 7816 file system. The image staging area can just be mapped as a quite big (for smart cards) file.

Common Criteria Evaluation. A security target for a smart card product that features such update functionality can claim conformance to our CC protection profile package. It defines a common set of requirements to the update functions. To make this option achievable this package should be certified by an institution that can set industry standards.

9   Conclusion

We have presented a simple and safe update mechanism that is robust against interruptions on smart cards. It satisfies the necessary safety properties to guarantee a working device even if the update mechanism is attacked. The principal attack vector requires breaking the security of the operating system and therefore breaking the card.

We also described a draft of a Common Criteria protection profile package for such an algorithm. The package is general and abstract, so that different implementations may be used. It can serve as a template for adoption by a certification authority.

Acknowledgments. This work is funded through a grant by the Bundesdruckerei GmbH.

References

1. STMicroelectronics ST33F1M Smartcard MCU,
   http://www.st.com/internet/mcu/product/215291.jsp
2. Common Criteria for Information Technology Security Evaluation, Part 1: Introduction and General Model; CCMB-2012-09-001, Version 3.1, Revision 4 (September 2012)

3. Abrahamsson, D.: Security Enhanced Firmware Update Procedures in Embedded Systems. Master's thesis, Linköping University, Department of Computer and Information Science (2008)
4. Consortium, T.M.: The MULTOS Specification, http://www.multos.com
5. Corp., O.: Java Card, http://www.oracle.com/technetwork/java/javacard
6. Eurosmart: Protection Profile Security IC Platform Protection Profile developed by Atmel, Infineon Technologies AG, NXP Semiconductors, Renesas Technology Europe Ltd., STMicrocontrollers, Registered and Certified by Bundesamt für Sicherheit in der Informationstechnik (BSI) under Reference BSI-PP-0035, Version 1.0, 15.06 (June 2007), https://www.bsi.bund.de/SharedDocs/Zertifikate/PP/aktuell/PP_0035.html
7. Eurosmart: Security Integrated Circuit Platform Protection Profile with Augmentation Packages developed by Inside Secure, Infineon Technologies AG, NXP Semiconductors, STMicroelectronics, Registered and Certified by Bundesamt für Sicherheit in der Informationstechnik (BSI) under Reference BSI-CC-PP-0084-2014, Version 1.0, 19.02 (February 2014), https://www.bsi.bund.de/SharedDocs/Zertifikate/PP/aktuell/PP_0084.html
8. Giuffrida, C., Kuijsten, A., Tanenbaum, A.S.: Safe and automatic live update for operating systems. In: Proceedings of the Eighteenth International Conference on Architectural Support for Programming Languages and Operating Systems, ASPLOS 2013, pp. 279–292. ACM, New York (2013), http://doi.acm.org/10.1145/2451116.2451147
9. GlobalPlatform, I.: GlobalPlatform, http://www.globalplatform.org/
10. Lobdell, M.: Robust Over-the-Air Firmware Updates Using Program Flash Memory Swap on Kinetis Microcontrollers, http://cache.freescale.com/files/microcontrollers/doc/app_note/AN4533.pdf
11. Margraf, M.: The new german id card. In: Pohlmann, N., Reimer, H., Schneider, W. (eds.) ISSE 2010: Securing Electronic Business Processes (2011)
12. Noll, M.: System for a primary bios rom recovery in a dual bios rom computer system. US Patent 5,793,943 (August 11, 1998), http://www.google.com/patents/US5793943
13. Noubissi, A.C., Iguchi-Cartigny, J., Lanet, J.L.: Hot updates for java based smart cards. In: 22nd International Conference on Data Engineering Workshops, pp. 168–173 (2011)
14. Rankl, W., Effing, W.: Smart Card Handbook, 4th edn. Wiley Publishing (2010)
15. Skorobogatov, S., Woods, C. In: the blink of an eye: There goes your aes key. Cryptology ePrint Archive, Report 2012/296 (2012), http://eprint.iacr.org/2012/296
16. Smith, S., Weingart, S.: Building a high-performance, programmable secure coprocessor. Comput. Netw. 31, 831–860 (1999), http://domino.research.ibm.com/comm/research_projects.nsf/pages/ssd_scop.pubs.html
17. Torrance, R., James, D.: The state-of-the-art in IC reverse engineering. In: Clavier, C., Gaj, K. (eds.) CHES 2009. LNCS, vol. 5747, pp. 363–381. Springer, Heidelberg (2009), http://dx.doi.org/10.1007/978-3-642-04138-9_26

Discrete vs. Dense Times in the Analysis of Cyber-Physical Security Protocols

Max Kanovich[1,5], Tajana Ban Kirigin[2], Vivek Nigam[3],
Andre Scedrov[4,5], and Carolyn Talcott[6]

[1] Queen Mary, University of London & University College, UK
mik@dcs.qmul.ac.uk
[2] University of Rijeka, HR
bank@math.uniri.hr
[3] Federal University of Paraba, João Pessoa, Brazil
vivek@ci.ufpb.br
[4] University of Pennsylvania, Philadelphia, USA
scedrov@math.upenn.edu
[5] National Research University Higher School of Economics, Moscow, Russia
[6] SRI International, USA
clt@csl.sri.com

Abstract. Many security protocols rely on the assumptions on the physical properties in which its protocol sessions will be carried out. For instance, Distance Bounding Protocols take into account the round trip time of messages and the transmission velocity to infer an upper bound of the distance between two agents. We classify such security protocols as Cyber-Physical. Time plays a key role in design and analysis of many of these protocols. This paper investigates the foundational differences and the impacts on the analysis when using models with discrete time and models with dense time. We show that there are attacks that can be found by models using dense time, but not when using discrete time. We illustrate this with a novel attack that can be carried out on most distance bounding protocols. In this attack, one exploits the execution delay of instructions during one clock cycle to convince a verifier that he is in a location different from his actual position. We propose a Multiset Rewriting model with dense time suitable for specifying cyber-physical security protocols. We introduce Circle-Configurations and show that they can be used to symbolically solve the reachability problem for our model. Finally, we show that for the important class of balanced theories the reachability problem is PSPACE-complete.

1 Introduction

With the development of pervasive cyber-physical systems and consequent security issues, it is often necessary to specify protocols that not only make use of cryptographic keys and nonces, but also take into account the physical properties of the environment where its protocol sessions are carried out. We call such protocols *Cyber-Physical Security Protocols*. For instance, Distance Bounding Protocols [4] is a class of cyber-physical security protocols which infers an upper bound on the distance between two agents from the round trip time of messages. In a distance bounding protocol session, the verifier (V) and the prover (P) exchange messages:

© Springer-Verlag Berlin Heidelberg 2015
R. Focardi and A. Myers (Eds.): POST 2015, LNCS 9036, pp. 259–279, 2015.
DOI: 10.1007/978-3-662-46666-7_14

$$V \longrightarrow P : m$$
$$P \longrightarrow V : m'$$

(1)

where m is a challenge and m' is a response message (constructed using m's compo-nents). To infer the distance to the prover, the verifier remembers the time, t_0, when the message m was sent, and the time, t_1, when the message m' returns. From the difference $t_1 - t_0$ and the assumptions on the speed of the transmission medium, v, the verifier can compute an upper bound on the distance to the prover, namely $(t_1 - t_0) \times v$.

This is just one example of cyber-physical security protocols. Other examples in-clude Secure Neighbor Discovery, Secure Localization Protocols [5,29,31], and Secure Time Synchronization Protocols [14,30]. The common feature in most cyber-physical security protocols is that they mention cryptographic keys, nonces and time. (For more examples, see [2,24] and references therein.)

A major problem of using the traditional protocol notation for the description of dis-tance bounding protocols, as in Eg. 1, is that many assumptions about time, such as the time requirements for the fulfillment of a protocol session, are not formally specified. It is only informally described that the verifier remembers the time t_0 and t_1 and which exact moments these correspond to. Moreover, from the above description, it is not clear which assumptions about the network are used, such as the transmission medium used by the participants. Furthermore, it is not formally specified which properties does the above protocol ensure, and in which conditions and against which intruders.

It is easy to check that the above protocol is not safe against the standard Dolev-Yao intruder [10] who is capable of intercepting and sending messages anywhere at anytime. The Dolev-Yao intruder can easily convince V that P is closer than he actually is. The intruder first intercepts the message m and with zero transmission time sends it P. Then he intercepts the message m' and instantaneously sends it to V, reducing the round-trip-time $(t_1 - t_0)$. Thus, V will believe that P is much closer than he actually is. Such an attack does not occur in practice as messages take time to travel from one point to another. Indeed, the standard Dolev-Yao intruder model is not a suitable model for the analysis of cyber-physical protocols. Since he is able to intercept and send messages anywhere at anytime, he results faster than the speed of light. In fact, a major difference between cyber-physical protocols and traditional security protocols is that there is not necessarily a network in the traditional sense, as the medium is the network.

Existing works have proposed and used models with time for the analysis of dis-tance bounding protocols where the attacker is constrained by some physical properties of the system. Some models have considered dense time [2], while others have used discrete time [3]. However, although these models have included time, the foundational differences between these models and the impacts to analysis has not been investigated in more detail. For example, they have not investigated the fact that provers, verifiers, and attackers may have different clock rates, $i.e.$, processing speeds, affecting security. This paper addresses this gap. While studying this problem, we have identified a novel attack called *Attack In-Between-Ticks*. We believe it can be carried out on most distance bounding protocols. The main observation is that while the verifier uses discrete clock ticking and thus measures time in discrete units, the environment and the attacker is not limited by a particular clock. In fact, a key observation of this paper is that models with dense time abstract the fact that attacker clocks may tick at any rate. The attacker can mask his location by exploiting the fact that a message may be sent at any point between two clock ticks of the verifier's clock, while the verifier believes that it was sent at a particular time. Depending on the speed of the verifier, *i.e.*, its clock rate, the attacker can *in principle* convince the verifier that he is very close to the verifier (less than a meter) even though he is very far away (many meters away).

Interestingly, however, from a foundational point of view, there is no complexity increase when using a model with dense time when compared to a model with discrete time. In our previous work [18], we proposed a rewriting framework which assumed discrete time. We showed that the reachability problem is PSPACE-complete. Here we show that if we extend the model with dense time, the reachability problem is still PSPACE-complete. For this result we introduce a novel machinery called Circle-Configurations.

Section 2 contains two motivational examples, including the novel attack in-between-ticks. In Section 3 we introduce a formal model based on Multiset Rewriting (MSR) which includes dense time. We also show how to specify distance bounding protocols in this language. Section 4 introduces a novel machinery, called Circle-Configurations, that allow one to symbolically represent configurations that mention dense time. Section 5 proves that the reachability problem for timed bounded memory protocols [16] is PSPACE-complete. Finally, in Section 6, we comment on related and future work.

2 Two Motivating Examples

This section presents two examples of protocols to illustrates the differences between models with discrete and dense time. In the first example we present a timed version of the classical *Needham-Schroeder* protocol [25]. It shows that some attacks may only be found when using models with dense time. The second example is the novel attack in-between-ticks, which illustrates that for the analysis of distance bounding protocols it is necessary to consider time assumptions of the players involved.

2.1 Time-Bounding Needham-Schroeder Protocol

We first show some subtleties of cyber-physical protocol analysis by re-examining the original *Needham-Schroeder* public key protocol [25] (NS), see Fig 1a. Although this protocol is well known to be insecure [22], we look at it from another dimension, the dimension of time. We check whether Needham and Schroeder were right after all, in the sense that their protocol can be considered secure under some time requirements. In other words, we investigate whether NS can be fixed by means of time.

We timestamp each event in the protocol execution, that is, we explicitly mark the time of sending and receiving messages by a participant. We then propose a timed version of this protocol, called *Time-Bounding Needham-Schroeder Protocol* (Timed-NS), as depicted in Figure 1b. The protocol exchanges the same messages as in the original version, but the last protocol message, *i.e.* the confirmation message $\{N_B\}_{K_B}$, is sent by A only if the time difference $t_3 - t_0$ is smaller or equal to the given *response bounding time R*.

The protocol is considered *secure* in the standard way, that is, if the "accepted" N_A and N_B may never be revealed to anybody else except Alice and Bob. Recall that the well known Lowe attack on NS [22] involves a third party, Mallory who is able to learn

Fig. 1. Adding time to Needham-Schroeder Protocol

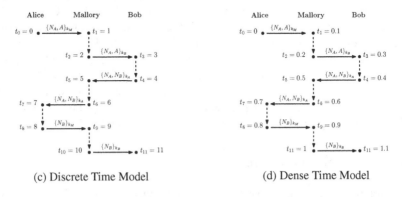

Fig. 2. Timed Version of Lowe Attack

Bob's nonce. At the same time Bob believes that he communicated with Alice and that only Alice learned his nonce.

The intriguing result of the analysis of Timed-NS is that one may not find an attack in the discrete time model, but can find one in the dense time model: Figure 2 depicts the Lowe attack scenario in Timed-NS. In particular, the attack requires that events marked with $t_0, \ldots, t_7$ take place and that the round trip time of messages, that is $t_7 - t_0$, does not exceed the given response bounding time R. Assuming that both network delay and processing time are non-zero, in the discrete time model the attack could be modeled only for response bounding time $R \geq 7$, see Figure 1c. In the discrete model, the protocol would seem safe for response bounding time $R < 7$. However, in the dense time model the attack is possible for any response bounding time R, see Figure 1d.

This simple example already illustrates the challenges of timed models for cyber-physical security protocol analysis and verification. No rescaling of discrete time units removes the presented difference between the models. For any discretization of time, such as seconds or any other infinitesimal time unit, there is a protocol for which there is an attack with continuous time and no attack is possible in the discrete case. This is further illustrated by the following more realistic example.

2.2   Attack In-Between-Ticks

Regardless of the design details of a specific distance bounding protocol a new type of anomaly can happen. We call it *Attack In-Between-Ticks*. This attack is particularly

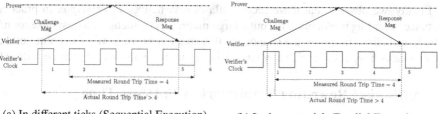

(a) In different ticks (Sequential Execution)   (b) In the same tick (Parallel Execution)

Fig. 3. Attack In-Between-Ticks. Here $R = 4$ ticks.

harmful when the verifier and the prover exchange messages using radio-frequency (RF), where the speed of transmission is the speed of light. In this case an error of a 1 nanosecond (ns) already results in a distance error of $30cm$.

Consider the illustrations in Figure 3. They depict the execution of instructions by the verifier. The verifier has to execute two instructions: (1) the instruction that sends the signal to the prover and (2) the instruction that measures the time when this message is sent. Figure 3a illustrates the case when the verifier is running a sequential machine (that is, a single processor), which is the typical case as the verifier is usually a not very powerful device, e.g., door opening device. Here we assume optimistically that an instruction can be executed in one cycle. When the first instruction is executed, it means that the signal is sent somewhere when the clock is up, say at time 0.6. In the following clock cycle, the verifier remembers the time when the message is sent. Say that this was already done at time 1.5. If the response message is received at time 5 it triggers an interruption so that the verifier measures the response time in the following cycle, i.e., at time 5.5. Thus the measured round time is $4 = 5.5 - 1.5 = R$ ticks. Therefore, the verifier grants access to the prover although the actual round trip is $5 - 0.6 = 4.4 > R = 4$ ticks. This means that the verifier is granting access to the prover although the prover's distance to the verifier may not satisfy the distance bound and thus is a security flaw.[1]

Depending on the speed of verifier's processor, the difference of 0.4 tick results in a huge error. Many of these devices use very weak processors. The one proposed in [28], for example, executes at a frequency of at most $24MHz$. This means a tick is equal to $41ns$ (in the best case). Thus, an error of 0.4 tick corresponds to an error of $16ns$ or an error of *4.8 meters* when using RF. In the worst case, the error can be of 1.5 ticks when the signal is sent at the beginning of the cycle, i.e., at time 0.5 tick, and the measurements at the end of the corresponding cycles, i.e., at times 2 and 6 ticks. An error of 1.5 tick ($61.5ns$) corresponds to an error greater than 18 *meters* when using RF.

Consider now the case when the verifier can execute both instructions in the same cycle. Even in this case there might be errors in measurement as illustrated in Figure 3b. It may happen that the signal is sent before the measurement is taken thus leading to errors of at most 0.5 ticks (not as great as in the sequential case). (Here we are again assuming optimistically that an instruction can be executed in one cycle.)

---

[1] Notice that inverting the order of the instructions, i.e., first collecting the time and then sending the signal, would imply errors of measurement but in the opposite direction turning the system impractical.

Finally, we observe that these security flaws may happen *in principle*. In practice, distance bounding protocols carry out a large number of challenge and response rounds which we believe mitigates the chances of this attack occurring. We also point out that these attacks have been inspired by similar issues in the analysis of digital circuits [1].

3   A Multiset Rewriting Framework with Dense Time

We assume a finite first-order typed alphabet, Σ, with variables, constants, function and predicate symbols. Terms and facts are constructed as usual (see [12]) by applying symbols with correct type (or sort). For instance, if P is a predicate of type $\tau_1 \times \tau_2 \times \cdots \times \tau_n \to o$, where o is the type for propositions, and $u_1, \ldots, u_n$ are terms of types $\tau_1, \ldots, \tau_n$, respectively, then $P(u_1, \ldots, u_n)$ is a *fact*. A fact is grounded if it does not contain any variables.

In order to specify systems that mention time, we use *timestamped facts* of the form $F@T$, where F is a fact and T is its timestamp. In our previous work [19], timestamps were only allowed to be natural numbers. Here, on the other hand, timestamps are allowed to be non-negative real numbers. We assume that there is a special predicate symbol *Time* with arity zero, which will be used to represent the global time. A configuration is a multiset of ground timestamped facts, $\{Time@t, F_1@t_1, \ldots, F_n@t_n\}$, with a single occurrence of a *Time* fact. Configurations are to be interpreted as states of the system. For example, the following configuration

$$\{Time@7.5, Deadline@10.3, Task(1, done)@5.3, Task(2, pending)@2.13\} \quad (2)$$

specifies that the current global time is 7.5, the Task 1 was performed at time 5.3, Task 2 is still pending and issued at time 2.13, and the deadline to perform all tasks is 10.3. We may sometimes denote the timestamp of a fact F in a given configuration as T_F.

3.1   Actions and Constraints

Actions are multiset rewrite rules and are either the time advancement action or instantaneous actions. The action representing the advancement of time, called *Tick Action*, is the following:

$$Time@T \longrightarrow Time@(T + \varepsilon) \quad (3)$$

Here ε can be instantiated by any positive real number specifying that the global time of a configuration can advance by any positive number. For example, if we apply this action with $\varepsilon = 0.6$ to the configuration (2) we obtain the configuration

$$\{Time@8.1, Deadline@10.3, Task(1, done)@5.3, Task(2, pending)@2.13\} \quad (4)$$

where the global time advanced from 7.5 to 8.1.

Clearly such an action is a source of unboundedness as time can always advance by any positive real number. In particular we will need to deal with issues such as Zeno Paradoxes when considering how time should advance.

The remaining actions are the Instantaneous Actions, which do not affect the global time, but may rewrite the remaining facts. They have the following shape:

$$Time@T, W_1@T_1, \ldots, W_k@T_k, F_1@T_1', \ldots, F_n@T_n' \mid C \longrightarrow$$
$$\exists X.[Time@T, W_1@T_1, \ldots, W_k@T_k, Q_1@(T + D_1), \ldots, Q_m@(T + D_m)]$$

where $D_1, \ldots, D_m$ are natural numbers and C is the guard of the action which is a set of constraints involving the time variables appearing in the pre-condition, *i.e.* the variables $T, T_1, \ldots, T_k, T'_1, \ldots, T'_n$. Constraints are of the form:

$$T > T' \pm D \quad \text{and} \quad T = T' \pm D \tag{5}$$

where T and T' are time variables, and D is a natural number.

An instantaneous action can only be applied if all the constraints in its guard are satisfied. We use $T' \geq T' \pm D$ to denote the disjunction of $T > T' \pm D$ and $T' = T' \pm D$.

Notice that the global time does not change when applying an instantaneous action. Moreover, the timestamps of the facts that are created by the action, namely the facts $Q_1, \ldots, Q_m$, are of the form $T + D_i$, where D_i is a natural number and T is the global time. That is, their timestamps are in the present or the future. For example, the following is an instantaneous action

$Time@T, Task(1, done)@T_1, Deadline@T_2, Task(2, pending)@T_3 \mid \{T_2 \geq T + 2\}$
$\longrightarrow Time@T, Task(1, done)@T_1, Deadline@T_2, Task(2, done)@(T + 1)$

which specifies that one should complete Task 2, if Task 1 is completed, and moreover, if the Deadline is at least 2 units ahead of the current time. If these conditions are satisfied, then the Task 2 will be completed in one time unit. Applying this action to the configuration (4) yields

$\{Time@8.1, Deadline@10.3, Task(1, done)@5.3, Task(2, done)@9.1\}$

where Task 2 will be completed by the time 9.1.

Finally, the variables X that are existentially quantified in the above action are to be replaced by fresh values, also called *nonces* in protocol security literature [6, 11]. For example, the following action specifies the creation of a new task with a fresh identifier *id*, which should be completed by time $T + D$:

$Time@T \longrightarrow \exists Id.[Time@T, Task(Id, pending)@(T + D)]$

Whenever this action is applied to a configuration, the variable *Id* is instantiated by a fresh value. In this way we are able to specify that the identifier assigned to the new task is different to the identifiers of all other existing tasks. In the same way it is possible to specify the use of nonces in Protocol Security [6, 11].

Notice that by the nature of multiset rewriting there are various aspects of non-determinism in the model. For example, different actions and even different instantiations of the same rule may be applicable to the same configuration S, which may lead to different resulting configurations S'.

3.2   Initial, Goal Configurations, The Reachability Problem and Equivalence

We write $S \longrightarrow_r S_1$ for the one-step relation where configuration S is rewritten to S_1 using an instance of action r. For a set of actions $\mathcal{R}$, we define $S \longrightarrow^*_{\mathcal{R}} S_1$ as the transitive reflexive closure of the one-step relation on all actions in $\mathcal{R}$. We elide the subscript $\mathcal{R}$, when it is clear from the context.

A *goal* S_G is a pair of a multiset of facts and a set of constraints:

$\{F_1@T_1, \ldots, F_n@T_n\} \mid C$

where $T_1, \ldots, T_n$ are time variables, $F_1, \ldots, F_n$ are ground facts and C is a set of constraints involving only $T_1, \ldots, T_n$. We call a configuration S_1 a *goal configuration* if there is a substitution σ replacing $T_1, \ldots, T_n$ by real numbers such that $S_G\sigma \subseteq S_1$ and all the constraints in $C\sigma$ are satisfied. The reachability problem, $\mathcal{T}$, is then defined for a given initial configuration S_I, a goal S_G and a set of actions $\mathcal{R}$ as follows:

Reachability Problem: Is there a goal configuration S_1, such that $S_I \longrightarrow_{\mathcal{R}}^* S_1$?

Such a sequence of actions is called a *plan*. We assume that goals are invariant to nonce renaming, that is, a goal S_G is equivalent to the goal S_G' if they only differ on the nonce names (see [15] for more discussion on this).

The following definition establishes the equivalence of configurations. Many formal definitions and results in this paper mention an upper bound D_{max} on the numeric values of a reachability problem. This value is computed from the given problem: we set D_{max} to be a natural number such that $D_{max} > n + 1$ for any number n (both real or natural) appearing in the timestamps of the initial configuration, or the Ds and D_is in constraints or actions of the reachability problem.

Definition 1. *Given a reachability problem $\mathcal{T}$, let D_{max} be an upper bound on the numeric values appearing in $\mathcal{T}$. Let*
$$S = Q_1@t_1, Q_2@t_2, \ldots, Q_n@t_n \qquad and \qquad \widetilde{S} = Q_1@\widetilde{t_1}, Q_2@\widetilde{t_2}, \ldots, Q_n@\widetilde{t_n}$$
be two configurations written in canonical way where the two sequences of timestamps $t_1, \ldots, t_n$ and $\widetilde{t_1}, \ldots, \widetilde{t_n}$ are non-decreasing. Then S and $\widetilde{S}$ are equivalent if they satisfy the same constraints, that is: $t_i > t_j \pm D$ iff $\widetilde{t_i} > \widetilde{t_j} \pm D$ and $t_i = t_j \pm D$ iff $\widetilde{t_i} = \widetilde{t_j} \pm D$, for all $1 \le i, j \le n$ and $D < D_{max}$.

The following proposition states that the notion of equivalence defined above is coarse enough to identify applicable actions and thus the reachability problem.

Proposition 1. *Let S and S' be two equivalent configurations for a given reachability problem $\mathcal{T}$ and the upper bound D_{max}. There is a transition $S \longrightarrow_r S_1$ for an action r in $\mathcal{T}$ if and only if there is a transition $S' \longrightarrow_r S_1'$ using a possibly different instance of the same action r and furthermore S_1 and S_1' are also equivalent.*

Theorem 1. *Let S_I and S_I' be two equivalent initial configurations, S_G be a goal and $\mathcal{R}$ a set of actions. Let D_{max} be an upper bound on the numbers in $\mathcal{R}$, S_I, S_I' and S_G. Then the reachability problem with S_I, S_G and $\mathcal{R}$ is solvable if and only if the reachability problem with S_I', S_G and $\mathcal{R}$ is solvable.*

3.3 Distance Bounding Protocol Formalization

To demonstrate how our model can capture the attack in-between-ticks, consider the following protocol, called DB, This protocol captures the time challenge of distance bounding protocols.[2] Verifier should allow the access to his resources only if the measured round trip time of messages in the distance-bounding phase of the protocol does not exceed the given bounding time R. We assume that the verifier and the prover have already exchanged nonces n_P and n_V:

$$V \longrightarrow P : n_P \qquad \text{at time } t_0$$
$$P \longrightarrow V : n_V \qquad \text{at time } t_1$$
$$V \longrightarrow P : OK(P) \qquad \text{iff } t_1 - t_0 \le R$$

---

[2] Another specification that includes an intruder model, keys, and the specification of the attack described in [2] can be found in our workshop paper [17].

$Time@T, V_0(P, N_P, N_V)@T_1, E@T_2, E@T_3 \longrightarrow$
$\qquad Time@T, V_1(pending, P, N_P, N_V)@T, N_V^S(N_P)@T, Start(P, N_P, N_V)@T$

$Time@T, V_1(pending, P, N_P, N_V)@T_1, Clock_V@T, P@T_2 \mid T \geq T_1 \longrightarrow$
$\qquad Time@T, V_1(start, P, N_P, N_V)@T, Clock_V@T, Start_V(P, N_P, N_V)@T$

$Time@T, P_0(V, N_V, N_P)@T_1, N_P^R(N_P)@T_2 \mid T \geq T_2 \longrightarrow Time@T, P_1(V, N_V, N_P)@T, N_P^S(N_V)@T$

$Time@T, V_1(start, P, N_P, N_V)@T_1, N_V^R(N_V)@T_2 \longrightarrow Time@T, V_2(pending, P, N_P, N_V)@T, Stop(P, N_P, N_V)@T$

$Time@T, V_2(pending, P, N_P, N_V)@T_1, Clock_V@T, E@T_2 \mid T \geq T_1 \longrightarrow$
$\qquad Time@T, V_2(stop, P, N_P, N_V)@T, Clock_V@T, Stop_V(P, N_P, N_V)@T$

$Time@T, Start_V(P, N_P, N_V)@T_1, Stop_V(P, N_P, N_V)@T_2, V_2(stop, P, N_P, N_V)@T_3 \mid T_2 - T_1 \leq R, T \geq T_3 \longrightarrow$
$\qquad Time@T, V_3(P)@T, N_V^S(Ok(P))@T, E@T$

Fig. 4. Protocol Rules for DB protocol

Encoding of verifier's clock The fact $Clock_V@T$ denotes the local clock of the verifier *i.e.* the discrete time clock that verifier uses to measure the response time in the distance bounding phase of the protocol.

We encode ticking of verifier's clock in *discrete units of time*. Action (6) represents the ticking of verifier's clock:

$$Time@T, \ Clock_V@T_1 \mid T = T_1 + 1 \longrightarrow Time@T, \ Clock_V@T \qquad (6)$$

Notice that if this action is not executed and T advances too much, *i.e.*, $T > T_1$, it means that the verifier clock stopped as it no longer advances.

Network Let $D(X, Y) = D(Y, X)$ be the integer representing the minimum time needed for a message to reach Y from X. We also assume that participants do not move. Rule (7) models network transmission from X to some Y:

$$Time@T, N_X^S(m)@T_1, E@T_2 \mid T \geq T_1 + D(X, Y) \longrightarrow Time@T, N_X^S(m)@T_1, N_Y^R(m)@T \quad (7)$$

Facts $N_X^S(m)$ and $N_X^R(m)$ specify that the participant X has sent and may receive the message m, respectively. Once X has sent the message m, that message can only be received by Y once it traveled from X to Y. The fact E is an empty fact which can be interpreted as a slot of resource. This is a technical device used to turn a theory balanced. It can safely be ignored until Section 5 (see as well [16]).

Measuring the round trip time of messages A protocol run creates facts denoting times when messages of the distance bounding phase are sent and received by the verifier. Predicates *Start* and *Stop* denote the actual (real) time of these events so that the round trip time of messages is $T_2 - T_1$ for timestamps T_1, T_2 in $Start(m)@T_1, Stop(m)@T_2$. On the other hand predicates $Start_V$ and $Stop_V$ model the verifier's view of time: $T_2 - T_1$, for T_1, T_2 in $Start_V(m)@T_1, Stop_V(m)@T_2$.

Protocol Theory Our example protocol *DB* is formalized in Figure 4. The first rule specifies that the verifier has sent a nonce and still needs to mark the time, specified by the fact $V_1(pending, P, N_P, N_V)@T$. The second rule specifies verifier's instruction of remembering the current time. The third rule specifies prover's response to the verifier's challenge. The fourth and fifth rules are similar to the first two, specifying when verifier actually received prover's response and when he executed the instruction to remember the time. Finally, the sixth rule specifies that the verifier grants access to the prover if he believes that the distance to the prover is under the given bound.

Attack In-Between-Ticks

We now show how attack in-between-ticks is detected in our formalization.

The initial configuration contains facts $Time@0$, $Clock_V@0$ denoting that global time and time on verifier's discrete time are initially set to 0.

Given the protocol specification in Figure 4, attack in-between-ticks is represented with the following configuration:

$$Start(P, N_P, N_V)@T_1, Stop(P, N_P, N_V)@T_2, \mathcal{N}_V^S(Ok(P))@T_3 \mid T_2 - T_1 > R$$

It denotes that in the session involving nonces N_P, N_V the verifier V has allowed the access to prover P although the distance requirement has been violated.

Notice that such an anomaly is really possible in this specification. Consider the following example: between moments 1.7 and 4.9, there would be 3 ticks on the verifier's clock. The verifier would consider starting time of 2 and finishing time of 5, and confirm with the time bound $R = 3$. Actually, the real round trip time is greater than the time bound, namely $4.9 - 1.7 = 3.2$. Following facts would appear in the configuration: $Start_V(n)@2, Stop_V(n)@5, Start(n)@1.7, Stop(n)@4.9$. Since $5 - 2 = 3$ the last rule from Figure 4, the accepting rule, would apply resulting in the configuration containing the facts: $Start(p, n_P, n_V)@1.7$, $Stop(p, n_P, n_V)@4.9$, $\mathcal{N}_V^S(Ok(p))@5$. Since $4.9 - 1.7 = 3.2$ is greater than $R = 3$, this configuration constitutes an attack.

Protocol Formalization in Maude We have formalized this scenario in an extension with SMT-solver of the rewriting logic tool, Maude. The tool was able to automatically find this attack. A main advantage of using an SMT solver in conjunction with Maude proof search is that one can reduce considerably the search-space involved. For example, when using the specification above, we do not provide a specific value for $D(p, v)$, but simply state that $D(p, v) > R$, that is, the prover is outside the distance bound. Due to space constraints, we do enter into the details of this implementation. We leave as future work the challenges of building a tool that can find verify cyber-physical protocols. We believe that we can integrate time constraints with the machinery used by MaudeNPA [13].

4   Circle-Configurations

This section introduces the machinery, called Circle-Configurations, that can symbolically represent configurations and plans that mention dense time. Dealing with dense time leads to some difficulties, which have puzzled us for some time now, in particular, means to handle Zeno paradoxes. When we use discrete domains to represent time, such as the natural numbers, time always advances by one, specified by the rule:

$$Time@T \longrightarrow Time@(T + 1)$$

There is no other choice.[3] On the other hand, when considering systems with dense time, the problem is much more involved, as the non-determinism is much harder to

---

[3] However, as time can always advance, a plan may use an unbounded number of natural numbers. This source of unboundedness was handled in our previous work [19]. This solution, however, does not scale to dense time.

deal with: the value that the time advances, the ε in $Time@T \longrightarrow Time@(T + \varepsilon)$ (Eq. 3), can be instantiated by any positive real number.

Our claim is that we can symbolically represent any plan involving dense time by using a canonical form called circle-configurations. We show that circle-configurations provide a sound and complete representation of plans with dense time (Theorem 2).

A circle-configuration consists of two components: a δ-*Configuration*, Δ, and a *Unit Circle*, $\mathcal{U}$, written $\langle \Delta, \mathcal{U} \rangle$. Intuitively, the former accounts for the integer part of the timestamps of facts in the configuration, while the latter deals with the decimal part of the timestamps.

In order to define these components, however, we need some additional machinery. For a real-number, r, $int(r)$ denotes the integer part of r and $dec(r)$ its decimal part. For example, $int(2.12)$ is 2 and $dec(2.12)$ is 0.12. Given a natural number D_{max}, the *truncated time difference* between two facts $P@t_P$ and $Q@t_Q$ such that $t_Q \geq t_P$ is defined as follows

$$\delta_{P,Q} = \begin{cases} int(t_Q) - int(t_P), & \text{if } int(t_Q) - int(t_P) \leq D_{max} \\ \infty, & \text{otherwise} \end{cases}$$

For example, if $D_{max} = 3$ and $F@3.12, G@1.01, H@5.05$, then $\delta_{F,H} = 2$ and $\delta_{G,H} = \infty$. Notice that whenever $\delta_{P,Q} = \infty$ for two timestamped facts, $P@t_P$ and $Q@t_Q$, we can infer that $t_Q > t_P + D$ for any natural number D in the theory. Thus, we can truncate time difference without sacrificing soundness and completeness. This was pretty much the idea used in [19] to handle systems with discrete-time.

δ-*Configuration* We now explain the first component, Δ, of circle-configurations, $\langle \Delta, \mathcal{U} \rangle$, namely the δ-configuration, to only later enter into the details of the second component in Section 4.1. Given a configuration $S = \{F_1@t_1, \ldots, F_n@t_n, Time@t\}$, we construct its δ-configuration as follows: We first sort the facts using the integer part of their timestamps, obtaining the sequence of timestamped facts $Q_1@t'_1, \ldots, Q_{n+1}@t'_{n+1}$, where $t'_i \leq t'_{i+1}$ for $1 \leq i \leq n + 1$ and $\{Q_1, \ldots, Q_{n+1}\} = \{F_1, \ldots, F_n, Time\}$. We then aggregate in classes facts with the same integer part of the timestamps obtaining a sequence of classes $\{Q_1^1, \ldots, Q_{m_1}^1\}, \{Q_1^2, \ldots, Q_{m_2}^2\}, \ldots, \{Q_1^j, \ldots, Q_{m_j}^j\}$, where $\delta_{Q_i^k, Q_1^k} = 0$ for any $1 \leq i \leq m_k$ and $1 \leq k \leq j$. The δ-configuration for S is then:

$$\Delta = \left\langle \{Q_1^1, \ldots, Q_{m_1}^1\}, \delta_{1,2}, \{Q_1^2, \ldots, Q_{m_2}^2\}, \ldots \{Q_1^{j-1}, \ldots, Q_{m_{j-1}}^{j-1}\}, \delta_{j-1,j}, \{Q_1^j, \ldots, Q_{m_j}^j\} \right\rangle$$

where $\delta_{i,i+1} = \delta_{Q_1^i, Q_1^{i+1}}$ is the truncated time difference between the facts in class i and class $i + 1$. For such a δ-configuration, Δ, we define

$$\Delta(Q_i^l, Q_j^h) = \begin{cases} \sum_{k=l}^{k=h-1} \delta_{k,k+1} & \text{if } h \geq l \\ -\sum_{k=h}^{k=l-1} \delta_{k,k+1} & \text{otherwise} \end{cases}$$

which is the truncated time difference between any two facts Q_i^l and Q_j^h from the classes l and h, respectively, of Δ. Here we assume ∞ is the addition absorbing element, *i.e.*, $\infty + D = \infty$ for any natural number D and $\infty + \infty = \infty$.

Notice that, for a given upper bound D_{max}, different configurations may have the same δ-configuration. For example, with $D_{max} = 4$, configurations

$$S_1 = \{M@3.01, R@3.11, P@4.12, Time@11.12, Q@12.58, S@14\} \quad \text{and} \tag{8}$$
$$S'_1 = \{M@0.2, R@0.5, P@1.6, Time@6.57, Q@7.12, S@9.01\}$$

have both the following δ-configuration: $\varDelta_{S_1} = \langle\{M, R\}, 1, \{P\}, \infty, \{Time\}, 1, \{Q\}, 2, \{S\}\rangle$. This δ-configuration specifies the truncated time differences between the facts. For example, $\varDelta_{S_1}(R, P) = 1$, that is, the integer part of the timestamp of the fact P is ahead one unit with respect to the integer part of the timestamp of the fact R. Moreover, the timestamp of the fact $Time$ is more than D_{max} units ahead with respect to the timestamp of P. This is indeed true for both configurations S_1 and S'_1 given above.

4.1   Unit Circle and Constraint Satisfaction

In order to handle the decimal part of the timestamps, we use intervals instead of concrete values. These intervals are represented by a circle, called Unit Circle, which together with a δ-configuration composes a circle-configuration. The unit circle of a configuration $S = \{F_1@t_1, \ldots, F_n@t_n, Time@t\}$ is constructed by first ordering the facts according to the *decimal part* of their timestamps, obtaining the sequence of facts $Q_1, \ldots, Q_{n+1}$, where $\{Q_1, \ldots, Q_{n+1}\} = \{F_1, \ldots, F_n, Time\}$. Then the unit circle of the given configuration S is obtained by aggregating facts that have the same *decimal part* obtaining a sequence of classes:

$$\mathcal{U} = [\{Q_1^0, \ldots, Q_{m_0}^0\}_Z, \{Q_1^1, \ldots, Q_{m_1}^1\}, \ldots, \{Q_1^j, \ldots, Q_{m_j}^j\}]$$

where the first class $\{Q_1^0, \ldots, Q_{m_0}^0\}_Z$, marked with the subscript Z contains all facts whose timestamp's decimal part is zero, *i.e.*, $dec(Q_i^0) = 0$ for $1 \le i \le m_0$. We call it the *Zero Point*. Notice that the zero point may be empty. For a unit circle, $\mathcal{U}$, we define: $\mathcal{U}(Q_j^i) = i$ to denote the class in which the fact Q_j^i appears in $\mathcal{U}$.

For example, the unit circle of configuration S_1 given in Eq. 8 is the sequence: $\mathcal{U}_{S_1} = [\{S\}_Z, \{M\}, \{R\}, \{P, Time\}, \{Q\}]$. Notice that P and $Time$ are in the same class as the decimal parts of their timestamps are the same, namely 0.12. Moreover, we have that $\mathcal{U}_{S_1}(S) = 0 < 2 = \mathcal{U}_{S_1}(R)$, specifying that the decimal part of the timestamp of the fact R is greater than the decimal part of the timestamp of the fact S.

We will graphically represent a unit circle as shown in Figure 5. The (green) ellipse at the top of the circle marks the zero point, while the remaining classes are placed on the circle in the (red) squares ordered clockwise starting from the zero point. Thus, from the above graphical representation, the decimal part of the timestamp of the fact Q_1^1 is smaller than the decimal of the timestamp of the fact Q_1^2, while the decimal part of the timestamps of the facts Q_1^i and Q_2^i are equal. The exact point where the squares are placed is not important, only their relative positions matter, *e.g.*, the square for the class containing the fact Q_1^1 should be placed on the circle somewhere in between the zero point and the square for the class containing the fact Q_1^2, clockwise.

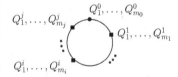

Fig. 5. Unit Circle

Constraint Satisfaction

A circle-configuration $\langle\varDelta, \mathcal{U}\rangle$ contains all the information needed in order to determine whether a constraint of the form given in Eq. 5 is satisfied or not. Consider the circle-configuration in Figure 6 which corresponds to configuration S_1,

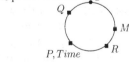

$\langle\{M, R\}, 1, \{P\}, \infty, \{Time\}, 1, \{Q\}, 2, \{S\}\rangle$

Fig. 6. Circle-Configuration

Eq. 8. To determine, for instance, whether $t_Q > t_{Time} + 1$, we compute the integer difference between t_Q and t_{Time} from the δ-configuration. This turns out to be 1 and means that we need to look at the decimal part of these timestamps to determine whether the constraint is satisfied or not. Since the decimal part of t_Q is greater then the decimal part of t_{Time}, as can be observed in the unit circle, we can conclude that the constraint is satisfied. Similarly, one can also conclude that the constraint $t_Q > t_{Time} + 2$ is not satisfied as $int(t_Q) = int(t_{Time}) + 1$. The following definition formalizes this intuition.

Definition 2. *Let $\langle \Delta, \mathcal{U} \rangle$ be a circle-configuration. We say that $\langle \Delta, \mathcal{U} \rangle$ satisfies the constraint involving the timestamps of two arbitrary facts P and Q in the circle-configuration, where D is a natural number, as defined by cases:*
- $t_P > t_Q + D$ *iff* $\Delta(Q, P) > D$ *or* $\Delta(Q, P) = D$ *and* $\mathcal{U}(P) > \mathcal{U}(Q)$;
- $t_P > t_Q - D$ *iff* $\Delta(P, Q) < D$ *or* $\Delta(P, Q) = D$ *and* $\mathcal{U}(P) > \mathcal{U}(Q)$;
- $t_P = t_Q + D$ *iff* $\Delta(Q, P) = D$ *and* $\mathcal{U}(Q) = \mathcal{U}(P)$;
- $t_P = t_Q - D$ *iff* $\Delta(P, Q) = D$ *and* $\mathcal{U}(Q) = \mathcal{U}(P)$;

Proposition 2. *For a given upper bound D_{max}, the configuration S satisfies a constraint c of the form $t_P > t_Q \pm D$ or $t_P = t_Q \pm D$, for any facts $P, Q \in S$ and $D \leq D_{max}$ iff its circle-configuration also satisfies the same constraint c.*

4.2 Rewrite Rules and Plans with Circle-Configurations

This section shows that given a reachability problem with a set of rules, $\mathcal{A}$, involving dense time, and an upper bound on the numbers appearing in the problem, D_{max}, we can compile a set of rewrite rules, C, over circle-configurations. Moreover, we show that any plan generated using the rules from $\mathcal{A}$ can be soundly and faithfully represented by a plan using the set of rules C. We first explain how we apply instantaneous rules to circle-configurations and then we explain how to handle the time advancement rule.

Instantaneous Actions

Let D_{max} be an upper bound on the numeric values in the given problem and let the following rule be an instantaneous rule (see Section 3.1) in the set of actions $\mathcal{A}$:

$$Time@T, W_1@T_1, \ldots, W_k@T_k, F_1@T'_1, \ldots, F_n@T'_n \mid C \longrightarrow$$
$$\exists X.[Time@T, W_1@T_1, \ldots, W_k@T_k, Q_1@(T + D_1), \ldots, Q_m@(T + D_m)]$$

The above rule is compiled into a sequence of operations that may rewrite a given circle-configuration $\langle \Delta, \mathcal{U} \rangle$ into another circle-configuration $\langle \Delta_1, \mathcal{U}_1 \rangle$ as follows:
1. Check whether there are occurrences of $W_1, \ldots, W_k$ and $F_1, \ldots, F_n$ in $\langle \Delta, \mathcal{U} \rangle$ such that the guard C is satisfied by $\langle \Delta, \mathcal{U} \rangle$. If it is the case, then continue to the next step; otherwise the rule is not applicable;
2. We obtain the circle-configuration $\langle \Delta', \mathcal{U}' \rangle$ by removing the occurrences $F_1, \ldots, F_n$ in $\langle \Delta, \mathcal{U} \rangle$ used in step 1, and recomputing the truncated time differences so that for all the remaining facts P and R in Δ, we have $\Delta'(P, R) = \Delta(P, R)$, i.e., the truncated time difference between P and R is preserved;
3. Create fresh values, e, for the existentially quantified variables X;
4. We obtain the circle-configuration $\langle \Delta_1, \mathcal{U}_1 \rangle$ by adding the facts $Q_1[e/X], \ldots, Q_m[e/X]$ to Δ' so that $\Delta_1(Time, Q_i) = D_i$ for $1 \leq i \leq m$ and that $\Delta_1(P, R) = \Delta'(P, R)$ for all the remaining facts P and R in Δ'. Moreover, we obtain $\mathcal{U}_1$ by adding $Q_1, \ldots, Q_m$ to the class of $Time$ in the unit circle $\mathcal{U}'$;

- **Time in the zero point and not in the last class in the unit circle, where $n \geq 0$:**

Rule 0:

- **Time alone and not in the zero point nor in the last class in the unit circle:**

Rule 1:

- **Time not alone and not in the zero point nor in the last class in the unit circle:**

Rule 2:

Fig. 7. Rewrite Rules for Time Advancement using Circle-Configurations

5. Return the circle-configuration $\langle \Delta_1, \mathcal{U}_1 \rangle$.

The sequence of operations described above has the effect one would expect: replace the facts $F_1, \ldots, F_n$ in the pre-condition of the action with facts $Q_1, \ldots, Q_m$ appearing in the post-condition of the action but taking care to update the truncated time differences in the δ-configuration. Moreover, all steps can be computed in polynomial time.

For example, consider the configuration S_1 given in Eq. 8 and the rule:
$$Time@T, R@T_1, P@T_2 \rightarrow Time@T, P@T_2, N@(T+2)$$
If we apply this rule to S_1, we obtain the configuration
$$S_2 = \{M@3.01, P@4.12, Time@11.12, Q@12.58, N@13.12, S@14\}.$$
On the other hand, if we apply the above steps to the circle-configuration of S_1, shown in Figure 6, we obtain the circle-configuration shown to the right. It is easy to check that this is indeed the circle-configuration of S_2. The truncated time differences are updated and the fact N is added to the class of $Time$ in the unit circle.

$$\langle \{\{M\}, 1, \{P\}, \infty, \{Time\}, 1, \{Q\}, 1, \{N\}, 1, \{S\}\rangle$$

Time Advancement Rule

Specifying the time advancement rule (Eq. 3 shown in Section 3.1) over circle-configurations is more interesting. This action is translated into the rules depicted in Figures 7 and 8. There are eight rules that rewrite a circle-configuration, $\langle \Delta, \mathcal{U} \rangle$, depending on the position of the fact $Time$ in $\mathcal{U}$.

Rule 0 specifies the case when the fact $Time$ appears in the zero point of $\mathcal{U}$. Then $\mathcal{U}$ is re-written so that a new class is created immediately after the zero point clockwise, and $Time$ is moved to that class. This denotes that the decimal part of $Time$ is greater than zero and less than the decimal part of the facts in the following class $G_1, \ldots, G_n$.

Rule 1 specifies the case when $Time$ appears alone in a class on the unit circle and not in the last class. This means that there are some facts, $F_1, \ldots, F_n$, that appear in a class immediately after $Time$, i.e., $\mathcal{U}(F_i) > \mathcal{U}(Time)$ and for any other fact G, such that $\mathcal{U}(G) > \mathcal{U}(Time)$, $\mathcal{U}(G) > \mathcal{U}(F_i)$ holds. In this case, then time can advance so that it ends up in the same class as F_i, i.e., time has advanced so much that its decimal part is the same as the decimal part of the timestamps of $F_1, \ldots, F_n$. Therefore a constraint of

- **Time not alone and in the last class in the unit circle which may be at the zero point:**

Rule 3: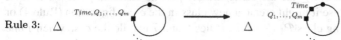

- **Time alone and in the last class in cnit circle - Case 1:** $m > 0, k \geq 0, n \geq 0$ and $\delta_1 > 1$:

Rule 4:

$$\Delta = \langle \ldots, \mathcal{P}_{-1}, \delta_{-1}, \{Time, Q_1, \ldots, Q_m\}, \delta_1, \mathcal{P}_1, \ldots, \mathcal{P}_k \rangle \quad \Delta' = \langle \ldots, \mathcal{P}_{-1}, \delta_{-1}, \{Q_1, \ldots, Q_m\}, 1, \{Time\}, \delta_1 - 1, \mathcal{P}_1, \ldots, \mathcal{P}_k \rangle$$

- **Time alone and in the last class in unit circle - Case 2:** $m > 0, k \geq 1$ and $n \geq 0$:

Rule 5: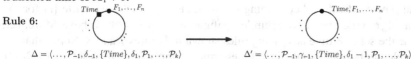

$$\Delta = \langle \ldots, \mathcal{P}_{-1}, \delta_{-1}, \{Time, Q_1, \ldots, Q_m\}, 1, \mathcal{P}_1, \ldots, \mathcal{P}_k \rangle \quad \Delta' = \langle \ldots, \mathcal{P}_{-1}, \delta_{-1}, \{Q_1, \ldots, Q_m\}, 1, \{Time\} \cup \mathcal{P}_1, \ldots, \mathcal{P}_k \rangle$$

- **Time alone and in the last class in unit circle - Case 3:** $k \geq 0, \delta_1 > 1$ and γ_{-1} is the truncated time of $\delta_{-1} + 1$:

Rule 6:

$$\Delta = \langle \ldots, \mathcal{P}_{-1}, \delta_{-1}, \{Time\}, \delta_1, \mathcal{P}_1, \ldots, \mathcal{P}_k \rangle \quad \Delta' = \langle \ldots, \mathcal{P}_{-1}, \gamma_{-1}, \{Time\}, \delta_1 - 1, \mathcal{P}_1, \ldots, \mathcal{P}_k \rangle$$

- **Time alone and in the last class in unit circle - Case 4:** $k \geq 1$ and γ_{-1} is the truncated time of $\delta_{-1} + 1$:

Rule 7:

$$\Delta = \langle \ldots, \mathcal{P}_{-1}, \delta_{-1}, \{Time\}, 1, \mathcal{P}_1, \ldots, \mathcal{P}_k \rangle \quad \Delta' = \langle \ldots, \mathcal{P}_{-1}, \gamma_{-1}, \{Time\} \cup \mathcal{P}_1, \ldots, \mathcal{P}_k \rangle$$

Fig. 8. (Cont.) Rewrite Rules for Time Advancement using Circle-Configurations

the form $T_{F_i} > T_{Time} + D$ that was satisfied by $\langle \Delta, \mathcal{U} \rangle$ might no longer be satisfied by the resulting circle-configuration, depending on D and the δ-configuration Δ.

Rule 2 is similar, but is only applicable when $Time$ is not alone in the unit circle class, *i.e.*, there is at least one fact F_i such that $\mathcal{U}(Time) = \mathcal{U}(F_i)$ and this class is not the last one, as in Rule 1. Rule 2 advances time enough so that its decimal part is greater than the decimal part of the timestamps of F_i, but not greater than the decimal part of the timestamps of the facts in the class that immediately follows on the circle.

For example, Rule 2 could be applied to the circle-configuration shown in Figure 6. We obtain the following circle-configuration, where the δ-configuration does not change, but the fact $Time$ is moved to a new class on the unit circle, obtaining the circle-configuration C_{S_2} shown to the right.

$$\langle \{M, R\}, 1, \{P\}, \infty, \{Time\}, 1, \{Q\}, 2, \{S\} \rangle$$

Rule 3 is similar to Rule 2, but it is applicable when $Time$ is in the last equivalence class, in which case a new class is created and placed clockwise immediately before the zero point of the circle.

Notice that the δ-configuration is not changed by Rules 0-3. The only rules that change the δ-configuration are the Rules 4, 5, 6 and 7, as in these cases $Time$ advances enough to complete the unit circle, *i.e.*, reach the zero point. Rules 4 and 5 handle the case when *Time* initially has the same integer part as timestamps of other facts $Q_1, \ldots, Q_m$, in which case it might create a new class in the δ-configuration (Rule 4) or merge with the following class $\mathcal{P}_1$ (Rule 5). Rules 6 and 7 handle the case when *Time* does not have the same integer part as the timestamp of any other fact, *i.e.*, it appears alone in $\varDelta$, in which case it might still remain alone in the same class (Rule 6) or merge with the following class $\mathcal{P}_1$ (Rule 7). Notice that the time difference, δ_{-1}, to the class, $\mathcal{P}_{-1}$, immediately before the class of *Time* is incremented by one and truncated by the value of D_{max} if necessary.

For example, it is easy to check that applying Rule 1, followed by Rule 3 to circle-configuration C_{S_2} shown above, we obtain a circle-configuration for which the Rule 7 is applicable. After applying Rule 7 we obtain the configuration shown to the right.

$$\langle \{M, R\}, 1, \{P\}, \infty, \{Time, Q\}, 2, \{S\} \rangle$$

Given a reachability problem $\mathcal{T}$ and an upper bound D_{max} on the numeric values of $\mathcal{T}$ with the set of rules $\mathcal{R}$ containing an instantaneous rule r, we write $[r]$ for the corresponding rewrite rule of r over circle-configurations as described above. Moreover, let *Next* be the set of 8 time advancing rules shown in Figures 7 and 8. Notice that for a given circle-configuration only one of these rules is applicable. We use $C \longrightarrow_{rl} C_1$ for the one-step reachability relation using the rewrite rule rl, *i.e.*, the circle-configuration C may be rewritten to the circle-configuration C_1 using the rewrite rule rl. Finally, $C \longrightarrow^* C_1$ (respectively, $C \longrightarrow^*_{\mathcal{R}'} C_1$) denotes the reflexive transitive closure relation of the one-step relation (respectively, using only rules in the set $\mathcal{R}' \subseteq \mathcal{R}$).

Lemma 1. *Let $\mathcal{T}$ be a reachability problem and D_{max} be an upper bound on the numeric values in $\mathcal{T}$. Let S_1 be a configuration, whose circle-configuration is C_1, and r be an instantaneous action in $\mathcal{T}$. Then $S_1 \longrightarrow_r S_2$ if and only if $C_1 \longrightarrow_{[r]} C_2$ and C_2 is the circle-configuration of S_2. Moreover, $S_1 \longrightarrow_{Tick} S_2$ if and only if $C_1 \longrightarrow^*_{Next} C_2$ and C_2 is the circle-configuration of S_2.*

Theorem 2. *Let $\mathcal{T}$ be a reachability problem, D_{max} be an upper bound on the numeric values in $\mathcal{T}$. Then $S_I \longrightarrow^* S_G$ for some initial and goal configurations, S_I and S_G, in $\mathcal{T}$ if and only if $C_I \longrightarrow^* C_G$ where C_I and C_G are the circle-configurationss of S_I and S_G, respectively.*

This theorem establishes that the set of plans over circle-configurations is a sound and complete representation of the set of plans with dense time. This means that we can search for solutions of problems symbolically, that is, without writing down the explicit values of the timestamps, *i.e.*, the real numbers, in a plan.

5   Complexity Results

This section details some of the complexity results for the reachability problem.

Conditions for Decidability

From the Literature, we can infer some conditions for decidability of the reachability problem in general:

1. *Upper Bound on the Size of Facts*: In general, if we do not assume an upper bound on the size of facts appearing in a plan, where the size of facts is the total number of predicate, function, constant and variable symbols it contains (*e.g.* the size of $P(f(a), x, a)$ is 5), then it is easy to encode the Post-Correspondence problem which is undecidable, see [6, 11].[4] Thus we will assume an upper bound on the size of facts, denoted by the symbol k.
2. *Balanced Actions*: An action is balanced if its pre-condition has the same number of facts as its post-condition [20]. The reachability problem is undecidable for (un-timed) systems with possibly unbalanced actions even if the size of facts is bounded [6, 11]. In a balanced system, on the other hand, the number of facts in any configuration in a plan is the same as the number of facts of the initial configuration, allowing one to recover decidability under some additional conditions. We denote the number of facts in the configuration by the symbol m.

   As all these undecidability results are time irrelevant, they carry over to systems with dense time.

Corollary 1. *The reachability problem for our model is undecidable in general.*

PSPACE-Completeness We show that the reachability problem for our model with dense time and balanced actions is PSPACE-complete. Interestingly, the same problem is also PSPACE-complete when using models with discrete time [18].

Given the machinery in Section 4, we can re-use many results in the Literature to show that the reachability problem is also PSPACE-complete for balanced systems with dense time that can create fresh values, given in Section 3, assuming an upper bound on the size of facts. For instance, we use the machinery detailed in [15] to handle the fact that a plan may contain an unbounded number of fresh values.

The PSPACE lower bound can be inferred from [15]. The interesting bit is to show PSPACE membership of the reachability problem. The following lemma establishes an upper bound on the number of different circle-configurations:

Lemma 2. *Given a reachability problem $\mathcal{T}$ under a finite alphabet Σ, an upper bound on the size of facts, k, and an upper bound, D_{max}, on the numeric values appearing in $\mathcal{T}$, then the number of different circle-configurations, denoted by $L_{\mathcal{T}}(m, k, D_{max})$, with m facts (counting repetitions) is $L_{\mathcal{T}}(m, k, D_{max}) \leq J^m (D + 2mk)^{mk} m^m (D_{max} + 2)^{(m-1)}$, where J and D are, respectively, the number of predicate and the number of constant/function symbols in Σ.*

Intuitively, our upper bound algorithm keeps track of the length of the plan it is constructing and if its length exceeds $L_{\mathcal{T}}(m, k, D_{max})$, then it knows that it has reached the same circle-configuration twice. This is possible in PSPACE since the above number, when stored in binary, occupies only polynomial space with respect to its parameters. The proof of the result below is similar to the one in given in [15].

---

[4] We leave for Future Work the investigation of specific cases, *e.g.*, protocol with tagging mechanisms, where this upper bound may be lifted [27].

Theorem 3. *Let $\mathcal{T}$ be a reachability problem with balanced actions. Then $\mathcal{T}$ is in PSPACE with respect to m, k, and D_{max}, where m is the number of facts in the initial configuration, k is an upper bound on the size of facts, and D_{max} is an upper bound on the numbers appearing in $\mathcal{T}$.*

6 Related and Future Work

The formalization of timed models and their use in the analysis of cyber-physical security protocols has already been investigated. We review this literature.

Meadows *et al.* [24] and Pavlovic and Meadows in [26] propose and use a logic called Protocol Derivation Logic (PDL) to formalize and prove the safety of a number of cyber-physical protocols. In particular, they specify the assumptions and protocol executions in the form of axioms, specifying the allowed order of events that can happen, and show that safety properties are implied by the axiomatization used. They do not formalize an intruder model. Another difference from our work is that their PDL specification is not an executable specification, while we have implemented our specification in Maude [7]. Finally, they do not investigate the complexity of protocol analysis nor investigate the expressiveness of formalizations using discrete and continuous time.

Another approach similar to [24] in the sense that it uses a theorem proving approach is given by Schaller *et al.* [2]. They formalize an intruder model and some cyber-physical security protocols in Isabelle. They then prove the correctness of these protocols under some specific conditions and also identify attacks when some conditions are not satisfied. Their work was a source of inspiration for our intruder model specified in [17], which uses the model described in Section 3. Although their model includes time, their model is not refined enough to capture the attack in-between-ticks as they do not consider the discrete behaviour of the verifier.

Recently [3] proposed a discrete time model for formalizing distance bounding protocols and their security requirements. Thus they are more interested in the computational soundness of distance bounding protocols by considering an adversary model based on probabilistic Turing machines. They claim that their SKI protocol is secure against a number of attacks. However, their time model is discrete where all players are running at the same clock rate. Therefore, their model is not able to capture attacks that exploit the fact that players might run at different speeds.

The Timed Automata [1] (TA) literature contains models for cyber-physical protocol analysis. Corin *et al.* [8] formalize protocols and the standard Dolev-Yao intruder as timed automata and demonstrate that these can be used for the analysis. They are able to formalize the generation of nonces by using timed automata, but they need to assume that there is a bound on the number of nonces. This means that they assume a bound on the total number of protocol sessions. Our model based on rewrite theory, on the other hand, allows for an unbounded number of nonces, even in the case of balanced theories [15]. Also they do not investigate the complexity of the analysis problems nor the expressiveness difference between models with discrete and continuous time. Lanotte *et al.* [21] specify cyber-physical protocols, but protocols where messages can be re-transmitted or alternatively a protocol session can be terminated, *i.e.*, timeouts, in case a long time time elapses. They formalize the standard Dolev-Yao intruder. Finally, they also obtain a decidability result for their formalism and an EXPSPACE-hard lower bound for the reachability problem. It seems possible to specify features like timeouts and message re-transmission, in our rewriting formalism.

We also point out some important differences between our PSPACE-completeness proof and PSPACE-completeness proof for timed automata [1]. A more detailed account can be found in the Related Work section of [19]. The first difference is that we do not impose any bounds on the number of nonces created, while the TA proof normally assumes a bound. The second difference is due to the first-order nature of rewrite rules. The encoding of a first-order system in TA leads to an exponential blow-up on the number of states of the automata as one needs take into account all instantiations of rules. Finally, the main abstractions that we use, namely circle-configurations, are one-dimensional, while regions used in the TA PSPACE proof are multidimensional.

Malladi *et al.* [23] formalize distance bounding protocols in strand spaces. They then construct an automated tool for protocol analysis using a constraint solver. They did not take into account the fact that the verifier is running a clock in their analysis and therefore are not able to detect the attack in-betweeen-ticks.

Finally, [9] introduces a taxonomy of attacks on distance bounding protocols, which include a new attack called Distance Hijacking Attack. This attack was caused by failures not in the time challenges phase of distance bounding protocols, but rather in the autenthication phases. It would be interesting to understand how these attacks can be combined with the attack in-between-ticks to build more powerful attacks. We are investigating completeness theorems for the analysis of protocols against types of attacks in the taxonomy. For example, how many colluding intruders is enough.

Another well known formalism that involves time is Time Petri Nets and we plan to investigate the relationship to our model in the future.

Acknowledgments. Nigam is supported by the Brazilian Research Agencies CNPq and Capes. Talcott is partially supported by NSF grant CNS-1318848. Kanovich is supported in part by EPSRC. Scedrov is supported in part by the AFOSR MURI Science of Cyber Security: Modeling, Composition, and Measurement as AFOSR Grant No. FA9550-11- 1-0137. Additional support for Scedrov from ONR. Part of the work was done while Kanovich and Scedrov were visiting the National Research University Higher School of Economics, Moscow. They would like to thank Sergei O. Kuznetsov for providing a very pleasant environment for work.

References

1. Alur, R., Madhusudan, P.: Decision problems for timed automata: A survey. In: Bernardo, M., Corradini, F. (eds.) SFM-RT 2004. LNCS, vol. 3185, pp. 1–24. Springer, Heidelberg (2004)
2. Basin, D.A., Capkun, S., Schaller, P., Schmidt, B.: Formal reasoning about physical properties of security protocols. ACM Trans. Inf. Syst. Secur. 14(2), 16 (2011)
3. Boureanu, I., Mitrokotsa, A., Vaudenay, S.: Practical & provably secure distance-bounding. IACR Cryptology ePrint Archive, 2013:465 (2013)
4. Brands, S., Chaum, D.: Distance-bounding protocols (extended abstract). In: Helleseth, T. (ed.) EUROCRYPT 1993. LNCS, vol. 765, pp. 344–359. Springer, Heidelberg (1994)

5. Capkun, S., Hubaux, J.-P.: Secure positioning in wireless networks. IEEE Journal on Selected Areas in Communications 24(2), 221–232 (2006)
6. Cervesato, I., Durgin, N.A., Lincoln, P., Mitchell, J.C., Scedrov, A.: A meta-notation for protocol analysis. In: CSFW, pp. 55–69 (1999)
7. Clavel, M., Durán, F., Eker, S., Lincoln, P., Martí-Oliet, N., Meseguer, J., Talcott, C.: All About Maude - A High-Performance Logical Framework. LNCS, vol. 4350. Springer, Heidelberg (2007)
8. Corin, R., Etalle, S., Hartel, P.H., Mader, A.: Timed analysis of security protocols. J. Comput. Secur. 15(6), 619–645 (2007)
9. Cremers, C.J.F., Rasmussen, K.B., Schmidt, B., Capkun, S.: Distance hijacking attacks on distance bounding protocols. In: SP (2012)
10. Dolev, D., Yao, A.: On the security of public key protocols. IEEE Transactions on Information Theory 29(2), 198–208 (1983)
11. Durgin, N.A., Lincoln, P., Mitchell, J.C., Scedrov, A.: Multiset rewriting and the complexity of bounded security protocols. Journal of Computer Security 12(2), 247–311 (2004)
12. Enderton, H.B.: A mathematical introduction to logic. Academic Press (1972)
13. Escobar, S., Meadows, C., Meseguer Maude-NPA, J.: Cryptographic Protocol Analysis Modulo Equational Properties. In: Aldini, A., Barthe, G., Gorrieri, R. (eds.) FOSAD 2007. LNCS, vol. 5705, pp. 1–50. Springer, Heidelberg (2009)
14. Ganeriwal, S., Pöpper, C., Capkun, S., Srivastava, M.B.: Secure time synchronization in sensor networks. ACM Trans. Inf. Syst. Secur., 11(4) (2008)
15. Kanovich, M., Kirigin, T.B., Nigam, V., Scedrov, A.: Bounded memory Dolev-Yao adversaries in collaborative systems. Inf. Comput. (2014)
16. Kanovich, M., Ban Kirigin, T., Nigam, V., Scedrov, A.: Bounded memory protocols and progressing collaborative systems. In: Crampton, J., Jajodia, S., Mayes, K. (eds.) ESORICS 2013. LNCS, vol. 8134, pp. 309–326. Springer, Heidelberg (2013)
17. Kanovich, M.I., Kirigin, T.B., Nigam, V., Scedrov, A., Talcott, C.L.: Towards timed models for cyber-physical security protocols. Available on Nigam's homepage (2014)
18. Kanovich, M.I., Kirigin, T.B., Nigam, V., Scedrov, A., Talcott, C.L., Perovic, R.: A rewriting framework for activities subject to regulations. In: RTA, pp. 305–322 (2012)
19. Kanovich, M.I., Kirigin, T.B., Nigam, V., Scedrov, A., Talcott, C.L., Perovic, R.: A rewriting framework and logic for activities subject to regulations (2014), submitted, available on Nigam's homepage
20. Kanovich, M.I., Rowe, P., Scedrov, A.: Collaborative planning with confidentiality. J. Autom. Reasoning 46(3-4), 389–421 (2011)
21. Lanotte, R., Maggiolo-Schettini, A., Troina, A.: Reachability results for timed automata with unbounded data structures. Acta Inf. 47(5-6), 279–311 (2010)
22. Lowe, G.: Breaking and fixing the Needham-Schroeder public-key protocol using FDR. In: Margaria, T., Steffen, B. (eds.) TACAS 1996. LNCS, vol. 1055, pp. 147–166. Springer, Heidelberg (1996)
23. Malladi, S., Bruhadeshwar, B., Kothapalli, K.: Automatic analysis of distance bounding protocols, CoRR, abs/1003.5383 (2010)
24. Meadows, C., Poovendran, R., Pavlovic, D., Chang, L., Syverson, P.F.: Distance bounding protocols: Authentication logic analysis and collusion attacks. In: Secure Localization and Time Synchronization for Wireless Sensor and Ad Hoc Networks, pp. 279–298 (2007)
25. Needham, R.M., Schroeder, M.D.: Using encryption for authentication in large networks of computers. Commun. ACM 21(12), 993–999 (1978)
26. Pavlovic, D., Meadows, C.: Deriving ephemeral authentication using channel axioms. In: Christianson, B., Malcolm, J.A., Matyáš, V., Roe, M. (eds.) Security Protocols 2009. LNCS, vol. 7028, pp. 240–261. Springer, Heidelberg (2013)

27. Sarukkai, S., Suresh, S.P.: Tagging makes secrecy decidable with unbounded nonces as well. In: Pandya, P.K., Radhakrishnan, J. (eds.) FSTTCS 2003. LNCS, vol. 2914, pp. 363–374. Springer, Heidelberg (2003)
28. Ravi, K., Varun, G.H., Vamsi, P.T.: Rfid based security system. International Journal of Innovative Technology and Exploring Engineering 2 (2013)
29. Wang, M.-H.: Secure verification of location claims with simultaneous distance modification. In: Cervesato, I. (ed.) ASIAN 2007. LNCS, vol. 4846, pp. 181–195. Springer, Heidelberg (2007)
30. Sun, K., Ning, P., Wang, C.: Tinysersync: secure and resilient time synchronization in wireless sensor networks. In: CCS, pp. 264–277 (2006)
31. Tippenhauer, N.O., Čapkun, S.: ID-based secure distance bounding and localization. In: Backes, M., Ning, P. (eds.) ESORICS 2009. LNCS, vol. 5789, pp. 621–636. Springer, Heidelberg (2009)

Timing Attacks in Security Protocols: Symbolic Framework and Proof Techniques[*]

Vincent Cheval[1,2] and Véronique Cortier[1]

[1] LORIA, CNRS, France
[2] School of Computing, University of Kent, UK

Abstract. We propose a framework for timing attacks, based on (a variant of) the applied-pi calculus. Since many privacy properties, as well as strong secrecy and game-based security properties, are stated as process equivalences, we focus on (time) trace equivalence. We show that actually, considering timing attacks does not add any complexity: time trace equivalence can be reduced to length trace equivalence, where the attacker no longer has access to execution times but can still compare the length of messages. We therefore deduce from a previous decidability result for length equivalence that time trace equivalence is decidable for bounded processes and the standard cryptographic primitives.

As an application, we study several protocols that aim for privacy. In particular, we (automatically) detect an existing timing attack against the biometric passport and new timing attacks against the Private Authentication protocol.

1 Introduction

Symbolic models as well as cryptographic models aim at providing high and strong guarantees when designing security protocols. However, it is well known that these models do not capture all types of attacks. In particular, most of them do not detect *side-channel* attacks, which are attacks based on a fine analysis of *e.g.*, time latencies, power consumption, or even acoustic emanations [34,12]. The issue of side-channel attacks is well-known in cryptography. Efficient implementations of secure cryptographic schemes may be broken by a fine observation of the computation time or the power consumption. Of course, counter-measures have been proposed but many variations of side-channel attacks are still regularly discovered against existing implementations.

The same kind of issues occur at the protocol level as well. For example, the biometric passport contains an RFID chip that stores sensitive information such as the name, nationality, date of birth, etc. To protect users' privacy, data are never sent in the clear. Instead, dedicated protocols ensure that confidential data are sent encrypted between the passport and the reader. However, a minor variation in the implementation of the protocol in the French passport has led to a privacy flaw [9]. Indeed, by observing the error message when replaying some old message, an attacker could learn whether a given passport belongs to Alice or not. The attack has been fixed by unifying the error messages produced by the passports. However, it has been discovered [25] that *all*

---

[*] The research leading to these results has received funding from the European Research Council under the European Union's Seventh Framework Programme (FP7/2007-2013) / ERC grant agreement $n°$ 258865, project ProSecure.

R. Focardi and A. Myers (Eds.): POST 2015, LNCS 9036, pp. 280–299, 2015.
DOI: 10.1007/978-3-662-46666-7_15

biometric passports (from all countries) actually suffer from exactly the same attack as soon as the attacker measures the computation time of the passport instead of simply looking at the error messages.

The goal of the paper is to provide a symbolic framework and proof techniques for the detection of timing attacks on security protocols. Symbolic models for security protocols typically assume "the perfect encryption hypothesis", abstracting away the implementation of the primitives. We proceed similarly in our approach, assuming a perfect implementation of the primitives w.r.t. timing. It is well known that implementation robust against side-channel attacks should, at the very least, be "in constant time", that is, the execution time should only depend on the number of blocks that need to be processed. "Constant time" is not sufficient to guarantee against timing attacks but is considered to be a minimal requirement and there is an abundant literature on how to design such implementations (see for example the NaCl library [1] and some related publications [33,16]). One could think that side-channel attacks are only due to a non robust implementation of the primitives and that it is therefore enough to analyze in isolation each of the cryptographic operations. However, in the same way that it is well known that the perfect encryption assumption does not prevent flaws in protocols, a perfect implementation of the primitives does not prevent side-channel attacks. This is exemplified by the timing attack found against the biometric passport [25] and the timing attacks we discovered against the Private Authentication protocol [7] and several of its variants. These attacks require both an interaction with the protocol and a dedicated time analysis. Robust primitives would not prevent these attacks.

Our first contribution is to propose a symbolic framework that models timing attacks at the protocol level. More precisely, our model is based on the applied-pi calculus [4]. We equip each function symbol with an associated time function as well as a length function. Indeed, assuming a perfect implementation of the primitives, the computation time of a function typically only depends on the size of its arguments. Each time a process (typically a machine) performs an observable action (e.g., it sends out a message), the attacker may observe the elapsed time. Our model is rather general since it inherits the generality of the applied-pi calculus with e.g., arbitrary cryptographic primitives (that can be modeled through rewrite systems), possibly arbitrarily replicated processes, etc. Our time and length functions are also arbitrary functions that may depend on the machine on which they are run. Indeed, a biometric passport is typically much slower than a server. Moreover, a server usually handles thousands of requests at the same time, which prevents from a fine observation of its computation time. Our model is flexible enough to cover all these scenarios. Finally, our model covers more than just timing attacks. Indeed, our time functions not only model execution times but also any kind of information that can be leaked by the execution, such as power consumption or other "side-channel" measurements.

Our second main contribution is to provide techniques to decide (time) process equivalence in our framework. Equivalence-based properties are at the heart of many security properties such as privacy properties [29,9] (e.g., anonymity, unlinkability, or ballot privacy), strong secrecy [19] (i.e. indistinguishability from random), or game-based security definitions [5,27] (e.g., indistinguishability from an ideal protocol). Side channel attacks are particularly relevant in this context where the attacker typically tries to distinguish between two scenarios since any kind of information could help to make a distinction. Several definitions of equivalence have been proposed such as trace equivalence [4], observational equivalence [4], or diff-equivalence [18]. In this paper, we focus on trace equivalence. In an earlier work [24], we introduced length (trace) equivalence. It reflects the ability for an attacker to measure the length of a message but it does not let him access to any information on the internal computations of the processes.

Our key result is a generic and simple simplification result: time equivalence can be reduced to length equivalence. More precisely, we provide a general transformation such that two processes P and Q are in time equivalence if and only if their transformation $\tilde{P}$ and $\tilde{Q}$ are in length equivalence, that is $P \approx_{ti} Q \Leftrightarrow \tilde{P} \approx_{\ell} \tilde{Q}$. This result holds for an arbitrary signature and rewriting system, for arbitrary processes - including replicated processes, and for arbitrary length and time functions. The first intuitive idea of the reduction is simple: we add to each output a term whose length encodes the time needed for the intermediate computations. The time elapsed between two outputs of the same process however does not only depend on the time needed to compute the sent term and the corresponding intermediate checks. Indeed, other processes may run in parallel on the same machine (in particular other ongoing sessions). Moreover, the evaluation of a term may fail (for example if a decryption is attempted with a wrong key). Since we consider else branches, this means that an else branch may be chosen after a failed evaluation of a term, which execution time has to be measured precisely. The proof of our result therefore involves a precise encoding of these behaviors.

A direct consequence of our result is that we can inherit existing decidability results for length equivalence. In particular, we deduce from [24] that time equivalence is decidable for bounded processes and a fixed signature that captures all standard cryptographic primitives. We also slightly extend the result of [24] to cope with polynomial length functions instead of linear functions.

As an application, we study three protocols that aim for privacy in different application contexts: the private authentication protocol (PA) [7], the Basic Authentication Protocol (BAC) of the biometric passport [2], and the 3G AKA mobile telephony protocol [10]. Using the APTE tool [22] dedicated to (length) trace equivalence, we retrieve the flaw of the biometric passport mentioned earlier. We demonstrate that the PA protocol is actually not private if the attacker can measure execution times. Interestingly, several natural fixes still do not ensure privacy. Finally, we provide a fix for this protocol and (automatically) prove privacy. Similarly, we retrieve the existing flaw on the 3G AKA protocol.

Related work. Several symbolic frameworks already include a notion of time [15,30,26,31,32]. The goal of these frameworks is to model timestamps. The system is given a global clock, actions take some number of "ticks", and participants may compare time values. Depending on the approach, some frameworks (e.g. [15,30]) are analysed using interactive theorem provers, while some others (e.g. [26,32]) can be analysed automatically using for example time automata techniques [32]. Compared to our approach, the representation of time is coarser: each action takes a fixed time which does not depend on the received data while the attack on e.g. the biometric passport precisely requires to measure (and compare) the time of a given action. Moreover, these frameworks consider trace properties only and do not apply to equivalence properties. They can therefore not be applied to side-channel analysis.

On the other hand, the detection or even the quantification of information possibly leaked by side-channels is a subject thoroughly studied in the last years (see e.g. [35,13,37,17,11]). The models for quantifying information leakage are typically closer to the implementation level, with a precise description of the control flow of the program. They often provide techniques to *measure* the amount of information that is leaked. However, most of these frameworks typically do not model the cryptographic primitives that security protocols may employ. Messages are instead abstracted by atomic data. [35] does consider primitives abstracted by functions but the framework is dedicated to measure the information leakage of some functions and does not apply to the protocol level. This kind of approaches can therefore not be applied to protocols such as BAC or PA (or when they may apply, they would declare the flawed and fixed variants equally insecure).

Fewer papers do consider the detection of side-channel attacks for programs that include cryptography [36,8]. Compared to our approach, their model is closer to the implementation since it details the implementation of the cryptographic primitives. To do so, they over-approximate the ability of an attacker by letting him observe the control flow of the program, e.g. letting him observe whether a process is entering a then or an else branch. However privacy in many protocols (in particular for the BAC and PA) precisely relies on the inability for an attacker to detect whether a process is entering a then (meaning e.g. that the identity is valid) or an else branch (meaning e.g. that the identity is invalid). So the approach developed in [36,8] could not prove secure the fixed variants of BAC and PA. Their side-channel analysis is also not automated, due to the expressivity of their framework.

2   Messages and Computation Time

2.1   Terms

As usual, messages are modeled by terms. Given a *signature* $\mathcal{F}$ (*i.e.* a finite set of function symbols, with a given arity), an infinite set of *names* $\mathcal{N}$, and an infinite set of variables $\mathcal{X}$, the set of terms $\mathcal{T}(\mathcal{F}, \mathcal{N}, \mathcal{X})$ is defined as the union of names $\mathcal{N}$, variables $\mathcal{X}$, and function symbols of $\mathcal{F}$ applied to other terms. In the spirit of [6], we split $\mathcal{F}$ into two distinct subsets $\mathcal{F}_d$ and $\mathcal{F}_c$. $\mathcal{F}_d$ represents the set of *destructors* whereas $\mathcal{F}_c$ represents the set of *constructors*. We say that a term t is a *constructor term* if t does not contain destructor function symbol, *i.e.* $t \in \mathcal{T}(\mathcal{F}_c, \mathcal{N}, \mathcal{X})$. Intuitively, constructors stand for cryptographic primitives such as encryption or signatures, while destructors are operations performed on primitives like decryption or validity checks.

A term is said to be ground if it contains no variable. The set of ground terms may be denoted by $\mathcal{T}(\mathcal{F}, \mathcal{N})$ instead of $\mathcal{T}(\mathcal{F}, \mathcal{N}, \emptyset)$. The set of names of a term M is denoted by $names(M)$. $\tilde{n}$ denotes a set of names. Substitutions are replacement of variables by terms and are denoted by $\theta = \{^{M_1}/_{x_1}, \ldots, ^{M_k}/_{x_k}\}$. The application of a substitution θ to a term M is defined as usual and is denoted $M\theta$. The set of subterms of a term t is denoted $st(t)$. Given a term t and a position p, the subterm of t at position p is denoted $t|_p$. Moreover, given a term r, we denote by $t[r]_p$ the term t where its original subterm at position p is replaced by r.

Example 1. A signature for modelling the standard cryptographic primitives (symmetric and asymmetric encryption, concatenation, signatures, and hash) is $\mathcal{F}_{\text{stand}} = \mathcal{F}_c \cup \mathcal{F}_d$ where $\mathcal{F}_c$ and $\mathcal{F}_d$ are defined as follows (the second argument being the arity):

$$\mathcal{F}_c = \{\text{senc}/2,\ \text{aenc}/2,\ \text{pk}/1,\ \text{sign}/2,\ \text{vk}/1,\ \langle\rangle/2,\ \text{h}/1\}$$
$$\mathcal{F}_d = \{\text{sdec}/2, \text{adec}/2, \text{check}/2, \text{proj}_1/1, \text{proj}_2/1, \text{equals}/2\}$$

The function aenc (resp. senc) represents asymmetric (resp. symmetric) encryption with corresponding decryption function adec (resp. sdec) and public key pk. Concatenation is represented by $\langle\rangle$ with associated projectors proj_1 and proj_2. Signature is modeled by the function sign with corresponding validity check check and verification key vk. h represents the hash function. The operator equals models equality tests. These tests are typically hard-coded in main frameworks but we need here to model precisely the time needed to perform an equality test.

2.2   Rewriting Systems

The properties of the cryptographic primitives (e.g. decrypting an encrypted message yields the message in clear) are expressed through rewriting rules. Formally, we equip the term algebra with a *rewriting system*, that is a set $\mathcal{R}$ of *rewrite rules* $\ell \rightarrow r$ such that $\ell \in \mathcal{T}(\mathcal{F}, \mathcal{X}) \smallsetminus \mathcal{X}$ and $r \in \mathcal{T}(\mathcal{F}, vars(\ell))$. A term s is rewritten into t by a rewriting system $\mathcal{R}$, denoted $s \rightarrow_{\mathcal{R}} t$ if there exists a rewrite rule $\ell \rightarrow r \in \mathcal{R}$, a position p of s and a substitution σ such that $s|_p = \ell\sigma$ and $t = s[r\sigma]_p$. The reflexive transitive closure of $\rightarrow_{\mathcal{R}}$ is denoted by $\rightarrow_{\mathcal{R}}^*$.

A rewriting system $\mathcal{R}$ is *confluent* if for all terms s, u, v such that $s \rightarrow_{\mathcal{R}}^* u$ and $s \rightarrow_{\mathcal{R}}^* v$, there exists a term t such that $u \rightarrow_{\mathcal{R}}^* t$ and $v \rightarrow_{\mathcal{R}}^* t$. Moreover, we say that $\mathcal{R}$ is *convergent* if $\mathcal{R}$ is confluent and terminates.

A term t is in *normal form* (w.r.t. a rewrite system $\mathcal{R}$) if there is no term s such that $t \rightarrow_{\mathcal{R}} s$. Moreover, if $t \rightarrow_{\mathcal{R}}^* s$ and s is in normal form then we say that s is a normal form of t. In what follows, we consider only convergent rewriting system $\mathcal{R}$. Thus the normal form of a term t is unique and is denoted $t\!\downarrow$.

Example 2. We associate to the signature $\mathcal{F}_{\text{stand}}$ of Example 1 the following rewriting system:

$$\begin{array}{lll} \text{sdec}(\text{senc}(x,y),y) \rightarrow x & \text{check}(\text{sign}(x,y),\text{vk}(y)) \rightarrow x & \text{proj}_1(\langle x,y\rangle) \rightarrow x \\ \text{adec}(\text{aenc}(x,\text{pk}(y)),y) \rightarrow x & \text{equals}(x,x) \rightarrow x & \text{proj}_2(\langle x,y\rangle) \rightarrow y \end{array}$$

The two first rewriting rules on the left represent respectively symmetric and asymmetric encryption. The first two rules on the right represent the left and right projections. The rewriting rule $\text{check}(\text{sign}(x,y),\text{vk}(y)) \rightarrow x$ models the verification of signature: if the verification succeeds, it returns the message that has been signed. Finally, the equality test succeeds only if both messages are identical and returns one of the two messages.

A ground term u is called a *message*, denoted $\text{Message}(u)$, if $v\!\downarrow$ is a constructor term for all $v \in st(u)$. For instance, the terms $\text{sdec}(a, b)$, $\text{proj}_1(\langle a, \text{sdec}(a, b)\rangle)$, and $\text{proj}_1(a)$ are not messages. Intuitively, we view terms as modus operandi to compute bitstrings where we use the call-by-value evaluation strategy.

2.3 Length and Time Functions

We assume a perfect implementation of primitives and we aim at detecting side-channel attacks at the protocol level. In standard robust implementations of encryption, the time for encrypting is constant, that is, it does not depend on the value of the key nor the value of the message but only on the number of blocks that need to be processed. So the computation time of a function depends solely on the length of its arguments. For example, assuming the size of m and k to be a multiple of the size of one block, the time needed to compute $senc(m, k)$, the encryption of the message m over the key k, depends on the lengths of m and k. We thus introduce time functions as well as length functions.

Length Function. For any primitive $f \in \mathcal{F}$ of arity n, we associate a length function from $\mathbb{N}^n$ to $\mathbb{N}$. Typically, the length function of f indicates the length of the message obtained after application of f, based on the length of its arguments. Given a signature $\mathcal{F}$ and a set of length functions L associated to $\mathcal{F}$, we denote by len_L^f the length function in L associated to f. Moreover we consider that names can have different sizes. Indeed, an attacker can always create a bitstring of any size. Hence we consider an infinite partition of $\mathcal{N}$ such that $\mathcal{N} = \cup_{i \in \mathbb{N}} \mathcal{N}_i$ and each $\mathcal{N}_i$ is an infinite set of names of size i. To ease the reading, we may denote by n^i a name of $\mathcal{N}_i$.

The length of a closed message t, denoted $\text{len}_L(t)$, is defined as follows:

$$\text{len}_L(n^i) = i \qquad\qquad \text{when } n^i \in \mathcal{N}_i$$
$$\text{len}_L(f(t_1, \ldots, t_k)) = \text{len}_L^f(\text{len}_L(t_1), \ldots, \text{len}_L(t_k))$$

We say that a set of length functions L is polynomial if for all $f \in \mathcal{F}$, there exists a polynomial $P \in \mathbb{N}[X_1, \ldots, X_n]$ (*i.e.* a polynomial of n variables, with coefficients in $\mathbb{N}$) such that for all $x_1, \ldots, x_n \in \mathbb{N}$, $\text{len}_L^f(x_1, \ldots, x_n) = P(x_1, \ldots, x_n)$. The class of polynomial time functions is useful to obtain decidability of (timed) trace equivalence. A particular case of polynomial length functions are *linear* length functions, for which the associated polynomial is linear. Note that the linear length functions are so far the only functions that have been proved sound w.r.t. symbolic models [27].

Example 3. An example of set of length functions L associated to the signature $\mathcal{F}_c$ of Example 1 is defined as follows.

$$\text{len}_L^{senc}(x, y) = x \qquad \text{len}_L^{aenc}(x, y) = x + y \qquad \text{len}_L^{pk}(x) = x$$
$$\text{len}_L^{\langle\rangle}(x, y) = 1 + x + y \qquad \text{len}_L^{sign}(x, y) = x + y \qquad \text{len}_L^{vk}(x) = x$$

In this example, the length of a encrypted message is linear in the size of the original message and the length of the key. The concatenation of two messages is of length the sum of the lengths of its arguments, plus some constant size used to code the frontier between the two messages. Note that these length functions are polynomial and even linear. These length functions are rather simple and abstract away some implementation details such as padding but more complex functions may be considered if desired.

Time Function. For each primitive $f \in \mathcal{F}$ of arity n, we associate a *time function* from $\mathbb{N}^n$ to $\mathbb{N}$. Given a set of time functions T, we denote time_T^f the time function associated to f in T. Intuitively, $\text{time}_T^f(x_1, \ldots, x_n)$ determines the computation time of the application of f on some terms $u_1, \ldots, u_n$ assuming that the terms u_i are already computed and the length of u_i is x_i. Finally, we define a constant function modelling the computation time to access data such as the content of a variable in the memory, usually denoted $\text{time}_T^{\mathcal{X}}$.

Example 4. Coming back to the signature $\mathcal{F}_{\text{stand}}$ of Example 1, we can define the set T of time functions as follows:

$$\text{time}_T^{\mathcal{X}} = 1 \quad \text{time}_T^{\text{proj}_2}(x) = 1 \quad \text{time}_T^{\text{proj}_1}(x) = 1 \quad \text{time}_T^{\langle \rangle}(x, y) = 1$$
$$\text{time}_T^{\text{adec}}(x, y) = x \quad \text{time}_T^{\text{aenc}}(x, y) = x \quad \text{time}_T^{\text{equals}}(x, y) = x + y$$

In this example, concatenation and projections have constant computation time (e.g., concatenation and projections are done by adding or removing a symbolic link). The asymetric encryption of m by k linearly depends on the size of m. We ignore here the complexity due to the size of the key since key size is usually fixed in protocols. Note it would be easy to add a dependency. Finally the time for an equality test is the sum of the length of its arguments. This corresponds to a naive implementation. We could also choose $\text{time}_T^{\text{equals}}(x, y) = \max(x, y)$. Our framework does not allow to model efficient implementations where the program stops as soon as one bit differs. However, such efficient implementations leak information about the data tested for equality and are therefore not good candidates for an implementation robust against side-channel attacks. Again, other time functions may of course be considered.

The computation time of a term is defined by applying recursively each corresponding time function. More generally, we define the computation time of a term $t\sigma$ assuming that the terms in σ are already computed.

Definition 1. *Let $\mathcal{F}$ be a signature, let L be a set of length functions for $\mathcal{F}$ and let T be a set of time functions for $\mathcal{F}$. Consider a substitution σ from variables to ground constructor terms. For all terms $t \in \mathcal{T}(\mathcal{F}, \mathcal{N}, \mathcal{X})$ such that $vars(t) \subseteq \text{dom}(\sigma)$, we define the computation time of t under the substitution σ and under the sets L and T, denoted $\text{ctime}_{L,T}(t, \sigma)$, as follows:*

$$\text{ctime}_{L,T}(t, \sigma) = \text{time}_T^{\mathcal{X}} \qquad \qquad \textit{if } t \in \mathcal{X} \cup \mathcal{N}$$
$$\text{ctime}_{L,T}(f(u_1, \ldots, u_n), \sigma) = \text{time}_T^f(\ell_1, \ldots, \ell_n) + \sum_{i=1}^{n} \text{ctime}_{L,T}(u_i, \sigma)$$
$$\textit{if } \ell_i = \text{len}_L((u_i\sigma)\downarrow) \textit{ and } \text{Message}(u_i\sigma) \textit{ is true } \forall i \in \{1, \ldots, n\}$$
$$\text{ctime}_{L,T}(f(u_1, \ldots, u_n), \sigma) = \sum_{i=1}^{k} \text{ctime}_{L,T}(u_i, \sigma)$$
$$\textit{if } \text{Message}(u_i\sigma) \textit{ is true } \forall i \in \{1, \ldots, k-1\} \textit{ and } \text{Message}(u_k\sigma) \textit{ is false}$$

Intuitively, $\text{ctime}_{L,T}(t, \sigma)$ represents the time needed to compute $t\sigma\downarrow$ when the terms of σ are already computed and stored in some memory. Therefore the computation time of a variable represents in fact the access time to the memory. We assume in this paper that all primitives are computed using the call-by-value evaluation strategy with a lazy evaluation when failure arises. Hence, when computing $f(u_1, \ldots, u_n)$ with the memory σ, the terms u_i are computed first from left to right. If all computations succeed then the primitive f is applied. In such a case, we obtain the computation time $\text{time}^f_T(\text{len}_L(u_1\sigma\downarrow), \ldots, \text{len}_L(u_n\sigma\downarrow)) + \sum_{i=1}^n \text{ctime}_{L,T}(u_i, \sigma)$. Otherwise, the computation of $f(u_1, \ldots, u_n)$ stops at the first u_k that does not produce a message. This yields the computation time $\sum_{i=1}^k \text{ctime}_{L,T}(u_i, \sigma)$. We assume here that names are already generated to avoid counting their generation twice. Hence the associated computation time is also time^X_T the access time to the memory. We will see later in this section how the computation time for the generation of names is counted, when defining the semantics of processes.

3 Processes

Protocols are modeled through processes, an abstract small programming language. Our calculus is inspired from the applied-pi calculus [4].

3.1 Syntax

The grammar of *plain processes* is defined as follows:

$$P, Q, R := 0 \mid P + Q \mid P \mid Q \mid \nu k.P \mid \, !P \mid$$
$$\text{let } x = u \text{ in } P \text{ else } Q \mid \text{in}(u, x).P \mid \text{out}(u, v).P$$

where u, v are terms, and x is a variable of $\mathcal{X}$. Our calculus contains the nil process 0, parallel composition $P \mid Q$, choice $P + Q$, input $\text{in}(u, x).P$, output $\text{out}(u, v)$, replication $\nu k.P$ that typically models nonce or key generation, and unbounded replication $!\, P$. Note that our calculus also contains the assignment of variables $\text{let } x = u \text{ in } P \text{ else } Q$. In many calculus, $\text{let } x = u \text{ in } P$ is considered as syntactic sugar for $P\{^u/_x\}$. However, since we consider the computation time of messages during the execution of a process, the operation $\text{let } x = u \text{ in } P$ is not syntactic sugar anymore. For example, the three following processes do not yield the same computation time even though they send out the same messages.

- $P_1 = \text{let } x = \text{senc}(a, k). \text{ in } \text{out}(c, h(n)).\text{out}(c, \langle x, x \rangle)$
- $P_2 = \text{out}(c, h(n)).\text{let } x = \text{senc}(a, k) \text{ in } \text{out}(c, \langle x, x \rangle)$
- $P_3 = \text{out}(c, h(n)).\text{out}(c, \langle \text{senc}(a, k), \text{senc}(a, k) \rangle)$

P_1 first computes $\text{senc}(a, k)$, and then outputs $h(n)$ and $\langle \text{senc}(a, k), \text{senc}(a, k) \rangle$. P_2 is very similar but outputs $h(n)$ before computing $\text{senc}(a, k)$ meaning that the output of $h(n)$ will occur faster in P_2 than in P_1, thus an attacker may observe the difference. Finally, P_3 computes $\text{senc}(a, k)$ twice and therefore takes twice more time.

The operation $\text{let } x = u \text{ in } P$ can also be used to change the default evaluation strategy of terms. As mentioned in the previous section, we assume that all primitives are computed using the call-by-value evaluation strategy with a lazy evaluation when a failure arises. For example, the eager evaluation of a message $\text{senc}(\text{sdec}(y, k), u)$ in the process $\text{let } x = \text{senc}(\text{sdec}(y, k), u) \text{ in } P \text{ else } Q$ can be modelled with the following process:

$\text{let } x_1 = \text{sdec}(y, k) \text{ in } \text{let } x = \text{senc}(x_1, u) \text{ in } P \text{ else } Q \text{ else } \text{let } x_2 = u \text{ in } Q \text{ else } Q$

In this process, even if the computation of sdec(y, k) fails (else branch), then u is still computed.

Note that the else branch in let $x = u$ in P else Q is used in case u cannot be computed. For example, let $x = $ sdec(a, a) in 0 else out(c, ok) would output ok. At last, note that the traditional conditional branching (If-then-else) is not part of our calculus. We use instead the assignment of variables and the destructor symbol equals. The traditional process if $u = v$ then P else Q is thus replaced by let $x = $ equals(u, v) in P else Q where x does not appear in P nor Q.

The computation time of some operation obviously depends on the machine on which the computation is performed. For example, a server is much faster than a biometric passport. We defined *extended processes* to represent different physical *machines* that can be running during the execution of a protocol. For example, biometric passports are distinct physical machines that can be observed independently. In contrast, a server runs several threads which cannot be distinguished from an external observer.

The grammar for our extended processes is defined as follows:

$$A, B := [P, i, T] \quad | \quad !A \quad | \quad A \| B$$

where P is a plain process, i is an integer, and T is a set of time functions. $[P, i, T]$ represents a machine with program P and computation time induced by T. The integer i represents the computation time used so far on that machine. Note that inside a machine $[P, i, T]$, there can be several processes running in parallel, *e.g.* $P_1 | \ldots | P_n$. We consider that their executions rely on a scheduling on a single computation machine and so the computation time might differ depending on the scheduling. The situation is different in the case of a real parallel execution of two machines, *e.g.* $A \| B$ where the attacker can observe the execution of A and B independently.

Messages are made available to the attacker through *frames*. Formally, we assume a set of variables $\mathcal{AX}$, disjoint from $\mathcal{X}$. Variables of $\mathcal{AX}$ are typically denoted $ax_1, \ldots, ax_n$. A frame is an expression of the form $\Phi = \{ax_1 \triangleright u_1; \ldots; ax_n \triangleright u_n\}$ where $ax_i \in \mathcal{AX}$ and u_i are terms. The application of a frame Φ to a term M, denoted $M\Phi$, is defined as for the application of substitutions.

Definition 2 (time process). *A time process is a tuple $(\mathcal{E}, A, \Phi, \sigma)$ where:*

- $\mathcal{E}$ *is a set of names that represents the private names of A;*
- Φ *is a ground frame with domain included in $\mathcal{AX}$. It represents the messages available to the attacker;*
- A *is an extended process;*
- σ *is a substitution of variables to ground terms. It represents the current memory of the machines in A.*

3.2   Semantics

The semantics for time processes explicits the computation time of each operation. In particular, for each operation, we define a specific time function representing its computation time standalone, *i.e.* without considering the computation time required to generate the messages themselves. Hence, given a set T of time functions associated a physical machine, $\text{t\_letin}_T(n)$ represents the computation time of the assignation of a message of length n to a variable, whereas t_letelse_T represents the computation time in the case the computation of the message fails; $\text{t\_in}_T(n)$ (resp. $\text{t\_out}_T(n)$) corresponds to the computation time of the input (resp. output) of a message of length n; and $\text{t\_comm}_T(n)$ corresponds to the computation time of the transmission of the message of length n through internal communication. At last, $\text{t\_restr}_T(n)$ represents the time needed to generate a fresh nonce of length n.

The semantics for time processes is similar to the semantics of the applied-pi calculus [4] and is given in Figure 1. For example, the label $\text{out}(M, ax_n, j)$ means that some message has been sent on a channel corresponding to M after some time j (j is actually the total computation time until this send action). This message is stored in variable ax_n by the attacker. Internal communications within the same machine (or group of machines connected through a local network) cannot be observed by an attacker, therefore the computation time of the corresponding machine increases but the transition is silent (τ action). No external machines can communicate secretly since we assume the attacker can control and monitor all communications (he can at least observe the encrypted traffic). Lastly, note that the choice, replication and parallel composition operators do not have associated time functions.

The $\xrightarrow{w}$ relation is the reflexive and transitive closure of $\xrightarrow{\ell}$, where w is the concatenation of all actions. Moreover, $\xRightarrow{\text{tr}}$ is the relation $\xrightarrow{w}$ where tr are the words w without the non visible actions (τ). The set of traces of a time process $\mathcal{P}$ is the set of the possible sequences of actions together with the resulting frame.

$$\text{trace}(\mathcal{P}) = \left\{ (\text{tr}, \nu\mathcal{E}'.\Phi') \,\middle|\, \mathcal{P} \xRightarrow{\text{tr}} (\mathcal{E}', A', \Phi', \sigma') \text{ for some } \mathcal{E}', A', \Phi', \sigma' \right\}$$

Example 5. Consider the signature $\mathcal{F}$, the set L of length functions of Example 3 and the set T of time functions of Example 4 and assume that for all $n \in \mathbb{N}$, $\text{t\_out}_T(n) = n$. Let $a, b \in \mathcal{N}_\ell$ and $k \in \mathcal{N}_{\ell_{pk}}$ with $\ell, \ell_{pk} \in \mathbb{N}$. Consider the time process $\mathcal{P} = (\emptyset, [\text{out}(c, \langle a, b\rangle), 0, T] \,\|\, [\text{out}(c, \text{aenc}(a, k)), 0, T], \emptyset, \emptyset)$. Since we have $\text{len}_L(\text{aenc}(a, k)) = \ell + \ell_{pk}, \text{len}_L(\langle a, b\rangle) = 2\ell + 1, \text{ctime}_{L,T}(\text{aenc}(a, b), \emptyset) = \ell \cdot \ell_{pk}^3 + 2$ and $\text{ctime}_{L,T}(\langle a, b\rangle, \emptyset) = 3$, the set $\text{trace}(A)$ is composed of four traces (s, Φ):

1. $s = \text{out}(c, ax_1, \ell \cdot \ell_{pk}^3 + \ell + \ell_{pk} + 3)$ and $\Phi = \{ax_1 \triangleright \text{aenc}(a, k)\}$
2. $s = \text{out}(c, ax_1, 2\ell + 5)$ and $\Phi = \{ax_1 \triangleright \langle a, b\rangle\}$
3. $s = \text{out}(c, ax_1, \ell \cdot \ell_{pk}^3 + \ell + \ell_{pk} + 3).\text{out}(c, ax_2, 2\ell + 5)$ and $\Phi = \{ax_1 \triangleright \text{aenc}(a, k); ax_2 \triangleright \langle a, b\rangle\}$
4. $s = \text{out}(c, ax_1, 2\ell + 5).\text{out}(c, ax_2, \ell \cdot \ell_{pk}^3 + \ell + \ell_{pk} + 3)$ and $\Phi = \{ax_1 \triangleright \langle a, b\rangle; ax_2 \triangleright \text{aenc}(a, k)\}$

Note that since each computation time is local to each machine, the last argument of the out action is not necessarily increasing globally on the trace, as exemplified by the third trace.

3.3 Example: The PA Protocol

We consider (a simplified version of) the Passive Authentication protocol (PA), presented in [7]. It is designed for transmitting a secret without revealing the identity of

$$(\mathcal{E}, [\text{let } x = u \text{ in } P \text{ else } Q \mid R, i, T] \parallel A, \Phi, \sigma) \xrightarrow{\tau} \qquad \text{(LET)}$$
$$(\mathcal{E}, [P \mid R, j, T] \parallel A, \Phi, \sigma \cup \{^{u\sigma\downarrow}/_x\})$$
$$\text{if Message}(u\sigma) \text{ with } j = i + \text{ctime}_{L,T}(u, \sigma) + \text{t\_letin}_T(\text{len}_L(u\sigma\downarrow))$$

$$(\mathcal{E}, [\text{let } x = u \text{ in } P \text{ else } Q \mid R, i, T] \parallel A, \Phi, \sigma) \xrightarrow{\tau} (\mathcal{E}, [Q \mid R, j, T] \parallel A, \Phi, \sigma) \qquad \text{(ELSE)}$$
$$\text{if } \neg\text{Message}(u\sigma) \text{ with } j = i + \text{ctime}_{L,T}(u, \sigma) + \text{t\_letelse}_T$$

$$(\mathcal{E}, [\text{out}(u, t).Q_1 \mid \text{in}(v, x).Q_2 \mid R, i, T] \parallel A, \Phi, \sigma) \xrightarrow{\tau} \qquad \text{(COMM)}$$
$$(\mathcal{E}, [Q_1 \mid Q_2 \mid R, j, T] \parallel A, \Phi, \sigma \cup \{^{t\sigma\downarrow}/_x\})$$
$$\text{if Message}(u\sigma), \text{Message}(v\sigma), \text{Message}(t\sigma) \text{ and } u\sigma\downarrow = v\sigma\downarrow \text{ with } j = i +$$
$$\text{ctime}_{L,T}(u, \sigma) + \text{ctime}_{L,T}(v, \sigma) + \text{ctime}_{L,T}(t, \sigma) + \text{t\_comm}_T(\text{len}_L(t\sigma\downarrow))$$

$$(\mathcal{E}, [\text{in}(u, x).Q \mid P, i, T] \parallel A, \Phi, \sigma) \xrightarrow{in(N,M)} (\mathcal{E}, [Q \mid P, j, T] \parallel A, \Phi, \sigma \cup \{^t/_x\}) \qquad \text{(IN)}$$
$$\text{if } M\Phi\downarrow = t, \text{fvars}(M, N) \subseteq \text{dom}(\Phi), \text{fnames}(M, N) \cap \mathcal{E} = \emptyset,$$
$$N\Phi\downarrow = u\sigma\downarrow, \text{Message}(M\Phi), \text{Message}(N\Phi), \text{ and Message}(u\sigma)$$
$$\text{with } j = i + \text{ctime}_{L,T}(u, \sigma) + \text{t\_in}_T(\text{len}_L(t))$$

$$(\mathcal{E}, [\text{out}(u, t).Q \mid P, i, T] \parallel A, \Phi, \sigma) \xrightarrow{out(M, ax_n, j)} \qquad \text{(OUT)}$$
$$(\mathcal{E}, [Q \mid P, j, T] \parallel A, \Phi \cup \{ax_n \triangleright t\sigma\downarrow\}, \sigma)$$
$$\text{if } M\Phi\downarrow = u\sigma\downarrow, \text{Message}(u\sigma), \text{fvars}(M) \subseteq \text{dom}(\Phi), \text{fnames}(M) \cap \mathcal{E} = \emptyset,$$
$$\text{Message}(M\Phi), \text{Message}(t\sigma) \text{ and } ax_n \in \mathcal{AX}, n = |\Phi| + 1$$
$$\text{with } j = i + \text{ctime}_{L,T}(t, \sigma) + \text{ctime}_{L,T}(u, \sigma) + \text{t\_out}_T(\text{len}_L(t\sigma\downarrow))$$

$$(\mathcal{E}, [P_1 + P_2 \mid R, i, T] \parallel A, \Phi, \sigma) \xrightarrow{\tau} (\mathcal{E}, [P_1 \mid R, i, T] \parallel A, \Phi, \sigma) \qquad \text{(CHOICE-1)}$$

$$(\mathcal{E}, [P_1 + P_2 \mid R, i, T] \parallel A, \Phi, \sigma) \xrightarrow{\tau} (\mathcal{E}, [P_2 \mid R, i, T] \parallel A, \Phi, \sigma) \qquad \text{(CHOICE-2)}$$

$$(\mathcal{E}, [\nu k.P \mid R, i, T] \parallel A, \Phi, \sigma) \xrightarrow{\tau} (\mathcal{E} \cup \{k\}, [P \mid R, j, T] \parallel A, \Phi, \sigma) \qquad \text{(RESTR)}$$
$$\text{with } j = i + \text{t\_restr}_T(\ell) \text{ and } k \in \mathcal{N}_\ell$$

$$(\mathcal{E}, [!\, P \mid R, i, T] \parallel A, \Phi, \sigma) \xrightarrow{\tau} (\mathcal{E}, [!\, P \mid P\rho \mid R, i, T] \parallel A, \Phi, \sigma) \qquad \text{(REPL)}$$

$$(\mathcal{E}, !\, A \parallel B, \Phi, \sigma) \xrightarrow{\tau} (\mathcal{E}, !\, A \parallel A\rho \parallel B, \Phi, \sigma) \qquad \text{(M-REPL)}$$

where u, v, t are ground terms, x is a variable and ρ is used to rename variables in $bvars(P)$ and $bvars(A)$ (resp. names in $bnames(P)$ and $bnames(A)$) with fresh variables (resp. names).

Fig. 1. Semantics

the participants. In this protocol, an agent A wishes to engage in communication with an agent B that is willing to talk to A. However, A does not want to compromise her privacy by revealing her identity or the identity of B more broadly. The participants A and B proceed as follows:

$$A \rightarrow B \;:\; \text{aenc}(\langle N_a, \text{pk}(sk_A)\rangle, \text{pk}(sk_B))$$
$$B \rightarrow A \;:\; \text{aenc}(\langle N_a, \langle N_b, \text{pk}(sk_B)\rangle\rangle, \text{pk}(sk_A))$$
$$else \quad \text{aenc}(N_b, \text{pk}(sk_B))$$

A first sends to B a nonce N_a and her public key encrypted with the public key of B. If the message is of the expected form then B sends to A the nonce N_a, a freshly generated nonce N_b and his public key, all of this being encrypted with the public key of A. If the message is not of the right form or if B is not willing to talk with A, then B sends out a "decoy" message $\mathsf{aenc}(N_b, \mathsf{pk}(sk_B))$. Intuitively, this message should look like B's other message from the point of view of an outsider. This is important since the protocol is supposed to protect the identity of the participants.

This protocol can be modeled in our process algebra as follows:

$$B(b, a) \stackrel{\text{def}}{=} \mathsf{in}(c, x).\mathsf{let}\ y = \mathsf{adec}(x, sk_b)\ \mathsf{in}$$
$$\mathsf{let}\ z = \mathsf{equals}(\mathsf{proj}_2(y), \mathsf{pk}(sk_a))\ \mathsf{in}\ \nu n_b.\mathsf{out}(c, \mathsf{aenc}(M, \mathsf{pk}(sk_a))).0$$
$$\mathsf{else}\ \nu n_{error}.\mathsf{out}(c, \mathsf{aenc}(n_{error}, \mathsf{pk}(sk_a))).0$$
$$\mathsf{else}\ 0.$$
$$A(a, b) \stackrel{\text{def}}{=} \nu n_a.\mathsf{out}(c, \mathsf{aenc}(\langle n_a, \mathsf{pk}(sk_a)\rangle, \mathsf{pk}(sk_b))).\mathsf{in}(c, z).0$$

where $M = \langle \mathsf{proj}_1(y), \langle n_b, \mathsf{pk}(sk_b)\rangle\rangle$. The process $A(a, b)$ represents the role A played by agent a with b while the process $B(b, a)$ represents the role B played by agent b with a.

4   Time Equivalence

Privacy properties such as anonymity, unlinkability, or ballot privacy are often stated as *equivalence properties* [29,9]. Intuitively, Alice's identity remains private if an attacker cannot distinguish executions from Alice from executions from Bob. Equivalence properties are also useful to express strong secrecy [19], indistiguishability from an ideal system [5], or game-based properties [27]. Several definitions of equivalence have been proposed such as trace equivalence [4], observational equivalence [4], or diff-equivalence [18]. In this paper, we focus on trace equivalence that we adapt to account for length and computation times.

The ability of the attacker is now characterized by three parameters: the set of cryptographic primitives, their corresponding length functions, and their corresponding computation times (w.r.t. the attacker). Later in the paper, for decidability, we will show that we can restrict the attacker to a finite set of names. So we define a *length signature*, usually denoted $\mathcal{F}_\ell$, as a tuple of a symbol functions signature $\mathcal{F}$, a set of names $\mathsf{N} \subseteq \mathcal{N}$, and a set of length functions L, *i.e.* $\mathcal{F}_\ell = (\mathcal{F}, \mathsf{N}, L)$. Similarly, we denote a *time signature*, usually denoted $\mathcal{F}_{ti}$, as a pair containing a length signature $\mathcal{F}_\ell$ and a set of time functions T corresponding to the signature in $\mathcal{F}_\ell$, *i.e.* $\mathcal{F}_{ti} = (\mathcal{F}_\ell, T)$.

4.1   Time Static Equivalence

The notion of static equivalence has been extensively studied (see *e.g.*, [3]). It corresponds to the indistinguishability of sequences of messages from the point of view of the attacker. In the standard definition of static equivalence [3,14,28], the attacker can only perform cryptographic operations on messages. [24] introduces *length static equivalence*, that provides the attacker with the ability to measure the length of messages. Intuitively, two frames are in length static equivalence if an attacker cannot see any difference, even when applying arbitrary primitives and measuring the length of the resulting messages. In this framework, we also provide the attacker with the capability to measure computation times. We therefore adapt the definition of static equivalence to account for both length and computation times.

Definition 3. *Let $\mathcal{F}_{ti} = (\mathcal{F}_\ell, T)$ be a time signature with $\mathcal{F}_\ell = (\mathcal{F}, \mathsf{N}, L)$. Let $\mathcal{E}, \mathcal{E}'$ two sets of names. Let Φ and Φ' two frames. We say that $\nu\mathcal{E}.\Phi$ and $\nu\mathcal{E}'.\Phi'$ are time statically equivalent w.r.t. $\mathcal{F}_{ti}$, written $\nu\mathcal{E}.\Phi \sim_{ti}^{\mathcal{F}_{ti}} \nu\mathcal{E}'.\Phi'$, when $\mathrm{dom}(\Phi) = \mathrm{dom}(\Phi')$, $fnames(\nu\mathcal{E}.\Phi, \nu\mathcal{E}'.\Phi') \cap (\mathcal{E}' \cup \mathcal{E}) = \emptyset$ and when for all $i, j \in \mathbb{N}$, for all $M, N \in \mathcal{T}(\mathcal{F}, \mathsf{N} \cup \mathcal{X})$ such that $fvars(M, N) \subseteq \mathrm{dom}(\Phi)$ and $fnames(M, N) \cap (\mathcal{E} \cup \mathcal{E}') = \emptyset$, we have:*

- Message$(M\Phi)$ *if and only if* Message$(M\Phi')$
- *if* Message$(M\Phi)$ *and* Message$(N\Phi)$ *then*
  1. *$M\Phi\!\downarrow = N\Phi\!\downarrow$ if and only $M\Phi'\!\downarrow = N\Phi'\!\downarrow$; and*
  2. *$\mathrm{len}_L(M\Phi\!\downarrow) = i$ if and only if $\mathrm{len}_L(M\Phi'\!\downarrow) = i$; and*
  3. *$\mathrm{ctime}_{L,T}(M, \Phi) = j$ iff $\mathrm{ctime}_{L,T}(M, \Phi') = j$*

Consider the length signature $\mathcal{F}_\ell$, we say that $\nu\mathcal{E}.\Phi$ and $\nu\mathcal{E}'.\Phi'$ are length statically equivalent w.r.t. $\mathcal{F}_\ell$, written $\nu\mathcal{E}.\Phi \sim_\ell^{\mathcal{F}_\ell} \nu\mathcal{E}'.\Phi'$, when $\nu\mathcal{E}.\Phi$ and $\nu\mathcal{E}'.\Phi'$ satisfy the same properties as above except Property 3.

4.2 Time Trace Equivalence

Time trace equivalence is a generalization of time static equivalence to the active case. It corresponds to the standard trace equivalence [4] except that the attacker can now observe the execution time of the processes. Intuitively, two extended processes $\mathcal{P}$ and $\mathcal{Q}$ are in time trace equivalence if any sequence of actions of $\mathcal{P}$ can be matched by the same sequence of actions in $\mathcal{Q}$ such that the resulting frames are time statically equivalent. It is important to note that the sequence of actions now reflects the computation time of each action. We also recall the definition of length trace equivalence introduced in [24], which accounts for the ability to measure the length but not the computation time. We denote by $=_{ti}$ the equality of sequences of labels, where the time parameters of outputs are ignored. Formally, we define $\ell_1 \ldots \ell_p =_{ti} \ell'_1 \ldots \ell'_q$ to hold when $p = q$ and

- for all $N, M, \ell_i = in(N, M)$ if and only if $\ell'_i = in(N, M)$; and
- for all $M, ax_n, \ell_i = out(M, ax_n, c)$ for some c if and only if $\ell'_i = out(M, ax_n, c')$ for some c'.

Definition 4. *Consider a time (resp. length) signature $\mathcal{F}$. Let $\mathcal{P}$ and $\mathcal{Q}$ be two closed time processes with $fnames(\mathcal{P}, \mathcal{Q}) \cap bnames(\mathcal{P}, \mathcal{Q}) = \emptyset$. $\mathcal{P} \sqsubseteq_{ti}^{\mathcal{F}} \mathcal{Q}$ (resp. $\mathcal{P} \sqsubseteq_\ell^{\mathcal{F}} \mathcal{Q}$) if for every $(tr, \nu\mathcal{E}.\Phi) \in \mathsf{trace}(\mathcal{P})$, there exists $(tr', \nu\mathcal{E}.\Phi') \in \mathsf{trace}(\mathcal{Q})$ such that $\nu\mathcal{E}.\Phi \sim_{ti}^{\mathcal{F}} \nu\mathcal{E}'.\Phi'$ and $tr = tr'$ (resp. $\nu\mathcal{E}.\Phi \sim_\ell^{\mathcal{F}} \nu\mathcal{E}'.\Phi'$ and $tr =_{ti} tr'$).*

Two closed time processes $\mathcal{P}$ and $\mathcal{Q}$ are time (resp. length) trace equivalent w.r.t. $\mathcal{F}$, denoted by $\mathcal{P} \approx_{ti}^{\mathcal{F}} \mathcal{Q}$ (resp. $\mathcal{P} \approx_\ell^{\mathcal{F}} \mathcal{Q}$), if $\mathcal{P} \sqsubseteq_{ti}^{\mathcal{F}} \mathcal{Q}$ and $\mathcal{P} \sqsubseteq_{ti}^{\mathcal{F}} \mathcal{Q}$ (resp. $\mathcal{P} \sqsubseteq_\ell^{\mathcal{F}} \mathcal{Q}$ and $\mathcal{P} \sqsubseteq_\ell^{\mathcal{F}} \mathcal{Q}$).

4.3 Timing Attacks against PA

We consider again the PA protocol described in Section 3.3. This protocol should in particular ensure the anonymity of the sender A. The anonymity of A can be stated as an equivalence property: an attacker should not be able to distinguish whether b is willing to talk to a (represented by the process $B(b, a)$) or willing to talk to a' (represented by the process $B(b, a')$), provided that a, a' and b are honest participants. This can be modeled by the following equivalence:

$$(\mathcal{E}, [B(b, a'), 0, T] \,\|\, [A(a', b), 0, T], \Phi, \emptyset) \overset{?}{\approx}_{ti}^{\mathcal{F}} (\mathcal{E}, [B(b, a), 0, T] \,\|\, [A(a, b), 0, T], \Phi, \emptyset)$$

with $\mathcal{E} = \{sk_a, sk_{a'}, sk_b\}$, $\Phi = \{ax_1 \rhd \mathsf{pk}(sk_a); ax_2 \rhd \mathsf{pk}(sk_{a'}); ax_3 \rhd \mathsf{pk}(sk_b)\}$.

In the literature, the Private Authentication protocol was proved [23] to preserve A's anonymity when considering standard trace equivalence, *i.e.* without length and time. However, an attacker can easily break anonymity by measuring the length of the messages. Indeed, it is easy to notice that the length of the decoy message is smaller than the size of the regular message. Therefore, an attacker may simply initiate a session with B in the name of A:

$$C(A) \to B \ : \ \mathsf{aenc}(\langle N_c, \mathsf{pk}(sk_A)\rangle, \mathsf{pk}(sk_B))$$

If the message received in response from B is "long", the attacker learns that B is willing to talk with A. If the message is "small", the attacker learns that A is not one of B's friends.

This attack can be easily reflected in our formalism. Consider the sequence of labels $\mathsf{tr}(j) = \mathsf{in}(c, \mathsf{aenc}(\langle n_i, ax_1\rangle, ax_3)).\mathsf{out}(c, ax_4, j)$ and the corresponding execution on $B(b, a)$, where b is indeed willing to talk with a.

$$(\mathcal{E}, [B(b, a), 0, T] \,\|\, [A(a, b), 0, T], \Phi, \emptyset) \overset{\mathsf{tr}(j)}{\Rightarrow} (\mathcal{E}', [A(a, b), 0, T], \Phi \cup \{ax_4 \rhd M\}, \sigma)$$

with $M = \mathsf{aenc}(\langle n_i, \langle n_b, \mathsf{pk}(sk_b)\rangle\rangle, \mathsf{pk}(sk_a))$ and $\mathcal{E}' = \mathcal{E} \cup \{n_b\}$ for some σ and j. On the other hand, when the communication is between a' and b then b detects that the public key does not correspond to a' and outputs the decoy message:

$$(\mathcal{E}, [B(b, a'), 0, T] \,\|\, [A(a', b), 0, T], \Phi, \emptyset) \overset{\mathsf{tr}(j')}{\Rightarrow} (\mathcal{E}', [A(a, b), 0, T], \Phi \cup \{ax_4 \rhd M'\}, \sigma')$$

with $M' = \mathsf{aenc}(n_{error}, \mathsf{pk}(sk_a))$ for some σ' and j'. If the attacker computes the length of the received message, he gets $\mathsf{len}_L(\mathsf{aenc}(\langle n_i, \langle n_b, \mathsf{pk}(sk_b)\rangle\rangle, \mathsf{pk}(sk_a))) = 2\ell + \ell_{pk} + 2$ and $\mathsf{len}_L(\mathsf{aenc}(n_{error}, \mathsf{pk}(sk_a))) = \ell$ with $n_i, n_b, n_{error} \in \mathcal{N}_\ell$ and $sk_b \in \mathcal{N}_{pk}$. Therefore the two resulting frames are not in length static equivalence, thus

$$(\mathcal{E}, [B(b, a'), 0, T] \,\|\, [A(a', b), 0, T], \Phi, \emptyset) \not\approx_{ti}^{\mathcal{F}} (\mathcal{E}, [B(b, a), 0, T] \,\|\, [A(a, b), 0, T], \Phi, \emptyset)$$

To repair the anonymity of the PA protocol, the decoy message should have the same length than the regular message.

PA-fix1. A first solution is to include N_a in the decoy message which is set to be $\mathsf{aenc}(\langle N_a, \mathsf{Error}\rangle, \mathsf{pk}(sk_A))$ where Error is a constant of same length than $\langle N_b, \mathsf{pk}(sk_B)\rangle$. However, this variant does not satisfy even trace equivalence since the attacker can now reconstruct $\mathsf{aenc}(\langle N_a, \mathsf{Error}\rangle, \mathsf{pk}(sk_A))$ when N_a has been forged by himself.

PA-fix2. To fix this attack, a natural variant is to set the decoy message to be aenc($\langle N_a, N_d \rangle$, pk(sk_A)), where N_d is a nonce of same length than $\langle N_b$, pk(sk_B)$\rangle$. However, this variant is now subject to a timing attack. Indeed, it takes more time to generate N_d than N_b since N_d is larger. Therefore an attacker may still notice the difference. Note that this attack cannot be detected when considering length trace equivalence only.

PA-fix3. Finally, a third solution is to set the decoy message to be the cipher aenc($\langle N_a, \langle N_b, \text{Error} \rangle$, pk($sk_A$)$\rangle$) where Error is a constant of same length than pk(sk_B). We show in Section 6 that due to our main result and thanks to the APTE tool, we are able to prove this version secure, assuming that public keys are of the same length (otherwise there is again a straightforward attack on privacy).

We will see in Section 6 that our tool detects all these attacks.

5 Reduction of Time Trace Equivalence to Length Equivalence

We focus in this section on the key result of this paper: time equivalence reduces to length equivalence. We show that this holds for arbitrary processes, possibly with replications and private channels (Theorem 1). This means that, from a decidability point of view, there is no need to enrich the model with time. We also prove that our result induces that time trace equivalence for processes without replication can also be reduced to length trace equivalence for processes without replication, even if we restrict the names of the attacker. Finally, applying the decidability result on length trace equivalence of [24], we can deduce decidability of trace equivalence for processes without replication and for a fixed signature that includes all standard cryptographic primitives (Theorem 2).

These three results rely on a generic transformation from a time process P to a process P' where the sole observation of the length of the messages exchanged in P' reflects both the time and length information leaked by P.

5.1 Representing Computation Time with Messages

The key idea to get rid of computation times is to attach to each term t a special message, called *time message*, whose length corresponds to the time needed to compute t. To that extent, we first need to augment the signature used to describe our processes. Given a time signature $\mathcal{F}_t = ((\mathcal{F}, \mathsf{N}, L), T)$, we extend it as $\overline{\mathcal{F}_t}^T = ((\overline{\mathcal{F}}^T, \mathsf{N}, \overline{L}^T), \overline{T}^T)$, which is defined as follows. We first add, for each function symbol f, a fresh function symbol $\overline{\mathsf{f}}$ whose length function is the time function of f, meaning that $\mathrm{len}_{\overline{L}^T}^{\overline{\mathsf{f}}} = \mathrm{time}_T^{\mathsf{f}}$. Similarly, for each action proc in the execution of a process, we add a new function symbol whose length function represents the computation time of proc, that is $\mathrm{len}_{\overline{L}^T}^{\mathsf{g_{proc}}} = \mathsf{t\_proc}_T$. Lastly, we consider two new symbol functions plus/1 and hide/2 where the resulting size of the application of plus is the sum of the size of its arguments, and hide reveals only the size of its first argument. Since these news function symbols should not yield information on the computation time other than by their size, we consider that all their time functions are the null function. With these extended time signature $\overline{\mathcal{F}_t}^T$, the time message of a term t, denoted $[t]_{L,T}$, can be naturally defined. For instance, if $t = f(t_1, \ldots, t_m)$ then $[t]_{L,T} = \mathsf{plus}([t_1]_{L,T}, \ldots \mathsf{plus}([t_m]_{L,T}, \bar{f}(t_1, \ldots, t_m)) \ldots)$. Thanks to the function symbol plus, the length of $[t]_{L,T}$ models exactly the computation time of t.

5.2 Transformed Processes

The computation time of a process becomes visible to an attacker only at some specific steps of the execution, typically when the process sends out a message. Therefore the corresponding time message should consider all previous actions since the last output. In case a machine executes only a sequential process (*i.e.* that does not include processes in parallel) then the computation time of internal actions is easy to compute. For example, given a process $P = \mathsf{in}(c, x).\nu k.\mathsf{out}(c, v)$, the computation time of P when v is output can be encoded using the following time message $\mathsf{plus}(m_{in}, \mathsf{plus}(g_{\mathsf{restr}}(k), m_{out}))$ where:

$$m_{in} = \mathsf{plus}([x]_{L,T}, \mathsf{plus}([c]_{L,T}, g_{\mathsf{in}}(x))) \quad m_{out} = \mathsf{plus}([v]_{L,T}, \mathsf{plus}([c]_{L,T}, g_{\mathsf{out}}(v)))$$

However, if a machine executes a process Q in parallel of P, then the time message m does not correspond anymore to the computation time when v is output since some actions of Q may have been executed between the actions of P. Therefore, we need to "store" the computation time that has elapsed so far. To do this, we introduce *cells* that can store the time messages of a machine and will be used as time accumulator. Formally, a cell is simply a process with a dedicated private channel defined as $Cell(c, u) = \mathsf{out}(c, u) \mid !\,\mathsf{in}(c, x).\mathsf{out}(c, x)$. Note that a cell can only alternate between inputs and outputs (no consecutive outputs can be done). Thanks to those cells, we can define a transformation for a time process P into an equivalent process w.r.t. to some cell d and some length and time functions L and T respectively, denoted $[P]_{L,T}^d$, where the computation time can now be ignored.

Intuitively, each action of a plain process first starts by reading in the cell d and always ends by writing on the cell the new value of the computation time. For instance, $[\nu k.P]_{L,T}^d = \mathsf{in}(d, y).\nu k.\mathsf{out}(d, \mathsf{plus}(y, g_{\mathsf{restr}}(k))).[P]_{L,T}^d$. Moreover, in the case of an output, $\mathsf{out}(u, v)$ is transformed to $\mathsf{out}(u, \langle v, \mathsf{hide}(t, k) \rangle)$ where t is the current value of the computation time of the plain process and k is a fresh nonce. Hence, the attacker gets information about the computation time of the process through the size of the second message of the output. The most technical case is for the process let $x = u$ in P else Q. Indeed, if u is not a message then the process executes Q instead of P. The main issue here is that the computation time of u depends on which subterm makes the computation fail. This, in turn, may depend on the intruder's inputs. Therefore we introduce below the process $\mathsf{LetTr}_T(c, t, [u], y)$ that determines which cryptographic primitive fails and then returns on channel c the computation time message that corresponds to the execution of u, added to the existing computation time message y and t being some initial parameters.

$\mathsf{LetTr}_T(c, t, \emptyset, u) = \mathsf{out}(c, \mathsf{plus}(u, t))$
$\mathsf{LetTr}_T(c, t, [t_1; \ldots; t_n], u) = \mathsf{LetTr}_T(c, t, [t_2; \ldots; t_n], \mathsf{plus}(u, [t_1]_{L,T}))$ if $t_1 \in \mathcal{N} \cup \mathcal{X}$
$\mathsf{LetTr}_T(c, t, [t_1; \ldots; t_n], u) = \mathsf{let}\ x = t_1\ \mathsf{in}$
$\quad \mathsf{LetTr}_T(c, t, [t_2; \ldots; t_n], \mathsf{plus}(u, [t_1]_{L,T}))\ \mathsf{else}\ \mathsf{LetTr}_T(c, t', [v_1; \ldots; v_m], u)$
$\qquad\qquad\qquad\qquad\qquad$ where $t_1 = \mathsf{f}(v_1, \ldots, v_m), t' = \bar{\mathsf{f}}(v_1, \ldots, v_m)$.

Thanks to this process, the transformed process $[\mathsf{let}\ x = u\ \mathsf{in}\ P\ \mathsf{else}\ Q]^d_{L,T}$ is defined as follows where $u = \mathsf{f}(v_1, \ldots, v_m), t = \bar{\mathsf{f}}(v_1, \ldots, v_m)$.

$\quad \mathsf{in}(d, y).\mathsf{let}\ x = u\ \mathsf{in}\ \mathsf{out}(d, \mathsf{plus}(\mathsf{plus}(y, \mathsf{g_{letin}}(x)), [u]_{L,T})).[P]^d_{L,T}$
$\quad\ \mathsf{else}\ \nu c.\left(\mathsf{LetTr}_T(c, t, [v_1; \ldots; v_m], \mathsf{plus}(y, \mathsf{g_{letelse}}))\ |\ \mathsf{in}(c, z).\mathsf{out}(d, z).[Q]^d_{L,T}\right)$

This transformation is naturally adapted to extended processes by introducing a cell for each extended process $A = [P, i, T]$, that is $[A]_L = [\nu d.(Cell(d, n^i)\ |\ [P]^d_{L,T}), i, T]$ for some $n^i \in \mathcal{N}$.

5.3   Main Theorem

We can finally state the main results of this paper. First, time equivalence can be reduced to length equivalence, for any two processes.

Theorem 1. Let $\mathcal{F}_{ti} = ((\mathcal{F}, \mathcal{N}, L), T)$ be a time signature. Intuitively, T is the set of time functions for the attacker. Consider two time processes $\mathcal{P}_1 = (\mathcal{E}_1, A_1, \Phi_1, \emptyset)$ and $\mathcal{P}_2 = (\mathcal{E}_2, A_2, \Phi_2, \emptyset)$ with $\mathrm{dom}(\Phi_2) = \mathrm{dom}(\Phi_1)$, built on $(\mathcal{F}, \mathcal{N}, L)$ and time functions sets $T_1, \ldots, T_n$. Let $\mathcal{P}'_1 = (\mathcal{E}_1, [A_1]_L, \Phi_1, \emptyset)$ and $\mathcal{P}'_2 = (\mathcal{E}_2, [A_2]_L, \Phi_2, \emptyset)$. Then

$$\mathcal{P}_1 \approx^{\mathcal{F}_{ti}}_{ti} \mathcal{P}_2 \text{ if, and only if, } \mathcal{P}'_1 \approx^{\overline{\mathcal{F}_{ti}}^{T, T_1, \ldots, T_n}}_{\ell} \mathcal{P}'_2$$

This theorem holds for arbitrary processes and for any signature and associated rewriting system. It is interesting to note that it also holds for arbitrary time functions. Moreover, the transformed processes $\mathcal{P}'_1$ and $\mathcal{P}'_2$ only add length functions which are either linear or are the same than the initial time functions. It therefore does not add any complexity. Note also that if $\mathcal{P}_1$ and $\mathcal{P}_2$ are two processes without replication then $\mathcal{P}'_1$ and $\mathcal{P}'_2$ are still processes with replication. For decidability in the case of processes without replication, we need to further restrict the number of names given to the attacker. We therefore refine our theorem for processes without replication with a slightly different transformation. Instead of adding cells of the form $\mathsf{out}(c, u)\ |\ !\mathsf{in}(c, x).\mathsf{out}(c, x)$, we unfold in advance the replication as much as needed in the extended process. As a consequence, and relying on the decidability of time trace equivalence described in [24], we can immediately deduce decidability of time trace equivalence for processes without replication and polynomial time functions.

Theorem 2. Let $\mathcal{F}_{ti} = ((\mathcal{F}, \mathcal{N}, L), T)$ be a time signature such that $\mathcal{F} = \mathcal{F}_{\mathsf{stand}} \uplus \mathcal{F}_o$ where $\mathcal{F}_o$ contains only one-way symbols, that are not involved in any rewrite rules. We assume that L and T contain only polynomial functions. Then time trace equivalence is decidable for time processes without replication.

Anonymity	Status	Execution time
PA-Original	timing attack	0.01 sec
PA-fix1	timing attack	0.01 sec
PA-fix2	timing attack	0.08 sec
PA-fix3	safe	0.3 sec

Unlinkability	Status	Execution time
BAC	timing attack	0.08 sec
AKA	timing attack	0.9 sec

Fig. 2. Timing attacks found with the APTE tool

6 Application to Privacy Protocols

The APTE tool [21,22] is a tool dedicated to the automatic proof of trace equivalence of processes without replication, for the standard cryptographic primitives. It has been recently extended to length trace equivalence [24]. We have implemented our generic transformation (Theorem 2) and thanks to this translator from time to length equivalence, APTE can now be used to check time trace equivalence. Using the tool, we have studied the privacy of three protocols:

PA. Our running example is the Private Authentication Protocol, described in Section 3.3. As explained in Section 4.3, this protocol suffers from length or time attacks for several versions of it, depending on the decoy message. With the APTE tool, we have found privacy attacks against all the fixes we first proposed. The APTE tool was able to show privacy of our last version of PA.

BAC. As explained in the Introduction, several protocols are embedded in biometric passports, to protects users' privacy. We have studied the *Basic Access Control protocol* (BAC). With the APTE tool, we have retrieved the timing attack reported in [25]. Note that this attack could not have been detected when considering length trace equivalence only. Indeed, the returned message does not vary. The only noticeable change is the time needed to reply. Even if APTE is guaranteed to always terminate (since it implements a decidable procedure [21]), the corrected version that includes a fake test was unfortunately out of reach of the APTE tool in its current version (we stopped the computation after two days). This is due to the fact that the BAC protocol contains several inputs and else branches which causes state-explosion in APTE.

3G AKA Protocol. The 3G AKA protocol is deployed in mobile telephony to protect users from being traced by third parties. To achieve privacy, it makes use of temporary pseudonyms but this was shown to be insufficient [10]. Indeed, thanks to error messages, an attacker may recognize a user by replaying an old session.

The suggested fix proposes to simply use a unique error message. However, the protocol then remains subject to potential timing attacks (as for the BAC protocol). The APTE tool is able to automatically detect this timing privacy attack.

Our study is summarized in Figure 2. The precise specification of the protocols and their variants can be found in [20].

References

1. http://nacl.cr.yp.to/
2. Machine readable travel document. Technical Report 9303, International Civil Aviation Organization (2008)
3. Abadi, M., Cortier, V.: Deciding knowledge in security protocols under equational theories. Theoretical Computer Science 387(1-2), 2–32 (2006)
4. Abadi, M., Fournet, C.: Mobile values, new names, and secure communication. In: 28th ACM Symp. on Principles of Programming Languages, POPL 2001 (2001)
5. Abadi, M., Gordon, A.: A calculus for cryptographic protocols: The spi calculus. In: 4th Conference on Computer and Communications Security (CCS 1997), pp. 36–47. ACM Press (1997)
6. Abadi, M., Blanchet, B.: Analyzing Security Protocols with Secrecy Types and Logic Programs. Journal of the ACM 52(1), 102–146 (2005)
7. Abadi, M., Fournet, C.: Private authentication. Theoretical Computer Science 322(3), 427–476 (2004)
8. Almeida, J.B., Barbosa, M., Barthe, G., Dupressoir, F.: Certified computer-aided cryptography: Efficient provably secure machine code from high-level implementations. In: 21st ACM Conference on Computer and Communications Security, CCS 2013 (2013)
9. Arapinis, M., Chothia, T., Ritter, E., Ryan, M.: Analysing unlinkability and anonymity using the applied pi calculus. In: 23rd IEEE Computer Security Foundations Symposium, CSF 2010 (2010)
10. Arapinis, M., Mancini, L.I., Ritter, E., Ryan, M., Golde, N., Redon, K., Borgaonkar, R.: New privacy issues in mobile telephony: fix and verification. In: ACM Conference on Computer and Communications Security, pp. 205–216 (2012)
11. Backes, M., Doychev, G., Köpf, B.: Preventing side-channel leaks in web traffic: A formal approach. In: Network and Distributed System Security Symposium, NDSS 2013 (2013)
12. Backes, M., Duermuth, M., Gerling, S., Pinkal, M., Sporleder, C.: Acoustic emanations of printers. In: 19th USENIX Security Symposium (2010)
13. Backes, M., Köpf, B., Rybalchenko, A.: Automatic discovery and quantification of information leaks. In: Symposium on Security and Privacy, S&P 2009 (2009)
14. Baudet, M., Cortier, V., Delaune, S.: YAPA: A generic tool for computing intruder knowledge. ACM Transactions on Computational Logic 14 (2013)
15. Bella, G., Paulson, L.C.: Kerberos version IV: Inductive analysis of the secrecy goals. In: Quisquater, J.-J., Deswarte, Y., Meadows, C., Gollmann, D. (eds.) ESORICS 1998. LNCS, vol. 1485, pp. 361–375. Springer, Heidelberg (1998)
16. Bernstein, D.J., Chou, T., Schwabe, P.: Mcbits: Fast constant-time code-based cryptography. In: Bertoni, G., Coron, J.-S. (eds.) CHES 2013. LNCS, vol. 8086, pp. 250–272. Springer, Heidelberg (2013)
17. Biondi, F., Legay, A., Malacaria, P., Wąsowski, A.: Quantifying information leakage of randomized protocols. In: Giacobazzi, R., Berdine, J., Mastroeni, I. (eds.) VMCAI 2013. LNCS, vol. 7737, pp. 68–87. Springer, Heidelberg (2013)

18. Blanchet, B., Abadi, M., Fournet, C.: Automated Verification of Selected Equivalences for Security Protocols. In: 20th Symposium on Logic in Computer Science, LICS 2005 (2005)

19. Blanchet, B.: Automatic proof of strong secrecy for security protocols. In: Symposium on Security and Privacy (S&P 2004), pp. 86–100. IEEE Comp. Soc. Press (2004)

20. Cheval, V.: APTE (Algorithm for Proving Trace Equivalence) (2013),
    http://projects.lsv.ens-cachan.fr/APTE/

21. Cheval, V., Comon-Lundh, H., Delaune, S.: Trace equivalence decision: Negative tests and non-determinism. In: 18th ACM Conference on Computer and Communications Security, CCS 2011 (2011)

22. Cheval, V.: Apte: an algorithm for proving trace equivalence. In: Ábrahám, E., Havelund, K. (eds.) TACAS 2014. LNCS, vol. 8413, pp. 587–592. Springer, Heidelberg (2014)

23. Cheval, V., Blanchet, B.: Proving more observational equivalences with proverif. In: Basin, D., Mitchell, J.C. (eds.) POST 2013. LNCS, vol. 7796, pp. 226–246. Springer, Heidelberg (2013)

24. Cheval, V., Cortier, V., Plet, A.: Lengths may break privacy – or how to check for equivalences with length. In: Sharygina, N., Veith, H. (eds.) CAV 2013. LNCS, vol. 8044, pp. 708–723. Springer, Heidelberg (2013)

25. Chothia, T., Smirnov, V.: A traceability attack against e-passports. In: Sion, R. (ed.) FC 2010. LNCS, vol. 6052, pp. 20–34. Springer, Heidelberg (2010)

26. Cohen, E.: Taps: A first-order verifier for cryptographic protocols. In: 13th IEEE Computer Security Foundations Workshop (CSFW 2000). IEEE Computer Society Press, Los Alamitos (2000)

27. Comon-Lundh, H., Cortier, V.: Computational soundness of observational equivalence. In: 15th Conf. on Computer and Communications Security, CCS 2008 (2008)

28. Cortier, V., Delaune, S.: Decidability and combination results for two notions of knowledge in security protocols. Journal of Automated Reasoning, 48 (2012)

29. Delaune, S., Kremer, S., Ryan, M.D.: Verifying privacy-type properties of electronic voting protocols. Journal of Computer Security (4), 435–487 (2008)

30. Evans, N., Schneider, S.: Analysing time dependent security properties in CSP using PVS. In: Cuppens, F., Deswarte, Y., Gollmann, D., Waidner, M. (eds.) ESORICS 2000. LNCS, vol. 1895, pp. 222–237. Springer, Heidelberg (2000)

31. Gorrieri, R., Locatelli, E., Martinelli, F.: A simple language for real-time cryptographic protocol analysis. In: Degano, P. (ed.) ESOP 2003. LNCS, vol. 2618, pp. 114–128. Springer, Heidelberg (2003)

32. Jakubowska, G., Penczek, W.: Modelling and checking timed authentication of security protocols. Fundamenta Informaticae, 363–378 (2007)

33. Käsper, E., Schwabe, P.: Faster and timing-attack resistant aes-gcm. In: Clavier, C., Gaj, K. (eds.) CHES 2009. LNCS, vol. 5747, pp. 1–17. Springer, Heidelberg (2009)

34. Kocher, P.C.: Timing attacks on implementations of diffie-hellman, RSA, DSS, and other systems. In: Koblitz, N. (ed.) CRYPTO 1996. LNCS, vol. 1109, pp. 104–113. Springer, Heidelberg (1996)

35. Köpf, B., Basin, D.: An information-theoretic model for adaptive side-channel attacks. In: 14th ACM Conf. on Computer and Communications Security, CCS 2007 (2007)

36. Molnar, D., Piotrowski, M., Schultz, D., Wagner, D.: The program counter security model: Automatic detection and removal of control-flow side channel attacks. In: Won, D.H., Kim, S. (eds.) ICISC 2005. LNCS, vol. 3935, pp. 156–168. Springer, Heidelberg (2006)

37. Phan, Q.-S., Malacaria, P., Tkachuk, O., Pasareanu, C.S.: Symbolic quantitative information flow. ACM SIGSOFT Software Engineering Notes (2012)

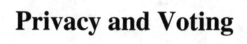

Privacy and Voting

Type-Based Verification of Electronic Voting Protocols

Véronique Cortier[1], Fabienne Eigner[2], Steve Kremer[1],
Matteo Maffei[2], and Cyrille Wiedling[3]

[1] LORIA, CNRS & INRIA & University of Lorraine, France
[2] CISPA, Saarland University, Germany
[3] Université Catholique de Louvain, Belgium

Abstract. E-voting protocols aim at achieving a wide range of sophisticated security properties and, consequently, commonly employ advanced cryptographic primitives. This makes their design as well as rigorous analysis quite challenging. As a matter of fact, existing automated analysis techniques, which are mostly based on automated theorem provers, are inadequate to deal with commonly used cryptographic primitives, such as homomorphic encryption and mix-nets, as well as some fundamental security properties, such as verifiability.

This work presents a novel approach based on refinement type systems for the automated analysis of e-voting protocols. Specifically, we design a generically applicable logical theory which, based on pre- and post-conditions for security-critical code, captures and guides the type-checker towards the verification of two fundamental properties of e-voting protocols, namely, vote privacy and verifiability. We further develop a code-based cryptographic abstraction of the cryptographic primitives commonly used in e-voting protocols, showing how to make the underlying algebraic properties accessible to automated verification through logical refinements. Finally, we demonstrate the effectiveness of our approach by developing the first automated analysis of Helios, a popular web-based e-voting protocol, using an off-the-shelf type-checker.

1 Introduction

Cryptographic protocols are notoriously difficult to design and their manual security analysis is extremely complicated and error-prone. As a matter of fact, security vulnerabilities have accompanied early academic protocols like Needham-Schroeder [49] as well as carefully designed de facto standards like SSL [56], PKCS #11 [18], and the SAML-based Single Sign-On for Google Apps [4]. E-voting protocols are particularly tricky, since they aim at achieving sophisticated security properties, such as verifiability and coercion-resistance, and, consequently, employ advanced cryptographic primitives such as homomorphic encryptions, mix-nets, and zero-knowledge proofs. Not surprisingly, this makes the attack surface even larger, as witnessed by the number of attacks on e-voting protocols proposed in the literature (see e.g., [36,30,45]).

This state of affairs has motivated a substantial research effort on the formal analysis of cryptographic protocols, which over the years has led to the development of several automated tools based on symbolic abstractions of cryptography. *Automated theorem provers* build on a term-based abstraction of cryptography and proved successful in the enforcement of various trace properties [16,6,9,33] and even observational

© Springer-Verlag Berlin Heidelberg 2015
R. Focardi and A. Myers (Eds.): POST 2015, LNCS 9036, pp. 303–323, 2015.
DOI: 10.1007/978-3-662-46666-7_16

equivalence relations [17,25,26]. While some of these tools have also been used in the context of e-voting [43,8,53,3], they fall short of supporting the cryptographic primitives and security properties specific of this setting. For instance, none of them supports the commutativity property of homomorphic encryption that is commonly exploited to compute the final tally in a privacy-preserving manner (e.g., [27,32,2]), and the proof of complex properties like verifiability or coercion-resistance must be complemented by manual proofs [34,53] or encodings [8] respectively, which are tedious and error-prone.

Another line of research has focused on the design of *type systems* for cryptographic protocol analysis. Refinement type systems, in particular, allow for tracking pre- and post-conditions on security-sensitive code, and thus enforcing various trace properties, such as authentication [40,23,24,19,20,5,37], classical authorization policies [7,14,10], and linear authorization policies [21,22]. Type systems proved capable to enforce even observational equivalence relations, such as secrecy [38], relational properties [55], and differential privacy [35]. Type systems are to some extent less precise than theorem provers and are not suitable to automatically report attacks, in that they do not explicitly compute abstractions of execution traces, but they are modular and therefore scale better to large-scale protocols. Furthermore, by building on a code-based, as opposed to term-based, abstraction of cryptography, they enable reasoning about sophisticated cryptographic schemes [38,10]. Although they look promising, type systems have never been used in the context of e-voting protocols. This task is challenging since, for guiding the type-checking procedure, one needs to develop a dedicated logical theory, capturing the structure of e-voting systems and the associated security and privacy properties.

Our Contributions. We devise a novel approach based on refinement type systems for the formal verification of e-voting protocols. Specifically,

- we design a generically applicable logical theory based on pre- and post-conditions for security-critical code, which captures and guides the type-checker towards the verification of two fundamental properties, namely, vote privacy and verifiability;
- we formalize in particular three different verifiability properties (i.e., individual, universal, and end-to-end verifiability), proving for the first time that individual verifiability plus universal verifiability imply end-to-end verifiability, provided that ballots cannot be confused (no-clash property [45]);
- we develop a code-based cryptographic abstraction of the cryptographic primitives commonly used in e-voting protocols, including homomorphic encryption, showing how to make its commutativity and associativity properties accessible to automated verification through logical refinements;
- we demonstrate the effectiveness of our approach by analyzing Helios [2], a popular, state-of-the-art, voting protocol that has been used in several real-scale elections, including elections at Louvain-la-Neuve, Princeton, and among the IACR [41]. We analyze the two main versions of Helios that respectively use homomorphic encryption and mix-net based tally. For this we use F* [55], an off-the-shelf type-checker supporting the verification of trace properties and observational equivalence relations, as required for verifiability and vote privacy, through refinement and relational types, respectively. Analyzing Helios with homomorphic encryption was out of reach of existing tools due to the need of a theory that reflects the addition of the

votes. A strength of our approach is that proof obligations involving such theories can be directly discharged to SMT solvers such as Z3 [51].

Related Work. Many symbolic protocol verification techniques have been applied to analyze e-voting systems [43,8,34,53,44,30,31,3]. In all of these works, the cryptographic primitives are modeled using terms and an equational theory, as opposed to the code-based abstractions we use in this paper. While code-based abstractions of cryptography may look at a first glance more idealized than the modeling using equational theories, they are actually closer to ideal functionalities in simulation-based cryptographic frameworks. Although a formal computational soundness result is out of the scope of this work, the code-based abstractions we use are rather standard and computational soundness results for similar abstractions have been proven in [12,38].

One of the main advantages of symbolic protocol verification is the potential for automation. However, current automated protocol verification tools are not yet mature enough to analyze most voting protocols. Firstly, existing tools do not support equational theories modeling homomorphic encryption. Thus, existing analyses of systems that rely on homomorphic tallying all rely on hand proofs [30,31,44], which are complicated and error-prone due to the complexity of the equational theories. Secondly, most current automated tools offer only limited support for verifying equivalence properties, which is required for verifying vote privacy. For instance, in [8] the analysis of Civitas using ProVerif relies on manual encodings and many other works, even though the equational theory is in the scope of the tools, again rely on hand proofs of observational equivalences [43,34]. Although some recent tools, such as AKiSs [25] succeed in analyzing simple protocols such as [39], more complicated protocols are still out of reach. In [3], the privacy of the mix-net based version of Helios was shown using AKiSs, but mix-nets were idealized by simply outputting the decrypted votes in a non-deterministic order. In contrast, our model manipulates lists to express the fact that a mix-net produces a permutation. ProVerif was used to check some cases of verifiability [53], but automation is only supported for protocols without a homomorphic tally.

Other work on e-voting protocols considers definitions of privacy [46,15] and verifiability [42,47,29] in computational models. However, no computer aided verification techniques have yet been applied in this context. Furthermore, prior work [48] demonstrated that individual and universal verifiability in general do not imply end-to-end verifiability, not even by assuming the no-clash property, using as an example the Three-Ballot voting system [52]. In this paper, we show on the contrary that individual and universal verifiability do imply end-to-end verifiability. This is due to the fact that our individual verifiability notion is actually stronger and assumes that the board can be uniquely parsed as a list of ballots. This is the case for many voting systems but not for ThreeBallot where each ballot is split into three components.

2   Background

We review the fundamental concepts underlying the typed-based analysis of security protocols and we present the Helios e-voting protocol that constitutes our case study.

2.1   Refinement Types for Cryptographic Protocols

Computational RCF. The protocols we analyze are implemented in Computational RCF et al. [38], a λ-calculus with references, assumptions, and assertions. We briefly review below the syntax and semantics of the language, referring to the long version [28] for more details. Constructors, ranged over by h, include inl and inr, which are used to construct tagged unions, and fold, which is used to construct recursive data structures. Values, ranged over by M, N, comprise variables x, y, z, the unit value (), pairs (M, N), constructor applications $h\ M$, functions fun $x \rightarrow A$, and functions read_a and write_a to read from and write to a memory location a, respectively. The syntax and semantics of expressions are mostly standard. $M\ N$ behaves as $A\{N/x\}$ (i.e., A where x is replaced by N) if $M = \text{fun } x \rightarrow A$, otherwise it gets stuck; let $x = A$ in B evaluates A to M and then behaves as $B\{M/x\}$; let $(x, y) = M$ in A behaves as $A\{N/x, N'/y\}$ if $M = (N, N')$, otherwise it gets stuck; match M with $h\ x$ then A else B behaves as $A\{N/x\}$ if $M = h\ N$, as B otherwise; ref M allocates a fresh label a and returns the reading and writing functions $(\text{read}_a, \text{write}_a)$. The code is decorated with assumptions assume F and assertions assert F. The former introduce logical formulas that are assumed to hold at a given program point, while the latter specify logical formulas that are expected to be entailed by the previously introduced assumptions.

Definition 1 (Safety). *A closed expression A is safe iff the formulas asserted at runtime are logically entailed by the previously assumed formulas.*

The code is organized in *modules*, which are intuitively a sequence of function declarations. A module may export some of the functions defined therein, which can then be used by other modules: we let $B \cdot A$ denote the composition of modules B and A, where the functions exported by B may be used in A.

Types and Typing Judgements. Table 1 shows the syntax of types. Types bool for boolean values and bytes for bitstrings can be constructed from unit by encoding[1]. The singleton unit type is populated by the value (); $\mu\alpha.T$ describes values of the form fold M, where M has the unfolded type $T\{\mu\alpha.T/\alpha\}$; $T + U$ describes values of the form inl M or inr M, where M has type T or U, respectively; the dependent type $x : T * U$ describes pairs of values (M, N), where M has type T and N has type $U\{M/x\}$; the dependent type $x : T \rightarrow U$ describes functions taking as input a value M of type T and returning a value of type $U\{M/x\}$; the dependent refinement type $x : T\{F\}$ describes values M of type T such that the logical formula $F\{M/x\}$ is entailed by the active assumptions. Notice that a refinement on the input of a function expresses a pre-condition, while a refinement on the output expresses a post-condition.

The typing judgement $I \vdash A : T$ says that expression A can be typed with type T in a typing environment I. Intuitively, a typing environment binds the free variables and labels in A to a type. The typing judgement $I \vdash B \rightsquigarrow I'$ says that under environment I module B is well-typed and exports the typed interface I'.

Modeling the Protocol and the Opponent. The protocol is encoded as a module, which exports functions defining the cryptographic library as well as the protocol parties. The latter are modeled as cascaded functions, which take as input the messages

---

[1] E.g., boolean values are encoded as true $\triangleq$ inl () and false $\triangleq$ inr ().

Table 1. Syntax of types

$T, U, V ::=$		type
	unit	unit type
	α	type variable
	$\mu\alpha.T$	iso-recursive type (α bound in τ)
	$T + U$	sum type
	$x : T * U$	dependent pair type (x bound in U)
	$x : T \rightarrow U$	dependent function type (x bound in U)
	$x : T\{F\}$	dependent refinement type (x bound in F)

received from the network and return the pair composed of the value to be output on the network and the continuation code [2]. Concurrent communication is modeled by letting the opponent, which has access to the exported functions, act as a scheduler.

Modeling the Cryptographic Library. We rely on a sealing-based abstraction of cryptography [50,54]. A seal for a type T consists of a pair of functions: the sealing function of type $T \rightarrow$ bytes and the unsealing function of type bytes $\rightarrow T$. The sealing mechanism is implemented by storing a list of pairs in a global reference that can only be accessed using the sealing and unsealing functions. The sealing function pairs the payload with a fresh, public value (the handle) representing its sealed version, and stores the pair in the list. The unsealing function looks up the public handle in the list and returns the associated payload. For symmetric cryptography, the sealing and unsealing functions are both private and naturally model encryption and decryption keys, respectively: a payload of type T is sealed to type bytes and can be sent over the untrusted network, while a message retrieved from the network with type bytes can be unsealed to its correct type T. Different cryptographic primitives, like public key encryptions and signature schemes, can be encoded in a similar way, by exporting the function modeling the public key to the opponent. We will give further insides on how to build sealing-based abstractions for more sophisticated cryptographic primitives, such as homomorphic encryptions and proofs of knowledge in Section 4.

Type-Based Verification. Assumptions and assertions can be used to express a variety of trace-based security properties. For instance, consider the very simple e-voting protocol below, which allows everyone in possession of the signing key k_V, shared by all eligible voters, to cast arbitrarily many votes.

$$V \qquad\qquad\qquad\qquad\qquad T$$

$$\text{assume Cast}(v)$$

$$\text{sign}(k_V, v) \qquad\qquad\qquad >$$

$$\text{assert Count}(v)$$

The assumption $\text{Cast}(v)$ on the voter's side tracks the intention to cast vote v. The authorization policy $\forall v.\text{Cast}(v) \Rightarrow \text{Count}(v)$, which is further defined in the system as a global assumption expresses the fact that all votes cast by eligible voters should be counted. Since this is the only rule entailing $\text{Count}(v)$, this rule actually captures a correspondence assertion: votes can be counted only if they come from eligible voters.

---

[2] For the sake of readability we use the standard message-passing-style syntax in our examples and some additional syntactic sugar (e,g., sequential let declarations) that are easy to encode.

The assertion assert Count(v) on the tallying authority's side expresses the expectation that vote v should be counted.

In order to type-check the code of authority T, it suffices to prove Cast(v) on the authority's side, which entails Count(v) through the authorization policy. Since the type-checking algorithm is modular (i.e., each party is independently analyzed) and Cast(v) is assumed on the voter's side, this formula needs to be conveyed to T. This is achieved by giving the vote v the *refinement type* x : bytes{Cast(x)}. In order to type v on the voter's side with such a type, v needs to be of type bytes and additionally, the formula Cast(v) needs to be entailed by the previous assumptions, which is indeed true in this case. In our sealing-based library for signatures signing corresponds to sealing a value and verification is modeled using the unsealing function and thus the types of signing and verification are sigkey(T) $\triangleq$ T $\to$ bytes and verkey(T) $\triangleq$ bytes $\to$ T, while the types of the signing and verification functions are sig : sigkey(T) $\to$ T $\to$ bytes and ver : verkey(T) $\to$ bytes $\to$ T, respectively.[3] Here T is x : bytes{Cast(x)}, thereby imposing a pre-condition on the signing function (before signing x, one has to assume the formula Cast(x)) and a post-condition on the verification function (after a successful verification, the formula Cast(x) is guaranteed to hold for the signed x).

When reasoning about the implementations of cryptographic protocols, we are interested in the safety of the protocol against an arbitrary opponent.

Definition 2 (Opponent and Robust Safety). *A closed expression O is an opponent iff O contains no assumptions or assertions. A closed module A is robustly safe w.r.t. interface I iff for all opponents O such that $I \vdash O : T$ for some type T, $A \cdot O$ is safe.*

Following the approach advocated in [38], the typed interface I exported to the opponent is supposed to build exclusively on the type bytes, without any refinement. This means that the attacker is not restricted by any means and can do whatever it wants with the messages received from the network, except for performing invalid operations that would lead it to be stuck (e.g., treating a pair as a function). In fact, the well-typedness assumption for the opponent just makes sure that the only free variables occurring therein are the ones exported by the protocol module. Robust safety can be statically enforced by type-checking, as stated below.

Theorem 1 (Robust Safety). *If $\emptyset \vdash A \rightsquigarrow I$ then A is robustly safe w.r.t. I.*

2.2 Helios

Helios [2] is a verifiable and privacy-preserving e-voting system. It has been used in several real-life elections such that student elections at the University of Louvain-la-Neuve or at Princeton. It is now used by the IACR to elect its board since 2011 [41]. The current implementation of Helios (Helios 2.0) is based on homomorphic encryption, which makes it possible to decrypt only the aggregation of the ballots as opposed

---

[3] We note that the verification function only takes the signature as an input, checks whether it is indeed a valid signature and if so, retrieves the corresponding message that was signed. This is a standard abstraction and used for convenience, an alternate approach would be to have verification take both the signature and message as an input and return a boolean value. The sealing-based library functions for both versions are very similar.

to the individual ballots. Homomorphic tally, however, requires encrypted ballots to be split in several ciphertexts, depending on the number of candidates. For example, in case of 4 candidates and a vote for the second one, the encrypted ballot would be $\{0\}_{\mathsf{pk}}^{r_1}, \{1\}_{\mathsf{pk}}^{r_2}, \{0\}_{\mathsf{pk}}^{r_3}, \{0\}_{\mathsf{pk}}^{r_4}$. In case the number of candidates is high, the size of a ballot and the computation time become large. Therefore, there exists a variant of Helios that supports mix-net-based tally: ballots are shuffled and re-randomized before being decrypted. Both variants co-exist since they both offer advantages: mix-nets can cope with a large voting space while homomorphic tally eases the decryption phase (only one ballot needs to be decrypted, no need of mixers). We present here both variants of Helios, which constitute our case studies. For simplicity, in the case of homomorphic tally, we assume that voters are voting either 0 or 1 (referendum).

The voting process in Helios is divided in two main phases. The bulletin board is a public webpage that starts initially empty. Votes are encrypted using a public key pk. The corresponding decryption key dk is shared among trustees. For privacy, the trust assumption is that at least one trustee is honest (or that the trustees do not collaborate).

Voting Phase. During the voting phase, each voter encrypts her vote v using the public key pk of the election. She then sends her encrypted vote $\{v\}_{\mathsf{pk}}^{r}$ (where r denotes the randomness used for encrypting), together with some auxiliary data aux, to the bulletin board through an authenticated channel. In the homomorphic version of Helios, aux contains a zero-knowledge proof that the vote is valid, that is 0 or 1. This avoids that a voter gives e.g. 100 votes to a candidate. In the mix-net variant of Helios, aux is empty. Provided that the voter is entitled to vote, the bulletin board adds the ballot $\{v\}_{\mathsf{pk}}^{r}$, aux to the public list. The voter should check that her ballot indeed appears on the public bulletin board.

The voter's behavior is described in Figure 1. It corresponds to the mix-net version but could be easily adapted to the homomorphic version. Note that this description contains assume and assert annotations that intuitively represent different states of the voter's process. These annotations are crucially used to state verifiability, cf Section 3.

The voting phase also includes an optional audit phase allowing the voter to audit her ballot instead of casting it. In that case, her ballot and the corresponding randomness are sent to a third party that checks whether the correct choice has been encrypted. We do not model here the auditing phase, since a precise characterization would probably require probabilistic reasoning, which goes beyond the scope of this paper.

Tallying Phase. Once the voting phase is over, the bulletin board contains a list of ballots $\{v_1\}_{\mathsf{pk}}^{r_1}, \ldots, \{v_n\}_{\mathsf{pk}}^{r_n}$ (we omit the auxiliary data). We distinguish the two variants.
- *Homomorphic tally.* The ballots on the bulletin board are first homomorphically combined. Since $\{v\}_{\mathsf{pk}}^{r} * \{v'\}_{\mathsf{pk}}^{r'} = \{v + v'\}_{\mathsf{pk}}^{r+r'}$ anyone can compute the encrypted sum of the votes $\{\sum_{i=1}^{n} v_i\}_{\mathsf{pk}}^{r*}$. Then the trustees collaborate to decrypt this ciphertext. Their computation yields $\sum_{i=1}^{n} v_i$ and a proof of correct decryption.
- *Mix-net tally.* Ballots are shuffled and re-randomized, yielding $\{v_{i_1}\}_{\mathsf{pk}}^{r'_1}, \ldots, \{v_{i_n}\}_{\mathsf{pk}}^{r'_n}$ with a proof of correct permutation. This mixing is performed successively by several mixers. For privacy, the trust assumption is that as least one mix-net is honest (that is, will not leak the permutation). Then the trustees collaborate to decrypt each (re-randomize) ciphertext and provide a corresponding proof of correct decryption.

$$\begin{aligned}
\text{Voter}(id, v) = \; &\text{assume Vote}(id, v); && \text{send(net}, b); \\
&\text{let } r = \text{new() in} && \text{let } bb = \text{recv(net) in} \\
&\text{let } b = \text{enc(pk}, v, r) \text{ in} && \text{if } b \in bb \text{ then} \\
&\text{assume MyBallot}(id, v, b); && \text{assert VHappy}(id, v, bb)
\end{aligned}$$

Fig. 1. Modeling of a voter

3   Verifiability

Verifiability is a key property in both electronic as well as paper-based voting systems. Intuitively, verifiability ensures that the announced result corresponds to the votes such as intended by the voters. Verifiability is typically split into several sub-properties.

- *Individual verifiability* ensures that a voter is able to check that her ballot is on the bulletin board.
- *Universal verifiability* ensures that any observer can verify that the announced result corresponds to the (valid) ballots published on the bulletin board.

Symbolic models provide a precise definition of these notions [44].

The overall goal of these two notions is to guarantee *end-to-end verifiability*: if a voter correctly follows the election process her vote is counted in the final result. In our terminology, *strong end-to-end verifiability* additionally guarantees that at most k dishonest votes have been counted, where k is the number of compromised voters. This notion of strong end-to-end verifiability includes the notion of what is called *eligibility verifiability* in [44]. For simplicity, we focus here on end-to-end verifiability.

We will now explain our modeling of individual, universal, and end-to-end verifiability. One of our contributions is a logical formalization of these properties that enables the use of off-the-shelf verification techniques, in our case a type system, at least in the case of individual and universal verifiability. End-to-end verifiability may be more difficult to type-check directly. Instead, we formally prove for the first time that individual and universal verifiability entail end-to-end verifiability provided that there are no "clash attacks" [45]. A clash attack typically arises when two voters are both convinced that the same ballot b is "their" own ballot. In that case, only one vote will be counted instead of two. The fact that individual and universal verifiability entail end-to-end verifiability has two main advantages. First, it provides a convenient proof technique: it is sufficient to prove individual and universal verifiability, which as we will show can be done with the help of a type-checker. Second, our results provide a better understanding of the relation between the different notions of verifiability.

Notations. Before presenting our formal model of verifiability we introduce a few notations. Voting protocols aim at counting the votes. Formally, a *counting function* is a function $\rho : \mathbb{V}^* \to R$, where $\mathbb{V}$ is the vote space and R the result space. A typical voting function is the number of votes received by each candidate. By a slight abuse of notation, we may consider $\rho(l)$ where l is a list of votes instead of a sequence of votes.

If l is a list, $\#l$ denotes the size of l and $l[i]$ refers to the ith element of the list. $a \in l$ holds if a is an element of l. Given $a_1, \ldots, a_n$, we denote by $\{\!| a_1, \ldots, a_n |\!\}$ the corresponding multiset. $\subseteq_m$ denotes multiset inclusion. Assume l_1, l_2 are lists; by a slight abuse of notation, we may write $l_1 \subseteq_m l_2$ where l_1, l_2 are viewed as multisets. We also write $l_1 =_m l_2$ if the two lists have the same multisets of elements.

In order to express verifiability and enforce it using a type system, we rely on the following assumptions:

- assume $\mathsf{Vote}(id, v, c)$ means that voter id intends to vote for c possibly using some credential c. This predicate should hold as soon as the voter starts to vote: he knows for whom he is going to vote.
- assume $\mathsf{MyBallot}(id, v, b)$ means that voter id thinks that ballot b contains her vote v. In case votes are sent in clear, b is simply the vote v itself. In the case of Helios, we have $b = \{v\}_{\mathsf{pk}}^{r}, \mathsf{aux}$. Typically, this predicate should hold as soon as the voter (or her computer) has computed the ballot.

An example of where and how to place these predicates for Helios can be found in Figure 1. The credential c is omitted since there is no use of credentials in Helios.

3.1   Individual Verifiability

Intuitively, individual verifiability enforces that whenever a voter completes her process successfully, her ballot is indeed in the ballot box. Formally we define the predicate VHappy as follows:

$$\text{assume } \mathsf{VHappy}(id, v, c, bb) \Leftrightarrow \mathsf{Vote}(id, v, c) \wedge \exists b \in bb. \mathsf{MyBallot}(id, v, b)$$

This predicate should hold whenever voter id has finished her voting process, and believes she has voted for v. At that point, it should be the case that the ballot box bb contains the vote v (in some ballot). We therefore annotate the voter function with the assertion assert $\mathsf{VHappy}(id, v, c, bb)$. This annotation is generally the final instruction, see Figure 1 for the Helios example.

Definition 3 (Individual Verifiability). *A protocol with security annotations*
- *assume* $\mathsf{Vote}(id, v, c)$, *assume* $\mathsf{MyBallot}(id, v, b)$;
- *and* assert $\mathsf{VHappy}(id, v, c, bb)$
as described above guarantees individual verifiability *if it is robustly safe.*

3.2   Universal Verifiability

Intuitively, universal verifiability guarantees that anyone can check that the result corresponds to the ballots present in the ballot box. Formally, we assume a program $\mathsf{Judge}(bb, r)$ that checks whether the result r is valid w.r.t. ballot box bb. Typically, Judge does not use any secret and could therefore be executed by anyone. We simply suppose that Judge contains assert $\mathsf{JHappy}(bb, r)$ at some point, typically when all the verification checks succeed. For Helios, the Judge program is displayed Figure 2. We first introduce a few additional predicates that we use to define the predicate JHappy.

Good Sanitization. Once the voting phase is closed, the tallying phase proceeds in two main phases. First, some "cleaning" operation is performed in bb, e.g., invalid ballots (if any) are removed and duplicates are weeded, resulting in the sanitized valid bulletin board vbb. Intuitively, a good cleaning function should not remove ballots that correspond to honest votes. We therefore define the predicate $\mathsf{GoodSan}(bb, vbb)$ to hold if the honest ballots of bb are not removed from vbb.

$$\text{assume } \mathsf{GoodSan}(bb, vbb) \Leftrightarrow \forall b.[(b \in bb \wedge \exists id, v.\mathsf{MyBallot}(id, v, b)) \Rightarrow b \in vbb]$$

$$\begin{aligned}
&\mathsf{Judge}(bb, r) = \mathsf{let}\ vbb = \mathsf{recv}(\mathsf{net})\ \mathsf{in} \\
&\quad \mathsf{let}\ zkp = \mathsf{recv}(\mathsf{net})\ \mathsf{in} \\
&\quad \mathsf{if}\ vbb = \mathsf{removeDuplicates}(bb) \wedge \mathsf{check\_zkp}(zkp, vbb, r)\ \mathsf{then} \\
&\quad \mathsf{assert}\ \mathsf{JHappy}(bb, r)
\end{aligned}$$

Fig. 2. Judge function for Helios

Good Counting. Once the ballot box has been sanitized, ballots are ready to be tallied. A good tallying function should count the votes "contained" in the ballots. To formally define that a vote is "contained" in a ballot, we consider a predicate $\mathsf{Wrap}(v, b)$ that is left undefined, but has to satisfy the following properties:

- any well-formed ballot b corresponding to some vote v satisfies:
  $\mathsf{MyBallot}(id, v, b) \Rightarrow \mathsf{Wrap}(v, b)$
- a ballot cannot wrap two distinct votes: $\mathsf{Wrap}(v_1, b) \wedge \mathsf{Wrap}(v_2, b) \Rightarrow v_1 = v_2$

If these two properties are satisfied, we say that Wrap is *voting-compliant*. For a given protocol, the definition Wrap typically follows from the protocol specification.

Example 1. In the Helios protocol, the Wrap predicate is defined as follows.

$$\mathsf{assume}\ \mathsf{Wrap}(v, b) \Leftrightarrow \exists r.\ \mathsf{Enc}(v, r, \mathsf{pk}, b)$$

where $\mathsf{Enc}(v, r, \mathsf{pk}, b)$ is a predicate that holds if b is the result of the encryption function called with parameters pk, v and r. It is easy to see that Wrap is voting-compliant and this can in fact be proved using a type-checker. It is sufficient to add the annotations

- assert $\mathsf{MyBallot}(id, v, b) \Rightarrow \mathsf{Wrap}(v, b)$ and
- assert $\forall v_1, v_2.\ \mathsf{Wrap}(v_1, b) \wedge \mathsf{Wrap}(v_2, b) \Rightarrow v_1 = v_2$

to the voter function (Figure 1) just after the MyBallot assumption. The second assertion is actually a direct consequence of our modeling of encryption which implies that a ciphertext cannot decrypt to two different plaintexts.

We are now ready to state when votes have been correctly counted: the result should correspond to the counting function ρ applied to the votes contained in each ballot. Formally, we define $\mathsf{GoodCount}(vbb, r)$ to hold if the result r corresponds to counting the votes of $rlist$, i.e., the list of votes obtained from the ballots in vbb'. The list vbb' is introduced for technical convenience and either denotes the list of valid votes vbb itself (in the homomorphic variant) or any arbitrary permutation of vbb (for mix-nets).

$$\begin{aligned}
\mathsf{assume}\ \mathsf{GoodCount}(vbb, r) \Leftrightarrow \exists vbb', rlist.\ [\ &\#vbb = \#rlist \wedge vbb =_m vbb' \wedge \\
&\forall b, i.[vbb'[i] = b \\
&\Rightarrow \exists v.(\mathsf{Wrap}(v, b) \wedge (rlist[i] = v))] \wedge \\
&r = \rho(rlist)\ ]
\end{aligned}$$

Note that the definition of $\mathsf{GoodCount}$ is parameterized by the counting function ρ of the protocol under consideration. We emphasize that for $\mathsf{GoodCount}(vbb, r)$ to hold, the sanitized bulletin board may only contain correctly wrapped ballots, i.e., we assume that the sanitization procedure is able to discard invalid ballots. In the case of mix-net-based Helios we therefore require that the sanitization discards any ballots that do not decrypt. This can for instance be achieved by requiring a zero knowledge proof that the submitted bitstring is a correct ciphertext. We may however allow that a ballot decrypts to an invalid vote, as such votes can be discarded by the tallying function.

Universal Verifiability. Finally, universal verifiability enforces that whenever the verification checks succeed (that is, the Judge's program reaches the JHappy assertion), then GoodSan and GoodCount should be guaranteed. Formally, we define the predicate

$$\text{assume JHappy}(bb, r) \Leftrightarrow \exists vbb. \ (\text{GoodSan}(bb, vbb) \ \wedge \ \text{GoodCount}(vbb, r))$$

and add the annotation assert JHappy(bb, r) at the end of the judge function.

Definition 4 (Universal Verifiability). *A protocol with security annotations*
- assume MyBallot(id, v, b), *and*
- assert JHappy(bb, r)

as described above guarantees universal verifiability *if it is robustly safe and the predicate* Wrap(v, b) *is voting-compliant.*

3.3 End-to-End Verifiability

End-to-end verifiability is somehow simpler to express. End-to-end verifiability ensures that whenever the result is valid (that is, the judge has reached his final state), the result contains at least all the votes of the voters that have reached their final states. In other words, voters that followed the procedure are guaranteed that their vote is counted in the final result. To formalize this idea we define the predicate EndToEnd as follows:

$$\text{assume EndToEnd} \Leftrightarrow \forall bb, r, id_1, \ldots, id_n, v_1, \ldots, v_n, c_1, \ldots, c_n.$$
$$(\text{JHappy}(bb, r) \wedge \text{VHappy}(id_1, v_1, c_1, bb) \wedge \ldots \wedge \text{VHappy}(id_n, v_n, c_n, bb))$$
$$\Rightarrow \exists rlist. \ r = \rho(rlist) \wedge \{v_1, \ldots, v_n\} \subseteq_m rlist$$

To ensure that this predicate holds we can again add a final assertion assert EndToEnd.

Definition 5 (End-to-End Verifiability). *A protocol with security annotations*
- assume Vote(id, v, c), assume MyBallot(id, v, b);
- *and* assert VHappy(id, v, c, bb), assert JHappy(bb, r), assert EndToEnd

as described above guarantees end-to-end verifiability *if it is robustly safe.*

For simplicity, we have stated end-to-end verifiability referring explicitly to a bulletin board. It is however easy to state our definition more generally by letting bb be any form of state of the protocol. This more general definition does not assume a particular structure of the protocol, as it is also the case in a previous definitions of end-to-end verifiability in the literature [47].

It can be difficult to directly prove end-to-end verifiability using a type-checker. An alternative solution is to show that it is a consequence of individual and universal verifiability. However, it turns out that individual and universal verifiability are actually not sufficient to ensure end-to-end verifiability. Indeed, assume that two voters id_1 and id_2 are voting for the same candidate v. Assume moreover that they have built the same ballot b. In case of Helios, this could be the case if voters are using a bad randomness generator. Then a malicious bulletin board could notice that the two ballots are identical and could display only one of the two. The two voters would still be "happy" (they can see their ballot on the bulletin board) as well as the judge since the tally would correspond to the bulletin board. However, only one vote for v would be counted instead of two. Such a scenario has been called a clash attack [45].

We capture this property by the predicate NoClash defined as follows.

$$\text{NoClash} \Leftrightarrow \forall id_1, id_2, v_1, v_2, b. \text{MyBallot}(id_1, v_1, b) \land \text{MyBallot}(id_2, v_2, b)$$
$$\Rightarrow id_1 = id_2 \land v_1 = v_2$$

The assertion assert NoClash is then added after the assumption MyBallot.

Definition 6 (No Clash). *A protocol with security annotations*
- assume MyBallot(id, v, b) *and*
- assert NoClash

as described above guarantees no clash *if it is robustly safe.*

We can now state our result (proved in the long version [28]) that no clash, individual, and universal verifiability entail end-to-end verifiability.

Theorem 2. *If a protocol guarantees individual and universal verifiability as well as no clash, then it satisfies end-to-end verifiability.*

3.4   Verifiability Analysis of Helios

Using the F* type-checker (version 0.7.1-alpha) we have analyzed both the mix-net and homomorphic versions of Helios. The corresponding files can be found in [1]. The (simplified) model of the voter and judge functions is displayed in Figures 1 and 2.

Helios with Mix-Nets. Using F*, we automatically proved both individual and universal verifiability. As usual, we had to manually define the types of the functions, which crucially rely on refinement types to express the expected pre- and post-conditions. For example, for universal verifiability, one has to show that GoodSan and GoodCount hold whenever the judge agrees with the tally. For sanitization, the judge verifies that vbb is a sublist of bb, where duplicate ballots have been removed. Thus, the type-checker can check that the function removeDuplicates(bb) returns a list vbb whose type is a refinement stating that $x \in bb \Rightarrow x \in vbb$, which allows us to prove GoodSan. Regarding GoodCount, the judge verifies a zero-knowledge proof that ensures that any vote in the final result corresponds to an encryption on the sanitized bulletin board. Looking at the type of the check_zkp function we see that this information is again conveyed through a refinement of the boolean type returned by the function:

$$\text{check\_zkp} : zkp : \text{bytes} \rightarrow vbb : \text{list ballot} \rightarrow res : \text{result} \rightarrow b : \text{bool}\{b = \text{true} \Rightarrow \varphi\}$$

$$\text{where } \varphi \triangleq \exists vbb'. [\ \#vbb = \#res \ \land \ vbb =_m vbb' \ \land$$
$$\forall b, i.[vbb'[i] = b \Rightarrow \exists v, r.(\text{Enc}(v, r, \text{pk}, b) \ \land \ (res[i] = v))] \ ]$$

In the case where check_zkp returns true we have that the formula φ holds. The formula φ is similar to the GoodCount predicate (with ρ being the identity function for mix-net based Helios) except that it ensures that a ballot is an encryption, rather than a wrap. This indeed reflects that the zero-knowledge proof used in the protocol provides exactly the necessary information to the judge to conclude that the counting was done correctly.

The *no clash* property straightforwardly follows from observing that the logical predicate MyBallot(id, v, b) is assumed only once in the voter's code, that each voter has a distinct id, and that, as argued for Wrap(v, b), the same ciphertext cannot decrypt to two different plaintexts. By Theorem 2, we can conclude that the mix-net version of Helios indeed satisfies end-to-end verifiability.

Type-checkers typically support lists with the respective functions (length, membership test, etc.). As a consequence, we prove individual and universal verifiability *for an arbitrary number of dishonest voters*, while only a fixed number of dishonest voters can typically be considered with other existing protocol verification tools.

Helios with Homomorphic Tally. The main difference with the mix-net version is that each ballot additionally contains a zero-knowledge proof, that ensures that the ballot is an encryption of either 0 or 1. The judge function also differs in the tests it performs. In particular, to check that the counting was performed correctly, the judge verifies a zero-knowledge proof that ensures that the result is the sum of the encrypted votes that are on the sanitized bulletin board. This ensures in turn that the result corresponds to the sum of the votes. Considering the "sum of the votes" is out of reach of classical automated protocol verification tools. Here, F* simply discharges the proof obligations involving the integer addition to the Z3 solver [51] which is used as a back-end.

Finally, as for the mix-net based version, we proved individual and universal verifiability using F*, while the *no clash* property relies on (the same) manual reasoning. Again, we conclude that end-to-end verifiability is satisfied using Theorem 2.

4 Privacy

The secrecy of a ballot is of vital importance to ensure that the political views of a voter are not known to anyone. Vote privacy is thus considered a fundamental and universal right in modern democracies.

In this section we review the definition of vote privacy based on observational equivalence [34] and present a type-based analysis technique to verify this property using RF*, an off-the-shelf type-checker. We demonstrate the usefulness of our approach by analyzing vote privacy in the homomorphic variant of Helios, which was considered so far out of the scope of automated verification techniques.

4.1 Definition of Privacy

Observational Equivalence. We first introduce the concept of observational equivalence, a central tool to capture indistinguishability properties. The idea is that two runs of the same program with different secrets should be indistinguishable for any opponent. The definition is similar to the natural adaption of the one presented in [38] to a deterministic, as opposed to probabilistic, setting.

Definition 7 (Observational Equivalence). *For all modules A, B we say that A and B are observationally equivalent, written $A \approx B$, iff they both export the same interface I and and for all opponents O that are well-typed w.r.t the interface I it holds that $A \cdot O \to^* M$ iff $B \cdot O \to^* M$ for all closed values M.*

Here, $A \rightarrow^* N$ denotes that expression A eventually evaluates to value N, according to the semantic reduction relation.

Privacy. We adopt the definition of vote privacy presented in [43]. This property ensures that the link between a voter and her vote is kept secret. Intuitively, in the case of a referendum this can only be achieved if at least two honest voters exist, since otherwise all dishonest voters could determine the single honest voter's vote from the final tally by colluding. Furthermore, both voters must vote for different parties, thus counter-balancing each other's vote and ensuring that it is not known who voted for whom. Our definition of privacy thus assumes the existence of two honest voters Alice and Bob and two candidates v_1 and v_2. We say that a voting system guarantees privacy if a protocol run in which Alice votes v_1 and Bob votes v_2 is indistinguishable (i.e., observationally equivalent) from the protocol run in which Alice votes v_2 and Bob votes v_1.

In the following, we assume the voting protocol to be defined as fun $(v_A, v_B) \rightarrow$ S[Alice(v_A), Bob(v_B)]. The two honest voters Alice and Bob are parameterized over their votes v_A and v_B. Here, S[•, •] describes a two-hole context (i.e., an expression with two holes), which models the behavior of the cryptographic library, the public bulletin board, and the election authorities (i.e., the surrounding system).

Definition 8 (Vote Privacy). $P =$ fun $(v_A, v_B) \rightarrow$ S[Alice(v_A), Bob(v_B)] *guarantees vote privacy iff for any two votes* v_1, v_2 *it holds that* $P(v_1, v_2) \approx P(v_2, v_1)$.

4.2   RF*: A Type System for Observational Equivalence Properties

To prove privacy for voting protocols we rely on RF*, an off-the-shelf existing type-checker that can be used to enforce indistinguishability properties. RF* was introduced by Barthe et al. [13] and constitutes the relational extension of the F* type-checker [55]. The core idea is to let refinements reason about two runs (as opposed to a single one) of a protocol. Such refinements are called *relational refinements*. A relational refinement type has the form $x : T\{|F|\}$, where the formula F may capture the instantiation of x in the left run of the expression that is to be type-checked, denoted L x, as well as the instantiation of x in the right run, denoted R x. Formally, $A : x : T\{|F|\}$ means that whenever A evaluates to M_L and M_R in two contexts that provide well-typed substitutions for the free variables in A, then the formula $F\{M_L/_{\text{L } x}\}\{M_R/_{\text{R } x}\}$ is valid. We note that relational refinements are strictly more expressive than standard refinements. For instance, $x :$ bytes$\{H(x)\}$ can be encoded as $x :$ bytes$\{|H(\text{L } x) \wedge H(\text{R } x)|\}$. A special instance of relational refinement types is the so-called *eq-type*. Eq-types specify that a variable is instantiated to the same value in both the left and the right protocol run. Formally, eq $T \triangleq x : T\{|\text{L } x = \text{R } x|\}$. The authors show how such types can be effectively used to verify both non-interference and indistinguishability properties.

4.3   Type-Based Verification of Vote Privacy

In the following, we show how to leverage the aforementioned technique to statically enforce observational equivalence and, in particular, vote privacy. The key observation is that whenever a value M is of type eq bytes it can safely be published, i.e., given to the opponent. Intuitively, this is the case since in both protocol runs, this value will be

Alice $v_A =$
let $b_A = $ create_ballot$_A(v_A)$ in
send(c_A, b_A)

Bob $v_B =$
let $b_B = $ create_ballot$_B(v_B)$ in
send(c_B, b_B)

Fig. 3. Model of Alice   **Fig. 4.** Model of Bob

the same, i.e., the opponent will not be able to observe any difference. Given that both runs consider the same opponent O, every value produced by the opponent must thus also be the same in both runs, which means it can be typed with eq bytes.

We denote typed interfaces that solely build on eq bytes by I_{eq} and following the above intuition state that if a voting protocol can be typed with such an interface, the two runs where (i) Alice votes v_1, Bob votes v_2 and (ii) Alice votes v_2, Bob votes v_1 are observationally equivalent, since no opponent will be able to distinguish them.

Theorem 3 (Privacy by Typing). *For all* $P = $ fun $(v_A, v_B) \rightarrow S[\text{Alice}(v_A), \text{Bob}(v_B)]$ *and all* M, M', v_1, v_2 *such that* $M : x : $ bytes$\{\!| L\ x = v_1 \wedge R\ x = v_2 |\!\}$ *and* $M' : x :$ bytes$\{\!| L\ x = v_2 \wedge R\ x = v_1 |\!\}$ *it holds that if* $\emptyset \vdash P(M, M') \rightsquigarrow I_{eq}$, *then* P *provides vote privacy.*

Modeling a Protocol for Privacy Verification. We demonstrate our approach on the example of Helios with homomorphic encryption. For simplicity, we consider one ballot box that owns the decryption key dk and does the complete tabulation. An informal description of Alice and Bob's behavior is displayed in Figures 3 and 4, respectively. The voters produce the relationally refined ballots using the ballot creation functions create_ballot$_A$, create_ballot$_B$ respectively. The ballots b_A, b_B consist of the randomized homomorphic encryption of the votes and a zero-knowledge proof of correctness and knowledge of the encrypted vote. The ballots are then sent to the ballot box over secure https-connections c_A and c_B respectively.

The behavior of the ballot box is described in Figure 5. For the sake of simplicity, we consider the case of three voters. The ballot box receives the ballots of Alice and Bob and publishes them on the bulletin board. It then receives the ballot of the opponent and checks that the proofs of validity of all received ballots succeed. Furthermore, it checks that all ballots are distinct before performing homomorphic addition on the ciphertexts. The sum of the ciphertexts is then decrypted and published on the bulletin board.

Intuitively, all outputs on the network are of type eq bytes, since (i) all ballots are the result of an encryption that keeps the payload secret and thus gives the opponent no distinguishing capabilities, and (ii) the homomorphic sum of all ciphertexts $b_{ABO} = \{v_A + v_B + v_O\}_{pk}$ is the same in both runs of the protocol up to commutativity. Indeed, L $b_{ABO} = \{v_1 + v_2 + v_O\}_{pk}$ and R $b_{ABO} = \{v_2 + v_1 + v_O\}_{pk} = $ L b_{ABO}.

However, since the application of the commutativity rule happens on the level of plaintexts, while the homomorphic addition is done one level higher-up on ciphertexts, we need to guide the type-checker in the verification process.

Sealing-Based Library for Voting. While privacy is per se not defined by logical predicates, we rely on some assumptions to describe properties of the cryptographic library, such as homomorphism and validity of payloads, in order to guide the type-checker in

BB $\doteq$ let $b_A = \text{recv}(c_A)$ in   match check_zkp(b_B) with true then
        let $b_B = \text{recv}(c_B)$ in   match check_zkp(b_O) with true then
        send(net, (b_A, b_B));   match $(b_A \neq b_O \wedge b_A \neq b_B \wedge b_B \neq b_O)$ with true then
        let $b_O = \text{recv}(\text{net})$ in   let $b_{AB} = \text{add\_ballot}(b_A, b_B)$ in
        if check_zkp(b_A) true then   let $b_{ABO} = \text{add\_ballot}(b_{AB}, b_O)$ in
                                                                              let $result = \text{dec\_ballot}(b_{ABO})$ in
                                                                              send(net, $result$)

Fig. 5. Model of the ballot box

the derivation of eq-types. The (simplified) type of the sealing reference for homomorphic encryption with proofs of validity is given below:[4]

$$m : \text{bytes} * c : \text{eq bytes}\{|\text{Enc}(m, c) \wedge \text{Valid}(c) \wedge$$
$$(\text{FromA}(c) \vee \text{FromB}(c) \vee (\text{FromO}(c) \wedge \text{L } m = \text{R } m))|\}$$

Here, predicates FromA, FromB, FromO are used to specify whether an encryption was done by Alice, Bob or the opponent, while $\text{Enc}(m, c)$ states that c is the ciphertext resulting from encrypting m and $\text{Valid}(c)$ reflects the fact that the message corresponds to a valid vote, i.e., a validity proof for c can be constructed. Note that if a ballot was constructed by the opponent, the message stored therein must be the same in both runs (L m = R m), i.e., the message must have been of type eq bytes. These logical predicates are assumed in the sealing functions used by Alice, Bob, and the opponent, respectively. These functions, used to encode the public key, share the same code, and in particular they access the same reference, and only differ in the internal assumptions.

Similarly, there exist three ballot creation functions create_ballot$_A$, create_ballot$_B$, and create_ballot$_O$, used by Alice, Bob and the opponent, respectively, only differing in their refinements and internal assumptions. Their interfaces are listed below:

$$\text{create\_ballot}_A : m : x : \text{bytes}\{|\text{L } x = v_1 \wedge \text{R } x = v_2|\} \rightarrow$$
$$c : \text{eq bytes}\{|\text{Enc}(m, c) \wedge \text{FromA}(c)|\}$$
$$\text{create\_ballot}_B : m : x : \text{bytes}\{|\text{L } x = v_2 \wedge \text{R } x = v_1|\} \rightarrow$$
$$c : \text{eq bytes}\{|\text{Enc}(m, c) \wedge \text{FromB}(c)|\}$$
$$\text{create\_ballot}_O : = \text{eq bytes} \rightarrow \text{eq bytes}$$

Notice that, as originally proposed in [13], the result of probabilistic encryption (i.e., the ballot creation function) is given an eq bytes type, reflecting the intuition that there always exist two randomnesses, which are picked with equal probability, that make the ciphertexts obtained by encrypting two different plaintexts identical, i.e., probabilistic encryption does not leak any information about the plaintext.

The interfaces for the functions dec_ballot, check_zkp, add_ballot for decryption, validity checking of the proofs, and homomorphic addition are listed below. The public interfaces for the latter two functions, built only on eq-types, are exported to the opponent. The interface for decryption is however only exported to the ballot box.

---

[4] The actual library includes *marshaling* operations, which we omit for simplicity.

dec_ballot : c : eq bytes $\rightarrow$ privkey $\rightarrow m$: bytes$\{\!|\forall z.\mathsf{Enc}(z, c) \Rightarrow z = m|\!\}$
check_zkp : c : eq bytes $\rightarrow b$: bool$\{\!| b = \mathsf{true} \Rightarrow (\mathsf{Valid}(c) \wedge (\exists m.\mathsf{Enc}(m, c)) \wedge$
$\qquad\qquad\qquad\qquad (\mathsf{FromA}(c) \vee \mathsf{FromB}(c) \vee (\mathsf{FromO}(c) \wedge \mathsf{L}\ m = \mathsf{R}\ m)))|\!\}$
add_ballot : c : eq bytes $\rightarrow c'$: eq bytes $\rightarrow$
$\qquad\qquad c''$: eq bytes$\{\!|\forall m, m'.(\mathsf{Enc}(m, c) \wedge \mathsf{Enc}(m', c')) \Rightarrow \mathsf{Enc}(m + m', c'')|\!\}$

Intuitively, the type returned by decryption assures that the decryption of the ciphertext corresponds to the encrypted message. The successful application of the validity check on ballot c proves that the ballot is a valid encryption of either v_1 or v_2 and that it must come from either Alice, Bob, or the opponent. In the latter case it must be the same in both runs. When homomorphically adding two ciphertexts, the refinement of function add_ballot guarantees that the returned ciphertext contains the sum of the two. The implementation of dec_ballot is standard and consists of the application of the unsealing function. The implementation of check_zkp follows the approach proposed in [10,11]: in particular, the zero-knowledge proof check function internally decrypts the ciphertexts and then checks the validity of the vote, returning a boolean value. Finally, the add_ballot homomorphic addition function is implemented in a similar manner, internally decrypting the two ciphertexts and returning a fresh encryption of the sum of the two plaintexts.

Global Assumptions. In order to type-check the complete protocol we furthermore rely on three natural assumptions:
- A single ciphertext only corresponds to one plaintext, i.e., decryption is a function:
    assume $\forall m, m', c.(\mathsf{Enc}(m, c) \wedge \mathsf{Enc}(m', c)) \Rightarrow m = m'$
- Alice and Bob only vote once:
    assume $\forall c, c'.(\mathsf{FromA}(c) \wedge \mathsf{FromA}(c')) \Rightarrow c = c'$
    assume $\forall c, c'.(\mathsf{FromB}(c) \wedge \mathsf{FromB}(c')) \Rightarrow c = c'$

Modeling revoting would require a bit more work. Revoting requires some policy that explains which ballot is counted, typically the last received one. In that case, we would introduce two types depending on whether the ballot is really the final one (there is a unique final one) or not.

4.4   Privacy Analysis of Helios

Using the RF* type-checker (version 0.7.1-alpha) we have proved privacy for the homomorphic version of Helios. The corresponding files can be found in [1]. Our implementation builds on the above defined cryptographic library and global assumptions as well as Alice, Bob, and the ballot box BB as defined in the previous section.

We briefly give the intuition why the final tally $result = \mathsf{dec\_ballot}(b_{ABO})$ can be typed with type eq bytes, i.e., why both runs return the same value by explaining the typing of the ballot box BB.
- The ballots b_A, b_B, b_O that are received by the ballot box must have the following types (by definition of the corresponding ballot creation functions):

$$b_A : c : \text{eq bytes}\{\!|\mathsf{Enc}(v_A, b_A) \wedge \mathsf{FromA}(b_A)|\!\}$$
$$b_B : c : \text{eq bytes}\{\!|\mathsf{Enc}(v_B, b_B) \wedge \mathsf{FromB}(b_B)|\!\}$$
$$b_O : \text{eq bytes}$$

- Adding b_A and b_B together using add_ballot thus yields that the content of the combined ciphertext corresponds to $v_A + v_B$ and in particular, due to commutativity, this sum is the same in both protocol runs.
- The most significant effort is required to show that the payload v_O contained in b_O is indeed of type eq bytes, i.e., $L\ v_O = R\ v_O$, meaning the sum of $v_A + v_B + v_O$ is the same in both runs. Intuitively, the proof works as follows: From checking the proof of b_O it follows that there exists v_O such that $\mathsf{Enc}(v_O, b_O) \wedge (\mathsf{FromA}(b_O) \vee \mathsf{FromB}(b_O) \vee (\mathsf{FromO}(b_O) \wedge L\ v_O = R\ v_O))$. From checking the distinctness of the ciphertexts we furthermore know that $b_A \neq b_O \neq b_C$. Given $\mathsf{FromA}(b_A)$ and $\mathsf{FromB}(b_B)$, the second and third global assumptions imply that neither $\mathsf{FromA}(b_O)$ nor $\mathsf{FromB}(b_O)$ hold true. Thus, it must be the case that $\mathsf{FromO}(b_O) \wedge L\ v_O = R\ v_O$.

5   Conclusion

In this paper we proposed a novel approach, based on type-checking, for analyzing e-voting systems. It is based on a novel logical theory which allows to verify both verifiability and vote privacy, two fundamental properties of election systems. We were able to put this theory into practice and use an off-the-shelf type-checker to analyze the mix-net-, as well as homomorphic tallying-based versions of Helios, resulting in the first automated verification of Helios with homomorphic encryption. Indeed, the fact that the type-checker can discharge proof obligations on the algebraic properties of homomorphic encryption to an external solver is one of the strengths of this approach. Providing the right typing annotations constitutes the only manual effort required by our approach: in our analysis this was, however, quite modest, in our analysis, thanks to the support for type inference offered by RF*.

As a next step we are planning to extend our theory to handle *strong* end-to-end verifiability, which additionally takes the notion of eligibility verifiability into account. This stronger notion is not satisfied by Helios, but the Helios-C protocol [29] was designed to achieve this property, providing an interesting case study for our approach.

We also plan to apply our approach to the e-voting protocol recently deployed in Norway for a political election. The privacy of this protocol was analyzed in [31], but due to the algebraic properties of the encryption, the proof was completely done by hand. Our approach looks promising to enable automation of proofs for this protocol.

Acknowledgements. This work was supported by the German research foundation (DFG) through the Emmy Noether program, the German Federal Ministry of Education and Research (BMBF) through the Center for IT-Security, Privacy and Accountability (CISPA), the European Research Council under the EU 7th Framework Programme (FP7/2007-2013) / ERC grant agreement no 258865 and the ANR project Sequoia ANR-14-CE28-0030-01.

References

1. http://sps.cs.uni-saarland.de/voting
2. Adida, B.: Helios: Web-based Open-Audit Voting. In: USENIX 2008, pp. 335–348 (2008)

3. Arapinis, M., Cortier, V., Kremer, S., Ryan, M.D.: Practical Everlasting Privacy. In: POST 2013, pp. 21–40 (2013)
4. Armando, A., Carbone, R., Compagna, L., Cuellar, J., Tobarra, L.: Formal analysis of SAML 2.0 web browser single sign-on: breaking the SAML-based single sign-on for Google Apps. In: FMSE 2008, pp. 1–10 (2008)
5. Backes, M., Cortesi, A., Focardi, R., Maffei, M.: A calculus of challenges and responses. In: FMSE 2007, pp. 51–60 (2007)
6. Backes, M., Cortesi, A., Maffei, M.: Causality-based abstraction of multiplicity in security protocols. In: CSF 2007, pp. 355–369 (2007)
7. Backes, M., Grochulla, M.P., Hritcu, C., Maffei, M.: Achieving security despite compromise using zero-knowledge. In: CSF 2009, pp. 308–323 (2009)
8. Backes, M., Hriţcu, C., Maffei, M.: Automated Verification of Remote Electronic Voting Protocols in the Applied Pi-calculus. In: CSF 2008, pp. 195–209 (2008)
9. Backes, M., Lorenz, S., Maffei, M., Pecina, K.: The CASPA Tool: Causality-Based Abstraction for Security Protocol Analysis. In: Gupta, A., Malik, S. (eds.) CAV 2008. LNCS, vol. 5123, pp. 419–422. Springer, Heidelberg (2008)
10. Backes, M., Hriţcu, C., Maffei, M.: Union and Intersection Types for Secure Protocol Implementations. In: Mödersheim, S., Palamidessi, C. (eds.) TOSCA 2011. LNCS, vol. 6993, pp. 1–28. Springer, Heidelberg (2012)
11. Backes, M., Maffei, M., Hriţcu, C.: Union and Intersection Types for Secure Protocol Implementations. JCS, 301–353 (2014)
12. Backes, M., Maffei, M., Unruh, D.: Computationally Sound Verification of Source Code. In: CCS 2010, pp. 387–398 (2010)
13. Barthe, G., Fournet, C., Grégoire, B., Strub, P., Swamy, N., Béguelin, S.Z.: Probabilistic Relational Verification for Cryptographic Implementations. In: POPL 2014, pp. 193–206 (2014)
14. Bengtson, J., Bhargavan, K., Fournet, C., Gordon, A.D., Maffeis, S.: Refinement Types for Secure Implementations. TOPLAS 33(2), 8 (2011)
15. Bernhard, D., Cortier, V., Pereira, O., Smyth, B., Warinschi, B.: Adapting Helios for provable ballot secrecy. In: Atluri, V., Diaz, C. (eds.) ESORICS 2011. LNCS, vol. 6879, pp. 335–354. Springer, Heidelberg (2011)
16. Blanchet, B.: An Efficient Cryptographic Protocol Verifier Based on Prolog Rules. In: CSFW 2001, pp. 82–96 (2001)
17. Blanchet, B., Abadi, M., Fournet, C.: Automated Verification of Selected Equivalences for Security Protocols. JLAP 75(1), 3–51 (2008)
18. Bortolozzo, M., Centenaro, M., Focardi, R., Steel, G.: Attacking and Fixing PKCS#11 Security Tokens. In: CCS 2010, pp. 260–269 (2010)
19. Bugliesi, M., Focardi, R., Maffei, M.: Analysis of typed-based analyses of authentication protocols. In: CSFW 2005, pp. 112–125. IEEE (2005)
20. Bugliesi, M., Focardi, R., Maffei, M.: Dynamic types for authentication. JCS 15(6), 563–617 (2007)
21. Bugliesi, M., Calzavara, S., Eigner, F., Maffei, M.: Resource-aware Authorization Policies in Statically Typed Cryptographic Protocols. In: CSF 2011, pp. 83–98 (2011)
22. Bugliesi, M., Calzavara, S., Eigner, F., Maffei, M.: Logical Foundations of Secure Resource Management in Protocol Implementations. In: Basin, D., Mitchell, J.C. (eds.) POST 2013. LNCS, vol. 7796, pp. 105–125. Springer, Heidelberg (2013)
23. Bugliesi, M., Focardi, R., Maffei, M.: Principles for entity authentication. In: Broy, M., Zamulin, A.V. (eds.) PSI 2003. LNCS, vol. 2890, pp. 294–306. Springer, Heidelberg (2003)
24. Bugliesi, M., Focardi, R., Maffei, M.: Authenticity by tagging and typing. In: FMSE 2004, pp. 1–12 (2004)

25. Chadha, R., Ciobâcă, Ş., Kremer, S.: Automated verification of equivalence properties of cryptographic protocols. In: ESOP 2012, pp. 108–127 (2012)

26. Cheval, V.: APTE: an Algorithm for Proving Trace Equivalence. In: Ábrahám, E., Havelund, K. (eds.) TACAS 2014. LNCS, vol. 8413, pp. 587–592. Springer, Heidelberg (2014)

27. Cohen, J.D., Fischer, M.J.: A Robust and Verifiable Cryptographically Secure Election Scheme. In: FOCS 1985, pp. 372–382 (1985)

28. Cortier, V., Eigner, F., Kremer, S., Maffei, M., Wiedling, C.: Type-Based Verification of Electronic Voting Protocols. Cryptology ePrint Archive, Report 2015/039 (2015)

29. Cortier, V., Galindo, D., Glondu, S., Izabachène, M.: Election Verifiability for Helios under Weaker Trust Assumptions. In: Kutyłowski, M., Vaidya, J. (eds.) ICAIS 2014, Part II. LNCS, vol. 8713, pp. 327–344. Springer, Heidelberg (2014)

30. Cortier, V., Smyth, B.: Attacking and fixing Helios: An analysis of ballot secrecy. In: CSF 2011, pp. 297–311 (2011)

31. Cortier, V., Wiedling, C.: A formal analysis of the Norwegian E-voting protocol. In: POST 2012, pp. 109–128 (2012)

32. Cramer, R., Gennaro, R., Schoenmakers, B.: A Secure and Optimally Efficient Multi-Authority Election Scheme. In: Fumy, W. (ed.) EUROCRYPT 1997. LNCS, vol. 1233, pp. 103–118. Springer, Heidelberg (1997)

33. Cremers, C.: The Scyther Tool: Verification, Falsification, and Analysis of Security Protocols. In: CAV 2008, pp. 414–418 (2008)

34. Delaune, S., Kremer, S., Ryan, M.D.: Verifying privacy-type properties of electronic voting protocols. JCS 17(4), 435–487 (2009)

35. Eigner, F., Maffei, M.: Differential Privacy by Typing in Security Protocols. In: CSF 2013, pp. 272–286. IEEE (2013)

36. Estehghari, S., Desmedt, Y.: Exploiting the Client Vulnerabilities in Internet E-voting Systems: Hacking Helios 2.0 as an Example. In: EVT/WOTE 2010 (2010)

37. Focardi, R., Maffei, M.: Types for security protocols. In: Formal Models and Techniques for Analyzing Security Protocols. IOS (2011)

38. Fournet, C., Kohlweiss, M., Strub, P.: Modular Code-Based Cryptographic Verification. In: CCS 2011, pp. 341–350 (2011)

39. Fujioka, A., Okamoto, T., Ohta, K.: A Practical Secret Voting Scheme for Large Scale Elections. In: Zheng, Y., Seberry, J. (eds.) AUSCRYPT 1992. LNCS, vol. 718, pp. 244–251. Springer, Heidelberg (1993)

40. Gordon, A.D., Jeffrey, A.: Types and effects for asymmetric cryptographic protocols. JCS 12(3), 435–484 (2004)

41. IACR. Elections page at http://www.siacr.org/elections/

42. Juels, A., Catalano, D., Jakobsson, M.: Coercion-Resistant Electronic Elections. In: Chaum, D., Jakobsson, M., Rivest, R.L., Ryan, P.Y.A., Benaloh, J., Kutylowski, M., Adida, B. (eds.) Towards Trustworthy Elections. LNCS, vol. 6000, pp. 37–63. Springer, Heidelberg (2010)

43. Kremer, S., Ryan, M.D.: Analysis of an Electronic Voting Protocol in the Applied Pi Calculus. In: Sagiv, M. (ed.) ESOP 2005. LNCS, vol. 3444, pp. 186–200. Springer, Heidelberg (2005)

44. Kremer, S., Ryan, M., Smyth, B.: Election verifiability in electronic voting protocols. In: Gritzalis, D., Preneel, B., Theoharidou, M. (eds.) ESORICS 2010. LNCS, vol. 6345, pp. 389–404. Springer, Heidelberg (2010)

45. Küsters, R., Truderung, T., Vogt, A.: Clash Attacks on the Verifiability of E-Voting Systems. In: S&P 2012, pp. 395–409 (2012)

46. Küsters, R., Truderung, T., Vogt, A.: A Game-Based Definition of Coercion-Resistance and its Applications. In: CSF 2010, pp. 122–136 (2010)

47. Küsters, R., Truderung, T., Vogt, A.: Accountabiliy: Definition and Relationship to Verifiability. In: CCS 2010, pp. 526–535 (2010)

48. Küsters, R., Truderung, T., Vogt, A.: Verifiability, Privacy, and Coercion-Resistance: New Insights from a Case Study. In: S&P 2011, pp. 538–553 (2011)
49. Lowe, G.: Breaking and Fixing the Needham-Schroeder Public-Key Protocol using FDR. In: Margaria, T., Steffen, B. (eds.) TACAS 1996. LNCS, vol. 1055, pp. 147–166. Springer, Heidelberg (1996)
50. Morris, J.: Protection in Programming Languages. CACM 16(1), 15–21 (1973)
51. de Moura, L., Bjørner, N.: Z3: An efficient SMT solver. In: Ramakrishnan, C.R., Rehof, J. (eds.) TACAS 2008. LNCS, vol. 4963, pp. 337–340. Springer, Heidelberg (2008)
52. Rivest, R.L.: The threeballot voting system, unpublished draft (2006)
53. Smyth, B., Ryan, M., Kremer, S., Kourjieh, M.: Towards automatic analysis of election verifiability properties. In: Armando, A., Lowe, G. (eds.) ARSPA-WITS 2010. LNCS, vol. 6186, pp. 146–163. Springer, Heidelberg (2010)
54. Sumii, E., Pierce, B.: A Bisimulation for Dynamic Sealing. TCS 375(1-3), 169–192 (2007)
55. Swamy, N., Chen, J., Fournet, C., Strub, P.Y., Bhargavan, K., Yang, J.: Secure Distributed Programming with Value-Dependent Types. In: ICFP 2011, pp. 266–278 (2011)
56. Wagner, D., Schneier, B.: Analysis of the SSL 3.0 protocol. In: USENIX Workshop on Electronic Commerce, pp. 29–40 (1996)

Composing Security Protocols: From Confidentiality to Privacy[*]

Myrto Arapinis[1], Vincent Cheval[2,3], and Stéphanie Delaune[4]

[1] School of Informatics, University of Edinburgh, UK
[2] LORIA, CNRS, France
[3] School of Computing, University of Kent, UK
[4] LSV, CNRS & ENS Cachan, France

Abstract. Security protocols are used in many of our daily-life applications, and our privacy largely depends on their design. Formal verification techniques have proved their usefulness to analyse these protocols, but they become so complex that modular techniques have to be developed. We propose several results to safely compose security protocols. We consider arbitrary primitives modeled using an equational theory, and a rich process algebra close to the applied pi calculus.

Relying on these composition results, we derive some security properties on a protocol from the security analysis performed on each of its sub-protocols individually. We consider parallel composition and the case of key-exchange protocols. Our results apply to deal with confidentiality but also privacy-type properties (*e.g.* anonymity) expressed using a notion of equivalence. We illustrate the usefulness of our composition results on protocols from the 3G phone application and electronic passport.

1 Introduction

Privacy means that one can control when, where, and how information about oneself is used and by whom, and it is actually an important issue in many modern applications. For instance, nowadays, it is possible to wave an electronic ticket, a building access card, a government-issued ID, or even a smartphone in front of a reader to go through a gate, or to pay for some purchase. Unfortunately, as often reported by the media, this technology also makes it possible for anyone to capture some of our personal information. To secure the applications mentioned above and to protect our privacy, some specific cryptographic protocols are deployed. For instance, the 3G telecommunication application allows one to send SMS encrypted with a key that is established with the *AKA* protocol [2]. The aim of this design is to provide some security guarantees: *e.g.* the SMS exchanged between phones should remain confidential from third parties.

Since security protocols are notoriously difficult to design and analyse, formal verification techniques are important. These techniques have become mature and

[*] The research leading to these results has received funding from the project ProSecure (ERC grant agreement $n°$ 258865), and the ANR project VIP $n°$ 11 JS02 006 01.

© Springer-Verlag Berlin Heidelberg 2015
R. Focardi and A. Myers (Eds.): POST 2015, LNCS 9036, pp. 324–343, 2015.
DOI: 10.1007/978-3-662-46666-7_17

have achieved success. For instance, a flaw has been discovered in the Single-Sign-On protocol used by Google Apps [6], and several verification tools are nowadays available (e.g. ProVerif [9], the AVANTSSAR platform [7]). These tools perform well in practice, at least for standard security properties (e.g. secrecy, authentication). Regarding privacy properties, the techniques and tools are more recent. Most of the verification techniques are only able to analyse a bounded number of sessions and consider a quite restrictive class of protocols (e.g. [18]). A different approach consists in analysing a stronger notion of equivalence, namely diff-equivalence. In particular, ProVerif implements a semi-decision procedure for checking diff-equivalence [9].

Security protocols used in practice are more and more complex and it is difficult to analyse them altogether. For example, the UMTS standard [2] specifies tens of sub-protocols running concurrently in 3G phone systems. While one may hope to verify each protocol in isolation, it is however unrealistic to expect that the whole application will be checked relying on a unique automatic tool. Existing tools have their own specificities that prevent them to be used in some cases. Furthermore, most of the techniques do not scale up well on large systems, and sometimes the ultimate solution is to rely on a manual proof. It is therefore important that the protocol under study is as small as possible.

Related Work. There are many results studying the composition of security protocols in the symbolic model [15,13,12], as well as in the computational model [8,16] in which the so-called UC (universal composability) framework has been first developed before being adapted in the symbolic setting [10]. Our result belongs to the first approach. Most of the existing composition results are concerned with trace-based security properties, and in most cases only with secrecy (stated as a reachability property), e.g. [15,13,12,14]. They are quite restricted in terms of the class of protocols that can be composed, e.g. a fixed set of cryptographic primitives and/or no else branch. Lastly, they often only consider parallel composition. Some notable exceptions are the results presented in [17,14,12]. This paper is clearly inspired from the approach developed in [12].

Regarding privacy-type properties, very few composition results exist. In a previous work [4], we considered parallel composition only. More precisely, we identified sufficient conditions under which protocols can "safely" be executed in parallel as long as they have been proved secure in isolation. This composition theorem was quite general from the point of view of the cryptographic primitives allowed. We considered arbitrary primitives that can be modelled by a set of equations, and protocols may share some standard primitives provided they are tagged differently. We choose to reuse this quite general setting in this work, but our goal is now to go beyond parallel composition. We want to extend the composition theorem stated in [4] to allow a modular analysis of protocols that use other protocols as sub-programs as it happens in key-exchange protocols.

Our Contributions. Our main goal is to analyse privacy-type properties in a modular way. These security properties are usually expressed as equivalences between processes. Roughly, two processes P and Q are equivalent ($P \approx Q$) if, however they behave, the messages observed by the attacker are indistinguishable. Actually, it is well-known that:

$$\text{if } P_1 \approx P_2 \text{ and } Q_1 \approx Q_2 \text{ then } P_1 \mid P_2 \approx Q_1 \mid Q_2.$$

However, this parallel composition result works because the processes that are composed are disjoint (*e.g.* they share no key). In this paper, we want to go beyond parallel composition which was already considered in [4]. In particular, we want to capture the case where a protocol uses a sub-protocol to establish some keys. To achieve this, we propose several theorems that state the conditions that need to be satisfied so that the security of the whole protocol can be derived from the security analysis performed on each sub-protocol in isolation. They are all derived from a generic composition result that allows one to map a trace of the composed protocol into a trace of the disjoint case (protocol where the sub-protocols do not share any data), and conversely. This generic result can be seen as an extension of the result presented in [12] where only a mapping from the shared case to the disjoint case is provided (but not the converse).

We also extend [12] by considering a richer process algebra. In particular, we are able to deal with protocols with else branches and to compose protocols that both rely on asymmetric primitives (*i.e.* asymmetric encryption and signature).

Outline. We present our calculus in Section 2. It can be seen as an extension of the applied pi calculus with an assignment construction. This will allow us to easily express the sharing of some data (*e.g.* session keys) between sub-protocols. In Section 3, we present a first composition result to deal with confidentiality properties. The purpose of this section is to review the difficulties that arise when composing security protocols even in a simple setting. In Section 4, we go beyond parallel composition, and we consider the case of key-exchange protocols. We present in Section 5 some additional difficulties that arise when we want to consider privacy-type properties expressed using trace equivalence. In Section 6, we present our composition results for privacy-type properties. We consider parallel composition as well as the case of key-exchange protocols. In Section 7, we illustrate the usefulness of our composition results on protocols from the 3G phone application, as well as on protocols from the e-passport application. We show how to derive some security guarantees from the analysis performed on each sub-protocol in isolation. The full version of this paper as well as the ProVerif models of our case studies can be found at http://www.loria.fr/~chevalvi/other/compo/.

2   Models for Security Protocols

Our calculus is close to the applied pi calculus [3]. We consider an assignment operation to make explicit the data that are shared among different processes.

2.1   Messages

As usual in this kind of models, messages are modelled using an abstract term algebra. We assume an infinite set of *names* $\mathcal{N}$ of *base type* (used for representing keys, nonces, ...) and a set $\mathcal{Ch}$ of names of *channel type*. We also consider a set of *variables* $\mathcal{X}$, and a signature Σ consisting of a finite set of *function symbols*. We rely on a sort system for terms. The details of the sort system are unimportant, as long as the base type differs from the channel type, and we suppose that function symbols only operate on and return terms of base type.

Terms are defined as names, variables, and function symbols applied to other terms. The set of terms built from $\mathsf{N} \subseteq \mathcal{N} \cup \mathcal{Ch}$, and $\mathsf{X} \subseteq \mathcal{X}$ by applying function symbols in Σ (respecting sorts and arities) is denoted by $\mathcal{T}(\Sigma, \mathsf{N} \cup \mathsf{X})$. We write $fv(u)$ (resp. $fn(u)$) for the set of variables (resp. names) occurring in a term u. A term u is *ground* if it does not contain any variable, *i.e.* $fv(u) = \emptyset$.

The algebraic properties of cryptographic primitives are specified by the means of an *equational theory* which is defined by a finite set E of equations $u = v$ with $u, v \in \mathcal{T}(\Sigma, \mathcal{X})$, *i.e.* u, v do not contain names. We denote by $=_\mathsf{E}$ the smallest equivalence relation on terms, that contains E and that is closed under application of function symbols and substitutions of terms for variables.

Example 1. Consider the signature $\Sigma_{\mathsf{DH}} = \{\mathsf{aenc}, \mathsf{adec}, \mathsf{pk}, \mathsf{g}, \mathsf{f}, \langle\ \rangle, \mathsf{proj}_1, \mathsf{proj}_2\}$. The function symbols $\mathsf{adec}, \mathsf{aenc}$ of arity 2 represent asymmetric decryption and encryption. We denote by $\mathsf{pk}(sk)$ the public key associated to the private key sk. The two function symbols f of arity 2, and g of arity 1 are used to model the Diffie-Hellman primitives, whereas the three remaining symbols are used to model pairs. The equational theory E_{DH} is defined by:

$$\mathsf{E}_{\mathsf{DH}} = \left\{ \begin{array}{ll} \mathsf{proj}_1(\langle x, y \rangle) = x & \mathsf{adec}(\mathsf{aenc}(x, \mathsf{pk}(y)), y) = x \\ \mathsf{proj}_2(\langle x, y \rangle) = y & \mathsf{f}(\mathsf{g}(x), y) = \mathsf{f}(\mathsf{g}(y), x) \end{array} \right.$$

Let $u_0 = \mathsf{aenc}(\langle n_A, \mathsf{g}(r_A) \rangle, \mathsf{pk}(sk_B))$. We have that:

$$\mathsf{f}(\mathsf{proj}_2(\mathsf{adec}(u_0, sk_B)), r_B) =_{\mathsf{E}_{\mathsf{DH}}} \mathsf{f}(\mathsf{g}(r_A), r_B) =_{\mathsf{E}_{\mathsf{DH}}} \mathsf{f}(\mathsf{g}(r_B), r_A).$$

2.2   Processes

As in the applied pi calculus, we consider *plain processes* as well as *extended processes* that represent processes having already evolved by *e.g.* disclosing some terms to the environment. *Plain processes* are defined by the following grammar:

$P, Q := 0$	null	$P \mid Q$	parallel
$\mathbf{new}\ n.P$	restriction	$!P$	replication
$[x := v].P$	assignment	$\mathbf{if}\ \varphi\ \mathbf{then}\ P\ \mathbf{else}\ Q$	conditional
$\mathbf{in}(c, x).P$	input	$\mathbf{out}(c, v).Q$	output

where c is a name of channel type, φ is a conjunction of tests of the form $u_1 = u_2$ where u_1, u_2 are terms of base type, x is a variable of base type, v is a term of base type, and n is a name of any type. We consider an assignment operation that instantiates x with a term v. Note that we consider private channels but we do not allow channel passing. For the sake of clarity, we often omit the null process, and when there is no "**else**", it means "**else** 0".

Names and variables have scopes, which are delimited by restrictions, inputs, and assignment operations. We write $fv(P)$, $bv(P)$, $fn(P)$ and $bn(P)$ for the sets of *free* and *bound variables*, and *free* and *bound names* of a plain process P.

Example 2. Let $P_{\mathsf{DH}} = \mathsf{new}\, sk_A.\mathsf{new}\, sk_B.(P_A \mid P_B)$ a process that models a Diffie-Hellman key exchange protocol:

- $P_A \stackrel{\text{def}}{=} \mathsf{new}\, r_A.\mathsf{new}\, n_A.\mathsf{out}(c, \mathsf{aenc}(\langle n_A, \mathsf{g}(r_A)\rangle, \mathsf{pk}(sk_B))).\mathsf{in}(c, y_A).$
  $\quad \mathsf{if}\ \mathsf{proj}_1(\mathsf{adec}(y_A, sk_A)) = n_A\ \mathsf{then}\ [x_A := \mathsf{f}(\mathsf{proj}_2(\mathsf{adec}(y_A, sk_A)), r_A)].0$
- $P_B \stackrel{\text{def}}{=} \mathsf{new}\, r_B.\mathsf{in}(c, y_B).\mathsf{out}(c, \mathsf{aenc}(\langle \mathsf{proj}_1(\mathsf{adec}(y_B, sk_B)), \mathsf{g}(r_B)\rangle, \mathsf{pk}(sk_A))).$
  $\qquad\qquad\qquad\qquad\qquad\qquad [x_B := \mathsf{f}(\mathsf{proj}_2(\mathsf{adec}(y_B, sk_B)), r_B)].0$

The process P_A generates two fresh random numbers r_A and n_A, sends a message on the channel c, and waits for a message containing the nonce n_A in order to compute his own view of the key that will be stored in x_A. The process P_B proceeds in a similar way and stores the computed value in x_B.

Extended processes add a set of restricted names $\mathcal{E}$ (the names that are *a priori* unknown to the attacker), a sequence of messages Φ (corresponding to the messages that have been sent so far on public channels) and a substitution σ which is used to store the messages that have been received as well as those that have been stored in assignment variables.

Definition 1. *An extended process is a tuple $(\mathcal{E}; \mathcal{P}; \Phi; \sigma)$ where $\mathcal{E}$ is a set of names that represents the names that are restricted in $\mathcal{P}$, Φ and σ; $\mathcal{P}$ is a multiset of plain processes where null processes are removed and such that $fv(\mathcal{P}) \subseteq \mathrm{dom}(\sigma)$; $\Phi = \{w_1 \rhd u_1, \ldots, w_n \rhd u_n\}$ and $\sigma = \{x_1 \mapsto v_1, \ldots, x_m \mapsto v_m\}$ are substitutions where $u_1, \ldots, u_n, v_1, \ldots, v_m$ are ground terms, and $w_1, \ldots, w_n, x_1, \ldots, x_m$ are variables.*

For the sake of simplicity, we assume that extended processes are *name and variable distinct*, *i.e.* a name (resp. variable) is either free or bound, and in the latter case, it is at most bound once. We write $(\mathcal{E}; \mathcal{P}; \Phi)$ instead of $(\mathcal{E}; P; \Phi; \emptyset)$.

The semantics is given by a set of labelled rules that allows one to reason about processes that interact with their environment (see Figure 1). This defines the relation $\xrightarrow{\ell}$ where ℓ is either an input, an output, or a silent action τ. The relation $\xrightarrow{\mathsf{tr}}$ where tr denotes a sequence of labels is defined in the usual way whereas the relation $\xRightarrow{\mathsf{tr}'}$ on processes is defined by: $A \xRightarrow{\mathsf{tr}'} B$ if, and only if, there exists a sequence tr such that $A \xrightarrow{\mathsf{tr}} B$ and tr' is obtained by erasing all occurrences of the silent action τ in tr.

Example 3. Let $\Phi_{\mathsf{DH}} \stackrel{\text{def}}{=} \{w_1 \rhd \mathsf{pk}(sk_A), w_2 \rhd \mathsf{pk}(sk_B)\}$. We have that:

$(\{sk_A, sk_B\}; P_A \mid P_B; \Phi_{\mathsf{DH}})$
$$\xrightarrow{\nu w_3.\mathsf{out}(c, w_3).\mathsf{in}(c, w_3).\nu w_4.\mathsf{out}(c, w_4).\mathsf{in}(c, w_4)} (\mathcal{E}; \emptyset; \Phi_{\mathsf{DH}} \uplus \Phi; \sigma \cup \sigma')$$

where $\Phi =_{\mathsf{E_{DH}}} \{w_3 \rhd u_0, w_4 \rhd \mathsf{aenc}(\langle n_A, \mathsf{g}(r_B)\rangle, pk_A)\}, \mathcal{E} = \{sk_A, sk_B, r_A, r_B, n_A\}$, $\sigma =_{\mathsf{E_{DH}}} \{y_A \mapsto \mathsf{aenc}(\langle n_A, \mathsf{g}(r_B)\rangle, pk_A), y_B \mapsto \mathsf{aenc}(\langle n_A, \mathsf{g}(r_A)\rangle, pk_B)\}$, and lastly $\sigma' =_{\mathsf{E_{DH}}} \{x_A \mapsto \mathsf{f}(\mathsf{g}(r_B), r_A), x_B \mapsto \mathsf{f}(\mathsf{g}(r_A), r_B)\}$. We used pk_A (resp. pk_B) as a shorthand for $\mathsf{pk}(sk_A)$ (resp. $\mathsf{pk}(sk_B)$).

$$(\mathcal{E}; \{\texttt{if } \varphi \texttt{ then } Q_1 \texttt{ else } Q_2\} \uplus \mathcal{P}; \varPhi; \sigma) \xrightarrow{\tau} (\mathcal{E}; Q_1 \uplus \mathcal{P}; \varPhi; \sigma) \qquad (\textsc{Then})$$
$$\text{if } u\sigma =_\mathsf{E} v\sigma \text{ for each } u = v \in \varphi$$

$$(\mathcal{E}; \{\texttt{if } \varphi \texttt{ then } Q_1 \texttt{ else } Q_2\} \uplus \mathcal{P}; \varPhi; \sigma) \xrightarrow{\tau} (\mathcal{E}; Q_2 \uplus \mathcal{P}; \varPhi; \sigma) \qquad (\textsc{Else})$$
$$\text{if } u\sigma \neq_\mathsf{E} v\sigma \text{ for some } u = v \in \varphi$$

$$(\mathcal{E}; \{\texttt{out}(c, u).Q_1; \texttt{in}(c, x).Q_2\} \uplus \mathcal{P}; \varPhi; \sigma) \xrightarrow{\tau} (\mathcal{E}; Q_1 \uplus Q_2 \uplus \mathcal{P}; \varPhi; \sigma \cup \{x \mapsto u\sigma\})(\textsc{Comm})$$

$$(\mathcal{E}; \{[x := v].Q\} \uplus \mathcal{P}; \varPhi; \sigma) \xrightarrow{\tau} (\mathcal{E}; Q \uplus \mathcal{P}; \varPhi; \sigma \cup \{x \mapsto v\sigma\}) \qquad (\textsc{Assgn})$$

$$(\mathcal{E}; \{\texttt{in}(c, z).Q\} \uplus \mathcal{P}; \varPhi; \sigma) \xrightarrow{\texttt{in}(c, M)} (\mathcal{E}; Q \uplus \mathcal{P}; \varPhi; \sigma \cup \{z \mapsto u\}) \qquad (\textsc{In})$$
$$\text{if } c \notin \mathcal{E}, \ M\varPhi = u, \ fv(M) \subseteq \mathrm{dom}(\varPhi) \text{ and } fn(M) \cap \mathcal{E} = \emptyset$$

$$(\mathcal{E}; \{\texttt{out}(c, u).Q\} \uplus \mathcal{P}; \varPhi; \sigma) \xrightarrow{\nu w_i . \texttt{out}(c, w_i)} (\mathcal{E}; Q \uplus \mathcal{P}; \varPhi \cup \{w_i \triangleright u\sigma\}; \sigma) \qquad (\textsc{Out-T})$$
$$\text{if } c \notin \mathcal{E}, \ u \text{ is a term of base type, and } w_i \text{ is a variable such that } i = |\varPhi| + 1$$

$$(\mathcal{E}; \{\texttt{new } n.Q\} \uplus \mathcal{P}; \varPhi; \sigma) \xrightarrow{\tau} (\mathcal{E} \cup \{n\}; Q \uplus \mathcal{P}; \varPhi; \sigma) \qquad (\textsc{New})$$

$$(\mathcal{E}; \{!Q\} \uplus \mathcal{P}; \varPhi; \sigma) \xrightarrow{\tau} (\mathcal{E}; \{!Q; Q\rho\} \uplus \mathcal{P}; \varPhi; \sigma) \qquad (\textsc{Repl})$$
$$\rho \text{ is used to rename } bv(Q)/bn(Q) \text{ with fresh variables/names}$$

$$(\mathcal{E}; \{P_1 \mid P_2\} \uplus \mathcal{P}; \varPhi; \sigma) \xrightarrow{\tau} (\mathcal{E}; \{P_1, P_2\} \uplus \mathcal{P}; \varPhi; \sigma) \qquad (\textsc{Par})$$

where n is a name, c is a name of channel type, u, v are terms of base type, and x, z are variables of base type.

Fig. 1. Semantics of extended processes

2.3 Process Equivalences

We are particularly interested in security properties expressed using a notion of equivalence such as those studied in *e.g.* [5,11]. For instance, the notion of *strong unlinkability* can be formalized using an equivalence between two situations: one where each user can execute the protocol multiple times, and one where each user can execute the protocol at most once.

We consider here the notion of *trace equivalence*. Intuitively, two protocols P and Q are in trace equivalence, denoted $P \approx Q$, if whatever the messages they received (built upon previously sent messages), the resulting sequences of messages sent on public channels are indistinguishable from the point of view of an outsider. Given an extended process A, we define its set of traces as follows:

$$\mathrm{trace}(A) = \{(\texttt{tr}, \texttt{new } \mathcal{E}.\varPhi) \mid A \xRightarrow{\texttt{tr}} (\mathcal{E}; \mathcal{P}; \varPhi; \sigma) \text{ for some process } (\mathcal{E}; \mathcal{P}; \varPhi; \sigma)\}.$$

The sequence of messages $\varPhi$ together with the set of restricted names $\mathcal{E}$ (those unknown to the attacker) is called the *frame*.

Definition 2. *We say that a term u is* deducible *(modulo* E*) from a frame* $\phi = \texttt{new}\mathcal{E}.\varPhi$, *denoted* $\texttt{new}\mathcal{E}.\varPhi \vdash u$, *when there exists a term M (called a* recipe*) such that* $fn(M) \cap \mathcal{E} = \emptyset$, $fv(M) \subseteq \mathrm{dom}(\varPhi)$, *and* $M\varPhi =_\mathsf{E} u$.

Two frames are indistinguishable when the attacker cannot detect the difference between the two situations they represent.

Definition 3. *Two frames ϕ_1 and ϕ_2 with $\phi_i = new\mathcal{E}.\Phi_i$ ($i \in \{1,2\}$) are statically equivalent, denoted by $\phi_1 \sim \phi_2$, when $\mathrm{dom}(\Phi_1) = \mathrm{dom}(\Phi_2)$, and for all terms M, N with $fn(\{M,N\}) \cap \mathcal{E} = \emptyset$ and $fv(\{M,N\}) \subseteq \mathrm{dom}(\Phi_1)$, we have that:*

$$M\Phi_1 =_\mathsf{E} N\Phi_1, \text{ if and only if, } M\Phi_2 =_\mathsf{E} N\Phi_2.$$

Example 4. Consider $\Phi_1 = \{w_1 \triangleright \mathsf{g}(r_A), w_2 \triangleright \mathsf{g}(r_B), w_3 \triangleright \mathsf{f}(\mathsf{g}(r_A), r_B)\}$, and $\Phi_2 = \{w_1 \triangleright \mathsf{g}(r_A), w_2 \triangleright \mathsf{g}(r_B), w_3 \triangleright k\}$. Let $\mathcal{E} = \{r_A, r_B, k\}$. We have that $new\,\mathcal{E}.\Phi_1 \sim new\,\mathcal{E}.\Phi_2$ (considering the equational theory $\mathsf{E_{DH}}$). This equivalence shows that the term $\mathsf{f}(\mathsf{g}(r_A), r_B)$ (the Diffie-Hellman key) is indistinguishable from a random key. This indistinguishability property holds even if the messages $\mathsf{g}(r_A)$ and $\mathsf{g}(r_B)$ have been observed by the attacker.

Two processes are trace equivalent if, whatever the messages they sent and received, their frames are in static equivalence.

Definition 4. *Let A and B be two extended processes, $A \sqsubseteq B$ if for every $(\mathsf{tr}, \phi) \in trace(A)$, there exists $(\mathsf{tr}', \phi') \in trace(B)$ such that $\mathsf{tr} = \mathsf{tr}'$ and $\phi \sim \phi'$. We say that A and B are trace equivalent, denoted by $A \approx B$, if $A \sqsubseteq B$ and $B \sqsubseteq A$.*

This notion of equivalence allows us to express many interesting privacy-type properties *e.g.* vote-privacy, strong versions of anonymity and/or unlinkability.

3   Composition Result: A Simple Setting

It is well-known that even if two protocols are secure in isolation, it is not possible to compose them in arbitrary ways still preserving their security. This has already been observed for different kinds of compositions (*e.g.* parallel [15], sequential [12]) and when studying standard security properties [13] and even privacy-type properties [4]. In this section, we introduce some well-known hypotheses that are needed to safely compose security protocols.

3.1   Sharing Primitives

A protocol can be used as an oracle by another protocol to decrypt a message, and then compromise the security of the whole application. To avoid this kind of interactions, most of the composition results assume that protocols do not share any primitive or allow a list of standard primitives (*e.g.* signature, encryption) to be shared as long as they are tagged in different ways. In this paper, we adopt the latter hypothesis and consider the fixed common signature:

$$\Sigma_0 = \{\mathsf{sdec}, \mathsf{senc}, \mathsf{adec}, \mathsf{aenc}, \mathsf{pk}, \langle, \rangle, \mathsf{proj}_1, \mathsf{proj}_2, \mathsf{sign}, \mathsf{check}, \mathsf{vk}, \mathsf{h}\}$$

equipped with the equational theory $\mathsf{E_0}$, defined by the following equations:

$$\mathsf{sdec}(\mathsf{senc}(x,y),y) = x \qquad \mathsf{check}(\mathsf{sign}(x,y),\mathsf{vk}(y)) = x$$
$$\mathsf{adec}(\mathsf{aenc}(x,\mathsf{pk}(y)),y) = x \qquad \mathsf{proj}_i(\langle x_1, x_2 \rangle) = x_i \text{ with } i \in \{1,2\}$$

This allows us to model symmetric/asymmetric encryption, concatenation, signatures, and hash functions. We consider a type *seed* which is a subsort of the base type that only contains names. We denote by $\mathsf{pk}(sk)$ (resp. $\mathsf{vk}(sk)$) the public key (resp. the verification key) associated to the private key sk which has to be a name of type *seed*. We allow protocols to both rely on Σ_0 provided that each application of aenc, senc, sign, and h is tagged (using disjoint sets of tags for the two protocols), and adequate tests are performed when receiving a message to ensure that the tags are correct. Actually, we consider the same tagging mechanism as the one we have introduced in [4] (see Definitions 4 and 5 in [4]). In particular, we rely on the same notation: we use the two function symbols $\mathsf{tag}/\mathsf{untag}$, and the equation $\mathsf{untag}(\mathsf{tag}(x)) = x$ to model the interactions between them. However, since we would like to be able to iterate our composition results (in order to compose *e.g.* three protocols), we consider a family of such function symbols: $\mathsf{tag}_i/\mathsf{untag}_i$ with $i \in \mathbb{N}$. Moreover, a process may be tagged using a subset of such symbols (and not only one). This gives us enough flexibility to allow different kinds of compositions, and to iterate our composition results.

Example 5. In order to compose the protocol introduced in Example 2 with another one that also relies on the primitive aenc, we may want to consider a tagged version of this protocol. The tagged version (using $\mathsf{tag}_1/\mathsf{untag}_1$) of P_B is given below (with $u = \mathsf{untag}_1(\mathsf{adec}(y_B, sk_B))$):

$$
\left\{
\begin{array}{l}
\mathsf{new}\, r_B.\mathsf{in}(c, y_B).\\
\mathsf{if}\ \mathsf{tag}_1(\mathsf{untag}_1(\mathsf{adec}(y_B, sk_B))) = \mathsf{adec}(y_B, sk_B)\ \mathsf{then}\\
\mathsf{if}\ u = \langle \mathsf{proj}_1(u), \mathsf{proj}_2(u)\rangle\ \mathsf{then}\\
\mathsf{out}(c, \mathsf{aenc}(\mathsf{tag}_1(\langle \mathsf{proj}_1(u), \mathsf{g}(r_B)\rangle), \mathsf{pk}(sk_A))).[x_B := \mathsf{f}(\mathsf{proj}_2(u), r_B)].0
\end{array}
\right.
$$

The first test allows one to check that y_B is an encryption tagged with tag_1 and the second one is used to ensure that the content of this encryption is a pair as expected. Then, the process outputs the encrypted message tagged with tag_1.

3.2   Revealing Shared Keys

Consider two protocols, one whose security relies on the secrecy of a shared key whereas the other protocol reveals it. Such a situation will compromise the security of the whole application. It is therefore important to ensure that shared keys are not revealed. To formalise this hypothesis, and to express the sharing of long-term keys, we introduce the notion of *composition context*. This will help us describe under which long-term keys the composition has to be done.

A *composition context* C is defined by the grammar:

$$C := \_ \mid \mathsf{new}\ n.\ C \mid !C \qquad \text{where } n \text{ is a name of base type.}$$

Definition 5. *Let C be a composition context, A be an extended process of the form $(\mathcal{E}; C[P]; \Phi)$, $key \in \{n, \mathsf{pk}(n), \mathsf{vk}(n) \mid n \text{ occurs in } C\}$, and c, s two fresh names. We say that A reveals key when*

$$(\mathcal{E} \cup \{s\}; C[P \mid \mathit{in}(c, x).\ \mathit{if}\ x = key\ \mathit{then}\ \mathit{out}(c, s)]; \Phi) \overset{\mathsf{tr}}{\Longrightarrow} (\mathcal{E}'; \mathcal{P}'; \Phi'; \sigma')$$

for some $\mathcal{E}'$, $\mathcal{P}'$, Φ', and σ' such that $\mathsf{new}\ \mathcal{E}'.\Phi' \vdash s$.

3.3   A First Composition Result

Before stating our first result regarding parallel composition for confidentiality properties, we gather the required hypotheses in the following definition.

Definition 6. *Let C be a composition context and $\mathcal{E}_0$ be a finite set of names of base type. Let P and Q be two plain processes together with their frames Φ and Ψ. We say that P/Φ and Q/Ψ are composable under $\mathcal{E}_0$ and C when $fv(P) = fv(Q) = \emptyset$, $\mathrm{dom}(\Phi) \cap \mathrm{dom}(\Psi) = \emptyset$, and*

  1. *P (resp. Q) is built over $\Sigma_\alpha \cup \Sigma_0$ (resp. $\Sigma_\beta \cup \Sigma_0$), whereas Φ (resp. Ψ) is built over $\Sigma_\alpha \cup \{\mathsf{pk}, \mathsf{vk}, \langle \, \rangle\}$ (resp. $\Sigma_\beta \cup \{\mathsf{pk}, \mathsf{vk}, \langle \, \rangle\}$), $\Sigma_\alpha \cap \Sigma_\beta = \emptyset$, and P (resp. Q) is tagged;*
  2. *$\mathcal{E}_0 \cap (fn(C[P]) \cup fn(\Phi)) \cap (fn(C[Q]) \cup fn(\Psi)) = \emptyset$; and*
  3. *$(\mathcal{E}_0; C[P]; \Phi)$ (resp. $(\mathcal{E}_0; C[Q]; \Psi)$) does not reveal any key in*

  $$\{n, \mathsf{pk}(n), \mathsf{vk}(n) \mid n \ occurs \ in \ fn(P) \cap fn(Q) \cap bn(C)\}.$$

Condition 1 is about sharing primitives, whereas Conditions 2 and 3 ensure that keys are shared via the composition context C only (not via $\mathcal{E}_0$), and are not revealed by each protocol individually.

We are now able to state the following theorem which is in the same vein as those obtained previously in *e.g.* [15,13]. However, the setting we consider here is more general. In particular, we consider arbitrary primitives, processes with else branches, and private channels.

Theorem 1. *Let C be a composition context, $\mathcal{E}_0$ be a finite set of names of base type, and s be a name that occurs in C. Let P and Q be two plain processes together with their frames Φ and Ψ, and assume that P/Φ and Q/Ψ are composable under $\mathcal{E}_0$ and C. If $(\mathcal{E}_0; C[P]; \Phi)$ and $(\mathcal{E}_0; C[Q]; \Psi)$ do not reveal s then $(\mathcal{E}_0; C[P \mid Q]; \Phi \uplus \Psi)$ does not reveal s.*

As most of the proofs of similar composition results, we show this result going back to the *disjoint case*. Indeed, it is well-known that parallel composition works well when protocols do not share any data (the so-called *disjoint case*). We show that all the conditions are satisfied to apply our generic result (presented only in the full version of this paper) that allows one to go back to the disjoint case. Thus, we obtain that the disjoint case $D = (\mathcal{E}_0; C[P] \mid C[Q]; \Phi \uplus \Psi)$ and the shared case $S = (\mathcal{E}_0; C[P \mid Q]; \Phi \uplus \Psi)$ are in trace equivalence, and this allows us to conclude.

4   The Case of Key-Exchange Protocols

Our goal is to go beyond parallel composition, and to further consider the particular case of key-exchange protocols. Assume that $P = \mathsf{new}\,\tilde{n}.(P_1 \mid P_2)$ is a protocol that establishes a key between two parties. The goal of P is to establish a shared session key between P_1 and P_2. Assume that P_1 stores the key in the variable x_1, while P_2 stores it in the variable x_2, and then consider a protocol Q that uses the values stored in x_1/x_2 as a fresh key to secure communications.

4.1   What Is a Good Key Exchange Protocol?

In this setting, sharing between P and Q is achieved through the composition context as well as through assignment variables x_1 and x_2. The idea is to abstract these values with fresh names when we analyse Q in isolation. However, in order to abstract them in the right way, we need to know their values (or at least whether they are equal or not). This is the purpose of the property stated below.

Definition 7. *Let C be a composition context and $\mathcal{E}_0$ be a finite set of names. Let $P_1[\_]$ (resp. $P_2[\_]$) be a plain process with a hole in the scope of an assignment of the form $[x_1 := t_1]$ (resp. $[x_2 := t_2]$), and Φ be a frame.*
We say that $P_1/P_2/\Phi$ is a good key-exchange protocol under $\mathcal{E}_0$ and C when $(\mathcal{E}_0; P_{\text{good}}; \Phi)$ does not reveal bad where P_{good} is defined as follows:

$P_{\text{good}} = new\,bad.newd.\big(C[newid.(P_1[out(d, \langle x_1, id\rangle)])\mid P_2[out(d, \langle x_2, id\rangle)])]\big)$
$\mid in(d,x).in(d,y).if\,\mathsf{proj}_1(x) = \mathsf{proj}_1(y) \wedge \mathsf{proj}_2(x) \neq \mathsf{proj}_2(y)\,then\,out(c, bad)$
$\mid in(d,x).in(d,y).if\,\mathsf{proj}_1(x) \neq \mathsf{proj}_1(y) \wedge \mathsf{proj}_2(x) = \mathsf{proj}_2(y)\,then\,out(c, bad)$
$\mid in(d,x).in(c,z).if\,z \in \{\mathsf{proj}_1(x), \mathsf{pk}(\mathsf{proj}_1(x)), \mathsf{vk}(\mathsf{proj}_1(x))\}\,then\,out(c, bad))$

where bad is a fresh name of base type, and c, d are fresh names of channel type.

The expressions $u \neq v$ and $u \in \{v_1, \ldots, v_n\}$ used above are convenient notations that can be rigorously expressed using nested conditionals. Roughly, the property expresses that x_1 and x_2 are assigned to the same value if, and only if, they are joined together, *i.e.* they share the same id. In particular, two instances of the role P_1 (resp. P_2) cannot assign their variable with the same value: a fresh key is established at each session. The property also ensures that the data shared through x_1/x_2 are not revealed.

Example 6. We have that $P_A/P_B/\Phi_{\mathsf{DH}}$ described in Example 2, as well as its tagged version (see Example 5) are *good* key-exchange protocols under $\mathcal{E}_0 = \{sk_A, sk_B\}$ and $C = \_$. This corresponds to a scenario where we consider only a single execution of the protocol (no replication).

Actually, the property mentioned above is quite strong, and never satisfied when the context C under study ends with a replication, *i.e.* when C is of the form $C'[!\_]$. To cope with this situation, we consider another version of this property. When C is of the form $C'[!\_]$, we define P_{good} as follows (where r_1 and r_2 are two additional fresh names of base type):

$new\,bad, d, r_1, r_2.\big(C'[new\,id.!(P_1[out(d, \langle x_1, id, r_1\rangle)]\mid P_2[out(d, \langle x_2, id, r_2\rangle)])]\big)$
$\mid in(d,x).in(d,y).if\,\mathsf{proj}_1(x) = \mathsf{proj}_1(y) \wedge \mathsf{proj}_2(x) \neq \mathsf{proj}_2(y)\,then\,out(c, bad)$
$\mid in(d,x).in(d,y).if\,\mathsf{proj}_1(x) = \mathsf{proj}_1(y) \wedge \mathsf{proj}_3(x) = \mathsf{proj}_3(y)\,then\,out(c, bad)$
$\mid in(d,x).in(c,z).if\,z \in \{\mathsf{proj}_1(x), \mathsf{pk}(\mathsf{proj}_1(x)), \mathsf{vk}(\mathsf{proj}_1(x))\}\,then\,out(c, bad))$

Note that the id is now generated before the last replication, and thus is not uniquely associated to an instance of P_1/P_2. Instead several instances of P_1/P_2 may now share the same id as soon as they are identical. This gives us more flexibility. The triplet $\langle u_1, u_2, u_3\rangle$ and the operator $\mathsf{proj}_3(u)$ used above are convenient notations that can be expressed using pairs. This new version forces distinct values in the assignment variables for each instance of P_1 (resp. P_2) through the 3rd line. However, we do not fix in advance which particular instance of P_1 and P_2 should be matched, as in the first version.

Example 7. We have that $P_A/P_B/\Phi_{\mathsf{DH}}$ as well as its tagged version are good key-exchange protocols under $\mathcal{E}_0 = \{sk_A, sk_B\}$ and $C = !\,\_.$

4.2   Do We Need to Tag Pairs?

When analysing Q in isolation, the values stored in the assignment variables x_1/x_2 are abstracted by fresh names. Since P and Q share the common signature Σ_0, we need an additional hypothesis to ensure that in any execution, the values assigned to the variables x_1/x_2 are not of the form $\langle u_1, u_2 \rangle$, $\mathsf{pk}(u)$, or $\mathsf{vk}(u)$. These symbols are those of the common signature that are not tagged, thus abstracting them by fresh names in Q would not be safe. This has already been highlighted in [12]. They however left as future work the definition of the needed hypothesis and simply assume that each operator of the common signature has to be tagged. Here, we formally express the required hypothesis.

Definition 8. *An extended process A satisfies the* abstractability property *if for any $(\mathcal{E}; \mathcal{P}; \Phi; \sigma)$ such that $A \overset{\mathsf{tr}}{\Longrightarrow} (\mathcal{E}; \mathcal{P}; \Phi; \sigma)$, for any $x \in \mathrm{dom}(\sigma)$ which corresponds to an assignment variable, for any u_1, u_2, we have that $x\sigma \neq_\mathsf{E} \langle u_1, u_2 \rangle$, $x\sigma \neq_\mathsf{E} \mathsf{pk}(u_1)$, and $x\sigma \neq_\mathsf{E} \mathsf{vk}(u_1)$.*

Note also that, in [12], the common signature is restricted to symmetric encryption and pairing only. They do not consider asymmetric encryption, and signature. Thus, our composition result generalizes theirs considering both a richer common signature, and a lighter tagging scheme (we do not tag pairs).

4.3   Composition Result

We retrieve the following result which is actually a generalization of two theorems established in [12] and stated for specific composition contexts.

Theorem 2. *Let C be a composition context, $\mathcal{E}_0$ be a finite set of names of base type, and s be a name that occurs in C. Let $P_1[\_]$ (resp. $P_2[\_]$) be a plain process without replication and with an hole in the scope of an assignment of the form $[x_1 := t_1]$ (resp. $[x_2 := t_2]$). Let Q_1 (resp. Q_2) be a plain process such that $fv(Q_1) \subseteq \{x_1\}$ (resp. $fv(Q_2) \subseteq \{x_2\}$), and Φ and Ψ be two frames. Let $P = P_1[0] \mid P_2[0]$ and $Q = \mathsf{new}\ k.[x_1 := k].[x_2 := k].(Q_1 \mid Q_2)$ for some fresh name k, and assume that:*

1. *P/Φ and Q/Ψ are composable under $\mathcal{E}_0$ and C;*
2. *$(\mathcal{E}_0; C[Q]; \Psi)$ does not reveal k, $\mathsf{pk}(k)$, $\mathsf{vk}(k)$;*
3. *$(\mathcal{E}_0; C[P]; \Phi)$ satisfies the abstractability property; and*
4. *$P_1/P_2/\Phi$ is a good key-exchange protocol under $\mathcal{E}_0$ and C.*

If $(\mathcal{E}_0; C[P]; \Phi)$ *and* $(\mathcal{E}_0; C[Q]; \Psi)$ *do not reveal* s *then* $(\mathcal{E}_0; C[P_1[Q_1] | P_2[Q_2]]; \Phi \uplus \Psi)$
does not reveal s.

Basically, we prove this result relying on our generic composition result. In [12], they do not require P to be good but only ask for secrecy of the shared key. In particular they do not express any freshness or agreement property about the established key. Actually, when considering a simple composition context without replication, freshness is trivial (since there is only one session). Moreover, in their setting, agreement is not important since they do not have else branches. The analysis of Q considering that both parties have agreed on the key corresponds to the worst scenario. Note that this is not true anymore in presence of else branches. The following example shows that as soon as else branches are allowed, as it is the case in the present work, agreement becomes important.

Example 8. Consider a simple situation where:

- $P_1[0] = \mathsf{new}\, k_1.[x_1 := k_1].0$ and $P_2[0] = \mathsf{new}\, k_2.[x_2 := k_2].0$;
- $Q_1 = \mathsf{if}\ x_1 = x_2\ \mathsf{then}\ \mathsf{out}(c, \mathsf{ok})\ \mathsf{else}\ \mathsf{out}(c, s)$ and $Q_2 = 0$.

Let $\mathcal{E}_0 = \emptyset$, and $C = \mathsf{new}\, s.\_$. We consider the processes $P = P_1[0] \mid P_2[0]$, and $Q = \mathsf{new}\, k.[x_1 := k].[x_2 := k].(Q_1 \mid Q_2)$ and we assume that the frames Φ and Ψ are empty. We clearly have that $(\mathcal{E}_0; C[P]; \Phi)$ and $(\mathcal{E}_0; C[Q]; \Psi)$ do not reveal s whereas $(\mathcal{E}_0; C[P_1[Q_1] \mid P_2[Q_2]]; \Phi \uplus \Psi)$ does. The only hypothesis of Theorem 2 that is violated is the fact that $P_1/P_2/\Phi$ is not a good key-exchange protocol due to a lack of agreement on the key which is generated (*bad* can be emitted thanks to the 3rd line of the process P_{good} given in Definition 7).

Now, regarding their second theorem corresponding to a context of the form $\mathsf{new}\, s.\,!\_$, as before agreement is not mandatory but freshness of the key established by the protocol P is crucial. As illustrated by the following example, this hypothesis is missing in the theorem stated in [12] (Theorem 3).

Example 9. Consider $A = (\{k_P\}; \mathsf{new}\, s.\,!([x_1 := k_P].0 \mid [x_2 := k_P].0); \emptyset)$, as well as $B = (\{k_P\}; \mathsf{new}\, s.\,!Q; \emptyset)$ where $Q = \mathsf{new}\, k.[x_1 := k].[x_2 := k].(Q_1 \mid Q_2)$ with

$$Q_1 = \mathsf{out}(c, \mathsf{senc}(\mathsf{senc}(s, k), k)); \text{ and } Q_2 = \mathsf{in}(c, x).\mathsf{out}(c, \mathsf{sdec}(x, k)).$$

Note that neither A nor B reveals s. In particular, the process Q_1 emits the secret s encrypted twice with a fresh key k, but Q_2 only allows us to remove one level of encryption with k. Now, if we plug the key-exchange protocol given above with no guarantee of freshness (the same key is established at each session), the resulting process, *i.e.* $(\mathcal{E}_0; C[P_1[Q_1] \mid P_2[Q_2]]; \emptyset)$ does reveal s.

Note that this example is not a counter example of our Theorem 2: $P_1/P_2/\emptyset$ is not a good key-exchange protocol according to our definition.

5 Dealing with Equivalence-Based Properties

Our ultimate goal is to analyse privacy-type properties in a modular way. In [4], we propose several composition results w.r.t. privacy-type properties, but for parallel composition only. Here, we want to go beyond parallel composition, and consider the case of key-exchange protocols.

5.1 A Problematic Example

Even in a quite simple setting (the shared keys are not revealed, protocols do not share any primitives), such a sequential composition result does not hold. Let $C = $ new k.! new k_1.! new k_2. _ be a composition context, yes/no, ok/ko be public constants, $u = $ senc($\langle k_1, k_2 \rangle, k$), and consider the following processes:

$$Q(z_1, z_2) = \text{out}(c, u).\text{in}(c, x).\text{if } x = u \text{ then } 0 \text{ else}$$
$$\text{if proj}_1(\text{sdec}(x, k)) = k_1 \text{ then out}(c, z_1) \text{ else out}(c, z_2)$$

$$P[\_] = \text{out}(c, u).(\_ \mid \text{in}(c, x).\text{if } x = u \text{ then } 0 \text{ else}$$
$$\text{if proj}_1(\text{sdec}(x, k)) = k_1 \text{ then out}(c, \text{ok}) \text{ else out}(c, \text{ko}))$$

We have that $C[P[0]] \approx C[P[0]]$ and also that $C[Q(\text{yes}, \text{no})] \approx C[Q(\text{no}, \text{yes})]$. This latter equivalence is non-trivial. Intuitively, when $C[Q(\text{yes}, \text{no})]$ unfolds its outermost ! and then performs an output, then $C[Q(\text{no}, \text{yes})]$ has to mimic this step by unfolding its innermost ! and by performing the only available output. This will allow it to react in the same way as $C[Q(\text{yes}, \text{no})]$ in case encrypted messages are used to fill some input actions. Since the two processes $P[0]$ and $Q(\text{yes}, \text{no})$ (resp. $Q(\text{no}, \text{yes})$) are almost "disjoint", we could expect the equivalence $C[P[Q(\text{yes}, \text{no})]] \approx C[P[Q(\text{no}, \text{yes})]]$ to hold. Actually, this equivalence does *not* hold. The presence of the process P gives to the attacker some additional distinguishing power. In particular, through the outputs ok/ko outputted by P, the attacker will learn which ! has been unfolded. This result holds even if we rename function symbols so that protocols P and Q do not share any primitives. The problem is that the two equivalences we want to compose hold for different reasons, *i.e.* by unfolding the replications in a different and incompatible way. Thus, when the composed process $C[P[Q(\text{yes}, \text{no})]]$ reaches a point where $Q(\text{yes}, \text{no})$ can be executed, on the other side, the process $Q(\text{no}, \text{yes})$ is ready to be executed but the instance that is available is not the one that was used when establishing the equivalence $C[Q(\text{yes}, \text{no})] \approx C[Q(\text{no}, \text{yes})]$. Therefore, in order to establish equivalence-based properties in a modular way, we rely on a stronger notion of equivalence, namely *diff-equivalence*, that will ensure that the two "small" equivalences are satisfied in a compatible way.

Note that this problem does not arise when considering reachability properties and/or parallel composition. In particular, we have that:

$$C[P[0] \mid Q(\text{yes}, \text{no})] \approx C[P[0] \mid Q(\text{no}, \text{yes})].$$

5.2 Biprocesses and Diff-Equivalence

We consider pairs of processes, called *biprocesses*, that have the same structure and differ only in the terms and tests that they contain. Following the approach of [9], we introduce a special symbol diff of arity 2 in our signature. The idea being to use this diff operator to indicate when the terms manipulated by the processes are different. Given a biprocess B, we define two processes fst(B) and snd(B) as follows: fst(B) is obtained by replacing each occurrence of diff(M, M') (resp. diff(φ, φ')) with M (resp. φ), and similarly snd(B) is obtained by replacing each occurrence of diff(M, M') (resp. diff(φ, φ')) with M' (resp. φ').

The semantics of biprocesses is defined as expected via a relation that expresses when and how a biprocess may evolve. A biprocess reduces if, and only if, both sides of the biprocess reduce in the same way: a communication succeeds on both sides, a conditional has to be evaluated in the same way in both sides too. For instance, the **then** and **else** rules are as follows:

$$(\mathcal{E}; \{\text{if diff}(\varphi_L, \varphi_R) \text{ then } Q_1 \text{ else } Q_2\} \uplus \mathcal{P}; \Phi; \sigma) \xrightarrow{\tau}_{\text{bi}} (\mathcal{E}; Q_1 \uplus \mathcal{P}; \Phi; \sigma)$$
if $u\sigma =_\mathsf{E} v\sigma$ for each $u = v \in \varphi_L$, and $u'\sigma =_\mathsf{E} v'\sigma$ for each $u' = v' \in \varphi_R$

$$(\mathcal{E}; \{\text{if diff}(\varphi_L, \varphi_R) \text{ then } Q_1 \text{ else } Q_2\} \uplus \mathcal{P}; \Phi; \sigma) \xrightarrow{\tau}_{\text{bi}} (\mathcal{E}; Q_2 \uplus \mathcal{P}; \Phi; \sigma)$$
if $u\sigma \neq_\mathsf{E} v\sigma$ for some $u = v \in \varphi_L$, and $u'\sigma \neq_\mathsf{E} v'\sigma$ for some $u' = v' \in \varphi_R$

When the two sides of the biprocess reduce in different ways, the biprocess blocks. The relation $\xrightarrow{\text{tr}}_{\text{bi}}$ on biprocesses is defined as for processes. This leads us to the following notion of *diff-equivalence*.

Definition 9. *An extended biprocess B_0 satisfies* diff-equivalence *if for every biprocess $B = (\mathcal{E}; \mathcal{P}; \Phi; \sigma)$ such that $B_0 \xrightarrow{\text{tr}}_{\text{bi}} B$ for some trace* tr, *we have that*

1. *new $\mathcal{E}.\mathsf{fst}(\Phi) \sim$ new $\mathcal{E}.\mathsf{snd}(\Phi)$*
2. *if $\mathsf{fst}(B) \xrightarrow{\ell} A_L$ then there exists B' such that $B \xrightarrow{\ell}_{\text{bi}} B'$ and $\mathsf{fst}(B') = A_L$ (and similarly for* snd*).*

The notions introduced so far on processes are extended as expected on biprocesses: the property has to hold on both $\mathsf{fst}(B)$ and $\mathsf{snd}(B)$. Sometimes, we also say that the biprocess B is in trace equivalence instead of writing $\mathsf{fst}(B) \approx \mathsf{snd}(B)$.

As expected, this notion of diff-equivalence is actually stronger than the usual notion of trace equivalence.

Lemma 1. *A biprocess B that satisfies diff-equivalence is in trace equivalence.*

6   Composition Results for Diff-Equivalence

We first consider the case of parallel composition. This result is in the spirit of the one established in [4]. However, we adapt it to diff-equivalence in order to combine it with the composition result we obtained for the the case of key-exchange protocol (see Theorem 4).

Theorem 3. *Let C be a composition context and $\mathcal{E}_0$ be a finite set of names of base type. Let P and Q be two plain biprocesses together with their frames Φ and Ψ, and assume that P/Φ and Q/Ψ are composable under $\mathcal{E}_0$ and C.*

If $(\mathcal{E}_0; C[P]; \Phi)$ and $(\mathcal{E}_0; C[Q]; \Psi)$ satisfy diff-equivalence (resp. trace equivalence) then the biprocess $(\mathcal{E}_0; C[P \mid Q]; \Phi \uplus \Psi)$ satisfies diff-equivalence (resp. trace equivalence).

Proof. (sketch) As for the proof for Theorem 1, parallel composition works well when processes do not share any data. Hence, we easily deduce that $D = (\mathcal{E}_0; C[P] \mid C[Q]; \Phi \uplus \Psi)$ satisfies the diff-equivalence (resp. trace equivalence).

Then, we compare the behaviours of the biprocess D to those of the biprocess $S = (\mathcal{E}_0; C[P \mid Q]; \Phi \uplus \Psi)$. More precisely, this allows us to establish that $\mathsf{fst}(D)$ and $\mathsf{fst}(S)$ are in diff-equivalence (as well as $\mathsf{snd}(D)$ and $\mathsf{snd}(S)$), and then we conclude relying on the transitivity of the equivalence. $\square$

Now, regarding sequential composition and the particular case of key-exchange protocols, we obtain the following composition result.

Theorem 4. *Let C be a composition context and $\mathcal{E}_0$ be a finite set of names of base type. Let $P_1[\_]$ (resp. $P_2[\_]$) be a plain biprocess without replication and with an hole in the scope of an assignment of the form $[x_1 := t_1]$ (resp. $[x_2 := t_2]$). Let Q_1 (resp. Q_2) be a plain biprocess such that $fv(Q_1) \subseteq \{x_1\}$ (resp. $fv(Q_2) \subseteq \{x_2\}$), and Φ and Ψ be two frames. Let $P = P_1[0] \mid P_2[0]$ and $Q = new\ k.[x_1 := k].[x_2 := k].(Q_1 \mid Q_2)$ for some fresh name k, and assume that:*

1. *P/Φ and Q/Ψ are composable under $\mathcal{E}_0$ and C;*
2. *$(\mathcal{E}_0; C[Q]; \Psi)$ does not reveal k, $\mathsf{pk}(k)$, $\mathsf{vk}(k)$;*
3. *$(\mathcal{E}_0; C[P]; \Phi)$ satisfies the abstractability property; and*
4. *$P_1/P_2/\Phi$ is a good key-exchange protocol under $\mathcal{E}_0$ and C.*

Let $P^+ = P_1[out(d, x_1)] \mid P_2[out(d, x_2)] \mid in(d, x).in(d, y).if\ x = y\ then\ 0\ else\ 0$. If the biprocesses $(\mathcal{E}_0; new\ d.C[P^+]; \Phi)$ and $(\mathcal{E}_0; C[Q]; \Psi)$ satisfy diff-equivalence then $(\mathcal{E}_0; C[P_1[Q_1] \mid P_2[Q_2]]; \Phi \uplus \Psi)$ satisfies diff-equivalence.

We require $(\mathcal{E}_0; \mathbf{new}\ d.C[P^+]; \Phi)$ to be in diff-equivalence (and not simply $(\mathcal{E}_0; C[P]; \Phi)$). This ensures that the same equalities between values of assignment variables hold on both sides of the equivalence. Actually, when the composition context C under study is not of the form $C'[!\_]$, and under the hypothesis that $P_1/P_2/\Phi$ is a good key-exchange protocol under $\mathcal{E}_0$ and C, we have that these two requirements coincide. However, the stronger hypothesis is important to conclude when C is of the form $C'[!\_]$. Indeed, in this case, we do not know in advance what are the instances of P_1 and P_2 that will be "matched". This is not a problem but to conclude about the diff-equivalence of the whole process (*i.e.* $(\mathcal{E}_0; C[P_1[Q_1] \mid P_2[Q_2]]; \Phi \uplus \Psi)$), we need to ensure that such a matching is the same on both sides of the equivalence. Note that to conclude about trace equivalence only, this additional requirement is actually not necessary.

7   Case Studies

Many applications rely on several protocols running in composition (parallel, sequential, or nested). In this section, we show that our results can help in the analysis of this sort of complex system. Our main goal is to show that the extra hypotheses needed to analyse an application in a moduar way are reasonnable.

7.1   3G Mobile Phones

We look at confidentiality and privacy guarantees provided by the *AKA* protocol and the Submit SMS procedure (*sSMS*) when run in composition as specified by the 3GPP consortium in [2].

Protocols Description. The *sSMS* protocol allows a mobile station (MS) to send an SMS to another MS through a serving network (SN). The confidentiality of the sent SMS relies on a session key ck established through the execution of the *AKA* protocol between the MS and the SN. The *AKA* protocol achieves mutual authentication between a MS and a SN, and allows them to establish a shared session key ck. The *AKA* protocol consists in the exchange of two messages: the *authentication request* and the *authentication response*. The *AKA* protocol as deployed in real 3G telecommunication systems presents a linkability attack [5], and thus we consider here its fixed version as described in [5]. At the end of a successful execution of this protocol, both parties should agree on a fresh ciphering key ck. This situation can be modelled in our calculus as follows:

$$\text{new } sk_{SN}. \text{ !new } IMSI. \text{ new } k_{IMSI}. \text{ !new } sqn. \text{ new } sms.$$
$$(AKA^{SN}[sSMS^{SN}] \mid AKA^{MS}[sSMS^{MS}])$$

where sk_{SN} represents the private key of the network; while $IMSI$ and k_{IMSI} represent respectively the long-term identity and the symmetric key of the MS. The name sqn models the sequence number on which SN and MS are synchronised. The two subprocesses AKA^{MS} and $sSMS^{MS}$ (*resp. AKA^{SN}, and $sSMS^{SN}$*) model one session of the MS's (*resp.* SN's) side of the *AKA*, and *sSMS* protocols respectively. Each MS, identified by its identity $IMSI$ and its key k_{IMSI}, can run multiple times the *AKA* protocol followed by the *sSMS* protocol.

Security Analysis. We explain how some confidentiality and privacy properties of the *AKA* protocol and the *sSMS* procedure can be derived relying on our composition results. We do not need to tag the protocols under study to perform our analysis since they do not share any primitive but the pairing operator. Note that the *AKA* protocol can *not* be modelled in the calculus given in [12] due to the need of non-trivial else branches. Moreover, to enable the use of ProVerif, we had to abstract some details of the considered protocols that ProVerif cannot handle. In particular, we model timestamps using nonces, we replace the use of the xor operation by symmetric encryption, and we assume that the two parties are "magically" synchronised on their counter value.

Strong unlinkability requires that an observer does not see the difference between the two following scenarios: *(i)* a same mobile phone sends several SMSs; or *(ii)* multiple mobile phones send at most one SMS each. To model this requirement, we consider the composition context[1]:

$$C_U[\_] \stackrel{\text{def}}{=} \text{!new } IMSI_1. \text{ new } k_{IMSI1}. \text{ !new } IMSI_2. \text{ new } k_{IMSI2}.$$
$$\text{let } IMSI = \text{diff}[IMSI_1, IMSI_2] \text{ in let } k_{IMSI} = \text{diff}[k_{IMSI1}, k_{IMSI2}] \text{ in}$$
$$\text{new } sqn. \text{ new } sms. \ \_$$

To check if the considered 3G protocols satisfy strong unlinkability, one needs to check if the following biprocess satisfies diff-equivalence ($\Phi_0 = \{w_1 \rhd \mathsf{pk}(sk_{SN})\}$):

$$(sk_{SN}; C_U[AKA^{SN}[sSMS^{SN}] \mid AKA^{MS}[sSMS^{MS}]]; \Phi_0)$$

---

[1] We use let $x = M$ in P to denote the process $P\{M/x\}$.

Hypotheses (1-4) stated in Theorem 4 are satisfied, and thus this equivalence can be derived from the following two "smaller" diff-equivalences:

$$(sk_{SN}; \text{new } d.\ C_U[AKA^+]; \Phi_0) \quad \text{and} \quad (sk_{SN}; C'_U[sSMS]; \emptyset)$$

- $sSMS \stackrel{\text{def}}{=} sSMS^{SN} \mid sSMS^{MS}$,
- $AKA^+ \stackrel{\text{def}}{=} AKA^{SN}[\text{out}(d, xck_{SN})] \mid AKA^{MS}[\text{out}(d, xck_{MS})] \mid$
  $\text{in}(d, x).\ \text{in}(d, y).\ \text{if } x = y \text{ then } 0 \text{ else } 0$
- $C'_U[\_] \stackrel{\text{def}}{=} C_U[\text{new } ck.\text{let } xck_{SN} = ck \text{ in let } xck_{MS} = ck \text{ in } \_]$.

Weak secrecy requires that the sent/received SMS is not deducible by an outsider, and can be modelled using the context

$$C_{WS}[\_] \stackrel{\text{def}}{=} !\text{new } IMSI.\ \text{new } k_{IMSI}.\ !\text{new } sqn.\text{new } sms.\_.$$

The composition context C_{WS} is the same as $\text{fst}(C_U)$ (up to some renaming), thus Hypotheses (1-4) of Theorem 2 also hold and we derive the weak secrecy property by simply analysing this property on AKA and $sSMS$ in isolation.

Strong secrecy means that an outsider should not be able to distinguish the situation where sms_1 is sent (resp. received), from the situation where sms_2 is sent (resp. received), although he might know the content of sms_1 and sms_2. This can be modelled using the following composition context:

$$C_{SS}[\_] \stackrel{\text{def}}{=} !\text{new } IMSI.\ \text{new } k_{IMSI}.\ !\text{new } sqn.\ \text{let } sms = \text{diff}[sms_1, sms_2] \text{ in } \_$$

where sms_1 and sms_2 are two free names known to the attacker. Again, our Theorem 4 allows us to reason about this property in a modular way.

Under the abstractions briefly explained above, all the hypotheses have been checked using ProVerif. Actually, it happens that ProVerif is also able to conclude on the orignal protocol (the one without decomposition) for the three security properties mentioned above. Note that a less abstract model of the same protocol (*e.g.* the one with the xor operator) would have required us to rely on a manual proof. In such a situation, our composition result allows us to reduce a big equivalence that existing tools cannot handle, to a much smaller one which is a more manageable work in case the proof has to be done manually.

7.2   E-passport Application

We look at privacy guarantees provided by three protocols of the e-passport application when run in composition as specified in [1].

Protocols Description. The information stored in the chip of the passport is organised in data groups (dg_1 to dg_{19}): dg_5 contains a JPEG copy of the displayed picture, dg_7 contains the displayed signature, whereas the verification key $\text{vk}(sk_P)$ of the passport, together with its certificate $\text{sign}(\text{vk}(sk_P), sk_{DS})$ issued by the Document Signer authority are stored in dg_{15}. For authentication purposes, a hash of all the dgs together with a signature on this hash value are stored in a separate file, the Security Object Document:

$$sod \stackrel{\text{def}}{=} \langle \text{sign}(\text{h}(dg_1, \ldots, dg_{19}), sk_{DS}), \text{h}(dg_1, \ldots, dg_{19}) \rangle.$$

The ICAO standard specifies several protocols through which this information can be accessed [1]. First, the *Basic Access Control (BAC)* protocol establishes a key seed *kseed* from which a session key *kenc* is derived. The purpose of *kenc* is to prevent skimming and eavesdropping on the subsequent communication with the e-passport. The security of the *BAC* protocol relies on two master keys, *ke* and *km*. Once the *BAC* protocol has been successfully executed, the reader gains access to the information stored in the RFID tag through the *Passive Authentication (PA)* and the *Active Authentication (AA)* protocols that can be executed in any order. This situation can be modelled in our calculus:

$$P \stackrel{\text{def}}{=} \text{new } sk_{DS}. \ !\text{new } ke. \ \text{new } km. \ \text{new } sk_P. \text{new } id. \ \text{new } sig. \ \text{new } pic. \ \ldots$$
$$!(BAC^R[PA^R \mid AA^R] \mid BAC^P[PA^P \mid AA^P])$$

where $id, sig, pic, \ldots$ represent the name, the signature, the displayed picture, *etc* of the e-passport's owner, *i.e.* the data stored in the *dgs* (1-14) and (16-19). The subprocesses BAC^P, PA^P and AA^P (*resp.* BAC^R, PA^R and AA^R) model one session of the passport's (*resp.* reader's) side of the *BAC*, *PA* and *AA* protocols respectively. The name sk_{DS} models the signing key of the Document Signing authority used in all passports. Each passport (identified by its master keys *ke* and *km*, its signing key sk_P, the owner's name, picture, signature, ...) can run multiple times the *BAC* protocol followed by the *PA* and *AA* protocols.

Security Analysis. We explain below how *strong anonymity* of these three protocols executed together can be derived from the analysis performed on each protocol in isolation. In [4], as sequential composition could not be handled, the analysis of the e-passports application had to exclude the execution of the *BAC* protocol. Instead, it was assumed that the key *kenc* is "magically" pre-shared between the passport and the reader. Thanks to our Theorem 4, we are now able to complete the analysis of the e-passport application.

To express strong anonymity, we need on the one hand to consider a system in which the particular e-passport with publicly known id_1, sig_1, pic_1, etc. is being executed, while on the other hand it is a different e-passport with publicly known id_2, sig_2, pic_2, etc. which is being executed. We consider the context:

$$C_A[\_] \stackrel{\text{def}}{=} !\text{new } ke. \ \text{new } km. \ \text{new } sk_P.\text{let } id = \text{diff}[id_1, id_2] \text{ in } \ldots ! \ \_$$

This composition context differs in the e-passport being executed on the left-hand process and on the right-hand process. In other words, the system satisfies anonymity if an observer cannot distinguish the situation where the e-passport with publicly known id_1, sig_1, pic_1, etc. is being executed, from the situation where it is another e-passport which is being executed. To check if the tagged version of the e-passport application (we assume here that *BAC*, *PA*, and *AA* are tagged in different ways) preserves strong anonymity, one thus needs to check if the following biprocess satisfies diff-equivalence (with $\Phi_0 = \{w_1 \triangleright \text{vk}(sk_{DS})\}$):

$$(sk_{DS}; C_A[BAC^R[PA^R \mid AA^R] \mid BAC^P[PA^P \mid AA^P]]; \Phi_0)$$

We can instead check whether *BAC*, *PA* and *AA* satisfy anonymity in isolation, *i.e.* if the following three diff-equivalences hold:

$$(sk_{DS}; \text{new } d. \; C_A[BAC^+]; \emptyset) \; (\alpha) \qquad \begin{array}{l} (sk_{DS}; C'_A[PA^R \mid PA^P]; \Phi_0) \; (\beta) \\ (sk_{DS}; C'_A[AA^R \mid AA^P]; \emptyset) \; (\gamma) \end{array}$$

where

- $BAC^+ \stackrel{\text{def}}{=} BAC^R[\text{out}(d, xkenc_R)] \mid BAC^P[\text{out}(d, xkenc_P)]$
  $\mid \text{in}(d, x). \; \text{in}(d, y). \; \text{if } x = y \text{ then } 0 \text{ else } 0;$
- $C'_A[\_] \stackrel{\text{def}}{=} C_A[C''_A[\_]];$ and
- $C''_A[\_] \stackrel{\text{def}}{=} \text{new } kenc. \; \text{let } xkenc_R = kenc \; \text{in let } xkenc_P = kenc \; \text{in } \_.$

Then, applying Theorem 3 to (β) and (γ) we derive that the following biprocess satisfies diff-equivalence:

$$(sk_{DS}; C'_A[PA^R \mid AA^R \mid PA^P \mid AA^P]; \Phi_0) \quad (\delta).$$

and applying Theorem 4 to (α) and (δ), we derive the required diff-equivalence:

$$(sk_{DS}; C_A[BAC^R[PA^R \mid AA^R] \mid BAC^P[PA^P \mid AA^P]]; \Phi_0)$$

Note that we can do so because Hypotheses (1-4) stated in Theorem 4 are satisfied, and in particular because $BAC^R/BAC^P/\emptyset$ is a good key-exchange protocol under $\{sk_{DS}\}$ and C_A. Again, all the hypotheses have been checked using ProVerif. Actually, it happens that ProVerif is also able to directly conclude on the whole system.

Unfortunately, our approach does not apply to perform a modular analysis of strong unlinkability. The BAC protocol does not satisfy the diff-equivalence needed to express such a security property, and this hypothesis is mandatory to apply our composition result.

8   Conclusion

We investigate composition results for reachability properties as well as privacy-type properties expressed using a notion of equivalence. Relying on a generic composition result, we derive parallel composition results, and we study the particular case of key-exchange protocols under various composition contexts.

All these results work in a quite general setting, *e.g.* processes may have non trivial else branches, we consider arbitrary primitives expressed using an equational theory, and processes may even share some standard primitives as long as they are tagged in different ways. We illustrate the usefulness of our results through the mobile phone and e-passport applications.

We believe that our generic result could be used to derive further composition results. We may want for instance to relax the notion of being a *good protocol* at the price of studying a less ideal scenario when analysing the protocol Q in isolation. We may also want to consider situations where sub-protocols sharing some data are arbitrarily interleaved. Moreover, even if we consider arbitrary primitives, sub-protocols can only share some standard primitives provided that they are tagged. It would be nice to relax these conditions. This would allow one to compose protocols (and not their tagged versions) or to compose protocols that both rely on primitives for which no tagging scheme actually exists (*e.g.* exclusive-or).

References

1. PKI for machine readable travel documents offering ICC read-only access. Technical report, International Civil Aviation Organization (2004)
2. 3GPP. Technical specification group services and system aspects; 3G security; security architecture (release 9). Technical report, 3rd Generation Partnership Project (2010)
3. Abadi, M., Fournet, C.: Mobile values, new names, and secure communication. In: Proc. 28th Symposium on Principles of Programming Languages, POPL 2001 (2001)
4. Arapinis, M., Cheval, V., Delaune, S.: Verifying privacy-type properties in a modular way. In: Proc. 25th IEEE Computer Security Foundations Symposium, CSF 2012 (2012)
5. Arapinis, M., Mancini, L.I., Ritter, E., Ryan, M., Golde, N., Redon, K., Borgaonkar, R.: New privacy issues in mobile telephony: fix and verification. In: ACM Conference on Computer and Communications Security (2012)
6. Armando, A., Carbone, R., Compagna, L., Cuéllar, J., Tobarra, M.L.: Formal analysis of SAML 2.0 web browser single sign-on: breaking the SAML-based single sign-on for google apps. In: Proc. 6th ACM Workshop on Formal Methods in Security Engineering, FMSE 2008 (2008)
7. Armando, A., et al.: The AVANTSSAR Platform for the Automated Validation of Trust and Security of Service-Oriented Architectures. In: Flanagan, C., König, B. (eds.) TACAS 2012. LNCS, vol. 7214, pp. 267–282. Springer, Heidelberg (2012)
8. Barak, B., Canetti, R., Nielsen, J., Pass, R.: Universally composable protocols with relaxed set-up assumptions. In: Proc. 45th Symposium on Foundations of Computer Science, FOCS 2004 (2004)
9. Blanchet, B., Abadi, M., Fournet, C.: Automated verification of selected equivalences for security protocols. Journal of Logic and Algebraic Programming (2008)
10. Böhl, F., Unruh, D.: Symbolic universal composability. In: Proc. 26th Computer Security Foundations Symposium, CSF 2013 (2013)
11. Bruso, M., Chatzikokolakis, K., den Hartog, J.: Formal verification of privacy for RFID systems. In: Proc. 23rd Computer Security Foundations Symposium, CSF 2010 (2010)
12. Ciobâcă, Ş., Cortier, V.: Protocol composition for arbitrary primitives. In: Proc. of the 23rd IEEE Computer Security Foundations Symposium, CSF 2010 (2010)
13. Cortier, V., Delaune, S.: Safely composing security protocols. Formal Methods in System Design 34(1), 1–36 (2009)
14. Groß, T., Mödersheim, S.: Vertical protocol composition. In: Proc. 24th Computer Security Foundations Symposium, CSF 2011 (2011)
15. Guttman, J.D., Thayer, F.J.: Protocol independence through disjoint encryption. In: Proc. 13th Computer Security Foundations Workshop, CSFW 2000 (2000)
16. Küsters, R., Tuengerthal, M.: Composition Theorems Without Pre-Established Session Identifiers. In: Proc. 18th Conference on Computer and Communications Security, CCS 2011 (2011)
17. Mödersheim, S., Viganò, L.: Secure pseudonymous channels. In: Backes, M., Ning, P. (eds.) ESORICS 2009. LNCS, vol. 5789, pp. 337–354. Springer, Heidelberg (2009)
18. Tiu, A., Dawson, J.E.: Automating open bisimulation checking for the spi calculus. In: Proc. 23rd Computer Security Foundations Symposium, CSF 2010 (2010)

PriCL: Creating a Precedent, a Framework for Reasoning about Privacy Case Law

Michael Backes, Fabian Bendun, Jörg Hoffmann, and Ninja Marnau

CISPA, Saarland University
{backes,bendun,hoffmann,marnau}@cs.uni-saarland.de

Abstract. We introduce PriCL: the first framework for expressing and automatically reasoning about privacy case law by means of precedent. PriCL is parametric in an underlying logic for expressing world properties, and provides support for court decisions, their justification, the circumstances in which the justification applies as well as court hierarchies. Moreover, the framework offers a tight connection between privacy case law and the notion of norms that underlies existing rule-based privacy research. In terms of automation, we identify the major reasoning tasks for privacy cases such as deducing legal permissions or extracting norms. For solving these tasks, we provide generic algorithms that have particularly efficient realizations within an expressive underlying logic. Finally, we derive a definition of deducibility based on legal concepts and subsequently propose an equivalent characterization in terms of logic satisfiability.

1 Introduction

Privacy regulations such as HIPAA, COPPA, or GLBA in the United States impose legal grounds for privacy [25,30,31]. In order to effectively reason about such regulations, e.g., for checking compliance, it is instrumental to come up with suitable formalizations of such frameworks along with the corresponding automated reasoning tasks.

There are currently two orthogonal approaches to how regulations are expressed and interpreted in real life that both call for such a formalization and corresponding reasoning support. One approach is based on explicit rules that define what is allowed and what is forbidden. The alternative is to consider precedents, which is the approach predominantly followed in many countries such as the US. Precedents are cases that decide a specific legal context for the first time and thus serve as a point of reference whenever a future similar case needs to be decided. Moreover, even judges in countries that do not base their legal system on precedents often use this mechanism to validate their decision or shorten the process of argumentation.

Case law is particularly suitable for resolving vague formulations that naturally occur in privacy regulations like the definition of 'disclosure' in COPPA. Here, case law could reference decisions that define what circumstances are qualified as a non-identifiable form of personal data, thereby aiding the user by providing judicially accurate interpretation of such terms.

© Springer-Verlag Berlin Heidelberg 2015
R. Focardi and A. Myers (Eds.): POST 2015, LNCS 9036, pp. 344–363, 2015.
DOI: 10.1007/978-3-662-46666-7_18

While rule-based frameworks have received tremendous attention in previous research (see the section on related work below) there is currently no formalization for case law that is amenable to automated reasoning.

Our Contribution. Our contribution to this problem space is threefold:
- We derive important legal concepts from actual judicial processes and relevant requirements from related work. The resulting framework PriCL, can be applied to the judicature of many different countries as it does not assume any specific argumentation.
- We tailor the framework for privacy regulations. In particular, our privacy specific case law framework is compatible with former policy languages since it has only minimal requirements regarding the logic. Therefore, it is possible to embed other formalizations into our framework.
- We define the major reasoning tasks that are needed to apply the framework to privacy cases. In particular, these tasks allow us to derive requirements for the underlying logic which we analyze. Several logics allow an embedding of the reasoning tasks by giving an equivalent characterization of the tasks. Consequently, we are able to select a well suited logic.

Related Work. There are plenty of privacy regulations that companies are required to comply with. In the US there are regulations for specific sectors, e.g., HIPAA for health data, COPPA for children's data, or GLBA and RFPA for financial data. In the EU, the member states have general data protection codes. The legislative efforts to harmonize these national codes via the EU Data Protection Regulation [18] are proceeding and already provide for identifying legislative trends. The importance and impact of these privacy regulations has brought the interpretation thereof to the attention of more technically focused privacy research [22,8,2,17,13,26].

Policy languages were mainly developed in order to model these regulations and to reflect companies' policies. Many of the modern logics modeling regulations are based on temporal logic [19,10,15,29,9] and were successfully used to model HIPAA and GLBA [16]. While these logics focus on expressiveness in order to reflect the regulations, the logics for company policies focus on enforcement [7,3] and thus also on authorization [1,3]. Consequently, company policies are mostly based on access control policies [24,21].

Bridging the gap between the regulation policies and the company's policies leads to automating compliance checks [28]. For many deployed policies, i.e., the ones that are efficiently enforceable, this is currently not possible due to the lack of decidability regarding the logics used to formalize regulations. However, for these cases there exist run-time monitoring tools that allow compliance auditing on log files [8,19,11,10]. In particular, such auditing was invented for HIPAA [19].

A different approach for achieving compliance is guaranteeing privacy-by-design [23,14,20]. However, the policy of these systems still needs to be checked for compliance with the relevant privacy regulations.

2   Ingredients

In the first step we illustrate which components are essential for a case law framework. To that end, we analyze actual judicial processes and derive ingredients for the framework from the relevant legal principles. Hence, in the following, we analyze a representative court decision[1] and discuss the implications for our framework.

The Conflict. *"This matter involves three certified questions from the Circuit Court of Harrison County regarding whether applicable state and federal privacy laws allow dissemination of confidential customer information [...] during the adjustment or litigation of an insurance claim."*

Every case reaching a court is based on a conflict, i.e., there is some question, as the one above, for which different parties have different opinions on its truth value. As a requirement for the framework, we can conclude that there has to be a conflict that needs to be resolved by a decision. This decision can be an arbitrary statement; hence, we call it a *decision formula*.

Sub-cases. A decision's justification usually involves decisions of several *sub-cases* in order to arrive at the final decision formula, e.g. the court needs to decide whether a specific law is applicable before examining what follows from its application. Each of these individual sub-case decisions may become a precedent for decisions which deal with a similar sub-case.

The Circumstances. *"[The plaintiff] concedes that under the definitions of the GLBA [...] information he requests is technically nonpublic personal information of a customer which the Act generally protects from disclosure[...]."*

Every case contains some factual background. These facts constitute some statements which are not under discussion but measurably true, e.g., that an address is nonpublic personal information. We summarize these facts in a *case description*.

Referencing Related Court Decisions. *"[T]he United States District Court for the Southern District of West Virginia handed down an opinion in Marks v. Global Mortgage Group, Inc., 218 F.R.D. 492 (S.D.W.Va.2003), providing us with timely and pertinent considerations."*

The key of case law is referencing other cases in order to derive statements. In the example case, this capability is used to introduce an argumentation from a different court. This mechanism is also used when statements are derived from regulations. Consequently, the framework has to be capable of introducing statements during the case justification by *references* to their origin.

Argumentation Structure of the Justification. *"[The] GLBA provides exceptions to its notification and opt-out procedures, including [...]"*

---

[1] The quotes are taken from MARTINO v. BARNETT, Supreme Court of Appeals of West Virginia, No. 31270, Decided: March 15, 2004. The decision text is public at http://caselaw.findlaw.com/wv-supreme-court-of-appeals/1016919.html

The argumentation structure of the justification is not linear, i.e., of the form $A \Rightarrow B \Rightarrow \ldots \Rightarrow$. But the arguments can be ordered in a tree form. The exceptions stipulated by the GLBA are enumerated and then discussed in the case justification. If more than one is applicable, these may serve as *independent decision grounds*, each being a potential precedent in its own right.

World Knowledge. *"[We] conclude that nonpublic personal information may be subject to release pursuant to judicial process."*

In the argumentation, the court leaves to the reader's knowledge that the plaintiff's litigation actually is a "judicial process". These open ends in the argumentation are neither explicitly covered by a decision nor by a case reference. Therefore, we need some world knowledge KB_W that will cover these axiomatic parts of the argumentation.

Precedents and Stare Decisis. The doctrine of *stare decisis* (to stand by things decided) or binding precedents is unique to common law systems. The decisions of superior courts are binding for later decisions of inferior courts (*vertical stare decisis*). These binding precedents are applied to similar cases by analogy.

In addition to the binding precedent, there also exists the persuasive precedent: *"While we recognize that the decision of the Marks court does not bind us, we find the reasoning in Marks regarding a judicial process exception to the GLBA very persuasive and compelling"*.

Stare decisis does not apply in civil law systems, like those of Germany or France. However, these systems have a *jurisprudence constante*, facilitating predictable and cohesive court decisions. Though civil law judges are not obliged to follow precedents, they may use prior decisions as persuasive precedents and oftentimes do so.

Material Difference. Stare decisis only applies if the subsequent court has to decide on a case or sub-case that is similar to the precedent. Therefore, if the court finds *material difference* between the cases, it is not bound by stare decisis. In practice, judges may claim material difference on unwarranted grounds, which may lead to conflicting decisions of analoguous cases within our framework. Thus, we need to be able to account for *false material difference*.

Involving Court Hierarchies. *"[W]e look initially to federal decisions interpreting the relevant provisions of the GLBA for guidance with regard to the reformulated question. However, the issue proves to be a novel one in the country since few courts, federal or state, have addressed the exceptions to the GLBA."*

For our framework we need to take into account court hierarchies to identify binding precedents. In common law jurisdictions, inferior courts are bound by the decisions of superior courts; in civil law jurisdictions superior courts usually have higher authority without being strictly binding. In federal states like the USA or Germany we need to account for parallel hierarchies on state and on federal levels. This complex hierarchy has significant implications on stare decisis.

Hence, in our framework every case needs to be annotated by a court which is part of a *court hierarchy*, to identify the character of precedents, binding or potentially persuasive.

Ratio Decidendi and Obiter Dicta. Regarding the court's decision text, we need to differentiate between two types of statements. The actual binding property of a precedent has only those statements and legal reasoning that are necessary for the rationale of the decision. These necessary statements as called *ratio decidendi* and constitute the binding precedent. Further statements and reasoning that are not essentially necessary for the decision are called *obiter dicta*. These are not binding but can be referenced as persuasive precedents.

For our reasoning framework we need to differentiate and annotate statements into these two different categories to correctly identify binding precedents.

3   Defining the PriCL Framework

Reflecting the observations just made, we define cases (Section 3.1) and case law databases (Section 3.2). Thereby we also explain how to model the legal principles described in Section 2. Then, we define how the database can be used in order to deduce facts outside the framework (Section 3.3). We analyze our framework, validating a number of basic desirable properties of case law databases (Section 3.4). We finally show, for privacy regulations specifically, that our framework matches the requirements identified by previous work [8] (Section 3.5).

Throughout this section, we assume an underlying logic in which world properties are expressed and reasoned about. Our framework is parametric with respect to the precise form of that logic. The requirements the logic has to fulfill are interpreting predicates as relations over objects, supporting universal truth/falseness (denoted respectively as $\top$ and $\bot$), conjunction (denoted $\wedge$), entailment (denoted $A \models B$ if formula A entails formula B), and monotonicity regarding entailment, i.e., if $A \models B$ then $A \wedge C \models B$ for any formula C. As an intuition when reading the following, the reader may assume we are using a first-order predicate logic.

3.1   Introducing Cases

As we have seen, a case consists of a decision formula, a case description, a court, and a proof tree. The first three components are straightforward to capture formally (courts are represented by a finite set Courts of court identifiers). Designing the proof tree is more involved since it needs to capture the judge's justification. We distinguish between different kinds of nodes in the tree depending on the role the respective statements play in the justification: Does a sentence make an axiomatic statement, or form part of the case description? Does it refer to a previous case, adopting a decision under particular prerequisites? Does it make an assessment on the truth of a particular statement (e.g., that a particular piece of information is or is not to be considered private) under particular prerequisites?

We therefore reflect these "standalone" statements in the leaf nodes of the proof tree, categorized by the three different types of statements mentioned.

The inner nodes of the tree perform logical deductions from their children nodes, representing the reasoning inherent in the justification, i.e., the conclusions that are made until finally, in the tree root, the decision formula is reached. We differentiate between two kinds of reasoning steps, AND-steps and OR-steps. The OR-steps reflect the principle of *independent decision grounds*. The AND-step is the natural conclusion steps that is used to ensure that the decision made is reached through the argumentation.

In order to avoid a recursive definition, we need a (possibly infinite) set of case identifiers C_I. Throughout the paper we assume a fixed given set C_I.

Definition 1 (Case). *A case C is a tuple* (df, CaseDesc, ProofTree, crt) *s.t.*
- *df is a formula that we call the* decision formula *of C.*
- *CaseDesc is a formula describing the case's circumstances.*
- *ProofTree is a (finite) tree consisting of formulas f where the formula of the root node is df. Inner nodes are annotated with AND or OR and leaves are annotated with $l \in \{Axiom, Assess\} \cup \{Ref(i) \mid i \in C_I\}$. Leaf formulas l are additionally associated with a* prerequisite *formula* **pre**. *For leaves annotated with Axiom, we require that pre $= l$.*
- *crt $\in$ Courts.*

For leaf formulas l, we refer to l as the node's fact, and we will often write these nodes as pre $\to$ fact *where* fact $= l$.

By the prerequisites *of an inner node n with children nodes $n_1, \ldots, n_k$, denoted as* pres(n), *we refer to $\bigvee_{1 \leq i \leq k}$ pres(n_i) if n is annotated by OR and $\bigwedge_{1 \leq i \leq k}$ pres(n_i) if n is annotated by AND. The prerequisites of a case C are the prerequisites of the root node and denoted by pres$_C$. We define analogously the facts of a node and a case. We will often identify formulas with proof tree nodes. Given a case C, by df$_C$ we denote the decision formula of C.*

Let $\mathbf{C}$ be a set of cases and $\mu : \mathbf{C} \to C_I$ a function. If for every reference Ref(i) in $\mathbf{C}$, there is an $D \in \mathbf{C}$ with $\mu(D) = i$, we call the set $\mathbf{C}$ closed under μ.

We assume *world knowledge* common to all cases. In the example of argumentation ends in Section 2, it is assumed that the reader knows that the predicate is_judical_process holds for any case. Formally, the world knowledge is a formula KB_W (naturally, a conjunction of world properties) in the underlying logic.

Definition 1 is purely syntactic, imposing no restrictions on how the different elements are intended to behave. We will fill in these restrictions one by one as part of spelling out the details of our framework, forcing cases to actually decide a conflict and behave according to the legal principles. One thing the reader should keep in mind is that pre $\to$ fact is *not* intended as a logical implication. Rather, pre are the prerequisites that a judge took into account when making the assessment that fact (e.g., the privacy status of a piece of information) is considered to be true under the circumstances CaseDesc $\models$ pre. This solely captures human decisions such as trade-off decisions. However, the frameworks allows reasoning about consequence of such decisions. The formulas pres$_C$, and respectively facts$_C$, collect all prerequisites needed to apply the proof tree, and respectively all facts needed to execute the proof tree; axiom leaves act in both roles.

In principle, a case has the purpose to decide a formula df. However, while justifying that a formula holds, e.g., that a telecommunication company has to delete connection data after a certain amount of time, the court might decide other essential subquestions. This concept is conveniently captured through the notion of *subcases*.

Definition 2 (Subcase). *Let* $C = (df, \mathsf{CaseDesc}, \mathsf{ProofTree}, crt)$ *be a case and* $n \in \mathsf{ProofTree}$ *a node. Let* $\mathsf{sub}(n)$ *be the subtree of* $\mathsf{ProofTree}$ *with root node* n. *The case* $\mathsf{sub}(C, n) := (n, \mathsf{CaseDesc}, \mathsf{sub}(n), crt)$ *is a subcase of* C.

Another aspect that is of interest when referencing cases is the degree of abstraction. For example, one case could decide that a specific telecommunication company C has to delete connection information D of some user U after a specific time period t. The question of how this decision can be used in order to decide the question for different companies C' or different information D' is covered by the legal concept of material difference. For this work, we assume that a judge specifies the allowed difference in the prerequisites of a decision.

Our definition of cases, so far, is generic in the sense that it may be applied to any domain of law. To configure our framework to privacy regulations more specifically, a natural approach is to simply restrict the permissible forms of decision formulas. We explicitly leave out legal domains such as individualized sentencing or measuring of damages. Decisions in the privacy context are about whether or not a particular action is legal when executed on particular data. We capture this by assuming a dedicated predicate is_legal_action, and restricting the decision formula to be an atomic predicate of the form is_legal_action(a), where a is an action from an underlying set Actions of possible actions treated as objects (constants) in the underlying logic. This can also be used in other legal domains, but it turns out to be sufficient to connect our formalization of privacy cases with other policy based approaches. Note that, in contrast to other policy frameworks, we do not need to add the context to the predicate, as the context is contained in the case, via nodes of the form *"if the transfer-action a has purpose marketing and the receiver is a third party, then ¬is_legal_action(a)"*. As decisions about the legality of actions are not naturally part of the common world knowledge KB$_W$, nor of the case description CaseDesc itself, our modeling decision is to disallow the use of is_legal_action predicates in these formulas. In other words, the world and case context describe the circumstances which are relevant to determining action legality, but they do not define whether or not an action is legal.

Definition 3 (Privacy Case). *Given world knowledge* KB$_W$ *and action set* Actions, *a case* $C = (df, \mathsf{CaseDesc}, \mathsf{ProofTree}, crt)$ *is a privacy case if* $df \in \{\neg\mathsf{is\_legal\_action}(a), \mathsf{is\_legal\_action}(a)\}$ *for some action* $a \in$ Actions, *where the* is_legal_action *predicate is not used in either of* KB$_W$ *or* CaseDesc.

Starting to fill in the intended semantics of cases, we first capture the essential properties a case needs to have to "make sense" as a stand-alone structure. Additional properties regarding cross-case structures will be considered in the next subsection. We will use the word "consistency" to denote this kind of property. The following definition captures the intentions behind cases:

Definition 4 (Case Consistency). *Let $C = (df,\ CaseDesc,\ ProofTree,\ crt)$ be a case. C is* consistent *if the following holds (for all nodes n where $n_1, \ldots, n_k$ are its child nodes)*

(i) $KB_W \wedge CaseDesc \not\models \bot$ *(ii) $KB_W \wedge CaseDesc \models pres_C$*

(iii) $KB_W \wedge CaseDesc \wedge facts_C \not\models \bot$

(iv) $\bigwedge_{1 \leq i \leq k} n_i \models n$ if n is an AND step   and $\bigvee_{1 \leq i \leq k} n_i \models n$ if n is an OR step

Regarding (i), if the world knowledge contradicts the case description, i.e., $KB_W \wedge CaseDesc \models \bot$, then the case could not have happened. Similarly, (iii) the case context must not contradict the facts that the proof tree makes use of (this subsumes (i), which we kept as it improves readability). As for (ii), the case context must imply the axioms as well as the prerequisites which the present judge (assessments) or other judges (references to other cases; see also Definition 7) assumed to conclude these facts. (iv) says that inner nodes must represent conclusions drawn from their children.

The OR nodes of the proof tree reflect the legal argumentation structure of *independent decision grounds*, the judge gives several arguments. If the judge of a later case decides that one of these arguments is invalid for the conclusion, he needs to be able to falsify only one of the branches and not the whole tree.

3.2   Combining Cases to Case Law Databases

The quintessential property of case law is that cases make references to other cases. These references are necessary to formulate several legal principles.

The legal principles *false material difference* and *reversing decisions* define requirements for when not to reference a case, either because it contains a mistake or because the opinion has changed over time. Therefore, we consider the design cleaner if both principles are covered by the same mechanism of the framework and hence we denote single Assess nodes as unwarranted, i.e., to forbid the reference to be used thereafter.

We require a different mechanism to differentiate cases we must agree with and cases which we may use as reference. Unwarranting rather defines which decisions must not be referenced. In particular, we need to differentiate between assessments coming from the legal principles *ratio decidendi* and *obiter dicta*. While the part of the decision following *ratio decidendi* leads to a binding precedent, the *obiter dicta* part is not binding. Thus, we introduce predicates may-ref and must-agree. It also provides a mechanisms to respect the *court hierarchy*. Intuitively, may-ref(C_1, C_2) denotes the circumstances that case C_1 may reference case C_2; must-agree(C_1, C_2) analogously denotes that C_1 must agree with C_2.

In addition, we need to introduce the concept of time by a total order $\leq_t$ over cases. This concept allows us to formulate the requirement that references can only point to the past.

Definition 5 (Case Law Database (CLD)). *A case law database is a tuple* $DB = (\mathbf{C}, \leq_t, \text{must-agree}, \text{may-ref}, \mu, U)$ *such that:*

- $\mathbf{C}$ *is a set of cases. We will also write* $C \in DB$ *for* $C \in \mathbf{C}$.
- $\mu : \mathbf{C} \to \mathcal{C}_\mathbf{I}$ *is an injective function such that* $\mathbf{C}$ *is closed under* μ. *In the following we will also write* Ref(D) *for* Ref(i) *if* $\mu(D) = i$.
- *Let* $<_{ref} := \{(C, D) \mid D$ *contains a* Ref(C) *node}* *and* $\leq_t$ *is an order that we call* time order *of the cases. It has to hold:*

$$\text{must-agree} \underset{<_{ref}\subseteq}{\subseteq} \text{may-ref} \subseteq \leq_t \subseteq \mathbf{C} \times \mathbf{C}$$

- U *specifies the unwarranted nodes, i.e.,* $U : \mathbf{C} \to \mathbf{N}$ *is function such that*
  - $\mathbf{N}$ *is a subset of the nodes labelled with* Assess *or* Ref *in the cases* $\mathbf{C}$.
  - *The set increases monotonic, i.e.,* $C \leq_t D \implies U(C) \subseteq U(D)$.

  We denote the unwarranted *nodes of* DB *by* $U(DB) := \bigcup_{C \in \mathbf{C}} U(C)$.

The function μ is used to remove the recursive definition of a case and enables us to connect cases via their individual semantics.

Regarding the relations must-agree and the may-ref we made two design decisions. First, we require to not link must-agree and the actual references $<_{ref}$. On the one hand, there might be precedents which are not applicable, but on the other hand, we want the freedom to define must-agree and may-ref only depending on the court hierarchy. The second design decision is to base these relations on cases instead of decision nodes. As for the first decision, the purpose is to make an instantiation of the definition only depending on the court, but we need to be careful regarding the principles *ratio decidendi* and *obiter dicta*. Since one of them is not binding, i.e., a must-agree and the other is. This differentiation can be achieved by replacing every case with a set of cases. We require this to be part of the modeling process. We did not add further restrictions since they may depend on local law.

Example 1 (Must-agree and may-references for a court hierarchy). Assume the set of courts Courts is partially ordered by $\leq_\S$, i.e., there is a court hierarchy. In this case, we could model must-agree by
must-agree $= \{(C_1, C_2) \mid C_i = (\text{df}_i, d_i, p_i, \text{crt}_i), i \in \{1, 2\}, C_1 \leq_t C_2,$
                    and $\text{crt}_1 \leq_\S \text{crt}_2\}$.

It is easy to see that the must-agree predicate actually only depends on the crt and not on the other parameters of the proof. We call this property *court-dependency*.

The key property of unwarranted decisions is that they are time dependent. In order to only use warranted decisions when referencing, we define warranted subcases as follows:

Definition 6 (Warranted Subcase). *A subcase* $(df, \mathsf{CaseDesc}, \mathsf{ProofTree}, crt)$
is warranted with respect to a set N *of nodes if the case*
$(df, \mathsf{CaseDesc}, \mathsf{ProofTree'}, crt)$ *is consistent where* $\mathsf{ProofTree'}$ *is derived from*
$\mathsf{ProofTree}$ *by replacing every precondition of a node* $n \in N$ *by* $\perp$.

It remains to define when a case law database can be considered to be consistent. To that end, we consider case references and conflicts between cases. Starting with the former, we obtain:

Definition 7 (Correct Case Reference). *Let* DB *be a case law database and* $C = (df, \mathsf{CaseDesc}, \mathsf{ProofTree}, crt)$ *a case in* DB. *A leaf node* $\mathsf{pre} \to \mathsf{fact}$ *in* $\mathsf{ProofTree}$ *annotated with* $\mathsf{Ref}(D)$ *references correctly if* $D_u = (\mathsf{fact}, \mathsf{CaseDesc}_D, \mathsf{ProofTree}_D, crt_D)$ *is a warranted subcase of a case* $D \in DB$ *w.r.t.* $U(C)$, $\mathsf{may\text{-}ref}(C, D)$ *holds and* $\mathsf{KB}_W \wedge \mathsf{pre} \models \mathsf{pres}_D$. C *references correctly if all its leaves annotated with* $\mathsf{Ref}(D)$ *reference correctly.*

Consider that, when referencing a (sub)case D as $\mathsf{pre} \to \mathsf{fact}$ from our case C at hand, we are essentially saying that the same argumentation applied in D can be applied in our case, to prove fact under circumstances pre. So we need to show that this applicability of arguments is actually given. This is ensured by $\mathsf{KB}_W \wedge \mathsf{pre} \models \mathsf{pres}_D$ because pres_D collects all prerequisites, axioms and otherwise, needed to apply D. Note that, if C is consistent, by Definition 4 (ii) it holds that $\mathsf{KB}_W \wedge \mathsf{CaseDesc} \models \mathsf{pre}$ and thus $\mathsf{KB}_W \wedge \mathsf{CaseDesc} \models \mathsf{pres}_D$. As the same applies recursively to the case references made in D, we know that pre (given KB_W and $\mathsf{CaseDesc}$) entails *all* judge decisions underlying the assessment fact.

We are now almost in the position to define consistency of the entire case law database. The last missing piece in the puzzle is to identify when cases should be considered to be in conflict — which naturally occurs in case law databases where judges may make different decisions. We capture this through pairs of cases whose prerequisites are compatible, while their facts are contradictory:

Definition 8 (Case Conflict). *Let* C_1 *be a case in* DB *and* C_2 *be a warranted case w.r.t.* $U(C_1)$. *We say that* C_1 *is in conflict with* C_2 *if and only if*
   (i) $\mathsf{KB}_W \wedge \mathsf{pres}_{C_1} \wedge \mathsf{pres}_{C_2} \not\models \perp$ (ii) $\mathsf{KB}_W \wedge \mathsf{facts}_{C_1} \wedge \mathsf{facts}_{C_2} \models \perp$
   (iii) $\mathsf{must\text{-}agree}(C_1, C_2)$
A case C *is in conflict with* DB *if there is a* $D \in DB$ *s.t.* C *is in conflict with* D.

We ignore the case descriptions here, other than what is explicitly employed as axioms in the proof trees: we consider cases to be in conflict if one *could* construct a case (e.g., $\mathsf{pres}_{C_1} \wedge \mathsf{pres}_{C_2}$) which would make it possible to come to a contradictory decision. We define case law database consistency as follows:

Definition 9 (Case law database consistency). *A case law database* $DB = (\mathbf{C}, \leq_t, \mathsf{must\text{-}agree}, \mathsf{may\text{-}ref}, \mu, U)$ *is*
  (i) case-wise consistent *if every* $C \in DB$ *is consistent,*
  (ii) referentially consistent *if every* $C \in DB$ *references correctly, and*
  (iii) hierarchically consistent *if every* $C \in DB$ *is not in conflict with* DB.

(iv) warrants consistently *if for every C holds: U(C) contains all* Ref*(D) nodes where D is an unwarranted subcase w.r.t. U(C).*

We call *DB* consistent *if it warrants consistently and is hierarchically, referentially and case-wise consistent.*

3.3   Deriving Legal Consequences: Deducibility and Permissibility

In the following we assume that the predicates may-ref and must-agree of the DB do not depend on the case description, the decision formula or the proof tree, but are only court dependent, cf. Example 1. As a consequence, we know the value of these predicates for formula values and case descriptions which are not contained as a case in the database given only the court level of the case. In other words, we require an operation DB $\cup$ {C} that puts C at the end of the timeline regarding $\leq_t$, assigns a fresh identifier $i \in \mathcal{C}_I$ to C with μ, uses as $U(C) := U(\text{DB})$, and adopts must-agree, may-ref appropriately and is independent of the decision formula and the proof tree. This operation is needed to apply the framework to situations not contained in the database.

Obvious applications of our framework are advanced support for case search, and consistency checking. A more advanced task is to evaluate the legality of actions given the cases reflected in the database. For example, when designing a course administration system, one may ask "Am I allowed to store students' grades in the system?" Our formalism supports this kind of question at different levels of strength, namely:

Definition 10 (Deducibility and Permissibility). *Let* DB $=$ $(\mathbf{C}, \leq_t$, must-agree, may-ref, $\mu, U)$ *be a consistent CLD, and f a formula. We say that f is* permitted *in DB under circumstances* CaseDesc *and court* crt *if there exists a case* $C = (f, \text{CaseDesc}, \text{ProofTree}, \text{crt})$ *such that* ProofTree *does not contain nodes labeled with* Assess, *and* DB $\cup$ {C} *is consistent (where C is inserted at the end of the timeline $\leq_t$). We say that f is* uncontradicted *in DB under* CaseDesc *and* crt *if* $\neg f$ *is not permitted under* CaseDesc *and* crt. *We say that f is* deducible *if it is permitted and uncontradicted.*

For sets F of formulas, we say that F is permitted *in DB under* CaseDesc *and* crt *if there exists a set of cases* {$C_f = (f, \text{CaseDesc}, \text{ProofTree}_f, \text{crt}) \mid f \in F$} *such that every* ProofTree$_f$ *does not contain nodes labeled with* Assess, *and* DB $\cup$ {$C_f \mid f \in F$} *is consistent (where the C_f are inserted in any order at the end of the timeline $\leq_t$).*

It might be confusing at first why we attach to f the weak attribute of being "permitted" if we can construct a case supporting it. The issue is, both f and $\neg f$ may have such support in the same database. This follows directly from the freedom of different courts to contradict each other. If two courts at the same level decide differently on the same issue, then that is fine by our assumptions. Hence, to qualify a formula f for the strong attribute of being "deducible", we require the database to permit f and to not permit its contradiction.

The concept of deducibility of a *set F* of formulas is interesting because, in general, this is not the same as deducing each formula in separation. In particular, while each of f and $\neg f$ may be permitted in the same database, $\{f, \neg f\}$ is never permitted because adding the hypothetical supporting cases necessarily incurs a hierarchical conflict. Permissibility of F is also not the same as permissibility of $\bigwedge_{f \in F} f$ because the latter makes a stronger assumption: all cases referred to in order to conclude $\bigwedge_{f \in F} f$ must have compatible prerequisites. So deducibility of formula sets forms a middle ground between individual and conjunctive deducibility.

Theorem 1. *There is a consistent case law database DB, case description CaseDesc and court crt, such that there is a set F of formulas for each of the following properties (in DB under circumstances CaseDesc and court crt):*

(i) For every $f \in F$, f is permissible and F is not permissible.
(ii) F is permissible, but $\bigwedge_{f \in F} f$ is not permissible.

The proof and the details of all other proofs are given in the long version [6].

Characterizing Deducibility. Deducibility is the central concept for answering questions that are not explicitly answered by the database. However, Definition 10 does not give an algorithmic description of how to decide whether some formula is deducible. It is also inconvenient for proving properties about permissibility and deducibility.

Intuitively, a formula should be permissible if there is a set of warranted decisions which allow us to conclude the predicate and a formula f should be deducible if in addition no set of decisions contradicts f. We will first define *supporting sets* and then prove that the intuition matches the definitions of permissibility and deducibility.

Definition 11 (Supporting set). *Let $DB = (\mathbf{C}, \leq_t, \text{must-agree}, \text{may-ref}, \mu, U)$ be a consistent case law database, f a formula, CaseDesc a case description and crt a court. A set $\mathcal{A}$ of leaf nodes in DB that are labeled with Assess is a supporting set for formula f if the following holds:*

(1) $KB_W \wedge CaseDesc \models \bigwedge_{(pre \rightarrow fact) \in \mathcal{A}} pre$
(2) $KB_W \wedge CaseDesc \wedge \bigwedge_{(pre \rightarrow fact) \in \mathcal{A}} fact \models f$
(3) $KB_W \wedge CaseDesc \wedge \bigwedge_{(pre \rightarrow fact) \in \mathcal{A}} fact \not\models \bot$

A supporting set is unwarranted if it contains an unwarranted node w.r.t. any $C \in \mathbf{C}$. If it is not unwarranted it is warranted.

A supporting set is consistent with DB if $DB \cup \{(\top, CaseDesc, ProofTree, crt)\}$ is consistent, where ProofTree consists of a root node with annotation $\top$ and leaf nodes with annotation $Ref(C_n)$ for $n \in \mathcal{A}$, where C_n is the case that contains node n.

Note that a supporting set that is consistent with the DB leads to consistency, and correct referencing, and does not create any conflicts. The properties required in the definition are a consequence of the definition of database consistency. A case constructed from a supporting set would simply refer to all decisions and place the formula at the root.

The following theorem characterizes permissibility and deducibility using supporting sets. This characterization suggests an algorithmic way of deciding the properties and gives a tool for proving properties about case law databases.

Theorem 2. *Let DB be a consistent case law database, f a formula, CaseDesc a case description and crt a court. The following holds:*

1. *$C \in DB$ with warranted node $f \Rightarrow \exists \mathcal{A}$ that supports f*
2. *f is permitted (under circumstance CaseDesc and court crt) $\Leftrightarrow \exists \mathcal{A}$ that supports f, is warranted, and is consistent with DB*
3. *f is deducible $\Leftrightarrow \exists \mathcal{A}$ that supports f and is consistent with DB, and $\forall \mathcal{B}$ it holds that $\mathcal{B}$ does not support $\neg f$, is unwarranted, or is not consistent with DB*

3.4   General Properties of Case Law Databases

Introducing a new framework always comes with the risk of modeling errors. A method for alleviating that risk is to prove properties that the framework is expected to have. In order to validate the framework introduced here, we have proven that (i) case references do not influence decisions (Theorem 2); in this subsection we also prove that (ii) consistency is necessary for property (i) (Theorem 3), and that (iii) neither $\bot$ nor $\{f, \neg f\}$ are ever permitted (Theorem 4).

Regarding (i), we have shown that every formula f in the database can be derived from a supporting set of previous decisions (Theorem 2) with the case description and world knowledge. Hence there is no possible interplay between case references that would make it possible to prove something not backed up by judges' decisions.

Regarding (ii), Theorem 2 implies immediately that, whenever a formula f is deducible, then it follows from decisions made by judges in previous cases. It is easy to verify that our restrictions are necessary to ensure this, i.e., that this property gets lost if we forsake either case-wise or referential consistency:

Theorem 3. *Let DB be a case law database, and let f be any formula that does not entail $\bot$. Then there exist cases C_1 and C_2, each with root node f and the empty case desc $\top$, such that (inserting C_i at the end of the timeline $\leq_t$):*

- *If DB is case-wise consistent, then so is $DB \cup \{C_1\}$.*
- *If DB is referentially consistent, then so is $DB \cup \{C_2\}$.*
- *If there is a crt such that must-agree(crt) $= \emptyset$, then in addition this holds: for each of $i = 1, 2$, if DB is hierarchically consistent, then so is $DB \cup \{C_i\}$.*

We remark that, by restricting the formula f only slightly, the proof of Theorem 3 can be strengthened so as not to have to rely on a maximal court for ensuring hierarchical consistency. In particular, if f is made of predicates that do not occur anywhere in the case law database, then the cases C_1 and C_2 as constructed cannot be in conflict with any other cases, thus preserving hierarchical consistency for arbitrary courts crt. We finally prove (iii), non-permissibility of either $\bot$ or $\{f, \neg f\}$:

Theorem 4. *The formula* $\bot$ *is not permitted in any case law database DB, under any circumstances* CaseDesc *and court* crt. *The same holds for* $\{f, \neg f\}$ *if* $crt \in$ must-agree(crt).

3.5   Privacy Cases and Norms

We now point out an interesting property of privacy cases, and of databases consisting only of such cases. We call such databases *privacy case law databases.*

Rule based privacy policies are a well established and widely used concept. The rules that are used are usually reflected by norms defining privacy regulations. However, neither rules nor norms are reflected in the case law framework. In this subsection, we show that we can use a natural definition of norms that can be extracted from privacy cases. In addition, it is possible to transform a privacy case to a normal form such that a norm that decides the case is represented.

At the core of privacy regulations are positive and negative norms, as introduced by [8]. Positive norms are permissive in the sense that they describe conditions that allow transactions with personal data ($\phi \Rightarrow$ is_legal_action(a)). Negative norms, in contrast, define necessary conditions for such transactions, i.e., they forbid transactions with personal data unless certain conditions are met ($\phi \Rightarrow \neg$is_legal_action(a)).

Definition 12 (Norms). *Let* $a \in$ Actions. *A norm is a formula that has the form* $\phi \Rightarrow p$ *where* is_legal_action(a) *does not occur in* ϕ. *The norm is a positive norm, denoted* ϕ^+, *if* $p =$ is_legal_action(a) *and a negative norm, denoted* ϕ^-, *if* $p = \neg$is_legal_action(a). *A norm* ϕ *decides* p *given* f *if* $KB_W \wedge f \models \phi$.

In the case law framework, norms are hidden by judges' assessments. However, in the spirit of Theorem 2, norms are reflected by sets of cases that could be referenced in order to support either the legality of an action (positive norm) or its illegality (negative norm). In the following theorem, we show that we can extract a norm for every privacy case avoiding the recursion of Theorem 2.

Theorem 5. *Let* DB *be a consistent privacy case law database and* $C = ($df, CaseDesc, ProofTree, crt$) \in$ DB. *Then there is a norm* ϕ *that decides* df *given* CaseDesc. *In particular, there are formulas* ϕ_W, ϕ_S *such that* is_legal_action(a) *does not occur in these formulas and*
(1) facts$_C \Rightarrow \phi_W \wedge (\phi_S \Rightarrow$ df$)$ *(2)* $\phi_W \wedge (\phi_S \Rightarrow$ df$) \Rightarrow$ df

The formulas ϕ_W and ϕ_S can be used to construct a normal form of privacy cases. In particular, this normal form is consistent and allows reading off norms.

Corollary 1 (Normal forms). *Let* $DB = (\mathbf{C}, \leq_t,$ must-agree, may-ref, $\mu, U)$ *be a privacy case law database,* $C = ($df, CaseDesc, ProofTree, crt$) \in$ DB *be a case, and* D *be the set of* C's *leaf nodes.* $N(C)$ *is the case that consists of a root node* df, *two inner nodes* ϕ_w *and* $\phi_S \Rightarrow$ df *and the leaf nodes* D *as children of both inner nodes. We call* $N(C)$ *the normal form of* C. *If DB is consistent, then* $(\mathbf{C} \backslash \{C\} \cup \{N(C)\}, \leq_t)$ *is also consistent (where* $N(C)$ *is placed at the position of* C *w.r.t.* $\leq_t$).

In order to define $N(C)$, we need to duplicate the leaf nodes since the transformations to get ϕ_W and ϕ_S ignore which fact is needed to get the corresponding formula. Thus, a leaf node's fact could end up in both formulas ϕ_W and ϕ_S.

In conformance with [8], we can conclude from deducibility of an action that there is a positive norm supporting it and show that no negative norm can be applied, i.e., all negative norms are respected (Theorem 4).

4   Reasoning Tasks

We now discuss the reasoning tasks associated with our framework — how to answer questions such as "are we allowed to send data D to some party P?" — in more detail, giving an algorithm sketch and brief complexity analysis (in terms of the number of reasoning operations required) for each.

Consistency. Analyzing and keeping the state of the case law database consistent is of vital importance for its usefulness; cf. Theorem 4. As in the definition of consistency, we split the task of checking consistency into case-wise, referential, and hierarchical consistency. Due to their simplicity, we postpone the detailed description of their algorithms to the long version [6].

All of these properties are defined per case, i.e., the case wise check of the corresponding property has to be repeated |DB| times. Following the respective definition, checking case consistency costs |ProofTree + 1| entailment operations and checking correct referencing for C costs references(C) where references(C) is the number of nodes in C annotated by Ref(D). Hierarchical consistency can be checked along the time line $\leq_t$ only testing for conflicts with earlier cases. So for the i-th case, we need at most $(i-1) \cdot 2$ entailment checks, since every conflict check requires 2. Consequently, we require $|DB| \cdot (|DB| + 1)$ entailment checks.

Deducibility and Permissibility. As deducibility amounts to two consecutive permissibility checks, we consider the latter exclusively. We are given a database DB, a formula whose permissibility should be checked, as well as a case description CaseDesc and a court crt forming the circumstances. Permissibility is equivalent to the existence of a supporting set $\mathcal{A}$ for f that is consistent with DB. Thus the task of permissibility can be reduced to checking the existence of a suitable set $\mathcal{A}$. If the answer is "yes", we can also output a witness, i.e., a hypothetical case C showing permissibility. A straightforward means for doing this is to set $C := (f, \mathsf{CaseDesc}, \mathsf{ProofTree}, \mathsf{crt})$ where ProofTree consists of root node f, one leaf node l labeled with Ref(D) for every $D \in \mathcal{A}$, as well as one leaf node $\mathsf{KB}_W \wedge \mathsf{CaseDesc}$ labeled with Axiom. For convenience, we will denote this construction by $C(\mathcal{A})$. See Algorithm 1.

The correctness of the algorithm is shown by Theorem 2. In contrast to our previous algorithms, deducibility checking as per Algorithm 1 requires an exponential number of entailment checks in the worst case. This raises the questions (1) whether or not this exponential overhead is inherent in the complexity of deciding permissibility, and (2) whether it is possible to encode the permissibility test directly into the logic instead.

Algorithm 1. Permissibility

Input : A formula f, case description CaseDesc, court crt, and a consistent
CLD DB

Output: A case $C = (f, \text{CaseDesc}, \text{ProofTree}, \text{crt})$ such that $\text{DB} \cup \{C\}$ is
consistent (where C is set to be the maximum w.r.t. $\leq_t$), or $\bot$ if no
such C exists

1 Test whether $\text{KB}_W \wedge \text{CaseDesc} \models \bot$. If so, output $\bot$.
2 Test whether $\text{KB}_W \wedge \text{CaseDesc} \models f$. If so, output
   $(f, \text{CaseDesc}, \text{ProofTree}, \text{crt})$ where ProofTree is the proof tree consisting of a
   leaf node labeled by Axiom containing f.
3 Set $\mathcal{N} := \emptyset$.
4 **for** every $D \in DB$ and every $(\text{pre} \to \text{fact}) \in D$ labeled **Assess do**
5 $\quad$ Check if $\text{KB}_W \wedge \text{CaseDesc} \models \text{pre}$
6 $\quad$ Check if $\text{KB}_W \wedge \text{CaseDesc} \wedge \text{fact} \not\models \bot$
7 $\quad$ If both checks succeed, set $\mathcal{N} := \mathcal{N} \cup \{(\text{pre} \to \text{fact})\}$.
8 **end**
9 **for** $\mathcal{A} \in 2^{\mathcal{N}}$ **do**
10 $\quad$ Check that $\text{KB}_W \wedge \text{CaseDesc} \models \bigwedge_{(\text{pre} \to \text{fact}) \in \mathcal{A}} \text{pre}$
11 $\quad$ Check that $\text{KB}_W \wedge \text{CaseDesc} \wedge \bigwedge_{(\text{pre} \to \text{fact}) \in \mathcal{A}} \text{fact} \models f$
12 $\quad$ Check that $\text{KB}_W \wedge \text{CaseDesc} \wedge \bigwedge_{(\text{pre} \to \text{fact}) \in \mathcal{A}} \text{fact} \not\models \bot$
13 $\quad$ **for** every $E \in DB$ with $\text{crt} <_\S \text{crt}_E$ **do**
14 $\quad\quad |$ Check that E and $C(\mathcal{A})$ are not in conflict.
15 $\quad$ **end**
16 $\quad$ If all three tests succeed, go on with step 18, otherwise continue with
   the next $\mathcal{D}$.
17 **end**
18 If a set $\mathcal{A}$ succeeded, output $C(\mathcal{A})$, otherwise output $\bot$.

The answer to (1) is a qualified "yes" in the sense that permissibility checking
essentially pre-fixes entailment checks with an existential quantifier. As entailment checks correspond to universal quantification, this intuitively means that
for permissibility we need to test the validity of a $\exists\forall$ formula, instead of a $\forall$
formula for entailment. So we add a quantifier alternation step, which typically
does come at the price of increased complexity. This line of thought also immediately provides an intuitive answer to question (2), namely "yes but only if the
underlying logic contains $\exists\forall$ quantification".

Of course, both these answers are only approximate and only speak in broad
terms. Whether each is to be answered with "yes" or "no" depends on the precise
form of the logic, and on what kind of blow-up we are willing to tolerate. To
make matters concrete, we now consider three particular logics, namely first-
order predicate logic, description logic (more specifically a particular version
of $\mathcal{ALC}$) and propositional logic (i.e., first-order predicate logic given a finite
universe and without quantification). We start with the latter.

In what follows, say we need to check whether formula f is permitted in
DB under circumstances CaseDesc. We abstract from the complications entailed
by maintaining hierarchical consistency, and assume that for crt, it holds that
must-agree(crt) $= \emptyset$.

Theorem 6. *For propositional logic, deciding permissibility is Σ_2^p-complete.*

Proof sketch. The set $\Sigma_2^p = \mathbf{NP^{NP}}$, so containment is shown by guessing a supporting set and verifying its properties using an **NP** oracle. For the hardness we encode an QBF formula $\exists x \forall y : \phi(x,y)$ in permissibility request for case law database. We do this by encoding all possible values for x in the database and asking for the permissibility of $\phi(x,y)$. Details can be found in [6].

As entailment testing in propositional logic is only **coNP**-complete, Theorem 6 answers question (1) with "yes", and answers question (2) with "no, unless we are willing to tolerate worst-case exponentially large formulas".

Theorem 7. *Permissibility is equivalent to satisfiability of a formula whose size is polynomial in the size of DB, CaseDesc, and f for*
(1) first-order logic.
*(2) the description logic $\mathcal{ALC}$ with concept constructors **fills** and **one-of** by role constructors **role-and, role-not, product**, and **inverse**.[2]*

Proof sketch. The result in [12] shows equality of expressivity of first-order logic with at most two free variables. Thus we construct a suitable formula for the first part. We do this by using existantial quantification in order to choose a warranted supporting set and then design the formula such that it is satisfiable if and only if the consistency properties of the case holds that can be constructed from that supporting set (i.e., the case potentially output by Algorithm 1). All parts that are not choosen by the existential quantifier will be equivalent to $\top$. Details can be found in [6].

Norm Extraction. As seen in Section 3.5, privacy cases induce normative rules. The format of rules gives the advantage that these are easy to enforce and bridge the gap towards privacy policies. As shown by Theorem 5 we extract a norm for every case in the database. The algorithm is postponed to the long version [6]. It basically turns the proof of Theorem 5 into an algorithm transforming the logical formula of the case's facts.

Let f be the size of the biggest formula in the leaves of C and n the number of nodes in C. Then the size of the norm can become $\mathcal{O}(2^f \cdot n + |\mathsf{pre}_C|)$. The computation needs operations linear in that size.

5 Logic Selection

For modeling purposes as well as for computational purposes the choice of logic is, of course, of paramount importance. The only hard requirement ("must have") that the logic, $\mathcal{L}$, must meet is:
(i) **Sufficient expressivity** to tackle our framework and reasoning tasks. Precisely, the minimal requirement is for $\mathcal{L}$ to provide a language $\mathcal{L}_{\mathcal{F}}$ for formulas, with reasoning support for tests of the form (a) $\bigwedge_{\phi \in \Phi} \models \bot$ and (b)

---

[2] For details on this instance of $\mathcal{ALC}$, please consult [12].

$\bigwedge_{\phi \in \Phi} \models \psi$: These are the only tests our reasoning tasks demand from the underlying logic. If $\mathcal{L}_{\mathcal{F}}$ is closed under conjunction and contains $\bot$ (as will be the case in our logic of choice), the requirement simply becomes to be able to test whether $\phi \models \psi$.

The soft requirements ("nice to have") on the logic are:
(ii) **Suitable for modeling real-world phenomena and knowledge**, ideally an established paradigm for such modeling tasks.
(iii) **Decidability, and as low complexity as possible**, of the relevant reasoning (e.g., satisfiability checks; cf. (i)).
(iv) **Effective tool support** established and available.

What we have just outlined is essentially a "wanted poster" for *description logic (DL)* [4]. This is a very well investigated family of fragments of first-order logic, whose mission statement is to provide a language for modeling real-world phenomena and knowledge (ii), while retaining decidability and exploring the trade-off of expressivity vs. complexity (iii). Effective tool support (iv) has been an active area for two decades. Every DL provides a language to describe "axioms", and even the most restricted DLs make it possible to answer queries about the truth of an axiom relative to a conjunction of axioms, which is exactly the test we require.

We briefly consider the description logic *attributive concept language with complements*, for short $\mathcal{ALC}$ [27,5], which is widely regarded as the canonical "basic" description logic variant (most other DLs extend $\mathcal{ALC}$, in a variety of directions). Description logic is a form of predicate logic that considers only 1-ary and 2-ary predicates, referred to as *concepts* and *roles*, respectively. Assuming a set N_C of concept names and a set N_R of role names, DL makes it possible to construct *complex concepts*, which correspond to a particular subset of predicate-logic formulas with exactly one free variable. For $\mathcal{ALC}$, the set of complex concepts is the smallest set s.t.

1. $\top, \bot$ and every concept name $A \in N_C$ are complex concepts, and
2. if C and D are complex concepts and $r \in N_R$, then $C \sqcap D$, $C \sqcup D$, $\neg C$, $\forall r.C$, and $\exists r.C$ are complex concepts.

Here, $\sqcap$ denotes concept intersection (logical conjunction), $\sqcup$ denotes concept union (logical disjunction), and $\neg C$ denotes concept complement (logical negation). $\forall r.C$ collects the set of all objects x such that, whenever x stands in relation r to y, $y \in C$. Similarly, $\exists r.C$ collects the set of all objects x such that there exists y where x stands in relation r to y and $y \in C$.

$\mathcal{ALC}$ allows *concept inclusion* axioms, of the form $C \sqsubseteq D$, where C, D are complex concepts, meaning that C is a subset of D (universally quantified logical implication). $\mathcal{ALC}$ furthermore allows *assertional* axioms, of the form $x : C$ or $(x, y) : r$, where C is a complex concept, r is a role, and x and y are individual names (i.e., constants). An $\mathcal{ALC}$ knowledge base consists of finite sets of concept inclusion axioms and assertional axioms (called the *TBox* and *ABox* respectively, interpreted as conjunctions. The basic reasoning services provided by $\mathcal{ALC}$ (and most other DLs) are testing whether a knowledge base KB is satisfiable, and testing whether KB $\models \phi$ where ϕ is an axiom. These decision problems are decidable, and more precisely, ExpTime-complete for $\mathcal{ALC}$.

For our purposes, we can assume as our formulas $\mathcal{L}_\mathcal{F}$ conjunctions of axioms, i.e., the smallest set that contains $\perp$, all axioms of the underlying DL (e.g., $\mathcal{ALC}$), as well as $\phi \wedge \psi$ if ϕ and ψ are members of $\mathcal{L}_\mathcal{F}$. In order to test whether $\phi \models \psi$, we then simply call the DL reasoning service "$\phi \models \psi_i$?" for every conjunct ψ_i of ψ and return "yes" iff all these calls did. In other words, we may use conjunctions of DL axioms in the knowledge base, case descriptions, and proof tree nodes.

6 Conclusion

In this paper, we introduced PriCL, the first framework for automated reasoning about case law. We showed that it complies with natural requirements of consistency. Moreover, we showed a tight connection between privacy case law and the notion of norms that underlies existing rule-based privacy research. We identified the major reasoning tasks such as checking the case law database for consistency, extracting norms and deducing whether an action is legal or not. For all these tasks, we gave algorithms deciding them and we did an analysis that leads to $\mathcal{ALC}$ as a suitable instantiation for the logic.

Acknowledgements. We want to thank the anonymous reviewer for their valuable feedback. We tried to incorporate the feedback as much as possible. Due to space constraints, parts of the feedback was only used for the long version [6].

This work was supported by the German Ministry for Education and Research (BMBF) through funding for the Center for IT-Security, Privacy and Accountability (CISPA).

References

1. Anderson, A.: A comparison of two privacy policy languages: EPAL and XACML (2005)
2. Annas, G.J.: Hipaa regulations-a new era of medical-record privacy? New England Journal of Medicine 348(15), 1486–1490 (2003)
3. Ashley, P., Hada, S., Karjoth, G., Powers, C., Schunter, M.: Enterprise privacy authorization language (EPAL 1.2). Submission to W3C (2003)
4. Baader, F., Calvanese, D., McGuinness, D.L., Nardi, D., Patel-Schneider, P.F. (eds.): The Description Logic Handbook: Theory, Implementation, and Applications. Cambridge University Press (2003)
5. Baader, F., Horrocks, I., Sattler, U.: Description Logics. In: Handbook of Knowledge Representation, ch. 3, pp. 135–180. Elsevier (2008)
6. Backes, M., Bendun, F., Hoffman, J., Marnau, N.: PriCL: Creating a Precedent. A Framework for Reasoning about Privacy Case Law (Extended Version) (2015), http://arxiv.org/abs/1501.03353
7. Backes, M., Karjoth, G., Bagga, W., Schunter, M.: Efficient comparison of enterprise privacy. In: Proc. of Symposium on Applied Computing, pp. 375–382. ACM (2004)
8. Barth, A., Datta, A., Mitchell, J.C., Nissenbaum, H.: Privacy and contextual integrity: Framework and applications. In: Proc. of S&P, p. 15. IEEE (2006)

9. Barth, A., Mitchell, J.C., Datta, A., Sundaram, S.: Privacy and utility in business processes. In: CSF, vol. 7, pp. 279–294 (2007)
10. Basin, D., Klaedtke, F., Marinovic, S., Zălinescu, E.: Monitoring compliance policies over incomplete and disagreeing logs. In: Qadeer, S., Tasiran, S. (eds.) RV 2012. LNCS, vol. 7687, pp. 151–167. Springer, Heidelberg (2013)
11. Basin, D.A., Klaedtke, F., Müller, S., Pfitzmann, B.: Runtime monitoring of metric first-order temporal properties. In: Proc. of FSTTCS, pp. 49–60 (2008)
12. Borgida, A.: On the relative expressiveness of description logics and predicate logics. Artificial Intelligence 82(1), 353–367 (1996)
13. Breaux, T.D., Antón, A.I.: Analyzing regulatory rules for privacy and security requirements. IEEE Trans. on Software Engineering 34(1), 5–20 (2008)
14. Cavoukian, A.: Privacy by design. Report of the Information & Privacy Commissioner Ontario, Canada (2012)
15. Datta, A., Blocki, J., Christin, N., DeYoung, H., Garg, D., Jia, L., Kaynar, D., Sinha, A.: Understanding and protecting privacy: formal semantics and principled audit mechanisms. In: Jajodia, S., Mazumdar, C. (eds.) ICISS 2011. LNCS, vol. 7093, pp. 1–27. Springer, Heidelberg (2011)
16. DeYoung, H., Garg, D., Kaynar, D., Datta, A.: Logical specification of the glba and hipaa privacy laws. CyLab, p. 72 (2010)
17. Duma, C., Herzog, A., Shahmehri, N.: Privacy in the semantic web: What policy languages have to offer. In: Proc. of POLICY, pp. 109–118. IEEE (2007)
18. European Commission. General data protection regulation, http://ec.europa.eu/justice/data-protection/document/review2012/com_2012_11_en.pdf
19. Garg, D., Jia, L., Datta, A.: Policy auditing over incomplete logs: theory, implementation and applications. In: Proc. of CCS, pp. 151–162. ACM (2011)
20. Gürses, S., Gonzalez Troncoso, C., Diaz, C.: Engineering privacy by design. Computers, Privacy & Data Protection (2011)
21. Karat, J., Karat, C.-M., Bertino, E., Li, N., Ni, Q., Brodie, C., Lobo, J., Calo, S., Cranor, L., Kumaraguru, P., Reeder, R.: Policy framework for security and privacy management. IBM Journal of Research and Development 53(2), 4 (2009)
22. Lämmel, R., Pek, E.: Understanding privacy policies. Empirical Software Engineering 18(2), 310–374 (2013)
23. Maffei, M., Pecina, K., Reinert, M.: Security and privacy by declarative design. In: Proc. of CSF, pp. 81–96. IEEE (2013)
24. Ni, Q., Bertino, E., Lobo, J., Brodie, C., Karat, C.-M., Karat, J., Trombeta, A.: Privacy-aware role-based access control. Proc. of TISSEC 13(3), 24 (2010)
25. Office for Civil Rights, U.S. Department of Health and Human Services. Summary of the HIPAA privacy rule (2003)
26. Oh, S.E., Chun, J.Y., Jia, L., Garg, D., Gunter, C.A., Datta, A.: Privacy-preserving audit for broker-based health information exchange. In: Proc. of Data and Application Security and Privacy, pp. 313–320. ACM (2014)
27. Schmidt-Schauß, M., Smolka, G.: Attributive concept descriptions with complements. Artificial Intelligence 48(1), 1–26 (1991)
28. Sen, S., Guha, S., Datta, A., Rajamani, S.K., Tsai, J., Wing, J.M.: Bootstrapping privacy compliance in big data systems. In: Proc. of S& P
29. Tschantz, M.C., Datta, A., Wing, J.M.: Formalizing and enforcing purpose restrictions in privacy policies. In: Proc. of S& P, pp. 176–190. IEEE (2012)
30. United States Congress. Financial services modernization act of 1999 (2010)
31. United States federal law. Children's Online Privacy Protection Act (1998)

Author Index

.